THE METHUEN DRAMA GUIDE TO CONTEMPORARY BRITISH PLAYWRIGHTS

Martin Middeke holds the Chair of English Literature at the University of Augsburg and is Visiting Professor of English at the University of Johannesburg. He is Co-Editor of *Anglia* and General Editor of the CDE book series. Recent book publications include *Literature and Circularity* (2009), *The Methuen Drama Guide to Contemporary Irish Playwrights* (2010) and *The Literature of Melancholia: Early Modern to Postmodern* (2011).

Peter Paul Schnierer read English, German, Political Sciences and Philosophy at the universities of London, Greenwich and Tübingen. He has taught full-time at the universities of Greenwich, Buckingham, Tübingen, Northern Arizona, Maryland and Vienna, and he currently holds the Chair of English Literature at the University of Heidelberg.

His publications on contemporary drama include two books and three edited or co-edited collections, including *The Methuen Drama Guide to Contemporary Irish Playwrights* (2010). He has also published a monograph on literary demonization since the Renaissance.

Aleks Sierz FRSA is Visiting Professor at Rose Bruford College, and author of *In-Yer-Face Theatre: British Drama Today* (Faber, 2001), *The Theatre of Martin Crimp* (Methuen Drama, 2006), *John Osborne's Look Back in Anger* (Continuum, 2008) and most recently *Rewriting the Nation: British Theatre Today* (Methuen Drama, 2011). He also works as a journalist, broadcaster, lecturer and theatre critic.

in the same series from Methuen Drama:

The Methuen Drama Guide to Contemporary Irish Playwrights
Edited by Martin Middeke and Peter Paul Schnierer

THE METHUEN DRAMA
GUIDE TO CONTEMPORARY
BRITISH PLAYWRIGHTS

Edited and with an introduction by Martin Middeke,
Peter Paul Schnierer and Aleks Sierz

B L O O M S B U R Y
LONDON · NEW DELHI · NEW YORK · SYDNEY

Bloomsbury Methuen Drama

An imprint of Bloomsbury Publishing Plc

50 Bedford Square	1385 Broadway
London	New York
WC1B 3DP	NY 10018
UK	USA

www.bloomsbury.com

Bloomsbury is a registered trade mark of Bloomsbury Publishing Plc

First published in Great Britain in 2011 by Methuen Drama
Reprinted by Bloomsbury Methuen Drama 2014

© 2011 by Martin Middeke, Peter Paul Schnierer and Aleks Sierz

British Library Cataloguing-in-Publication Data
A catalogue record for this book is available from the British Library.

ISBN: PB: 978-1-4081-2278-5

Library of Congress Cataloging-in-Publication Data
A catalog record for this book is available from the Library of Congress.

Typeset by SX Composing DTP, Rayleigh, Essex
Printed and bound in Great Britain

CONTENTS

INTRODUCTION

Martin Middeke, Peter Paul Schnierer and Aleks Sierz

This collection surveys twenty-five representative playwrights of contemporary British drama, with an emphasis on those whose work first appeared during the 1980s or later. The chapters are written by a team of internationally renowned specialists from the UK, USA, Canada, France, Greece, Austria and Germany. Each chapter has a four-part structure: an introduction which includes a short biographical sketch of each playwright; a concise analysis of the major work of the respective author in chronological order; a summary of the playwright's particular contribution to contemporary British theatre, including an assessment of their characteristic themes, stylistic features and the critical reception of their work; and, finally, a bibliography of primary texts and a selection of critical material. The twenty-five chapters in this volume discuss a total of 133 plays in detail (while many more are mentioned on the way) – an abundant body of work, which enables conclusions to be drawn about the state of affairs in contemporary British playwriting and provides helpful suggestions for further research. The plays under scrutiny span 1981 (Sarah Daniels's *Ripen Our Darkness*) to 2010 (Jonathan Harvey's *Canary*). The vast majority were written during the boom in new playwriting during the past two decades; more than half of the plays discussed in detail were staged in the first decade of the twenty-first century.

British playwriting has historically had a close affinity not only with its material base (the theatre system that stages the plays), but also with the structures of British society, and especially with a more general discussion of economic, social and political issues. Since the advent of Ibsen in the late nineteenth century, and the adoption of naturalism as the ruling aesthetics of much socially engaged and pro-gressive drama, truthfulness in new playwriting has been intimately related to work which has aimed not only to represent society accurately, but also to offer solutions to social problems. This process received a powerful shot in the arm from George Bernard Shaw (not for the first or last time, it was an Irish playwright who defined a hegemonic strand in British playwriting). Although much commercial playwriting continued to aspire to entertain as much as instruct, the independent theatres of the 1890s produced new work with a literary or artistic value. Because the Independent Theatre Society, the Stage Society and the New Century Theatre were dependent on subscriptions rather than box-office and, as theatre clubs, managed to avoid censorship by the Lord Chamberlain, their activities focused on 'the search for new playwrights', and this trend culminated in the Harley Granville Barker and J. E. Vedrenne seasons, three of which were produced at the Court Theatre (later renamed Royal Court) in 1904–07.[1] Significantly, regional repertory companies outside London also helped to promote the new drama. In the post-war era, these tendencies were revived and a mixture of naturalism and a socially progressive social realism became, to a greater or lesser extent, the main aesthetic criteria of the UK's theatre. Playwrights sought both to mirror society, and to change it.

In the past three decades, which are the subject of this book, there have been enormous changes in British society. The long reign of Conservative Prime Minister Margaret Thatcher, which started in May 1979 and ended in November 1990, deliberately broke up the economic, social and political consensus of post-war Britain, introducing the ideology of monetarism, the practice of privatisation and the rule of the market into many corners of society, from selling off the public utilities to freeing the financial sector from restraint in the City of London's Big Bang of 1986. The concomitant battles with trade unions, symbolised by the exceptionally bitter Miners' Strike of 1984–85, changed relations between the classes, while conditions at work were also reformed in favour of the employers. Unemployment became a permanent condition of life for millions in the 1980s. One historian sums up her impact on British society: 'Thatcher achieved her victories at terrible cost, usually borne by others. By any test, from statistical surveys of relative incomes to the striking reappearance of beggars on the street, Britain became a more unequal society.'[2]

So powerful were these changes, which are often called Thatcherism, that not only did the Conservative administrations of Prime Minister John Major (1990–97) continue with them, privatising, for example, the railways in 1993, but the arrival of New Labour in 1997 did little to significantly reverse these processes, despite a handful of liberal reforms such as the introduction of a national minimum wage in 1999. The New Labour governments of Prime Ministers Tony Blair and Gordon Brown substantially built on the legacy of Thatcher, and even in foreign policy Blair proved as bellicose as the Iron Lady. The Iraq War of 2003 was particularly contentious. In general, Thatcherism had enormous and long-lasting effects on the culture of the UK. Nor could theatre remain immune from these changes. In the 1980s, the obsession with the market meant that money distributed by the Arts Council (a body which is at 'arm's length' from the government and chooses which theatres to fund) for theatre was repeatedly cut. It was not until the 2000s that, following the Boyden Report, New Labour belatedly reversed this trend and pumped £25 million extra into the beleaguered theatre system nationwide. The result was a boom in new writing in the first decade of the new millennium.

All the playwrights in this volume belong to a distinct genre in British theatre: new writing. Since the premieres of John Osborne's *Look Back in Anger* and Samuel Beckett's *Waiting for Godot* in the mid-1950s, the idea of new writing has developed into a particular tradition. It is a genre characterised by plays which are contemporary in their language, contemporary in their subject matter and often contemporary in their attitude to theatre form (all experiments in dramatic structure implicitly question the past forms of theatrical storytelling). Occasionally, these plays have been confrontational and provocative; often, they have had something urgent to say about life, whether in its political or personal aspects, or indeed both. They are usually distinguished from other new plays such as populist comedies, adaptations of novels or history plays by their seriousness of purpose and occasionally by the difficulty of their writing. But the most important thing to understand about new writing is its material basis. Because these playwrights were and are consciously writing in opposition to the populist and commercial West End theatre, all of them have depended on those metropolitan theatres which are funded by state subsidy. Distributed by the Arts Council, such subsidies have sustained specialist new writing theatres (which usually produce only contemporary new work), and these institutions have been responsible for developing the country's playwriting. Clearly, the advantage of a theatre specialising in new writing is that it can develop the play-reading, dramaturgical and directorial talent needed to find the best contemporary new plays and to give such new work its best productions. It can also devote resources to finding, nurturing and developing new playwrights.

As far as specialised new writing theatres in the first decade covered by this book are concerned, the most important venue in the 1980s was the Royal Court, London, with its main stage (audience capacity of about 350) and Theatre Upstairs (a studio space which seated about seventy). This small but iconic theatre was justly proud of its heritage as a promoter of provocative plays such as Osborne's debut in 1956 or Edward Bond's scandalous *Saved* (1965), both of which divided the critics. Under artistic director Max Stafford-Clark (1979–93), the Royal Court developed the workshop method pioneered by his Joint Stock company in the 1970s and the accolade of being a Royal Court writer – someone regularly staged at this venue – became increasingly valued as a mark of artistic success. But other venues were equally important: Christopher Hampton describes the 1980s as the 'decade of exploding outlets'.[3] In Edinburgh, the Traverse Theatre premiered work by both Scottish and English writers. In London, equally important were three other venues: the Bush Theatre, a tiny pub theatre in west London, the Hampstead Theatre, a small prefab hut in north London, and the Soho Poly Theatre. During this time, the National Theatre also contributed to the staging of some new plays along with its repertoire of classical revivals. Outside London, only Live Theatre in Newcastle upon Tyne specialised in new writing (unusual for theatres outside the metropolis), establishing itself on the city's quayside in the early 1980s, 'long before the area became a symbol of cultural renaissance'.[4] Other theatres outside London, as for example the Royal Exchange in Manchester or the Octagon in Bolton, also staged the occasional new play. Equally significant were the completely unfunded fringe venues in the metropolis, such as the Finborough Theatre. Likewise, subsidised touring companies like Paines Plough also specialised in contemporary new plays; feminist groups such as Monstrous Regiment helped nurture women playwrights.

Following the election of Thatcher as prime minister, the ideology of Thatcherism influenced not only the policies of the Arts Council, but also the subject matter of many individual playwrights. For the theatre system in general the most obvious effect of Thatcherism was cuts to state subsidy for the arts, but the profoundest result was the gradual commercialisation of this whole cultural sector. In the words of Keith Peacock, there was a shift from theatre being a contributor to 'the political, social, personal and moral changes taking place' in Britain, to that of 'an entertainment industry'.[5] During the 1980s, theatres slowly became businesses as well as arts organisations. They rebranded themselves, acquired logos, formulated mission statements, learnt to use niche marketing, made sponsorship deals, redesigned their foyers and expanded their bar sales. Audiences became customers, shows became product, and the box-office ruled. Due to Thatcherite market pressures, the mixed economy of funding – part state subsidy, part business sponsorship and part box-office – tilted decisively in favour of the commercial.[6] Despite their initial resistance, even the specialised new writing theatres were affected by these changes. Subsidised companies had to become successful businesses, and they gradually became dependent for about 30–40 per cent of their income on the box-office. Of course, all this had an aesthetic effect: the repertoire gradually narrowed and the space for artistic experiment contracted.

But theatres and arts policies did not remain static over the period covered by this book. Although state subsidies for theatres contracted in the 1980s, the 1990s saw the first stirrings of expansion. In 1994, the National Lottery was created by John Major's Conservative government, and very soon its funds were available to pay for ambitious theatre-building projects. All of the main new writing theatres were transformed by this largesse. The Royal Court, under the artistic directors Stephen Daldry (1993–98) and Ian Rickson (1998–2006), was refurbished, increasing its seating capacity – especially in its Theatre Upstairs – and accentuating its cool image. While building works continued, Daldry rented out two West End theatres (the Duke of York's and the Ambassadors) where three stages were available for new productions. It was in these theatres that iconic productions such as Mark Ravenhill's *Shopping and Fucking* (1996) and Sarah Kane's *Cleansed* (1998) were staged. Similarly, during the 2000s, the Bush Theatre – under Mike Bradwell (1996–2007) – was refurbished, while the Soho Theatre – under Abigail Morris (1992–2006) – found brand-new premises in a former synagogue in Dean Street, Soho, in 2000, ending a decade of peregrination from one temporary venue to another. Likewise, the Hampstead – under Jenny Topper (1988–2003) – moved into an entirely new, purpose-built venue in 2003. Long before these metropolitan changes, in 1992, the Traverse – under Ian Brown (1989–96) – also acquired a new building, with two new stages. Live Theatre – under Max Roberts – was also substantially refurbished, in various phases, the most recent project being completed in 2008. If, after the departure of Thatcher in 1990, theatres improved, then so did state subsidies. The New Labour government of Tony Blair, elected in 1997, made more money available to theatres in the 2000s.[7]

The subjects that new writers addressed also changed over the three decades from the 1980s to the 2000s. Following the schema adopted by playwright David Edgar, the story of British new writing from 1980 to 2010 is something of a three-act drama.[8] In Act One, new writing is under pressure from an unsympathetic nanny, Thatcher, but responds by offering more opportunities for minority voices. In these years, women playwrights such as Caryl Churchill and Timberlake Wertenbaker – as well as new arrivals such as Sarah Daniels, April De Angelis and Andrea Dunbar – were promoted by the Royal Court. Black and Asian playwrights such as Hanif Kureishi and Winsome Pinnock were also staged. As well as the Royal Court, smaller theatres such as the Bush helped Terry Johnson and Kevin Elyot at the start of their careers. Jonathan Harvey started at the Liverpool Playhouse before his Royal Court debut in 1988 with *Mohair*. In the 1980s, Martin Crimp's early work was staged by the Orange Tree pub theatre in Richmond, south London. Anthony Clark, the director of Crimp's first play, eventually became artistic director of the Hampstead in 2003. In the 1980s, Jim Cartwright – a playwright sceptical of the social policies of Thatcherism – enjoyed productions at the Royal Court and the National. But the embattled feeling due to cuts in state subsidy did have a demoralising effect on theatres and directors. By the end of the 1980s, there was talk of an enormous crisis in new writing.

In Act Two, new writing revives but turns its back on politics, retiring into privacy. Starting with playwrights such as Philip Ridley (staged by Dominic Dromgoole at the Bush and Jenny Topper at the Hampstead) and Anthony Neilson (staged at the Traverse, Finborough and Royal Court), a new sensibility developed in British theatre. While the moment of 'in-yer-face theatre' – raw, uncompromising plays that smashed taboos and provoked audiences – was rather short-lived, spanning the four years between the arrival of Sarah Kane's notorious debut *Blasted* at the Royal Court in January 1995 and her suicide in February 1999, its effects were to change the face of British new writing. As well as promoting an older generation represented by Crimp and Johnson, the Royal Court under Daldry sponsored the work of a large number of new writers, such as Mark Ravenhill, Joe Penhall, Jez Butterworth and Judy Upton. The emergence of other talents such as David Eldridge, Phyllis Nagy, Rebecca Prichard, Martin McDonagh, Patrick Marber and Nick Grosso suggested a renaissance in new writing. Some critics even spoke of a new golden age. From Scotland came David Greig and David Harrower, encouraged by the Traverse under Philip Howard (1996–2007). Shelagh Stephenson was promoted by the Hampstead Theatre, and Roy Williams and Tanika Gupta moved across the wide theatrical spectrum from writing plays about their Caribbean and Bengali heritage to penning dramas about contemporary Britain. Both had work staged at the Royal Court and National. Once again, smaller venues made an equally important contribution. The Bush, for example, staged Jonathan Harvey's feel-good play, *Beautiful Thing*. In these exciting years, many new writers abandoned political subjects, and focused on personal feelings and intimate relationships. Most were interested in tackling the overarching subject of masculinity in crisis.

In Act Three, the 2000s, as state funding for theatre rose, new writing multiplied in its practitioners and diversified in its subjects – and the 'children' of 1990s new writing rediscovered overtly political concerns. In the aftermath of 9/11, it was hard to avoid politics, and the fashion for verbatim theatre influenced even fictional stories. Simon Stephens and Richard Bean were two of the most prolific and powerful new voices to emerge in this decade. Similarly, in Scotland, Gregory Burke joined David Greig and David Harrower as a chronicler of the new millennium, while new black playwrights such as Kwame Kwei-Armah and debbie tucker green were staged at the National and Royal Court theatres in London. While in England older playwrights continued to add to the huge variety of new plays that characterised the first decade of the new millennium, the subject matter of this great outpouring of new work spanned the whole gamut of possibilities, from large state-of-the-nation dramas to small intimate stories. Typical themes included the War on Terror and the culture of fear, the social problems of poverty and violence, the effects of migration from the EU and beyond, the disaffection of segregated communities, and the domestic issues of abuse and infidelity. In the 2000s, the family once more became interesting to young playwrights, as did plays about teenage angst. The increased numbers of dystopic visions of the future testify to the creativity and imagination of these playwrights, who were now joined by a new crop of talents, such as Dennis Kelly, Tim Crouch, Steve Waters, Bola Agbaje, Chloe Moss, Polly Stenham, Laura Wade and Mike Bartlett, all of whom together ensured that the 2000s were a remarkable decade for British new writing.

A survey of the twenty-five chapters illustrates the major thematic and aesthetic trends in British new writing.[9] With regard to both form and content, contemporary drama oscillates between the aesthetic extremes of political drama and experimental self-reflexivity. On the one hand, since Osborne's *Look Back in Anger* even the most experimental plays of the new British drama have featured recognisable traits of everyday life, language and images and thus have retained a thoroughly political concern; on the other hand, even the most political plays have been characterised by a heightened realism that went beyond social realism and the didacticism of a Brechtian *Lehrstück*. New writing has therefore maintained a middle ground between such self-reflexive movements of drama in the twentieth and twenty-first century as the Theatre of the Absurd, Metadrama, or Postdramatic Theatre and the more overtly political intentions of Epic Theatre while creatively adopting issues and techniques from both directions. The narrator in Jim Cartwright's *Road* is one case in point, and another is David Greig, whose work thoroughly exhibits epic features with a Brechtian coinage but whose imagery often recalls the more hermetic and self-reflexive language of Howard Barker. On a psychological basis, a view of modern subjectivity has been attached to a sense of community; this sense of society and responsible interaction has also never been seen apart from the vital interests of the imaginative potential of human individuality.

A central political concern of contemporary British drama has obviously been Thatcherite politics. Playwrights have laid bare the disenchantment with old political certainties, witnessing the failure of party politics and, especially, the inadequacies of both communism and capitalism. The utopian socialist vision of the 1970s has turned stale, and plays such as Philip Ridley's *The Pitchfork Disney* or *Brokenville* instead envisage scenarios of nuclear, military, terroristic or ecological catastrophe, which threaten the sense of community, public welfare and solidarity. A very potent image of this conflict has been the image of the market. Plays like Martin Crimp's *Dealing with Clair* or, more overtly, David Eldridge's *Market Boy*, unmask the social changes brought about by Thatcherite politics and the ensuing process of dehumanisation. This also entails plays that have focused on working-class conditions, unemployment, bourgeois decay, the decline of heavy industries, and violence.

One of the locations of these issues in contemporary British drama has been the battlefield of war. As the character Keith in Richard Bean's *The God Botherers* points out: 'The last war's fucked everything, and the next war will fuck everything else' (p. 145). The invasion of Iraq by the USA and Britain in 2003 is reflected upon in Gregory Burke's *Black Watch*, April De Angelis's *Amongst Friends*, and Simon Stephens's *Motortown*. Sarah Kane's *Blasted* famously was a response to the war in Bosnia, and in particular the attack on Srebrenica.

The 1990s also staged plays which question globalisation and multiculturalism – both extremely productive issues for the contemporary British stage. Mark Ravenhill's work springs to mind, or the provocative satires of Bean, whose *In the Club* is rather Eurosceptic and whose controversial *England People Very Nice* appears as an account of the problems involved in multiculturalism as well as a criticism of Muslim fundamentalism. Likewise, Burke's *Gagarin Way* gives insight into the way global capitalism neutralises any opposition by rendering everyone complicit in its mechanisms. In Burke, again, a sense of deeply rooted alienation is paired with a desire for community and communication. David Harrower's *Kill the Old Torture Their Young* is likewise characterised by a sense of urban isolation. The global may also be set against ethnic contexts. Tanika Gupta's portrayal of Indian myths and their vivid imagery is juxtaposed with ideas about the uprootedness of human beings in contemporary urban Britain.

Related to the challenges of globalisation are issues about post-colonialism and cultural hybridity, as well as questions about national identity, immigration and citizenship. Gupta has portrayed South Asian communities in Britain and her plays reflect on historical as well as socio-sexual realities that usually have been hushed up in those communities. Winsome Pinnock's *Leave Taking* epitomises questions of the post-colonial and also addresses the black subject and questions of migration, thus paving the way for a transnational feminism. The concerns of immigrants, and of the second and third generations have been central topics in the work of Roy Williams, especially as regards stereotypes and racial discrimination. Citizenship, migration and the question of what it means to be 'British' permeate the plays of Kwame Kwei-Armah. Related topics that surface again and again are ethnicity and Englishness or, as its variant, Scottishness. The work of Bean, for instance, or plays by Harrower, Greig and Burke emphasise that the idea of national identity denotes a work in progress, a state of flux, and that identity formation in an absolute sense is doomed to fail. A bitter example is Williams's *Sing Yer Heart Out for the Lads*, which portrays football fervour turning into racist hysteria. Racism is an important issue in a wide range of plays from Joe Penhall's *Blue/Orange*, Kwei-Armah's *Statement of Regret*, Williams's *Fallout*, to works by debbie tucker green, Pinnock or Gupta.

On a more abstract note, many plays have dealt with the problem of history and the relation of past and present. Harrower in *Dark Earth*, for example, has shown a contiguity between the present and the past; a key motif of Kwei-Armah's plays is the threatening impact of an unfinished or psychologically undigested past on the psychic stability of his characters. Pinnock's plays feature a melancholy sense of the past reflected in a guilty conscience as one of their central concerns. In Shelagh Stephenson's *An Experiment with an Air Pump* historicism is a means of defamiliarising the present through the perspective of the past.

One of the most important sociological facts in recent Western European history is the collapse of the traditional family unit and the redefinition of family values – both also vital issues on the contemporary stage. Stephenson's *Mappa Mundi* depicts tensions and complications in family life, and the sphere of the domestic is also highlighted in Eldridge's *Incomplete and Random Acts of Kindness* as well as in Greig's *The Architect*. Even more pressingly, green's *Born Bad*, *Stoning Mary* and *Random* provide frightening views of a deteriorating family, threatened by violence and hatred. The topic of the family in crisis connects with issues of psychology, dissolving identities, madness, trauma, and especially the concern with gender and gender-performativity. Many playwrights have made it clear that gender identity is not an ontological category, but that it is achieved through institutionalised repetitions of physical acts. This stance, theoretically elucidated by Judith Butler, underlies, for instance, the way that the construction of both femininity and masculinity appears in contemporary new writing. Bean and Eldridge's work (most notably in the latter's *Serving It Up*) illustrate masculinity in crisis, and Kwei-Armah and Williams's plays approach a redefinition of masculinity in their portrayals of generational conflicts among black males. Masculinity and sexual indisposition are highlighted in Terry Johnson's work, and both in Sarah Daniels and in Kane men turn out to be actual as well as potential rapists. Insincerity as well as repression are presented as two sides of masculinity in Penhall's *Love and Understanding*. Male brutalism and authoritarianism, abuse and violence in marriage, are questioned in Bean's *Under the Whaleback* and green's *Dirty Butterfly*. While Jez Butterworth's *The Night Heron*, by contrast, concentrates on male friendship, a central theme of his *Mojo* is father-and-son relationships.

Many plays highlight the role of women from feminist to post-feminist angles. Daniels was one of the first to link this perspective to questions of sexism, male gaze and also to the structures of marriage. Daniels's *Masterpieces* lays bare the connection between the porn industry and violence against women. De Angelis's *2006* centres on the escape of the Austrian Natascha Kampusch from her tormentor. Under the male gaze female sexuality has become little more than a commodity, a debased instrument of male pleasure and power. In a slightly different vein, Stephenson in *The Memory of Water* has reflected a post-Thatcher society, which presents women trying to bridge the gaps between economic success and family bonds. Gupta's *Sugar Mummies* and green's *Trade* both cast a critical glance at female sex tourism. Here, romance has degenerated into a business trans-action, but then, what the female protagonists seek abroad is sadly lacking in their lives at home. Pinnock's *Talking in Tongues* defies easy categorisation between white and black, and also reverses gender politics in that women exploit men. Mother–daughter relationships are investigated in plays such as Daniels's *Neaptide* or green's *Born Bad*. Different from second-generation feminist drama, *Born Bad* focuses on women's intra-sexual behaviour while still challenging post-feminist beliefs. The depiction of both male and female homo-sexuality and, especially, the topic of AIDS, has been an important kindred issue. Notable plays dealing with this are Cartwright's *Hard*

Fruit, Kevin Elyot's *My Night with Reg* and *Coming Clean*, green's *Stoning Mary*, and also Jonathan Harvey's *Beautiful Thing* and *Canary*. Sexuality and the depiction of gay sex on stage are so omnipresent that it is pointless to single out particular plays and instances. Such portrayals include taboo areas such as paedophilia and child abuse (from Elyot's *Mouth to Mouth* to Harrower's *Blackbird*) as well as incestuous relationships.

Much of contemporary new writing has extensively grappled with the issue of postmodernism and postmodern society, especially the aspect that conveys the impression of the dissolution of the autonomous self. Crimp's *The Treatment* and *Attempts on Her Life*, for instance, have portrayed a world of multiple, media-induced perspectives which suggest an excess of meanings and a breakdown of communication. In much the same vein, Ravenhill has commented on the dissolution of the grand narratives in favour of micro-narratives in *Shopping and Fucking*. In Ravenhill's *Product* both society and each individual are a mere commodity, easily bought, sold or consumed. His entire work embodies an attack on a particular, media- and consumerism-orientated depthlessness while, at the same time, his plays decisively defend a humanist stance amid the alienation that surrounds contemporary life. Money, it seems, is an insufficient simulacrum after all, and the nightmarish ending of Crimp's *The Country* has the female protagonist imagine that the rest of her life might be a simulation of love, which in turn appeals to love as a transcending force that can leave hatred and violence behind – a humanist feeling that Crimp definitely shares with Ravenhill and with many other British playwrights.

The reaction against the alienating forces of capitalism and materialism explains the recent interest in ecology and the environment. In a way, the moment of 'in-yer-face theatre' could be read as a visceral reaction that makes us see how nature creeps back and how our natural impulses can surprise us. Concrete environmental concerns can be traced in the work of Simon Stephens and his elaborated visions of an ecological apocalypse in plays such as *Herons*, *Punk Rock* and *Marine Parade*. Recent examples of plays that address the issue of climate change include Moira Buffini, Matt Charman,

Penelope Skinner and Jack Thorne's co-authored *Greenland* (National Theatre, 2011) or Bean's *The Heretic* (Royal Court, 2011).

As regards the formal developments of contemporary new writing, the oscillation between the traditional realist mode and the more experimental open forms of drama resists easy pigeonholing. There are still traces of social realism to be found, for instance, in Gupta's plays. While the vast majority of contemporary British plays strongly resist closure, they still employ teleological plotlines, which set out to untangle their twisted strands. Remnants of the well-made play can also be found in Bean's early kitchen-sink comedies or in Elyot's *Coming Clean*. It has been a trademark of naturalism to connect minutely observed examinations of social milieu and human behaviour with the grander scale of cultural, social or political change. Naturalist aesthetics dominate the work of Burke and Butterworth. Kwei-Armah's *Elmina's Kitchen* links the examination of urgent social issues with the ethical concern to reveal black humanity through art. Realism – itself a much debated, contradictory and multi-faceted aesthetic term – also includes a range of varieties such as the emotional realism of Daniels, the heightened naturalism of Penhall, or the good-natured didacticism of Harvey. Gupta's *Gladiator Games* mixes fiction with verbatim theatre, a method which also characterises Burke's *Black Watch*.

Traditional forms on the contemporary British stage include the widespread predilection for satire and farce: laughter is directed against 'correct' positions and against any fundamentalism, and is to be found in writers as diverse as Bean, Crimp or Penhall. The farcical hyperbole that exposes a loss of control, panic and the breakdown of a moral status quo is characteristic of, for example, the work of Johnson. In Johnson and elsewhere the farcical for the most part seamlessly merges with the more self-reflexive, experimental modes of surrealism and the grotesque. Ridley's *The Pitchfork Disney* is a case in point. 'In-yer-face theatre' has been characterised by omnipresent incidents of verbal, physical and structural violence which as a whole blend with the surreal and grotesque in order to produce thoroughly paradoxical and sublime effects that range from an emotional allurement to an abject distancing. Rather than providing us with messages,

Anthony Neilson's nightmarish shock-fests, the grotesque violence in Ridley, or Kane's superbly poetic heightening of graphic violence, move away from explicit political commentary and towards ambiguous imagery which works on the imagination and provokes reflection rather than easy answers.

The more experimental plays are characterised by a high degree of self-consciousness and intertextuality which, as a rule, echoes the problematic stance postmodern drama takes towards history. Elyot's interest in intermediality as well as intertextuality may spring to mind here, as well as much of De Angelis's work. Metadramatic and metatheatrical devices are ubiquitous and may even be found in realist surroundings where social-realist intentions are self-reflexively broken, as, for instance, in De Angelis's *A Laughing Matter* or in Bean's *England People Very Nice*. Many of these intertextual plays are engaged in demythologising mythic unities: Butterworth's *The Winterling* or *Jerusalem*, for example, continue the great tradition of questioning the idea of the romantic pastoral, as do Harrower's *Dark Earth* and Crimp's *The Country*. Ancient myths themselves and their closed systems of truth have been subjected to criticism, as Kane's *Phaedra's Love* or Stephens's *Harper Regan* have proved.

On an even more abstract formal level a number of experimental plays have pushed their forms to the borderline of the post-dramatic. This move in many instances makes theatre aesthetics approximate performance art and generates a creative mix of drama, narrative and poetry. All these aesthetically hybrid forms take a most decisive turn away from issue-based drama in favour of the phenomenological perspectives of human consciousness and perception. Parallel monologues in Cartwright's *I Licked a Slag's Deodorant* produce a creative emphasis on theatricality; Crimp's phenomenological spaces in his more daring plays such as *Attempts on Her Life* and *Fewer Emergencies* produce an impression of epistemological as well as ontological uncertainty. green's black urban stories are experiential spaces mixing elliptical strains of language in order to produce disturbing effects. Kane's *4:48 Psychosis* is not a description of a psychotic state of mind but rather tries to make this state of mind a vital experience for the audience. The site of Neilson's dark vision in

The Censor is arguably the subconscious, and the inner world of the mentally disturbed protagonist is a major concern of his *The Wonderful World of Dissocia*. While phenomenological drama of this kind obviously centres on the conflicts between the real and the imaginary, Crimp, Kane, Ravenhill, Stephens and green are arguably the most minimalist voices on the experimental side of contemporary British drama.

All in all, these transgressions of the traditional boundaries of theatre amount to a series of alternative ways of looking at twenty-first-century life. And as, year after year, new playwrights continue to emerge, the story of British new writing – in its most traditional forms as well as in its most experimental – continues to develop. We can easily appreciate the way that these playwrights responded to the New Labour era: it will be interesting to see how they react to the new age of austerity inaugurated by the present Coalition government of David Cameron and Nick Clegg. The future is all to play for.

Martin Middeke, Peter Paul Schnierer and Aleks Sierz
Augsburg, Heidelberg and London, March 2011

Bibliography

Aragay, Mireia, Hildegard Klein, Enric Monforte and Pilar Zozaya (eds), *British Theatre of the 1990s: Interviews with Directors, Playwrights, Critics and Academics* (Basingstoke: Palgrave Macmillan, 2007).

Aston, Elaine, *Feminist Views on the English Stage: Women Playwrights, 1990–2000* (Cambridge: CUP, 2003).

Billingham, Peter, *At the Sharp End: Uncovering the Work of Five Leading Dramatists* (London: Methuen Drama, 2007).

Billington, Michael, *State of the Nation: British Theatre Since 1945* (London: Faber & Faber, 2007).

Bull, John, *Stage Right: Crisis and Recovery in British Contemporary Mainstream Theatre* (Basingstoke: Macmillan, 1994).

D'Monté, Rebecca and Graham Saunders (eds), *Cool Britannia? British Political Drama in the 1990s* (Basingstoke: Palgrave Macmillan, 2008).

Dromgoole, Dominic, *The Full Room: An A–Z of Contemporary Playwriting*, 2nd edn (London: Methuen Drama, 2002).

Edgar, David (ed.), *State of Play: Playwrights on Playwriting* (London: Faber, 1999).

Goddard, Lynette, *Staging Black Feminisms: Identity, Politics, Performance* (Basingstoke: Palgrave Macmillan, 2007).

Godiwala, Dimple (ed.), *Alternatives within the Mainstream: British Black and Asian Theatres* (Newcastle: Cambridge Scholars, 2006).

Griffin, Gabriele, *Contemporary Black and Asian Women Playwrights in Britain* (Cambridge: CUP, 2003).

Hewison, Robert, *Culture and Consensus: England, Art and Politics Since 1940*, rev. edn (London: Methuen, 1997).

Howe Kritzer, Amelia, *Political Theatre in Post-Thatcher Britain: New Writing 1995–2005* (Basingstoke: Palgrave Macmillan, 2008).

Lane, David, *Contemporary British Drama* (Edinburgh: EUP, 2010).

Rabey, David Ian, *English Drama Since 1940* (Harlow: Longman, 2003).

Rebellato, Dan, *Theatre & Globalization* (Basingstoke: Palgrave Macmillan, 2009).

Shellard, Dominic, *British Theatre Since the War* (New Haven, CT: Yale University Press, 1999).

Sierz, Aleks, *In-Yer-Face Theatre: British Drama Today* (London: Faber & Faber, 2001).

——, *Rewriting the Nation: British Theatre Today* (London: Methuen Drama, 2011).

Wallace, Clare, *Suspect Cultures: Narrative, Identity and Citation in 1990s New Drama* (Prague: Litteraria Pragensia, 2006).

Wandor, Michelene, *Post-War British Drama: Looking Back in Gender* (London: Routledge, 2001).

Wyllie, Andrew, *Sex on Stage: Gender and Sexuality in Post-War British Theatre* (Bristol: Intellect, 2009).

Notes

1. Stage Society quoted in Ian Clarke, *Edwardian Drama: A Critical Study* (London: Faber, 1989), p. 16; see also pp. 12–21.
2. Peter Clarke, *Hope and Glory: Britain 1900–2000* (London: Penguin, 2004), p. 400.
3. In the early 1960s the Royal Court was the main new writing theatre, but by the 1980s many more theatres were staging new work (Hampton quoted in Aleks Sierz, Interview with Max Stafford-Clark, London, 17 November 2010).
4. Arts Council England, *Capital Case Study: Live Theatre Newcastle* (London: Arts Council England, 2009), p. 4.
5. D. Keith Peacock, *Thatcher's Theatre: British Theatre and Drama in the Eighties* (Westport, CT: Greenwood Press, 1999), p. 215.
6. See Baz Kershaw, 'British Theatre, 1940–2002: An Introduction', in Baz Kershaw (ed.), *The Cambridge History of British Theatre: Vol. 3, Since 1895* (Cambridge: Cambridge UP, 2004), pp. 313–14.

7. See Aleks Sierz, *Rewriting the Nation: British Theatre Today* (London: Methuen Drama, 2011).

8. See David Edgar, 'Provocative Acts', in David Edgar (ed.), *State of Play: Playwrights on Playwriting* (London: Faber, 1999), pp. 3–34.

9. The German Society for Contemporary Theatre and Drama in English (CDE) publishes both the proceedings of the annual CDE conference and monographs on aspects of contemporary playwriting. Many of these relate to the playwrights covered in this volume. See the CDE website, <http://www.contemporarydrama.de>.

1 RICHARD BEAN

Eckart Voigts-Virchow

Toast; Under the Whaleback; Smack Family Robinson; The God Botherers; Honeymoon Suite; Harvest; England People Very Nice

Introduction

It is not just because his origins are less than glamorous that Hull-born playwright Richard Bean (born in 1956) appears as the odd man out among successful British playwrights of the past decade. When he was awarded the George Devine Award in 2002 and hailed as a young, up-and-coming playwright, he pointed out the irony in his acceptance speech that a forty-six-year-old playwright was still referred to as 'young'.[1] The son of a policeman and a hairdresser, Bean's upbringing was lower-middle-class and his Hull-based plays reflect the experience of tattooed north-eastern working-class masculinity, from the eighteen months he worked in a bread plant after school in *Toast* (Royal Court, 1999) to the fishermen in *Under the Whaleback* (Royal Court, 2003), the inmates in a 1976 prison riot in *Up on Roof* (Hull Truck, 2006) or, more recently, the pub quiz team in recession-hit Hull in *Pub Quiz is Life* (Hull Truck, 2009). He has admitted that his plays focus very much on male camaraderie, but also claims that his subsequent education – he studied social psychology at Lough-borough University in the 1970s and worked as an occupational psychologist for a telephone company in the 1980s – has changed his attitudes towards gender issues:

> My life has been a blokey life. I went to a boys' school, I played a lot of sports, all very blokey. Then I went to university, and became a born-again feminist.[2]

Bean came to the performing arts erratically and almost without prior grooming through his work as a stand-up comedian in the late 1980s and early 1990s, and after he won a drama competition at a night class at Middlesex University. Subsequently, he worked as writer and performer for the Writers Guild-nominated BBC radio sketch comedy *Control Group Six* and wrote the libretto for Terence McNeff's opera *Paradise for Fools* (Canal Café, 1995). Several years after his first full-length play *Of Rats and Men* (Canal Café, 1992), Bean's debut success was *Toast*. Since then, Bean has produced plays at a steady rate, winning the George Devine Award for *Under the Whaleback* and the Pearson Award for Best New Play for *Honeymoon Suite* in 2002 as well as the Critics' Circle Best New Play Award for *Harvest* (Royal Court, 2005), with three volumes of collected plays in print and no sign of diminishing activities. With the grand, if controversial, success of *England People Very Nice* (National Theatre, 2009), it seems that he has finally delivered on the promise of the Monsterists group that he co-founded (with Moira Buffini, David Eldridge, Colin Teevan, Roy Williams and Sarah Woods) in 2002. According to Aleks Sierz, the 'Monsterists, a group of writers determined to change the landscape of new writing', sought to 'promote new writing of large-scale work in the British theatre', to liberate new writing 'from the ghetto of the studio black box to the main stage', and demanded 'equal access to financial resources for a play being produced by a living writer'.[3] Taking their name from a portmanteau word ('monster', large, and *'montrer'*, to show), the Monsterists' plea to open the main stages for their 'big' plays was nourished under Nicholas Hytner's reign at the National Theatre.

Bean's early work is best described as kitchen-sink comedy with a firm regional north-eastern footing. His farcical, occasionally pitch-black workplace comedies *Toast*, *Under the Whaleback* and *Harvest* reminded critics of the kitchen-sinks of David Storey and Arnold Wesker; these 'work' plays established Bean as a chronicler of industrial bread plants, Hull trawlers and east Yorkshire pig farms. While he keeps returning to less than flattering portrayals of working-class prejudice as well as resilience, more recent plays have proved Bean to be far more versatile than just that. His dramatic repertoire has considerably expanded, for instance, to foul-mouthed and sharp-edged farces such as *Smack Family Robinson* (Live Theatre, Newcastle upon Tyne, 2003) and *In the Club* (Hampstead Theatre, 2007) that invite comparison with Monty Python and Joe Orton. *In the Club*, a Strasbourg-set Eurosceptic farce, toured Britain in 2008. Interestingly, it received large-scale transfers in other Eurosceptic countries such as Slovenia and Denmark.[4] A play such as *Honeymoon Suite* suggested the influence of Alan Ayckbourn's stagecraft, while the two-hander *The Mentalists* (National Theatre, 2002) analysed the warped male psyche in almost 'absurdist' fashion as 'a deliberate homage to Pinter's *The Dumb Waiter*'.[5]

His latest projects for autumn 2010, *The Big Fellah*, a new play focusing on New York IRA supporters, for veteran director Max Stafford-Clark's touring company Out of Joint, and a stage adaptation of David Mamet's film *House of Cards* for the Almeida Theatre, are both set in urban America and prompted Bean to reflect in his e-mail announcement on being pigeonholed as a regional British working-class dramatist: 'I promise that there will be more plays set in East Hull in the near future.'[6] *The God Botherers* (Bush Theatre, 2003), a play about the absurdities of relief work set in the fictional African country Tambia, paved Bean's way towards his more recent *England People Very Nice* (National Theatre, 2009), his highly controversial, large-scale dismissal of multiculturalism on the large Olivier stage of the National Theatre. Both *The God Botherers* and *England People Very Nice* expose the absurdities of radical multiculturalism and appear to be the work of a pro-Israeli assimilationist. This is diametrically opposed to the pro-Palestinian political sentiments of Caryl Churchill (*Seven Jewish Children*, 2009), David Hare (*Via Dolorosa*, 1999; *Berlin/Wall*, 2009) or Katherine Viner/Alan Rickman (*My Name is Rachel Corrie*, 2005), prompting Jewish theatre critic John Nathan to call Bean '[t]he only prominent British playwright who is prepared to challenge left-wing orthodoxy'.[7] Plays such as *Harvest* or *England People Very Nice* and titles such as *Mr England* (Crucible Theatre, Sheffield, 2000) or *The English Game* (Headlong, 2008) are indicative of Bean's aspiration to create theatre on a grand scale and to write 'state-of-the-nation' farces in ways vastly different from the 'playwright laureate' David Hare.[8] Interestingly, his parochial comic epics on Englishness do not seem to invite continental transfers.

The Plays

Toast (1999)

Written in 1997 and having been sent as an unsolicited script to several theatres, it took two years for Bean's second play *Toast* to arrive at the Royal Court, where it opened on 12 February 1999. Jack Bradley has recalled how Bean's script travelled from a recommendation by his assistant, who happened to keep score for Bean's cricket team, via an arduous reading process to the Royal Court Upstairs at the New Ambassadors in 1999.[9] Originally entitled *Wonderloaf,* the title had to be changed after the owner of the brand name threatened litigation. The play, directed by Richard Wilson, was well received by the critics as 'one of the most truly original comedies of the late Nineties', firmly within the tradition of socialist stage realism.[10] Having seen a revival of David Storey's *The Changing Room* at the Royal Court, Bean had the idea to set his play in the canteen of a Hull bakery threatened by closure in 1975. In terms of structure, the play is simple – a cast of seven in a unified, linear plot, covering a single day in a single, naturalistically designed setting, with an ending that brings closure. Clocks in the minutely outlined stage design mark the short gaps in between the scenes from a day's shift. The all-male play's focus is on middle-aged, unskilled labourers in the throes of industrial food production. Having been pushed around from a dying industry (fishing) to the next in the post-industrial decline of northern England in the 1970s and 1980s, the men depend on their oven to keep working and prevent the imminent closure of the plant. The daily routines are – just as in the nineteenth-century 'industrial' literature – governed by service to the machine. As one of the workers says, 'We work a six-day week. Nights is three till finish. Finish can be anywhere between eleven at night to three in't morning' (p. 28). The thudding of the industrial bread plant oven is incessant and the scenario of male relations is harsh, peppered by cruel jokes and aggressive pranks. Men such as Dezzie or Cecil are on the brink – pressed for money, fatigued by years of monotonous work, always in danger of being stripped of masculine pride and under pressure from their wives and partners. Workers' solidarity is tested by rivalry for the job of chargehand and by the demands of the management. The action is propelled to a crisis when the emotionally unstable 'student' Lance appears as 'flier' (invariably called 'spare wank', p. 23) and the oven gets jammed. This is a major crisis as any loss of bread orders is likely to result in imminent closure and permanent joblessness. In the dénouement, it turns out that one of the workers, Colin, intentionally jammed the oven in order to put the blame on the chargehand Blakey. Working-class boys need not be noble painters manqué (Lee Hall, *The Pitman Painters*, 2007); in this play, they are more likely to be nasty, sexist, ex-convict bullies.

Under the Whaleback (2003)

The award-winning *Under the Whaleback* clearly expands the scale of the work play formula Bean had found in *Toast*. When he adapted this conception of interrogating male camaraderie to a group of Hull trawlermen for the Royal Court Theatre Upstairs, Richard Wilson's production – which opened on 10 April 2003 – garnered almost unanimously positive reviews. Among accolades ranging from 'tough, harrowing but beautiful' (John Peter), 'subtly engrossing' (Kate Bassett) and 'enthralling' (Nicholas de Jongh) to 'thrilling, savagely funny and deeply affecting' (Charles Spencer), Michael Billington praised it as 'impressive in its sense of lived experience'.[11] As a play that illustrates the impact of neoconservative economic policies on male working-class communities it probably needed this kind of support. It could hardly be expected to court either West End success or celebrity attention, as Bean himself concedes:

These days, I suppose producers think audiences expect a West End play to mean witty lines delivered by Ralph Fiennes – they don't want five tattooed Hull trawler-men dying.[12]

Both Paul Miller and Charles Spencer noted the influence of Eugene O'Neill's one-act sea plays, but Bean introduced a three-act structure set on the eponymous bow deck ('under the whaleback') of three different trawlers in 1965, 1972 and, finally, 2002, when fishing has deteriorated to a museum piece and the harrowing storm of the central act has been replaced with a jaded loop tape. Separated thirty years from a harrowing accident of the auspiciously named *James Joyce*, the plot sees this pale simulation of trawler life disrupted by Pat, who seeks revenge for the death of his father on the seaman-turned-museum guard, Darrel. Having his hand nailed to the table by Pat, Darrel explains that Pat is the offspring from his mother's affair with his father's mate. This revelation equals Darrel's own earlier conflict with the 'mythic' old reprobate Cassidy, who claims he has 'fathered' Darrel. Darrel survived the sinking of the *James Joyce* by putting on the 'duck suit' given to him by Cassidy – so at least in this sense he indeed becomes an ersatz father to Darrel, who comes to accept his role as Cassidy's surrogate son. Cassidy and the tall tales that surround him epitomise the male pride and tradition of seamanship, of forcefully and tragically fighting the elements. At the same time he is part of a legacy of sad brutality – which finally emerges in Darrel's story of how Cassidy killed his twin sons as he did not want them to die at sea the way his own fathers died. Darrel is precariously positioned in the crossfire of this transition from the tragic heights of the early seventies to the sad museum-piece working class of the millennium. Comic lines such as Pat's 'I've always been against the death penalty, unless it's for something really serious' (p. 125) cleverly expose the internal contradictions of male brutalism and authoritarianism.

Smack Family Robinson (2003)

This play, which opened at the Live Theatre, directed by Jeremy Herrin, on 20 May 2003, is yet again typical in its regional anchoring. Bean may be described as a playwright bent on sociological accuracy and, accordingly, the play is prefaced with a minute description of the John Lewis-style decor in the gorgeously crude and funnily immoral drug dealer's family. True, a Mercedes and an Alfa are in the drive, but the moral co-ordinates of the family in this gangster farce have gone awry. There are no ethical qualms about providing the Whitley Bay community (near Newcastle) with drugs, but exchanging shoes for slippers in the house is a clear moral imperative. The family is headed by ageing semi-retired drug-dealing couple Catherine and Gavin, with two sons, the retarded Robert and the unscrupulous Sean. The plot focuses on the murder of Tammy, Robert's junkie wife, and ends on the retributive matricide of Catherine at the hands of Robert. In between, there is much dark humour, plenty of casual, ridiculous and exaggerated violence and the racket, now masterminded by young Cora and Sean, is shared with, and farmed out to the incoming Russian Mafia:

> **Catherine** What the fucking hell's factoring?
> **Gavin** Do you know what factoring is Robert?
> **Robert** Yeah.
> **Sean** If you're a printer, and some bastard owes you four grand, you sell the debt to a factoring consultant for three grand – cash. He makes a grand when he collects [. . .]
> (p. 161)

Cora, the aspiring, well-educated eighteen-year-old daughter, would have been the focus of hope in a sentimental plot, but Bean is happy to provide an extremely funny, overblown farce of northern crime and moral abyss worthy of a Martin McDonagh.

The God Botherers (2003)

Cynicism and despair in the face of a world gone mad continue in *The God Botherers*, this time with the absurdity of NGO relief work as a target and Bean's signature criticism of fanatic Muslim fundamentalists. Critics stressed the riskiness of this 'freewheeling satire on worldwide political correctitude' (Patrick Marmion), which opened, again during Bean's *annus mirabilis* 2003, on 21 November in William Kerley's production for the Bush Theatre.[13] The scene is the fictional African country Tambia, later Tambekistan – a nightmare state marked by tribalism, anarchy, religious fundamentalism, clitoridectomy and the interests of Western oil conglomerates. Keith is a disillusioned relief worker, rocked out of complacency by the arrival of the hands-on enthusiasm of mid-twenties new arrival Laura. He thinks that Tambia is a 'male-dominated, tradition-oriented, patriarchal society, i.e.: it's fucked' (p. 145). The excited Laura appears in a Gucci hijab and, introducing narrative elements to the play, regularly 'posts' her experience and her obsession with puerile celebrity magazines back to her boring, nondescript Britain represented by places such as Burton Latimer or Kettering. Having taken in the clichés of political correctness from *The Idiot's Guide to Islam*, her adaptive progress comes in the shape of an ingenious scheme to provide local women with Tambia Cell mobile phones. The madness of cultural incongruity arrives in the shape of the predicament of local lady Ibrahima. Wearing a burka, the mother of three also flirts with Keith and surreptitiously reads *Cosmopolitan*. She is being threatened with murder at the hands of her husband in case her fourth child turns out to be a girl. Having cast a vote against her husband's will, she becomes the mad culture's prime victim: she is set on fire and burnt badly – but her child turns out to be a boy. The play revels in the contradictions between indigenous culture and global capitalist consumerism: when Ibrahima seeks contact with the Earth Spirit, her mobile goes off. The name of the local bodyguard Monday suggests Defoe's key Western tale of successful colonisation. In this case, however, it is colonisation gone hybrid that has generated no end of contradictions. Harking back to the good old days of his Poro tribal roots (mandatory fornication and cannibalism), Monday is flogged for drinking and also wears a t-shirt that announces 'Dip Me in Honey and Throw Me to the Lesbians'. Eventually, Ibrahima has a boy and Keith, who may have interfered with Laura after a drinking bout, is presumably killed by the Diesel Boys, a gang of Muslim marauders. Having learnt the lessons of futility and having accepted the incongruities of Tambekistan, Laura marries Monday, to be replaced by yet another enthusiastic, this time Anglo-Indian girl. Being a pragmatist, Bean argues, Monday is the least ridiculous character in a ridiculous world.[14] Tambia is going to continue to be with or without the British NGO arrivals, a country where, as Keith puts it, 'the last war's fucked everything, and the next war will fuck everything else' (p. 145).

Honeymoon Suite (2004)

Bean's debut on the main stage of the Royal Court Theatre on 8 January 2004, directed by Paul Miller, is another departure, replacing his 'blokey' work plays with a literary marriage comedy well established in the West End. Critics seemed divided, but all of them noted the rich dramatic ancestry of Alan Ayckbourn, Neil Simon (Aleks Sierz), Tom Stoppard (Kate Bassett), Caryl Churchill's *Hotel* (Paul Taylor) and Albee's *Three Tall Women* (Nicholas de Jongh).[15] The three-act structure of temporal ellipses is similar to *Under the Whaleback* and pointing forward to *Harvest* – Bean describes it as a set of separate one-act plays punctured by gaps. This time, however, the plays are woven into a temporal palimpsest that has three stages in the development of the relationship between Eddie and Irene, from 1955 to the 1980s and, finally, the present – a device that only gradually dawns on the audience. The setting is a Bridlington seaside hotel bedroom, and both the device of the co-presence of the actors and the old-fashioned portrayal of bourgeois decay recall J. B. Priestley or Alan Ayckbourn – a singularly alien presence in the Royal Court. This time, Bean not only expands the class range of his characters and his technical ingenuity, he also escapes from his signature male ghettoes. The tentative unity of the newly-weds unsurprisingly diverges – in the 1980s he is a bankrupt arsonist and she a night-school adulteress and, finally, she has become a wealthy and successful Labour baroness while he is solitary and suicidal. His comment to her sums up his resentment: 'Council are tekking me to court. It needs new guttering. I can afford the guttering, but not the scaffolding to put it up. Your lot, Labour. None of them have ever done a day's work in their lives' (p. 230). While Bean has varied his writing technique and personnel, his focus is yet again on masculinity in crisis – at the losing end after decades of empowering women.

Harvest (2005)

If *Honeymoon Suite* seemed slightly derivative of established comedy writers, the three-hour, three-act 'comic epic' (Bean), *Harvest* revisited *Under the Whaleback*. Expanding the ellipses in the temporal structure rendered the play less realist and more experimental, as well as more expansively representative of rural life in the UK.[16] Again, the critical response to Wilson Milam's production for the Royal Court (opening on 2 September 2005) was mostly positive, stressing Bean's intimate knowledge of the subject and arguing that, for a main stage Royal Court play, the pro-farming message seemed 'refreshingly unaligned'.[17] Whereas the east Yorkshire pig farm is a stable spatial setting, the temporal gaps take the plot from 1914 to 2008, with the central character William as a link, aged nineteen in the first scene and 109 in the final one. The second Bean play to open on the theatre's main stage, its affirmative depiction of rural Englishness seems unusual for the Royal Court. He parades two brothers (William and Albert), rivals for the attentions of Maudie and exposed to the vagaries of two world wars that render William legless and Albert accidentally shot dead by a female neighbour. Quirky characters are paraded, such as Lord Agar in an Inuit bearskin coat, or Titch, a crude new pig man in Status Quo jeans gear. The farm is taken over by a niece (Laura) and a German Luftwaffe pilot (Stefan) who is gradually assimilated into Yorkshire-ness. Stefan having died from emphysema, the foul-mouthed Titch takes over, and answers Stef's farming expert's questions about his qualifications in a job interview with a typically blunt: 'Fuck off! I like pigs' (p. 61). Bean sets out to take the more conventional 'in-yer-face' staging of a crime-ridden and morally corrupt country from its conventional urban settings to the countryside – particularly in the last scene. When the farm is attacked by two thugs – one of them grotesquely abject and the other one surprisingly knowledgeable about food processing – the old man kills one of them, whereas the other continues the farming tradition as new 'pig man'. Bean clearly takes the rugged Yorkshire farm to be metonymic for Englishness and the Harrison pig farming team to represent residual 'family values' to be preserved from the ills of an abject modernity. As William says, 'I don't wanna be the Harrison who sold his inheritance and left the Harrisons with nowt to work. If I do that they'll tek me portrait off the landing and stick it in the scullery.' When Agar asks incredulously whether he really has a portrait he replies: 'I thought you of all people'd spot a metaphor' (p. 53). In the play's final lines, the 'ancient' William becomes the spokesman of an ironic 'gentlemanliness' in pig farming:

> Could you make love to your wife? [. . .] You could adore her; worship her; and make her feel beautiful and blessed and glad she married a pig farmer and not James Bond. (p. 87)

England People Very Nice (2009)

England People Very Nice is Bean's most ambitious, most successful and at the same time his most controversial play to date. Premiered on the largest stage of the National Theatre on 4 February 2009, it played to packed houses. It may be seen as part of Nicholas Hytner's agenda for the National Theatre, offering 'a promiscuous combination of the popular, the political and the classical'.[18] In this instance, Hytner's multi-national theatre, reaching out to younger, ethnically more diverse audiences, however, provoked angry comment from the multi-ethnic east London community, when, for the first time ever, a platform discussion at the National Theatre was invaded, by teacher Keith Kinsella and Tower Hamlets playwright Ismail Hussein, calling Bean 'racist'. Hussein had previously articulated his criticism, arguing that the play 'simply reinforces racist myths more commonly found in the gutter press'[19] and threatening the season sponsor Travelex with boycott action. Similarly, Anwar Akhtar, the former chief executive of the Cultural Industries Development Agency who has also held positions at Arts Council England and the Rich Mix Cultural Foundation, deemed the play 'anti-multicultural', and 'infuriating' and noted stereotypes of 'Muslim radicals, extremists, assorted fruit cakes and bigots from the downright evil to the "look at me" theatricals of preacher Abu Hamza al-Masri, aka Captain Hook himself'. John Bull called it a 'confused play, unclear in its intentions, and by no means consensual in its reception', but also argued that 'it is precisely this lack of ideological clarity that makes it such an important event in England's National Theatre'.[20]

The play has a framing device: it is cast as an amateur performance by immigrants in detention – therefore its crude humour can easily be laid at the feet of popular perceptions of immigration rather than being equated with the playwright's humour.[21] We do indeed get racist one-liners as this one ascribed to Laurie: 'That's the worst mix – Irish and Jewish. You end up with a family of pissed-up burglars run by a clever accountant' (p. 77) – without, however, an indignant audience response on behalf of either the Jews or the Irish. Bean argues that the outrage was primarily a political move; he points out a positive review in the *Bangla Times* and enthusiastic response from an ethnically expanded National Theatre audience.[22] Audience reaction to the 'single story' of ethnic stereotypes is clearly a measure of the confidence and vulnerability of the ethnic group at the receiving end of the joke – and some Muslim communities continue to be sensitive. Interestingly, the frame narrative had already foreseen the kind of criticism Anwar Akhtar voiced with reference to the play's Abu Hamza character – clearly a yellow press stereotype regularly encountered in the pages of the *Sun* and the *Star*:

> **Taher** The group turned my imam into a stereotype – mad, blind, hooks for hands. The imam will be better without the beard and the beard wig.
>
> **Tatyana** It's not a stereotype, they've all got beards. (p. 12)

The framing device clearly highlights the performative aspects of ethnicity. The fact that a professional multi-ethnic cast plays a multi-ethnic amateur cast playing a set of multi-ethnic characters results in a palimpsestic 'colourdiverse' array of multiple subjectivities. This gesture towards instable, performative subject positions contributes to the play's essential point, namely that ethnic and cultural identities are subject to permanent change and prone to being used for politically unsavoury reasons. 'Tribal' cultural and religious identity is rendered as a perverse joke if pitted against universalised Western values (liberal, Enlightenment, rationalist). The play makes this point in the comic epic mode familiar from *Under the Whaleback* or *Harvest*. The scene is a Spitalfields pub, with the pub landlords Laurie and Ida as trans-historical chorus. We witness a recurring, simple 'Romeo and Juliet' pattern between a 'boy lover' (Norfolk Danny, Carlo, Aaron, Mushi) and a 'girl lover' (Camille, Mary, Ruth, Deborah), an assimilationist pattern variously enacted among waves of East End immigrants, from Huguenot Protestants, Jews and Irish Catholics to Bangladeshi Muslims. The play's conflicting narratives are first, a celebration of hyphenated identity, hybridity and ethnic diversity, and second a destructive play of caricatured essentialisms and a satire on cultural fundamentalisms that establish civic Englishness as limiting diversity. Successful integration of immigrants invariably enriches a culture: the Huguenot Camille invents denim jeans, the Jew Aaron invents the biro and the Bangladeshi Mushi invents chicken tikka masala. However, both integration and the ideal of East End Englishness are not without problems:

> **Laurie** How's a Muslim woman gonna integrate round here?
> **Ida** Get your arse tattooed, a crack habit and seven kids by seven dads! (p. 94)

The key witness for the pattern of assimilation and the universalist civic Englishness is Daniel Defoe:

> I only infer that an Englishman, of all men, ought not to despise foreigners as such, and I think the inference is just, since what they are to-day, we were yesterday, and to-morrow they will be like us. (Daniel Defoe, 'The True-Born Englishman', 1701)

Bean is clear about this: 'Us' is diverse rather than monolithic and also includes the assimilation towards 'tattooed arses, crack habits and seven kids by seven dads'. Bean's Englishness, therefore, is far from sentimental or idealised, and when he is charged with disparaging ethnic minorities and reiterating dominant ethnic discourses, one may look at his equally stereotypical Englishmen from Yorkshire and elsewhere. Criticism that requires balance in humour has no concept of how comedy works.

When Mushi – just arrived in London – sucks up to the new host nation exhibiting the alarming eponymous linguistic inadequacy (**Mushi** 'England people very nice!'), the Constable's bland relativist reply ('There's good and bad in all', p. 74), however, does not seem entirely flat and ironic. In the framing device, the play can meta-theatrically reflect on the simplicity of its own underlying pattern, ending on its very limitations and drawbacks by highlighting the persistence of Taher's stereotypes:

> **Taher**   The play is like four Romeo and Juliets, but what does it matter? I worry we have made the play too light [. . .] why is it so important?
>
> **Philippa**   We discussed this during research. The truest measure of racial and cultural integration in any society is the rate of inter-marriage [. . .]
>
> **Taher**   Yes. Only love can free humanity from the shackles of history. And that is exactly what those bastard Israelis will never understand! (p. 69)

The disavowal of religion also transcends historical, ethnic and cultural specificity, as the quip 'There is no hell! Nor heaven! This [Bethnal Green] is the only paradise any of you will ever know' is repeated in a variety of historical and ethnic contexts (pp. 30, 63, 85). Variously, Bean's spokespersons can be detected in the play, such as publican Laurie, who argues that 'love laughs at the manufactured made-up madness of religion and culture' (p. 113). An 'objective correlative' of this madness is the beard of asylum seeker Iqbal, who is cast as the mad imam, but subsequently shaves it off and puts on a beard wig ('The reason I am seeking asylum in this country is because Hamas want to kill me for not having a beard'). Beards are OK as performative props and the subject of laughter, but not as divisive essences of a cultural identity. Iqbal testifies to the global attraction of Western liberalism:

> I left Yemen to seek asylum in England. I am not here to turn England into Yemen. If England ever does become Yemen, I will have to seek refuge in another country. (p. 123)

Clearly, anti-assimilation positions are the butt of Bean's satire. Having briefly paraded a number of mad ethnic purists and isolationists, Bean trusts that yet another anti-integration speech by a radical imam (p. 120) will be equally futile. Typically, the imam's feeble attempt at a joke ('*Jew York*') misfires in the performative inadequacy of having to explain it. As Osama bin-Laden's close ally Aymen al-Zawahiri argued in 2005:

> The Sharee'ah brought down by Allah is the Sharee'ah which must be followed. [. . .] it is a matter that can only be received very seriously because it doesn't accept jokes.[23]

Essentialists are no fun, culture is farce, but Bethnal Green humour is Englishness universalised. Or, as a philippic by the English director Philippa has it: 'It's my English humour not your Gaza Strip humour!' (p. 72).

Summary

This passage from *England People Very Nice* raises interesting questions about the author's position in the discourse about multi-cultural Britain. First of all, humour and satire seem particularly problematic and dangerous in intercultural discourse. As Susanne Reichl and Mark Stein have argued, in the post-colonial situation there has been a curious piety, silence and reluctance on the part of cultural criticism to even address questions of humour.[24] Both Nicholas Hytner and Bean himself have defended the 'un-embedded' plays, arguing that Bean's 'state-of-the-nation' comedy is about the

English rather than about an ethnic community.[25] The pro-hybridity position, it seems, is more consensually articulated by more 'embedded' playwrights. After all, in 1981, Hanif Kureishi's *Borderline* was tactically positioned to attract the Asian community to the Royal Court. Ethnically diverse 'specialists' (*Goodness Gracious Me*, BBC Radio 4 and BBC2, 1996–2001) can be trusted with ethnic humour – Gurinder Chadha, Hanif Kureishi, Ayub Khan-Din, Tanika Gupta, Omid Djalili or Meera Syal. Bean, however, is attacked by John Bull as 'an asylum tourist in a strange country'.[26]

Becoming increasingly outspoken in political and public affairs, Bean's demythologised view of the lower classes seems at odds with nostalgic visions popularised by Ken Loach, and the sentimentalism profitably exploited by Lee Hall. Currently, he is formally and socially versatile in his comic epics, with clever verbal and structural designs, with aspirations towards larger themes and audiences as well as with his anti-multiculturalist dissent. Arguing that 'we are all racist' and that we 'have to manage our racism', he challenges the consensus voiced by leading socialist veteran playwrights such as Caryl Churchill or David Hare – disparagingly referred to by Bean as 'the Hampstead Hamas'.[27] Generally, he is no formal innovator and professes to like the well-made play and to not understand Martin Crimp, but Bean is a significant voice in contemporary British theatre – one that would have deserved a mention in recent editions on contemporary British theatre and drama.[28]

This is not to say that his plays on Englishness are unproblematic. The simplistic Huguenot–Irish–Jewish–Bangladeshi parallelism in *England People Very Nice* irons out the cultural specificity of all of these groups, when the fact that the Bangladeshi Muslims get the most extensive coverage by far in Act 4 of *England People Very Nice* implicitly acknowledges the special problems of current issues of communal multiculturalism. Bean participates in what Edward Said has described as the European fear of Muslim culture. Finally, when Bean describes himself as a 'liberal hawk' this is a contradiction in terms, as liberalism must necessarily be tolerant of intolerance.[29] Kwame Anthony Appiah makes a similar point in his championing of 'partial', rooted cosmopolitanism of continuing conversation and tentative relativism. It is precisely the absence of this conversation, however, that Bean laments.[30] From the perspective of a cultural ethnographer, Appiah maintains, genital 'cutting' is defensible, reminding us that erroneous universal moral claims often mask local preferences. Appiah argues that the global neofundamentalists are championing a malign universalism without toleration or cultural awareness: 'They have no need of national loyalties or cultural traditions.'[31] Far from being manufactured madness, then, cultural practice is inevitable and needs protection from universalism without tolerance. The community of 'free-born Englishmen' praised in Bean's plays may be an entirely 'imagined community' (Benedict Anderson) and the paternalism of education – subaltern Londoners in need of a lesson in integration – may be misplaced.

Bean is an 'in-yer-face' comedian. His jokes are his trademark, and he has said that he is a comedy writer, not a playwright or poet. The punchline, 'the full stop', is what dissociates him from the overlapping dialogue of a writer like David Mamet, whose (fittingly 'blokey') *Glengarry Glen Ross* he admires.[32] Unlike Bean himself, I would argue that his 'black' or 'gallows' humour is the very core of his aesthetics, as it acts as corrosive to political orthodoxy and social consensus. Bean himself is wary of a humour that rendered not only his 'multi-culturalist' plays controversial, prompting the rejection of a play satirising suicide bombers by the Soho Theatre,[33] but also preventing a BBC radio adaptation of *Smack Family Robinson*:

> I get criticised for having too many jokes in my plays. It's something I've had to look at. I don't want to give people an excuse not to take me seriously. I always want to say the unpalatable thing – that's what fascinates me. For example, I want to know whether women wearing full burkas are allowed to drive big lorries.[34]

It seems to me that Bean should take his own jokes more seriously. First of all, the laughter and stereotypes shared with an audience are seismographic. Christie Davies argues:

> To become angry about jokes and to seek to censor them
> because they impinge on sensitive issues is about as sensible as
> smashing a thermometer because it reveals how hot it is.[35]

Attacking the vice and folly of immorality and multicultural relativism, Bean's humour is clearly powerfully satiric as he seeks to reinforce pride in dominant British culture. At his best, however, Bean laughs at the power centre from the weak margins, as he self-deprecatingly manages to attack and interrogate its own moral ground through black humour, that is: hopeless wit and ridicule in the face of despair. His plays fulfil the classic functions of humour, some of them problematic: psychic expenditure, cognitive rehearsal, spiritual equipoise, group cohesion, reduction of anxiety, control of deviance, warding off danger, rebellion against authority, relief from routine, defusing tension, overcoming taboos (anti-social safety valve), reinforcing centrality: marginalisation.[36] On some occasions, Bean's comedy provides the disparaging laughter of superiority, but we may also see in his work an attack on the corrosive piety of politically correct positions and the rigidity of global fundamentalisms, a non-evaluative celebration of cosmopolitan laughter as absolute comedy.

Primary Sources

Works by Richard Bean

Plays One: The Mentalists, Under the Whaleback, The God Botherers (London: Oberon Books, 2006).

Plays Two: Toast, Smack Family Robinson, Mr. England, Honeymoon Suite (London: Oberon Books, 2007).

Plays Three: Harvest, In the Club, The English Game, Up on Roof (London: Oberon Books, 2009).

England People Very Nice (London: Oberon Books, 2009).

Pub Quiz is Life (London: Oberon Books, 2009).

Secondary Sources

Anderson, Benedict, *Imagined Communities: Reflections on the Origins and Spread of Nationalism* (London: Verso, 1991).

Appiah, Kwame Anthony, *Cosmopolitanism: Ethics in a World of Strangers* (New York: Norton, 2007).

Baluch, Lalayn, 'Arts Chief Akhtar Criticises "Right Wing" Bean Play', *The Stage*, 5 May 2009 <http://www.thestage.co.uk/news/newsstory.php/24309/arts-chief-akhtar-criticises-right-wing>

Bean, Richard, 'House of Games / The Big Fellah', e-mail newsletter, 25 August 2010.

—, Personal Interview, Hull, 3 March 2010.

Bradley, Jack, 'Introduction', in Richard Bean, *Plays Two*, pp. 7–13.

Bull, John, '*England People Very Nice*: Intercultural Confusions at the National Theatre, London', in Werner Huber et al. (eds), *Staging Interculturality* (Trier: WVT, 2010), pp. 123–43.

Campbell, Christopher, 'Introduction', in Richard Bean, *Plays Three*, pp. 7–9.

Cavendish, Dominic, 'Richard Bean: Blurred Boundaries', *Daily Telegraph*, 10 May 2008 <http://www.telegraph.co.uk/culture/theatre/drama/3673273/Richard-Bean-blurred-boundaries.html>

Costa, Maddy, 'Truth and Taboos', *Guardian*, 28 January 2009 <http://www.guardian.co.uk/stage/2009/jan/28/richard-bean-taboo-playwright-theatre>

Davies, Christie, *Ethnic Humour Around the World* (Bloomington, IN: Indiana UP, 1990).

Deeney, John, 'National Causes / Moral Clauses?: The National Theatre, Young People and Citizenship', *Research in Drama Education*, Vol. 12, No. 3 (2007), pp. 331–47.

Devine, Harriet, 'Richard Bean', in *Looking Back: Playwrights at the Royal Court* (London: Faber & Faber, 2006), pp. 43–53.

Holdsworth, Nadine (ed.), *A Concise Companion to Contemporary British and Irish Drama* (Malden, MA: Blackwell, 2008).

Hussein, Ismail, 'Why the National Theatre's New Play is Racist and Offensive', *Guardian Theatre Blog*, 13 February 2009 <http://www.guardian.co.uk/stage/theatreblog/2009/feb/13/national-theatre-play-racist>

Luckhurst, Mary (ed.), *A Companion to Modern British and Irish Drama* (Oxford: Blackwell, 2006).

Nathan, John, 'Interview: Richard Bean', *Jewish Chronicle*, 29 January 2009 <http://www.thejc.com/arts/arts-interviews/interview-richard-bean>

Palmer, Jerry, *Taking Humour Seriously* (London: Routledge, 1994).

Parekh, Bhikhu, *Rethinking Multiculturalism: Cultural Diversity and Political Theory* (Cambridge, MA: Harvard UP, 2000).

Reichl, Susanne and Mark Stein (eds), *Cheeky Fictions: Laughter and the Postcolonial* (Amsterdam: Rodopi, 2005).

Shantz, Jeff, 'Richard Bean', in Gabrielle H. Cody and Evert Sprinchorn (eds), *Columbia Encyclopedia of Modern Drama* (New York: Columbia UP, 2007), pp. 125–6.

Sierz, Aleks, 'theartsdesk Q&A: Playwright Richard Bean', *The Arts Desk website*, 20 September 2009 <http://www.theartsdesk.com/index.php?option=com_k2&view =item&id=186:playwright-richard-bean-interview&Itemid=80>
—, 'Richard Bean in Conversation with Aleks Sierz', in Christoph Henke and Martin Middeke (eds), *Drama and/after Postmodernism* (Trier: WVT, 2006), pp. 351–61.
—, 'Beyond Timidity', *PAJ: A Journal of Performance and Art*, Vol. 27, No. 3 (2005), pp. 55–61.

Notes

1. Aleks Sierz, 'Richard Bean in Conversation', p. 352. See also Devine, 'Richard Bean'.
2. Sierz, 'Richard Bean in Conversation', p. 354.
3. Aleks Sierz, 'Beyond Timidity', pp. 55–61.
4. Richard Bean, Personal Interview.
5. Sierz, 'Richard Bean in Conversation', p. 355. In the Personal Interview, Bean said that Morrie is based on the tall tales of his former hairdresser and Ted on a crank who produced a video, arguing that Hitler is a Plymouth-born Englishman still alive in 1956.
6. Richard Bean, 'House of Games / The Big Fellah'.
7. John Nathan, 'Interview: Richard Bean'.
8. The frequency of the word 'England' or its derivatives in Bean's titles has been noted by Christopher Campbell, 'Introduction', p. 9.
9. Jack Bradley, 'Introduction', pp. 7–9. At the time, the Royal Court was in the West End while its Sloane Square base was being refurbished.
10. Sheridan Morley, *The Spectator, Theatre Record*, Vol. XVIII, No. 4 (1999), p. 210.
11. *Theatre Record*, Vol. XXIII, No. 8 (2003), pp. 476–80.
12. Dominic Cavendish, 'Richard Bean: Blurred Boundaries'.
13. *Theatre Record*, Vol. XXIII, No. 25/26 (2003), p. 1595.
14. Bean, Personal Interview.
15. *Theatre Record*, Vol. XXIV, No. 1–2 (2004), pp. 48–53.
16. Sierz, 'Richard Bean in Conversation', p. 357. He confirmed during the Personal Interview that the tripartite temporal structure was his way of avoiding the problem of providing a satisfying closure.
17. Michael Coveney, *Independent, Theatre Record*, Vol. XXV, No. 18 (2005), p. 1125.
18. John Deeney, 'National Causes / Moral Clauses?', p. 333.
19. Ismail, Hussein, *Guardian Theatre Blog*.
20. John Bull, *'England People Very Nice'*, p. 130.
21. In the Personal Interview, Bean called the framing device 'absolutely crucial. The key thing about the framing device is that it allows for extreme stereotypes because these guys know nothing about the Irish, the Jewish, or indeed, the English.'

22. Bean, Personal Interview.

23. Quoted in Appiah, *Cosmopolitanism*, p. 146. Bean has directly attacked sharia law in Britain (Nathan, 'Interview').

24. They even ask if humour is 'an abomination in postcolonial studies?' (Susanne Reichl and Mark Stein, 'Introduction', *Cheeky Fictions*, p. 2).

25. Nick Hytner, quoted in Nathan, 'Interview', 2009; Bean, quoted in Maddy Costa, 'Truth and Taboos'.

26. Bull, 'Intercultural Confusions', p. 141.

27. Bean, Personal Interview; quoted by Bull, 'Intercultural Confusions', p. 140.

28. Bean is a glaring omission in the recent collections edited by Mary Luckhurst, *A Companion to Modern British and Irish Drama*, and Nadine Holdsworth, *A Concise Companion to Contemporary British and Irish Drama*.

29. Bhikhu Parekh, *Rethinking Multiculturalism*, p. 113.

30. Bean, quoted in Nathan, 'Interview'.

31. Appiah, *Cosmopolitanism*, p. 140.

32. Bean, Personal Interview.

33. See Nathan, 'Interview'.

34. Aleks Sierz, 'theartsdesk Q&A: Playwright Richard Bean'.

35. Christie Davies, *Ethnic Humour Around the World*, p. 9.

36. Jerry Palmer, *Taking Humour Seriously*, pp. 57ff.

2 GREGORY BURKE

David Pattie

Gagarin Way; The Straits; On Tour; Black Watch; Hoors

Introduction

Gregory Burke has written two of the most significant plays of the early twenty-first century: *Gagarin Way* (Traverse, 2001) and *Black Watch* (National Theatre of Scotland, 2006). The impact of his work is even more notable when we consider that not only was *Gagarin Way* his first play text, but that prior to writing it he had no relation to the theatre at all. Burke was born into a working-class Scottish family in Dumfermline, Fife, in 1968: his father worked in the naval dockyard in Rosyth, on the Firth of Forth. Burke grew up in the working-class communities of Rosyth and Dumfermline; his residence in Scotland was interrupted in the late 1970s – his father was posted to Gibraltar for six years, and the family returned to Scotland in 1984, when Burke was sixteen. Burke went to the University of Stirling to study economics, but he found the experience alienating; he felt out of place (as one of the few working-class undergraduates), and was disciplined after a violent encounter with another student. After dropping out of Stirling, Burke took a number of poorly paid, menial jobs; these carried him through his twenties:

> The reason I did all these rubbish jobs is because I had to – there was no choice. I worked on the production line in a factory, as a dishwasher, as a porter in a hospital – all sorts. Never again. You meet brilliant people in these jobs and you have a brilliant laugh and sometimes you think, why are you here as well. That experience influences everything I do now, it teaches you to get on with it.[1]

One of the things that Burke 'just got on with' was the first draft of *Gagarin Way*: he has said that he found himself writing drama, rather than prose, because he couldn't be bothered describing things (a typically ironic self-judgement). The play was sent to the Traverse Theatre, Scotland's most significant new writing venue: this venue produced the play (in conjunction with the National Theatre's Springboard scheme for new playwrights), and Burke found himself, almost instantly, a successful playwright. He later said that 'I wouldn't have tried to write anything ever again if it hadn't been put on by the Traverse'.[2] The production marked the beginning of a long association with John Tiffany, who directed *Gagarin Way*. Tiffany has gone on to direct two more of Burke's plays – *The Straits* (Paines Plough, 2003) and *Black Watch* – one of the few modern plays that can properly, with no sense of hyperbole, be described as phenomenally successful. It toured extensively and visited London repeatedly. Burke has also written two other full-length plays: *On Tour* (Royal Court, 2005) and *Hoors* (Traverse, 2009). In addition, he has written a number of works for young actors: *Debt* (National Theatre, 2004), *Liar* (Galway Youth Theatre, 2006) and *Battery Farm* (Oran Mor, 2010).

The Plays

Gagarin Way (2001)

This rather bald summary of Burke's life does not really convey the influence of his background on his work: a serious omission, given that Burke's great strength as a writer is his ability to link minutely observed examinations of social (and predominantly male) behaviour with larger cultural, social and political changes. In particular, he is fascinated by the way in which apparently immutable social structures can simply be swept away, apparently overnight, leaving those caught up in those structures bereft, and unable to respond effectively. As Burke put it in the Preface to *Gagarin Way*, which was first performed on 12 July 2001, directed by John Tiffany:

> Economics decides the fate of people, not their politicians.
> Governments are powerless when up against a multi-national,
> the vagaries of the stock market and history. But the people
> remain. That's the constant. We remain and we find other
> things to keep ourselves amused. (p. iv)

This process was something that Burke experienced at first hand. As
noted above, the family returned to Fife in 1984 – a crucial period in
the recent history of that area, and of Scotland: the heavy industries
that had sustained the Scottish economy for most of the nineteenth
and much of the twentieth century were in terminal decline (indeed,
many of them disappeared during the decade); and in their place
much of the old industrial areas of the country became the preferred
location for a number of global corporations, mostly specialising in
newer, hi-tech industries such as IT. These new companies, however,
part as they were of larger, multinational corporations, were prone to
disappear as their parent companies found cheaper, more flexible
workforces elsewhere: an economy which had seemed rooted, however
damagingly, in particular communities, organised and socialised in
particular ways, was replaced by an economy where everything was
unsure: where the firm that employed you might very well disappear
at the first indication that the economic grass might be greener
elsewhere. At the same time, in a profoundly ironic development not
lost on Burke or his characters, something changed in the state of
Scotland. The country rejected, more and more clearly, the
Conservative governments of the 1980s and early 1990s; at the same
time, and decisively influenced by the country's rejection of
Thatcherism, a groundswell of Scottish opinion built up behind the
idea that the country should take some measure of control over its own
destiny. When the Labour Party came to power in 1997, they held a
referendum in Scotland; and the Scottish electorate voted for partial
self-government. Perhaps uncharitably, one might say that the new
parliament gave Scots the illusion of control over their own destinies,
at a time when economic control over the country had moved
offshore.[3]

Gagarin Way explores this paradox. The central action of the play (in which two disaffected factory workers kidnap an executive, finding, to their considerable surprise, that he is not Japanese but from the same part of Scotland as they are) takes place in the storeroom of one of the new types of factories that had replaced the old heavy industries, in Fife and elsewhere. The action takes place against the backdrop of the early years of the new parliament, but its powers are mocked; real power, the play argues, is not located in any national government but in international capital. Against these overwhelming, ever-changing forces, Burke opposes two representatives of a rooted Scottishness. The two kidnappers – Gary and Eddie – are versions of two Scottish character types; Gary is the militant left-wing activist, the kind lauded in plays by Bill Bryden (*Willie Rough*, 1972) and in the work of companies like 7:84 and Wildcat in the 1970s and 1980s. Eddie, who begins the play arguing about Sartre with the security guard Tom, is an updated version of the lad o' pairts – the working-class autodidact, whose native intelligence and thirst for knowledge allows him to debate with his apparent betters on equal terms. Indeed, it could be said that the man they kidnap, Frank, is himself another archetype – the Red Scot, to borrow Christopher Harvie's term:[4] the man who can flourish only outside of the confines of his native land.

However, there is more to the play than an encounter between varying archetypes of Scottishness: the territory under each of the characters has shifted – the apparently solid working-class culture that could support the activism of a Gary has disappeared: the cultural framework that would prize the efforts of an autodidact like Eddie no longer exists; and Frank is not the driven, entrepreneurial Scotsman on the make, but an easily replaceable apparatchik, shuffled around the globe at the company's behest. The activist and the autodidact are, in their various ways, figures of resistance: the activist seeks a better world for himself and his fellows, and the autodidact uses learning as a way of contesting his place in society. As Frank points out, neither can flourish in a world which, by its very nature, closes down any chance of opposition: not through oppression, but by extending its logic through every part of society. Global capitalism, essentially, neutralises opposition by making everyone caught up in it complicit in its workings:

> **Frank** If you want me to say I've exploited and robbed
> honest, working people? Caused my fair share of
> suffering? Destroyed the environment? Fine. I've done it.
> So has everybody else. You want arrogance? Greed?
> Stupidity? Look around. There's no need for defences
> when something's everywhere. (p. 86)

What is worse is that both the representatives of traditional Scottish radical values are compromised from the start. Gary is an ineffectual revolutionary; the autodidact Eddie, far from possessing the requisite attachment to Enlightenment humanism, is a cynical, destructive nihilist. The welter of violence that ends the play (Eddie, who has been clear throughout about the attraction that violence holds for him, knifes both Frank and Tom) achieves nothing. Conceived initially as a grand, anarchistic gesture that would, through its very audacity, inspire others, Frank's murder is rendered the more horrible because it is completely drained of significance – a sign as empty as the road sign that gives the play its name. The strongly left-wing working-class community of Lumphinnans named one of the village's streets Gagarin Way to commemorate the flight of the first Soviet cosmonaut; the Soviet Union has gone, the Fife coalfields have gone, and the little communist enclave in Lumphinnans has disappeared. All that is left is the empty signifier of the road sign: Gagarin Way, in the context of early-twenty-first-century Scotland, is a meaningless name, a road that no longer leads anywhere.

The Straits (2003)

Burke's next play, *The Straits*, was first produced by Paines Plough on 1 August 2003: auspiciously for Burke's development as a writer, the company was led at that time by Vicky Featherstone (who later on became the artistic director of the National Theatre of Scotland). The play was directed by John Tiffany; interestingly, given the importance of the movement sequences in *Black Watch*, the production also employed Steven Hoggett from the company Frantic Assembly as a movement coach. According to Aleks Sierz, his input gave the original production a 'dreamlike feel'; as with *Black Watch*, this provided an interesting and effective counterpoint to the scrupulous realism of the dialogue.[5] *The Straits* is set in Gibraltar in 1982: according to Burke, the play is about being in a gang, and feeling part of a group. And in times of crisis, people create a threat even when there isn't one, and this reinforces their identity. The reinforced identity also perpetuates the threat. If you feel besieged, as people in Gibraltar did during the Falklands conflict, you lash out.[6]

If *Gagarin Way* is about the dissolution of social bonds, *The Straits* is about their formation; however, just as Burke's first play casts a rather jaundiced eye over the Scottish communities that are disappearing, so his second play is a harsh analysis of one of the strongest social bonds tying new or emerging societies together – national identity.

The Straits is a coming-of-age tale: a teenager, Darren, new to Gibraltar at the play's beginning, has problems in establishing himself; but by the play's end he is an accepted part of the British community. To prove himself, he has to do something which can be accepted by his peers as in the best interests of that community: once he has done this, he has proved himself, not only to his peers, but to himself. He gains their acceptance by killing a native Gibraltarian, apparently by accident, although the way in which he and his friends talk about the event is disturbingly callous:

> **Doink**   Silly spic shouldn't have been scuba-divin at night.
>   He wouldn't have drowned otherwise.
> **Doink** *looks away from* **Darren**. **Darren** *has to look away too.*
> *They are suppressing giggles.*
> **Jock**   It ain't fuckin funny.
> *They laugh.*
> **Darren**   Oh come on. It is a bit funny. (p. 94)

Such callousness is even more worrying, given that the action of the play takes place against the backdrop of the Falklands War – which, for the teenagers in the play, is a conflict conducted in a way that is exactly analogous to Darren's actions. Darren demonstrates his suitability as a community member by indiscriminately killing a Spaniard: Britain rediscovers its greatness by reasserting its military might, even if that means destroying Argentinean ships that pose no danger to British troops. As Doink puts it:

> It goes all the way back, don't it? England an fightin an that. War's what we do, innit. What we do best. Don't matter who we fight either. Spics or Germans or French or whatever. Reckon we'll always be at war with someone and we always win. (p. 34)

Darren has proved himself worthy, not only by the terms laid out by his contemporaries, but in the terms defined for him (and for them) by the history of their nation. The Spaniard's death is a necessary sacrifice, to enable this particular part of the Gibraltar community to accept and welcome someone new.

Burke's portrait of this community is however rather more nuanced than the discussion so far might suggest. Darren uses his part in the Spaniard's death as a way of turning his back on parts of his life that he would like to forget (he was bullied at his school in England). For him, accepting the identity laid out for him by Doink is simpler than coming to terms with the more painful parts of his life. For the other male characters, an identity forged in conflict similarly simplifies and clarifies their experience of the world; but, as with Darren, it does so at a cost. The imperial role that Doink tries to claim for the group and for his country no longer exists: it is an identity that has to be laboriously and painfully constructed. The male characters gleefully participate in acts of violence against the local population (who are treated as surrogate Argentineans); they ape military behaviour, putting themselves through the kind of training regimes used to inure troops to the hardships of conflict; they police themselves and each other for the slightest sign of weakness towards the enemy – as Doink says to Jock: 'You've been actin like you'd rather be hangin about with spics ever since you started playin football with them' (p. 49). The attractions of this simplified version of their identities is obvious for each of the male characters: it gives them a place in the world, it gives them an easily accessible group identity, and it gives them ready-made enemies against whom they can define themselves. By the play's end, the teenagers have accepted that the only way that they, as young British men, can deal with the world is through violence; the problem is that this acceptance traps them, allowing them only a very small repertoire of responses to the rest of the world, and the rest of their lives.

On Tour (2005)

Doink in *The Straits* might think of England as primarily a nation of fighters: H, in Burke's next play (*On Tour*, co-produced by the Royal Court and the Liverpool Everyman, first performed on 7 October 2005, and directed by Matt Wilde) has a different view of his country's inherent nature:

> Our history. We're a nation of criminals. Always have been. Outlaws. The highwayman. Pirates. They're the folk heroes of this country. (*Beat*) You look back to the Elizabethans [. . .] people are startin to explore the unknown parts of the world. Some countries, they used to send people out to convert the infidel. They were doin it for God. Not us, though. This country was only ever interested in the bottom line. (p. 37)

H, rather like Eddie in *Gagarin Way* and Doink in *The Straits*, has chosen a worldview that allows him to justify his actions, no matter how callous they might be. Unlike those two characters, though, the rationale he has adopted leaves him without the dubious consolations that Eddie and Doink are able to call on (in Eddie's case, an absolute cynicism that downgrades everything; in Doink's, an ersatz community based on the idea of defensive violence). If the logic of H's argument is taken to its conclusion, then it leaves him in a world where there can be no such thing as trust or communal endeavour; a world that is governed by the simplest, most basic version of market forces: that anything that turns a profit is by its very nature worthwhile.

The plot of *On Tour* is simple. H, a criminal who smuggles goods across Europe, using the chaos created by English football fans to disguise his activities, recruits Daz, an ex-soldier he meets in prison, to help him steal drugs and money from Ray, a dealer with whom H used to do business. By the play's end, however, we have learned that Ray, who used to work on his own, now works for a cartel run by ex-members of the IRA; Daz has, in fact, been employed by the cartel to kill Ray – but at the play's end, following the logic of the bottom line, he ties up both Ray and H, and escapes with the money and drugs. The mechanism that drives the story is that of the double-cross: H plots to double-cross Ray; left alone in their Amsterdam hotel room, H and Ray plan to double-cross Daz; and finally Daz double-crosses them both. What gives the operation of this mechanism a greater resonance is that the characters are adrift: the structures that supported communities (no matter how destructive and warped) in Burke's previous two plays no longer fulfil this function. Football, the army, political activism, nationality: all hold out the promise of connection with others; for H, Daz and Ray, such connections are deemed unnecessary. H (who seems to have read as widely as Eddie in *Gagarin Way*, although from a different ideological angle) delivers a coke-fuelled eulogy to the work of Robert Nozick, whose writing embodies the kind of neoliberalism that underpinned political and especially economic thinking in Britain and the USA during the decade:

> People are entitled to anything they acquire in a just way. An anything you acquire from someone who acquired it in a just way is justly acquired. Anything which ain't has to be restored to their rightful owners. What he calls a justice-preserving transaction [. . .] Now what I say, and Nozick sort of agrees, is if everythin in the world, everythin, every single fuckin thing, was initially acquired by force, which it was [. . .] then all initial acquisitions are illegitimate. No fucker legally owns anythin. An if they're unjustly acquired then they can be transferred in an unjust way. (pp. 48–9)

H's appropriation of Nozick's ideas might provide him with a spurious legitimation for his activities; however, its weakness is that it can be turned against him – and this is exactly what Daz does.

On Tour is not as successful a play as either *Gagarin Way* or *The Straits*; the integration of the characters' actions into their wider context is not as carefully worked out as it is in *The Straits*, and none of its characters has the same sense of dramatic dynamism and surprise as Eddie. It is, though, an interesting play, because it reverses the situation of his previous works: H, Ray and Daz live in a world which is socially, culturally and economically chaotic, without even the shreds of older, more communal ways of living to cling on to. Each of them, in their various ways, attempts to come to terms with this world; but the only reckoning with the dynamics of the neoliberal market place comes through a complete acceptance of its logic – even if that logic destroys any possibility of community. As H puts it, the apparent chaos of the market place gives opportunities to those who can see them; but those opportunities, by their very nature, can be taken up only by one person, acting alone and against his fellows.

Black Watch (2006)

In 2003, the new Scottish government finally began to create something that had been the subject of passionate debate in the Scottish theatre community for much of the twentieth century: they funded the development of a Scottish national theatre. The new company, headed by Vicky Featherstone was, however, rather different from its counterpart in London. For one thing, it was not building-based: a national theatre, the reasoning went, should be able to tour productions around Scotland and to collaborate with already existing theatre companies in the country. The new National Theatre of Scotland began to produce work in early 2006; *Black Watch*, commissioned by Featherstone in 2005 and based on interviews with soldiers of the Black Watch regiment, was first staged by the NTS at that year's Edinburgh festival, on 5 August 2006, directed by John Tiffany. It is fair to say that *Black Watch* rapidly became as iconic a production for the NTS as John McGrath's *The Cheviot, the Stag and the Black, Black Oil* was for 7:84 in the 1970s, or *The Steamie* was for Wildcat in the 1980s, but its impact was felt far beyond Scotland; the

31

show had an extremely successful run in London, and went on an extensive international tour which included a successful run in New York. Barry Didcock in the *Glasgow Herald* went so far as to call *Black Watch* the first cultural landmark of the twenty-first century; and Burke himself commented on the depth of the reactions the play produced:

> There seem to be two different audiences for the play. Those who are thrilled by the theatricality of the play and show their appreciation immediately and the people who take a little bit of time to give you a reaction, particularly if they've been crying.[7]

In part, as Burke pointed out, this was because of the visceral impact of the staging: as with *The Straits*, Tiffany (who had joined the NTS soon after its formation) employed Steven Hoggett to create movement pieces that grew from and complemented the dialogue. In one particularly striking, low-key piece of staging, the soldiers received and read 'blueys' – airmail letters from home: as they read the letters, they began to mime actions suggested by the letters and their character's reactions to them. The actions are silent; the thoughts and emotions conjured up by the letters remain hidden – and the audience has to work to infer the nature of the actions, and their import.

Powerful moments such as this (and others: troops slicing their way through the baize surface of a pool table, the history of the regiment staged as a parade, with the narrator Cammy dressed and undressed by the other characters in versions of the regimental uniform from the eighteenth century to the present, the slow-motion staging of an explosion near the play's end) do not, however, explain the impact of the play on their own. Nor does the fact that it discussed one of the most controversial issues of the day – the invasion of Iraq by the USA and Britain in 2003 – from the soldiers' perspective; a perspective lacking in other dramatic analyses of the conflict (such as David Hare's *Stuff Happens*). Rather, the play's impact comes from the fact that it is based on a series of painful ironies. At the time that Burke was researching the play, it was announced that the Black Watch was to be absorbed into a new, amalgamated Scottish regiment; for the soldiers currently serving in Iraq, this meant that a crucial part of their communal identity (described in the play as the *'Golden Thread'*, binding the current regiment to its history) would disappear. Behind this, there was a deeper historical irony:

> Greg felt that the Black Watch regiment was an example of Scottish history in relation to English history, in terms of all the [. . .] imperialist attacks that Britain has undertaken, and the irony of using the Scottish Highland warrior to do that. And at the final moment you leave them in the biggest foreign policy disaster ever.[8]

The soldiers, in other words, had been betrayed; but that betrayal was only one in a long-running series. The soldiers weren't sheep, going in to the army because they had no other choice, and nor were they heroes, doing their duty for their country; they were part of a community that had been used, over and over again, as fodder, for factories, for the mines, and for the forces. As Burke put it in the play's Introduction:

> The Black Watch is a tribe. It is also, overwhelmingly, a working-class institution. As much part of the social history of Scotland as mining, ship-building or fishing. Indeed, soldiering, like banking, is arguably the only significant indigenous industry to have lasted into the twenty-first century. Whether it lasts much longer, now that all the Scottish regiments have been amalgamated [. . .] remains to be seen. (p. viii)

The army, like the working-class communities that have disappeared before the beginning of *Gagarin Way*, provides those caught up in it with a history, a culture and a community; these benefits are, however, balanced against costs – and the play does not shy away from dramatising them. For example, we learn near the play's end that one of the characters, Stewarty, was drafted back to Iraq on the regiment's second tour of duty even though he had been diagnosed as suffering from depression: the army, Cammy tells us, had, typically, lost his papers: 'If they need you, they'll lose your paperwork' (p. 65). The soldiers might want, for various reasons, to do their best by the army; the army might very well not return the favour.

The play sets up a dichotomy between the traditions of the army and the experience of the soldier in its opening minutes: the play is to be performed in a transverse stage, which recalls the esplanade below Edinburgh Castle where the military tattoo that closes the Festival takes place. As the audience settle, the music swells, and a voice tells us to expect 'the unforgettable first sight and sound of the massed pipes and drums. Ladies and Gentlemen, may we now present the Black Watch' (p. 3). Then the door at the far end of the stage opens, to reveal not the military display the voice invokes, but one former soldier, Cammy, in civilian dress. A comically handled recruitment scene, in which Lord Elgin seeks to galvanise a new generation of soldiers into joining the regiment, balances Elgin's appeal to the spirit of Robert the Bruce with the potential recruits' deflating question, 'How much?' (p. 26); Elgin is only able to gain their attention by promising them foreign travel and 'guns and football and drink and exotic poontang and that' (p. 28).[9] Other ironies are far more painful; the soldiers tell their stories to a writer (a satirically handled version of Burke, solidly middle-class rather than working-class); although the writer claims to understand them, he ends the play as uncomprehending, and as distanced from the soldiers as he was at the beginning. One of the few violent scenes in the play is not sparked by a confrontation with terrorists but by an argument between the soldiers over the meals they will have when they get home – a fight that has more to do with their sense of helpless isolation, trapped in an armoured personnel carrier, exposed on a main road. And the final irony; the deaths of three soldiers in a suicide bombing is prefaced by a scene where their fellows engage in the kind of bantering dialogue that has been their default conversational setting since the play's opening. This ending has been foreshadowed, and we as an audience know what is coming – the soldiers do not.

Critiques of *Black Watch* that take it to task for missing out parts of the history of the regiment, or for ignoring the plight of ordinary Iraqis, rather miss the point.[10] The play, like *Gagarin Way*, is primarily about the effect on people when apparently rooted, immutable institutions disappear: all the things associated with them – all the glory, all the stupidity, all the bravery, and all the waste – disappear too. The link between the two plays is made explicit in one of the final dialogue exchanges between Cammy, on the point of resigning from the regiment, and an officer who accounts for his involvement in the Black Watch by invoking the Golden Thread, and its link to a proud history. Cammy's reply could have come from *Gagarin Way*:

> **Cammy** People have said that about a lot of things. The
> shipyards, the pits. They can have all the adverts they
> want, but if cunts like me are sacking it, it's [. . .]
> **Officer** It's a fucking shame.
> **Cammy** It's fucking knackered. (p. 71)

At the end of the play, the regiment has reached the same state as the street in Limphinnans that gives its name to Burke's first play; the title simply means something that has now receded into irrecoverable history, leaving those who have invested meaning in the name and what it represented damaged, bitter and adrift.

Hoors (2009)

Burke's follow-up to *Black Watch* was produced at the Traverse theatre on 1 May 2009 (directed by Jimmy Fay in a co-production by the Traverse and Theatre Royal, Bath). In interviews before the production, Burke had described *Hoors* as the 'disappointing follow-up to *Black Watch*'.[11] And after the first performances, it was easy to find critics who agreed with him (the *Guardian*'s Euan Ferguson, for example, described the play as 'technically very competent': it is rather hard to think of a more unemphatic compliment).[12] Such judgements were perhaps inevitable: after the global success of *Black Watch*, almost any subsequent work would have been disappointing. It is, however, fair to say that *Hoors* is the least theatrically effective of Burke's full-length dramas: the situation it describes (four characters holding an attenuated wake for a man who died of a heart attack during his stag weekend) is static, and the organisation of the plot (essentially a series of two-handed, blackly comic dialogues between various permutations of the two men and the two women) is rather schematic, especially when compared to the scope of *Black Watch* or the dynamism of *Gagarin Way*.

However, the fact that the play is not Burke's best work does not mean that it is without interest. For one thing, it shows Burke broadening his analysis of contemporary Scotland. *Hoors* moves away from the working- and ex-working-class communities that have populated Burke's work from his first play onwards: the four characters are all part of the twenty-first-century Scottish middle class. They can afford to buy designer clothes and accessories; they can stump up for stag weekends in Hamburg and Amsterdam. However, as with *On Tour*, the four characters in *Hoors* (Vicky, the dead man's fiancée; Nikki, her sister; and the dead man's friends Stevie and Tony) are socially rootless; both Stevie and Tony are distanced from their children, and Vicky reacts to the death of her future husband with relief. Despite various attempts, none of the characters manages to have sex in any form; and none of them knows how to acknowledge and deal with the fact that there is a dead body in the house. And yet each one of them is ostensibly reasonably successful; they have done well for themselves, in a society which seems (as was the case during the early years of this century) to be growing steadily more prosperous for reasons no one can quite put their finger on. The experience of this wealth is rather unsettling, for the male characters in particular; as Tony puts it, 'I prefer it when Scotland's poor' (p. 60).

In an unmissably ironic symbol, a large print of Titian's allegorical painting 'The Three Ages of Man' hangs on the back wall of the living room (in the original production the set was on a revolve, with the living room and bedroom on either side). The painting is there, however, not as a *memento mori* or an invitation to ponder the journey of life; as Tony and Vicky construe it, Titian's masterpiece is the illustration of a blunt, sexual demand. The man and woman in the right foreground of the painting are about to make love; and the woman is warning the man that, if he can't perform, he will be replaced. This misreading is intentional, and played for comic effect; but it does demonstrate the level of relationship the characters prefer. They all fight shy of self-exposure; they are all concerned not to give too much of themselves away. They do not connect with each other, not because (as in previous plays) the tides of social change are pulling them apart, but because, cocooned as they are in a comfortable, credit-fuelled world, they are happier with the idea of relationships as commodities which require little investment, and are easily replaceable.

Summary

In 2003, the *Guardian* ran a series of articles on contemporary political theatre, and, unsurprisingly, Burke was asked to contribute.[13] *Gagarin Way* had been a major international success, and Burke was able to reflect on his experience of seeing the show produced across the world. What amused and interested him, he wrote, was the fact that his play, rooted in post-industrial Fife, seemed to be extremely adaptable; it could be co-opted into any number of local political debates (in Warsaw, it was seen as an attack on globalisation; in Montreal, an examination of national identity, and so on). All of the various interpretations, however, seemed to circle around a central theme. As Burke put it:

> Wherever I go, I've found that people relate to one thing: that *Gagarin Way* is set in a recognisable community [. . .] a community that adhered to a certain brand of leftwing politics while the world transformed itself into a much more complex place.[14]

Gagarin Way might have been a black comedy about the death of socialist communities, rather than a lament for their passing; but the comedy was based on an acute analysis of the relation between major historical and economic forces and the people caught up in them:

> In her essay on political theatre [. . .] Naomi Wallace talked about recording the ghosts our governments are creating in Iraq. She is right: they should be recorded. But what really interests me is the ghosts that our governments have always created, and continue to create, in communities here.[15]

It could be said that this is the theme that ties all of Burke's full-length plays together; Eddie and Gary, the boys in *The Straits*, and the soldiers in *Black Watch* are uncomfortably aware that they face a rapidly changing world with mindsets, ways of defining themselves, that are no longer relevant. In *On Tour* and *Hoors*, the characters lack this awareness; but their acceptance of the world as it is also condemns them to irrelevance; in simply going along with the spirit of the times they deny themselves the possibility of community and social identity. They are ghosts too; the affluent Fifers in *Hoors* are as lost as the failed revolutionaries in *Gagarin Way* – the only difference being that they have yet to realise it.

Burke's work, then, catches Scottish (and British) society in a moment of transition; apparently impregnable political and social certainties – the narratives that came to define the Scottish nation through much of the nineteenth and twentieth centuries – have simply disappeared. Thus Burke's characters find themselves, in many cases, condemned to actions without meaning because the narratives that they once used to define themselves either do not work or do not provide them with the communal identity that could allow them structure and meaning. The kidnapping in *Gagarin Way* is an empty act; the killing of the Spaniard in *The Straits* simply cannot bear the symbolic weight that the boys try to load on it; the characters' apparently ringing endorsement of capitalism as theft in *On Tour* leaves them damagingly isolated; the weight of history and tradition in *Black Watch* is not enough to compensate for the realities of global politics; and, in *Hoors*, the characters find it impossible to communicate with each other, even about the immutable reality of death.

This process can be seen at work in the writing of Burke's con-temporaries: David Greig and David Harrower, for example, have also written about the destabilising effect that the end of old narratives has had on Scotland's sense of itself. However, it is in Burke's plays that the most incisive analysis of this process can be found.

As Antonia Kearton has argued, contemporary visions of the Scottish nation tend to imagine the country as the product of three national narratives: the idea that Scotland is a civic society, rather than an atavistic nation; that Scotland is territorially determined (that is, that Scots are people who live in Scotland, rather than people who can claim to an ethnically pure Scottishness – whatever such an unlikely thing might be); and that Scotland's identity is expressed through civic institutions: the Church, the education system, the legal system, and now the devolved parliament.[16] Taken together, these narratives combine to create the image of a nation which is inclusive, liberal, tolerant and uses the mechanisms of the state as a bulwark against the worst depredations of the free market. In Burke's plays, however, this comforting image of the nation is thoroughly debunked; and as *The Straits* and *On Tour* demonstrate, the same forces that are trans-forming Scotland are at work everywhere. For all that *Gagarin Way* deals with the death of the socialist alternative (itself a very powerful narrative in Scottish culture), it could be said that Burke's work as a whole bears out one of the central tenets of the Marxist analysis of capitalism. It is only in the early years of the twenty-first century that we have reached the point at which capitalism truly has the power to transform social relations globally; to make, in Marx's phrase, all that is solid melt into air. And, as Burke demonstrates, the apparent solidities of civic, institutional, political and nationalist identities dis-appear, so characters are reduced to the status of atomised individuals – unable (or unwilling) to link their lives together in community. In David Lane's words, 'The sense of self is no longer secure.'[17] As Burke puts it in his *Guardian* article, individuals are reduced (or they reduce themselves) to the status of ghosts, unable to exert any meaningful pressure on the system that shapes their lives.

Primary Sources

Works by Gregory Burke

Gagarin Way (London: Faber & Faber, 2001).
The Straits (London: Faber & Faber, 2003).
On Tour (London: Faber & Faber, 2005).
Black Watch (London: Faber & Faber, 2006).
Hoors (London: Faber & Faber, 2009).

Secondary Sources

Archibald, David, ' "We're Just Big Bullies . . ." Gregory Burke's Black Watch', *The Drouth*, No. 26 (2008), pp. 8–13.
Burke, Gregory, 'Black Watch: The Toast of New York', *Daily Telegraph*, 7 November 2007 <http://www.telegraph.co.uk/culture/theatre/3669088/Black-Watch-The-toast-of-New-York.html>
—, 'Funny Peculiar', *Guardian*, 12 April 2003 <http://www.guardian.co.uk/stage/2003/apr/12/theatre.artsfeatures1>
—, '20 Questions with . . . Gregory Burke', *What's On Stage*, 4 March 2002 <http://www.whatsonstage.com/interviews/theatre/london/E8821014992446/20+Questions+with...Gregory+Burke.html>
Didcock, Barry, 'His Play Black Watch Has Become the First Cultural Landmark of the 21st Century. So What Inspired Gregory Burke to Take on the Army?', *Herald*, 3 March 2007 <http://www.heraldscotland.com/his-play-black-watch-has-become-the-first-cultural-landmark-of-the-21st-century-so-what-inspired-gregory-burke-to-take-on-the-army-1.836303>
Featherstone, Vicky, 'Black Watch: A Soldier's Tale', interview, *Artworks Scotland*, BBC Scotland, 16 March 2010.
Harvie, Christopher, *Scotland and Nationalism* (London: Routledge, 2004).
Holdsworth, Nadine, 'Travelling Across Borders: Re-Imagining the Nation and Nationalism in Contemporary Scottish Theatre', *Contemporary Theatre Review*, Vol. 13, No. 2 (2003), pp. 25–39.
Howe Kritzer, Amelia, *Political Theatre in Post-Thatcher Britain* (Basingstoke: Palgrave, 2008).
Kearton, Antonia, 'Imagining the "Mongrel Nation": Political Uses of History in the Recent Scottish Nationalist Movement', *National Identities*, Vol. 7, No. 1 (2005), pp. 23–50.
Lane, David, *Contemporary British Drama* (Edinburgh: EUP, 2010).
Leach, Robert, 'The Short, Astonishing History of the National Theatre of Scotland', *New Theatre Quarterly*, Vol. 23, No. 2 (2007), pp. 171–83.
Pattie, David, 'Mapping the Territory: Modern Scottish Drama', in Rebecca D'Monté and

Graham Saunders (eds), *Cool Britannia? British Political Drama in the 1990s* (Basingstoke: Palgrave, 2007), pp. 143–57.

Ross, Peter, 'Gregory Burke Interview: Once More unto the Breach', *Scotland on Sunday*, 19 April 2009 <http://scotlandonsunday.scotsman.com/sos-review/Gregory-Burke-interview-Once-more.5182112.jp>

Sierz, Aleks, 'Beyond Timidity? The State of British New Writing', *Performing Arts Journal*, Vol. 27, No. 3 (2005), pp. 55–61.

—, 'Interview with Gregory Burke', *In-Yer-Face Theatre* website, 29 October 2003 <www.inyerface-theatre.com/archive9.html#g>

—, '"Can Old Forms be Reinvigorated?" Radical Populism and New Writing in British Theatre Today', *Contemporary Theatre Review*, Vol. 16, No. 3 (2006), pp. 301–11.

Stark, Kathleen, 'Battlefield "Body": Gregory Burke's *Gagarin Way* and Anthony Neilson's *Stitching*', in Hans-Ulrich Mohr and Kerstin Machler (eds), *Extending the Code: New Forms of Dramatic and Theatrical Expression* (Trier: WVT, 2004), pp. 171–9.

Various Authors, 'Pipes and Drums: Responses to *Black Watch*', *Contemporary Theatre Review*, Vol. 18, No. 2 (2008), pp. 272–9.

Notes

1. Gregory Burke, '20 Questions with'.
2. Barry Didcock, 'His Play Black Watch'.
3. See also Amelia Howe Kritzer, *Political Theatre*, pp. 208–10.
4. See Christopher Harvie, *Scotland and Nationalism*.
5. Aleks Sierz, '"Can Old Forms be Reinvigorated?"', p. 304.
6. Aleks Sierz, 'Interview with Gregory Burke'.
7. Gregory Burke, 'Black Watch: The Toast of New York'.
8. Vicky Featherstone, 'Black Watch: A Soldier's Tale'.
9. Note that Elgin's speech patterns, redoubtably upper-class when he first enters, have slipped into the demotic.
10. See David Archibald, '"We're Just Big Bullies . . ."'.
11. Burke quoted in Peter Ross, 'Gregory Burke Interview'.
12. Euan Ferguson, *Observer*, *Theatre Record*, Vol. XXIX, No. 9 (2009), p. 505.
13. See Sierz, '"Can Old Forms be Reinvigorated?"'
14. Gregory Burke, 'Funny Peculiar'.
15. Ibid.
16. Antonia Kearton, 'Imagining the "Mongrel Nation"'.
17. David Lane, *Contemporary British Drama*, p. 39.

3 JEZ BUTTERWORTH

Aleks Sierz

Mojo; The Night Heron; The Winterling; Parlour Song; Jerusalem

Introduction

One of the most distinctive playwrights to emerge from the mid-1990s moment of 'in-yer-face theatre', Jeremy Penfold Butterworth was born in 1969, and grew up in St Albans. Nicknamed Jez, he went to a comprehensive school and then St John's, Cambridge, where he read English, his contemporaries including actor Rachel Weisz, director David Farr and *Times* editor James Harding. His siblings are also in show business: Tom and John Henry are screenwriters, Steve a film producer, and Joanna a registrar at LAMDA. Along with his older brother Tom, who was his mentor, Butterworth has been writing since his late teens, as often for film as for the stage. Although the sudden appearance of the exciting *Mojo* (Royal Court, 1995) was seen as an example of the individual genius's stunning debut, the truth is that Butterworth served an apprenticeship, and has always been a collaborative writer. With Tom, he wrote an adaptation of veteran journalist Katharine Whitehorn's *Cooking in a Bedsitter* (Edinburgh, 1991). With James Harding, he wrote four shorts under the title *I Believe in Love* (Etcetera Theatre, 1992). Then came *Huge* (Edinburgh and King's Head, 1993), about two failed comedy writers, a play he wrote with Simon Godley and Ben Miller (who also took the stage in this two-hander). With Tom, he then wrote *The Census Man* as part of Carlton Television's New Writers Course, which led to their being commissioned to make *The Night of the Golden Brain* (Carlton, 1994), a short film about a pub quiz team. Helped by his brother, Butterworth wrote *Mojo* in a cottage in Wiltshire. This debut was hyped as the first time since John Osborne's *Look Back in Anger* that a first play was put on the Royal Court's main stage.[1] It won the Olivier, *Evening Standard*, George Devine, Critics' Circle and Writers' Guild awards. Versions of the play were produced in New York, Chicago, Johannesburg and Sydney, its popularity making it one of the most significant plays of the decade.

Meanwhile, Jez and Tom Butterworth wrote *Christmas* (FilmFour, 1996), a story about a teenager. A year later, their film version of *Mojo* (Portobello Pictures, 1997), with Harold Pinter in the cast, premiered at the Venice Film Festival, but got mixed reviews. Their *Birthday Girl* (Channel 4, 2002), about a bank clerk who acquires a Russian bride, starred Nicole Kidman, and was more successful, but because the star was often absent during the shooting Jez had time to write *The Night Heron* (Royal Court, 2002). Most significantly, he then moved to Somerset, where he lives on a smallholding with his wife Gilly and two children. His *The Winterling* (Royal Court, 2006) was condemned by critics as being too derivative of Pinter. In 2007, he was awarded the E. M. Forster Award by the American Academy of Arts and Letters. With Tom, he adapted Valerio Massimo Manfredi's novel about the Roman Empire, *The Last Legion* (Dino De Laurentiis, 2007). With his brother John Henry, he scripted *Fair Game* (River Road, 2010), based on the story of CIA agent Valerie Plame. His *Parlour Song* (Atlantic, 2008; Almeida, 2009) and *Jerusalem* (Royal Court, 2009) re-established his theatre presence, and the latter, helped by an extraordinary performance by Mark Rylance, transferred to the West End and was also immensely successful in New York. It won Olivier, *Evening Standard* and Critics' Circle and Tony awards.

The Plays

Mojo (1995)

Mojo opened at the Royal Court on 14 July 1995. Set in Ezra's Atlantic Club in Soho, during the summer of 1958, the play begins with the sound of drums, bass and guitar chords, and the image of Silver Johnny, a seventeen-year-old rock 'n' roll protégé and the talismanic magic charm of the title, dancing across the stage. Then two twentysomething petty villains – Sweets and Potts – introduce us to this criminal milieu. It's a great double act. Then they are joined by other small-time crims, Skinny, and Baby, who is the son of Ezra, their boss. Baby enjoys tormenting, even torturing, Skinny. While the youngsters mess about, a sinister gangster, Sam Ross, kills Ezra, and takes Silver Johnny. Terrified, the gang, now led by Mickey (Ezra's number two) barricade themselves in the club, and prepare for an attack. Although he is Ezra's son and heir, Baby realises that Mickey is now in charge and suggests they run the club together, but Mickey rejects him. When the lights go up for the final scene, however, everything has changed. Baby is back: he has killed Sam Ross and retrieved Silver Johnny. Now he unmasks Mickey as the man who betrayed Ezra to Ross. When Skinny sides with Mickey, Baby shoots him dead and then beats up Mickey. As dawn breaks, Baby takes Silver Johnny for a walk.

What is immediately compelling about Butterworth's play is his thrilling and imaginative use of language, a mixture of quick-fire jokes and baroque elaboration. The following exchange, talking of Silver Johnny's audience, is typical:

Sweets Micks.
Potts Do me a favour.
Sweets Micks and Paddies.
Potts Do me a clean turn.
Sweets Micks and Paddies and wops who fuck dogs. (p. 9)

The speed of the dialogue is emphasised by the fact that Sweets and Potts are high on amphetamines, but the structure of the thinking is based on repetition, reiteration and exaggeration. 'Micks' and 'Paddies' are synonyms for Irish people, and 'Do me a clean turn' offers an elaborated restatement of 'Do me a favour' (p. 9). Typically, Butterworth first sets up a situation in plain language, then repeats it using a striking metaphor. For example, Silver Johnny is described as a marketable commodity first because he makes girls 'shit when he sings', and next because he 'makes polite young ladies come their cocoa in public' (p. 5). Another device is the constant use of verbal tags, such as 'fish are jumping' (pp. 11–14), and visual puns, such as when Sweets asks Baby if he can ask him a question, Baby points a gun at him and says: 'Fire away' (p. 69). Most reviewers remembered lines of dialogue such as 'when Silver Johnny sings the song my pussyhair stands up' (p. 4) and 'There's nothing like someone cutting your dad in two for clearing the mind' (p. 59).

In terms of character, the play is about the transformation of a lazy hedonistic joker into an avenging psychotic leader – Shakespeare's Prince Hal is surely a template – and Baby grows into his inheritance. But he is insensate: 'I feel completely numb' (p. 77). When told of his father's death, he changes the subject (p. 31). Sweets explains why: 'There's dads and dads. You're thinking of a *dad*. Like in a book. Fucking figure of something.' But Baby's dad was different, a 'bloke' who 'waits for you [to] come home from school [and] stuffs his hands down your pants' (p. 44). Baby is a victim of abuse, and he has now become an abuser. In one of the play's longest speeches, he remembers his terror when Ezra took him for a drive in the country. He was nine and, noticing a 'bag of sharp knives' on the front seat, was convinced his father meant to kill him. But Ezra has other ideas. He kills a cow and cuts it up for sale. Baby remembers being 'covered in blood' (pp. 66–8).

Mojo's central theme is father-and-son relationships. It is a story about masculine desire: the desire for sex, the desire to succeed, and the need for fatherhood. But if the play shows how a wayward son takes on his father's mantle, Ezra never appears on stage. Early on, Butterworth realised that in a play 'the real juice lies in the tension between what's onstage and what's off. It's what's left *off* that ignites what's *on*.'[2] We never see either Ezra or Sam Ross; we just hear about their meeting from Sweets and Potts, and then about Ezra's death from Mickey and Sam Ross's death from Baby. This is dramatically effective, but it does mean that the audience sees only Baby's side of the father–son relationship. In other words, it never sees the relationship but only its effects on Baby. Instead of Ezra, there is a parade of surrogate fathers led by Mickey, whose maturity is finally revealed as based on lies and betrayal. Similarly, Skinny's hero-worship of Baby is a form of displaced father love from a boy whose real father has been replaced by an 'uncle' at home (pp. 46–50). *Mojo* is a study of absent fathers.

In this all-male world, the men play all the parts, mothers as well as fathers. When Potts makes a steam treatment for Mickey's head cold, he sounds like a wife (p. 66). But the play also reveals that men are just boys. Their incessant chatter is both an effect of amphetamine use and a way of fending off fear: these lads are gangsters but unsuccessful ones. Their grown-up masculinity is usually undercut by adolescent behaviour. Baby's joke at the expense of Sweets – 'You only hang around Sid all the time because you want his cock up your arse' (p. 70) – is an example of juvenile homoeroticism, and the playground banter – including Skinny's calling the others 'sissy' and Baby a 'Jew' (p. 78) – suggests that all these boys have never grown up.

Directed by Ian Rickson, and designed by Ultz, *Mojo* had a flair for vivid visual images. Ezra's dead body has been dumped in two dustbins, which are dragged on stage in a grim parody of Beckett. At one point, Baby comes in, holding five toffee apples, his childish glee juxtaposed with the fact that he is about to be told that his father is dead; at another point, a big box is delivered, sparking off a panic: is Silver Johnny's head inside? No, it is just his silver suit. Then, in the last scene, when he is hung up by the ankles, Silver Johnny looked like a piece of meat. Other visual gags include the gang's newly acquired Derringer pistol, which turns out to be a tiny revolver, a sharp contrast to Baby's vicious cutlass. The play's design – glitzy jackets, noir shadows, glittering sequins and rock music – was as much a part of its impact as its language. *Mojo* was rapidly restaged in October 1996, with a new cast and a slightly rewritten text, transferring to the Royal Court's temporary base at the Duke of York's Theatre in the West End. Although the critics were enthusiastic, some perceived a moral void at the heart of the story, most made comparisons with the films of Quentin Tarantino and the plays of Harold Pinter, and many thought that the play was an example of style being more important than content.[3]

The Night Heron (2002)

First staged at the Royal Court on 11 April 2002, *The Night Heron* was Butterworth's first play after a gap of seven years. Directed by Ian Rickson, who was now the artistic director of this theatre, its staging represented an act of faith in the playwright. *The Night Heron* is set in the Cambridgeshire marshes in January and, like *Mojo*, begins with a duologue. The characters are two unemployed Cambridge gardeners: Wattmore, a suicidal religious fanatic, and Griffin, a more down-to-earth criminal type. To make money, they rent a room to Bolla, a female ex-con. Then it turns out that Wattmore is being blackmailed for a paedophile act, and that he believes that Bolla is a witch. Griffin tries to raise money to pay off the blackmail by mugging people in the marshes, while Bolla aims to help her hosts win a poetry competition by kidnapping a Cambridge student. Finally, a local religious sect, led by Dougal, arrives and attempts to discover if Wattmore and Bolla are embodiments of evil. In the end, Bolla leaves, Griffin settles the blackmail and Wattmore hangs himself. Hovering over the action is the visit of a night heron, a rare bird which attracts attention to the area.

The central theme of the play is male friendship, and the intense loyalty of Griffin for the crazed Wattmore is its emotional heart. With their mutual need, exasperation and knowledge, it feels as if the two men are an old married couple. Griffin's 'I'm not stupid Wattmore. Grant me *some* noodles' (p. 8) is typical. With the exception of Bolla, this is an exclusively male world and one full of religious imaginings: the set is dominated by a huge iconostasis, which 'depicts the Lord and the Saints at the final judgment' (p. 15), and the earthly judgment of Wattmore on himself is self-destruction. The theme of Christian redemption turns pagan, tragic. His religious delusions are resonant of Protestantism, Bunyan and English culture: 'Send a Guardian and light braziers . . . and mark the path through Disturbance. Display the dark path to everlasting Peace' (p. 12). Here the myth of the Expulsion from the Garden of Eden is reworked for a contemporary world of local radio, newspapers and sound recording. The rural imagery is often humorous: 'he hasn't got the brains of a bucket of frogs' (p. 50).

The symbolic heron, a continental bird that has been blown off course, is, like the main characters, stranded in a hostile environment. Chief among the comic flights of the play, whose dialogue is much more mature and less flashy than that of *Mojo*, is Griffin's story of Wattmore's wild religious behaviour at a meeting of the cubs: 'it's all passed off as normal when this one starts pointing at Warren Lee saying he's The Devil's last son' (p. 34). There is a running joke about the 'mongol' Dougal who has started a cult (pp. 10, 34–5, 75–80). And Bolla turns out to have studied Marvell's poetry in prison, while the naked kidnapped student recites a Shelley poem. The elaborately polite dialogue between Griffin and Bolla contrasts comically with their characters, and her transformation into a miniskirted chav is hilarious. Designed by Ultz, *The Night Heron* was set in a memorably mildew-timbered barn, atmospherically doomy, and featuring the iconostasis – made up of photocopied pages. Critics were sceptical about the production's deep Fenland accents, obscure background narrative and baffling symbolism, but recognised the comic and imaginative quality of the play.[4]

The Winterling (2006)

The Winterling was first performed at the Royal Court on 2 March 2006. Set in an abandoned Dartmoor farmhouse, it is about West, a former gangster in exile from London. When his old mate, Wally, and his gobby stepson, the twenty-five-year-old Patsy, visit, a territorial struggle rapidly develops. It emerges that West summoned former friends Wally and Jerry, but that Jerry is now dead. Towards the end of the long first act, West interrogates Patsy about a nearby ancient hillfort and Patsy asks West about a young woman he has glimpsed at the window. Act Two jumps back a year, and shows West, as a broken man, meeting Draycott, a vagrant who lives in the farmhouse. Through him, he meets Lue, an unusual young woman. It emerges that West was once a hitman, and that he was tortured by Wally and Jerry for falling asleep on a job. He dispossesses Draycott and makes a deal with Lue. Act Three returns to the present, and shows how Wally has planned for Patsy to kill West. But although West sends Lue off, Patsy can't kill him despite the fact that he accepts his role as a sacrifice.

This is a play about archetypal fathers and sons, male friendship and male competition, and about rites of passage. Wally is Patsy's surrogate father, and he has brought his 'son' into the wilderness to make him a man. There are several mentions of masculinity, the most explicit being West's 'Father and son. Man and boy' (p. 19) and Patsy's point that 'Men who love each other [. . .] are not benders' (p. 42). The three criminal men – West, Wally and Jerry – are companions, both heroic 'three Musketeers' and comic 'Three Stooges' (p. 31). With irony, Patsy calls Wally 'Daddy' when they argue (pp. 22, 25). It is also a tale of betrayal, and of role reversal. But, as well as the story of the blooding of a youngster, this is also the tale of another, equally primitive, ritual: the ancient hillfort, once the scene of human sacrifice, now a tourist attraction with an Information Centre, suggests the beating of a mythic heart, and a shape to destiny that is easier to see in the mud of the countryside than in the bright lights of the city. A winterling is a one-year-old animal, and this refers to a running joke about West's puppy dog, and to the fact that he has dwelt for only a year in the countryside.

Written with all of Butterworth's characteristically high-octane flair, the text flashes with jokes and oozes menacing charm. Patsy's sarcasm is typical:

> Who minds driving six hours, breathing your guffs, when you get here and it's this lovely? The crumbling walls. The overpowering smell of shit. And the dead fox on the doorstep. Always a welcoming touch. (p. 11)

The countryside is deliberately anti-romantic: West says, 'You fall asleep out here, something creeps up and eats you' (p. 30). Similarly, Draycott's account of his fight with a badger – 'Lost five pints of blood to it. And two toes' (p. 50) – and his other escapades show rural life to be violent, uneasy. Significantly, Lue wants West to sign her passport form: she dreams of escape. But although the atmosphere of menace is clear, the keynote is ambiguity: Lue remains mysterious, Patsy's future is uncertain.

Directed by Ian Rickson, and designed by Ultz, *The Winterling* was a deliciously doomy production, whose soundscape included both the overhead crash of passing military jets (a modern military base) and the hypnotic thump of distant drums (an ancient hillfort). It seemed to realise Butterworth's idea of his play as something of a dream. As the playwright says, '*The Winterling* was written mainly at night, with Dartmoor at my back. Writing at night puts you in a slightly odd state of mind. It feels like you're dreaming.'[5] This is a dream of Deep England, and its effect on urban criminals, who come across as eccentric, volatile and profane. Critical reaction was mainly mixed, with the playwright admired for being entertaining, but attacked for being too Pinteresque.[6]

Parlour Song (2008)

Parlour Song opened at the Atlantic Theater, New York, directed by Neil Pepe, before being revived at the Almeida Theatre in north London, this time directed by Ian Rickson, on 19 March 2009. It is the slightest of Butterworth's plays and the most compressed in its claustrophobia and ambiguity. On a new estate, bordering suburbia and the countryside, Ned, a demolition expert, and Joy, his wife of eleven years, find their relationship under strain. After Ned confides in his neighbour Dale, Dale has a brief affair with Joy. At the same time, Ned is tormented by the disappearance of various prized possessions from his home, from gold cufflinks to a tandem bicycle (symbolic of their relationship). But while Dale and Joy's plan to run away together is never realised, the text specifies that Ned kills Joy by attacking her with a cricket bat. Partly a painfully beautiful and excruciatingly agonised meditation on the business of living, partly a bizarrely hilarious comedy of suburban life, and partly a lament for the disappearance of England's nature in the face of new housing developments, this is a nightmarish play. It is never really clear why Joy has been disposing of Ned's belongings, or which elements of the play are dream, and which reality.

Unlike his other work, *Parlour Song* (whose title refers to 'an Anglicisation of a Negro spiritual, ballad or work song')[7] includes direct address to the audience by all three characters. In a typical one, Dale comments on the new estate: 'It's a nice area. Young couples. Families. You've not got to drive far to see a cow' (p. 21). Although this device allows us to get inside the heads of the characters, Joy, who remains an enigma (with shades of Pinter's Ruth from *The Homecoming*), has only one monologue (p. 62). The main theme of the play is the same as the blues murder ballads: the revenge of a betrayed man on his wife. But the prime emotional dynamic is not between Ned and Joy, but between Ned and Dale: this is about male competition, male suspicion of women and male anger. Likewise, nature, the menacing primal forest, is very close. One aspect of the play is its implied green agenda – our materialist society ruins nature, but nature creeps back. And our natural impulses surprise us.

Directed by Ian Rickson, designed by Jeremy Herbert, and with video projections of wild woods, some scenes were wildly hilarious – for example, when Ned tries to improve his cunnilingus technique or when he attempts a gymnastic workout. In one scene, Dale and Joy play Scrabble, a symbolic game of words that is a prelude to their adultery. In another, Ned tells one of many extraordinary stories about buying a birdbath for Joy in Gloucester. All in all, this was an emotionally intense account of an unhappy marriage, but its zany imagination was also a slap in the face of British new writing's default mode of literal naturalism.

As in *The Winterling*, a lot of critical comment discussed Butterworth's debt to Pinter. John Stokes analysed how he uses Estuary English 'in a Pinteresque way', 'making theatre out of absence' by using 'withheld information' and 'unseen characters':

> Dale not only has a wife we never see, he also, it turns out, has two adored children who are mentioned for the very first time only a matter of minutes before the end of the play. [Pinter's influence] is there in the adulterous, role-play sex (*The Lover*), in the accumulation of junk (*The Caretaker*), in the male bonding (*Betrayal*).[8]

Other reviews also noted the same influence.[9]

Jerusalem (2009)

Jerusalem opened at the Royal Court on 10 July 2009. The third and best of his rural plays, and one in which he shook off the influence of Pinter, is set on St George's Day and shows what happens when Kennet and Avon Council comes to evict Johnny 'Rooster' Byron, who lives in a battered mobile home in a Wessex wood opposite a new estate (reminiscent of *Parlour Song*).[10] In Ian Rickson's production, the stage was hidden by a curtain made of a faded flag of St George, which was parted by fifteen-year-old Phaedra, who comes out front to sing the hymn 'Jerusalem'. This evocation of traditional Deep England, with its words by William Blake, contrasts with the opening scene, a nocturnal bacchanalia of house music, gyrating girls and drug-addled wildness. The stage direction is succinct: '*England at midnight*' (p. 6). Johnny, an ex-stunt driving Romany, deals drugs, lives on the dole and is a magnet for local kids. It is the day of the annual Flintlock Fair, but the May Queen, Phaedra, is missing. When Dawn, the mother of Johnny's six-year-old child Marky, pays him a visit, it is clear that she has left him because of his juvenile behaviour – his inability to live up to his responsibilities as a parent. Then Troy, Phaedra's father, comes looking for her, and punishes Johnny by beating him up and branding him with a red-hot iron. At the end of the play, visited for the last time by Marky, Johnny decides to burn down his mobile home.

Johnny is a symbol of the contemporary freeborn Englishman, a roaring mix of skiving wastrel and Pied Piper. His Romany blood gives him outsider status, but he is no foreigner. As he doles out booze, drugs and tall tales to his hangers-on, who include some young teens, this larger-than-life figure is gradually revealed to have some deeply unattractive features. He is an absent father, incompetent male, and has a liking for young girls. He is also a hippie anarchist who seems to be directly plugged into an olde myth of Deep England, rural, pagan and dreamy. The lord of misrule and his beggars' banquet is attended by a band of eccentrics: Ginger, a lanky loser who acts as Johnny's questioning sceptic, Lee, a gormless lad on the eve of migrating to Australia, Davey, a parochial abattoir worker, and the mind-addled

Professor. All are vividly drawn individuals, Johnny's court of acolytes. There are also two sixteen-year-olds, Pea and Tanya. In the background of the action, but always intruding, is the Flintock Fair, a local celebration that was once a rural carnival but is now commercialised. Wesley, the village pub landlord, has been required by his distant brewery owners to dress up as a traditional Morris Dancer. His contempt for this articulates Butterworth's criticism of the invention of rural 'traditions', which are now money-making enterprises.

In this perspective, the enemy is modernity, represented also by the New Estate and the local council. Of course, in political terms, Butterworth's text sails dangerously close to those reactionary newspaper columnists, such as Richard Littlejohn in the *Sun*, who complain about governmental legislation, progressive or not. But Butterworth silences such doubts with the humour, bravado and sheer excess of his vision. The highpoints of the play are Johnny's rhetorical flights of fantasy. Typical is his address: 'Friends! Outcasts. Leeches. Undesirables. A blessing on you [. . .] I, Rooster Byron, your merciless ruler, have decreed that today all my bounty is bestowed upon you, gratis' (p. 50). The mix of Shakespearean allusion with legal language and Latin is hilariously playful. At one point, he describes his own fantasy virgin birth, due to a bullet – fired by a vengeful wife – passing through his philandering father's gonads:

> The bullet passes clean through his scrotum, bounces off the bedpost, zings out of the window, down the high street to the crossroads, where it hits the number 87 tram to Andover. The bullet passes through two inches of rusty metal, clean through an elderly lady's packed lunch and lodges in my sweet mother's sixteen-year-old womb. (p. 48)

In a playwriting culture that favours naturalism, this is a rare example of an impressively unchained imagination. Equally amazing is Johnny's story of his encounter with a hundred-foot giant who 'built Stonehenge' (p. 57) and who gives him a 'golden drum' that was hanging from 'his right ear' (p. 58). To clinch the truth of the story, Johnny shows his listeners the drum, and then, having been beaten up at the end of the play, bangs it to summon help from his ancestors and the country's mythic past. An equally hilarious, if more contemporary, tall tale is his account of being kidnapped by 'four big Nigerians [. . .] traffic wardens' (p. 68). But Johnny is not the only one to use narrative to explain, entertain and amaze. For example, Ginger tells how Johnny jumped over twenty buses on a bike in 1981, 'died' and then came back to life (pp. 31–2). In this play, narrative is the playwright's dramaturgical tool of choice.

As its title reminds us, *Jerusalem* is a lament for a freewheeling England whose time is up: as Johnny says about his birth, 'This one – me – he sits up, wipes the dew from his eyes and calls, "Mother, what is this dark place?" And she replied, "'Tis England, my boy. England"' (p. 49). Butterworth explains, 'I'm half-Irish but I feel very English. It's always been a struggle for me to work out exactly what that meant.'[11] Here, English identity means being drunken, drug-addled and sex-mad. As Stokes says, 'The prevailing "condition of England" is stoned.'[12] Through this deliciously fuzzy optic, national self-consciousness is in crisis. In this England all traditions are modern inventions, and the relentless march of commerce is altering the countryside beyond recognition. It also shows a rural location which is just as crime-ridden, drug-infested and dangerous as any inner city. But the play is more than just a state-of-the-nation pastoral, it is also about change: for most of the characters, the next day will be different from today.

Jerusalem transferred to the Apollo Theatre in the West End on 28 January 2010, to generally ecstatic reviews (none of which mentioned Pinter).[13] It starred Mark Rylance, who memorably started off by doing a handstand in a drinking trough, then downing a drink of raw eggs, alcohol and amphetamine. His mesmerising stage presence did much to create the play's legendary status. At the end, as the tang of petrol filled the air, Rylance's utterly convincing performance almost made you hope that Johnny, and his England, might be saved.[14]

Summary

From the beginning, Butterworth has been a controversial figure in the field of new writing for the British stage. As well as generating excitement in the media, his debut also divided critics and commentators. Playwright David Edgar saw *Mojo* as an example of typical 1990s plays which 'address masculinity and its discontents'.[15] And it was easy to see Butterworth as a laddish writer whose sensibility was similar to other emerging 'in-yer-face' playwrights: *Mojo* features in my *In-Yer-Face Theatre*'s chapter on 'Boys Together'. Seen as one of 'Mrs Thatcher's disorientated children' by critic Benedict Nightingale, Butterworth was part of a new generation of 'significant talents'.[16] But reaction against this kind of instant praise was equally swift. Peter Ansorge calls *Mojo* 'breathtaking' but only as 'an exercise in style': '*Mojo* tells us nothing new about Soho in the 1950s', and is 'purely' designed to delight a 'young audience weaned on *Reservoir Dogs*'.[17] Similarly, Vera Gottlieb dismissed Butterworth as 'strongly influenced by Pinter's language and style – but he remains essentially a stylist, lacking in content', trendy but lightweight.[18]

Laddism (which can be defined as a reactionary anti-feminist masculinity) became a central issue, largely because Butterworth was seen as part of a group of male playwrights who were being promoted by new writing theatres as a reaction against the women playwrights of the 1980s. Although she doesn't mention *Mojo*, the play is surely behind playwright Phyllis Nagy's criticism that in the mid-1990s there was a masculine laddish hegemony: 'this ridiculous promotion of men and bad plays and misogyny'.[19] Timberlake Wertenbaker agreed, saying about the Royal Court that 'suddenly they were hungry for a different kind of play: male violence, homoerotica'.[20] Here, aesthetic choices function, in the words of Elaine Aston and Janelle Reinelt, 'as a form of censorship', excluding other sensibilities.[21] Central to laddism was a tendency to, in Graham Saunders's words, 'fetishize violence, often by referencing it within a framework derived from films such as *The Long Good Friday* (1980) and *Reservoir Dogs* (1992)'.[22] A focus on masculinity and violence tended to obscure the virtues of Butterworth's writing, and his skill in alluding to older theatrical traditions. Dan Rebellato, for example, points out that *Mojo* 'almost effortlessly creates a convincing period slang, with witty, theatrical wisecracking dialogue, and an almost classical deployment of violence and tragedy'.[23] Dominic Dromgoole adds to the debate not merely by characterising Butterworth's linguistic style as having a 'Byronic dash in the way he maintains a mock-heroic high style over almost epic distances', but also by emphasising his use of 'one of the most potent metaphors for a particular nineties condition – the way that everyone tries to fuck talent up the arse'.[24] He also argues that part of the reason for *Mojo*'s success was the play's form: 'it is close enough to a well-made play', as well as the fascination of its portrait of a psychopath, a favourite theme in 1990s media.[25] Finally, Michael Billington sees *Mojo* as 'a jazzily written, biliously funny attack on a violent, patriarchal culture'.[26]

The controversy over Butterworth's laddishness gradually abated, aided by the long gap between his debut and his follow-up plays. On closer scrutiny, academics have viewed his work with increasing subtlety. David Ian Rabey, for example, observes that *Mojo* 'is a postmodern, blackly humorous melodrama celebrating masculine performative duels of charismatic and intimidating but defensive style', and emphasising the talismanic symbolism of the silver jacket that both Johnny and Baby wear, 'like a superhero costume'.[27] Rabey implicitly detects Pinter's influence in this 'comedy of menace' and interprets Baby as 'a mid-1990s refraction of the Coriolanus complex [. . .] an imperfectly individuated manchild who interprets neo-parental injunctions to maturity in self-consciously shockingly excessive actions'.[28] Although many reviewers criticised *The Winterling* for its excessive stylistic debt to Pinter, perhaps it's the absence of fully rounded female characters in all of Butterworth's work that most recalls the early Pinter oeuvre. Both playwrights share a love of mysterious female characters.

More recently, it is Butterworth's ability to create an image of national identity that has impressed critics. For example, his film *Birthday Girl* (2002), in the words of Steve Blandford, was 'crudely satirising the mores of contemporary England', and articulated 'contemporary xenophobic fears'.[29] In a similar vein, Amelia Howe

Kritzer interprets *Mojo* as a state-of-the-nation play, 'a metaphor of post-Thatcher politics', in which an older generation bases 'its success on exploitation of the young [. . .] they lose their power not through an uprising of the younger generation but through the breakdown of loyalty among themselves'.[30] She further argues that masculine rivalry is imagined as 'primal' and that the world of the play resembles a Hobbesian environment where the life of man is 'solitary, poor, nasty, brutish and short', the 'ultimate Thatcherite fantasy, in which there really is no such thing as society'.[31]

The Night Heron and *The Winterling* represent a break with the urban noir of *Mojo* and although they are characterised by a similar black hilarity, they are also rich texts, glowing with symbolism, buzzing with humour and aching with human frailty. Full of bizarre characters and crazy situations, they are shot through with Butterworth's highly individual voice. If it is too early for *The Night Heron* and *The Winterling* to be considered in depth as examples of a new kind of contemporary rural play, the former has been interpreted as an instance of a 'magic realist' sensibility that occasionally infil-trates, and questions, the hegemony of the mainstream naturalistic aesthetic that dominates British theatre.[32] But if the originality of writing plays set in a rural context – and its challenge to new writing's urban metro-centricism – has been as yet under-appreciated, *Jerusalem* was quickly recognised as a picture of the nation. Not only did most critics appreciate the play's portrait of a contemporary pastoral, but some commentators went further. In the programme for the West End transfer, Paul Kingsnorth asked, 'What are the foundation myths of the English?', and argued that the ancient narratives of Olde England are 'so common as to go unnoticed unless we go out and search for them'.[33] Likewise, Stokes points out that Byron 'sees himself as the embodiment of a lost England, and the play encourages us to recall a range of possible precursors', from St George to Falstaff.[34] One blogger, for example, noted that the play presented 'a vision of Englishness' which conjured up a historical seventeenth-century dimension: 'the Levellers, the Diggers, the wonderful and outré sects thrown up by the English revolution'.[35] Of course, it also evokes Shakespeare:

The most important reason, though, that I find Butterworth's vision of Englishness so compelling is the way it plays with other texts. The action is set on St George's Day, 23 April, and that, of course, is a thumping great clue to lead us to Shakespeare (birthday: 23 April). Byron (that name is another great big literary signpost, of course) is Falstaff to his chaotic band of hangers-on [. . .] Perhaps, too, there is also a touch of the Prospero about Byron, though a Prospero infused with the spirit of Caliban.[36]

In the *Daily Telegraph*, Dominic Cavendish also described *Jerusalem* as 'a state-of-the-nation drama with an incendiary difference. It speaks about a nation that has almost forgotten it is a nation – England.'[37] Pointing out that all the characters are white, and culturally homogeneous, he argues that it is 'an explosive whiff away from the sentiment: "England for the English!"', and wonders why there has been so little debate about its politics and its reactionary vision of Englishness.[38] Certainly, the play's high profile means that these debates will surface in the future.

In general, Butterworth has not experimented much with theatre form, and his plays are usually linear dramas with short lapses of time between the scenes or acts (*The Winterling* and *Parlour Song* are exceptions). He has developed a highly individual voice: while the rhythm of *The Winterling*'s 'pop them off' (p. 20) echoes *Mojo*'s 'kiss my pegs' (p. 37), he uses other devices such as repetition and stichomythia for both comic and sinister effect. Overall, he is a master of the tall tale and the narrative monologue. His obsession is male experience and he mixes laugh-aloud comedy with melancholy subtext. By exploiting the tension between what happens on- and off-stage, he represents mythic relationships (fathers and sons), symbolic nature, supernatural beings, and dark images of the countryside and nation. Increasingly, his subject has become national identity.

Primary Sources

Works by Jez Butterworth

Mojo (London: Nick Hern, 1996).
Mojo & A Film-maker's Diary (London: Faber & Faber, 1998).
The Night Heron (London: Nick Hern, 2002).
The Winterling (London: Nick Hern, 2006).
Parlour Song (London: Nick Hern, 2009).
Jerusalem (London: Nick Hern, 2009).

Secondary Sources

Anon., 'Jez Butterworth (Writer) and Ian Rickson (Director) in Conversation', *Parlour Song* programme, Almeida Theatre, March 2009.

Ansorge, Peter, *From Liverpool to Los Angeles: On Writing for Theatre, Film and Television* (London: Faber & Faber, 1997).

Aston, Elaine, *Feminist Views on the English Stage: Women Playwrights 1990–2000* (Cambridge: CUP, 2003).

Aston, Elaine and Janelle Reinelt (eds), *The Cambridge Companion to Modern British Women Playwrights* (Cambridge: CUP, 2000).

Billington, Michael, *State of the Nation: British Theatre Since 1945* (London: Faber & Faber, 2007).

Blandford, Steve, *Film, Drama and the Break-Up of Britain* (Bristol: Intellect, 2007).

Butterworth, Jez, 'Interview', *The Review Show*, BBC2, 12 February 2010.

Cavendish, Dominic, 'Jerusalem: Why No Fuss About This Radical Play?', *Daily Telegraph*, 23 February 2010 <http://www.telegraph.co.uk/culture/theatre/7265867/Jerusalem-why-no-fuss-about-this-radical-play.html>

Dromgoole, Dominic, *The Full Room: An A–Z of Contemporary Playwriting* (London: Methuen Drama, 2002).

Edgar, David (ed.), *State of Play* (London: Faber & Faber, 1999).

Gottlieb, Vera, 'Lukewarm Britannia', in Vera Gottlieb and Colin Chambers (eds), *Theatre in a Cool Climate* (Oxford: Amber Lane, 1999), pp. 201–12.

Higgins, Charlotte, 'Jez Butterworth's Jerusalem: A Vision of Englishness I'll Happily Sign Up to', *Guardian on Culture Blog*, 12 February 2010 <http://www.guardian.co.uk/culture/charlottehigginsblog/2010/feb/12/jerusalem-jez-butterworth-mark-rylance-englishness-shakespeare>

Howe Kritzer, Amelia, *Political Theatre in Post-Thatcher Britain: New Writing 1995–2005* (Basingstoke: Palgrave Macmillan, 2008).

Kingsnorth, Paul, 'Oak, Ash and Thorn', *Jerusalem* programme, Apollo Theatre, January 2010.

Nightingale, Benedict, *The Future of Theatre* (London: Phoenix, 1998).

Rabey, David Ian, *English Drama Since 1940* (Harlow: Longman, 2003).

Rebellato, Dan, 'Jez Butterworth', in Colin Chambers (ed.), *The Continuum Companion to Twentieth Century Theatre* (London: Continuum, 2002), p. 121.

Rickson, Ian, 'Interview: Ian Rickson', *theatreVOICE* website, 22 February 2010 <http://www.theatrevoice.com/listen_now/player/?audioID=828>

Saunders, Graham, 'Introduction', in Rebecca D'Monté and Graham Saunders, *Cool Britannia?: British Political Drama in the 1990s* (Basingstoke, 2008), pp. 1–18.

Sierz, Aleks, '"Art Flourishes in Times of Struggle": Creativity, Funding and New Writing', *Contemporary Theatre Review*, Vol. 13, No. 1 (2003), pp. 33–45.

—, *In-Yer-Face Theatre: British Drama Today* (London: Faber & Faber, 2001).

—, 'Happily Counting His Chickens', *Daily Telegraph*, 27 February 2006 <http://www.telegraph.co.uk/culture/theatre/drama/3650552/Happily-counting-his-chickens.html>

—, 'The Write Stuff', *Independent*, 9 April 1997 <http://www.independent.co.uk/arts-entertainment/the-write-stuff-1266024.html>

Stephenson, Heidi and Natasha Langridge, *Rage and Reason: Women Playwrights on Playwriting* (London: Methuen Drama, 1997).

Stokes, John, 'Country Matters', *The Times Literary Supplement*, 7 August 2009, p. 21.

—, 'The City Inside Me', *The Times Literary Supplement*, 10 April 2009, p. 17.

Trueman, Matt, 'Making a Stink About the Royal Court's *Jerusalem*', *Guardian theatre blog*, 20 July 2009 <www.guardian.co.uk/stage/theatreblog/2009/jul/20/royal-court-jerusalem>

Notes

1. See Aleks Sierz, *In-Yer-Face Theatre*, pp. 161–7, 236.
2. Jez Butterworth, 'A Film-maker's Diary', *Mojo & A Film-maker's Diary*, p. 147.
3. For reviews see *Theatre Record*, Vol. XV, No. 15 (1995), pp. 954–8; Vol. XVI, No. 21 (1996), pp. 1316–18.
4. For reviews see *Theatre Record*, Vol. XXII, No. 8 (2002), pp. 478–82.
5. Quoted in Aleks Sierz, 'Happily Counting His Chickens'.
6. For reviews see *Theatre Record*, Vol. XXVI, No. 5 (2006), pp. 266–8.
7. Anon., 'Jez Butterworth (Writer) and Ian Rickson (Director) in Conversation'.
8. John Stokes, 'The City Inside Me'.
9. For reviews see *Theatre Record*, Vol. XXIX, No. 7 (2009), pp. 336–40.
10. For the relationship between the two plays see Ian Rickson, 'Interview: Ian Rickson'.
11. Jez Butterworth, 'Interview', *The Review Show*.

12. John Stokes, 'Country Matters'.
13. For reviews see *Theatre Record*, Vol. XXIX, No. 14 (2009), pp. 767–71; Vol. XXX, No. 3 (2010), pp. 122–5.
14. For the controversial use of a petrol smell see Matt Trueman, 'Making a Stink about the Royal Court's *Jerusalem*'.
15. David Edgar, *State of Play*, p. 27. See also Aleks Sierz, 'The Write Stuff'.
16. Benedict Nightingale, *The Future of Theatre*, pp. 20, 22.
17. Peter Ansorge, *From Liverpool to Los Angeles*, p. 60.
18. Vera Gottlieb, 'Lukewarm Britannia', p. 211.
19. Quoted in Heidi Stephenson and Natasha Langridge, *Rage and Reason*, p. 28.
20. Quoted in ibid., p. 137.
21. Elaine Aston and Janelle Reinelt, *The Cambridge Companion to Modern British Women Playwrights*, p. 16. See also Aston, *Feminist Views on the English Stage*, p. 5.
22. Graham Saunders, 'Introduction', p. 7.
23. Dan Rebellato, 'Jez Butterworth', p. 121.
24. Dominic Dromgoole, *The Full Room*, pp. 43, 42.
25. Ibid., p. 42.
26. Michael Billington, *State of the Nation*, p. 359.
27. David Ian Rabey, *English Drama Since 1940*, pp. 198–9.
28. Ibid., p. 199.
29. Steve Blandford, *Film, Drama and the Break-Up of Britain*, p. 44.
30. Amelia Howe Kritzer, *Political Theatre in Post-Thatcher Britain*, p. 60.
31. Ibid., pp. 60, 61.
32. Aleks Sierz, '"Art Flourishes in Times of Struggle"', p. 45.
33. Paul Kingsnorth, 'Oak, Ash and Thorn'.
34. Stokes, 'Country Matters'.
35. Charlotte Higgins, 'Jez Butterworth's Jerusalem'.
36. Ibid.
37. Dominic Cavendish, 'Jerusalem'.
38. Ibid.

4 JIM CARTWRIGHT

Anette Pankratz

Road; Bed; The Rise and Fall of Little Voice; I Licked a Slag's Deodorant; Hard Fruit

Introduction

Born and still living in Lancashire, Jim Cartwright seems easy to locate. His plays, however, are difficult to place: very often representing northern English working-class life, and yet performed all over the world; politically committed, but funnier than Edward Bond, gruffer than Alan Ayckbourn, but equally imbued with wit and style; containing elements of the surreal and absurd, but more realistic than Samuel Beckett. Although many of Cartwright's dramas have won awards and some have been turned into movies, they are usually conspicuously absent from standard monographs or anthologies on British drama.

Born in Farnworth, Lancashire, in 1958, and also educated there, Cartwright decided to go to the Royal Academy of Dramatic Art in London. After graduating he founded a performance group called Acme Acting, which offered to bring plays to people's homes, foreshadowing the innovative use of theatrical space in his dramatic works.[1] His first play, *Road*, first performed in a promenade production at the Royal Court in 1986, established his reputation as playwright with an ear for authentic (northern) dialogue and experimental forms of representation. *Road* won the Samuel Beckett Award, *Drama Magazine*'s Best New Play Award, the George Devine Award and the *Plays and Players* Award. One year later, the TV version produced by the BBC won the Monte Carlo Golden Nymph Award. Max Stafford-Clark, who had been Artistic Director of the Royal Court in the 1980s, directed a revival of the play for Out of

Joint in 1994, and a later production at the Lyric, Hammersmith in 2003 attempted to adapt the play to post-Thatcherite times.

The main subsequent plays, *Bed* (National Theatre, 1989), *To/Two* (Octagon, Bolton, 1989) and *The Rise and Fall of Little Voice* (National Theatre, 1992) substantiated Cartwright's standing. Many critics ranked him as writing in the tradition of John Osborne, some saw in him the legitimate successor of Tennessee Williams or Samuel Beckett. Dominic Dromgoole sees him as:

> The king of the wordsmiths [. . .] Cartwright dived down into the underclass and found together with an unspeakable pain, a richness, a vitality, a toughness, an imagination and a romance that took the breath away.[2]

Cartwright worked at the National Theatre, the Royal Court and was writer in residence at the Octagon Theatre, Bolton, from 1989 to 1991. In the late 1980s and early 1990s he was awarded the *Manchester Evening News* Best Play Award (for *Two*), the *Evening Standard* Award for Best Comedy of the Year and the Laurence Olivier Award for Best Comedy (for *The Rise and Fall of Little Voice*).

While the earlier plays quickly became classics and sure box-office successes, his new work could not sustain this kind of critical and commercial attention. Not least because of its enigmatically provocative title, *I Licked a Slag's Deodorant* (Royal Court, 1996) was compared with 'in-yer-face' plays such as Mark Ravenhill's *Shopping and Fucking* (1996) or Martin McDonagh's *The Beauty Queen of Leenane* (1996), and found slightly wanting. What had initially been deemed an innovative success formula in *Road*, the mixture of vignettes of northern working-class life and an episodic structure, was considered as a nostalgic succession of clichés in *Hard Fruit* (Royal Court, 2000), the last published play to date. With *Kiss the Sky* (Bush, 1996), Cartwright continued his experimentation with the musical form, begun with *The Rise and Fall of Little Voice*, but without its wide acclaim.[3] Probably due to the less enthusiastic reception of his dramas in the 1990s, he started to diversify, working as director (very often of his own plays), writing for television and film, and publishing his first novel, *Supermarket Supermodel*, in 2008.

With growing temporal distance, Cartwright's earlier plays are perceived less as politically relevant statements about working-class life in Britain, than as popular entertainment full of local colour and comedy. *Road*, *The Rise and Fall of Little Voice* and *Two* (set in a pub and designed for two actors who embody all the characters) give the performers great opportunities to demonstrate their versatility, which makes them apt and sought-after star vehicles.[4] Thus, Ian Dury took over the part of Scullery for the production of *Road* in the Royal Court's main auditorium in 1987. *The Rise and Fall of Little Voice* originally provided both Jane Horrocks and Alison Steadman with great performance pieces. In the movie version, titled *Little Voice* (Miramax, 1998), Horrocks acts in a star cast together with Brenda Blethyn, Ewan McGregor and Michael Caine (who won a Golden Globe in 1999 for his portrayal of Ray). In the 2009 revival at the Vaudeville Theatre directed by Terry Johnson, *X-Factor* star Diana Vickers played Little Voice next to Cartwright's son James's Billy.[5]

The Plays

Road (1986)

Premiering at the Royal Court Theatre Upstairs on 22 March 1986 and later transferring to the main auditorium, *Road* established Cartwright as an important young dramatist.[6] The play was part of a trilogy about the North produced at the Royal Court (the other two plays were Terry Heaton's *Short Change* and Andrea Dunbar's *Shirley*).[7] It tells the story of a Lancashire town in the 1980s, hit by economic change and Thatcherite policies. In the first production (and most performances afterwards) the theatrical space extended beyond the confines of the stage. The Royal Court (including the bar and the street outside) became the acting space with the main plots presented as a promenade performance; the audience did not sit on chairs watching from a safe distance, but followed the characters on a typical night out on the eponymous road, from the ritual preparations at home to the disorderly drunken return after closing time, often accompanied by someone picked up in the pub or on the road.[8] This tight, almost Aristotelian temporal structure is undercut by a series of fragmented scenes, which move from glimpses into the characters' homes to events in the disco, pub, chip shop and road.

The bits and pieces are held together by the roguish Scullery. A cross between a lord of misrule, a Brechtian narrator and the stage manager of Thornton Wilder's *Our Town* (1938), he welcomes the audience and takes them on a journey through the supposedly unknown territory:[9]

> Wid' your night yous chose to come and see us. Wid' our night as usual we's all gettin' ready and turning out for a drink. THIS IS OUR ROAD! But tonight it's your road an' all! Don't feel awkward wi' us, make yourselves at home. You'll meet 'all-sorts' down here, I'm telling you, love. An' owt can happen tonight [. . .] Let's shove off downt' Road and find out! We'll go down house by house. Hold tight! Here we go! Come on! (p. 9)

Scullery's extroverted showmanship stands in contrast to an atmosphere of stasis and despair. Most people have lost their jobs and have to get by on social security. Boozing, smoking and quick sex at the end of the evening briefly and only superficially cover up their hopelessness. As the characters point out in direct addresses to the audience: 'Fucking long life in' it' (pp. 11, 15). Monologues further accentuate their isolation and often juxtapose the dire economic and political situation of 1980s Britain with a past of affluence and class solidarity. Middle-aged Jerry reminisces:

> There was so many jobs then. [. . .] You had the hit parade. Holidays in the Isle of Man or Blackpool. *'Volare'*. We all felt special but safe at the same time. (pp. 30–1)

The members of the younger generation do not even have the option to take refuge in their memories – they are living in a present without a hopeful future.

The seemingly random life on and around the road culminates in two scenes at the end of Acts One and Two: the death of Joey and his girlfriend Clare, and the performative outbursts by Louise, Carol, Brick and Eddie.[10] According to Joey, 'The world's a fat toilet. [. . .] Madhouse in' it this nineteen eighty-seven. Packed with muck. There's no jobs. I was robbed of mine. My future snatched' (pp. 33–4). This is why he decides to stay in bed and refuses to eat and drink. Here *Road* breaks up its strict temporal pattern and follows 'JOEY'S STORY' (p. 33), as Scullery introduces it to the audience, over a period of two weeks. Joey and Clare, who joins him out of love, die without having found the wished-for revelation: 'Look at me I am the solution. There is no solution' (p. 46).

While Act One ends with Joey and Clare's deaths, Act Two offers an imaginative and performative alternative to their utter desolation. Louise, Carol, Brick and Eddie at first seem to perpetuate the usual ritual that follows closing time: going home, drinking some more and having sex. But Carol upsets the awkward automatism, demanding, 'I want somethin' else to happen for a change' (p. 78), and the two young men initiate the women into their strategy for 'when outside gets to you' (p. 78). After getting seriously drunk and listening to Otis Redding's 'Try a Little Tenderness', all four emit cathartic rants in which they let out their anger and frustration.[11] The refrain 'If I keep shouting somehow a somehow I might escape' (p. 83) does not provide solutions either, but in contrast to Joey and Clare, it leaves the young people with a glimmer of hope, in the words of Simon Jones, 'a poetic space where the characters might imagine a transcendence of their cultural, political and social conditions, beyond any conception of class'.[12] The original casting highlighted the connectedness of the two sequences as the roles of Joey and Brick as well as that of Clare and Louise were played by the same actors.

On the meta-level, *Road* can be seen as a dramatised, prolonged version of this angry shout despite, or because of, the fact that it lacks any concrete solutions. It presents an imaginative and critical portrait of Britain in the 1980s, imbued with the vitality of northern working-class life. Its innovative use of theatrical space and the emphasis on performativity turned it into both a critical and financial success. At the time of its first performance critics hailed it as one of the most significant and incisive statements about Thatcherite, post-industrial Britain, styling Cartwright as the 'voice for the Eighties'.[13] Nowadays, the play is considered a modern classic and revived regularly.[14]

Bed (1989)

Bed premiered on 8 March 1989 at the National Theatre. It not only continues the monosyllabic titles of Cartwright's early plays, it also offers yet another fresh approach towards theatrical space. The bed of the title dominates the stage; behind it are a *'mountain of armchairs'* (p. 93) and a similarly alpine chest of drawers.[15] In this Brobdignagian setting, seven characters sleep and act out their lives and dreams. Unlike *Road*, the action of the play resembles a surreal tale: after the characters have settled in the huge bed and fallen asleep, they are woken up by the insomniac Sermon Head. The dust he, she or it blows into the general direction of the sleepers wakes up Marjorie, who desperately needs water. The Couple goes on an expedition, but eventually returns empty-handed and frustrated. The Spinster digs out a box, which contains objects over which the others break out in tears and which in turn fill Marjorie's glass. *'Soft white feathers begin to fall'* (p. 121).

Around this plot, Cartwright weaves a structure of solos and ensemble pieces that explore the possibilities of the theatre. With the exception of the altruistic Couple in search for water, all the characters remain fixed in the bed, and yet, at the same time, they travel through space and time, sometimes together, sometimes alone. Similar to Thornton Wilder's *A Happy Journey to Trenton and Campden* (1931), Charles sets off on a trip through England's countryside (and implicitly from pre-war culture through the 1960s to the 1970s) with the help of words and mime, gradually joined by the others. Sitting in bed, they overtake an invisible car, catch a bird, have a picnic, sing the Beatles' 'A Hard Day's Night', drive through the night – with the help of two *'little torches under the sheet'*, which serve as headlights (p. 100) – and end up at a disco. Although the characters all seem past their prime, in this scene they are rejuvenated by the communal experience. Moments of elation like these are countered by traumatic events such as the Captain's shipwreck (which is also re-enacted in the huge bed), the Couple getting lost or Marjorie's memories of her stale marital routine with her husband and the stillbirth of her child (pp. 120–1).

The oscillations between stage reality and memory, moments of distress and happiness, are punctuated and controlled by the rants of Sermon Head. This non-human, but not really inhuman, figure watches over the characters, envious of their sleep:

> Zedding hogs. Sleep sippers and spitters. [. . .] You cannot get a good English sleep these days. I can't even get a takeaway. They're not worthy of sleep them snore hogs. I am. So am. Number one sleep fan, student, swot. I've grasped all its degrees. I've got Forty Winks after me name. I've classified every type. One's sleep is well used. Another second hand. One's is brittle. One's is see-through. One's is alchemical. One's is passed around. One's a sleepskin rug.
> (pp. 109–10)

Sermon Head's logorrhoea anatomises sleep and atomises language. Puns, rhymes, half-rhymes, one-liners and word associations follow the logic of dreams. The monologues keep the characters from sleeping and trigger most of the fantastic bursts of activity on stage. It is uncertain whether we see the extended dream of one of the characters, the fusion of their individual dreams or an amalgam of archetypal situations. Unlike *Road*, *Bed* forgoes specificity and clear referentiality. The characters are types, as is clear from their names: Spinster, Captain, Couple, Bosom Lady and Sermon Head. Even the 'real' names of Charles and Marjorie point towards their roles as embodiments of typical middle-class Englishness. Superficially, the characters fulfil all the comical (stage) stereotypes. The Spinster loves to clean and hates her body; the Captain is gruff and the Bosom Lady's life 'has been just one long feather boa continually in the air!' (p. 118).

But beneath the surface, there is a common paradoxical pattern of varying states of isolation and community, of dancing and crying together about one's loneliness and loss.

Bed intrigued its first critics with poetic imagery, surrealism and a cast of mainly octogenarians, but the reviews also remarked on the play's lack of focus and structure. For quite a few, the dreamlike atmosphere bordered on the boring.[16]

The Rise and Fall of Little Voice (1992)

The Rise and Fall of Little Voice (first performed on 16 June 1992 at the National Theatre) reframes the setting of *Road* as a fairy tale. The play takes place in a northern town and portrays lower-class life in Britain in a way which does not offer much hope. And yet, the faint note of optimism in *Road* reappears in *The Rise and Fall of Little Voice* in a more sustained fashion. Title character Little Voice (LV) gradually finds herself through the medium of song, with the help of the big voices of the 1950s and 1960s, the repertoire of Shirley Bassey, Judy Garland, Marilyn Monroe, Edith Piaf and Gracie Fields. In contrast to *Road* and *Bed*, this play employs a clear-cut, and realistic, well-made plot, focusing on LV: her fraught life with her mother, her brief rise as a singer in Mr Boo's club and a happy ending with Billy after her supposed 'fall'.

The exposition contrasts LV and her mother Mari, the 'Merry Widow' (p. 183) who lives according to the motto 'Live while you can' (p. 182), drinking, dancing and having affairs in order to forget about her drab life. LV and she are complete opposites: where Mari acts extrovertedly and larger than life, LV retreats into silence. Openly aggressive sexuality meets solipsistic shyness; big mouth counters Little Voice. This initial situation is broken up when Mari's latest love interest, Ray, a rather seedy ex-bookie-turned-manager, hears LV singing in her bedroom. Awestruck, he sees his opportunity to get very rich very fast.

Act One teems with Mari's witty one-liners, her energy and the dramatic irony that arises when she mistakes Ray's ostentatious interest in LV for a proposal of marriage (or at least a long-term relationship):

Ray I'm so excited, it's like at the races when you've found
yourself a little nag no one's noticed but you know you're
on to a certainty and you're feeling, this is it! She is the
one. Do you know what I mean?

Mari Go on, yes! Yes! I'm with you lad. Yes [. . .]
(pp. 199–200)

Despite the comedy, the scene already bears the seeds of the more
sombre and tense second act. To Ray it does not matter who brings
him success: a racing 'nag', one of his striptease dancers or a singer.
Cajoled by him, LV agrees to sing in public and becomes an instant
success. In their triumph, Ray, Mari and club owner Mr Boo do not
notice LV's collapse, and make plans for a glamorous future (p. 236).
The situation comes to a crisis when Ray drops his mask, brutally
renounces Mari and tries to force LV on to the stage by slapping her.
The violence triggers LV's cathartic breakdown. Speaking and singing
in the voices of Monroe, Garland, Piaf and Bassey, she first knocks
Ray down the stairs, later she takes her mother to account and thereby
starts to find her own voice: 'I couldn't speak up to you, cause I could
never get a word in! [. . .] These become my tongues. [. . .] And now
they've gone, I don't know where this is coming from' (p. 259).

The only person who genuinely seems to care for the frail young
woman is Billy. This shy, awkward phone engineer complements LV.
Her private singing matches Billy's secret enthusiasm for lighting
design. At the end of the play, the pair have fled into the empty club.
When Billy starts his elaborate light show, LV sings in her own voice.

The Rise and Fall of Little Voice juxtaposes the grimy realism also
prevalent in *Road* and controls it with a melodramatic plot (in the
truest meaning of the word), which proves that 'the meek shall inherit
the earth' (p. 239). While Mr Boo quotes the Sermon on the Mount
in order to give his greed a humanist cache, the play has the meek, shy
and quiet win by turning the private public with the help of the fourth
wall. Despite her breakdown, LV triumphs in the eyes (and ears) of the
audience. Her nervous breakdown turns into a brilliant theatrical *tour
de force*, when the actress playing LV switches from one classic to the
next:

(*as Marilyn Monroe*) 'But baby I like it hot.' (*as Judy Garland*) 'Glory, glory, hallelujah, glory, glory, hallelujah, his truth is marching on.' 'I'm frightened Auntie Em, I'm frightened' 'There's no place like home. There's no place like home.' (p. 250)

The fusion of opposites also lends depth and dignity to Mari. Extroverted, witty and callous, she has to live through 'the famous "Tart's end"' (p. 260) when Ray rejects her. Balancing the comical tartness with Mari's frustrations, the play forgoes too facile stereotypes: 'Well, some might say I've got what I deserve. But that's the problem, I've never had what I deserved. I was more than this dump I had to live in' (p. 257). As with LV, on the performative level Mari indeed is more 'than this dump', she is a great role for a comic actress, another reason why the play was turned into a movie, transferred to the West End, was performed on Broadway and is regularly revived. The high praise heaped on the play at its premiere, setting the story of shy Little Voice on a par with Tennessee Williams's *A Glass Menagerie* (1944) or the plays of Eugene O'Neill, has given way to the acknowledgement of the piece's theatrical dimensions and its potential to provide the audience with an amusing night out.[17]

I Licked a Slag's Deodorant (1996)

Although Cartwright belongs to the generation of politically committed playwrights of the 1980s, the explicitness and post-dramatic experimentations of *I Licked a Slag's Deodorant*, first performed at the Royal Court on 27 November 1996 (directed by Cartwright himself), come closer to the then new 'in-yer-face' drama than to the plays of David Hare, Howard Brenton or David Edgar written at about the same time.[18] Set in contemporary London, *I Licked a Slag's Deodorant* depicts urban seediness and ennui. Like in Mark Ravenhill's *Shopping and Fucking*, human relationships have become either transactions or addictions or both: Slag works in a 'Fuck factory' (p. 5) to finance her crack addiction. Man is initially one of her customers, later moves in with her and eventually '*lives under the bed*' (p. 17). Where *Road* and

The Rise and Fall of Little Voice bustled with energy despite the characters' social deprivation, *I Licked a Slag's Deodorant* is shaped by apathy and isolation. Man and Slag do not interact, they deliver their personal stories mainly by way of parallel monologues which reflect on past events.

The play opens with Man telling the audience about the title-giving incident: 'The carpet was damp. I was cold in my vest. I licked her deodorant while she was out the room' (p. 1). Man's monologue switches from the narrative reconstruction of the evening to memories of childhood and adolescence. These are intercut by Slag's not very complimentary comments on their encounter – 'soft twat' (p. 4) – and her craving for crack.

Over the course of the play, Man's former life with his mother is gradually transposed into his life with Slag: 'Our flat was damp. We never moved. We kept ourselves to ourselves. We had the occasional visitor. We had a relative. Uncle Cigburns' (p. 5). In the present, the not-so-occasional visitors pay for sex with Slag and the relative is 'Uncle Crack' (p. 5). The monotony of Man's life is enhanced by his descriptions of private spaces. Everyone he knows – his mother, his dead neighbour, Slag, he himself – lives in the same uniform space, characterised by damp, squalor, dust, 'a bucket under the sink' (pp. 1, 8, 14), sparse furniture and 'the telly' (pp. 5, 7, 8).

Gradually, the realism prevalent in the narratives gives way to the Kafkaesque situation of Man living under Slag's bed together with 'Uncle' (p. 18) and 'other creatures' (p. 17). This can be interpreted as symbolic of his death-like life or as an indication of his status as a talking corpse who was killed by Slag's pimp Fatman and now exists only in Slag's drug-induced fantasy. This would reiterate the fate of one of Man's neighbours, who was found dead 'in his flat, covered in dust and beetles' (p. 2) with the television still running, 'one programme after another. Then going round again and again, and he's just the same, dead in the corner, or is it me!' (p. 8).

Slag's detailed information on her work only superficially counters Man's dusty existence. In her perspective, the joys of sex turn into a depersonalised routine: 'I hate every man jack the same. All get equal measure. As you give me your spunk I give you the whore's spit but you don't know it' (p. 15). Her direct communication with the audience focuses on the financial transactions, the money she needs and the services she can offer for it.

Critics acknowledged the power of the performances by Tim Potter (Man) and especially Polly Hemingway (Slag), as well as indicating the emotional impact of the play. But it compared unfavourably to Martin McDonagh's *The Beauty Queen of Leenane*, performed at the Royal Court during *I Licked a Slag's Deodorant*'s first run, because Cartwright's trademark surrealism lacked direction and the elements of 'in-yer-face' writing appeared as unnecessary nods towards the then current dramatic fashions.[19]

Hard Fruit (2000)

First performed at the Royal Court on 31 March 2000 (directed by James Macdonald), *Hard Fruit* shows the last day in the life of the repressed homosexual Choke, at first sight a rather untypical topic for Cartwright. In a mixture of symbolist dream play, physical theatre and heightened realism, Choke is dying of cancer, and his obsession with martial arts and his refusal to come out are interwoven. The regular command to 'Shut gate [tight] ahind ya!' (pp. 3, 7, 9, 12, 17, 31) not only indicates the old man's wish to be left alone, it also sums up his life. Feeling physically attracted to men, he does not give in to his desires, but tries to control them, living on the margins both of mainstream society and of the gay subculture. This is set parallel to Choke's lethal illness. When he turned away from his friend, not daring to kiss him, 'Maybe that's when the cancer cell doubled up and the cancer first began to crawl' (p. 41).

Choke's reticence and self-loathing are offset by a group of friends and acquaintances. Sparring partner Sump cherishes his life as an old-age pensioner who indulges in the mundane, albeit the mundane with some queer twists:

> Have a read and a chat down the library by the warm pipes. Have a walk through the park about ten miles per flower. I buy meself a cassette or LP from the charity shop

> every week, sometimes it's a good un like Boy George and I make up a dance in the kitchen. I sometimes pop in the Lesbian café where they shave my head for me and give me a hot pot, else a slap-up curry from Paki Miranda. I'll take a pint at night or go round someone's [. . .] At weekends I go to a club with the young uns. I just do what I want. (p. 29)

So do Yacky and Silver, a mixed-aged couple, and Friar Jiggle, the bouncer at a gay nightclub. All of them enjoy both the comforts of the gay community and the growing acceptance of their lives by society at large.

Despite its focus on queer history, *Hard Fruit* resembles Cartwright's other plays in its nostalgic perspective on northern working-class life. For example, Choke's athleticism and his tough 'Samurai love' (p. 41) are presented as forgotten or ignored facets of 1950s working-class culture. The men Choke remembers have nothing in common with the stereotypical images of (upper-class) effeminacy usually associated with male homosexuality:[20]

> [T]hey was big, like Rock Hudson, a bigness soft-weighted. They looked after their own. I'm talking about pubs wi' sawdust on the floor, I'm talking about vaults, false teeth on the table, smoke holding the place up, the beer in chunks. Hard places. [. . .] You might just still see that type today, older, grey, they wouldn't be able to stand the word gay. You might see 'em in a Berni Inn, Sunday cardigans on, four men having a meal, signet rings, good heads of hair. They're dying out together, that breed, end of an era. (p. 41)

Choke's suicide seems to mark the end of another era. *Hard Fruit* depicts him as the last closeted man of his generation (although all his friends and neighbours seem to know about his homosexuality), while his peers enjoy life uninhibited by the taboos and legal restrictions prevalent in the 1950s and 1960s. But the nostalgic reminiscences of the 'tender tough men' (p. 41) who appear more authentic than the present sauna-and-gym culture undercut this narrative of progress. So do the instances of homophobia. Yack's partner Silver wants to learn karate in order to defend himself from attacks, and Choke is pelted with half-bricks by the young people from the neighbourhood (p. 31).

The play ends with Choke's ambivalent death and symbolic resurrection. After finally confessing his desires and feelings to Friar Jiggle, following a long choreographed fight with Sump, he kisses his friend on the mouth and strangles himself in true Samurai fashion. In the last scene, after the funeral, men in overalls clean up the cluttered backyard. Choke's karate machine remains on the empty stage. It turns itself on, '*beautiful, precision engineering in motion*' (p. 57). Even when thrown into the skip, it keeps on whirring, just as Choke had kept on fighting as 'hard fruit'.

Many reviewers were moved by the portrayal of Choke's life and dying, highlighting the impressive performances of Nicholas Woodeson (Choke) and Richard Hope (Sump), especially in the demanding and physically trying wrestling and dancing scenes. But some also criticised the heavy symbolism which often verges on the stereotypical and the all-too-obvious.[21]

Summary

Although Cartwright's plays reflect the *zeitgeist* of life in Britain from the 1980s to 2000, they often run counter to the prevalent dramatic and theatrical trends. In contrast to politically committed 'state-of-the-nation' plays such as Caryl Churchill's *Serious Money* (1987) or Howard Brenton and David Hare's *Pravda* (1985), which take Thatcher's neoliberal politics to task and implicitly or explicitly offer socialist alternatives,[22] Cartwright's dramas forgo any direct criticism.[23] Thatcher and her Conservative Party are never mentioned, nor do the characters favour political means of resistance. In *Road* Jerry complains about his lack of purpose after he lost his job, but he cannot say why or 'how that time could turn into this time. So horrible for me and so complicated for me. And being poor and no good, no use' (p. 31).[24] Unlike the communist Phil Bott, Joey cannot envisage a clear political change either: 'I tried all that for a bit. I went with Phil to his meetings, but still I cun' decide who to attack. There's not one thing to blame. There's not just good and bad, everything's deeper' (p. 39).

Clare and Joey's hunger strike and death do not necessarily serve as the 'one true gesture of true revolt against the grim reality of *Road*' as Una Chaudhuri assumes,[25] but rather seem to be an indication of the futility of revolt, maybe part of a de-politicised 'fate', the term used by Mari in *The Rise and Fall of Little Voice* to comment on her 'Tart's end':

> I knew in my true heart there were nothing else for it, no matter how hard I tried I could not avoid what fate had reserved for me all along [. . .] an old girl left dirty on her belly in an alley, homeless and juiceless and tootless [sic] and solid stone cold alone. (p. 260)

Joey and Clare, the characters in *Bed*, Mari, the Man, Slag and Choke all end up in a fatal cul-de-sac: either dead or alive in a lethal state of emptiness, echoing the beginning of Beckett's *Waiting for Godot* (1953) in the textbook phrase: 'Nothing to be done'.

Eschewing political solutions, some characters find salvation in their private lives and the discovery of their true selves. Little Voice triumphs over both her mother and her manager, elopes with Billy and at the very end of *The Rise and Fall of Little Voice* she actually rises into the bright lights of Billy's laser show, singing in her newly found authentic voice (p. 261). Most of Cartwright's plays, however, end on a more ambivalent note. Man in *I Licked a Slag's Deodorant* breaks his isolation and lives – more or less contentedly – with Slag, albeit stuck under her bed. Choke refuses to go to hospital to get treatment for his cancer and strangles himself, but not without realising (and partly compensating for) what he has missed in his life:

> I keep dreaming of him lately, he's as in youth, he's radiant in a perfect white judo gi. I'm so glad to see him, I can't help myself and try to hold him but the white light of his suit stops me at every try. The only place I can enter is his lips. (p. 42)

Ambivalence, uncertainty and the retreat into the private sphere instead of a clear political stance relate Cartwright's dramas to the plays of the post-Thatcher generation. But although *I Licked a Slag's Deodorant* looks at the seedier side of urban life and in its parallel monologues employs post-dramatic techniques, it lacks the provocative 'in-yer-face' aesthetics 'that takes the audience by the scruff of the neck and shakes it until it gets the message'.[26] On the contrary, Man and Slag's narratives emphasise distance and the poeticism of the absurd.

Instead of concrete solutions which could alleviate the bleak status quo, most of the plays operate with nostalgic images of the times when working-class culture offered authenticity, dignity and class solidarity, 'True good, a 1950s good you don't feel now' as Choke puts it in *Hard Fruit* (p. 49).[27] The theme of a better England of the past permeates *Road*, reconstructed by the Professor's file cards and tapes, celebrated both in Jerry's monologue and Old Molly's memories and folk songs. Likewise, the opposition between a deficient present and a paradisiacal past returns in *Bed* in the characters' miming of a drive down country lanes, meeting the vicar and buying strawberry jam (p. 95). Charles's 'poem' cherishes the 'Lassie and Laddie and Lord Land' (p. 99). His comments on the negative changes of the last thirty years are later taken up by the Spinster. In contrast to Charles's lyricisms, her speech uses vitriol and sarcasm, bemoaning Britain's loss of power and tradition: 'Putrification. | England hangs off the map | half scrounger, half whore. | Oh Britannia | doing anything to get fat' (p. 113). Even in the upbeat and optimistic *The Rise and Fall of Little Voice* the title character gains her strength from memories of her dead father and his record collection, which consists of past stars from the 1950s and 1960s.

Little Voice signals hope by finding her own voice; so do Louise, Carol, Brick and Eddie in *Road* (again significantly after completely immersing themselves in Otis Redding's soul music). Cartwright regularly employs performance and performativity, literature and the arts as direct or indirect means to escape the present impasse. In *Road*, it is not only the young people's outburst which implicitly correlates agency with theatricality. Scullery holds the piece together by means of his bravado performances. His sexual energy at least temporarily challenges the characters' passivity; his wit and dexterity provide comic relief and counterpoint the general doom and gloom; his cheeky addresses and explanations give the audience some guidance through the seemingly random and chaotic action. While Scullery is mainly situated in the 'here and now' of *Road*, Friar Jiggle's paintings in *Hard Fruit* again link personal fulfilment with preserving the past. Drawing serves him as a means for articulation, 'No reada-writa, just draw' (p. 38). The portraits he does for a stained-glass pub window, moreover, reconstruct and preserve queer working-class culture. He intends to create a historical document on a par with the Bayeux Tapestry (p. 43): 'All the peepoh who suffered for all the peepoh who now enjoy' (p. 38).

Cartwright's emphasis on creativity and theatricality as a means of escape indirectly and on the meta-level also applies to his plays. Breaking up the confines of fourth-wall realism is usually seen as subversion and empowerment in the tradition of Brecht's Epic Theatre. Some critics claim that Cartwright even goes beyond Brecht. According to Una Chaudhuri, *Road*'s textual and theatrical strategy is the deconstruction of environmental theatre by a series of 'otherings'. In the intricate web of performance traces, appropriation of liminal spaces within the theatre and by blurring the boundaries between auditorium and stage, the play supposedly undermines a range of theatrical conventions from naturalism and realism to Brechtian alienation and performative experiments:

> The theatre's investment in presence, visibility, and display is
> revealed in *Road* to be an illusion, a fantasy of anthropological
> dimensions that seeks to vanquish otherness without the pain
> of being othered oneself.[28]

In an alternative reading, however, one could interpret Scullery's commentaries as a comforting gesture for a typical Royal Court audience to find their way around the venue. At no point are middle-class certainties undermined or questioned.[29] On an epistemological and structural level, *Road*'s and *Bed*'s use of overtly theatrical means to stage a search for meaning resemble the iconography of existential faultlines presented in Beckett's plays: Winnie in *Happy Days* (1961) covered by sand resembles Joey and Clare dying in bed as well as Sermon Head's monologues in *Bed*; Krapp listening to and commenting on his tapes as acts of futile documentation comes close to the Professor's notes in *Road*. Most of the plays advocate an attitude of resignation and 'Nothing to be done', occasionally undercut by an un-Beckettian emphasis on the potential bliss of private lives. One could interpret this as an indication of the plays' timelessness and universality. On a more critical note, the continuing popularity, especially of *Road* and *The Rise and Fall of Little Voice*, can be seen as fulfilling the expectations of the mainstream: criticism with a feel-good factor providing the audience, in Simon Jones's words, 'a voyeuristic (and safely distanced) account of the new poor',[30] plus offering a nostalgic look back in therapeutic anger at a time when it was still almost possible to divide the world into 'us' and 'them'.

Primary Sources

Works by Jim Cartwright

Plays One: Road, Bed, Two, The Rise and Fall of Little Voice (London: Methuen Drama, 1996).
I Licked a Slag's Deodorant (London: Methuen Drama, 1996).
Hard Fruit (London: Methuen Drama, 2000).

Secondary Sources

Billington, Michael, 'Cartwright, Jim', in K. A. Berney (ed.), *Contemporary British Dramatists* (London: St James Press, 1994), pp. 119–21.
Bradwell, Mike, *The Reluctant Escapologist: Adventures in Alternative Theatre* (London: Nick Hern, 2010).
Chaudhuri, Una, *Staging Place: The Geography of Modern Drama* (Ann Arbor: Michigan UP, 1997).
Cohn, Ruby, *Retreats from Realism in Recent English Drama* (Cambridge: CUP, 1991).

Davies, Stevie, 'Class Act', *Guardian*, 2 August 2008 <http://www.guardian.co.uk/books/2008/aug/02/fiction8/print>

Dromgoole, Dominic, *The Full Room: An A–Z of Contemporary Playwriting* (London: Methuen Drama, 2002).

Gottlieb, Vera, '1979 and After: A View', in Baz Kershaw (ed.), *The Cambridge History of British Theatre Volume 3: Since 1895* (Cambridge: CUP, 2004), pp. 412–25.

Jones, Simon, 'New Theatre for New Times: Decentralisation, Innovation and Pluralism, 1975–2000', in Baz Kershaw (ed.), *The Cambridge History of British Theatre Volume 3: Since 1895* (Cambridge: CUP, 2004), pp. 448–69.

Peacock, D. Keith, *Thatcher's Theatre: British Theatre and Drama in the Eighties* (Westport, CT: Greenwood Press, 1999).

Piper, Frances, 'Jim Cartwright', *British Council: Contemporary Writers* <http://www.contemporarywriters.com/authors/?p=auth252>

Roberts, Philip, *The Royal Court Theatre and the Modern Stage* (Cambridge: CUP, 1999).

Sadler, Geoff, '*Road* by Jim Cartwright', in K. A. Berney (ed.), *Contemporary British Dramatists* (London: St James Press, 1994), pp. 805–7.

Sierz, Aleks, *In-Yer-Face Theatre: British Drama Today* (London: Faber & Faber, 2001).

Sinfield, Alan, *The Wilde Century: Effeminacy, Oscar Wilde and the Queer Moment* (New York: Columbia UP, 1994).

Stafford-Clark, Max and Philip Roberts, *Taking Stock: The Theatre of Max Stafford-Clark* (London: Nick Hern, 2007).

Notes

1. Stevie Davies, 'Class Act'; Michael Billington, 'Cartwright'; Frances Piper, 'Jim Cartwright'.
2. Dominic Dromgoole, *The Full Room*, p. 49.
3. See the account of *Kiss the Sky* in Mike Bradwell, *The Reluctant Escapologist*, pp. 211–12.
4. D. Keith Peacock, *Thatcher's Theatre*, p. 194.
5. Michael Billington, *Guardian, Theatre Record*, Vol. XXIX, No. 21 (2009), p. 1117.
6. Peacock, *Thatcher's Theatre*, p. 192. Some reviewers even praised him as the legitimate successor of 'Angry Young Man' John Osborne.
7. Philip Roberts, *The Royal Court Theatre*, p. 192.
8. Ruby Cohn, *Retreats from Realism*, p. 47.
9. Cohn, *Retreats from Realism*, p. 45; Una Chaudhuri, *Staging Place*, p. 47.
10. Cohn, *Retreats from Realism*, p. 45; Simon Jones, 'New Theatre for New Times', pp. 455–6.
11. Chaudhuri, *Staging Place*, p. 51.
12. Jones, 'New Theatre for New Times', p. 456.

13. Alex Renton, *Independent, London Theatre Record,* Vol. VII, No. 2 (1987), pp. 86–7.

14. Roberts, *The Royal Court Theatre,* p. 194; Max Stafford-Clark, *Taking Stock,* p. 173.

15. Cohn, *Retreats from Realism,* p. 17.

16. Nicholas de Jongh, *Guardian;* Christopher Edwards, *The Spectator, London Theatre Record,* Vol. IX, No. 5 (1989), pp. 287–91.

17. Nicholas de Jongh, *Evening Standard; Theatre Record,* Vol. XII, No. 12 (1992), pp. 726–30; Michael Coveney, *Observer, Theatre Record,* Vol. XII, No. 13 (1992), p. 795.

18. American and German reviews especially tend to present Cartwright as part of the younger generation of playwrights such as Sarah Kane, Mark Ravenhill, Martin McDonagh or Jez Butterworth.

19. James Christopher, *Sunday Express;* John Gross, *Sunday Telegraph, Theatre Record,* Vol. XVI, No. 25 (1996), pp. 1554–7.

20. Alan Sinfield, *The Wilde Century,* pp. 140–1.

21. See, for example, Nick Curtis, *Evening Standard;* Michael Coveney, *Daily Mail;* Susannah Clapp, *Observer, Theatre Record,* Vol. XX, No. 7 (2000), pp. 415–18.

22. Jones, 'New Theatre', p. 450; Vera Gottlieb, '1979 and After', pp. 414, 419–20.

23. Jones, 'New Theatre', p. 454; Peacock, *Thatcher's Theatre,* p. 192.

24. Geoff Sadler, '*Road* by Jim Cartwright', p. 806.

25. Chaudhuri, *Staging Place,* p. 30.

26. Aleks Sierz, *In-Yer-Face Theatre,* p. 4.

27. Peacock, *Thatcher's Theatre,* p. 191.

28. Chaudhuri, *Staging Place,* p. 53.

29. Peacock, *Thatcher's Theatre,* p. 192.

30. Jones, 'New Theatre for New Times', p. 454. Jones used the quoted sentence to describe the impact of Andrea Dunbar's *Rita, Sue and Bob Too* (1982), another northern play presenting working-class life, but it seems applicable to Cartwright's plays as well. For instance, both Victoria Radin (for the *Guardian*) and Michael Ratcliffe (for the *Observer*) highlighted the voyeuristic atmosphere of *Road; London Theatre Record,* Vol. VI, No. 7 (1986), pp. 312–13.

5 MARTIN CRIMP

Martin Middeke

Dealing with Clair; The Treatment; The Misanthrope; Attempts on Her Life; The Country; Fewer Emergencies

Introduction

Martin Crimp is one of the most versatile, creative and aesthetically prolific and challenging playwrights of our time. Reminiscent of Samuel Beckett, whom Crimp has identified as one of his major influences and who once declared that his central aim was to make fiction and drama turn away from the well-trodden paths and 'puny exploits' of traditional realist form, Crimp has spent his career in search of new forms of aesthetic expression.[1] He has produced an impressive oeuvre that includes eleven major plays, four unpublished ones, accomplished stage adaptations, meticulous translations of European playwrights such as Chekhov, Marivaux, Genet, Ionesco and Koltès, as well as two prizewinning radio plays, an unpublished novel, and various other writings.[2]

Crimp certainly belongs among those writers whose life *is* their work. Characteristically, he appears to have never really lost an epistemological scepticism about (auto-)biographical truth, an attitude that both implicitly and explicitly permeates Crimp's entire work.

> Whatever I say to you [. . .] you will go away and make a shape from it. That shape will be definitive in the way that the relationship between you and I can never be. [. . .] You will undertake a shaping process . . . in which I as a person will be misinterpreted.[3]

Crimp was born in Dartford, Kent, on 14 February 1956. A year later his family moved to York. He read English at St Catharine's College, Cambridge, and after graduating moved to Richmond in Surrey. Crimp joined the writers' group at the Orange Tree Theatre in Richmond where he became Thames TV Writer-in-Residence in 1988–89. The Orange Tree premiered six of his plays over the next few years, thoroughly absurdist pieces such as *Living Remains* (1981), *Four Attempted Acts* (1984), *A Variety of Death-Defying Acts* (1985), or *Definitely the Bahamas* (1986) and the popular *Dealing with Clair* (1988) as well as the more experimental *Play with Repeats* (1989). The year 1990 marked a major step in Crimp's career when *No One Sees the Video* was premiered at the Royal Court Theatre Upstairs. *Getting Attention*, written before *No One Sees the Video*, was produced by the West Yorkshire Playhouse in 1991. A three-week stay in New York City during a Royal Court exchange programme resulted in *The Treatment* (1993), which was premiered at the Royal Court and directed by Lindsay Posner, winning the John Whiting Award. Crimp then adapted Molière's *The Misanthrope* (1996). In 1997 *Attempts on Her Life* was premiered at the Royal Court. This widely acclaimed play secured him a place among the most challenging experimental playwrights in the world. Other major Royal Court plays include *The Country* (2000), *Fewer Emergencies* (2005) and *The City* (2008).

The Plays

Dealing with Clair (1988)

Dealing with Clair was first performed on 14 October 1988. Since then, it was broadcast by the BBC in 1991, and frequently revived. The sparse plot centres on the estate agent Clair, who is about to sell Mike and Liz Walsum's suburban house to James, a sophisticated cash buyer. The unexpected offer of cash creates a dilemma for the couple as they have already accepted an offer from an elderly Shropshire couple. They emphasise repeatedly that they intend to 'behave honourably in this' (p. 15) yet, of course, they also do not mind cashing in on their luck. Critics have readily agreed that the play is a satire on 'the state of the market society', 'modern manners', or 'yuppie moral and emotional bankruptcy'.[4] Indeed, Liz and Mike's greed satirises the practice of gazumping during the house-buying and -selling craze at the end of the 1980s. The comedy of manners, however, is flanked by two major twists of plot that add mystery and thriller elements to the play. Clair, otherwise icily professional and enthusiastic about her job, seems much frailer when she is perceived on her own. A telephone conversation with her mother ends on a rather pensive note: 'Who knows *what* I'll do? Maybe make a killing and just . . . disappear. (*Laughs.*) That's right. Vanish' (p. 9). Ironically, her remark turns out a proleptic one as, in the second twist of plot, James changes into a sinister character who preys on Clair's privacy and ultimately, as another rather uncanny telephone call between James and Clair's mother lets shine through, seems very likely to have murdered her.

Crimp very loosely takes his cue from the case of the British estate agent Suzy Lamplugh, reported missing in 1986, and later declared dead, presumed murdered. The thriller elements of the plot, the satirical debunking of Thatcherite England and the subliminal feeling of betrayal between the married couple, who consider Clair both an object of desire and a threat, produce a lingering Pinteresque air of unease, menace and bad faith that permeates their interaction. The house, itself an object of desire, becomes a central symbol of the perverted, decaying system of 'Thatcher's ideology of a property-owning democracy'.[5] Ironically, yet quite tellingly, the builder Ashley in a minor scene points out that there is something very wrong with the structure of the house. Symbolically, thus, Crimp acidly asserts that something is indeed rotten in the state of Britain that will sooner rather than later pull the rug from under a nation's feet: 'I mean what we're talking about here is serious timber decay, we're talking about the structure, you with me?' (p. 47).

The Treatment (1993)

The Treatment was first performed on 15 April 1993 at the Royal

Court. The complex play is set in New York City, and it focuses on Anne, a young woman who has left her husband Simon, who has kept her in their home and allegedly taped her mouth to keep her silent. Jennifer and Andrew, a married couple of film producers, have bought Anne's life story in order to turn it into a major film. They give Anne's story a 'treatment', that is, they construct a marketable plotline. Yet it quickly turns out that the story Anne has to tell is by no means sensational enough in order to be likely to attract a film audience. Accordingly, Jennifer and Andrew hire Clifford, a forgotten play-wright, who once had a couple of Broadway hits and who would 'like to introduce a Shakespearean element' (p. 325) to Anne's story. In order to jolly Anne along, Andrew has casual and brutal sex with her, an act that he makes Clifford watch. Anne is shocked and in the course of the play reluctantly witnesses how her 'story' gets more and more 'treated', that is truncated and adapted to the violent and voyeuristic appeal of mass audiences. In the course of the action, Clifford is dismissed and Anne dropped from the project. In an act of irrational cruelty that is meant to take revenge on his eye-witnessing of her sex with Andrew, Anne makes Simon stab Clifford's eyes with a silver fork. The fourth act, in which the plot moves one year ahead, shows Anne having returned to Simon. Andrew leaves Jennifer in order to search for Anne, only to find her tied again to a chair with her mouth taped. He does not realise the strange sado-masochistic attraction that complementarily binds Anne and Simon to one another. Jennifer comes to look for Andrew and accidentally shoots Anne dead in the darkness. In the final scene of the play, the blind writer Clifford gets into a taxi steered by a blind taxi driver. The blind leading the blind is an obvious intertextual reference to *King Lear*, and, quite symbolically, the car and its blind passengers move through Manhattan:

Clifford Where is this? Where are we going?
Driver I've no idea, Clifford. (p. 389)

New York City and its 'labyrinthine strangeness' become synecdoches of the mediatised city in a play that is Crimp's relentless satire on the image-producing industry of film business.[6] Similar to *No One Sees the Video*, where the criticism is directed against the simulacra produced by market research, Crimp portrays a Baudrillardian world in which an essence or truth of a life is displaced into a kaleidoscopic myriad of perspectives and shapes, thus emphasising that an excess of technological communication has brought about a proliferation of (virtual) meanings. This impression is enhanced by the contradictory information that Anne herself provides about her life. As Aleks Sierz writes: 'How can you object to someone's life being stolen if they insist on giving it away?'[7] Here, in Baudrillard's words, the sign 'has no relation to any reality whatsoever; it is its own pure simulacrum'.[8] Andrew amply comments on this condition of hyperreality:

> **Andrew** The words, just the words, brought the emotion
> into being, and look at me – I have no control at all. Is it
> because you're real? We don't often meet real people here.
> We ourselves have no memories or stories. No enchant-
> ment, Anne. We are the disenchanted. We started out
> real, but the real-ness has burned out of us. (pp. 351–2)

Stylistically, the play features characteristic elements of Crimp's dramaturgy: subjectively shaped, surreal imagery; a precise sense of rhythm and atmosphere in the text as commas denote meticulously placed pauses, oblique strokes indicate points of interruption in overlapping dialogue, and brackets, for instance, refer to momentary changes of tone.[9] Overlapping dialogues and, as an augmentation of this, simultaneous conversations are indicative of Crimp's deep distrust of human communication. On the one hand, these scenes, again, function as synecdoches of the informational overkill in a hyperreal world; on the other hand, they are governed by the fact that the rationality that determines the characters' actions is notably of a purely strategic or instrumental rather than communicative nature.[10]

The Misanthrope (1996)

Compared to *The Treatment* and his subsequent plays, Crimp's virtuosic adaptation of Molière's classic seems like a playful finger exercise. 'The Misanthrope,' Crimp stated in an interview, 'was written entirely for my own amusement and enjoyment, just to get me out of a kind of black hole – if you like – of writing.'[11] While Molière's plot is set among fops, buffoons and spinsters, Crimp relocates it to a contemporary London scene that focuses on journalists, critics, agents, actors and film producers. Crimp turns Molière's tragi-comic hero Alceste into an acrimonious, self-righteous playwright and Célimène into Jennifer, a young and attractive, flirtatious, and cocaine-consuming Hollywood actress. In either play Célimène and Jennifer represent anything that both Alceste's high moral standards and demands would utterly have to despise, and yet they madly fall for. When Alceste in Molière brusquely ridiculed Oronte's clumsy attempt at verse, Crimp's Alceste likewise relentlessly attacks the attempt at a play by the notorious critic Covington – a portmanteau word of the names of two of the leading London theatre critics. In Crimp's play, the major satirical targets of Alceste's rage are 'sycophants, compromise, hypocrites, nepotism, betrayal, vested interests' (p. 109) and particularly the insensitivity of audiences 'gratefully reacting to yet another tour de force of classic over-acting' (p. 161). A musical by Andrew Lloyd Webber is likened to a 'natural disaster' (p. 119), and Alceste can hardly bear thinking what it takes 'to sit through another play by Stoppard or by David fucking Hare' (p. 161) – the plotline of Covington's play, by the way, ironically recalls Hare's Skylight (1995). The self-righteousness, though, with which Alceste in Crimp's adaptation carries his contempt forward, makes his ultimate defeat seem deserved. Of course, one is tempted to think, Jennifer must reject his offer to walk out on the people she is surrounded by and desert her career to follow Alceste into the prison-house of country loneliness and isolation.

The best lines of a veritable firework display of delightful and wittily crafted verses, though at times they plunge into doggerel, go to Alceste's friend John.

John   I have to say that this so-called rage
        Would make more sense on the seventeenth-century stage.

> And surely as a playwright you're aware
> Of sounding like something straight out of Molière. (p. 109)

Somewhat differently from Philinte in Molière, John does neither boundlessly demonstrate the very ideal which Alceste believes he is embodying himself, nor is he Crimp's mouthpiece. Like Philinte, however, John is able to effect that common-sense compromise which social interaction always entails without losing his inner freedom and independence (as his close friendship to Alceste enduringly proves). Whereas Molière's Alceste at least touches the tragic dimension of human failure, Crimp's Alceste is but a mere laughing stock when he leaves his society at the end of the play. Michael Billington is right when he argues that the modern media world which the play satirises is 'too flimsy to justify the weight of Alceste's wrath' and that, quite simply and much different from Molière's times, 'nothing vital seems at stake'.[12] The Western world, John seems to say, may be corrupt, pretentious, fashion-ridden, or dishonest, but then it is the only world that we inhabit. It is a world without a clear-cut borderline between right and wrong, good and evil, which, in his view, we had better encounter with a pinch of self-irony.

> **John**   [. . .] It's hard to be 'enraged'
> if one is philosophically disengaged.
> And the human animal looks far less fearsome
> through the prism
> of postmodernism.
> The world's a mess. Absolutely. We've fucked it.
> So why not just sit back and deconstruct it? (p. 112)

Attempts on Her Life (1997)

Attempts on Her Life was originally intended as 'a kind of grotesque footnote' to *The Treatment*.[13] Indeed, the plays have elements in common. They share the name of their main protagonist Anne, and one of their central topics is the limits of our comprehending another person to the full. The formal experiment with which Crimp encounters this topic in *Attempts*, however, is aesthetically so innovative, impressively daring and courageous that it has rightly taken Crimp to new heights of international stardom. Sierz goes as far as to call *Attempts* 'the best play of the decade', and Mary Luckhurst, in an analysis that is otherwise thoroughly critical, argues that the play is 'the most radically interrogative work in western mainstream theatre since Beckett'.[14] Shaun Usher compares the play to the innovation brought about by Pirandello and finds that Crimp 'goes even farther, doing away with character as such, not to mention a recognisable plot'.[15]

Crimp prefixes his play with a quotation by Jean Baudrillard, and the paratext neatly sets up our reception: 'No one will have directly experienced the actual cause of such happenings, but everyone will have received an image of them' (p. 198). Stephen Dedalus's maxim in Joyce's *A Portrait of the Artist as a Young Man* that absence is the highest form of presence might also well be preluding form and contents of *Attempts*. It is impossible to summarise what Crimp has named 'Seventeen Scenarios for the Theatre' which 'redefine the concepts of subject, author, and gender' and which turn drama and the theatre into phenomenological spaces of perception and fluxus and epistemological as well as even ontological uncertainty.[16]

Each of these scenarios, in which we encounter messages, elliptic sentences, advertising copy and patter, stage directions, non-sequential, hermetic and also highly poetic clusters of words and collage-like snapshot images, presents seventeen opposing or unrelated outlines for the life of someone called Anne (or Anya, Annie, Anny and Annushka) and in which the ever absent 'protagonist' adopts such diverse roles as those of a film heroine, a civil war victim, a megastar, an international terrorist, an artist, a survivalist, a porn star, or even a car or a victim of aliens. Such apparent arbitrariness notwithstanding, each scenario presents us with incoherent, albeit thoroughly recognisable images of everyday life. As minimalist in concept and as carefully crafted as these are, they are reminiscent of the ready-mades of conceptual art, as Clara Escoda Agustí has shown, or of Minimal Art.[17] Yet the realm of everyday life that Crimp's images derive from makes *Attempts* also thoroughly different from, for instance, Samuel Beckett's minimalist later works.[18] In Scenario 1, audiences and readers face eleven messages on Anne's answering machine giving contradictory information from which we can but infer contexts which, like leitmotifs, seem to be taken up by other scenarios later on: The lover (?), who is only 'pretty sure it's Prague' he's calling from; her mother (and a broken family home); somebody telling her that an (explosive?) device is in a small truck; the car dealer wanting her to collect a new vehicle; (death) threats such as 'We know where you live you fucking bitch. You're dead, basically' (p. 204); somebody praising a work (of art?) of hers; and the lover again (?), who imagines a scenario that she might be lying dead on the floor. Scenarios 2, 3 and 17 metafictionally centre on the development of plotlines for film scripts; structurally, the absent plot which we hear developed or 'treated' is deflected into discourse or narrative, a strategy which Crimp has employed in *The Treatment* before and again in other plays after *Attempts*, but which appears much more radicalised here as there are no more characters but only nameless voices the exact number of which is entirely open.[19] This renunciation of teleology and causal coherence stresses the self-reflexive, autopoietic force of the play. The result is a metafictional structure of a complex *mise en abyme* of ([an-opaque-story-] within-an-opaque-dialogue) that runs nowhere and remains inconclusive. The whole play resembles a collage of disjointed and fragmented images, which in their entirety render Anne a paradoxical presence/absence in a veritable Tower of Babel of discourse.

It is certainly one of the great accomplishments of the play that Crimp succeeds in turning the fragments of his collage of umpteen discursive versions of Anne into a serious meta-biographical statement. In the rhymed Scenario 5 'The Camera Loves You' an amorphous 'we' seems to comment on the megastar status of Anne.

> We're talking of a plan to be
> OVERWHELMED by the sheer totality
> And utterly believable three-dimensionality
> THREE DIMENSIONALITY
> of all the things that Anne can be
> ALL THE THINGS THAT ANNE CAN BE. (p. 223)

On the one hand, this is a satirical debunking of what Fredric Jameson calls the 'cultural logic of late capitalism' and the postmodern merging of all discourse into an undifferentiated text or textuality-process which results in an overkill, a new depthlessness, and an obsession with mere surface.[20] On the other hand, 'all the things that Anne can be' means all the things that Anne can be *in the eyes of others*, the possibilities of fictions, interpretations, and constructions of her life (or of any life in the eyes of others) are limitless. In Scenario 6, 'Mum and Dad', in which voices talk about photographs of her from different places, even the deictic reference of the voices makes it impossible to decide if these voices are actually Anne's parents, or whether these voices merely fictionalise Anne's parents reasoning as to why she has committed suicide.

> *They laugh all through next passage:*
> [. . .]
> She says she's not a real character, not a real character like you
> get in a book or on TV, but a *lack* of character, an *absence* she
> calls it, doesn't she, of character.
>   An absence of character, whatever *that* means . . . (p. 229)

The strange and almost tender poetic beauty of this passage reflects that Anne's life, her self, her individual 'I' is alleged to be seen by herself as a mere projection area. What she says, in fact, is itself but a reflection in a broken mirror as it is embedded in the memories of unknown voices that recall or fictionalise on what Anne's Mum and Dad remember that she said. Again, what we have in front of us here is an intricate Chinese box, another *mise en abyme* of <([memory] within memory) within dialogue between obscure voices> and, thus, an impressive structural analogy of the bottomless pit of epistemo-logical nothingness. Biographical truth hence turns out to be a mere chimera as the object of biography is a subject without a kernel, the search for which would resemble Peer Gynt's absurd peeling of the onion in search for its ideal core. Anne/Annie/Anya/Anny/Annushka are uncannily floating signifiers that have lost their (transcendental) signified. Who Anne *is*, who *anyone* is, what a self or what an identity *is* is ultimately unaccountable, Crimp seems to say. Whoever Anne *really is* can appear only as a 'trace', in Derrida's phrasing, as a paradoxical presence/absence and as an irreconcilable difference that also inevitably turns any interpretation into a misinterpretation. The ambiguous title of the play itself already exhibits this meta-biographical deconstruction of the self: whoever would even try to pin a life down to an *essence* or an *absolute* truth would go way towards murdering it. This epistemological depth renders *Attempts on Her Life*, both in its groundbreaking form and content, a true and lasting masterpiece of contemporary drama worldwide.

The Country (2000)

In *The Country*, which was first performed at the Royal Court on 11 April 2000, Crimp returns into the calmer, even if, it seems to me, more shallow waters of mainstream theatre.[21] With an ironic glance back at *The Misanthrope* it becomes fairly understandable why Jennifer rejects Alceste's offer of becoming a country wife: Crimp's countryside is no place of idyll. *The Country* comprises five scenes that seem loosely connected slices of life, and by degrees a comprehensible plotline unravels. Richard, a GP, and his wife Corinne, both in their forties, have moved to the country with their children, because he is fleeing from his drug addiction. One night, he brings to their home Rebecca, a young American girl he says he has found unconscious by the road. Corinne is suspicious from the start and in a conversation with Rebecca finds out that not only has Rebecca been having an affair with Richard, who has bought her an expensive watch, but also that he has brought her home because she overdosed on drugs that he had given her. Corinne also learns that it was for Rebecca's sake that they moved to the country in the first place. It further turns out that while Richard was taking care of Rebecca after the overdose he neglected looking after a patient who, as a consequence, died. In the final scene of the play, which is set two months later, Richard and Corinne celebrate her birthday. Richard has bought her a pair of expensive shoes, the high heels of which seem sadly out of place in that vicinity. She tells him that she went to the spot in the woods where

Rebecca had overdosed before and that she met Morris, who had found Rebecca's watch.

The plotline is deliberately left inconclusive since the fate of Rebecca is entirely left open: the watch Morris found might be an indicator that 'Richard is still meeting her, or it is simply a reminder of her existence', as Sierz suggests.[22] The prevailing atmosphere of an intriguing, creepy menace is generated by such Pinteresque devices as the intrusion of a stranger (Rebecca), an unseen character (Morris) or by the clipped dialogue which is rackingly stichomythic and in which, as critics have aptly observed, single words such as 'solicitous' or 'clean' acquire a 'sinister resonance' and produce an 'enigmatic inscrutability'.[23] Billington is right when he claims that the major topic of the play is the 'assault on the pastoral myth'.[24] Rebecca self-consciously mentions the Virgilian rural ideal of 'the harmonious . . . of the order of things, of the orderly cultivation of things' (p. 324). Much in this vein, the five-scene structure is an ironical echo of the five-act structure of classical tragedy, the ostensible order and unity of which has become a subject of Crimp's detached irony as the children's hand game of rock-paper-scissors determines the succession of the scenes. Crimp makes every scene end with a little parenthetical note which, seen as a whole, produces an ultimately inconclusive sequence of 'scissors – stone – paper – scissors – stone'.

The children's game is an acid comment on the power games taking place in Richard and Corinne's dying marriage, which seems utterly corroded by suspicion and betrayal. It is Corinne who, in a final conversation with Richard, envisions a nightmare future in which she would have to spend the rest of her life 'simulating love' (p. 366). The play ends in a Beckettian fashion as a cul-de-sac situation of paralysis:

Kiss me.
The phone continues to ring.
I have kissed you.
Then kiss me again.
Neither moves. The phone continues to ring.
(. . . stone) (p. 366)

Fewer Emergencies (2005)

Fewer Emergencies is a trilogy of short plays, which was first performed as a complete trilogy at the Royal Court Theatre Upstairs on 8 September 2005. The structure recalls Crimp's earlier unpublished *Four Attempted Acts*. Written as a companion piece to the third part of the trilogy, *Fewer Emergencies*, *Face to the Wall* was first co-staged with John Fosse's *nightsongs* at the Royal Court in 2002. The British premiere took place after Crimp had written a 'prequel' to the two already existing pieces, *Whole Blue Sky*.[25] With this trilogy Crimp continues the minimalist aesthetics of *Attempts on Her Life* only to exacerbate the process of aesthetic reduction and concentration. The central concern of the play is a formal one: fragments, or rather rudiments of a recognisable plot are entirely channelled into narrative. Crimp ascertains the gender of Speaker 1 in *Whole Blue Sky* as female, and of Speaker 1 in *Face to the Wall* as male (in order to make sure they cannot be seen as identical), but narrative context, identity or situation of the nameless speakers in all three short plays remain completely opaque, much enhanced by the carefully and intentionally placed blanks about time and place of the pieces. Crimp, thus, transfers the reception and interpretation of the plays completely into the realm of phenomenological perception and association. Whether we witness 'a script meeting, a brainstorming session, a rehearsal, or even a performance', or whether the voices are 'inside the writer's own head or those of the actors' remains open to conjecture.[26]

In *Whole Blue Sky*, the absent protagonist within the fictionalisation of the four voices is a woman. She married 'very young' (p. 7), presumably too young, and although she loves her husband the marriage seems to be 'a mistake' (p. 7). She might leave, but apparently decides to stay, becomes pregnant, yet cannot love the baby, although the baby 'cements the marriage' (p. 9) and seems to complete an idyllic family picture that includes the three of them in a fiction of wholeness and clichéd middle-class success of money and property constituting indeed an iconic 'blue sky':

Bought him pets, built him snowmen, assembled his jigsaws

late at night so that in the morning he'd come down the spiral stairs to find the sky, and I mean the whole blue sky completed, cut the crusts off his sandwiches and taken / the cheese out. (p. 18)

Under the surface of the family pastoral, however, violence is lurking: there's screaming, violent beating, insults, and the woman's refusal to sing 'Mummy and Daddy's private song' (p. 20) to the child, Bobby – a last disharmonious note that unmasks the artificial fiction of material comfort established before as a simulacrum of happiness and as an indication of a sham existence.

Violence becomes the central motif of the second short play, *Face to the Wall*. The narrative by the male Speaker 1 centres on the description of a school massacre. The deflection of action into narrative excellently succeeds in diverting both representation and perception of graphic violence into the realm of the imagination – a strategy that does not make the violence seem any less disturbing but rather creates an atmosphere of spellbinding emotional intensity. Characteristically, the dialogue of the four speakers sets out to run through potential motivations of the killer which is a metadramatic reflex of our own search for meaning in the play, which is, naturally, frustrated: 'Life's treating him well' (p. 28) and there are no clichéd traumata at the basis of the massacre, the killer was neither 'tortured' nor 'abused' nor 'fucked up the arse as a child' (p. 32) – far too easy explanations for Crimp, so it seems. The arbitrary chain of potential motivations brainstormed in the play gets as far as the absurd observation that the postman is sometimes late, which makes the killer angry. Here, the narrative changes its focus and rests on the postman whom his son wakes up in the morning, on which the postman throws 'hot tea RIGHT IN HIS FACE' (p. 35) before turning back to the wall. Crimp formally answers the change in narrative focus by an intermedial change of medium as he has the play end on a 'Twelve-Bar Delivery Blues' (pp. 34–6). The steady rhythm of the song and the rhyming stanzas produce a disturbing friction with the contents of the song: 'Hey sonny, / If there's one thing I've learned / It's don't rub on butter / When your skin is all burned' (p. 35).

The third piece of the trilogy, *Fewer Emergencies*, centres on the child Bobby. The narrative sets off from the observation that there are actually fewer emergencies and that things are in fact improving. But this, it turns out, is only a red herring, a riot starts in the streets and Bobby, who is locked in at home as his parents have gone for a boat ride, is injured by a stray bullet. The play ends on the wounded child painfully crawling up the spiral staircase in order to reach for the key that would open the door, a symbolic action that Crimp again leaves inconclusive:

> That's right, Bobby-boy. Watch the key. Watch the key swinging. (p. 49)

Crimp's minimalist aesthetics, the nameless speakers, the bare stage, the non-existence of an identifiable setting and time, the stream of images, and the fluidity and ambiguity of the dialogue make *Fewer Emergencies* look like an abstract, self-reflexive installation which can only suggest a meaning. But then, the self-reflexive structure of the narratives is tied to the icily dry humour of Crimp's satire evolving a characteristic feeling of angst and imminence that constitutes, as Sierz has argued with reference to Frank Furedi, a critical comment on a 'culture of fear' that pervades life in the twenty-first century.[27]

Summary

Crimp's work oscillates between the extreme of biting social satire and minimalist experiment. Indeed each extreme can never quite do without the other. On the one hand, and, for instance, quite unlike Beckett's, the minimalism in Crimp, its ambiguities and carefully crafted receptional blanks are always recognisably grounded in contemporary life; on the other hand, the satirical castigation of seemingly deficient moral characteristics of contemporary life always seems self-reflexively broken and far too disjointed to form a reliable moral judgement. The interlacing of the satirical and the self-reflexive, minimalist modes is indicative of Crimp's phenomenological aesthetics and an accordingly decisive turn of drama towards perception.

Esse est percipi (vel percipere) – to be is to be perceived (or to perceive): this proto-constructivist dictum by George Berkeley may well stand at the beginning of each analysis of Crimp's work. Thus, even in those plays that seem fairly grounded in reality, the recipient encounters ambiguous, menacing, often opaque and surreal, never conclusive yet always disturbing sceneries, dreamscapes, or frescoes of the skull and, for the most part, achronologically ordered, subjectively experienced slices of life that appear perceived through the reflector instance of human consciousness. The charge of 'obscurantism' that critics have occasionally levelled at Crimp ignores the fact that, quite simply, human consciousness does not proceed in an ordered way and that, accordingly, in phenomenological aesthetics *normative* expectations in traditional stage plays and in teleological and causal developments of their plotlines are insistently contradicted and frustrated.[28]

As to the critical reception of Crimp's work, Sierz's book-length study *The Theatre of Martin Crimp* must be considered the starting point of every analysis of the plays. Sierz identifies such significant major topics as consumerism, cruel interpersonal relationships, precarious marriages, distorted family structures, victimised children, crisis-laden constructions of the modern subject, prevalent power games, gender issues and, particularly, the male gaze as recurrent topics in Crimp's work. Important scholarly essays by David Barnett, Clara Escoda Agustí, Heiner Zimmermann and Eckart Voigts-Virchow have related the aesthetics of Crimp's most experimental work to what Hans-Thies Lehmann calls 'Postdramatic Theatre'.[29] This is as justified as it is problematic. Of course, in plays such as *Attempts* and *Fewer Emergencies* post-dramatic elements are manifest: the lack of dramatis personae, the deconstruction of character, the conflagration of discourse that leads nowhere, the often even inter-medial switch of genres, the generic inseparability of dialogue and narrative, the disjointed collage of images, the scepticism about meaning and semantics in favour of the self-referential and autopoietic forces of drama and theatre. On the other hand, even though *Attempts* possesses sections – most notably perhaps the examples of concrete poetry in Scenario 11 or the overkill of simultaneous discourse in various languages in Scenario 16 – which border on what Elfriede Jelinek conceived of as 'expanses of speech' ('*Sprachflächen*'), by far the largest part of Crimp's language is the everyday speech of dialogue of 'real people' that seems fairly grounded in the tradition of British drama.[30]

No matter whether one adheres to the term 'post-dramatic' or not, Crimp's plays highlight the *performative* aspects of both language and identity-construction; in fact, Crimp's work self-reflexively turns these aspects into major topics. The fluidity and radical openness of Crimp's phenomenological aesthetics may therefore well be called *meta-performative*. The way Crimp sees, for instance, the categories of 'gender' and 'identity' comes closest to the position brought forward by Judith Butler, who argues that gender identity is not based on ontological categories but achieved through institutionalised repetitions of bodily acts.[31] The 'Pornó' scenario in *Attempts* and the various deconstructions of the male gaze in Crimp's work are towering examples of how such institutionalising of gender construction in Crimp (as in Butler) is thwarted and rejected.

As Erika Fischer-Lichte has aptly pointed out, 'theatre spaces, whether they are permanently installed or merely provisional, are always performative spaces'.[32] Again, Crimp's work appears meta-performative in so far as, for example, the blanks of time and place and the emphasis on rhythm and atmosphere in Crimp's more experi-mental pieces reflect on this very performative potential of drama as they open possibilities and avenues for the negotiation of the relationships between text, performance, characters/actors, audience perception and reader response. The open character of these nego-tiations runs against any sense of continuity or the idea of stable and fixed identities. Even the symbolic qualities of metaphorical reference in the more traditional plays of Crimp's become deflected into the realm of the allegorical in pieces such as *Attempts* or *Fewer Emergencies*. In allegory, as Walter Benjamin has pointed out, 'any person, any object, any relationship can mean absolutely anything else'.[33] In Crimp, likewise, 'materiality, signifier, and signified diverge'.[34]

The key phenomenon of the construction of all performatives in culture, speech, as well as in Crimp's work is repetition. As Gilles Deleuze has argued, in a Platonic understanding, repetition rests on consensus.[35] As leitmotifs, such ambiguous signifiers as 'treatment' and 'attempts', to name but two of the most productive, that run through Crimp's work at least hint at the desire for such consensus. A Nietzschean view of repetition, by contrast, considers the notions of similarity and identity as derivational and conceivable only on the foundation of an all-encompassing difference. Crimp's work embodies an interlacing of the Platonic and the Nietzschean mode of repetition, with a clear emphasis, however, on difference. In a philosophically still quite harmless way, the protagonist of Crimp's *Play with Repeats* has to learn that life is irreversible. In a more complex way, Anne/Anya/Annie/Anny/Annushka in *Attempts*, to give one final example, constitutes, after all, an empty signifier that impressively stresses what Jacques Derrida called the 'iterability of the signifier', stressing that signifiers lack in ultimate authority.[36] For Derrida, and for Crimp, the iterability of a sign implies that each sign or each written syntagma could be isolated from the sequence or chain of written speech in which it appears and be 'grafted' on to other sequences, other chains.[37] No context surrounding a sign could ever capture it completely. It is precisely this radical openness that displaces representation, meaning, and (complete) understanding in Crimp into an ineluctable presence/absence.

It is due to the satirical elements in Crimp that, by definition, must be grounded in real-life contexts that a critical cultural stance does not peter out in mere self-reflexivity. One of the main targets of Crimp's critical thinking is, in his own words, a 'Culture of Contentment'.[38] The openness of his aesthetics and the perceptual multistability it provokes arouses the *activity* rather than the *contentment* of the recipient. A minimum of coherence implies a maximum of associative richness. The chains of association that Crimp's plays set in motion on the part of the recipient, therefore, possess a decisively ethical potential and appeal. Crimp's ethics, however, are not the ethics of moral finger-wagging, but the ethics of a brilliantly incoherent art.

Primary Sources

Works by Martin Crimp

Plays One: *Dealing with Clair, Play with Repeats, Getting Attention, The Treatment* (London: Faber & Faber, 2000).

Plays Two: No One Sees the Video, The Misanthrope, Attempts on Her Life, The Country (London: Faber & Faber, 2005).

Fewer Emergencies (London: Faber & Faber, 2005).

The City (London: Faber & Faber, 2008).

Secondary Sources

Barnett, David, 'When is a Play Not a Drama? Two Examples of Postdramatic Theatre Texts', *New Theatre Quarterly*, Vol. 24, No. 1 (2008), pp. 14–23.

Baudrillard, Jean, 'The Precession of Simulacra', *Simulacra and Simulation*, trans. Sheila Faria Glaser (Ann Arbor: University of Michigan Press, 1994), pp. 1–42.

Beckett, Samuel, 'Three Dialogues', *Disjecta: Miscellaneous Writing and a Dramatic Fragment*, ed. Ruby Cohn (London: Calder, 1983), pp. 138–45.

Benjamin, Walter, *The Origin of German Tragic Drama*, trans. J. Osborne (London: Verso, 1998).

Butler, Judith, 'Performative Acts and Gender Constitution: An Essay in Phenomenology and Feminist Theory', in Sue-Ellen Case (ed.), *Performing Feminism, Feminist Critical Theory and Theatre* (Baltimore, MD: Johns Hopkins UP, 1990), pp. 270–82.

Deleuze, Gilles, *Difference and Repetition*, trans. Paul Patton (New York: Columbia UP, 1994).

Dennewald, Martine, 'An den Rändern der Identität: Überindividuelle Figurenkonzeptionen bei Crimp, Kane, Abdoh und Foreman', *Forum Modernes Theater*, Vol. 19, No. 1 (2004), pp. 43–71.

Derrida, Jacques, 'Signature Event Context', in Derrida, *Limited Inc.*, ed. Gerald Graff (Evanston, IL: Northwestern UP, 1988), pp. 1–21.

Escoda Agustí, Clara, '"head green water to sing": Minimalism and Indeterminacy in Martin Crimp's *Attempts on Her Life*', in Christoph Henke and Martin Middeke (eds), *Drama and/after Postmodernism*, Contemporary Drama in English 14 (Trier: WVT, 2007), pp. 149–63.

Fischer-Lichte, Erika, *The Transformative Power of Performance: A New Aesthetics*, trans. Saskya Iris Jain (London: Routledge, 2008).

Habermas, Jürgen, *The Theory of Communicative Action*, 2 Vols (Cambridge: Polity Press, 1984).

Jameson, Fredric, *Postmodernism, or, The Cultural Logic of Late Capitalism* (Durham, NC: Duke UP, 1991).

Lehmann, Hans-Thies, *Postdramatic Theatre*, trans. Karen Jürs-Mundby (London: Routledge, 2006).

Luckhurst, Mary, 'Political Point-Scoring: Martin Crimp's *Attempts on Her Life*', *Contemporary Theatre Review*, Vol. 13, No. 1 (2003), pp. 47–60.

Middeke, Martin, 'Minimal Art: On the Intermedial Aesthetic Context of Samuel Beckett's Late Theatre and Drama', *Anglia*, Vol. 123, No. 3 (2005), pp. 359–80.

Sierz, Aleks, *The Theatre of Martin Crimp* (London: Methuen Drama, 2006).

—, 'NTQ Checklist: Martin Crimp', *New Theatre Quarterly*, Vol. 22, No. 4 (2006), pp. 352–60.

—, '"Form Follows Function": Meaning and Politics in Martin Crimp's *Fewer Emergencies*', *Modern Drama*, Vol. 50, No. 3 (2007), pp. 375–93.

—, '"D'You Really Give My Scribbling That Much Thought?" Narrative Games in the Plays of Martin Crimp', in Merle Tönnies and Christina Flotmann (eds), *Narrative in Drama*, Contemporary Drama in English 18 (Trier: WVT, 2011), pp. 257–79.

Voigts-Virchow, Eckart, 'Postdramatisches Theater: Martin Crimp', in Merle Tönnies (ed.), *Das englische Drama der Gegenwart: Kategorien – Entwicklungen – Modellinterpretationen* (Trier: WVT, 2010), pp. 158–71.

Zimmermann, Heiner, 'Martin Crimp, *Attempts on Her Life*: Postdramatic, Postmodern, Satiric?', in Margarete Rubik and Elke Mettinger-Schartmann (eds), *Discontinuities: Trends and Traditions in Contemporary Theatre and Drama in English*, Contemporary Drama in English 9 (Trier: WVT, 2002), pp. 105–24.

Notes

1. Samuel Beckett, 'Three Dialogues', p. 139.
2. Aleks Sierz, *The Theatre of Martin Crimp*, pp. 252–6, and Sierz, 'NTQ Checklist: Martin Crimp'.
3. John O'Mahony, 'Writers' Crimp', *Guardian*, 20 April 1993, quoted in Sierz, *Theatre of Martin Crimp*, p. 5.
4. Jack Tinker, *Daily Mail*, 3 November 1988; Jim Hiley, *Listener*, 27 October 1988; Georgina Brown, *Independent*, 18 October 1988; *Theatre Record*, Vol. VIII, No. 21 (1988), pp. 1443–5.
5. Sierz, *Theatre of Martin Crimp*, p. 24.
6. Michael Billington, *Guardian*, 22 April 1993, *Theatre Record*, Vol. XIII, No. 8 (1993), p. 434.
7. Aleks Sierz, *Tribune*, 30 April 1993, *Theatre Record*, Vol. XIII, No. 8 (1993), p. 431.
8. Jean Baudrillard, 'The Precession of Simulacra', p. 6.

9. David Nathan, *Jewish Chronicle*, 30 April 1993; Neil Smith, *What's On*, 24 April 1993; *Theatre Record*, Vol. XIII, No 8 (1993), pp. 431–4.

10. Jürgen Habermas, *The Theory of Communicative Action*.

11. Quoted in Sierz, *Theatre of Martin Crimp*, p. 45.

12. Michael Billington, *Guardian*, 15 February 1996, *Theatre Record*, Vol. XVI, No. 4 (1996), p. 205.

13. Crimp quoted in Heiner Zimmermann, 'Martin Crimp', p. 108.

14. Sierz, *Theatre of Martin Crimp*, p. 49; Mary Luckhurst, 'Political Point-Scoring', p. 49.

15. Shaun Usher, *Daily Mail*, 14 March 1997, *Theatre Record*, Vol. XVII, No. 6 (1997), pp. 312–13.

16. Clara Escoda Agustí, '"head green water to sing"', p. 149.

17. Ibid., passim.

18. See Middeke, 'Minimal Art'.

19. See Sierz, 'Narrative Games', and, for the profusion of discourse, Martine Dennewald, 'An den Rändern der Identität'.

20. See Fredric Jameson, *Postmodernism*.

21. See Sierz, *Theatre of Martin Crimp*, p. 56.

22. Ibid, p. 59.

23. Charles Spencer, *Daily Telegraph*, 18 May 2000; Nicholas de Jongh, *Evening Standard*, 15 May 2000; *Theatre Record*, Vol. XX, No. 10 (2000), pp. 616–17.

24. Michael Billington, *Guardian*, 17 May 2000, *Theatre Record*, Vol. XX, No. 10 (2000), p. 618.

25. See Sierz, '"Form Follows Function"', p. 378.

26. Ibid.

27. Ibid, pp. 386–91.

28. Alastair Macaulay, *Financial Times*, 15 March 1997, *Theatre Record*, Vol. XVII, No. 6 (1997), p. 313.

29. See Hans-Thies Lehmann, *Postdramatic Theatre*; Sierz, '"Form Follows Function"'; David Barnett, 'When is a Play Not a Drama?'; Escoda Agustí, '"head green water to sing"'; Eckart Voigts-Virchow, 'Postdramatisches Theater: Martin Crimp'; Zimmermann, 'Martin Crimp'.

30. See Sierz, '"Form Follows Function"', p. 380.

31. See Judith Butler, 'Performative Acts and Gender Constitution', p. 270, and Erika Fischer-Lichte, *The Transformative Power of Performance*, p. 27.

32. Fischer-Lichte, *Transformative Power*, p. 107.

33. Walter Benjamin, *The Origin of German Tragic Drama*, p. 175.

34. Fischer-Lichte, *Transformative Power*, p. 145.

35. See Gilles Deleuze, *Difference and Repetition*.

36. See Jacques Derrida, 'Signature Event Context'.

37. Ibid., p. 9.

38. Crimp quoted in Sierz, '"Form Follows Function"', p. 386.

6 SARAH DANIELS

Nicole Boireau

Ripen Our Darkness; *Masterpieces*; *Neaptide*; *Head-Rot Holiday*;
Broken Wings

Introduction

Sarah Daniels was born in 1956 in London. She made a name for
herself as an innovative playwright in 1981 with *Ripen Our Darkness*
(Royal Court) and *Ma's Flesh is Grass* (Crucible, Sheffield), two
spirited plays committed to feminism. She was immediately
recognised by critics as 'a woman who will say anything in public; a
sort of feminist Joe Orton [. . .] who writes so vehemently and
passionately she's worth having'.[1] *The Devil's Gateway* (Royal Court,
1983) completed the satire of ordinary sexism, and Daniels reached
consecration with *Masterpieces* (Royal Exchange, Manchester, 1983),
a controversial play about pornography, which won two Most
Promising Playwright awards, the London Theatre Critics' Award and
the *Drama Magazine* Award. A worldwide success, *Masterpieces* was
selected in 1999 by the National Theatre as one of the best plays of the
twentieth century. Daniels was Resident Dramatist at the Royal Court
in 1984–85. Year after year she has enlarged her terrain of observation
of women's condition, with *Neaptide* (National Theatre), which deals
with lesbian mothers and won the George Devine Award in 1986. In
the same year, *Byrthrite* (Royal Court) scrutinised the way medical
power interferes with childbirth. Daniels has left no area of women's
experience unexplored. The Victorian working-class world is central
to *The Gut Girls* (1988), which premiered at the Albany Empire,
where she was Resident Dramatist in 1989–90.

Daniels's exploratory drama applies to many types of power
situations and ethical dilemmas. Her experience of social work also

comes out forcefully in her plays. *Beside Herself* (Royal Court, 1990), *Head-Rot Holiday* (BAC, 1992) and *The Madness of Esme and Shaz* (Royal Court, 1994) are based on the issue of women and madness. A versatile writer, Daniels has adapted books for the stage, such as Pat Barker's 1984 novel, *Blow Your House Down* (Live Theatre, Newcastle upon Tyne, 1995), and *Flying Under Bridges* (Palace Theatre, Watford, 2005), a 2001 novel by comedienne and novelist Sandi Toksvig, which contains similar themes to *Ripen Our Darkness*. The more recent stage plays are focused on youngsters, such as *Taking Breath* (National Theatre, 1999), *Best Mates* (National Theatre, 2000), *Morning Glory* (Palace Theatre, Watford, 2001), *Dust* (National Theatre, 2003) and *Broken Wings* (American Conservatory Theatre, 2008).

Since 2002, Daniels has been more and more involved in radio drama. Her talent for short, densely packed sequences that resonate with emotion is given free rein in her radio plays. *Cross My Heart and Hope to Fly* (BBC, 2002) won the 2003 Bronze Sony Award. Her radio work specialises in strong subjects. *The Long Wait* (BBC, 2004) was commissioned for the sixtieth anniversary of D-Day. A review of *Sound Barriers* (BBC, 2005) is clear about Daniels's expertise:

> Sarah Daniels's drama inventively explored themes of sound and silence and moved into heavier terrain. It did so with such skill in tone and pace [. . .] that it should be required listening for aspiring radio dramatists [. . .] tremendous emotional realism.[2]

'Emotional realism' is an apt phrase to describe Daniels's distinctive style. *Soldiers' Wives* (BBC, 2006) is a gripping five-part series based on interviews with wives of servicemen fighting in Iraq. *Humanly Possible* (BBC, 2010) tackles an ethical dilemma.[3] The play describes a gruelling day in a neonatal intensive care unit, with very humane although very busy staff, worried parents and new babies: a couple has to face the harrowing situation of a baby with a damaged cortex. She has also adapted major feminist books for radio: *The Women's Room* by Marilyn French (BBC, 2006) and *The Golden Notebook* by Doris Lessing (BBC, 2008).

With eighteen stage plays, most of them produced in major London venues (National Theatre, Royal Court), sixteen scripts and adaptations for BBC radio, and her extensive work as a writer for television series (*Grange Hill, EastEnders*), Daniels is a major figure of the British scene, unanimously considered as one of the wittiest and most gifted of contemporary dramatists. Her accomplished plays, for the stage and for BBC radio, have received huge critical acclaim. They achieve the right balance between emotion and laughter, comedy and tragedy, distance and catharsis. Most of all, Daniels's works radically, and usefully, undermine ready-made frames of perception.

The Plays

Ripen Our Darkness (1981)

First presented at the Royal Court Theatre Upstairs on 7 September 1981, *Ripen Our Darkness* introduces a lower-middle-class family, composed of Mary, the downtrodden mother, David, her domineering churchwarden husband, Paul, the tyrannical, lazy son, and Anna, the teacher daughter dearly loved by her mother but considered a disgrace by her father on account of her being a lesbian. Slowly cracking up under the strain of domestic life, Mary is driven to despair and eventually suicide. Out of the simple storyline Daniels builds a devastating play. The structure is linear and the fourteen scenes are so many realistic vignettes boldly exposing traditional sexist attitudes. Her pompous, unfeeling and sarcastic husband keeps her on the lowest level of communication:

> **David** Mary, I don't like to mention it but it took me almost seven minutes to locate my underpants this morning. [. . .] And perhaps next time you reorganise the bedroom you would leave me a little plan or map as a guide, then I might be able to negotiate my way around the furniture, ha, ha. (pp. 3–4)

The crisp dialogues poignantly capture Mary's slow deterioration. Thanks to the moral support of her daughter, Mary realises that something is amiss in her life. She also develops her own wry sense of humour, a way of distancing herself from her domestic hell. To her son, who asks her, 'How long's dinner anyway?', audacious Mary replies on impulse: 'Four inches – it's a sausage' (p. 7). Paul ignores the joke and puts his mother down; women are expected to conform, not to have a sense of humour: 'Please don't try to be funny, Mummy. It doesn't suit you' (p. 7).

Daniels explores the subversive potential of laughter to the full. Each verbal confrontation throws light on a moral point, showing the mechanism of oppression and, simultaneously, giving the female protagonist a chance to resist verbally. Such moments give the spectator the relief of laughter with the shock of recognition. Mary's sense of humour makes her gradually aware of her condition: 'Why does my life seem like a half-finished jigsaw while everybody else seem to have completed their pictures?' (p. 11). As she seems clinically depressed, David refers her to Marshall, a psychiatrist, whose simplistic Freudian approach she derides. When he reads out 'penis running dry', a scrawl on a piece of paper she had thrown away when writing a letter to her daughter, Mary corrects him: 'pen is running dry' (p. 61). Marshall's answer to what he considers an attempt at castrating her son is the mental hospital. Distraught at the prospect, Mary puts everything in order and leaves a note on the kitchen table:

> **Mary** (*writing new letter*)   Dear David, your dinner and my head are in the oven.
> *She crosses to the cooker, finds a comfortable position, turns on the gas and puts her head in the oven. Fade. Black out.* (p. 64)

The play ends with Mary in heaven, in good female company. From above she helps her husband, engaged in a game of Monopoly with Marshall, whose wife has unsurprisingly ended up in a mental hospital. Instead of closing the play on a downbeat naturalistic note, Daniels introduces a theatrical twist. More than a surreal victory over her repressive male-dominated household, Mary's escape to heaven confirms the intimations of change present in the play, with Anna and other women, who find their own way in life. Breaking through the barriers of realism opens up new perspectives. Both terrifying and hilarious, *Ripen Our Darkness* is a tragi-comedy of domestic manners.

Carole Hayman's efficient directing of 'an ebullient cast' was praised by all critics, as well as Daniels's style, 'mingling Ortonesque elegance, self-deprecating female humour and music hall turns with outrageous flashes of *grand guignol*. [. . .] There is great spirit there.'[4] The 'first play by a girl of 24 [. . .] lively and irreverent', *Ripen Our Darkness* heralded a bright future.[5]

Masterpieces (1983)

First performed at the Royal Exchange Theatre, Manchester, on 31 May 1983, then transferred to the Royal Court Theatre Upstairs, on 7 October 1983, *Masterpieces* denounces the connection between the pornography industry and violence against women in all its forms. The play involves three middle-class liberal couples, living in London. The three women have varying degrees of awareness as regards feminism: Rowena, a social worker in her thirties, is hesitant and sometimes angry; Yvonne, a teacher and a convinced feminist, is embittered and permanently depressed; Jennifer, Rowena's extrovert mother, is married to an obnoxious young man and loves anti-male jokes. The action again is simple: the cumulative effect of porn-ography on Rowena's subconscious is such that, one evening, when a man tries to address her on a tube platform, she pushes him under the oncoming train. The man is killed. Rowena receives a prison sentence.

The tightly constructed play falls into seventeen scenes. The time structure moves back and forth, dislocating the chronological order, compressing or extending the flow of time. Cerebral agility is required from the spectator, for on the axis of realistic time, each scene either precedes or follows the previous one, revealing a crisis, which fore-shadows or explains a past event. The future is inscribed in the past. The alternation of flashbacks and flash-forwards intensifies the argumentative power of the play.

After an impersonal prologue, with a man making easy money

selling pornographic material, the first scene portrays the three couples in a restaurant. It is the chronological starting point, anchoring the play in a real past and articulating the underlying conflicts. The conversation hinges on male fantasies. Scene Two, Scene Sixteen (the logical continuation of Scene Two) and Scene Seventeen take place in a crown court. The actual enactment of the 'crime' is mimed (Scene Fourteen). The scenes in between throw light on what has been going on in Rowena's life and mind to result in her committing such an impulsive action. The construction serves an explanatory function, keeping the reader/spectator critically active.

In her social work, Rowena has befriended Hilary, a young single mother desperate for employment. Treated as a 'slag' at school, by her parents, by men, by her employers, Hilary has a low self-image but a strong sense of humour. Rowena finds her a job with Ron, Yvonne's husband, who needs a secretary. Ron becomes her boss and harasses her sexually. Hilary leaves her job. A sequence shows Rowena and her husband Trevor having an argument about pornography. In the next scene, we learn that they have split. The other couples follow suit. In Scene Thirteen, the three women are having a picnic and planning a holiday in Greece. Scene Fifteen reveals what actually took place in what was anticipated in Scene Twelve. On the axis of objective time Scene Fifteen antedates Scene Twelve. In Scene Sixteen, Rowena presents her own defence. Before she committed the crime she had been upset by a snuff video, the horrific contents of which she reveals to the policewoman, who takes her to prison (Scene Seventeen).

In *Masterpieces*, the significance of the demonstration lies in the play's form. Its clarity of construction and its use of distancing devices make for clear thinking about the issues. Monologues overlap, with voices coming over on tape. Scenes fade into one another. Hilary's famous solo performance about her zany experience of contraception was a memorable theatrical moment for all critics, and for playwright David Edgar: 'Hilary's description of an attempt to use Coca-Cola as a contraceptive, [. . .] is one of the funniest scenes written in English in my lifetime.'[6] Actress Patti Love, who doubled for Yvonne and Hilary (two contrasting parts), gave a stunning performance of what has become a 'classic monologue'.[7]

Daniels's talent for witty repartee with a moral edge works full scale when the three couples exchange jokes. The men relish the misogynist ones of the hackneyed variety, with nuns dreaming of being raped. Yvonne, poised for immediate retaliation, turns the tables: 'How many men does it take to tile a bathroom? Three if you slice them thinly' (p. 169). The punchline had a chilling effect on the audience.

The play was seen as 'an extraordinary play and a major work of drama', beautifully served by Jules Wright's perfect directing and an excellent cast.[8] Despite its technical brilliance, it made a number of male critics uncomfortable.[9] Strangely enough it was not so much the hard-hitting description of male chauvinism that was criticised, as the 'false connections' the author was said to make between pornography and violence, which was considered a weakness in the argument.[10] Opinions were divided. Some critics even unjustly thought Daniels was pleading for censorship.[11] Yet, the point of such a clever, controversial play should not be missed: *Masterpieces* is not about innate hostility between the sexes; it has nothing to do with turning men into enemies, nothing to do with human species or with nature. It has to do with social constructs, with what conditions the male gaze. *Masterpieces* is a rigorous deconstruction of the cultural.

Neaptide (1986)

Premiered at the National Theatre on 26 June 1986, *Neaptide* revisits the Demeter and Persephone myth, transposed to the twentieth century.[12] The action focuses on the custody of children by lesbian mothers. The story involves a mother, Joyce, and her three daughters. One of them, Claire, is divorced and her ex-husband wants custody of their daughter, Poppy, which he will probably get through the law on grounds of Claire's lesbianism. At the end, Claire runs away to America, with her mother and daughter.

In *Neaptide* the mother–daughter relationship covers three generations. Sweet little Poppy prefers the story of Demeter, the loving mother pining away for Persephone, to the usual fairy tales with their cruel stepmothers. Poppy also notices that '"god" spells "dog" backwards' (p. 246). Quite conventional in her views at the beginning, Joyce slowly gets to understand Claire. A long monologue shows her becoming more tolerant of her daughter. She also realises that she has to master a new vocabulary to grasp the changes in life:

> **Joyce** [. . .] Well, my vocabulary has had a lot of new words prised into it over the years, and you have to be careful because there's a lot of difference between 'going out' and 'coming out'. (p. 284)

Neaptide breaks the taboo of the heterosexual family.[13] Claire living with a lesbian teacher colleague of hers introduces an alternative lifestyle, which Daniels is careful not to portray as being perfect. The play does not plead for difference to the point of 'separatism', as was originally said, but for the need to survive, to keep one's sanity as an individual, to raise a family in peace and love, whatever the gender or sex of the parents.[14] The play goes far beyond the taboo-breaking stage, since lesbian mothers and family set-ups with women only are far from being new themes in drama.[15] Daniels's purpose in introducing sexual self-determination for mothers is to examine the legal side of the situation. Margarete Rubik's criticism that the play was 'designed for the consumption of a mainstream audience' should therefore be taken as a compliment.[16] The wider the audience, the better.

If Daniels does not idealise alternative lifestyles, she also avoids easy caricature. Although he is portrayed as a brutish male chauvinist, Claire's ex-husband is shown to be genuinely missing his daughter. The pain of the situation is palpable on all sides. Overlapping scenes and voiceovers make the situation more general, and the play more analytical. John Burgess's award-winning, sensitive production did justice to a courageous play where combative energy is the rule throughout.

Head-Rot Holiday (1992)

Head-Rot Holiday was first performed at Battersea Arts Centre on 13 October 1992. Daniels was commissioned by Clean Break, the first theatre group for women ex-prisoners, to write a play on a mental institution for criminal women: 'Clean Break set up a research period, during which I was able to talk to ex-patients, psychiatrists, clinical psychologists, social workers and solicitors.'[17] Daniels's thorough research explains 'the play's potent docudrama authenticity'.[18] Three patients, mentally disturbed women prisoners (Dee, Ruth, Claudia), three nurses (Jackie, Sharon, Barbara), a social worker (Chris) and Helen, Ruth's stepmother, are the main characters. Jackie describes the place as violent and calls it 'Head-rot Hotel'. The first part of the play describes the organisation of the 'special hospital', definitely 'a corner of British life that needs inspecting', the second one scrutinises the patients' mental world.[19] The structure is linear, but frequent soliloquies open up secret areas, giving access to the inner worlds of patients and staff. Daniels breaks the realistic conventions with an angel, visible to the audience, a character in its own right, who plays for Dee the part of the *alter ego*, as Eve does for Evelyn in *Beside Herself*. Ruth hears voices. We see her in seclusion fighting them off; the scene is up-front and distressing, but avoids pathos. Although the play depicts the excruciating pain of mental illness, it never becomes voyeuristic. The case in point is not so much the disease as its possible causes, the way it develops through victimisation and, lastly, the way it has to be faced.

Daniels's approach to her characters is compassionate, yet never patronising. Victims though they may be, patients (and staff too) are also meant to play an active part in their own salvation. Ruth and Dee inflict injuries on themselves. Ruth, who was sexually abused by her father, hates her stepmother, Helen, who comes out with a revelation about her own 'denial' of the incestuous situation going on at home. Ruth stabbed Helen, which is the reason why she was sent to the 'Special Hospital':

> **Helen** Now it's really hard to discern what I denied and what I didn't. [. . .] When she stabbed me it was like, like she was trying to stab some life into me. [. . .] It was so frenzied. (pp. 244–5)

Helen, like Ruth, gradually sees the light about herself. Whereas Ruth has stabbed life into her stepmother, Helen's compelling monologue stabs life into the spectator to the same degree. The play ends on an ambivalent note. Unlike Ruth, who comes to life and will soon be able to leave the place, Dee remains unwell and has to stay.

Daniels tactfully controls the note of despair underlying *Head-Rot Holiday*. The swift-moving rhythm of the sequences counteracts the general oppressive atmosphere. The list of dramatis personae shows that doubling was systematically used for nurses and patients, both groups sharing equally the burden of received and inflicted violence.[20] The 'superb performances' were said to serve the 'in-depth exploration of the fine line between "sanity" and "madness"'.[21] We can speak here again of a combative dramaturgy, turning the pain of being 'beside oneself' into a source of knowledge and personal development.

Broken Wings (2007)

Broken Wings was co-commissioned by two companies for young people working in partnership, the American Conservatory Theater Young Conservatory, of San Francisco, and the Egg Theatre in Bath (Theatre Royal's Young People's Theatre).[22] The play was first produced in San Francisco in November 2007, and in Bath on 7 August 2008. Daniels moves away from the strictly feminist field to address tactfully the agonies of youngsters: Tiffany (aged nineteen), an American girl living in England, David (aged twenty-one) and Josh (sixteen years old). Tiffany has come to live with David's parents, Helen and Phil, her aunt and uncle (officially). Her now dead mother was Helen's sister. The two sisters, half-sisters rather, for Helen was an adopted child, were not on speaking terms. Josh met Tiffany at a therapy group. He has also lost his mother. David spends his days in his room, engrossed in the construction of cardboard wings. Tiffany encourages him to enter a flying competition at a seaside resort. Kinship and a sense of dissolving identity are the dominant themes of this disturbing play. The nine scenes go backwards in time, from autumn 2007 to 26 December 2004, with a quick fade back to autumn 2007 at the very end. Both reversed and circular, the time structure is emotionally compelling.

In the dramatic first scene, David is ready for the competition, but Tiffany demolishes the wings. Her acid comments are suggestive of fraught family relations, which come into sharp focus as the scenes go backwards in time. The action sticks to the metaphorical title: eager to fly away, David builds himself a pair of wings. Realising that his dream is both foolish and dangerous, Tiffany smashes them. We learn that David is Tiffany's half-brother since Phil, David's father, is also Tiffany's biological father, a well-known fact covered up by everyone, including Helen. In Scene One, Tiffany tells Josh that David is her brother, whereas Helen had told him previously (Scene Two) that he was her cousin. Tiffany also refers to Phil as her 'uncle', whereas he later turns out to be her father, a fact she knew and boldly confirms in a text message she sends Phil in the middle of a 'family' lunch. Josh and Tiffany tell everyone their respective mothers died of cancer. The truth comes out later: they had both committed suicide. Josh himself was a test-tube baby. A short-lived romance between Tiffany and David is nipped in the bud by David's parents. According to Phil's callous analysis of Tiffany: 'She is trouble. Just steer clear' (p. 25). Indeed, David is her half-brother, which he has suspected all along. The last scene conjures up a 'family' holiday with Tiffany, her mother and stepfather Bob, in the Maldives for Christmas 2004. On 26 December, Tiffany is bored and irritable. About Bob she says: 'He's not my parent. My dad was a true English gentleman' (p. 55). Then the tsunami breaks, engulfing her stepfather. Thence, probably, her mother's subsequent suicide. When the last scene fades back into the present (autumn 2007), Tiffany expresses her fear of the future.

Uncertain parentage, sibling rivalry, bereavement and grief are the stuff the family is made of in *Broken Wings*. Such a burden would be more than enough to clip anybody's wings, break anybody's back, smash anybody's heart and sense of identity. Doubling is part of the significance of this haunting play, where wholeness is what Tiffany is after. About herself and David she says they are 'the part of each other that's missing' (p. 19). She has to dismantle the mythical wings, the part of him that was her. Tiffany breaks through the prison of myths for everyone to be able to move on. Acted by and aimed at young people, the subtle production was enthusiastically received by audiences in both countries.

Summary

Daniels's rich output covers a wide territory and, when it comes to evaluating her works in relation to feminist drama, categorisation is not easy. Her commitment to the feminist cause subsumes all trends: radical, bourgeois, socialist, classical and neo-feminist.[23] To critics claiming that she tends to separate female oppression from the social dynamic of capitalism, it can be argued that Daniels's plays operate a perfect symbiosis between a realistic representation of society and the more abstract exposure of its underlying mechanisms.[24] Her drama has gone further than anyone else's in its exploration of the feminist terrain. Yet Daniels restricts her research to what she knows well, the repressive patterns of her own Western culture; she does not venture on to foreign territory.

Beyond the female condition, a strong sense of history runs through the plays. *Byrthrite* takes place in the seventeenth century, during the Civil War, and shows a female community on the warpath to reclaim women from an excess of medical authority, men doctors taking control over women's bodies. *The Gut Girls* scrutinises the grim condition of women working in a Victorian gutting shed. The gutsy, spirited, often saucy but realistic women, who love their drink after work, enjoy a freer life than the ones in service in bourgeois families. Focused on ecology, *Taking Breath*, a surreal play for young people, plunges back into a mythical past. *The Devil's Gateway* contains a criticism of post-war meritocracy, seen as 'illusions of upward mobility' (p. 90). Ivy's racy monologue grasps the nature of social change in Britain:

> **Ivy** We had a great time round here in the war. [. . .] Every
> Saturday there was a party 'cos you didn't know which
> house would be flattened next. [. . .] Women became

strong. [. . .] We ran the country and when it was over we
could see the way things were going and that it was a bit
late for us but we invested our dreams and hopes and
plans in our daughters, only to see them evaporate like pee
in the lift on a hot day. Having kids is important, but
having a washing machine, a television and a car became
more important. And a husband with a steady job was set
up as number one main aim. Bloody silly values for a
country what was s'posed to be embarking on freedom.
(pp. 139–40)

Ivy perceives the way the class struggle is progressively being eroded by
materialistic values. Daniels's well-researched plays articulate a
critique of the class-ridden society. The social spectrum is represented
with sociological accuracy, down to the 'gentrification' of some areas:
'This must be getting into a trendy area, can always tell when the
Citroëns are double-parked,' says Sid in *Neaptide* (p. 249). Domestic
scenes resonate with echoes from the outside world; cultural
differences are perceived at all levels.

In *Masterpieces*, *Neaptide* and *Broken Wings*, the characters are
clearly middle-class. *The Devil's Gateway* introduces a different social
stratum, with the unemployed father who goes moonlighting, the
grandmother who cheats the social services, the educated daughter
who has married a priggish solicitor, and the social worker who shares
her life with a female partner from a working-class background
seeking to better herself at the Open University. Some of the working-
class women in *Blow Your House Down* are prostitutes. When it comes
to repressive sexist patterns, women share the same plight, irrespective
of their social origins, but even within the competitive context of the
1980s, Daniels will always show women fighting back, taking their
lives in hand, with the support of other women. Written with an
exhilarating sense of humour, the early dark comedies satirise with
lucidity all aspects of the patriarchal order women have been subjected
to for centuries: the church, the law, medical authority.

The tone is much more intense when the delicate issue of sexual
abuse within the family is approached, as well as the entrapment of

women in the concept of mental illness, a theme common to *Ripen Our Darkness* and to the madness trilogy. Conventional psychiatry and sexual taboos are derided with a maximum degree of irreverence by the female characters.[25] The romantic veil of marriage cannot withstand the abrasive effect of Daniels's wit; love and sex are buoyantly de-sacralised. In *Ripen Our Darkness*, Rene has to endure a difficult marital situation. A newspaper article makes her think:

> **Rene** (*starts reading from* Woman's Own *aloud*)   Dear Mary Grant, My wife and I make love about five times a week, which suits me down to the ground, but she will insist on watching telly over my shoulder. I don't mind this so much, but she will keep one hand free so she can switch stations with the remote control. (p. 16)

We can agree with Michael Billington that 'Ms Daniels often aims squarely below the belt', but it should be stressed that there is method in the irreverent jokes of the early plays.[26] Indeed, the triumphant feminism of the 1980s and 1990s is less central to Daniels's more recent stage works. *Broken Wings* is youth-orientated. *Who's Afraid of Virginia's Sister* (Chicken Shed Theatre, 2006) was written for and played by a young woman with cerebral palsy, who uses a communication board (as does Stephen Hawking). Debbie, the vivacious main character, 'is a living reminder that a disabled body does not signal a disabled mind. And Debbie's mind is gimlet-sharp. [. . .] She also has a ruthless sense of humour.'[27] Like all her sisters Debbie fights her way along with panache.

When it comes to placing Daniels's works in a wider sociological perspective, what belonged to the realm of 'utopia' in the plays of the late twentieth century, such as alternative lifestyles for lesbians, has now become a reality. The related themes of sexual self-determination and the advent of a sisterhood are present in the plays well into the twenty-first century. If lesbianism is not a new theme in modern drama, especially seen from the viewpoint of social opprobrium, Daniels contextualises the issue to bring out its complexity.[28] The angle she has chosen to tackle the subject in her plays proves to be the right one.[29] Her viewpoint is pragmatic, especially when parenthood is involved. Carina Bartleet analyses the way the problem is approached in *Flying Under Bridges*:

> Daniels opts to explore the very real distress caused by the lack of legal rights accorded to lesbian and gay couples before the enactment of civil partnerships in 2004.[30]

More generally, the emphasis on female solidarity, on tenderness and trust between mothers and daughters, has been in itself a major breakthrough. In *The Devil's Gateway*, three generations of East End women unite. They leave their families to join the women's peace camp at Greenham Common. In *Byrthrite*, two women become soldiers, one becomes a preacher and another one writes plays. They head for London where they join other women demonstrating against war. The same team spirit is at work in *Neaptide* and in *The Madness of Esme and Shaz*, where aunt Esme retrieves her niece from prison to take her away to run a pizzeria in Greece. All ages, across the social spectrum, club together to build a new world. In *Morning Glory*, the resourceful, elderly women are perfectly able to defend themselves and teach the teenage thugs a lesson. Written like a sitcom, the play also reads like a comic strip. Never unduly optimistic as to the state of the world, Daniels's plays nevertheless point the way forward.

Daniels's skilful dramaturgy can be seen as strategy. With her flair for dramatic construction and verbal comedy, she reveals the truth at the heart of painful situations. The tight construction informs the moral argument. The stage plays are sharply focused comedies, often breaking away from realistic conventions. Different genres are combined and transcended: argumentative satirical comedies of manners, comedies of ideas, tragi-comedies, dark comedies of sexist manners, surreal dramas. The intertext is made of recognisable classical forms, of popular culture, well-known songs, television sitcoms, from which she borrows the cinematographic fluidity, the broken sequences, the use of voiceovers and fade-ins. Although she is part of the great British tradition of realism, Daniels has moved ahead developing her own brand, partly visionary, partly emotional, when necessary, and always functional.

Distancing devices paradoxically intensify the reality effects, like the monologues, which are directly addressed to the audience and inspired by stand-up comedy. In the way they relate past and present, anachronisms are also creative of comedy, like the Biblical prologue with Eve, Jezebel, Mrs Lot and Delilah in *Beside Herself,* or the leaps in time in *Byrthrite.* About the thatched roof that needs mending, Grace cracks the expected joke: 'Thatcher don't care 'bout poor folk on parish welfare' (p. 345).

Doubling is a prerequisite in Daniels's plays: far from being a way of restricting the number of actors, doubling is conducive to critical distance. It bypasses an essentialist approach to characters, making them less individualised. It serves the overall significance of a play, enhancing the similarity of the protagonists, thus universalising their plight and, lastly, showing that all situations can be reversed and ultimately changed. An overtly theatrical device, doubling contributes to making a play somewhat abstract, therefore sharpening its moral edge, heightening its argumentative effect.

According to one critic of *Head-Rot Holiday,* Daniels has a keen 'ear for authentic dialogue'.[31] The creative power of speech gathers its own momentum in her plays. Rhetoric is used to combat repressive ideologies. In the early plays, the viewpoint is never reductive for either of the sexes, for conditioning alone is the butt of the satire, a point often missed by critics. Puns and witticisms always illuminate a moral point: 'offal by name, awful by nature' says Polly about her place of work in *The Gut Girls* (p. 3). Finding the words to name the pain is a way of winning the battle. Laughter helps to defuse, therefore to control emotion. The road to a new life involves the mastery of language. A fulfilling sense of anarchy emerges from *The Madness of Esme and Shaz,* where prim aunt Esme, a convinced Christian, learns to speak differently and to open up to a new, and perhaps to an even more Christian, frame of mind. Comedy explodes the limits of harsh reality.

Revisited within the broader context of modern and contemporary British drama, Daniels holds a major, if not canonical, position. If the early plays are tinted with Joe Orton's stylish outrageousness and Oscar Wilde's aphoristic brilliance, all the works contain echoes of

George Bernard Shaw's pedagogical determination. Their privileged terrain being human rights, they fit in the political and feminist theatre of the 1980s and 1990s. Far less strident, yet much more efficiently demonstrative than the more recent 'in-yer-face' phenomenon, Daniels's plays discuss what it implies to be a human being and to act as one. It seems difficult to go farther than she already has in terms of consciousness-raising, a possible reason for her stage plays being less frequent of late, whereas her highly polished, versatile radio work is what she seems to go for, a medium which ensures a more effective 'cultural penetration' of all milieus.[32]

Daniels's works invite multiple critical perspectives, starting with feminist theory and gender studies, which cover body-related issues, such as violence against women (*Masterpieces, Blow Your House Down, Morning Glory* and *Dust*).[33] Well-informed and perceptive of social changes, in keeping with the times and with her ear to the ground, Daniels outdistances theoretical discourses. In Daniels's truthful approach, ethical integrity goes with artistic coherence. Her plays are first and foremost forceful poetic constructions of a world vision. If the task of art is to unlock systems, to fulfil a moral purpose, Daniels's prophetic drama provides the keys.

Primary Sources

Works by Sarah Daniels

Plays One: Ripen Our Darkness, The Devil's Gateway, Masterpieces, Neaptide, Byrthrite (London: Methuen Drama, 1991).

Plays Two: The Gut Girls, Beside Herself, Head-Rot Holiday, The Madness of Esme and Shaz (London: Methuen Drama, 1994).

Taking Breath (London: Samuel French, 1999).

Morning Glory (London: Faber & Faber, 2001).

Dust, in *Shell Connections 2003: New Plays for Young People* (London: Faber & Faber, 2003).

Blow Your House Down, in Sharon Moneith, Margaretta Jolly, Nahem Yousaf and Ronald Paul (eds), *Critical Perspectives on Pat Barker* (Columbia: South Carolina UP, 2005).

Secondary Sources

Abdollahzadeh, Jale, 'De-constructing and Re-constructing the Gendered Gaze in Lesbian Theatre', in *Contemporary Drama in English*, No. 4 (Trier: WVT, 1996), pp. 25–34.

Aston, Elaine, 'Daniels in the Lion's Den: Sarah Daniels and the British Backlash', *Theatre Journal*, Vol. 47, No. 3 (1995), pp. 393–403.

—, *Feminist Views on the English Stage 1990–2000* (Cambridge: CUP, 2003).

Bartleet, Carina, 'Eve's Side of It: Sarah Daniels' Biblical Revision', in Colette Rayment and Mark Levon Byrne (eds), *Seeking the Centre: 2001 International Religion, Literature and the Arts Conference Proceedings* (Sydney: RLA Press, 2002), pp. 191–203.

—, 'Sarah Daniels' Hysteria Plays: Re-presentation of Madness', *Modern Drama*, Vol. 46, No. 2 (2003), pp. 241–60.

—, 'Bringing the House Down: Pat Barker, Sarah Daniels and the Dramatic Dialogue', in Sharon Moneith et al. (eds), *Critical Perspectives on Pat Barker* (Columbia: South Carolina UP, 2005).

—, 'Sarah Daniels: Feminist Enque(e)ry within the Mainstream', *New Theatre Quarterly*, Vol. 46, No. 102 (2010), pp. 145–60.

Boireau, Nicole, 'La comédie selon Sarah Daniels ou l'éloge de la raison', *Études Anglaises*, Vol. 52, No. 2 (1999), pp. 225–36.

—, 'Le théâtre féministe des années 80 en Angleterre: voix transgressives, voies de la transgression', *L'Annuaire théâtral: Revue québécoise d'études théâtrales*, No. 38 (2005), pp. 27–39.

Brenton, Howard, 'The Red Theatre Under the Bed', *New Theatre Quarterly*, Vol. 3, No. 11 (1987), pp. 195–206.

Daniels, Sarah, 'Introduction', *Plays Two* (London: Methuen Drama, 1994), pp. ix–xi.

Davis, Tracy C., '*Extremities* and *Masterpieces*: A Feminist Paradigm of Art and Politics', in Helene Keyssar (ed.), *Feminist Theatre and Theory* (London: Macmillan, 1996), pp. 137–54.

Debling, Heather, '"How Will They Ever Heal . . .?" Bearing Witness to Abuse and the Importance of Female Community in Sarah Daniels's *Beside Herself, Head-Rot Holiday*, and *The Madness of Esme and Shaz*', *Modern Drama*, Vol. 51, No. 2 (2008), pp. 259–72.

Dymkowski, Christine, 'Questioning Comedy in Daniels, Wertenbaker and Churchill', *Contemporary Drama in English*, No. 1 (Trier: WVT, 1993), pp. 33–44.

—, 'Breaking the Rules: The Plays of Sarah Daniels', *Contemporary Theatre Review*, Vol. 5, No. 1 (1996), pp. 63–75.

Edgar, David, *How Plays Work* (London: Nick Hern, 2009).

Godiwala, Dimple, *Breaking the Bounds: British Feminist Dramatists Writing in the Mainstream since c. 1980* (New York: Peter Lang, 2003).

Goodman, Lizbeth, 'Representing Gender/Representing Self: A Reflection on Role Playing in Performance Theory and Practice', in Nicole Boireau (ed.), *Drama on Drama:*

Dimensions of Theatricality on the Contemporary British Stage (London: Macmillan, 1997).

Griffin, Gabriele, 'Violence, Abuse and Gender Relations in the Plays of Sarah Daniels', in Elaine Aston and Janelle Reinelt (eds), *The Cambridge Companion to Modern British Women Playwrights* (Cambridge: CUP, 2000), pp. 194–209.

Griffiths, Trevor, 'Le théâtre politique en Angleterre', in Nicole Boireau (ed.), *Actes du colloque de Metz, Coup de Théâtre*, No. 6 (1986), pp. 161–6.

Haedicke, Susan C., 'Doing the Dirty Work: Gendered Versions of Working Class Women in Sarah Daniels' *The Gut Girls* and Israel Horovitz's *North Shore Fish*', *Journal of Dramatic Theory and Criticism*, Vol. 8, No. 2 (1994), pp. 77–88.

Minwalla, Framji, 'Sarah Daniels: A Woman in the Moon', *Theatre*, Vol. 21, No. 3 (1990), pp. 26–9.

O'Casey, Sean, *Juno and the Paycock*, in *Three Dublin Plays* (London: Faber & Faber, 1998).

Rubik, Margarete, 'Fringe or Mainstream? What is Marketable?', *Contemporary Drama in English*, No. 4 (Trier: WVT, 1996), pp. 15–24.

Wandor, Michelene, 'Culture, Politics and Values in Plays by Women in the 1980s', in Klaus Peter Müller (ed.), *Englisch Amerikanische Studien*, Vol. 3–4 (1986), pp. 441–8.

Notes

1. Irene McManus, *Morning Telegraph*, 27 November 1981.
2. Elizabeth Mahoney, *Guardian*, 31 October 2005.
3. The play was written for the 'Inside the Ethics Committee' series (BBC Radio 4).
4. Robert Cushman, *Observer*, 13 September 1981.
5. John Barber, *Daily Telegraph*, 8 September 1981.
6. David Edgar, *How Plays Work*, p. 179.
7. Elaine Aston, 'Daniels in the Lion's Den'.
8. Carole Woddis, *City Limits*, 21–27 October 1983.
9. See Christine Dymkowski, 'Questioning Comedy in Daniels, Wertenbaker and Churchill'.
10. Michael Billington, *Guardian*, 12 October 1983.
11. Milton Shulman, *Evening Standard*, 12 October 1983.
12. The second contemporary play by a woman playwright to be produced at the National Theatre, the first being *Watch on the Rhine* by Lillian Hellman in 1980.
13. See Aston, 'Daniels in the Lion's Den', p. 394, for Daniels's revision of 'familial politics'.
14. Howard Brenton, 'The Red Theatre Under the Bed', p. 201.
15. Already present in Michelene Wandor's *Aid Thy Neighbour* (New End Theatre, 1978). In Sean O'Casey's *Juno and the Paycock* (1924), to Mary, who laments not having a

father for her child, her mother answers: 'It'll have what's far betther – it'll have two mothers' (p. 146).

16. Margarete Rubik, 'Fringe or Mainstream? What is Marketable?', p. 15.

17. Sarah Daniels, 'Introduction', p. x.

18. Kate Bassett, *City Limits*, *Theatre Record*, Vol. XII, No. 21 (1992), p. 1229.

19. Benedict Nightingale, *The Times*, *Theatre Record*, Vol. XII, No. 21 (1992), p. 1230.

20. For further analysis of the cycle of violence, see Heather Debling, '"How Will They Ever Heal . . .?"'.

21. Caroline Rees, *What's On*, *Theatre Record*, Vol. XII, No. 21 (1992), p. 1230.

22. Unpublished typescript, courtesy of Sarah Daniels.

23. See Michelene Wandor, 'Culture, Politics and Values in Plays by Women in the 1980s'.

24. Ibid., p. 448.

25. Such irreverence is not uncommon: for examples, see Mary O'Malley, *Once a Catholic* (1977), Claire Luckham, *Trafford Tanzi* (1980), Nell Dunn, *Steaming* (1981) and Sharman MacDonald, *When I was a Girl I Used to Scream and Shout* (1984).

26. Michael Billington, *Guardian*, 12 October 1983.

27. Susan Elkin, *The Stage*, 17 March 2006.

28. *The Children's Hour* (1934) by Lillian Hellman and *The Killing of Sister George* (1965) by Frank Marcus are relevant examples.

29. Jale Abdollahzadeh, 'De-constructing and Re-constructing the Gendered Gaze in Lesbian Theatre'; Margarete Rubik, 'Fringe or Mainstream? What is Marketable?'; and Carina Bartleet, 'Sarah Daniels: Feminist Enque(e)ry within the Mainstream', argue that Daniels does not analyse the nature of lesbian identity.

30. Bartleet, 'Sarah Daniels: Feminist Enque(e)ry within the Mainstream', p. 158.

31. Rick Jones, *Evening Standard*, *Theatre Record*, Vol. XII, No. 21 (1992), p. 1229.

32. The phrase is from Trevor Griffiths, 'Le théâtre politique en Angleterre', in Nicole Boireau (ed.), 'Actes du colloque de Metz', *Coup de Théâtre*, No. 6 (1986), p. 162.

33. See Heather Debling, '"How Will They Ever Heal . . .?"', and Carina Bartleet, 'Sarah Daniels: Feminist Enque(e)ry within the Mainstream'.

7 APRIL DE ANGELIS

Rebecca D'Monté

Ironmistress; Hush; Playhouse Creatures; A Laughing Matter; Amongst Friends

Introduction

April De Angelis was born in London in 1960 to an English mother and Italian father. All the decisions she made about where to train and work, as well as her plays themselves, speak of her lifelong concerns with feminism, history and community, and her work is informed by connections between chronology and narration, power and subjugation. De Angelis was at the Old Vic Youth Theatre as a teenager, before studying at the East 15 Acting School in London. She joined Monstrous Regiment as an actress, then worked as actress/deviser with ReSisters theatre group, and it is no coincidence that the names of these companies also act as forceful political statements. Her first work was *Breathless* (Albany Empire, 1986), joint winner of the Second Wave Women's Writing Festival.[1] Then she wrote *Women in Law* (1987), followed by *Me* (1988), *Wanderlust* (1989) and *Bombshell* (1989). *Visitants* won the Young Writers for Radio Festival on BBC Radio 4 in 1988, with another radio play, *The Outlander*, appearing as a two-part serial for Radio 5 in 1991.[2] A year later she was Winner of the Writers' Guild Award.

Like many dramatists of her generation, De Angelis was deeply affected by the Thatcherite policies of the 1980s, and while her play *Ironmistress* (ReSisters, 1989) is set in the industrial Victorian age, it also comments on the 'ironmistress' Margaret Thatcher, then ruling the country. From *Hush* (Royal Court, 1992) onwards, De Angelis, along with many other of the earlier feminist playwrights, started to move beyond representing the oppression of women to a broader and more complex social and political agenda. If *Hush* charts a disengagement by younger people with the loss of direction by the left and the lack of anything to take its place, *The Positive Hour* (Out of Joint, 1997) shows the legacy of ideological feminism and failures of New Labour, while *Soft Vengeance* (Graeae, 1993), for the disabled-led theatre company, Graeae, melds the personal and political through the bomb injuries suffered by activist Albie Sachs in 1960s Apartheid South Africa.

In 1990 De Angelis became Writer-in-Residence at Paines Plough, with *Crux*, a play about Marguarite Porete and a group of free-thinking religious women in the medieval period. This continues her overt concern with history, invariably in the form of literary adaptations and real lives, as a way of showing connections of power dynamics across time, or exploring the invisibility of women: what early feminist critics have termed 'her-story'. Similar plays include *Frankenstein* (1989), *The Life and Times of Fanny Hill* (Red Shift, 1991), *A Warwickshire Testimony* (RSC, 1999) and *Wuthering Heights* (Birmingham Rep, 2008).

Perhaps her most celebrated work came in 1993, with *Playhouse Creatures*, produced by Sphinx at the Leicester Haymarket Theatre. This was about the difficulties faced by the first actresses to appear on the English stage: the film, *Shakespeare in Love* (1998), covered some of the same issues of gender, sexuality and the theatre, as did Nicholas Wright's stage work, *Warning, Boys at Play* (2000), which looked back to the early boy actors. Interest in aspects of theatre and performance continued in *A Laughing Matter* (Out of Joint, 2002), which is about the attempts of Oliver Goldsmith to have his play *She Stoops to Conquer* (1773) staged by David Garrick. The play won the Whatsonstage Theatregoers' Choice award for best new comedy and was presented by Max Stafford-Clark in tandem with Goldsmith's comedy, similar to the director's pairing of George Farquhar's *The Recruiting Officer* and Timberlake Wertenbaker's *Our Country's Good* in 1988. De Angelis's continued fascination with the meaning of theatre showed itself in *Aristophanes: The Gods are Laughing*, a commission for the British Film Industry and Channel 4 in 1995.

With *Wild East* (Royal Court, 2005), a disquieting look at the ways in which history works against three individuals, and *Headstrong* (National Theatre, 2004), set aboard an opium clipper in the China Seas, De Angelis's work endeavours to engage with topical events. She has also become further involved with collaborative projects, and in experimenting with different theatrical forms. *Catch* (Royal Court, 2006) is about identity theft and the violent repercussions felt in society when its youth feel disempowered. Written in conjunction with four other female playwrights – Stella Feehily, Tanika Gupta, Chloe Moss and Laura Wade – it was designed to celebrate fifty years of experimental work at the Royal Court, as well as to provide a homage to *Lay By* (1971) by Howard Brenton, Brian Clark, Trevor Griffiths, David Hare, Stephen Poliakoff, Hugh Stoddart and Snoo Wilson: the replacement of a group of male dramatists by female dramatists seems indicative of the gradual inroads women have made into British theatre during the past forty years. *2006* (2006) was part of Theatre 503's bringing together of ten playwrights in its Decade season: De Angelis's play depicts the escape of the Austrian Natascha Kampusch from her kidnapper. The interplay between imprisonment, security and fear is also taken up in the opera *Silent Twins* (Almeida, 2007), which explores the strange, silent world of arsonist twins in Broadmoor psychiatric hospital in the 1980s, and the gated residence in *Amongst Friends* (Hampstead Theatre, 2009) is emblematic of the results of years of materialism and indifference shown to social minorities, as well as the culture of paranoia engendered by the terrorist attacks of 11 September 2001 and 7 July 2005.

De Angelis has written three libretti, *Pig* (1992), *Greed* (1993) and *Flight* (1998), with composer Jonathan Dove. She has also taught playwriting at a number of institutions, including the University of Birmingham, the Royal Court's Young Writing Programme, and the Royal Court International in Cuba, India, Mexico and Africa.

The Plays

Ironmistress (1989)

Ironmistress, commissioned by ReSisters, and directed by Anna Birch at the Young Vic on 24 January 1989, was De Angelis's first important work, and the one that brought her to the attention of the main-stream. She notes that 'When I was writing it I was trying to break away from the issue-based, "agit-prop" style that a lot of theatre groups with strong political intentions had adopted for themselves'; instead, she wanted to write something deliberately 'theatrical' in style.[3] In her concern with nuances of gender and power, De Angelis wanted Martha Darby – based on a real-life nineteenth-century woman – to be unsympathetic and even 'blameworthy as a patriarchal figure'.[4] Taking over her husband's iron foundry after his death, Martha finally has power after years spent lying 'in a box. | Padded and quiet' (p. 41), but now her days are spent providing equipment for a war-making machine over which she has no control. The name of her daughter, Little Cog, symbolically describes the whole play, where in the global market place, everyone exists only as part of a 'giant machine' (p. 12). Although Margaret Thatcher is not mentioned, the play's poetic force suggests the debasement of society through capitalism and the search for a more empowering form of femininity.

This is dramatised through the games they play on the eve of Little Cog's wedding. The daughter's rich imagination, a symbol for the process of theatre itself, conjures up the subversive figure of Shanny Pinns, an exploited former foundry worker who has died of starvation. Little Cog sees her as the embodiment both of the limitations of women's lives and as the anarchic spirit of the underclass. Reinventing her as a highwaywoman, still free to roam the hills and to seek revenge against the rich, 'Little Cog transforms Shanny's life, at least in imagination, from one of helpless privation to a tale of heroic daring and rebellion'.[5]

In contrast, stuck in reality, Little Cog has come to understand that female sexuality has become debased, nothing more than a conduit for male pleasure and power. After the wedding, she describes how her husband treated her like a machine, and when her virginity was taken from her, the blood ran like 'melted iron' (p. 57). Shanny Pinns's body was used to mould an iron statue of a woman, represented on stage through the projection of Little Cog's shadow on corrugated iron, and although it is polished and loved, Shanny Pinns says, the face said: 'Nothing' (p. 49).

Male fantasy, social convention and global capitalisation are seen as imprisoning women, rendering them passive and silent; in contrast, female imagination has the power to liberate them. At the end, Little Cog – in the guise of Shanny Pinns – dreams of life in the next century, when metal birds will fly through the air, transporting her to a different kind of life. In this way, De Angelis gives voice to 'women marginalised and abandoned by mid-nineteenth-century industrial "progress"', while simultaneously providing caustic commentary on the contemporary situation at the time of writing.[6]

Hush (1992)

Premiering at the Royal Court on 6 August 1992, Hush was De Angelis's first experience of working with director Max Stafford-Clark, and his rigorous rehearsal practices forced her to think constantly about her characters' motivations.[7] The play represented a departure for De Angelis: she wanted 'to ask different questions' and to 'explore my response to Britain today from outside the spectrum of the position of women in society'.[8] Although still describing herself as a feminist, this work moved away from 'issue-based' theatre towards what Heidi Stephenson and Natasha Langridge call 'the inadequacy of individual responses and isolated, ideological solutions to the world problems we have today'.[9] Portraying the troubled lives of alienated young people, similar to those who haunt the works of Judy Upton, one of the key 'in-yer-face' dramatists of the 1990s, it takes as its central plotline the anniversary of Jo's disappearance, and the reminiscences of friends and family, particularly her daughter Rosa and sister Louise, who gather near to the shoreline where she has possibly drowned.

The stage area is divided into two parts, the house and the beach:

'*The rooms look dusty, unlived in. The beach may encroach upon the house surrealistically*' (p. 75), the first production using the sound of waves as a constant background. The setting is symbolic, with one character mentioning that 'A lot of rich bastards live round here. They creep down from the cities. To escape the mess they've made. It's like an infection' (p. 96). As with Upton, for whom the seaside 'represents escape. The sea is [. . .] literally, the end of the line,' De Angelis's play is populated by those who are similarly running from life.[10] The personal loss the group has suffered is set against individual disappointments; for example, Denise searches through Eastern religions and New Age philosophies to find answers, even though she is unable to articulate what the questions might be, and Rosa suffers the angst of being a motherless teenager. This represents the wave of political vacillation hanging over the 1990s. Jo's radical activism at Greenham Common is no longer seen as relevant, with Louise thinking her 'Reclaim the Night' banner would 'probably fetch something on the memorabilia market' (p. 104). Tony might say it is 'an amazing time to be living in. Huge empires are breaking up. It's like the end of the ice age' (p. 104), but he, like all the other characters in the play, can only cope through self-invested avoidance tactics. As Sarah Hemming's preview article asserted, Jo's

> disappearance takes on an allegorical dimension. You realise that the play is in part taking stock of the loss of direction and certainty in the Left, and that, through the character of Jo, De Angelis is assessing what society offers to a 15-year-old.[11]

Rosa and Dogboy, the unemployed tramp who hangs about the beach, are seen as disenfranchised and their lack of ability to articulate their needs is shown through the way in which the homeless boy is forced to assume the role of a dog in order to be heard by society. Equally, though, De Angelis's work suggests it is those of the left who have also been left without a say in present-day society. As in the later *The Positive Hour*, there is a concern with female power and an examination of the climate of increasing political and personal desperation that afflicted liberals, leftists and feminists from the 1980s onwards, witnessing the erosion of values of community and compassion for which they had so long struggled.[12]

Playhouse Creatures (1993)

Playhouse Creatures exists in at least three different versions. It was originally written for an all-female cast on 5 October 1993, directed by Sue Parrish at the Leicester Haymarket, with extra roles (including two male characters), added for Lynne Parker's revival at the Old Vic Theatre in 1997. It returns to a theme already explored in *The Life and Times of Fanny Hill*, namely the interplay between female sexuality and male predatory behaviour. This voyeuristic male gaze was an accepted part of the English theatre when professional actresses first appeared in 1660. At the beginning of the play, Doll Common, the chorus-like figure, comments on how 'Once this was a playhouse, and before that, a bear pit', where animals are baited and forced to fight to the death (p. 159). Doll can still hear 'their cries very faint and in the wind', and likewise, actresses of the Restoration period return to the old theatre to reminisce about their struggles to be taken seriously alongside their male counterparts (p. 159). The indignities of their daily lives are catalogued, a constant struggle of misogyny, physical and sexual abuse, and poverty. Having upset the Earl of Oxford, Rebecca Marshall is set upon by his men, who 'rubbed shit into my hair. To teach me my manners' (p. 189). When Mrs Farley becomes pregnant and is forced to give up the stage, she has to prostitute herself, learning 'The art of performance [. . .] You've got to act like you like it. Love it even' (p. 218). For De Angelis, Mark Fisher says, 'Such women were like Wild West pioneers, surviving on a dangerous frontier entirely through their own resourcefulness.'[13] Beyond this, though, there is an understanding of the delights the theatre can bring to performer and audience alike. Nell Gwyn feels loved by the crowds who watch her, and Mrs Barry describes how 'the world outside is grey and boring. But here, everything is different. It's magic. Magic' (p. 199).

Into this material, De Angelis weaves myths and fables about women. Jane de Gay argues that there has been a trend in women's drama to deconstruct

> the original stories in some way, drawing attention to the constructed nature of narrative, the fabricated nature of performance, to deny that such narratives have any relationship to reality.[14]

Nevertheless, when actresses appear in De Angelis's play dressed as Amazons and baring their breasts, this is designed to heighten 'the private and public aspects of women's status as objects of possession and exchange': these mythical creatures replicate in reality strong, adventurous women who enter and succeed in patriarchal spaces, even while being denied an equal status.[15] Mention is also made of women's perceived closeness to black magic, an area brought into a number of De Angelis's plays. Mrs Marshall sticks pins into a wax figure of her abusive lover, and with the rest dances around invoking the three witches' spells from *Macbeth*, a recurring motif in the play. Thomas Betterton, actor manager of the Duke's Company, never appears, but nevertheless rules over them. His wife, Mary Betterton, feels akin to Lady Macbeth, and tells Doll, 'I know why she went mad [. . .] It was the waiting, the waiting' (p. 227). Once educated by the other more cynical and worldly women, she begins to criticise Betterton's decisions and make demands of her own; indeed, in reality Mrs Betterton would take over her husband's job as theatre manager after his death. Although, as Ian Shuttleworth notes,

> her overall concern is with a number of women trying to do full justice to their individual potentials in a profession which requires them merely to be objects (whether to the audience in general or to particular spectators in private), De Angelis's principal tone is comic; camaraderies and rivalries alike are portrayed sardonically.[16]

Her lightness of touch avoids moralistic sermonising.

A Laughing Matter (2002)

Careful leavening of weighty manners through humour is also evident in *A Laughing Matter*, which arrived on tour at the National Theatre on 6 February 2003. This was another piece for Stafford-Clark's Out of Joint company, a witty dissection of debates about low vs sentimental comedy, and stylised vs naturalistic acting, put in motion by Goldsmith and Garrick. While some critics were dismayed by the farcical scenes within the play, this was an accurate portrayal of theatre of the time, when the new middle-class audiences had to be catered for by dividing up a straight drama with entr'actes and afterpiece entertainments, usually the less intellectually challenging songs, dances and pantomime. Garrick's legacy is generally seen as raising the standards of the theatre, but this is gently mocked through his rejection of Goldsmith's *She Stoops to Conquer* in place of a vicar's third-rate play, so as to please his benefactor: Garrick tells the dramatist, 'I have a responsibility to my theatre [. . .] I can't just put a play on because a man is poor' (p. 27). In this way, the play has at its heart eternal concerns about literary ambition and patronage of the arts, and the dichotomy between experimentation and commercialism, where the nurturing of future classics is rejected in place of an undemanding present. As Benedict Nightingale wrote:

> Comedy needn't be soft and comforting. It can be mischievous and subversive. You see the bind in which Jason Watkins's spirited yet sly Garrick finds himself, trapped as he is by economic, social and moral pressures. It's a bind his descendants know even today.[17]

Stafford-Clark's decision to run Goldsmith's *She Stoops to Conquer* alongside *A Laughing Matter* cleverly mimics, and upholds, De Angelis's central storyline – whether or not the play should be staged – and is itself an interesting comment on Out of Joint's own commitment to new writing. Rachel Halliburton enjoyed 'Julian McGowan's opulently cluttered set', which allowed 'a handful of the audience to sit in boxes built onto the stage, so that the sense of the theatre within a theatre casts its spell over scenes'.[18] This cleverly added to the production's authenticity, while also highlighting the whole project's metatheatricality. Double casting helped to delineate interesting comparisons and contrasts between the characters. Michael Coveney noted that

> Owen Sharpe plays Goldsmith [. . .] as a tolerated booby in the literary club of Burke and Johnson, then the energetic madcap Tony Lumpkin in *She Stoops* . . . It is a superb double of comic infiltration in plays that question the nature of performance.[19]

Similar comments can also be made about Ian Radford cast in the roles of the Old Tory Samuel Johnson and the old-fashioned Mr Hardcastle, and Jane Wood as the patroness Lady Kingston and upwardly mobile Mrs Hardcastle. The concerns of *She Stoops to Conquer* – anxiety about social change, class displacement, sexual behaviour – all find their way into De Angelis's affectionate pastiche, and, for Coveney, 'The overall effect is of a wide-ranging survey of English class and manners in the late eighteenth century, filtered through a sieve of contemporary high spirits and bawdiness.'[20]

Amongst Friends (2009)

Amongst Friends, directed by Anthony Clark at Hampstead Theatre on 21 May 2009, is a dark morality tale, dealing with the fallout from New Labour and the Iraq War. Labour MP Richard and tabloid journalist Lara live in an upmarket gated community in London, variously described as a 'compound', a 'Cunt', and 'a Complex. Once a psychological defence mechanism now a network of retail outlets and dwellings' (pp. 8, 9). Dominic Maxwell commented on the 'social schism that this armour-plated luxury represents', which in turn has been spawned by panic in the middle-class bourgeoisie over perceived social, religious, and racial difference: the title points out the insidious paranoia.[21] Ironically, therefore, into this sanctum these figures of the Establishment invite their previous neighbours, Joe and Caitlin, whose grandfather once worked in the building when it used to be a factory, contracting 'fuzzy lung [. . .] their term for respiratory sclerosis' (pp. 16–17). A malfunctioning entry phone also brings in Shelley from 'the other side of the roundabout', or as Lara calls it 'the sink estate' (p. 24). Claiming her son has died fighting in Basra, she berates Lara for her newspaper column supporting the war, and Richard for supplying inadequate military equipment.

During the play's inception, De Angelis recognised similarities with J. B. Priestley's *An Inspector Calls* (1946), which itself was written between 1944–45 to promote the ideology of the Labour Party on the eve of a General Election.[22] This was picked up on by Michael Coveney, who saw it as a 'J. B. Priestley set-up with satirical remarks about lifestyle', adding waspishly: 'There's even a lumpy reference to MPs' expenses that must have been pitched in last week.'[23] Each character begins to be implicated in the death of the son, whose name changes from Leigh (English) to Mukerjee (Asian) to Donal (Irish), and who may or may not exist. The ambiguity is important, as he comes to stand for all those who have no place in society, who belong to no one and everyone at the same time. The social and political satire prods at the impact of years of Thatcherite policies on the rise of New Labour, with Joe's bitter repetition of the 1997 mantra, 'Things can only get better' (p. 10), a hollow echo even before his suicide. The suggestion is that society has moved from one concerned with community and neighbourliness to one fuelled by ignorance, fear and hatred.

The original production placed the upwardly mobile Lara and Richard's flat against a dominant cityscape, with a blue lift rising and descending at the side. In this competitive, dog-eat-dog world, Lara feels smug in her view that envy is 'the Brits' disease' (p. 17), not seeing herself as part of the problem. As they look out from their self-sealed world – and it is significant that Lara suffers from agoraphobia – it is inevitable that it will be invaded by those they seek to leave behind in their scramble up the social ladder. The incursion of an outer, politically motivated world on an inner, complacently private one, is a standard of theatre. It was used to stunning effect in Sarah Kane's *Blasted* (1995), but the two plays could not be further apart in terms of technique, hinted at in Lyn Gardner's review, which thought the production opted 'for kitchen-chic realism rather than something more surreal and edgy'.[24] It is instructive that few women dramatists have presented political subjects beyond the domestic arena, or in an experimental way: works such as *Blasted*, Caryl Churchill's *Far Away* (2000), and Gillian Slovo's *Guantanamo* (2004) remain exceptions rather than the rule.

Summary

Claire Macdonald provides a useful commentary on De Angelis:

> Her work is interestingly positioned between a newer wave of 1990s playwrights – such as the late Sarah Kane and Phyllis Nagy – who may have benefited from the widening of conventional opportunities [. . .] and the earlier generation of writer-makers from Bryony Lavery to Deborah Levy whose work was forged through the process of hands-on theatre making within a radical theatre generation (or two).[25]

Certainly her career has followed the rapid shift in visibility of women dramatists during the latter half of the twentieth century and into the next millennium. From 1979, when there were arguably only two well-known figures, Pam Gems and Caryl Churchill, there are now dozens of women contributing to British theatre. As one of these, De Angelis has made a significant contribution in signalling some of the most important concerns of women's drama: the necessity for giving a voice to the marginalised and disaffected through a reassessment of history, the effects of patriarchy on the disempowerment of women, and a belief in the strength of female creativity. Cheryl Robson notes that 'Since women's perspectives on life differed from the norm, they were inevitably considered to be an attack on the established order,' and De Angelis has shown herself to be consistently aware of this, embracing her position 'outside the margins of conventional theatre', as well as putting women's prescribed lives under scrutiny.[26] However, it is important to note that she cannot and must not be defined solely in terms of gender, and indeed she has become increasingly involved in wider political issues; for example, the failure of capitalism, and of globalisation. De Angelis's work has also followed some of the most stylistically interesting changes in dramatic form and technique, including free-flowing and episodic scene shifts, non-realistic language and situations, and the use of strong visual and aural imagery.

Unlike many female dramatists of recent years, De Angelis has never been shy of labelling herself a feminist; indeed, the strength of her work has mainly sprung from her political stance, and the sense of identity she gained from belonging to a larger collective group. Apart from herself, the list of female dramatists spawned out of this time is impressive. As De Angelis so rightly states, 'It now seems impossible to imagine a theatre landscape without these people. They changed the way women wrote and the things they felt they could write about.'[27] Like many of her female contemporaries, she brought to notice women who had been, in Sheila Rowbotham's words, 'hidden from history', finding creative expression in revivifying these disordered and disorderly lives. In De Angelis's version, for example, Fanny Hill directs a reconstruction of her own life, demanding a reassessment of the 'autobiographical' novel John Cleland has forced her to write.

As this suggests, narrating female experience also required a different theatrical form and technique. De Angelis has spoken about not just the defining influence of Caryl Churchill on her work, but of how they both arrived at the same place almost simultaneously. Thus, *Ironmistress* was written before De Angelis saw *Top Girls*, but in retrospect she could immediately see the plays' similarities, with their overlayering of myth and reality, and chronologically displaced time sequences. If the traditional three-act structure represented male sexuality – 'it all builds up to one big bang and it's over' – women's plays could respond to their own sexuality, 'with lots of peaky bits'.[28] This has, inevitably, resulted in critics describing her work as episodic. So, while *Playhouse Creatures* generally garnered good reviews when it first appeared, one male theatre critic seemed unimpressed by Alison Peebles's revival at the Dundee Rep in 2007: '*Playhouse Creatures* is less a play than a collage of scenes [. . .] Into this, she weaves the women's backstage stories, which come momentarily to life but lack sustaining dramatic force.'[29] Similar remarks have been made of De Angelis's other work, but this was a deliberate technique of women's drama: to stitch together stories from myth, history and fiction, past and present, to present a patchwork of different women's lives, and a new way of speaking. Jane de Gay and Lizbeth Goodman theorise this response as taking

> its cue from Lacanian psychoanalytic approaches to language acquisition, in which entry into the symbol order of written language is figured as a male privilege: such language represents 'woman' as the desired other and thus fails to embody her. Language becomes a tool that objectifies women and cannot convey their perspectives or experiences. The search for a 'woman's language' may thus be seen as an attempt to circumvent this perceived problem.[30]

As a feminist writer, then, De Angelis has done much to put women centre stage, a place that historically has been difficult for them. This can be seen most literally by the large number of female roles she has created, which provide a counterbalance to the male-dominated theatre of Britain, but her use of symbolic language and minimal staging also draws attention to female oppression and the loss of their history. The final image of *Playhouse Creatures* is chilling in its positioning of the female struggle for freedom. Doll recollects how her father, as master of the bear pit, had a bear's claws and teeth ripped out when she tried to turn against her fate, and Doll had the warm blood smeared on her face so she would not forget this lesson; all the while, Mrs Barry continues to count out the theatre owner's takings from the performances by women in the same space. A revival at the Leeds Playhouse in 2003 set the action on a revolve, and the distorted rectangular proscenium and use of a see-through mirror between front and backstage areas highlighted the links between past and present, performance and voyeurism, financial remuneration and exploitation. It is unclear for the characters at the end whether women have swapped their role as orange-sellers – a seventeenth-century euphemism for prostitutes – for acting, only to find that they are one and the same. Unlike her contemporary Sarah Daniels, De Angelis moves beyond a negotiation of male exploitation to argue that 'feminist writing of the eighties has re-invented a place for women's sexuality on stage', which puts women in control, rather than turning them into victims.[31]

By the 1990s, though, De Angelis, along with other female dramatists, began to see the emphasis upon feminist issues such as women's oppression as repetitive and limiting, usurped by 'in-yer-face' drama. She confided, 'Truth be told, women's theatre had become passé [. . .] it felt like writing against the grain of the times.'[32] The new generation of dramatists, including Sarah Kane, Mark Ravenhill, Jez Butterworth and Judy Upton, were disenchanted by the old political certainties: as a generation they believed they had witnessed the failure of party politics, communism and capitalism, and therefore no longer had any sense of engagement with 'the utopian socialist visions of the 1970s and the satirical critiques of the 1980s'.[33] De Angelis's worry was that 'if you abandon the big idea do you then abandon the idea of humanism, which is progress is possible, change is possible, people are basically good?'[34]

This is tackled in De Angelis's work through her interrogation of the nexus between history, society and politics, one of the most notable features of her oeuvre being how many are set in the past, with a slippage between real and fictionalised selves: *Crux* in the thirteenth century, *Playhouse Creatures* in the seventeenth; *The Life and Times of Fanny Hill* and *A Laughing Matter* in the eighteenth; *Frankenstein*, *Wuthering Heights*, *Emma* and *Ironmistress* in the nineteenth; *Soft Vengeance* in the more recent past, and so on. These time slips became of interest to British dramatists in the 1970s and 1980s, as in the politically motivated works of David Edgar (*Destiny*) and Caryl Churchill (*Light Shining in Buckinghamshire, Cloud Nine, Top Girls*), or the more inter-generational concerns of Charlotte Keatley (*My Mother Said I Never Should*) or Sharman Macdonald (*When I was a Girl I Used to Scream and Shout*). There are also strong similarities with the work of Timberlake Wertenbaker (*The Grace of Mary Traverse, The Love of the Nightingale*) and Bryony Lavery (*Origin of the Species*,

Witchcraze, Ophelia), all of whom were part of a major trend towards the deconstruction of history and myth. In a simple way, De Angelis interrogates the relationship between people's lives and how this relates to the wider social and political forces around them, demonstrating the ease with which the individual or group can be erased from memory and therefore from history. Her Fanny Hill says, 'I seem to have forgot myself', having been turned into 'one big hole' (pp. 179–80) by male sexual fantasies. When Marguarite in *Crux* is being burnt at the stake, all she felt was a 'terrible fear | Of pain, Of dark nothing forever' (p. 87). Villagers in *A Warwickshire Testimony* are concerned that the developers are 'making up a village and plonking it down on top of the old one. It'll be like a grave with the wrong headstone' (p. 10).

More complexly, as David Edgar has pointed out, De Angelis 'continues not only to write history historically, but to treat the present in the same way'.[35] In 1998 she wanted to believe in history as 'a truth that is the sum of us and what's happened to us in our histories that will emerge and reveal who we are'. However, the impact of commercialism and globalisation is leading instead to 'an age of surface depthlessness', a realisation brought home to her by watching Martin Crimp's *Attempts on Her Life* (1997), with its lack of realistic characters and 'elaborate and sophisticated game with the audience's expectations of how scenes connect within narrative'.[36]

De Angelis herself displays the workings of history through her use of poetic narrative and form, which goes back to the earliest forms of drama, suggesting that the narration of people's stories and the unfolding of the weight of historical events is part of humanity's power to survive, and of theatre itself as a communal activity. This sense of communality also underpins her collaborative working methods, forged out of her early political experiences. 'How better to enter a new territory but together?' she asks. 'The Women's Movement has accentuated the personal as political.'[37] While this term has often been abused, it is one that suits her agenda, as she strives to show how individuals and communities have been radically changed by wider political forces. Of course, De Angelis at first hand experienced how Thatcherism had a devastating effect on new theatre writing in general, and women's drama in particular, noting that now 'the emphasis lay on the marketable product [. . .] small casts, compact sets and efficiency – rather than on process, experiment, collaboration and collectivity'.[38] Nevertheless, she has managed to fuse these seemingly oppositional viewpoints. Collaborations with, and commissions for some of the most important theatre companies of the past few decades, where economic restraints have been acute, have led to a sharpening of her creative responses: minimal staging allows a focus upon the visual image – Dorothy at the beginning of *A Warwickshire Testimony* sitting on a bare stage with a gun in her lap – or on language – Magda and Minna's recollection of their dreams in *Breathless*. In both *Soft Vengeance* and *Ironmistress* the impossibility to be given a larger cast led to her creating alter egos for her main characters as a way to engage with their inner life in an intensely dramatic way.[39]

De Angelis's work was born of 1970s female agit prop, or what she terms 'the "upfront" feminist/revolutionary mode', and became part of 'the emergence of more poetic, experimental and visual theatre female/ritualistic forms'.[40] Her comments on female oppression and historical dislocation are illuminating, and she has on the whole worked to dismantle existing form, language and meaning. It is no coincidence that she celebrates 'the notion of play, central to deconstruction', which 'challenges the fixed relationships between the sign/signifier and the signified of semiotics, asserting that any text is not a self-enclosed model, but the meaning is always deferred by the play of signification'.[41] Ultimately, throughout her work runs a fundamental belief in the power of imagination. Once she noted that

> really oppressive regimes like the one in Beijing have to be so oppressive if they are going to control people's thoughts. They have to be rigorous and violent because people don't want to be controlled in that way.[42]

De Angelis has refused to have her imagination curtailed by political doctrine, passing fashions, or existing conventions. In this way she has proved herself to be one of British theatre's most serviceable and trenchant dramatists.

Primary Sources

Works by April De Angelis

Women in Law (unpublished script, University of Bristol Theatre Collection, 1987).

The Visitants (unpublished script, University of Bristol Theatre Collection, 1988).

Breathless, in Frances Gray (ed.), *Second Wave Plays: Women at the Albany Empire* (Sheffield: Sheffield Academic Press, 1990).

Crux, in Cheryl Robson (ed.), *Seven Plays by Women* (Twickenham: Aurora Metro Publications, 1991).

The Life and Times of Fanny Hill, in Michael Fry (ed.), *Frontline Drama Four: Adapting Classics* (London: Methuen Drama, 1996).

Plays One: Ironmistress, Hush, Playhouse Creatures, The Positive Hour (London: Faber & Faber, 1999).

A Warwickshire Testimony (London: Faber & Faber, 1999).

A Laughing Matter (London: Faber & Faber, 2002).

Soft Vengeance, in Jenny Sealey (ed.), *Graeae Plays One: New Plays Redefining Disability* (Twickenham: Aurora Metro Press, 2002).

Wild East (London: Faber & Faber, 2005).

Catch, co-written with Stella Feehily, Tanika Gupta, Chloe Moss, Laura Wade (London: Oberon, 2006).

Wuthering Heights (London: Samuel French, 2009).

Amongst Friends (London: Faber & Faber, 2009).

Secondary Sources

Aston, Elaine, *Caryl Churchill* (Devon: Northcote House, 1997).

—, *Feminist Views on the English Stage: Women Playwrights 1990–2000* (Cambridge: CUP, 2003).

—, and Janelle Reinelt, *The Cambridge Companion to Modern British Women Playwrights* (Cambridge: CUP, 2000).

Cousin, Geraldine, *Women in Dramatic Place and Time: Contemporary Female Characters on Stage* (London: Routledge, 1996).

Croft, Susan, *She Also Wrote Plays: An International Guide to Women Playwrights from the 10th to the 21st Century* (London: Faber & Faber, 2001).

De Angelis, April, 'Introduction', in *Plays One* (London: Faber & Faber, 1999), pp. ix–xi.

—, 'Women and Theatre: The University of Birmingham MA in Playwriting Lecture', <http://www.robinkelly.btinternet.co.uk/angelis.htm>

—, 'Riddle of the Sphinx', *Guardian*, 10 September 2005 <http://www.guardian.co.uk/stage/2005/sep/10/theatre>

—, and Susan Croft, 'An Alphabet of Apocrypha: Collaborations and Explorations', in Trevor R. Griffiths and Margaret Llewellyn-Jones (eds), *British and Irish Women Dramatists Since 1958: A Critical Handbook* (Buckingham: Open UP, 1993), pp. 135–51.

De Gay, Jane, 'Seizing Speech and Playing with Fire: Greek Mythological Heroines and International Women's Performance', in Jane de Gay and Lizbeth Goodman (eds), *Languages of Theatre Shaped by Women* (Bristol: Intellect, 2003), pp. 11–36.

—, and Lizbeth Goodman (eds), 'Introduction: Speaking in Tongues', in *Languages of Theatre Shaped by Women* (Bristol: Intellect, 2003), pp. 1–9.

D'Monté, Rebecca and Graham Saunders (eds), *Cool Britannia: British Political Drama in the 1990s* (Basingstoke: Palgrave, 2007).

Edgar, David (ed.), *State of Play: Playwrights on Playwriting* (London: Faber & Faber, 1999).

Goodman, Lizbeth, *Contemporary Feminist Theatres: To Each Her Own* (London: Routledge, 1993).

Griffiths, Trevor R. and Margaret Llewellyn-Jones (eds), *British and Irish Women Dramatists Since 1958: A Critical Handbook* (Buckingham: Open UP, 1993).

Macdonald, Claire, 'Writing Outside the Mainstream', in Elaine Aston and Janelle Reinelt (eds), *The Cambridge Companion to Modern British Women Playwrights* (Cambridge: CUP, 2000), pp. 235–52.

Robson, Cheryl (ed.), 'Introduction', in *Seven Plays by Women: Fighting Voices, Fighting Lives* (London: Aurora Metro, 1991), pp. 5–9.

Sedgwick, Eve Kosofsky, *Between Men: English Literature and Male Homosocial Desire* (New York: Columbia UP, 1985).

Sierz, Aleks, 'Interview with April De Angelis', *Theatrevoice* website, 28 May 2009 <http://www.theatrevoice.com/listen_now/player/?audioID=689>

Stephenson, Heidi and Natasha Langridge, *Rage and Reason: Women Playwrights on Playwriting* (London: Methuen Drama, 1997).

Notes

1. Susan Croft, *She Also Wrote Plays*, p. 58.
2. Other plays for BBC Radio 4 include adaptations of *Black Narcissus* (1997) and *Emma* (2000), *Childless* (2006), *I Leap Over the Wall* (2006), *Cashcows* (2009), and *Counting* (2009).
3. April De Angelis, 'Introduction', p. ix.
4. Ibid.
5. Geraldine Cousin, *Women in Dramatic Place and Time*, p. 65.
6. Ibid., p. 60.
7. April De Angelis and Caryl Churchill have both noted their debt to Max Stafford-

Clark's working methods. See, for example, Elaine Aston, *Caryl Churchill*, p. 65.

8. Quoted in Heidi Stephenson and Natasha Langridge, *Rage and Reason*, p. 59.

9. Ibid.

10. Rebecca D'Monté and Graham Saunders, *Cool Britannia*, p. 91.

11. Sarah Hemming, 'New Stages in Writing the Wrongs: Hush – Don't Tell Anyone, but April De Angelis No Longer Sees Women as the Big Issue', *Independent*, 29 July 1992.

12. Croft, *She Also Wrote Plays*, p. 59.

13. Mark Fisher, *Guardian, Theatre Record*, Vol. XXVII, No. 22 (2007), p. 1333.

14. Jane de Gay, 'Seizing Speech and Playing with Fire', p. 15.

15. Eve Kosofsky Sedgwick, *Between Men*, p. 57.

16. Ian Shuttleworth, *Financial Times, Theatre Record*, Vol. XVII, No. 19 (1997), p. 1168.

17. Benedict Nightingale, *The Times, Theatre Record*, Vol. XXII, No. 25–6 (2002), p. 1701.

18. Rachel Halliburton, *Evening Standard, Theatre Record*, Vol. XXII, No. 25–6 (2002), p. 1702.

19. Michael Coveney, *Daily Mail, Theatre Record*, Vol. XXII, No. 25–6 (2002), p. 1701.

20. Ibid.

21. Dominic Maxwell, *The Times, Theatre Record*, Vol. XXIX, No. 11 (2009), p. 580.

22. Aleks Sierz, 'Interview with April De Angelis'.

23. Michael Coveney, *Independent, Theatre Record*, Vol. XXIX, No. 11 (2009), p. 581.

24. Lyn Gardner, *Guardian, Theatre Record*, Vol. XXIX, No. 11 (2009), p. 580.

25. Claire Macdonald, 'Writing Outside the Mainstream', p. 237.

26. Cheryl Robson, 'Introduction', p. 6.

27. April De Angelis, 'Riddle of the Sphinx'.

28. April De Angelis, 'Women and Theatre'.

29. Mark Fisher, *Guardian, Theatre Record*, Vol. XXVII, No. 22 (2007), p. 1333.

30. Jane de Gay and Lizbeth Goodman, 'Introduction', p. 5.

31. De Angelis, 'Women and Theatre'.

32. De Angelis, 'Riddle of the Sphinx'.

33. D'Monté and Saunders, *Cool Britannia*, p. 110.

34. De Angelis, 'Women and Theatre'.

35. David Edgar, *State of Play*, p. 18.

36. Ibid., pp. 77, 78. De Angelis provides a useful metaphor for the effacement of individuals by larger political forces when she says: 'Thinking about the Ogoni people and about when they struggled with Shell, the multinational company that has its tentacles everywhere, all that happened was the Ogoni leaders were murdered and the logo of Shell continued to shine out brightly over our world – and nothing happened' (p. 78).

37. April De Angelis and Susan Croft, 'An Alphabet of Apocrypha', p. 139.

38. Ibid., p. 146.

39. There is also interesting use of cast doubling in *Wuthering Heights* to show inter-generational connections through the characters of Cathy/Young Cathy and Hindley/Hareton.
40. De Angelis and Croft, 'An Alphabet of Apocrypha', p. 140.
41. Ibid., p. 141.
42. Quoted in Stephenson and Langridge, *Rage and Reason*, p. 56.

8 DAVID ELDRIDGE

Graham Saunders

Serving It Up; A Week with Tony; Under the Blue Sky; Incomplete and Random Acts of Kindness; Market Boy

Introduction

Near the end of David Eldridge's *Under the Blue Sky* (Royal Court, 2000), Robert, one of the six teachers in the play, declaims loudly to his Devon neighbours, 'I am from Essex and I am dancing!' (p. 259). Essex, both as physical location and site of memory, has also significantly informed a number of Eldridge's other plays, including *A Week with Tony* (Finborough Theatre, 1996), *Summer Begins* (Donmar Warehouse, 1997), *M.A.D.* (Bush Theatre, 2004) and *Market Boy* (National Theatre, 2006).

David Eldridge was born in Romford, Essex, in 1973. His family had moved to the area in 1970 from the East End of London, following the long pattern of migration since the Second World War. After winning a part scholarship and assisted place to an independent secondary school, Eldridge's teenage years were shaped by his ability to co-exist in two very different worlds – at weekends and holidays he would work alongside his father on a shoe stall in Romford Market before returning to a regime of prep, cricket and hymns in the school chapel. Eldridge has commented, in the Introduction to his *Plays One*, that 'this weird double life [. . .] largely informs the person I am and the plays I write' (p. viii), and perhaps explains why his drama can move from the council estates, kebab shops and childless playgrounds in *Serving It Up*, to the Conservative constituency barbecue of *A Week with Tony*. In fact, his career shows that he has been much more versatile and more able than his initial reception as, in director Dominic Dromgoole's words, 'The writer as bloke'.[1]

It was an encounter with Shakespeare on a school trip to the Royal Shakespeare Company in 1990 to see Nicholas Hytner's production of *King Lear* that started Eldridge's interest in theatre. With the encouragement of one of his tutors, Peter Thomson, while reading for a degree in English and Drama at the University of Exeter, Eldridge first started writing. An early short play *Cabbage for Tea, Tea, Tea* (1995) was staged at university, and after sending *Serving It Up* to several London theatres during his final undergraduate year, it was produced at the Bush Theatre in 1996.

Since then, Eldridge's career has been one of gradual progression through London's subsidised theatres, where between 1996–99 his work was performed at the Finborough, Donmar Warehouse and Hampstead theatres. The critical and popular success of the Royal Court production of *Under the Blue Sky* in 2000 marked something of a watershed, and it has been one of relatively few contemporary plays to be revived in the West End (in 2008). An indication of this embrace by the theatrical establishment can be gauged by *Market Boy* being the first new play to premiere on the National Theatre's largest stage, the Olivier, since Tom Stoppard's trilogy *The Coast of Utopia* in 2002.

At the same time Eldridge has continued to write more intimate work for smaller venues, returning to the Bush Theatre in 2004 with *M.A.D.* and *Incomplete and Random Acts of Kindness* at the Royal Court's Theatre Upstairs in 2005. His adaptation of the Dogme film *Festen* (Almeida Theatre, 2004) was a notable success, transferring to the West End, and Eldridge has subsequently produced three well-received versions of Ibsen – *The Wild Duck* (2005), *John Gabriel Borkman* (2007) and *The Lady from the Sea* (2010) – the first two at the Donmar Warehouse, and the last at the Royal Exchange, Manchester. He has also translated Jean-Marie Besset's *Babylone* at the Belgrade Theatre, Coventry in 2009. In 2010, Eldridge collaborated with two other playwrights – Robert Holman and Simon Stephens – on the play, *A Thousand Stars Explode in the Sky*, at the Lyric Hammersmith.

The Plays

Serving It Up (1996)

Eldridge's first professional play opened at the Bush Theatre London on 14 February 1996. Directed by Jonathan Lloyd, it was the second of three plays for its *London Fragments* season. *Serving It Up* concerns two friends, Nick and Sonny. Over the course of the play, we see their relationship deteriorate, partly through a divergence in aspirations, and later Sonny's discovery that his friend has been having an affair with his mother. This culminates in Sonny slashing his former friend's face with a knife.

Serving It Up shares affinities with two other well-known dramas about the East End of London – Arnold Wesker's *Chicken Soup with Barley* (1958) and Steven Berkoff's *East* (1975) – yet with one important difference. Whereas Wesker's and Berkoff's plays are historical reconstructions of the area, *Serving It Up* eschews nostalgia and portrays a 1990s East End, notwithstanding Sonny briefly recounting his father's stories of hop picking in Kent (p. 7). Yet Berkoff's dedication in *East* as 'an elegy for the East End | and its energetic waste', is also the major preoccupation of *Serving It Up*.[2] For instance, the play opens with its two young male protagonists, Nick and Sonny, sitting on a park bench fantasising about the nature of their deaths (p. 12), and in contrast to the splenetic energy and glamorisation of violence of *East*, *Serving It Up* depicts a London that is far bleaker and nihilistic.

The play also demonstrates a fidelity to realism, particularly through the characters' use of language. The opening scene for example quickly establishes Nick and Sonny's lifestyle and aspirations through the language they employ: women are either sexual threats – 'might've had a dose of the crabs' (p. 6) – or conquests – 'Cunt like a Big Mac' (p. 8); happiness is equated with oblivion – 'I was fucked on gear and drink, I puked out of me arse' (p. 8) and identity is based on casual violence and racism: 'Had a couple of rumbles an' all with the spics [. . .] beat the shit out of them' (p. 11).

With the play's title (and its slang reference to drug dealing), together with its four young central characters, unsurprisingly comparisons were made with Irvine Welsh's novel *Trainspotting* (1993), and the successful film version that came out the same year as *Serving It Up*. However, as Eldridge has commented, the play is also 'as much about disaffected middle age as youth'.[3] Unlike Berkoff's *East*, where the parental marriage is used as a vehicle for comedy, the relationship between Sonny's parents Val and Charlie is far more complex. Both plays show older women embarking on sexual encounters with youths; in Berkoff the episode where Mum inadvertently masturbates her own son in the darkness of a cinema is rendered comic (pp. 36–7), whereas Val's affairs with Sonny's friends are shown through the context of her marriage. For instance, while Charlie is aware that Val has strayed in the past (p. 16), his attitude is pragmatic: 'You just keep quiet about your stupid poxy men [. . .] You just make the dinner and bake the fucking cake. That's how it is' (p. 18). Moreover, despite her dissatisfaction with the marriage, at one point Val turns on Nick, with whom she is having an affair: 'You're a boy and you'll never be in the same league as my Charles' (p. 29).

Serving It Up also introduces a technique that Eldridge was to put to use in subsequent work: that of connecting character to image. The title of the play partly alludes to Val's habit of offering cake in order to establish human connections. While she offers Charlie a slice at the opening of Scene Two, and Nick a piece of apple pie when she is attempting to have sex with him (p. 27), both men reject these offers, and in Nick's case Val's physical advances. The motif is developed through the play, and the final scene concludes with Val '*break*[ing] *off handfuls of cake which she disturbingly stuffs in her mouth*' and her closing line is 'I want to eat cake' (p. 84). These actions also develop out of Sonny's attack on Nick, and Val's general sense of loneliness and unfulfilment. Eldridge's irritation when some audiences at the first production laughed at this scene not only came from his suspicion that it was prompted by 'the great tradition of British theatre to laugh at the working classes', but perhaps also from an unwillingness to make the necessary connections between character and action.[4]

Critical reaction to this new play by the twenty-two-year-old Eldridge was generally favourable. Michael Billington in the *Guardian* felt that 'something is definitely stirring' in playwriting culture, with Eldridge the newest example from a crop of young dramatists including Simon Bent, Jez Butterworth and Jonathan Harvey.[5] For others, however, this youthfulness also showed up flaws and several reviewers, including Clare Bayley and Ian Shuttleworth saw its 'juvenile comedy' and 'televisual scenic structure' as evidence of an apprentice piece.[6] However, others such as Robert Gore-Langton in the *Telegraph* not only admired the realism of its dialogue, but also noticed the 'almost poetic spring', which would be developed further in later work.[7] However, if critics were to believe that Eldridge was going to be the spokesman for what Nick Curtis called 'the Mile End's non-working classes', his next play was to prove to be a surprise.[8]

A Week with Tony (1996)

Written before *Serving It Up* was produced, *A Week with Tony* premiered at the Finborough Theatre on 19 June 1996. It was directed by Mark Ravenhill, just prior to his own play *Shopping and Fucking* premiering at the Royal Court that September. The play's concern is with the fortunes of its eponymous central figure who, following the recession of the early 1990s, is struggling to regain the former wealth and status he enjoyed when Thatcherism was at its height. Despite his working-class and East End origins, Tony continues to support the Tory Party. His daughter Elizabeth is engaged to be married to the son of the wealthy and well-connected chairman of his local constituency, and it is Tony's increasingly desperate efforts to fund the lavish wedding that bring about the crisis that exposes both his personal, class and political allegiances.

A Week with Tony displays a scale and ambition that was not only unusual for a playwright at the start of his career, but in theme and approach also set itself against the prevailing style of the times. With a cast that included Tory councillors and city bankers, the play almost deliberately sets itself apart from the world of *Serving It Up*. However, Eldridge has commented, in his Introduction to *Plays One*, that while they 'may not be brothers [. . .] these plays are blood relatives' (p. viii), and when considered together both provide starkly contrasting, yet complementary, narratives of mid-1990s Britain. Yet *A Week with Tony* parts company from *Serving It Up* in some important ways: for instance, its treatment of 1990s party politics and Tony's advocacy of Thatcherite ideology meant that it stood apart from other new plays of that year, including Jim Cartwright's *I Licked a Slag's Deodorant*, Nick Grosso's *Sweetheart* and perhaps most significantly *Shopping and Fucking*. While all three could loosely be seen as 'state of Britain' plays, they were without reference to any formerly established style of political drama; instead the characters' personal stories took precedence over doctrine.

In one interview, Eldridge has rejected the state of the nation model adopted in the 1970s and 1980s by dramatists such as David Hare and David Edgar, who he believes were primarily 'motivated by proving a thesis'.[9] However, *A Week with Tony* demonstrates a number of close affinities with the form, and climactic speeches such as Roger's impassioned castigation of Thatcherites such as Tony who 'have torn this country apart' (p. 132), would not have felt out of place in a play written by Hare or Edgar ten years earlier.

While Eldridge has criticised his own play for being too polemical (p. x), he nevertheless puts forward an advocacy for *A Week with Tony* and new writing in general in terms of 'the big play', rather than its state of the nation cousin: this is an important distinction to make.[10] While the 1996 plays of Cartwright, Grosso and Ravenhill had cast sizes ranging from two to six, *A Week with Tony* had a cast of thirteen. Not only did this anticipate both Eldridge's later involvement with the Monsterists group, who among other things called for more plays with larger casts, but also his own ambitious play *Market Boy* ten years later.

A Week with Tony was also notable for its analysis and forecast of economic and political trends. While predictions of a New Labour victory less than a year before the 1997 General Election were not entirely surprising, and its forecast of a single term in office only to be replaced by the Conservatives under 'Prime Minister Lilley, Chancellor Portillo and Foreign Secretary Redwood' (p. 107) fell rather wide of the mark, the play was remarkably prescient in its analysis of New Labour's appropriation of Thatcherite ideas. For instance, Joseph laments the *laissez faire* approach that Labour politicians are already displaying to the banking sector in the City (p. 140), and the play ends with Tony's boss Penny producing a glossy brochure entitled 'Business and New Labour' (p. 167). This, together with their closing kiss at the end of the play indicates that Tony is once again prepared to switch (and possibly betray) his personal and political allegiances.

Under the Blue Sky (2000)

Directed by Rufus Norris and the first of Eldridge's plays to be produced at the Royal Court, opening on 14 September 2000, *Under the Blue Sky* marked a significant career turning point. Assessing his work at the end of the 1990s, Aleks Sierz commented that the 'latest work hasn't yet found a really satisfying match between emotional content and theatrical form'.[11] *Under the Blue Sky* demonstrably answers such criticism directly with the connections it establishes; not only through dramatic form but also the means it finds to express the characters' feelings towards each other.[12]

Whereas work up until this point could loosely be described as examples of social realism, *Under the Blue Sky* was a surprising departure in a number of ways. Not only does a preoccupation with family structures now give way to a play that focused on group of teachers between the ages of twenty-seven and fifty-eight, but there is even a locational shift – while the first two acts take place within Eldridge's familiar epicentres of London and Essex, the final act concludes in rural Devon.

Under the Blue Sky also experimented formally. Eldridge has spoken of the contributions that Arthur Schnitzler's *La Ronde* (1897), Edward Albee's *Who's Afraid of Virginia Woolf?* (1962) and Robert Holman's *Making Noise Quietly* (1986) made to *Under the Blue Sky*, yet only minimal traces of these influences can be detected in its innovative structure.[13] On the surface, the play seems to comprise three separate scenes. In the first, Nick is preparing dinner for his colleague and friend (and occasional lover) Helen, but he is preparing to move away – both physically, to teach at another school, and emotionally. In the second scene we meet Michelle and Graham. Both teach at the new school Nick has moved to and Michelle is on the rebound after Nick has finished their relationship. Michelle is prepared to sleep with Graham in order to make Nick jealous. We hear about her sordid string of affairs that include pupils and their parents. After she rejects him mid-way through their sex game of playing wounded soldier and nurse, Graham uses his knowledge of these encounters to blackmail Michelle. The last scene takes place in Devon between another pair of teachers, Robert and Anne. Both knew Nick and Helen, and in the interim, we learn, Helen has been killed in a car accident. However, the play ends optimistically with Robert professing love for his friend and colleague, which is eventually reciprocated.

Many of the interconnections in the play are metaphoric, such as the public school chapel that Nick describes to Helen in Act One (p. 194), later becoming the site of her memorial (p. 256). This is reinforced earlier by Helen's recollection of a conversation at university about the significance of Remembrance Sunday and later Anne's story concerning her aunt and the sweetheart she nursed through his dying moments in France during 1917. The pathos of this story together with Helen's sombre consideration of those who died in the First World War, is made more apparent in the preceding scene where Graham and Michelle play out their facile sex game. Here, the *faux* roles they adopt of nurse and wounded soldier demean but also accentuate the pain of lost innocence at the end of the play.

Under the Blue Sky won the 2001 *Time Out* Award for Best Play. An indication of its continuing impact with critics and audiences can be gauged by its West End revival at the Duke of York's Theatre in July 2008, where it was directed by Anna Mackmin, with high-profile cast including Francesca Annis and Catherine Tate. This production, eight years after its Royal Court debut, was a rare example of a new play that had begun life in a studio theatre transferring on to a major stage. The intervening period also affected its reception by critics and audiences. Whereas the original production looked back to the 1990s and the First World War, the revival seemed more directly concerned with recent events in the millennial decade. For instance, the opening stage direction '*the long thunderous sound of a huge bomb*' and Helen's comment about 'the ceasefire' being 'over' (p. 187), was originally a reference to the IRA bombing of London's Canary Wharf in 1996: yet audiences and critics in 2008 interpreted the scene through the events of 11 September 2001 and the War on Terror that followed. This awareness was reinforced through the many references to the 1914–18 war, while the playing of the Last Post at the play's close was an additional reminder of more recent British casualties in Iraq and Afghanistan.

With its intricate plotting, attention to metaphor and subtext, together with moments of heightened emotional drama and triptych structure, *Under the Blue Sky* shares similarities with the later work of Ibsen. It is perhaps not coincidental that following its success Eldridge has gone on to adapt versions of *The Wild Duck*, *John Gabriel Borkman* and *The Lady from the Sea*. These techniques were also noted by Mogens Rukov, one of the makers of the Dogme film *Festen*. In Eldridge's account of their meeting for a proposed stage adaptation Rukov observed: 'You as a playwright are a meticulous builder; everything has its place. There is cause and effect for everything.'[14] While this statement was originally intended to question Eldridge's suitability for adapting *Festen*, his eventual involvement in the project led to a notable West End success in 2004, with the *Evening Standard* selecting *Festen* as the most significant theatre adaptation of the decade in its millennial review of British theatre.[15]

Incomplete and Random Acts of Kindness (2005)

Directed by Sean Holmes, *Incomplete and Random Acts of Kindness* saw Eldridge's return to the Royal Court Theatre Upstairs, where it opened on 7 May 2005, five years after the success of *Under the Blue Sky*. To date it has also been the most critically well received of Eldridge's plays, winning almost universal acclaim during its first production.[16]

Its central protagonist, Joey, who works as a banker, resembles earlier protagonists from *A Week with Tony* who have risen from their working-class origins. Yet the play is far removed from the social and political discourses of earlier work and is set entirely from Joey's perspective – a form of subjectivist drama – as he attempts to come to terms with both his mother's death and his father's ensuing relationship with the nurse who tended his mother during the last course of her illness. With its relatively large cast of eight, the play is reminiscent in scale of *A Week with Tony*, yet *Incomplete and Random Acts of Kindness* developed further the experimental approach begun with *Under the Blue Sky*. *Incomplete and Random Acts of Kindness* is most notable for the spareness of its dialogue. Whereas Eldridge's previous work contains a signature trait of eloquently impassioned central speeches from its characters, this play has dialogue refined to a minimalist form in a style reminiscent of Edward Bond's *Saved* (1965). Its experiments with rhythm also share similarities with Sarah Kane's last two plays, *Crave* (1998) and *4.48 Psychosis* (1999). The following exchange illustrates many of these features:

> **Kate** Let me go!
> **Joey** Who'd want your little bastards!
> *He lets her go. He's hurt her. Long pause.*
> Why are you going? Do you think I haven't got any pride. Why are you going? Why are you going? Why are you going? Come on, why are you going? Why are you going? Why are you going? Why are you going? (p. 18)

Like *4.48 Psychosis*, Eldridge's play consists of a series (thirty-eight) of short, apparently disconnected scenes that do not specify time or location. As Charles Spencer commented in his review, 'It is a play that requires both patience and concentration,' and like *Under the Blue Sky* it places demands on an audience to make their own connections independently.[17] Yet the play was not simply a case of Eldridge experimenting out of caprice: as in his other work, the choice of dramatic form fits the content. Joey's increasing sense of alienation and disconnection from those around him is represented by fractured exchanges of dialogue and ambiguity of physical space.

The concerns of family and relationship tensions from previous work can also be recognised in the estrangement between Joey's father and Joey's fiancée Kate. The relationship between the former is traced through the singer Marvin Gaye's death at the hands of his own father, while the latter is shown through the giving and eventual rejection of an engagement ring (an image Eldridge returned to after using it as the starting point for writing an earlier play, *Summer Begins*), in order to chart Joey and Kate's relationship and its subsequent break-up.

Market Boy (2006)

One of the dedications to *Serving It Up* goes to 'the Romford Market Boys, 1986–1992' (p. 3), and Eldridge's adolescence spent working there informed his next play *Market Boy*, which also saw him reunited with Rufus Norris, who had directed *Under the Blue Sky*. *Market Boy*'s premiere on 27 May 2006, at the Olivier, the largest of the National Theatre's stages, was in many respects a vindication of Eldridge's involvement in the Monsterists and more recently the smaller-scale Antelope Group. Formed in 2002, the Monsterists issued a manifesto which called for major theatre institutions such as the National to champion new writing further by taking it out of the small studio theatres and on to their main stages. New work should also be given access to increased resources, including the production budgets and cast sizes that came with these larger spaces. *Market Boy*, with its cast of thirty and premiere on the Olivier stage, not only seemed a demonstrable breakthrough for the principal aims of the Monsterists, but also indicated how far Eldridge's reputation had grown during the ten years since his debut.

The last time someone of Eldridge's generation had occupied one of the larger National Theatre spaces had been Mark Ravenhill's *Mother Clap's Molly House* at the Lyttelton in 2001. Both playwrights used the opportunity to experiment with other ways of working, and Eldridge has described the National's production of *Market Boy* as a 'show' rather than a traditional play.[18] While based on a published text, the performance itself draws extensively from music and the physical theatre (in which the services of Scott Graham and Steven Hogget from the company Frantic Assembly were employed), characterisation defined by reference to a broad variety of types, and where the numerous fast-moving scenes became reminiscent of Jonsonian City Comedy such as *Bartholomew Fair* (1614). Set in Essex in 1985, one of the heartlands of working-class Thatcherism, the play is a subjectivist drama that follows thirteen-year-old Boy, who starts work on the Trader's shoe stall. An autobiographical love letter to Romford Market, the play charts Boy's growing pains as the booming 1980s turn into 1990s recession. Boy learns his trade, quarrels with his Mum, and falls in love with a local Girl. An epic panorama of street-market life, which doubles as a metaphor for Mrs Thatcher's free-market policies, the play sprawled across the stage with a huge cast bringing its bustling story to life. Eldridge's text is both a primer of Essex slang and a wonderful evocation of the theatricality of the market trader, all persuasive patter and polished humour.

The overall effect breaks away from psychological verisimilitude. This use of stylisation and caricature was a new departure for Eldridge, and he has spoken of the challenges in presenting a figure such as The Most Beautiful Woman in Romford as a broad stereotype in certain scenes and psychologically realistic in others in order to demarcate how the performative mercantilism of the market dehumanises people.[19] Yet the play also offered a celebration of the 1980s decade and of working-class culture. In one memorable scene dozens of Union Jacks are unfurled, and Thatcher descends from the ceiling in the shape of a bat.

The public spectacle of the market was an ideal performative metaphor to demonstrate some of the rapid social changes that defined the 1980s. This is shown both through the celebration of Mrs Thatcher and by the positive picture given by the play of working-class culture. Her onstage appearance also sets out to demonstrate that Romford Market is a set piece in miniature for her experiment with popular capitalism. In a scene where a prospective Labour candidate has been jeered and pelted by the market traders who announce, 'We're with Maggie', Mrs Thatcher asserts, 'This is my market, do you understand me? Mine! No one preaches in this free market except me!' (p. 53). Writing with hindsight, Eldridge is also able to show the aftermath of Thatcherism and the economic recession of the early 1990s. This affects characters from the market, leading to the Meat Man's bankruptcy and eventual suicide, and to Snooks, the former London bond dealer, returning to plead for his old job after the collapse of the stock market. Yet *Market Boy* also ends on a note of optimism and self-recognition for the Boy. After leaving Romford Market, he summarises the events of his life so far: 'Retrained – joined an ad agency IT department. Second guessed the dotcom boom [. . .] and funded my own digital agency,' yet the Boy also recognises his good fortune and knows 'better than anyone there are limits to what the free market can achieve' (p. 126).[20]

Summary

Eldridge's early reputation was yoked around the work of a group of young playwrights including Nick Grosso, Mark Ravenhill and Che Walker who in turn became associated with the short-lived cultural moment known as 'Cool Britannia' that flourished roughly during the years 1994–99. Eldridge's inclusion in Aleks Sierz's *In-Yer-Face Theatre* reinforced the association, and until *Under the Blue Sky* in 2000, Eldridge was still largely defined by *Serving It Up*. Yet this perception failed to take account of his ambitious second political play *A Week with Tony* in which the reception by audiences and critics was summed up by Eldridge's wry remark: 'How can this *Trainspotting*-generation-Eastender really write about the conservative classes?'[21] *A Week with Tony* even contains a sardonic reference to the so-called 'in-yer-face' generation of playwrights when Henry, a stockbroker, recounts being taken to see a play he describes as 'All eye-gouging and buggery and not five minutes from the King's Road' (p. 91). In truth, Eldridge's inclusion within this group of dramatists has always been problematic. At one point in his book, Sierz criticises *A Week with Tony* and *Summer Begins* for 'cultivat[ing] compassion and humanity' as opposed to 'the edginess of early writing'.[22] However, by 2003 Sierz had recognised that Eldridge's work was more about 'other sensibilities' than 'in-yer-face' ones.[23] In terms of the themes that occupy his work, Eldridge's Introduction to *Plays One* provides a useful summary:

> People trying to assume or avoid responsibility and its consequences; the family; society changed by the 'victory' of

the West in the Cold War, and the legacy of Margaret Thatcher; sexual betrayal; Essex and the East End; class and classlessness; the redefinition of masculinity; and an affinity with the underdog. (p. xv)

While 'the self-destructive male' was Sierz's early assessment of *Serving It Up*, his subsequent work – as Eldridge points out – has attempted to look at other reconfigurations of masculinity.[24] For instance, we see a number of fathers throughout his work who are defined either by their weakness (Charlie in *Serving It Up*), absence (Gina and Sherry's father in *Summer Begins*), or struggle to maintain relationships with offspring (Tony in *A Week with Tony* and Ronnie in *Incomplete and Random Acts of Kindness*). Several of the plays also explore the process of adolescence as boys pass into adulthood (John in *M.A.D.* and Boy in *Market Boy*), or else men who make a late transition into emotional maturity during adulthood or fail to do so at all. *Under the Blue Sky* concerns itself with both these last two categories. While Robert in his early forties finally expresses his long-held love for Anne, in the previous scene Graham demands that Michelle 'make me a man. Teach me. Show me' (p. 235). Yet in his role as 'Captain Tibbotson' commanding the school cadet force, Graham's masculine identity still appears to reside in the childhood world of 'playing soldiers' (p. 230).

One notable feature of Eldridge's generation that manifested itself in plays ranging from Mark Ravenhill's *Shopping and Fucking* to Patrick Marber's *Closer* (1997), was the absence of traditional family, or its replacement by alternative structures. In contrast, family is a defining feature of Eldridge's plays and occupies a central position in his adaptations of Ibsen and *Festen*. Yet from *Serving It Up* onwards the plays have also regularly returned to the family as destructive site. As Amelia Howe Kritzer says about this play, 'Sonny founds his identity, racism, and belligerence on the ostensible rock of his family, but this rock has been turning into sand.'[25] Eldridge's debut could be seen as belonging to a group of plays including Richard Zajdlic's *Dogs Barking* (1999) and Rebecca Prichard's *Yard Gal* (1998) that depicted an underclass, where chronic generational unemployment resulted in a social group dislocated from societal norms. Ursula's insouciant question in *A Week with Tony*, 'D'you really think that there are any poor people any more?' (p. 90) is spoken at the Barbican, which is but a short walk from the East End of London of *Serving It Up* – yet Ursula's comment is indicative of the alienation between the classes and the very different worlds they inhabit in the two plays. Subsequent work, including *Summer Begins* and *M.A.D.*, are more closely wrought observations of white East End and Essex working-class life than an exposé of the underclass. *Market Boy* in particular sets out to depict working-class culture with a vibrant spirit of camaraderie.

Eldridge's own background, moving between public school and Romford Market throughout his adolescence, can also find a rough equivalent in several of his plays whose characters either attempt to escape their background, such as Nick in *Serving It Up*, or who remain trapped in the interstices. The main example of this is the eponymous Tony in *A Week with Tony* as the play traces the personal cost of attempting to shed class identity by putting on a 'stupid accent' (p. 100) and cutting off contact with his relatives. Yet despite these efforts, his daughter's friend Ursula is constantly alert to the family's working-class origins through her put-downs about those who are 'are still eating jellied eels' (p. 84) and smoke from 'green and gold ashtrays' (p. 156).

Eldridge's work to date has also been an ongoing chronicle of the 1980s and 1990s. While plays such as *Serving It Up*, *A Week with Tony*, *Summer Begins* and *Under the Blue Sky* articulated events in the 1990s as they were happening, more recent plays have gone back to the previous decade with particular emphasis on the impact of Thatcherism upon the lives of individual characters. While this interest can be traced back to his debut, Eldridge's approach has been different from his contemporaries', which mainly focus on the lingering after-effects of Mrs Thatcher's decade in power. Even in *A Week with Tony*, set in the summer of 1996, Malcolm, one of the Tory councillors, laments, 'If only Margaret was still in charge' (p. 108), as he recalls her resignation in 1990 with sadness. However, the play's central concern is to demonstrate how Tony has been shaped by Thatcherite doctrines during the 1980s. Here, Tony's 'taste for the good life' (p. 131) and advocacy of the free market, become representative of the way much of south-east England embraced Mrs Thatcher during her years in power. This same idea was returned to, and flamboyantly writ large, in *Market Boy*, a play that attempted a rambunctious large-scale re-evaluation of Thatcherism's impact on the Essex town of Romford during the 1980s.

Eldridge's interests in class structure and the social and political effects of Thatcherism further distinguish him from his contemporaries such as Kane and Marber, who in the 1990s shied away from directly addressing political concerns. As Eldridge has commented, his generation tended to react to Thatcherism's legacy in the 1990s 'with dismay and anger', rather than using overt political discourse.[26] However, it is telling that the original title for *Serving It Up* was going to be *1995 (Let Them Eat Cake)*, until its replacement (at the suggestion of the Bush's Artistic Director Dominic Dromgoole), by not only a less polemical title, but one that with its references to drug dealing seemed more contemporary and modish in the wake of *Trainspotting*. Yet, as Sierz points out, 'within the nineties boys' story' of *Serving It Up* 'lies a seventies state-of-the-nation play'.[27] As mentioned before, Eldridge believes that the term has been hijacked by a form of playwriting from the 1970s that was 'very often motivated by proving a thesis about society';[28] yet he has also described *A Week with Tony* as his very own state-of-the-nation play (p. x), and while at university, prior to writing *Serving It Up* had contemplated writing 'a big political play, influenced by writers like Griffiths, Edgar and Hare' (p. x).

So, whereas one gets the impression that Eldridge's contemporaries, and many of the subsequent generation of playwrights, often tack on a speech about political engagement, often these are little more than gestural tics, included perhaps at the behest of the resident dramaturg or director to lend a veneer of political engagement to plays that are mostly concerned with the personal lives of their characters (or 'me and my mates' plays as Sierz has unkindly termed them).[29] By contrast, much of Eldridge's work has been an ongoing attempt to articulate the crossover point where politics impinge on characters' emotional lives. Overall, it is this quality that best defines Eldridge's work: moments such as the final scene of *Serving It Up* with Val stuffing handfuls of cake into her mouth (p. 84) or Roger's castigation of Tony's Thatcherite beliefs in *A Week with Tony* (p. 132). Arguably, it is also these personal stories that interest Eldridge the most, and dominate over explicit politics or ideology. Yet it could be argued that here Eldridge sets himself a far more challenging task: attempting to articulate raw emotional truth, while at the same time avoiding cliché and melodramatic effect. Finding the truth of a particular moment – be it political or emotional – has been, and continues to be both a major goal and a major achievement in his drama. The 2010 collaboration with fellow writers Robert Holman and Simon Stephens on the play *A Thousand Stars Explode in the Sky* demonstrates that Eldridge continues to look for new ways to develop and take his writing forward on new trajectories. It will be fascinating to see where his drama will take him in the next decade.

Primary Sources

Works by David Eldridge

Serving It Up and *A Week with Tony* (London: Methuen Drama, 1997).
Plays One: Serving It Up, Summer Begins, Under the Blue Sky, M.A.D. (London: Methuen Drama, 2005).
Incomplete and Random Acts of Kindness (London: Methuen Drama, 2005).
Market Boy (London: Methuen Drama, 2006).
A Thousand Stars Explode in the Sky, co-written with Robert Holman and Simon Stephens (London: Methuen Drama, 2010).

Secondary Sources

Aragay, Mireia, Hildegard Klein, Enric Montforte and Pilar Zozaya (eds), *British Theatre of the 1990s: Interviews with Directors, Playwrights, Critics and Academics* (Basingstoke: Palgrave Macmillan, 2007).
Berkoff, Steven, *Plays One* (London: Methuen Drama, 2000).
Bradwell, Mike (ed.), *The Bush Theatre Book* (London: Methuen Drama, 1997).
Curtis, Nick, '10 Years of London Theatre', *Evening Standard Magazine*, 2 December 2009, p. 35.

Dromgoole, Dominic, *The Full Room: An A–Z of Contemporary Playwriting* (London: Methuen Drama, 2000).

Edgar, David (ed.), *State of Play: Playwrights on Playwriting* (London: Faber & Faber, 1999).

Eldridge, David, 'In-Yer-Face and After', *Studies in Theatre and Performance*, Vol. 23, No. 1 (2003), pp. 55–8.

—, 'A Way of Going On by Other Means', in Eckart Voights-Virchow and Monika Pietrzak-Franger (eds), *Adaptations – Performing Across Media and Genres*, CDE 16 (Trier: WVT, 2009), pp. 287–94.

—, Personal Interview, London, 22 July 2010.

Howe Kritzer, Amelia, *Political Theatre in Post-Thatcher Britain: New Writing 1995–2005* (Basingstoke: Palgrave Macmillan, 2008).

Little, Ruth and Emily McLaughlin, *The Royal Court Theatre: Inside Out* (London: Oberon, 2007).

Neill, Heather, 'Interview with David Eldridge (two parts)', *Theatrevoice* website, 30 July 2008 <http://www.theatrevoice.com/listen_now/player/?audioID=593>, <http://www.theatrevoice.com/listen_now/player/?audioID=592>

Sierz, Aleks, *In-Yer-Face Theatre: British Drama Today* (London: Methuen Drama, 2001).

—, '"Me and My Mates": The State of English Playwriting, 2003', *New Theatre Quarterly*, Vol. 20, No. 1 (2004), pp. 79–83.

—, 'Interview with David Eldridge', *Theatrevoice* website, 9 June 2006 <http://www.theatrevoice.com/listen_now/player/?audioID=400>

Spencer, Charles, 'A Talent to Treasure', *Daily Telegraph*, 18 May 2005 <http://www.telegraph.co.uk/culture/theatre/drama/3642270/A-talent-to-treasure.html>

Notes

1. Dominic Dromgoole, *The Full Room*, p. 79.
2. Steven Berkoff, *East*, *Plays One*.
3. Aleks Sierz, *In-Yer-Face Theatre*, p. 172.
4. David Eldridge, *Serving It Up* and *A Week with Tony*, p. vii.
5. Michael Billington, *Guardian*, *Theatre Record*, Vol. XVI, No. 4 (1996), p. 220.
6. Clare Bayley, *Independent*, Ian Shuttleworth, *Financial Times*, *Theatre Record*, Vol. XVI, No. 4 (1996), pp. 220–1.
7. Robert Gore-Langton, *Daily Telegraph*, *Theatre Record*, Vol. XVI, No. 4 (1996), pp. 220–1.
8. Nick Curtis, *Evening Standard*, *Theatre Record*, Vol. XVI, No. 4 (1996), pp. 221–2.
9. Aleks Sierz, 'Interview with David Eldridge'. Eldridge also comments that originally the Finborough Theatre wanted what he calls 'a big play in a small space' (Personal Interview, 2010).

10. Sierz, 'Interview with David Eldridge'.
11. Sierz, *In-Yer-Face Theatre*, p. 176. Sierz's study was published in 2001, but the assessment was written before *Under the Blue Sky* premiered.
12. See Ruth Little and Emily McLaughlin, *The Royal Court Theatre*, pp. 401–2.
13. Heather Neill, 'Interview with David Eldridge'.
14. David Eldridge, 'A Way of Going on by Other Means', p. 292.
15. Nick Curtis, '10 Years of London Theatre'.
16. For reviews see *Theatre Record*, Vol. XXV, No. 10 (2005), pp. 639–41.
17. Charles Spencer, 'A Talent to Treasure'.
18. Sierz, 'Interview with David Eldridge'.
19. Ibid.
20. Although this speech was cut after the first preview (Personal Interview, 2010).
21. Eldridge, *Serving It Up* and *A Week with Tony*, p. vii.
22. Sierz, *In-Yer-Face Theatre*, p. 176.
23. Mireia Aragay et al. (eds), *British Theatre of the Nineties*, p. 144.
24. Sierz, *In-Yer-Face Theatre*, p. 177.
25. Amelia Howe Kritzer, *Political Theatre in Post-Thatcher Britain*, p. 52.
26. David Eldridge, 'In-Yer-Face and After', pp. 55–8.
27. Sierz, *In-Yer-Face Theatre*, p. 174.
28. Sierz, 'Interview with David Eldridge'.
29. See Aleks Sierz, '"Me and My Mates"', pp. 79–83.

9 KEVIN ELYOT

Christina Wald

Coming Clean; My Night with Reg; The Day I Stood Still; Mouth to Mouth; Forty Winks

Introduction

Kevin Elyot was born in Birmingham in 1951. After studying drama at Bristol University, he worked as an actor at a number of theatres, including the Bush Theatre, the Royal Exchange Theatre in Manchester and the Globe Theatre. Elyot began writing plays in the 1980s and became a full-time writer after the production of *My Night with Reg*. His debut play, *Coming Clean* (1982), staged by the Bush Theatre, won the Samuel Beckett Award. He remembers the press night as 'memorable' because the stage manager forgot the first sound cue and lights: 'I was sitting in the darkness [. . .] wondering if my writing debut was ever going to be allowed to begin.'[1] *My Night with Reg* had originally been commissioned by the Hampstead Theatre in 1991, but was eventually produced by the Royal Court Theatre Upstairs in 1994, directed by Roger Michell. The play was awarded the Laurence Olivier Award for Best Comedy and the *Evening Standard* Prize for the Most Promising Playwright. It was the first production to be transferred directly from the Royal Court Theatre Upstairs to the West End, where it ran for almost a year. Elyot then adapted *My Night with Reg* for a BBC television production with the same cast and director, and this was broadcast in 1997. His next play, *The Day I Stood Still* (National Theatre, 1998), was directed by Ian Rickson. By 2001, Rickson had become artistic director of the Royal Court, where he directed *Mouth to Mouth* on the main stage. Again, the play transferred to the West End. Elyot's latest play, *Forty Winks*, was staged on the Court's main stage in 2004, directed by Katie Mitchell.

In addition to the five major plays which Elyot has written so far, his dramatic oeuvre includes the unpublished play *Consent* (1989) and adaptations, for instance of Alexander Ostrovsky's *Artists and Admirers* (RSC, 1992) and Agatha Christie's *And Then There were None* (Gielgud, 2005). After their British premieres, *My Night with Reg* was produced by The New Group in New York in 1997, as was *Mouth to Mouth* in 2008; it was also put on by Pittsburgh's Quantum Theatre in 2009. Apart from these performances, Elyot's plays have not been staged abroad – somewhat surprisingly, given that they are not concerned with issues specifically relating to British culture.

Elyot writes for radio and is also a renowned screenplay writer. His first television play, *Killing Time* (BBC, 1990), won the Writers' Guild Award. He adapted Wilkie Collins's *The Moonstone* (BBC, 1996), Ruth Rendell's *No Night is Too Long* (BBC/Alliance Atlantis, 2002), Patrick Hamilton's *Twenty Thousand Streets Under the Sky* (BBC, 2005) and several Agatha Christie murder mysteries for television. More recently, he wrote *Clapham Junction* (BBC, 2007) as a reaction to the homophobic murder of a twenty-four-year-old man on Clapham Common in 2005. The drama sheds light on the contradictory attitudes towards homosexuality in present-day England, which range from homophobic violence to legalising gay marriage.[2]

The Plays

Coming Clean (1982)

Set in 1982 in Kentish Town, *Coming Clean*, which was first produced by the Bush Theatre on 3 November 1982, depicts the life of a group of gay friends, focusing on a couple, Tony and Greg. The play starts with their fifth anniversary, but it soon becomes clear that their relationship is undergoing a crisis, and, at the end of the play, they have split up. The play's ambiguous title refers to the delicate balance between honesty and secrecy in non-monogamous relationships, or, as Andrew Wyllie puts it, 'the tension between sterile promiscuity on the one hand and stifling domesticity on the other'.[3] Additionally, the title might refer to the couple's erstwhile cleaner, Robert, who is, as it turns out, Greg's latest affair but means more to him than the occasional one-night stand – also called 'the odd stray fuck' (p. 35) by the bluntest character, William. At the play's turning point, when Tony catches Greg and Robert red-handed, their differing attitudes towards honesty clash:

Tony   But the whole point is that we shouldn't have to lie to each other.

Greg   The whole point is that we should stick together! And if that means we have to lie to each other, then that's fine by me! (p. 58)

In the final scene, Tony brings home a German man. The play's closing image almost makes the domestic intimacy Tony dreamed of come true with this inarticulate stranger: listening to Schubert, *'they remain still and close together in the warm glow of the electric fire. And, slowly, that fades to black'* (p. 72). However, their prior conversation focused on feelings of loneliness and desperation after having been left, and Jürgen claims to have completely lost faith in love. With hindsight, the massive number of losses caused by the impending AIDS crisis which the play is still ignorant of seems foreshadowed in Jürgen's untranslated observation which Tony cannot decipher, *'Schubert hat dieses Stück in seinem letzten Lebensjahr geschrieben, als er erst einunddreissig war. Unglaublich, nicht?'* (p. 72) [Schubert wrote this piece in the last year of his life when he was only thirty-one. Unbelievable, isn't it?]. As Elyot himself states in the Foreword to his collected plays, this 'final scene has an elegiac quality – in retrospect, almost a sense of foreboding' (p. x).

Coming Clean presents an unusual and daring topic in a conventional dramatic form, a one-act well-made play with seven scenes which focus on communication and character development. It reads like a witty Oscar Wilde drawing-room comedy whose queer subtext has been brought to the fore. Setting, time structure, scenery and language are realistic – which, due to the subject matter, means that the play includes detailed and frank discussions and depictions of gay sex on stage. Despite this provocation, most reviews of the play's first performance in London were favourable. They called Elyot's 'impressive debut' the 'first mature play about homosexuality' and praised its 'unusually unsentimental love story' and 'emotional labyrinth'.[4] A second production at Westcliff, however, elicited a straightforwardly homophobic response; reviewers felt 'ill' after this 'beastly filth' and 'perverted horror' – one spectator even reproduced the anti-theatrical and homophobic accusations once used as arguments against the Elizabethan convention of using boy actors: 'Whatever happens to actors who have to perform such scenes night after night? [. . .] Do they spoil their own souls in order to divert us?'[5]

My Night with Reg (1994)

Once again written in a realistic manner as a one-act-piece, *My Night with Reg* was first performed at the Royal Court Upstairs on 31 March 1994 with John Sessions, a well-known comedian, playing the part of Daniel. Praised by reviewers, it subsequently transferred to the Criterion Theatre and the Playhouse Theatre. This immensely successful play depicts the impact of AIDS, which is never explicitly mentioned, on a group of friends who meet three times over the course of several years in a flat in London. The first gathering is still wholeheartedly positive because Guy has invited his friends to a flat warming. One off-stage character, Reg, who is expected to join the party but never arrives, recurs in their conversations: adored by his partner Daniel, aka 'Monica Monogamy' ever since he met Reg (p. 101), Reg also encountered John, with whom Guy has been secretly in love ever since their school days. Already in the play's first scene, the issue of AIDS is raised, albeit in a comical manner, when the friends mock Guy's cautiousness:

> **Daniel** He's practically taken the veil, you know.
> **Guy** I haven't.
> **Daniel** He's taking safety to an extreme. You know he masturbates in Marigolds?

Guy This isn't true –
Daniel And he won't look at pornography without a
condom over his head. (p. 98)

During the party, Guy attempts to make up for 'the biggest regret of
my life' (p. 101) – not to have told John about his love – but John
reveals that he has a secret affair and is in love with Reg, although
Daniel is his best friend.

The play's second scene at first seems to be set a few moments later,
as the same characters are present and '*the rain is still pelting down*'
(p. 109). In the original production, this distortion of the chronology
was reinforced by no costume changes between the scenes, so that the
three separate gatherings, performed with brief blackouts between the
scenes but without an interval, felt like the same party.[6] However, six
years have passed and the reason for their reunion is Reg's funeral.
Guy, who is presented as a caring, sensitive character, has to comfort
Reg's bereaved lovers, who include, as it turns out, Benny. In addition
to their grief, the men are haunted by their fear of AIDS. Thus, Benny
admits:

> Every fucking morning, I wake up and check my body, inch
> by inch, to make sure something hasn't appeared during the
> night, and when I get back from work, the same routine. And
> any little cough, twinge or itch brings me out in a cold sweat.
> And then I start panicking about the fucking cold sweat. I tell
> you, if I haven't caught anything, it'll be a fucking miracle.
> (p. 117)

His partner Bernie, unaware of Benny's unfaithfulness, believes that
'two people should be sufficient unto themselves' (p. 119), but admits
one trespass – with Reg. When Guy reacts with panic to a song that
his young helpmate Eric plays because it reminds him of a former
lover, we suspect that Eric too had sex with Reg. By this point, Reg has
become an off-stage personification of the thrill and the threat of gay
sex. The play's title, invoking Eric Rohmer's film *My Night with
Maude* (1969), which Reg and John saw together, refers to all

characters but the protagonist Guy, who shares with the audience an insight into Reg's promiscuity and the dramatic irony ensuing from the ignorance of the other characters. Unexpectedly, the third act takes place after Guy's funeral – he has died of AIDS, which he contracted during a holiday shortly before the first scene. In the face of Guy's carefulness, this device demonstrates the 'indiscriminate nature of AIDS'.[7]

The discrepant awareness of the characters and the secret sexual affairs, which add up to a gay version of Schnitzler's *La Ronde* (1900), could also have been the basis of a 'typical British sex farce'.[8] However, as Peter Paul Schnierer has pointed out, AIDS becomes a too powerful antagonist of the play to allow for its defeat and hence a happy ending – the action turns into tragedy.[9] Because Guy has committed only one mistake which leads to his downfall, and is pitied and feared by the audience, he can be considered the hero of the tragi-comedy. Thus, the play 'achieves the delicate balance between pink comedy and black satire'.[10] Schnierer suggests a third generic source, the morality play. If one considers Reg the play's (absent) protagonist, he can be seen as an Everyman figure who reminds audiences of their own mortality – read in this light, AIDS stands for the *conditio humana*, and Reg/Death assumes a similar role to Godot in Beckett's play.[11] A more direct intertext is Euripides's *The Bacchae*, which Daniel, Guy and John have performed together at school; it is likewise concerned with issues of ecstasy, betrayal and death. The reviews praised the 'real dramatic cunning' of the piece, its 'camp merriment, plotted absurdities, and verbal acrobatics', beyond which lies 'a drama with a beating, breaking human heart' by which 'only the most blinkered of homophobes could fail to be moved'.[12]

The Day I Stood Still (1998)

First performed at the National's Cottesloe Theatre on 22 January 1998, *The Day I Stood Still* is again set in a London apartment, this time covering a time-span of several decades. The play's three scenes present moments in the life of Horace, including a flashback to his youth. In the play's first scene Horace is surprised by the visit of Judy (the first female character in Elyot's oeuvre) and her partner Guy. Judy is, as emerges during their conversation, the widow of Horace's erstwhile close friend Jerry, and Horace is the godfather of their son Jimi. Towards the end of the scene, a prostitute called Terence arrives, but leaves before he and Horace, who is, as he admits, sexually inexperienced, get together; Scene Three will show Terence as an aggressive, homophobic youth who breaks into Horace's apartment. In Scene Two, Horace is once again surprised, this time by Jimi who has escaped from his English boarding school to meet his godfather; he is devastated because he was left by his first love the same morning. Horace is taken aback by Jimi's presence, because he looks like the adolescent Jerry he was in love with; as the playtext's dramatis personae notes, Jimi and young Jerry, both shown at seventeen, are played by the same actor. Jimi tells Horace about a photo of Jerry and Horace which he saw and towards the end of the scene, he cracks a floorboard to find a chain underneath which Jerry had once given to Horace. Scene Three re-enacts the very afternoon when that image was taken and Jerry gave the chain to Horace. This day, Horace tells us, felt so 'complete' and happy to him that he has not got over it: 'When I'm dying, it's that moment that'll make me think it was all worthwhile. My life crystallised in the memory of a moment. It was like we were outside time' (p. 210). Ever since Horace was unable to touch Jerry at the decisive moment, his life has stood still; as Judy observes, he is at risk of being 'ossified' (p. 170).

The play, which is structured with almost mathematical precision, emphasises Horace's clinging to the past through a number of repetitions with a difference – reinforced by the revolving stage of the original production. For example, he re-enacts the attempted caressing of Jerry's head first on his own and finally with Jimi, a chair collapses in each scene, several chains are exchanged and a number of Mars bars eaten – gestures which some reviewers have compared to Proustian *madeleines*.[13] However, the repetition of these incidents and gestures produce only a very cautious sense of fulfilment. Chronologically seen, the play has an open, albeit faintly comforting ending, because Jimi requites the gesture which Horace once did not dare to act out (at the play's actual ending after Scene Three):

He goes over to **Horace** *and stands above him. Beat.* **Jimi** *very tentatively places a hand on* **Horace**'s *head, then gently strokes his hair. Beat.* **Horace** *very gently lets his head rest against* **Jimi**'s *thigh. The lights fade.* (p. 220)

The play's overall realism is undercut by the non-chronological time structure. It offers the *'urszene'* in a flashback: the originating moment of Horace's obsession with the past as well as the first encounter with Terence and, via its Hendrix soundtrack, the origin of Jimi's name. This flashback serves as a solution to the analytical play which is characterised by an Ibsenite interest for the secret of the protagonist's past. The play's second non-realist feature is the fact that the same actor plays father and son – a device which privileges Horace's subjective perception over objective probability. Both of these techniques will return in *Forty Winks*.

Mouth to Mouth (2001)

Mouth to Mouth was first performed on the Royal Court mainstage on 1 February 2001 and subsequently transferred to the Albery Theatre. It is Elyot's least realistic play so far, because the characters are more enigmatic, the play's time structure is more fractured, and it contains supernatural phenomena. It opens in a kitchen, where Frank, a playwright, talks to his old friend Laura about his recent operation. The way that the characters are introduced and the fact that Laura remains mute is reminiscent of Beckett's damaged characters: '**Frank** *has a huge bandage over his left eye.* **Laura**'s *wearing sunglasses*' (p. 255). They are presented as survivors, but the audience does not learn which disease Frank suffers from, and also the cause of Laura's devastation remains unclear.[14] Instead, their pain manifests itself in a table which shifts inexplicably: the house and its inhabitants are haunted by the past. The next scene cuts to a conversation between Frank and his doctor in a restaurant the day before, where Frank attempts to reveal the cause of his guilty feelings, but fails to do so, because the doctor is too preoccupied with the traumatising death of his partner.

Again, Elyot fuses analytical drama with flashbacks to unearth the '*urszene*' of Frank's guilt: the conversation is interrupted by two scenes which depict the events at Laura's house that took place a year earlier. Dennis and Laura celebrate the return of their fifteen-year-old son Phillip from vacation in Madrid, together with Frank, Dennis's brother Roger, and his pregnant wife, Cornelia. During the celebration, several secrets of the past are revealed to the audience: Roger and Laura had a relationship; Dennis, who has always felt unloved by his wife, has an affair with a colleague and is about to leave Laura. Additionally, it turns out that Frank has taken advantage of his role as friend of the family and French teacher of Phillip to sexually abuse the boy – an event which Frank himself presents as having saved Phillip's life when he was about to drown by giving him the kiss of life. Phillip, who is unusually self-confident and eloquent for a fifteen-year-old, attempts to convince Frank that he does not reciprocate his feelings, but Frank blackmails him to share one more intimate moment. After a return to the restaurant conversation, the play comes full circle by returning to Frank and Laura's conversation in which Frank does not manage to tell Laura, who is 'a shadow of her once vibrant self', about his sexual harassment of Phillip – Frank's name is far from telling.[15] We learn, however, that Phillip had a motorbike accident immediately after his encounter with Frank, and that his mother, who can only talk with a stammer, still wonders

> every dday – mminute – [. . .] if he mmeant to – or if he wwas doing it jjust for the ththrill . . . or if something had upset him and he'd chch-chchosen to – to . . . or was it an accident wwaiting to happen? [. . .] The ththought of him being in ddespair . . . I wanted him to know that life ccould be happy, but that sseems to be – the hardest lessons to learn. (p. 299)

When Roger arrives on the scene, the misery is increased: Cornelia had a miscarriage, and Roger accuses himself of never having acknowledged Phillip as his son. Dennis still lives with Laura and appears even more disturbed than she is, and there is further evidence of a ghost haunting the house.

The play is unusual for choosing an unlikeable protagonist who is incapable of facing up to his mistakes (he keeps maintaining that he has saved Phillip's life) and who romanticises his paedophilia. The fact that Frank, a gay playwright, is closest to the author and that he plans to transform his experiences with Phillip into a new play makes this portrayal even more daring. Audiences learn that Frank's *A Piece of Cake*, his only play so far, staged an encounter between him and Proust. In a sentence with ironic, self-referential potential for Elyot's writing, Roger remarks deprecatingly on Proust:

> Boring as batshit. [. . .] Someone should have shoved that Madeleine right up his fucking arse. [. . .] One of his sentences was so long, I'd grown half an inch by the time I reached the end of it. [. . .] Talk about ego! Jesus Christ! Always writing about himself. I mean, who gives a toss if a whiff of his Aunt Léonie's old knickers sent him off into a four-volume reverie? (pp. 274–5)

However, as the final scene shows, Roger himself will be caught in the remembrance of things past. The play's motto, taken from Proust's *In Search of Lost Time*, 'The whole art of living is to make use of the individuals through whom we suffer' (p. 251) turns out to be Frank's doubly cruel maxim, because he exploits Phillip sexually and artistically.

Forty Winks (2004)

Forty Winks was first staged by the Royal Court Theatre on 28 October 2004. Its action covers sixteen years, but the protagonist Don, in particular, still clings to the more distant past – to his teenage love for Diana, who left him for Howard, with whom she now, somewhat unhappily, lives in London. The play begins in a hotel room where Diana makes advances to Don after a funeral. The action cuts to an afternoon at Diana's house a week earlier, where Don – after an absence of fourteen years – surprises Diana, Howard, Charlie, Howard's brother, and Danny, Charlie's partner. During the characters' dialogue, Diana recounts how Don and she once kissed in the back row of a cinema screening Pasolini's *Theorem*. Don's visit stirs an erotic confusion in the family similar to that caused by the stranger in Pasolini's film – both Diana and Charlie are again attracted to Don, while Don is besotted by Diana's fourteen-year-old daughter Hermia, who looks just like young Diana.

Don is obsessed by his wish to 'step back' (p. 38) to the past and is haunted by memories: 'Diana – she was life and death to me. [. . .] (*Touching his head.*) She's here, all the time, just as she was' (p. 29). Don is featured as yet another Proustian character in search of lost time, and the play provides an uncanny solution for his impossible, melancholic desire. When he offers to take care of Hermia, who is unwilling to join the party for a concert, Diana's remark before leaving: 'Help yourself – to whatever' and Don's response 'Yes. I will' (p. 38) creates suspense for audiences who have witnessed Don's infatuation with Hermia and have heard that Hermia might have been sexually molested a year ago. Ever since that afternoon, Hermia has suffered from narcolepsy, during which she has visions of an angel who touches her and whispers in her ear, and Don likewise has sleeping problems. In contrast to Pasolini's *Theorem*, the play forgoes any spiritual sublimation of this bond by making fun of Charlie's attempt to write a play that is 'mysterious in a – spiritual way. Kind of – transcendent – sort of thing' (p. 21).

Scene Three cuts back to the hotel room, where, as it turns out, Hermia had hidden in the bathroom. Audiences learn that Charlie died, presumably because he witnessed a sexual encounter between Don and Hermia when he returned to the house. This is what audiences can conclude from the following dialogue, which contains a deeply disturbing Freudian slip:

Hermia He shouldn't have died.
Don No. But it happens.
Hermia Why does it happen? [. . .]
Don I don't know.
Hermia They had to turn back on the way to the concert, didn't they?
Don Yes.

Hermia Cos he'd forgotten something.

Don If you know what happened, why are you asking?

Hermia He needed a spray for his vagina –

Don Angina. He'd forgotten his angina spray.

Hermia – and he came in and saw something that surprised him, didn't he?

Don You tell me.

Hermia What was it? What did he see?

Don Don't play games, Hermia.

A passing, nerve-jangling police siren. [. . .]

Hermia It shouldn't have happened. He shouldn't have died. [. . .] We made it happen, didn't we? [. . .] It's all our fault, all our . . . (pp. 41–3)

As is typical of Elyot's analytical plays, audiences are implicated in the process of excavating a secret that lies in the past, and that seems to be the common reason for Charlie's death and Hermia's narcolepsy. At the end of the scene, Hermia reveals that she encountered Don twice on the Heath, and that he is the angel she has been dreaming about ever since. To Don, the encounter seemed like a realisation of his dreams. His obsession with the past and his inability to acknowledge the loss of his Diana were strong enough to make him take Hermia for Diana, he claims:

But then I saw you – asleep, on the Heath, all alone . . . For years I'd tried to get away, and out of the blue, there you were. You'd come back to me . . . [. . .] And again I tried, for a whole year I tried, but again you were there, playing with your friend, even more like the girl I knew. [. . .] You won't let me be. You'll always be there . . . [. . .] Diana, my Diana . . . (p. 47)

Don's conviction that Diana will 'always be there' is realised in the final brief scene, in which he returns to the home of Howard and Diana after another sixteen years. Meanwhile, Diana has left the family, but Hermia has a thirteen-year-old daughter, who looks exactly like her mother and grandmother. Because audiences are left unsure about the further progress of the relationship between Don and Hermia, it is not impossible that Celia is Don's daughter – just as it is not entirely impossible that Hermia herself is Don's daughter. Given this potentially incestuous desire, his paedophilia is even more disturbing. (In the face of Don's erotic attraction to Hermia, his sometime occupation as a teacher at a girls' school is likewise alarming.) The incestuous subtext as well as Hermia's name and the statue shown on the play's cover, which also served, as usual at the Royal Court, as the programme, links the play to a dramatic intertext, Shakespeare's *The Winter's Tale*. Here, Leontes after sixteen years first meets his daughter without recognising her. In Shakespeare's source, Robert Greene's *Pandosto*, Leontes falls in love with the young woman and commits suicide when he learns that she is his daughter. *The Winter's Tale* mitigates Leontes's incestuous desire but depicts him as obsessed with the past and his wish to recover his dead wife, Hermione. Eventually, an alleged statue of Hermione is animated in a theatrical show – a metatheatrical device which critics usually read as a celebration of the power of theatre. Likewise, *Forty Winks* contains a remark on the compensating, wish-fulfilling capacities of theatre which is uncanny in view of the play's content:

> **Danny**   Theatre! What's the fucking point?
> **Charlie**   The point is, it can give you what you can't actually
> have – that's the point! (p. 33)

Summary

In academic criticism, Elyot's plays are discussed almost exclusively as gay or queer plays, with *My Night with Reg* receiving most attention as the paradigmatic AIDS crisis play. However, with the exception of *Coming Clean*, the dominant theme of Elyot's dramatic oeuvre is not chiefly the depiction of gay life, but a melancholic obsession with the past. His memory plays deal with fixations about idealised teenage loves and regret for missed opportunities, which mix with a growing sense of mortality. That in both *The Day I Stood Still* and *Forty Winks* the teenage love is reincarnated by a child gives the plays a disturbing quality. The issue of sexual child abuse also appears in *Mouth to Mouth*, and here it is not related to a love in the past. The plays do not present the protagonists who fall in love with adolescent characters as villains, which makes their portrayal of sexual child abuse more complicated than in a number of feminist plays, such as Sarah Daniels's *Beside Herself* (1990) or Victoria Hardie's *Sleeping Nightie* (1989), which straightforwardly demonise the abuser figure.[16] This lack of condemnation might also have to do with the sex and age of two of the supposed victims. Both Jimi and Phillip are male and no longer children – they are seventeen and fifteen years old and characterised as self-confident young men who do not appear traumatised. With Hermia, the fourteen-year-old girl of *Forty Winks* (thirteen when she first met Don), the issue of sexual harassment has become more pressing. None the less, her idealisation of Don as an angel complicates the issue.

Katie Mitchell, the director of *Forty Winks*'s original production, argued in an interview that child molestation is only

> a by-product of watching the play, which is about how you cannot escape the past. But the idea is embodied in such a potent metaphor, particularly now, that it is very hard for the key idea of the play not to get lost.[17]

Similarly, Elyot himself described the decisive attitude of his plays as 'to do with an obsession – they're all obsessive, really – about the passing of time, and about mortality, and missing the moment of something'.[18] Yet, in Elyot's plays, sexual child abuse is more than a metaphor. It is a symptom – or, put in rhetorical terms, a synecdoche – of an unwholesome fascination with the past. With the exception of the debut play, this fixation on the past leads to an emotional stasis and solipsism of the protagonists which critics and reviewers have described as Chekhovian.[19] It also results in a rather negative view of relationships, be they homosexual or heterosexual, because Elyot never contrasts the emotional paralysis of the main figure with a longstanding, happy relationship. On the contrary, all his couples either split up (all the gay couples do in fact) or live in miserable marriages such as that of Laura and Dennis in *Mouth to Mouth* and Diana and Howard in *Forty Winks*; even the bliss of couples like Judy and Guy in *The Day I Stood Still* is reported to be over once they have become off-stage characters. Elyot's view of love is, to say the least, sceptical. More drastically, some reviewers have accused him of 'nihilism and cynicism about the possibility of human connection'.[20] Because of this lack of cheerfulness, the black humour of his plays and the paralysis of the main characters, Elyot has also been compared to Beckett, although Elyot's plays are much more realistic.[21]

This sceptical and melancholic attitude hardly fits the genre of affirmative gay action. None the less, *Coming Clean*, which itself drew on Joe Orton's plays and the fringe shows of the Gay Sweatshop, can be regarded as a trendsetter for plays which openly depicted homosexuality. As Andrew Wyllie observes,

> *Coming Clean* achieved both a repertory run and publication by a mainstream publisher, an achievement unmatched in Britain by any other robust gay play (if such existed) for at least a decade.[22]

This is in contrast to the USA, where plays such as the *Torch Song Trilogy* (1981) were openly negotiating gay issues.[23] With Jonathan Harvey's *Beautiful Thing* (1993) and *Babies* (1993), as well as the British premiere of Tony Kushner's epic *Angels in America* (1992), addressing issues about homosexual life began to be popular on London stages. However, despite being trendsetters for openly gay plays, Elyot's plays are far from promoting a positive sense of gay identity and community. Accordingly, *My Night with Reg* has been criticised for its lack of political empowerment, for revelling in 'mourning and a resigned acceptance of the effects of AIDS, instead of offering us valid and more energetic alternatives to fight against them'.[24] Alan Sinfield described the play as a 'purposefully un-American, unheroic version of AIDS – wry and understated, furtive and thwarted, class-conscious, and virtually without uplift'.[25]

Discussing *The Day I Stood Still*, John M. Clum argues that Elyot's play – despite its realism – has lost the lifelike and vibrant qualities which reviewers praised in *My Night with Reg* (for example, Sheridan Morley argued that it 'will tell you more about what it is like to be alive and gay at the end of this century than all the seven hours of the apocalyptic *Angels in America*'):[26]

> Elyot offers up existential despair rather than meaningful connections of any kind. Elyot is a clever writer, but he is becoming the gay Simon Gray, offering up literate boulevard tragicomedies of unrequited lust and chic despair. [. . .] *The Day I Stood Still* inhabits a hermetic world of post-Pinter British drama, echoing plays rather than life, disconnected from the real problems facing gay men.[27]

I think it goes too far, however, to claim that Elyot 'de-gays' his characters and his plays, that he erases gay identity by killing off gay characters – according to this logic, plays on the impact of AIDS on gay life would all have to do without deaths and would hence be both unrealistic and dramaturgically disappointing.[28]

Elyot's pieces share the depiction of sexuality, but not the emphasis on violence of the 1990s pieces which were labelled 'in-yer-face theatre'. Elyot himself has stressed in interviews that he does not see his plays as part of the in-yer-face vogue because he is more interested in subtle, enigmatic situations and complex characterisation: 'I always feel that undercutting the situation may be more enlightening than banging it out.'[29] In fact, Aleks Sierz's seminal study comments only very briefly on the 'close-range eroticism' of *Coming Clean*.[30] In a later article, Sierz explains: 'Some significant plays – such as Jonathan Harvey's *Beautiful Thing* (1993) and Kevin Elyot's *My Night with Reg* (1994) – are marginalised [from inclusion in the moment of in-yer-face theatre] because they lack in-yer-face aggression.'[31] Given their common interest in the depiction of gay issues, the comparison with Mark Ravenhill's plays is particularly productive. Monforte contrasts *My Night with Reg* and *Shopping and Fucking* (1996) to trace the movement from gay theatre, concerned with the search for definitions of gayness and the creation of a stable gay identity, to queer theatre, more concerned with contesting the established capitalist, patriarchal, sexist and homophobic orders by showing the disappearance of fixed, stable identities, and of the ideologies that support them in specific *fin-de-siècle* societies through the adoption of undoubtedly 'in-yer-face' techniques.[32]

One of the differences between gay and queer theatre is their class-bound vision of homosexuality. Despite the appearance of a few working-class characters (for example, Eric and Benny in *My Night with Reg*), Elyot's plays tend to depict the white 'gay bourgeoisie'.[33] As some critics have noted, *Shopping and Fucking* queered not only the content, but also the form of conventional drama, whereas Elyot's plays, as I have argued, dramaturgically and in terms of their realistic style remain indebted to the English tradition. The compressed, witty dialogue between the characters, the small number of settings and the overall realism of the plays might be typical of a playwright who has produced more screenplays than stage plays. Another quality the plays share with TV drama is the importance of soundtrack. Virtually all pieces open and end with a piece of music being played – with a wide range from Bach to Samuel Barber's string quartets to tango music to The Police's 'Every Breath You Take'.[34] At the same time, the use of music is part of Elyot's interest in intermediality and intertextuality. Many of the play texts put a literary quote in front, and the dialogues in all of them explicitly refer to particular films, plays or novels. Because of its thematic and atmospheric relevance, Proust's *In Search of Lost Time* can arguably be considered the paradigmatic intertext for Elyot's entire oeuvre.

In the more recent plays, Elyot has modified stage realism by fragmenting the time structure, thus reinforcing the protagonists' obsession with the past and letting audiences participate in their time-travelling minds. Elyot's analytical plays, which excavate the origin of the protagonists' wistful or guilt-ridden clinging to the past, present the key scene in the past either as a flashback at the end of the plays or, in the case of *Mouth to Mouth*'s structure of Chinese boxes, as the play's core. The analytical task and the fragmented time structure, which one critic described as jigsaw puzzle pieces, offer audiences hermeneutic pleasure – although their discoveries are hardly ever pleasant ones.[35] Because of the lack of emotional comfort in Elyot's plays, director Dominic Dromgoole characterised them as displaying 'almost Japanese precision and formal beauty, a cool understatement'.[36] The dialogue has been praised most of all for its 'mordant wit' which offers relief from the emotionally engaging action.[37] The topicality of Elyot's plays, their fine depiction of character and communication, their humour (including camp aphorisms in the manner of Wilde), and also their relatively traditional form, have all certainly contributed to Elyot's success as a playwright.

Primary Sources

Works by Kevin Elyot

Four Plays: Coming Clean, My Night with Reg, The Day I Stood Still, Mouth to Mouth (London: Nick Hern, 2004).
Forty Winks (London: Nick Hern, 2004).

Secondary Sources

Allen, Brooke, 'Theater: Off the Main Stem', *New Criterion*, Vol. 27, No. 5 (2009), pp. 43–6.
Clum, John M., *Still Acting Gay: Male Homosexuality in Modern Drama* (New York: St Martin's Press, 2000).
Dromgoole, Dominic, *The Full Room: An A–Z of Contemporary Playwriting* (London: Methuen Drama, 2000).
Elyot, Kevin, '[Untitled essay]', in Mike Bradwell (ed.), *The Bush Theatre Book* (London: Methuen Drama, 1997), pp. 65–6.
—, 'Foreword', in *Kevin Elyot, Four Plays* (London: Nick Hern, 2004), pp. ix–xiii.
—, 'Interview', in Harriet Devine, *Looking Back: Playwrights at the Royal Court, 1956–2006* (London: Faber & Faber, 2006), pp. 107–14.
—, 'Interview', in Aragay, Mireia, Hildegard Klein, Enric Montforte and Pilar Zozaya

(eds), *British Theatre of the 1990s: Interviews with Directors, Playwrights, Critics and Academics* (Basingstoke: Palgrave Macmillan, 2007), pp. 69–76.

—, 'Modern Homophobia', in Rosie Boycott and Meredith Etherington-Smith, *25x4: Channel 4 at 25* (London: Cultureshock, 2008), pp. 375–8.

Monforte, Enric, 'English Gay/Queer Theatre in the 1990s: Kevin Elyot's *My Night with Reg* and Mark Ravenhill's *Shopping and Fucking*', *Revista canaria de estudios ingleses*, No. 54 (2007), pp. 195–206.

Schnierer, Peter Paul, *Modernes Englisches Drama und Theater seit 1945: Eine Einführung* (Tübingen: Narr, 1997).

Shevtsova, Maria, 'On Directing: A Conversation with Katie Mitchell', *New Theatre Quarterly*, Vol. 22, No. 1 (2006), pp. 3–18.

Sierz, Aleks, *In-Yer-Face Theatre: British Drama Today* (London: Faber & Faber, 2001).

—, '"We All Need Stories": The Politics of In-Yer-Face Theatre', in Rebecca D'Monté and Graham Saunders (eds), *Cool Britannia: British Political Drama in the 1990s* (Basingstoke: Palgrave Macmillan, 2008), pp. 23–37.

Sinfield, Alan, *Out on Stage: Lesbian and Gay Theatre in the Twentieth Century* (New Haven, CT: Yale UP, 1999).

Stasio, Marilyn, 'Plenty of Irony in a Twisted "Mouth"', *Variety*, Vol. 412, No. 13 (2008), p. 47.

Wald, Christina, *Hysteria, Trauma and Melancholia: Performative Maladies in Contemporary Anglophone Drama* (Basingstoke: Palgrave Macmillan, 2007).

Wyllie, Andrew, *Sex on Stage: Gender and Sexuality in Post-War British Theatre* (Bristol: Intellect, 2009).

Notes

1. Kevin Elyot, '[Untitled essay]', p. 66.
2. See Kevin Elyot, 'Modern Homophobia', pp. 375–8.
3. Andrew Wyllie, *Sex on Stage*, p. 103.
4. John Elsom, *Mail on Sunday*; Rosalind Carne, *Financial Times*, *Theatre Record*, Vol. II, No. 23 (1982), p. 615.
5. Kevin Elyot, 'Foreword', p. xi.
6. John M. Clum, *Still Acting Gay*, p. 276.
7. Wyllie, *Sex on Stage*, p. 104.
8. Clum, *Still Acting Gay*, p. 276.
9. Peter Paul Schnierer, *Modernes Englisches Drama und Theater seit 1945*, p. 179.
10. Nicholas de Jongh, *Evening Standard*, *Theatre Record*, Vol. XIV, No. 24 (1994), p. 1457.
11. Schnierer, *Modernes Englisches Drama und Theater seit 1945*, p. 180.
12. Nicholas de Jongh, *Evening Standard*; Irving Wardle, *Independent on Sunday*; Charles Spencer, *Daily Telegraph*, *Theatre Record*, Vol. XIV, No. 24 (1994), pp. 1457, 1460–1.

13. For example, Alastair Macaulay, *Financial Times*, *Theatre Record*, Vol. XXVIII, No. 1–2 (1998), pp. 34–5.
14. Many reviewers of the British production identified Frank's disease as HIV, and the American production at New York's The New Group explicitly presented Frank as HIV positive; see Brooke Allen, 'Theater: Off the Main Stem', p. 46.
15. Marilyn Stasio, 'Plenty of Irony in a Twisted "Mouth"', p. 47.
16. See my *Hysteria, Trauma and Melancholia* on the sub-genre of contemporary drama which focuses on sexual child abuse, pp. 93–160.
17. Quoted in Maria Shevtsova, 'On Directing', p. 16.
18. Kevin Elyot, 'Interview', *Looking Back*, p. 112.
19. See Clum, *Still Acting Gay*, p. 276; Dominic Dromgoole, *The Full Room*, p. 84; Jane Edwardes, *Time Out*, *Theatre Record*, Vol. XIV, No. 24 (1994), p. 1457.
20. Clum, *Still Acting Gay*, p. 277.
21. Ibid., p. 283.
22. Wyllie, *Sex on Stage*, p. 103.
23. Schnierer, *Modernes Englisches Drama und Theater seit 1945*, p. 174.
24. Enric Monforte, 'English Gay/Queer Theatre in the 1990s', p. 199.
25. Alan Sinfield, *Out on Stage*, p. 328.
26. Sheridan Morley, *Spectator*, *Theatre Record*, Vol. XIV, No. 24 (1994), p. 1457.
27. Clum, *Still Acting Gay*, p. 279.
28. Monforte, 'English Gay/Queer Theatre in the 1990s', p. 201.
29. Kevin Elyot, 'Interview', *British Theatre of the 1990s*, p. 73.
30. Aleks Sierz, *In-Yer-Face Theatre*, p. 28.
31. Aleks Sierz, '"We All Need Stories"', p. 30.
32. Monforte, 'English Gay/Queer Theatre in the 1990s', p. 197.
33. Clum, *Still Acting Gay*, p. 266.
34. With the exception of the opening of *The Day I Stood Still* and the ending of *Forty Winks*. See Elyot's remarks on the meaning of music in *Forty Winks* ('Interview', *British Theatre of the 1990s*, pp. 72–3).
35. Stasio, 'Plenty of Irony in a Twisted "Mouth"', p. 47.
36. Dromgoole, *The Full Room*, p. 84.
37. Clum, *Still Acting Gay*, p. 261.

10 DEBBIE TUCKER GREEN

Elaine Aston

Dirty Butterfly; Born Bad; Trade; Stoning Mary; Generations; Random

Introduction

'One of the most assured and extraordinary new voices we've heard in a long while'; 'A distinctive talent'; 'Undoubtedly one of British theatre's most exciting new talents'.[1] So wrote several of the London theatre critics in the wake of debbie tucker green's debuts with *Dirty Butterfly* (Soho Theatre, 2003) and *Born Bad* (Hampstead Theatre, 2003) – tributes that were endorsed as *Born Bad* won her the Olivier Award for Most Promising Newcomer. What makes green's work 'extraordinary', 'exciting' and 'distinctive' is her *métissage*, her mix, of black cultural and white theatrical influences and resonances.[2] Think 'Mamet welded with Ntozake Shange' writes one critic; 'Black Pinter on speed' says another, while echoes of the late Sarah Kane are claimed by many others.[3] Her theatre is a black urban voicing of the experimental and the experiential; a scratching and mixing of elliptical strains and cruel sensations. Although she is seen by some as heir to the 'Cruel Britannia' lineage of Sarah Kane and Mark Ravenhill, it is also important, as Lynette Goddard argues, critically to situate her theatre as a black woman writer within black cultural contexts, influences and traditions where green locates her main inspirations as coming from black music, poetry and performance, particularly by women such as Jamaican poet Louise Bennett, African American poet-playwright Ntozake Shange, and rapper/singers such as Lauryn Hill, Beverly Knight and Jill Scott.[4]

In the role of black British *griotte* (female storyteller), green narrates her angry political objections to contemporary island mentalities;

seeks to dis-ease her spectators into viewing the dehumanising effects of an inability to care for 'others', locally and globally.[5] In this regard, she shares common ground with Caryl Churchill, whom green acknowledges as an important influence on her work.[6] At the Royal Court in 2008, directing a reading of her favourite Churchill play, *No More Sleepless Nights*, for the older playwright's seventieth birthday celebrations, green's aural choreographing of Churchill's elliptical lines gestured to the canvas of her own carefully crafted compositions. Where Churchill is the acknowledged doyenne of theatrical invention, green rapidly has earned critical praise for her 'linguistic invention'.[7]

Another similarity with Churchill is that green is an intensely private person, wanting critical interest to focus on her work and not on herself or her family. Akin to a character in one of her plays, her biographical backstory is, therefore, decidedly elliptical. Personally, little is known about the writer other than her British Jamaican roots, and her dislike of interviews.[8] Professionally, she is known to have had a ten-year career in stage management before turning to writing.[9] In addition to her playwriting, which includes *Trade* (RSC, 2004), *Stoning Mary* (Royal Court, 2005), *Generations* (Young Vic, 2005) and *Random* (Royal Court, 2008), green has also produced work for BBC radio – *Freefall* (2002), *To Swallow* (2003), *Handprint* (2006), *Truth* (2009) – television – *Spoil* (Channel 4, 2007) – and film: *Heat* (Hillbilly, Film London and UK Film Council, 2009).

The Plays

Dirty Butterfly (2003)

green's *Dirty Butterfly* opened at the Soho Theatre on 26 February 2003 (it was revived at the Young Vic in February 2008). The play, as its title suggests, is characteristic of the beautiful but brutal poetics depicting human frailty as it flutters to survive a soiled, abject contemporary world that green's theatre has come to represent. In this particular instance, three (butterfly) lives are scarred by an inability to transform the respective circumstances of their daily, 'dirty' living into something more hopeful. Jo (white and female) suffers domestic abuse at the hands of a routinely violent husband who figures as an absent but threatening presence. Living either side of her are Amelia and Jason, both of whom are black, and appear previously to have been in some kind of relationship, but are now estranged by the triangulated dynamics of the abuse situation. Unable to cope with the nightly ritual of abuse that she can hear through the paper-thin walls, Amelia has decamped downstairs and taken to sleeping in her living room. On the other hand, Jason is as much addicted to listening to, perhaps even getting sexually off on, the 'audio version' of abuse (p. 32), as Jo is enthralled by the abuser she finds impossible to leave. All three lives are poised in a precarious abusive balancing act: Jo with her husband, Jason listening to the marital mistreatment of Jo, and Amelia fortifying herself against the loss of Jason's affection and the sounds of cruelty coming from Jo's bedroom. All of this influenced the set design for the original production: a 'steeply sloping' arrangement that meant 'the characters [lay] like pinned butterflies or sprawled murder victims'.[10]

The abuse of Jo evidently is having a contagious, contaminating effect; the 'dirt' rubs off on and sticks to the other two. While abuse is the subject the characters converse into a dominant theme of the play, green eschews any kind of issue-based drama. Rather, the rhythms and repetitions of her spare, sparse, fragmented lines are core to her meaning-making tactics by which, as spectators, we come to feel the isolation, suffering and hardship of these abject lives. The 'incompleteness' of the dialogue makes for ambiguity rather than clarity; for a partial rather than complete knowledge of the 'bad butterflies going ballistic' (p. 23) inside each of the characters. This is further underscored by the way in which green instructs that the dialogue move at all times between the characters but never outwards to the audience, positioning her spectators as voyeuristic eaves-droppers. Equally, ambiguity is heightened by her explanation of how in the main part of the play *options can be taken regarding who is talking to who and when, with varying implications for the characters. The form of the piece has been left open for these choices to be made* (p. 2).

There is, however, a compositional shift from the main part of the play to the epilogue that presses the visceral buttons of *seeing* the effects of abuse. Here Jo seeks out Amelia in the public space of the café that she is employed to keep '*extremely shiny, clinically clean*' for the owners (p. 38). As a '*defiant*' Jo, '*weak*', '*damaged*', '*bleeding*' and '*wet*', trespasses into the newly cleaned space (p. 38), 'sparklin and ready for *them* to start *their* day' (p. 42), Amelia refuses the safe-making, woman-to-woman comforting that Jo craves. Her response is practical rather than loving. She offers Jo sanitary towels to keep her from further dirtying the space; hands her '*a clean glass of crisp water*' (p. 50) rather than making her the hot, milky comfort drink she would prefer. As Jo dirties Amelia's clean space, so Amelia unwittingly treads in the traces of Jo's filth (blood), leaving a bloody trail of footprints that figure her body as contaminated by Jo's and damaged by an inability to reach out of her 'well of loneliness' to another woman.

Born Bad (2003)

While *Dirty Butterfly* tackles domestic abuse through its trio of isolated, dysfunctional characters, *Born Bad*, which opened at the Hampstead Theatre on 29 April 2003, picks up the abuse narrative, but threads it through a family-based story of incest. Instead of neighbours living in close proximity to each other, *Born Bad* presents a '*blood-related black family*' (p. 2) – a Mum, a Dad, a Dawta, Sister 1, Sister 2 and Brother – whose closeness as a family unit is challenged by Dawta's desire to out the dark secrets of familial kinship.

The dramatic revelation of a dark and dangerous family secret has a significant ancestry in Western theatre. green's contribution to this, however, plays with the dramatic conventions of crisis revelation and aftermath restoration in ways that leave spectators with a *feeling* for rather than full knowledge of events from the past, for memories are represented variously as unreliable, faulty, repressed or contradictory. Sister 1 has 'bits' of bad memories that support the idea that both Dawta and Brother were sexually abused by their father. Sister 2, who counts on a rosier view of the past, counters that 'bits don't count'; 'the bits don't make the bulk and | the bulk don't mek the whole and the all a your bits | together don't make your versions true and never will' (p. 39). If there is a moment in which the 'bits' appear to confirm the truth, it is signed visually rather than verbally towards the close of the play: Dawta, who previously refused to sit down with the family group, is seen sitting with her family, not on a chair but on the floor between her father's legs (p. 48). As Dawta sings and hums the prayer 'What a Friend We Have in Jesus' (a reversal of the opening moments where the singing of the same prayer is assigned to Mum), Brother appears also to have revealed his story of abuse to their mother who '*cries oddly, silently. Awkward. It's been a while*' (p. 49).

For green the 'question at its [the play's] heart is: what did mother know? You sometimes hear in trials of abusers that the mother said she didn't know. And you ask yourself: "How come?"'[11] 'How come you played me like wifey when I shoulda stayed playin dawta?' is the question Dawta asks her mother (p. 32). Bad mouthing her first-born as the daughter who 'was born bad right from the beginning' (p. 33), Mum's slippery and cruel admission is that if it is true that she 'did mek a choice' about which of her daughters to make a sexual sacrifice of, then Dawta 'made it easy' (p. 34). Reversing the cultural-feminist heritage of plays that offer the primacy of mother–daughter relationships as an antidote to patriarchal oppression, *Born Bad* gestures to the cruelty of intra-sexual betrayal: to the maternal 'bitch', that Dawta cannot bring herself to call 'mum' (Scene Two), and the mother's image of Dawta as the 'bitch of the family' (Scene Seven).

The verbal lashings of abuse dished out to each other by the family members (with the exception of Dad, who for the most part remains a silent, presumed guilty presence) constitute the affective means by which spectators are drawn experientially into the drama as they are made to feel the familial trauma of 'growing up on eggshells' (p. 16). In the original production directed by Kathy Burke, the edgy feeling of being drawn into the darker side of family life was reinforced by the aural choreography of chair slamming (chairs being the only furniture to signify the domestic in an otherwise bare, white-screened space) and the sequences of silent, often confrontational, looking between different family members. Such silent gazing routines served to punctuate the volley of verbal exchanges in which the need to know the truth was as complicated and complex as the perverse sibling rivalries to be confirmed as the special, the chosen one.

Trade (2004–05)

A different set of all-female rivalries is explored in *Trade* and its treatment of the topical subject of female sex tourism. A version of the script was developed for the RSC's New Work Festival in 2004 (The Other Place, Stratford-upon-Avon), which transferred to the Soho Theatre in March 2005. A subsequent (the published) version of the script was performed at the RSC's New Work Festival at the Swan Theatre, opening on 25 October 2005.

The play is written to be performed by three black actresses. Initially, the actresses appear in character as women 'local' to an exotic, Caribbean holiday destination. One performer remains in the role of the Local – she plays a black woman who earns a living on the beach, braiding the hair of Western women holidaymakers. The other two actresses assume the roles of white women tourists: Regular, who is an old hand at the holiday-sex-tourist business, and Novice who is entirely new to the game. To have black performers play black women playing white tourist women and all of the other characters cast in green's sex tourism narrative, including Bumster, the Local's man who sex 'trades' with Regular and Novice, serves to signify the sexual and racial inequalities of female sex tourism in which Local is revealed as the most exploited.

Female sex tourism is a controversial issue on account of the complex layers of (s)exploitation it involves.[12] On the one hand it is argued by sex travellers like Jeannette Belliveau (*Romance on the Road*) that it is an opportunity for women to make good the disappointments and deficiencies of sex and romance in their regular, Western lives. In the play, despite the post-feminist protestations of the younger white woman Novice, her sexually liberated voicing of 'we don't get bossed it no more' (p. 25), it is clear that successful (hetero)sexual relations, pleasures, or romance are missing from life back home. As Local challenges both Novice and Regular: 'What – yu noh able to be the women yu | wanna be over your "there" or what? | That why you come over to our "here" is it?' (p. 30). On the other hand, the female sex tourist is also seen as someone who uses her white Western privilege to exploit economically disadvantaged men from tourist destinations; as someone who deludes herself into believing she is paid romantic compliments as opposed to paying for (sex) compliments. Or, as Local insists, when her man Bumster buys a white Western woman a drink this is not a romantic gesture but rather a 'high balled glass a flattery' (p. 17); it is not a signifier of romance but of an 'economic-transaction' (p. 21).

All three women are divided from each other by geographies of difference: of economics, class, culture and race. green 'trades' on these differences to fuel angry exchanges about 'who is fuckin who?' and 'who's been fucked (over) –?' (p. 59) in ways that are both highly comic, given how the women constantly rival each other on the bitch-o-meter, and politically hard-hitting as these build into the play's overriding call for women to be 'equal righted' not nationally, but transnationally. In the words of Local who contests the white Western gaze of the tourist women:

> Yu there lookin the kinda man you lookin
> to like / like to like / like likin our man's
> dem . . . right.
> Thass your . . . human right. Right?
> Where's mine. (p. 27)

Stoning Mary (2005)

Human rights are at the heart of *Stoning Mary*, the play that saw green making her professional Royal Court Theatre mainstage debut on 1 April 2005. The play has three story strands: about a couple who fight over a prescription to treat AIDS; about a boy soldier coming home to his parents, and the stoning of Mary. Initially, each story appears as though in isolation from the others. However, as the scenes unfold so too do the connections. In a revenge-styled chain of reactions, as the boy soldier kills the AIDS couple, it is their daughter, Mary, who kills the boy soldier, whose mother, as the play closes, is imaged as the person who '*picks up her first stone*' (p. 73) to kill Mary.

green's directions instruct that '*the play is set in the country it is performed in*' (p. 2). Yet as this synopsis suggests, limited access to life-saving medicines, the stoning of women and boys trained to be soldiers are not the kinds of atrocities associated with living in the UK. However, green's invitation to her audiences is to think: What if it were like this? What if we did not have enough medicine and had to fight to survive? How would we behave? What might we do? As the play's director Marianne Elliott explained, *Stoning Mary* is about our Western inability to imagine what it is like for people on another continent, in the poorest parts of Africa for instance, and

> about a malaise that might be happening within this country, about helping each other. All the characters in *Stoning Mary* are trying to fight to survive, they are living in much more extreme conditions than the way that we normally live our lives, but nevertheless we are able to see, because it is much more extreme, we are able to see quite how bad things are. They have to be pushed that far. How would we behave? What would the extreme version of how we behave now be, if we had to survive?[13]

Brechtian-styled titles present each scene, opening with the title '*The AIDS Genocide. The Prescription*' (p. 3), as the Husband and Wife, each accompanied by an Ego, fight over the prescription, 'that one prescription for life' (p. 13) when what they need is two. The scene works like a duel – like a western-styled stand-off where the question is who will be the first to draw the gun and kill the other; be the first to get to the prescription and be saved? This stand-off is partly realised through the motif of 'lookin'; through a choreography of looking and looking away, turning 'eyes to the skies'. Not that there is to be salvation from on high. There is no benign presence looking down and looking on. 'God got bored before we did,' claims the Husband (p. 17).

Meanwhile, in this godless, loveless world, the Mum and Dad of the boy soldier attempt to recollect the child they have lost to soldiering. The mother thinks of kissing, touching and holding her son in affection. But then, to 'hold', to 'touch', Dad reflects, is also to be held down, pinned down, to 'play hard, play dead' (p. 20). So the child is lost to his parents – lost to them or taken from them as the boy turns soldier and turns his machete on Mary's parents. The time for family talk or talking of family is well and truly past as the son no longer talks but 'barks his demands and shouts his | curses –' at Mum and Dad (p. 51).

An idea of the family undone by violence, killing and hatred, surfaces in the '*Stoning Mary*' scenes that begin mid-way through the play. Scene Eight features Mary locked up for avenging the killing of her parents, and visited by her Older Sister. Sisterly love and concern is in short supply, however, as Older Sister's conversation turns on her own worries, her own self-centred interests. For instance, Mary is now wearing glasses having had her eyes tested and her sight corrected. How unfair, Older Sister comments, when *her* eyesight might in fact be worse than her sister's. And how unfair of Mary, she observes, to have given up smoking when it was she who got her Older Sister started on cigarettes. Feeling that she is under no obligation to see Mary but that Mary should be concerned for her Older Sister's welfare, she declares:

> I didn't have to come did I? Did I. *Did I?*
> – No I did not – and I'm fine thanks –
> I'm fucking fine – I'm doin alright –
> Thanks. Thanks for askin. (p. 48)

As in *Born Bad*, sibling rivalry is laced through the lines which are delivered with lashings of brutal humour, slicing into selfish behaviours of a white Western world that fails to care for others. Ultimately, Older Sister fails Mary as she gives away her ticket for the stoning (a sold-out spectacle of cruelty) to the correction officer. And as Older Sister and her Boyfriend begin to mirror the selfish actions of the murdered parents, so the marital and familial cycles of empty promises begin all over again.

Generations (2005)

The need to think beyond national borders in terms of our

responsibility for and care of others is movingly represented in *Generations*, which takes the form of a lamentation for those dying of AIDS in Africa. Premiered at the National Theatre as a Platform performance (30 June 2005), it was revived at the Young Vic on 22 February 2007. For the revival, the Young Vic's studio space was given a Cape Town-styled South African makeover (brightly coloured walls stencilled or dotted over with township images, and a red sand coated floor) designed to transport its audience to another world. The space resonated with the gospel singing and chanting of a South African choir who occupied the perimeter of the studio, surrounding the audience who were seated on plastic stools or wooden crates set in the sand. The spectators in turn circled the central playing space, set as a functioning kitchen (food was cooked, dished out and eaten), where the actors acted out the cooking and romancing ritual passed down through the generations of a black South African family.

This domestic family scene is played out five times, though each repeat is shorter than the one that went before it because one more member of the family is gone, lost to poverty or AIDS. Not that AIDS is ever mentioned explicitly in the text. Only in the final sequence between the surviving Grandad and Grandma do you hear these lines from Grandad: 'This thing. This dying thing . . . This | unease. This dis-ease' (p. 89). Rather, the inference of disease and poverty throughout the play comes from the cooking and romancing ritual where from generation to generation, the mouth that eats and kisses also receives the kiss of death.

What makes the fabric of this play a powerful and moving experience in performance is the weaving between the personal and the epic; the domestic family scene and the choir. The names of the dead are lamented in the prologue, and as individual family members die they are called out of the central playing space to swell the ranks of the choir. The humming and chanting underscores the spoken text signifying death as a daily presence. Instead of a family tree branching out and growing, the family is cut back and cut down. Dying before their time, the youngest generations are among the first to leave the space.

Like *Stoning Mary*, *Generations* is a play that challenges an island mentality; it moves audiences to think beyond the borders of white, Western privilege. Both plays made timely interventions into the global, political debates on Africa, as reflected in this comment taken from the Royal Court's Education Resources on *Stoning Mary*, an observation that is equally applicable to *Generations*:

> In January of this year Tony Blair made a statement that resonates strongly with the central theme of Debbie Tucker Green's play[s]: '*If what was happening in Africa today was happening in any other part of the world, there would be such a scandal and clamour that governments would be falling over themselves to act in response.*' (World Economic Forum, Davos, January 2005)[14]

Random (2008)

In contrast to either the cyclical ritual of *Generations* or the three stories composition of *Stoning Mary*, *Random* takes the form of a single, linear narrative; it is a monologue to be performed by a solo black actress. Written in the summer of 2007, it was trialled in a Rough Cuts (works-in-progress) event at the Royal Court and given a full production in the Theatre Downstairs, opening on 7 March 2008. Performed as a solo piece on a stage without a set, sound or lighting design it was, as the show's director Sacha Wares explains, a bold decision to opt for a mainstage production, instead of a staging in the relative intimacy of the Theatre Upstairs studio. It was a decision, however, that reflected the Court's belief that the subject of *Random*, knife crime among teenagers, warranted reaching a larger audience.[15] The play since has reached an even larger audience after being broadcast on BBC Radio 3 (13 March 2010), while the Royal Court has revived the show for its new Theatre Local project, conceived with the aim of taking work out of the theatre and into alternative spaces.[16]

Around the time of *Random*'s premiere, British newspapers were headlining the dramatic increase in the number of under-eighteen-year-olds convicted of carrying knives and the escalation of teenage knife crime casualties and fatalities, many of them from black families.

To promote an anti-knife message, in May 2009 the Home Office launched its billboard and social networking campaign It Doesn't Have to Happen.[17] The campaign's name sums up the feeling of *Random* as it dramatises the effects of knife crime on the family whose son is the victim of a random stabbing during a school lunch break. Written in a form and style accessible to young audiences, *Random* offers its own kind of anti-knife campaigning.[18]

Random begins with an ordinary school and work day in the life of a black family. The solo actress (Nadine Marshall in the original production) is charged with the task of playing all of the characters, shifting across the roles, emotions and linguistic registers. She appears first as Sister, whose voice is pivotal to the telling of the tragic events and of the play's overwhelming sense of the 'shit' that just 'ent fair' (p. 50). As the play starts, Sister is heard complaining she would far sooner dive back under her duvet than get up for work. There's just the tiniest hint of 'somethin in the air – | in the room – | in this day – | mekin mi shiver –' (pp. 3–4), that is niggling Sister, but nothing that prepares her, or Mum and Dad, for the tragic loss that this ordinary day brings. 'Normal situations that become dark' are the kinds of situations that green finds 'intriguing' as a dramatist, and in *Random* what begins as 'normal' turns 'dark' with the random killing of Brother.[19] Hence, the ordinary everyday goodbyes – a 'Laters Mum' (p. 11) or a 'stink message' (p. 13) sent to Sister because her phone's switched off – are tragically transformed into words of final leave-taking. The comic observational humour of family life, or Sister criticising her work colleagues for the way they 'chat [their] shit' (p. 14), in the opening part gives way to grief-stricken tones of bewilderment.

Away from the street scene of the crime that is rapidly transforming into a public site of mourning, the trauma of Brother's fatal wounding plays out in the family's front room. For West Indian families, the front room historically has figured as a special space, as a childfree room for best: 'my visitor room –', explains Mum, 'my room fe best – | fe formal – | not even fe fambily' (p. 26).[20] The front room sanctuary is violated by the death of the child and the presence of the police officers who wear their 'outside shoes inside' (p. 32), breaking Dad's 'first law' of 'no Polices to my door' (p. 25). Seeking sanctuary from the grief in the front room, Sister retreats to the 'stink' of Brother's bedroom, drinking in what's left of the smell of him, and asking the all-important personal, and at the same time socially relevant and pressing question, 'How come | "random" haveta happen to him?' (p. 49).

Summary

As *Random* exemplifies, green's language is distinctive for its black British expressions, rhythms and slang. These vary according to the characters and contexts of particular plays. For instance, the familial voices of *Random* are individualised by notes of Jamaican generational ancestry (Mum), in contrast to the street registers of the young and talking-it-tough (Brother). In *Stoning Mary* the black-sounding white characters linguistically register the alienation between First World affluence and Third World poverty, whereas there is a black linguistic kinship to the blood-related family in *Born Bad*.

It is through language that green forms an experientially styled aural critique; a poetics of the beautiful but brutal lines of urban-speak that variously depict violent, domestic alienation; the vicious, senseless acts of 'random' street crime, or a contemporary world 'coloured' by social injustices and inequalities. Her lines are economical and elliptical. They often can consist of a single word and are frequently punctuated by silences during which meaning-making transfers to visual communication between the performers – the choreographies of gazing, or the beats and pauses in which characters physically convey their feelings for or attitudes towards each other. On the page, green has devised a convention for marking what she defines as '*active silences*', whereby she sets out the names of characters without accompanying dialogue, as in this example from *Dirty Butterfly*:

Jason . . . I'm not goin nowhere
Amelia
Jason

Jo

Jo Heard you the other side still, still trying not to be
heard . . . (p. 17)

As these moments cue silences as punctuating the verbal interactions,
they produce a halting yet intensifying effect. By contrast, green
frequently deploys the convention of overlapping dialogue (pioneered
by Churchill) in ways that up the tempo of an emotional overspill.[21]
Equally, it is the rhythms, resonances and repetitions of the lines that
drive the emotional patterning and texturing of her scripts. Repetition
is key to

> 'How people speak,' she says. 'Listen to a group of kids – just
> repeat and repeat and repeat.' She demonstrates with a little
> improvised exchange: 'It's hot outside . . . it's really hot, innit?
> I bet it's really hot.' Suddenly, 'you've got half a page of
> dialogue'.[22]

Her dialogue is not written to flesh out events, dramatic details or to
offer audiences fully rehearsed backstories to the characters cast more
often than not as unnamed daughters and sons, brothers and sisters,
or mothers and fathers. Instead, minimal and elliptical, the lines have
designs on the audiences' ability to navigate their way through the
emotional undercurrents of abuse, (s)exploitation, AIDS or knife
crime.

Equally, from a practical point of view, director Sacha Wares
explains how working on a green script is akin to working on a musical
score. The director of three of her plays – *Trade*, *Generations* and
Random – Wares describes the rehearsal process as concentrating very
much on an analysis of the language on the page. Commenting, for
example, on the rehearsal process for *Random* she explains:

> Debbie writes with an extremely pointed sense of two things:
> page layout and punctuation. And really it is like a musical
> score. The rhythm of the dialogue is really, really communi-
> cated to you through the page layout and the punctuation. So

a huge amount of the rehearsal time was spent literally on analysing that punctuation and on accuracy.[23]

For Wares, the detailed attention to language that green's scripts require is part of the appeal of the writer's work.[24] This also holds for performer Nadine Marshall who, in addition to *Random*, has appeared as Sister 2 in *Born Bad* and Novice in *Trade*. Wares explains how Marshall's 'hugely emotional' style in performance may belie the fact that her rehearsal process is 'very, very technical and extremely accurate'.[25] This attention to linguistic precision and accuracy is something actress and director have learnt to work on together through a process that also involves green as writer: 'She's very present in the rehearsal room and she asks a lot of everybody,' Wares explains. 'For me as a director that's just a joy.'[26]

As musical scores, green's scripts also represent a challenge for theatre critics. More specifically, the primacy of language in her work, her attention to how the word looks on the page and is to be heard in performance, has attracted critical doubts as to whether her plays generically meet the criteria to count as drama or in fact better qualify as poetry. *Dirty Butterfly* has been described as a 'voice poem' and there was critical speculation as to whether it 'should be a radio play'.[27] Despite an otherwise positive review of *Born Bad*, Ian Johns for *The Times* cautioned that a 'play defined by its linguistic invention can go only so far'.[28] Subsequently, on a more critical note, Johns objected to the 'writing' of *Stoning Mary* as being 'more like brutal tone poems than conversation', while Quentin Letts for the *Daily Mail* wrote of *Random*: 'This short event is not a play but it is certainly powerful theatre.'[29] Similarly, as a writer green attracts hybrid labelling such as 'poetic playwright' or 'theatrical poet'.

It is arguable that some critical anxieties stem, at least in part, from green's retreat from realism, from denying critics the comfort zone of social realism. In this regard, her theatre contrasts with that of Roy Williams and Kwame Kwei-Armah – two writers with whom she is frequently grouped to evidence a more optimistic outlook for black theatre, writers who show a preference for populating a familiar style of gritty, hard-times realism with black characters. This observation is not made to be critical of dramatic strategies that explore ways of black belonging from within a realist form and stage tradition, but to understand green's rejection of realism as fundamental to her presentational rather than representational style where, minimally rather than realistically set, the domestic transforms into the epic. For instance, instead of a domestic interior for *Born Bad*, she specifies '*a solitary chair*' (p. 3), to prop up the familial setting, to transform it into a dangerous child's game of musical chairs. Or, in *Stoning Mary* the rules of realism are undone through her instruction that the atrocities that 'belong' elsewhere relocate to the country the play is performed in.

Equally, her plays eschew the familiar dramatic conventions of exposition, crisis and resolution in favour of here and now reflections; the articulation of states of feeling bad about the futures lost to a monumental past of 'growin up on eggshells' (*Born Bad*, p. 16), of lives ending before their time of beginning (*Generations*, *Random*), or, alternatively, of lives 'fucked' through the 'mornin' that seemingly refuses to be the morning to end the cycle of all bad mornings (*Dirty Butterfly*, p. 50). Rather than plays soaked in lengthy dialogic exchange, the emotional truth of a moment is condensed into the linguistic lobbing of a single word, phrase or line – the 'eyes to the skies' in *Stoning Mary*, for example, that tell of the fatally selfish behaviours of the Husband and Wife. In *Dirty Butterfly*, mood setting does not take the form of detailed exposition but is captured in the alliterative phrasing of 'butterflies gone ballistic' (p. 4). Or in *Random*, a sense of a bad day dawning, of a comic-to-tragic world out of joint, registers in the 'birds bitchin their birdsong outside' (p. 3).

Rather than worry over or try to fix on generic categories, more critically progressive and productive lines of enquiry engage in looking to the politicising possibilities that arise from the generic and stylistic mix of a theatre between art forms. Ultimately, as a *métissage* at the crossroads of poetry and theatre, green mixes experimental, experiential and elliptical registers with black expressivity, in ways that can be claimed to effect a racial queering of the linguistic and cultural hegemony of English/ness. Moreover, it is also important to note the centrality of the female rather than the male characters to this *métissage*. For instance, as Jo drips menstrual (possibly foetal) blood on Amelia's floor in *Dirty Butterfly*, the figuring of a female experiential registers as core to the greenesque landscape of lives damaged by a self-harming inability to connect to others. This, along with other moments of a damaged feminine, argues for a feminist perspective to her work. In contrast to second-wave feminist theatre that often focused on the 'anti-man, anti-fam., lyin sentiment' that Sister 2 refuses to hear in *Born Bad* (p. 19), green offers a feminist scrutiny of women's intra-sexual behaviour, of their inability to be supportive of each other. Specifically, her work engages in criticism of post-feminism: it contests the idea that Western women are 'equal-righted' and no longer in need of a women's movement; it critiques the 'us and them' apartheid of a so-called emancipated, privileged West that ignores the struggles in 'other' parts of the world to be 'human-righted'. The sex 'trade' between the white women tourists, Regular and Novice, at the expense of the Local black woman is one clear example of this. Another is presented in *Stoning Mary* where a lack of affection between women is personalised in the story of Mary and her Older Sister, and politicised in Mary's solo outpouring as she discovers only twelve women have signed her protest petition:

> So what happened to the womanist
> bitches?
> . . . The feminist bitches?
> . . . The professional bitches.
> What happened to them? (p. 61)

The refrain of 'bitches' spills and distils into an angry lament over the lack of solidarity between women. If women are behaving like 'bitches' then they cannot be 'sisters'. Or, 'if yu lookin like a bitch' as *Born Bad*'s Dawta accuses, you do not deserve to be called 'mum' (pp. 4, 7).

The challenge of green's theatre comes from the challenge she sets herself to be formally and linguistically inventive. Hers is a theatre voice that renews with each play. It speaks to and through urban cultures of black British dispossession, historically marginalised, illegitimised, by traditions of white, middle-class theatre, and argues a transnational feminist political theatre that insists on the rights of *all* women, here and there, local and global, to be 'equal-righted'.

Primary Sources

Works by debbie tucker green

Born Bad (London: Nick Hern, 2003).
Dirty Butterfly (London: Nick Hern, 2003).
Stoning Mary (London: Nick Hern, 2005).
Trade and *Generations* (London: Nick Hern, 2005).
Random (London: Nick Hern, 2008).

Secondary Sources

Aston, Elaine, 'A Fair Trade? Staging Female Sex Tourism in *Sugar Mummies* and *Trade*', *Contemporary Theatre Review*, Vol. 18, No. 2 (2008), pp. 180–92.

Edwardes, Jane, '*Generations* at the Young Vic', *Time Out*, 26 February 2007 <http://www.timeout.com/london/theatre/features/2650/-Generations-at_the_Young_Vic.html>

Goddard, Lynette, *Staging Black Feminisms: Identity, Politics, Performance* (Basingstoke: Palgrave Macmillan, 2007).

—, '"Death Never Used to be for the Young": Grieving Teenage Murder in debbie tucker green's *Random*', *Women: A Cultural Review*, Vol. 20, No. 3 (2009), pp. 299–309.

Ifekwunigwe, Jayne O., 'Diaspora's Daughters, Africa's Orphans? On Lineage, Authenticity and "Mixed Race" Identity', in Heidi Safia Mirza (ed.), *Black British Feminism* (London: Routledge, 1997), pp. 127–52.

McMillan, Michael, *The Front Room: Migrant Aesthetics in the Home* (London: Black Dog Publishing, 2009).

Royal Court, Young Writers Programme, debbie tucker green, Education Resources, *Stoning Mary* <http://www.royalcourttheatre.com/files/downloads/StoningMary.pdf>

—, Young Writers Programme, debbie tucker green, Education Resources, '*Random* Background Pack',<http://www.royalcourttheatre.com/files/edufiles/Random%20 Background%20Pack%20FINAL.pdf>

Sierz, Aleks, 'debbie tucker green: "If You Hate the Show, At Least You Have Passion"', *Independent*, 27 April 2003 <http://www.independent.co.uk/arts-entertainment/ theatre-dance/features/debbie-tucker-green-if-you-hate-the-show-at-least-you-have-passion-596009.html>

—, 'Interview with Sacha Wares', *Theatrevoice* website, 20 March 2008 <http://www.theatrevoice.com/listen_now/player/?audioID=556>

—, 'Random, Royal Court Theatre at Elephant and Castle Shopping Centre', 11 March 2010 <http://www.theartsdesk.com/index.php?option=com_k2&view=item&id=1161:random-royal-court-theatre-review&Itemid=25>

Urban, Ken, 'Cruel Britannia', in Rebecca D'Monté and Graham Saunders (eds), *Cool Britannia: British Political Drama in the 1990s* (Basingstoke: Palgrave Macmillan, 2008), pp. 38–55.

Notes

1. Reviews of *Born Bad* in *Theatre Record*, Vol. XXIII, No. 9 (2003), pp. 548–9.
2. I borrow *métissage* from Jayne O. Ifekwunigwe, 'Diaspora's Daughters, Africa's Orphans?', pp. 130–2.
3. Reviews of *Dirty Butterfly* in *Theatre Record*, Vol. XXIII, No. 5 (2003), pp. 251–2.
4. See Ken Urban, 'Cruel Britannia'; Lynette Goddard, *Staging Black Feminisms*, p. 185.
5. Ifekwunigwe, 'Diaspora's Daughters', pp. 135–6.
6. See interview in Royal Court Education Resources, *Stoning Mary*.
7. Jenny Topper, artistic director of the Hampstead Theatre, is quoted as saying, 'She [debbie tucker green] has the three essential elements of a new voice: she is concerned with ideas, she is concerned with form, and she has the courage to stay true to her intuition and let her own linguistic invention come through' (quoted in Aleks Sierz, 'debbie tucker green').
8. See Jane Edwardes, '*Generations* at the Young Vic'.
9. Sierz, 'debbie tucker green'.
10. Kate Bassett, *Independent on Sunday*, *Theatre Record*, Vol. XXIII, No. 5 (2003), p. 251.
11. Sierz, 'debbie tucker green'.
12. For a discussion of female sex tourism in respect of *Trade* and Tanika Gupta's *Sugar Mummies*, see Elaine Aston, 'A Fair Trade?'
13. Royal Court Education Resources, *Stoning Mary*.
14. Ibid.
15. Aleks Sierz, 'Interview with Sacha Wares'.
16. The play was performed in a vacant shop unit at the Elephant and Castle Shopping Centre in March 2010, followed by a national tour. For details see Aleks Sierz, 'Random, Royal Court Theatre at Elephant and Castle Shopping Centre'.
17. See <http://www.bebo.com/itdoesnthavetohappen>.
18. For another contemporaneous example of a teenage knife crime drama, see Tanika Gupta's *White Boy* (National Youth Theatre, 2007–08).
19. green quoted in Sierz, 'debbie tucker green'.
20. For further details see Lynette Goddard, '"Death Never Used to be for the Young"',

pp. 301–2; Michael McMillan, *The Front Room*; and the BBC 4 documentary, *Tales from the Front Room* (2007).

21. It is interesting to note green's direction of Churchill's *Three More Sleepless Nights* in 2008 because this was the play in which Churchill first experimented with the overlapping dialogue technique.

22. green quoted in Sierz, 'debbie tucker green'.

23. Sierz, 'Interview with Sacha Wares'. See also Wares on punctuation and layout in the Royal Court's Background Pack on *Random*.

24. Ibid. She also talks of the challenge of green's scripts and of how she appreciates having enough rehearsal time, given the brevity of the plays, to explore the depth and the precise detail of the work.

25. Ibid.

26. Ibid.

27. See reviews in *Theatre Record*, Vol. XXIII, No. 5 (2003), pp. 251–2.

28. *Theatre Record*, Vol. XXIII, No. 9 (2003), p. 548.

29. *Theatre Record*, Vol. XXV, No. 7 (2005), p. 424; *Theatre Record*, Vol. XXVIII, No. 6 (2008), p. 284.

11 DAVID GREIG

Janelle Reinelt

The Architect; The Cosmonaut's Last Message to the Woman He Once Loved in the Former Soviet Union; Victoria; The American Pilot; Damascus

Introduction

Between 26 April and 13 May 2000, David Greig's most ambitious play to date, *Victoria*, had a short but fairly sweet London run. Commissioned by the RSC, in retrospect it seems practically incomprehensible that a play containing an internal trilogy, spanning sixty years and requiring considerable cast and staging resources should have such a brief exposure to public performance. This paradox, however, is part and parcel of Greig's career, which has been characterised both by and beyond his Scottish identity, and has benefited and suffered from these kinds of associations. Aleks Sierz, in his review of *Victoria*, states the paradox succinctly:

> Although undoubtedly the most versatile of the gang of young
> Scottish playwrights who have emerged in the last decade,
> David Greig has been undervalued because of a cultural
> north–south divide. Massive in Scotland, he's not very well
> known in London. But this production of his epic new play,
> *Victoria*, may change all that.[1]

Although it is arguable whether *Victoria* alone made the difference, Greig is certainly recognised by many today as a major accomplished playwright. If it is true that he has arrived for scholars, commentators, theatre workers and critics alike, his positioning as both a Scottish and a British writer lies at the heart of his artistic signature.

203

While he was born in Scotland in 1969, Greig was raised in Nigeria where his father was working in construction. He returned to Scotland in his adolescence, went to university at Bristol, and continued to travel when he could. If cosmopolitanism and an adult travel lust consolidated his outsider status within his birth culture, his local political commitments, plays specifically about Scotland (including *Victoria*, *Outlying Islands*, *Caledonia Dreaming*), and formal role in Scottish culture as dramaturg of the new National Theatre of Scotland constitute him as a self-consciously Scottish artist. After his studies, he returned to live in Scotland and formed the theatre group Suspect Culture with Graham Eatough. Some of his work has been devised and written through their workshop opportunities while he has simultaneously written individual plays produced at the Traverse, the Royal Shakespeare Company, or by the touring company Paines Plough.

As has often been observed about Greig's plays, the theme of living through globalisation and the international scope of his imagination (and his settings) tends to submerge, to some extent, Greig's connections to Scotland. However, underplaying this aspect of his work would be a mistake. Adrienne Scullion positions Greig firmly within the generation of new Scottish writers who are contributing to post-devolution drama, opening her survey essay on the topic with Greig's *The Speculator* (Traverse, 1999), a play ostensibly about the history of economic speculation in Paris in 1720, but in light of its production in tandem with the opening of the new Scottish parliament, also about the present local moment. Scullion reads the play as a metaphor for the new Scotland, and interprets Greig's thesis

to be that what matters most is the possibilities afforded by an aspirational future bold enough to confront and progress away from the assumptions and prejudices of the past.[2]

To be simultaneously about Europe or another elsewhere as well as Scotland has proven central to a number of his most important plays.

Greig has been one of the most influential, prolific and wide-ranging playwrights of his generation. His vast output includes *Europe*

(Traverse, 1994), *Caledonia Dreaming* (Traverse, 1997), *Casanova* (Tron, 2001), *Dr Korczak's Example* (Tag, 2001), *San Diego* (Tron, 2003), *8000m* (Suspect Culture, 2004), *Pyrenees* (Paines Plough, 2005), *Midsummer* (with Gordon McIntyre, Traverse, 2008) and *Dunsinane* (RSC, 2010). He has also adapted several classics, such as Jarry's *Ubu the King* (RSC, 1996), Camus's *Caligula* (Donmar, 2003), Euripides's *Bacchae* (NTS, 2007) and Strindberg's *Creditors* (Donmar, 2008). He has created stage versions of *When the Bulbul Stopped Singing* (Traverse, 2004), *Hergé's Adventures of Tintin* (Bite, 2005) and *Peter Pan* (NTS, 2010). His works for children include *Danny 306 + Me (4 ever)* (1999) and *Gobbo* (2006). His work with Suspect Culture includes *Local* (1998), *Mainstream* (1999) and *Futurology: A Global Revue* (with Dan Rebellato, 2007). Selecting just five pieces from his steady accelerating corpus of work (more than forty plays in two decades) is extremely difficult. I have chosen plays that chart his development over the past fifteen years, between the mid-1990s and 2010, and have mentioned several others. Because his internationalism and critique of globalisation seem to me to be some of the most important aspects of his oeuvre, I have privileged plays that overtly explore those themes, although I have also tried to respond to the important Scottish concerns of his work.

The Plays

The Architect (1996)

Among his early plays, *The Architect* – which opened on 23 February 1996 at the Traverse Theatre in Edinburgh – provides a concentrated preview of many of the images and themes that became central to Greig's work during the following decade: transportation systems and circuits; failed communication (both telematic and face to face); desperation manifested in self-harm, suicide or disappearance; and landscapes that alternate between entrapment and transcendence. The most domestic of his plays, *The Architect*, juxtaposes the home to the expressway, that anonymous conduit transporting goods between the crumbling towns of post-industrial Britain. Dorothy's night-time hitchhiking sorties with truck drivers recall Adele and Katia's response to the lure of the international express trains in *Europe*, and presage the stowaway journey of Daniel in *San Diego*, who catches the wheels of a departing aircraft to make his getaway. Most striking perhaps is the last image of *The American Pilot* in which the farm girl Evie hangs suspended with the Pilot from a rescue winch as her village is razed. Dan Rebellato has commented that 'the view from above is a common motif in David's work', pointing up the perspective of distance, oversight, isolation.[3] It also, however, figures escape attempts, the desire to transcend, and aspiration to reach an elsewhere.

In *The Architect*, the marriage of Leo to Paulina is alienated and failing, just as his grandly designed modernist housing project is now facing demolition because the people who actually live there detest it. This failed 'design for living' is evident in Keith and Vivienne's loveless marriage (*The Cosmonaut's Last Message*), and in the irony of Paul's phone calls to his wife on Valentine's Day (*Damascus*). Greig's universe is peopled by those who have failed at or lost intimacy and those others who deeply seek it; *The Architect* directly displays the anguish of both groups.

Paulina asks Leo to pave over their garden, and later to move out. 'When you leave you'll notice a wife-shaped space,' she tells him (p. 184). Sheena comes to see Leo, representing the tenants of 'Eden Court', a block of high-rise flats he designed about twenty years ago. She presents a petition to have the flats knocked down; Leo tells her the Council is going to refurbish them. The tenants do not want the flats remodelled, however; they want a new estate. Leo cannot understand why, since he thinks they were well-designed. He shows Sheena a model and she agrees it looks good – 'From above' (p. 164). She suggests he replace the green felt representing the grass with brown to represent the mud that actually collects there. She explains the lifts do not work, the flats are cold and infested with cockroaches. The tenants 'are unhappy. They get depressed. They get ill. The place they live in makes them depressed' (p. 165). By the end, Sheena has convinced Leo, and he decides to stay inside his flats and be blown up with them.

Leo's two grown children, Martin and Dorothy, deal with the situation as best they can. Martin refuses to work with his father, and yearns to leave the city and escape to the mountains, 'some wilderness'. He imagines learning to make furniture: 'If I go to the country somewhere. I could find some old guy in the mountains that does it' (p. 160). His lover Billy wants to come along, but Martin shuts him out; Billy throws himself off the roof. Dorothy has psychosomatic stomach trouble as a result of the upset going on in her home. She cannot make it better, so she tries to find love in the back of a lorry with a driver named Joe who is also estranged from his wife. Explaining that she waited for him at the side of the road but he did not come she says, 'I tried sending you dolphin calls. You mustn't have picked them up' (p. 199). The metaphor of the dolphin calls is established early in their encounters. Dorothy says she gets signals or warnings as an explanation for her stomach pain. Joe says perhaps he has been signalling her 'like dolphin calls across the ocean floor'. Both Martin and Dorothy yearn for other places and other people in place of their nuclear family melt-down; neither of them ultimately succeeds.[4]

The Cosmonaut's Last Message to the Woman He Once Loved in the Former Soviet Union (1999)

The play was first staged by Paines Plough on 15 April 1999. With his lengthy title, Greig conjures a narrative of allusive complexity, an intersecting series of what Clare Wallace, in her Brechtian reading of Greig, has called 'micronarratives, each with its own *gest* [. . .] gradually revealed as nodal points in a web-like plot structure'.[5] Two cosmonauts circle the earth endlessly in the space capsule Harmony. 'They've forgotten us,' Oleg repeats three times; Casimir tries to fix the radio (p. 209). A second dyad, Keith and Vivienne, live in an Edinburgh home with shutters closed, an insular life with a broken television set that shows only static. Fearful of the outside, they have little to say to each other inside. Keith is having an affair with Nastasja, who might be Casimir's daughter, as she tells Keith, 'He left to go into space when I was six [. . .] He never came back to earth' (p. 229). A chance encounter links Keith with Eric in a bar at Heathrow. Eric is Norwegian and works for the World Bank in conflict resolution; he negotiates peaceful change and convinces Keith,

> It's a matter of leaving things behind [. . .] There's no need for things to be difficult for you. There's no need for you to be unhappy. No need. (p. 239)

Keith subsequently fakes his own suicide and disappears. Eric, having become attracted to the recording of Nastasja's breathing that Keith played, seeks her out and offers to set her up in a flat in Oslo with her friend Sylvia, also an exotic dancer.

Vivienne goes to France looking for Keith, following the clue of a Cézanne tie he left behind. She meets Bernard, a former space scientist, now a UFO enthusiast, who is using his computer to try to make contact with beings in space: 'Is this harmony?' (p. 288). He has had a stroke and has a second stroke when there is a flash in the sky – perhaps the destruction of the space capsule. As Vivienne is a speech therapist, she can respond, 'I know. I know. It's OK. I understand' (p. 292). In the last scene, Sylvia, who has gone looking for Keith to retrieve the tape of Nastaja's breathing, finds him in a West Highlands bar. As she is played by the same actor who played Vivienne, the image is ambiguous. Asked what she wants, she answers, 'Only to talk' (p. 299).

Linked by desire for intimacy/communication and a pervading sense of alienation and loss, all the characters experience dislocation and rapid change. While not all of them obtain their love-objects, enough possibility exists to keep the impact of the play poised between hope and despair.[6]

Victoria (2000)

In his introduction to *Victoria*, Greig relates that he first began the play in 1996, when he got the idea from the image of a woman standing by a tree smoking and waiting, and from a visit to a west-coast island pub where he observed the varieties of his fellow drinkers and discovered the telephone directory for the village contained merely eighty names.[7] Filling a commission from the RSC, he imagined a three-part epic with more than forty characters for fourteen actors.

The play takes place in a rural locale on the coast of the Scottish Highlands, each part a different landmark moment: 1936, within the spectre of Nazism and the Spanish Civil War; 1974 when the discovery of North Sea oil began to radically change the economy and lives of coastal Scots; and 1996, as coming devolution and the forces of globalisation constructed a third crucible of change for the village. Although families and characters persist through the three parts, only one character (Oscar) appears in all three, and he changes radically through time. 'Victoria', the eponymous title character, is actually three different characters, played by the same actress. There are also characters of the same name but different generations: Euan in Part One, 'The Bride', goes off to the Spanish Civil War at the end of the play where he dies, while Euan in Part Two, 'The Crash', is Oscar's son, named in honour of the prior Euan, but completely different – an entrepreneur with little idealism who returns to Scotland from America to make money off the new oil business. In Part Three, 'The Mountain', he is the owner of a quarry seeking to expand his operations, taking granite from the large mountain. Greig has deliberately built the play to confound any simple generational continuity, or characterisation based on biology, or for that matter, any unambiguous character traits. His characters are driven by contradictory impulses, and as Nadine Holdsworth points out, 'Greig resists easy polarisations between right and wrong [. . .] Personal motivations, histories and politics are [deliberately] murky and ambiguous.'[8]

This dramaturgy serves Greig's purpose of exploring the open possibilities for alternative choices that such historical change makes available to individuals, while simultaneously marking the power of place and the relationship between people and their environment as constitutive of meaning, value and desire.[9] The Highlands are confining and provincial, but they are also beautiful and bounteous; characters are drawn to the terrain and also long to escape it. Most of the major characters are in transit, either going or coming, through much of the play. While *Victoria* is clearly Greig's most important play about Scottish identity and nation-building, it is far from insular, connecting Scotland to major world events and to shifts in global economics, political ideologies and popular culture.

In each part, a ruling order is challenged by a set of new ideas, as Greig himself has observed: '*Victoria* is about Utopias and there is a driving ideology behind each play that is shown to be problematic.'[10] In 'The Bride', Lord Allen represents the landed gentry, possessing a connection through his father to the Clearances. His son David and his fiancée, Margaret, return home to the manse bringing 'modern' ideas with more than a Nazi tinge into a community ruled by tradition and privilege. Eugenics, in particular, is David's answer to his self-perceived degeneracy and he proposes paying a farm worker (Euan) to be a sperm donor in his stead. When David rapes Shona, the locals decide the 'evil fascist cunt' must be punished and they shoot him and hang him from a butcher's hook (p. 62), forming the final image of the play, with the older gentry and Margaret looking on in horror. Oscar and Euan leave to fight in the Spanish Civil War. In 'The Crash', the estate is still owned by the family (Margaret and her son Jimmie), but they are selling it. There are several bidders: Oscar wants to buy it for the Council and turn it into a community resource – a school for adult education; Connolly, a visiting folk singer, wants to turn it into a hippie commune; Euan, who manages Connolly, arranges to have him shot in the hand in order to use the insurance money to outbid them both. Victoria, the geologist, decides to stay and partner with Euan in what will clearly be a base for North Sea oil exploration. The Thatcherite entrepreneurial revolution is on the doorstep, sweeping out both the last of the gentry and the communitarianism of Oscar's generation.

Part Three, 'The Mountain', pits Euan's desire for expansion of his quarry against the fledgling environmental movement that establishes a protest at the site. Euan hires a marketing consultant, Kirsty, to improve his image so he can win out against the protesters. She suggests he open a training centre in his father's memory (recalling Oscar's desire to turn the estate into a school for the community).

Peter Billingham shrewdly sees Greig's critique of New Labour spin in
the dramaturgy, and concludes:

> To suggest, as do Kirsty and Euan, that Oscar's revolutionary
> Socialism can be reworded and sanitised as 'increasing
> opportunity for all' reveals Greg with his finger very firmly on
> the pulse of the early-twenty-first-century capitalism and its
> methods of concealing its own economic self-interest under a
> guise of 'opportunity', 'choice' and 'community'.[11]

Victoria, the granddaughter who returns to visit at the beginning of
the play, but values little about the landscape, the past, or her own
wealth, ends the play with an ambivalent gesture. She digs up Oscar's
body in order to burn it, vowing to take his ashes to Spain to sprinkle
them on the places he recounts in his Civil War memoirs. But in the
fire she also burns his memoir and his documents as well as her own
wealth in a curious gesture of discarding history while honouring it.[12]

The American Pilot (2005)

The play was first staged by the RSC on 27 April 2005. On a remote
farm, 'in a country that has been mired in civil war and conflict for
many years' (p. 1), an American pilot has made a crash landing. He is
injured and is thrown on his host's mercy. The Farmer wishes he
would go away quickly; the Trader wants to take advantage of the
situation, if only he knew what that was. The Farmer's wife, Sarah,
does what duty and hospitality require: she feeds the Pilot and takes
care of his wounds. The Farmer's daughter, Evie, thinks he and the
Americans might save her village and rescue her from an unwanted
marriage. The Captain and the Translator view him as possible
collateral to leverage in the long civil conflict they have been fighting.

Because the Pilot does not speak their language, nor they his, most
communication is gestural or extremely basic. The Translator turns
out to be very weak in English, and mostly mistranslates or renders
only a few words to each side. The Pilot is like a fetish-object: the
Farmer calls him beautiful, his skin 'the colour of sand flecked with

gold' (p. 3). The Trader hits him, the Captain kicks him, and the Translator stabs him in the leg – perhaps to break his iconic aura. Over three days, the rural village people try to decide what to do with him and what advantage they might gain through him, while the American Pilot listens to hip-hop on his cassette player (before they take it from him) and suffers from pain and fear. Still, he believes they will come for him – his guys – and get him out of this place.

The themes of clashing cultures, the power of US imperialism, and questions of hospitality and ethics in a Levinasian encounter of face to face coalesce in the moments when the Pilot and the Farmer establish a kind of tentative rapport, sharing a joke about smoking, and making attempts to protect each other. (The Farmer gives the Pilot warm clothes and urges him to try to escape before he is killed by the Captain and the Translator; the Pilot tries to warn the Farmer and protect daughter Evie when the Americans storm the shelter with machine guns and hand grenades.) In this reciprocity is the affirmation of civil possibilities among strangers. However, the intent to kill the Pilot and use the video footage on TV, and the overwhelming force of US military might that bursts into the space killing everyone concerned but the Pilot and Evie (whom he clutches) suggest that such fragile possibilities for overcoming enmity are nothing compared to the violence of these darker forces of globalisation and local terror.

The play is largely about what dreams are imagined in the chasm of indeterminacy that opens up when something unexpected ruptures the everyday. The Captain had lost faith in his mission and his own leadership capacity, but comes to believe that the spectacle of Evie leading his army, proclaiming the American Pilot to be a messenger sent to save them, will rejuvenate his cause. Evie herself makes friends with the Pilot, and knows a little about America from watching TV at her friends' homes. When she faces pressure from her father and mother to marry the Translator, she refuses and instead insists that she has prayed and seen visions that tell her: 'We were lost but America sent him to tell us, we don't have to be alone any more' (p. 60).

However, the Trader does not believe in dreams; he betrays the Captain and notifies the Americans because, as he sees it,

The margin exists in the deal and the deal exists in the world
as it is – not a dream of the world, not in the world as you
would like it to be. (p. 66)

The response he triggers from the Americans, of course, goes beyond
what any of them has imagined. They simply wipe out the village. The
tentative negotiations of a small socius trying to understand and define
its relationships are brutally crushed by an incommensurate use of
force. Manoeuvring for position, the Trader, the Captain, and the
Translator lose all positions, and the Farmer and his wife are simply
collateral damage. As Peter Billingham has pointed out, Greig first
conceived the play before the anticipated invasion of Iraq, and the
videotaped execution of the Pilot that the Translator envisages
presaged the global transmission of beheadings of Western hostages
that followed in reality. Billingham concludes that Greig 'could not
have anticipated either the direction that war would take or the way
that terrorists or insurgents would react against the "liberators"'.[13]

Damascus (2007)

On first encounter, *Damascus* – which premiered on 27 July 2007
at the Traverse – is a mythical, dream-like text, but on careful
examination, it reveals a series of sharply etched scenes between
extremely concrete characters. The hinge-figure is a storyteller, the
pianist in the hotel bar: a Christian Marxist transsexual named Elena
– from Ukraine. She sees everything that goes on, and orchestrates a
good deal of it: 'In the afternoon I play film themes for lovers [. . .] I
play in order to make them feel sad. It amuses me' (p. 40). The hotel
lobby serves several functions as waiting and meeting space, as small
restaurant, and as bar and dance floor (Greig specifies a glitter ball).
From her vantage point at the piano, Elena observes the myriad
transactions that take place in these spaces. The play unfolds in
seeming present time, but Elena narrates some of the events in
retrospect, telling the audience in direct address: 'You want to know
what happened. I know. I was here at the beginning. I was here at the
end. I am always here. Always' (pp. 7–8).

With Elena as ironic and omniscient guide, the story told in the hotel lobby concerns the business transaction between a young Scotsman (Paul) who is selling English-language textbooks to Syrian educators, Muna and Wasim. The transaction is complicated because Wasim, the Dean, does not speak English while Paul speaks neither Arabic nor French, and because Wasim is not actually interested in the textbooks – he has used the occasion as a pretext for spending time with Muna, an old lover from years before when he was an inspired professor and poet and she was an idealistic student. The hotel porter, Zakaria, who completes the dramatis personae, is an aspiring writer, desperate for some new experiences, especially sexual adventures, and thinks Paul may be able to sell his autobiographical film script to Hollywood.

The play explores the initial relations among these people following two trajectories of intercultural encounter: the first is linguistic, the second is romantic. Through the misunderstandings arising from different languages and cultural contexts, Greig creates his typical world of near-miss connections between people. The product Paul is selling is 'Middleton Road', billed in its promotional materials as 'a completely integrated English language learning system' (p. 14). Paul has himself written this material, so when he puts it forward to Muna and Wasim, he is simultaneously selling himself. Although Wasim never has any intention of considering his texts, Muna does study the materials and takes the project seriously, leading to a critique of its contents in terms of Syrian culture. Some of her criticisms ring familiar, even stereotypical, such as objecting to a child's voiced disrespect to his mother, 'This cannot be read out in the classroom [. . .] It is too much disrespect between a child and an elder' (p. 44). However, Greig cleverly reverses the perception of what is progressive when Muna complains that Paul has portrayed a character in full niqab. Paul justifies the choice by saying that some women prefer to be covered because of their religious faith, but she rejoins that it is 'an issue of patriarchy', and insists he is portraying fundamentalism:

Maybe in England you want to throw away equality. Here we are trying to educate girls that they are equal. There are plenty of communities here where women are kept down by religion or tradition. If a woman teacher is in the classroom using this teaching material, her position will be undermined. (p. 42)

As Paul and Muna argue about the situations Paul has portrayed, a bond grows between them. Both tell each other something about why they are invested in the values they argue for, and they reach a kind of détente, although Paul concedes almost all Muna's points. In contrast to this deep engagement in exploring the meanings of language and its cultural entailments, when Wasim is present and Muna translates, Paul has little idea what he really says, including the insults Wasim directly asks Muna to translate. At the same time, Wasim and Muna conduct a personal conversation in front of Paul concerning their previous love affair and Muna's accusation that Wasim is a hypocrite.

This triangular exploration of language and culture is interwoven with Paul's relationship to Zakaria, who wants to pick up 'American girls' and gets Paul to do the talking, translating Zakaria's blunt request: 'Ask them if they want to sleep with me' into asking them to the hotel for a drink (p. 70). This comedy functions mostly at Paul's expense as Zakaria's intensity and despair is underscored by his suicide in the final scene after the two have engaged in a drunken night on the town and Paul has fallen asleep in the lobby waiting for his flight home, incapable of responding when Zakaria wants to talk, just before shooting himself.

The romantic intercultural encounters that structure the play are failures. Paul, exiled to Damascus on Valentine's Day, leaves voice mail for his wife, and when he eventually reaches her, wakes her and they argue. Paul falls for Muna, but things remain inconclusive, she telling him, 'Lover, you will never know you have been loved' – which appears to be true as he cannot comprehend or even remember the line. And Zakaria's American girls laugh and make fun of him and tell him curse words to 'practise English'. The taxi comes for Paul; he holds Zakaria's hand as he dies. Elena tells us she remembers the smell – blood and whisky.[14]

Summary

Numerous commentaries about Greig's work have now been published. His work has been discussed by scholars such as Dan Rebellato, David Pattie and Adrienne Scullion. 'One of the most important new playwrights to have emerged in contemporary British theatre over the last ten years,' writes Peter Billingham; 'Few writers in British theatre are as prolific or as thought-provoking as this 38-year-old Scot,' commented the *Daily Telegraph* critic Dominic Cavendish.[15] Amid all this interest, Greig might best be described as a poet in the theatre. He creates a tapestry of allusion and imagery through subtle effects in his dialogue, such as repetition, elaboration or reversal. His metaphoric structures usually form the primary architecture of his dramaturgy. A cluster of images in a number of plays that evoke being suspended in space simultaneously signify as consignment to oblivion or reaching for freedom; elements such as fire and water are figured to combine positive and negative valences within one event (*Victoria, Europe, San Diego*). Greig's skill lies in investing his writing with the desires of his characters, creating tangible, contagious feelings through language and imagery. In this regard, he shows the influence of Howard Barker, whom he acknowledges as an influence on his writing: 'He was terrifically important for me.'[16]

Greig also cites a second strong influence in Brecht, frequently mentioned by critics as well in their analysis of his work. Clare Wallace describes *Europe* as a *Lehrstück*, Nadine Holdsworth discerns an epic structure in *Victoria*, and I have also commented on the epic features of *Europe* and here, of *The American Pilot* and *Damascus*.[17] However, it seems to me that the early Brecht of *Baal* and *Jungle of Cities* might be closer to Greig's texture and impact than the later plays. Brecht's own poetry leads in those plays, and the myth or fable explored has little clear political moral. Further, the lonely characters that people the plays introduce desire and desperation into the dramaturgical equation in ways that match Greig's own dramatic world of longing and loss.

This distinction, placing Greig's work in relation to the early

Brecht, goes a long way towards placing him politically as well. Greig is certainly a political writer, but the 'term' political will need to be parsed to identify a number of ways in which Greig redefines the term for his generation and historical context. Greig's critique has no specific programme such as socialism at its forefront, but as was apparent in his Scottish colleague Gregory Burke's *Gagarin Way* (2001), there is a discernible lament for the failure of its political projects in *The Architect*, *Victoria* and *Damascus*. What is recognised and criticised throughout Greig's work is the damage to the environment, local economies and quality of everyday lives in the wake of neoliberalism and late capitalist expansion into globalisation. Anomie, rootlessness, commodification and destructive deeds for profit recur throughout the plays. However, in place of the objectivity or problem/solution perspective of an older group of writers, Greig is more focused on subjective experiences and individual ethics.

In particular, Greig dramatises how his characters react to the multiple possibilities and chance occurrences of their lives. He asks about responsibility for the suffering of others (as when Martin feels responsible for Billy's suicide; or when Paul's narcissism leads to personal blind spots that make him part of the problem in *Damascus*). The social, economic and political context is part of the situation in his plays, but it does not fully determine behaviour or outcome for his characters. The political questions asked in the texts take the current geopolitical situation as a given and ask how humans might/should react. He has a lot of sympathy for, and lacks harsh judgement of most of his characters, writing that he has to like a character in order to write the part.[18]

In his daily life, Greig's politics and his writing are visibly joined up. He travels widely, and has been influenced by his experiences to write about Eastern Europe, for example, and more recently about San Diego and Syria.[19] He has commented on his interest in the environmental movement and his own efforts to work out his position within it, and he mentioned in an interview that he participated in a local community effort to set up a co-op in place of shopping at the supermarkets.[20] Thus the kind of political theatre Greig writes is joined to his own quest to understand his times and what constitutes an appropriate way to live and to belong to an interconnected society such as exists in the early decades of this new century.

At the end of the 1990s, as he was just beginning to enjoy critical success, Greig commented directly on the question of politics in the theatre and his understanding of it:

> I think it's possible for writing about politics not to be political and I think it's possible for writing that is not about politics to be intensely political. What I would call political theatre makes interventions into ideology. It deals in ideology. It poses questions about society to which it does not already know the answer. And perhaps most importantly, political theatre has at its very heart the possibility of change.[21]

Of course, he was working on *Victoria* around this time, and ideology critique was very much on his mind, as noted earlier. However, it is fruitful to think about *The Cosmonaut's Last Message* as staging the clash of several exhausted ideologies as well, and more recent work such as *San Diego*, *The American Pilot* and *Damascus* reveal the limits of systems of values or ways of living when subjected to the pressures of transformed global circumstances and displaced identities.

The claim in Greig's statement – that the possibility of change is at political theatre's 'very heart', may explain why in spite of the down-beat endings of many of Greig's plays, the final notes are not fully despairing. In all his plays, Greig gives space to missed opportunities, possibilities without closure, and elusive moments of connection (Dorothy and Joe, the farmer and the pilot, even Muna and Paul). These encounters offer hope for change, or possibility that things might be otherwise, even in the midst of a lament for the concrete losses of the narratives. Greig's work, in other words, fulfils his own definition of political theatre.

Along with the critique of globalisation and the more local and personal politics staged in his works, David Greig is also a writer of romances. The desire for human intimacy, sexual longing and relationships that are marked by loss appear everywhere in his work. Physical distance is one concrete problem, as when the cosmonaut

Oleg poignantly tries to leave a message for Adrianna, the woman he once loved: 'I don't love you. Don't think that. I realise I will never see you again. I don't even want to talk to you face to face . . . if you don't' (p. 278). The tell-tale 'if you don't' undermines the message.

The play stages the transfer of affection of several of its characters to new loves. Vivienne starts out looking for her disappeared husband Keith but ends up caring for and about Bernard. Eric becomes attracted to Nastasja's breathing on the tape that Keith plays for him and tries to capture her, setting her up in a flat, but she eludes him: to fetishise is not to love. In *Damascus*, Paul and Muna make a genuine connection, but their different histories and cultures militate against anything more than an elusive moment of attraction and desire. Greig writes scenarios of romance but they are seldom sustained or mutual – the exception is perhaps the last scene of *Europe* when Katia and Adele start a sexual relationship with each other on a train leaving their town – a new beginning with an open-ended possibility. However, scenes of romantic longing serve a larger metonymic function in Greig's dramas – they stand in for or adjacent to an existential longing for belonging and connection that has become increasingly vanquished from our mobile and fragmented identities. The romantic attractions of the plays are symptoms, whether Eric's for Nastasja, or Evie's for the American pilot. The longing is for the concrete Other, but it is also for something to fill the void of contemporary existence, something more metaphysical than physical sex, more constant than habit or custom. The ache in the hole of existence manifests as romance, but its origin is ontological.

Greig writes romance but is not exactly a romantic writer – he punctures the idealism of his romantic scenarios, whether making fun of Paul's obsession with the smell of piss (because he is afraid he has lost the sense of smell), or in the bickering between the Cosmonauts over the naked-lady playing cards.[22] His romantic characters are often a little ridiculous and he undercuts with irony any sentimental sympathy his audience may feel too deeply. This is one of the best features of his writing: he maintains an edge or tension within characters who suffer and yearn, and who are nevertheless self-indulgent or misguided or just plain silly, like Paul. Yet his affection for these postmodern sojourners accompanies his dramatisation of their obsessions and blunders.

Greig is clearly a playwright growing into his maturity. His prolific output by a relatively young age means that he will continue to develop and shape his craft and his vision of the human landscape. His work is truly international – not just about a wider world of places and cultures, but also an interrogation of what it means to live between and among them. As his work continues to be produced abroad, the effect of the plays will be tested in front of audiences who live in the different parts of the world he joins up in his work.

Primary Sources

Works by David Greig

Victoria (London: Methuen Drama, 2000).
Plays One: Europe, The Architect, The Cosmonaut's Last Message to the Woman He Once Loved in the Former Soviet Union (London: Methuen Drama, 2002).
The American Pilot (London: Faber & Faber, 2005).
Damascus (London: Faber & Faber, 2007).

Secondary Sources

Billingham, Peter, *At the Sharp End: Uncovering the Work of Five Leading Dramatists* (London: Methuen Drama, 2007).
Cavendish, Dominic, 'Edinburgh Festival: *Damascus* Confirms Dramatist's Blinding Talent', *Daily Telegraph*, 7 August 2007 <http://www.telegraph.co.uk/culture/theatre/drama/3667037/Edinburgh-Festival-Damascus-confirms-a-dramatists-blinding-talent.html>
Greig, David, 'Plays on Politics', in David Edgar (ed.), *State of Play* (London: Faber & Faber, 1999), pp. 66–70.
—, 'Rough Theatre', in Rebecca D'Monté and Graham Saunders (eds), *Cool Britannia? British Political Drama in the 1990s* (Basingstoke: Palgrave Macmillan, 2008), pp. 208–21.
Higgins, Charlotte, 'Road to Damascus', *Guardian*, 16 February 2009 <http://www.guardian.co.uk/stage/2009/feb/16/david-greig-playwright-damascus>

Holdsworth, Nadine, 'Travelling Across Borders: Re-Imagining the Nation and Nationalism in Contemporary Scottish Theatre', *Contemporary Theatre Review*, Vol. 13, Issue 2 (May 2003), pp. 25–39.

—, 'The Landscape of Contemporary Scottish Drama: Place, Politics and Identity', in Nadine Holdsworth and Mary Luckhurst (eds), *A Concise Companion to Contemporary British and Irish Drama* (Oxford: Blackwell, 2008), pp. 125–45.

McDonald, Jan, 'Towards National Identities: Theatre in Scotland', in Baz Kershaw (ed.), *The Cambridge History of British Theatre Volume 3: Since 1895* (Cambridge: CUP, 2004), pp. 195–227.

Pattie, David, 'Mapping the Territory: Modern Scottish Drama', in Rebecca D'Monté and Graham Saunders (eds), *Cool Britannia? British Political Drama in the 1990s* (Basingstoke: Palgrave, 2007), pp. 143–57.

Rebellato, Dan, 'Introduction', in David Greig, *Plays One* (London: Methuen Drama, 2002), pp. ix–xxiii.

Reinelt, Janelle, 'Performing Europe: Identity Formation for a "New Europe"', *Theatre Journal*, Vol. 53, No. 3 (2001), pp. 365–87.

Scullion, Adrienne, 'Theatre in Scotland in the 1990s and Beyond', in Baz Kershaw (ed.), *The Cambridge History of British Theatre Volume 3: Since 1895* (Cambridge: CUP, 2004), pp. 470–84.

—, 'Devolution and Drama: Imagining the Possible', in Berthold Schoene (ed.), *The Edinburgh Companion to Contemporary Scottish Literature* (Edinburgh: EUP, 2007), pp. 68–77.

Wallace, Clare, *Suspect Cultures: Narrative, Identity and Citation in 1990s New Drama* (Prague: Litteraria Pragensia, 2006).

Notes

1. Aleks Sierz, *Tribune*, *Theatre Record*, Vol. XX, No. 9 (2000), p. 545.
2. Adrienne Scullion, 'Devolution and Drama', p. 71.
3. Dan Rebellato, 'Introduction', p. xvii.
4. Reviews of *The Architect* in *Theatre Record*, Vol. XVI, No. 4 (1996), p. 251.
5. Clare Wallace, *Suspect Cultures*, p. 294.
6. Reviews of *The Cosmonaut's Last Message* in *Theatre Record*, Vol. XIX, No. 10 (1999), pp. 609–11.
7. David Greig, 'Author's Note', *Victoria*, p. 6.
8. Nadine Holdsworth, 'The Landscape of Contemporary Scottish Drama', p. 135.
9. This coupling of the local with a broader commentary is reminiscent of his achievement in *The Speculator*.
10. Quoted in Billingham, *At the Sharp End*, p. 86.
11. Billingham, *At the Sharp End*, p. 118.

12. Reviews of *Victoria* in *Theatre Record*, Vol. XX, No. 9 (2000), pp. 545–9.
13. Billingham, *At the Sharp End*, pp. 120–1. Reviews of *The American Pilot* in *Theatre Record*, Vol. XXV, No. 9 (2005), pp. 587–9.
14. Reviews of *Damascus* in *Theatre Record*, Vol. XXVII, Edinburgh Fringe Supplement (2007), pp. 1174, 1184.
15. Peter Billingham, *At the Sharp End*, p. 94; Dominic Cavendish, 'Edinburgh Festival'.
16. Quoted in Billingham, *At the Sharp End*, p. 76.
17. Wallace, *Suspect Cultures*, p. 281; Holdsworth, 'The Landscape', p. 134; Janelle Reinelt, 'Performing Europe', p. 383.
18. Quoted in Billingham, *At the Sharp End*, p. 82.
19. He mentions travelling around Eastern Europe in 1991–92 and its effect on his writing (Billingham, *At the Sharp End*, p. 77); he draws on his experiences of teaching creative writing in Palestine and Syria for *Damascus* (Charlotte Higgins, 'Road to Damascus'); *San Diego* is a metatheatrical response to his first trip to California, marked by writing a character, called David Greig, into the opening of the play; see also David Greig, 'Rough Theatre'.
20. See Billingham, *At the Sharp End*, p. 89.
21. David Greig, 'Plays on Politics', p. 66.
22. His 2008 play, *Midsummer* (written with Gordon McIntyre), is a satire on rom-coms.

12 TANIKA GUPTA

Gabriele Griffin

Skeleton; The Waiting Room; Inside Out; Sanctuary; Fragile Land; Gladiator Games; Sugar Mummies

Introduction

Tanika Gupta belongs to the generation of playwrights who began to receive public recognition for their work in the 1990s. Born in Chiswick, London, in 1963, she was brought up in a Bengali household 'steeped in Indian arts – my father was a singer and actor and my mother a classical Indian dancer, so having the ambition to become a writer was encouraged by my parents'.[1] Following a degree in modern history at Oxford University, she worked at an Asian women's refuge in Manchester and as a community worker in Islington while beginning her career as a writer, initially for television, where she wrote episodes for soaps such as *Grange Hill, Crossroads, The Bill, EastEnders* and the Asian network soap *Silver Street.* She has also written extensively for BBC Radio.

From fairly early on, and unlike some of her contemporaries such as Meera Syal or Maya Chowdhry for example, Gupta refused to be classified as either a 'woman' writer or as an 'Asian' writer. Rather, she has argued repeatedly: 'Nobody goes round describing Harold Pinter as a Jewish white playwright, so why does everyone go round calling me an Asian woman playwright?'[2] But since her first three performed plays for theatre – *Voices on the Wind* (National Theatre Studio, 1995), *A River Sutra* (National Theatre Studio, 1997) and *Skeleton* (Soho Theatre, 1997) – were all set in India, it was difficult for her to escape that soubriquet. *Voices on the Wind* focused on the story of her great-uncle Dinesh Gupta, a fighter against British colonial rule in India.[3] *A River Sutra*, adapted from a collection of stories by Gita

Mehta, brought together the stories of various characters who live by that river. *Skeleton* depicts a medical student's obsession with a skeleton that comes to life at night and almost lures him to his death.

The shift away from 'writing about my Asian roots' came with her fourth play, *The Waiting Room* (National Theatre, 2000).[4] Although it centred on a Hindu family in the UK, thus also drawing on her Bengali heritage, this play marked a transition in her work in terms of setting – moving from India to Britain, where her subsequent theatre plays are all located. As she once noted,

> I love living in London and the cosmopolitan nature of the place. Yet, almost all my plays to date have been based around an Asian family/perspective/narrative. I use Indian myths and tales, imagery, poetry and language but I seem to often root my stories in the here and now.[5]

During the 2000s this rootedness in contemporary, cosmopolitan urban culture became increasingly prominent as one strand of Gupta's theatre work, centring predominantly on young people between their mid-teens and mid-thirties trying to negotiate dislocation, uprootedness and identity in multicultural urban Britain. *Inside Out*, commissioned in 2002 by Clean Break, a theatre company which works with women in the criminal justice system, was concerned with women from diverse backgrounds, and with 'how crime and punishment could affect a family', a theme that emerges repeatedly in Gupta's work.[6] *Sanctuary* (National Theatre, 2002), also concerned the theme of justice, here in the context of the guilt and innocence of male refugees from Rwanda and India, whose precarious life in London unravels as they face up to their and their countries' histories of violence, betrayal and victimisation.

Sanctuary featured one of Gupta's standard characters, the sassy urban teenager, familiar with violence, and with a sense of instability and provisionality. This figure resurfaces in many of her subsequent plays, possibly inspired by having teenage children herself. And her work has repeatedly been praised for its ability to get into the vernacular of teenagers. In many plays, such as *Fragile Land*

(Hampstead Theatre, 2003), *Gladiator Games* (Crucible, Sheffield, 2005), the multi-authored *Catch* (Royal Court, 2006), *Sugar Mummies* (Royal Court, 2006) and *Meet the Mukherjees* (Octagon, Bolton, 2008), Gupta juxtaposes teenagers with older women and men to analyse different takes on contemporary issues such as the (ab)use of technology, inter-racial relations, and the economies of sexual relations. In so doing she gives voice to an age group – young people – that has risen to theatrical prominence in the past fifteen years, partly because of the new focus on teenage peer group dynamics rather than on the individual teenager. This is as evident in Gupta's *White Boy* (National Youth Theatre, 2007) as it is in her *2 Young 2 Luv*, a play for the Birmingham Rep's youth theatre (2009). It is also evident in Gupta's adaptations of canonical plays from white into contemporary British Asian contexts, highlighting the ways in which such plays speak across cultural and temporal boundaries, possibly because of their focus on family dynamics and the difficulty of choices. Her versions of Brecht's *The Good Woman of Setzuan* (National Theatre, 2001; Haymarket Theatre, Leicester, 2006), Brighouse's *Hobson's Choice* (Young Vic, 2003) and Wycherley's *The Country Wife* (Watford Palace, 2004), as well as *Meet the Mukherjees*, are part of a more general post-2000 surge in such adaptations.

Gupta's work has also included the intermittent co-writing of plays such as *The Chain Play* (2001), co-written with a large number of other playwrights to commemorate the National Theatre's twenty-fifth anniversary; *Catch*, co-written with four other female playwrights for the Royal Court's fiftieth anniversary; and *Waiting for Leroy* (2007), co-written with Atiha Sen-Gupta for the Hampstead Theatre's new writing festival. Her prolific output also includes *Brood* (Soho Theatre, 2010). She has won significant awards for her work, including in 1998 the EMMA (BT Ethnic and Multicultural Media Award for Best Television Production) for *Flight*; the John Whiting Award in 2000 for *The Waiting Room*; the Asian Women of Achievement Award in the Arts category in 2003; the EMMA again in 2004 for *Hobson's Choice*; the Laurence Olivier Award for Outstanding Achievement in 2004; and the Amnesty International Media Award for her radio play *Chitra* (BBC, 2004). In 2008 she was awarded an MBE.

The Plays

Skeleton (1997)

Skeleton, the play that launched Gupta's career as a playwright, was first performed at the Soho Theatre on 29 May 1997. A two-act play set in Bengal, and inspired by a short story by Rabindranath Tagore, it draws on two myths widely present in a range of cultures, and much explored in the late nineteenth century.[7] The first is of the figure – here a skeleton – who comes back to life to haunt the living.[8] In this play Gopal, a medical student, returns to his village from the city during the vacation, to be given a skeleton to support his studies by his proud father. The skeleton turns out to be that of a beautiful woman seeking to lure Gopal to his death in order to join her for ever. The second myth is of the beautiful figure so infatuated with her or his own beauty that they will go to any length, including death, to preserve it.[9] *Skeleton* weaves together a narrative of female vanity with that of male vanity, the latter in the figure of Gopal, bewitched by urban life and his emerging status as a doctor, and hence dismissive of rural life. Gopal has always been the 'star pupil' (p. 9), and although he promised marriage to a local girl, Anju, on his return to his village he confesses to his friend Biju – a village schoolteacher – that he is now in love with the daughter of his professor. He tells Biju about city girls:

> They're more [. . .] refined; more dignified. Biju, I'm not talking about common rough village girls whose only aim in life is to please their husband, breed and get fat. They're special. (p. 11)

To which Biju responds: 'So they're not real flesh and blood' (p. 12). Underlying the play's exploration of the deathliness of perfection is a critique of gender roles, cross-generational expectations, and the urban/rural, educated/uneducated divide. All the female characters suffer from their confinement in patriarchal households, either their father's or their husband's, which allow them decorative status but not independence – their status is that of being someone's possession.

None the less the female characters dream – mistakenly, the play suggests – of the move from their father's to their husband's house as a moment of transformation.

> **Anju** I thought that by now I'd be married and that would free me. Free me from this village, my father and his endless demands, from having to be quiet and constrained all the time. (p. 53)

The reification of women leads to unrealistic expectations on the part of both women and men. It renders the latter by turns timid and impotent or overbearing and violent towards women. Significantly, the play's Shakespearean plot structure ends with the protagonist's social isolation while the characters from the subplot, Gopal's faithful friends Biju and Anju, are united in seemingly contented matrimony.[10]

The Waiting Room (2000)

First performed at the National Theatre on 25 May 2000, *The Waiting Room* centres on Priya, a fifty-three-year-old woman who has died unexpectedly of a stroke. As her body lies in waiting in their dining room, and her family – her husband Pradip, her daughter Tara and her son Akash as well as old family friend Firoz – gather to perform the funeral rites, Priya has three days as a spirit to roam the earth and confront her past before going to the 'waiting room', a kind of heaven. In this process she is supported by another spirit who appears to her, at her calling, in the shape of Dilip Kumar, a famous actor of Hindi or Bollywood movies.

Gupta has described this play in terms of working through the death of her father and his history of immigration.[11] It deals with a woman's transition from death into the afterlife, and her attempts to deal with her past before that transition. Shocked like her family by her unexpected death, Priya has difficulties coming to terms with her changed state, and takes some time to understand the opportunities offered to her by the possibility of entering her family members' dreams to deal with unresolved conflicts. Over two acts, these conflicts unravel and find resolution. They include Priya's sense of failure at never having made anything of herself except being a housewife, her affair and resultant child with Firoz, the death of that child in an accident involving Priya's son Akash when he was six, Akash's sense of guilt about this and his feelings of rejection by his mother, as well as the revelation that Pradip knew of Priya's affair with Firoz and that Tara, Priya's daughter, felt unable to tell her mother that she is a lesbian.

In common with *Skeleton* and many other contemporary plays by black and South Asian playwrights, this work naturalises the spirit world on stage, attempting to give equal status to material and immaterial bodies.[12] This poses a challenge on contemporary Western stages where, despite a tradition of such productions reaching back to Shakespeare and beyond, secularism has psychologised and thus interiorised the immaterial. *The Waiting Room* in fact gestures to varying extents towards three layers of im/materiality: the actual physical world (inhabited by Priya's surviving family and friends), Dilip's celluloid world (both 'real' and make-believe), and the afterlife (the realities of which, in keeping with this play as tragi-comedy, are constructed in rosy terms). It is Dilip's role to instruct Priya, and through her the audience, regarding what to expect. Many of the play's comic moments derive from Dilip making fun of earthly pre-conceptions of heaven and hell. Thus he tells Priya: 'I am here to guide, advise and comfort you. Some prefer Buddha, Mohammed, Jesus Christ, Lord Krishna; but you – you called for Dilip Kumar. So . . .' (p. 24). In keeping with the play's feelgood dimension, all family conflicts are ultimately successfully addressed, and heaven, or the waiting room, emerges as a desirable place where, as attachments to the earth begin to fade, Priya cannot wait to go.[13]

Inside Out (2002)

Gupta devised *Inside Out* while Writer-in-Residence for Clean Break at HMP Winchester West Hill Wing. The play was first performed at the Salisbury Playhouse on 16 October 2002. In her Preface to the published play text Gupta notes that 'almost all the women inmates

[. . .] were from impoverished backgrounds' and that she was 'shocked to see how many black women languished inside' (p. 7). Taking her cue from this, she centred her play on the lives of a thirty-two-year-old mother Chloe and her two daughters, seventeen-year-old, mixed-race Di and fifteen-year-old white Affy. Chloe works as a prostitute, pimped by her violent boyfriend Ed, known to the girls as 'Godzilla'. Chloe is unable to stand up to Ed who, with her knowledge, persistently assaults her and the girls, as well as making Di give blow jobs to punters from age thirteen. Di and Affy protect their mother and themselves from the prospect of foster homes by keeping quiet about what goes on at home, even when they need regular hospital treatment to deal with the physical effects of Ed's assaults.

Two of the play's key themes are women's relations with men and women's relations with each other. Both are constructed as highly fraught. Chloe was a teenage mum, abandoned by the fathers of her children. She remains locked in an adolescent state and thus in need of parenting. It falls to her daughters to protect her from men who are ready to exploit her need for cash and affection. Tellingly, the stage directions indicate that she tends to lounge in front of the television with her thumb in her mouth. She expresses her dependency on her daughters by turns through verbally abusing them, in the case of Di in racist terms, and appealing to them to stay with her. Di and Affy cling together, making plans to move away from their violent present. When Affy escapes by tracking down her biological father Di is left with their mother, who readmits Ed into their lives. For Di this is the final straw and as she seeks to leave, her mother attacks her in order to force her to stay. Di stabs Chloe to death. Five years later, fresh out of prison, Di tracks down Affy, now herself a teenage mum of two children and thus replicating Chloe's pattern. The difference is that in trying to have the family life she never had Affy cohabits with the father of her children, Sean, who works all hours to make ends meet. But Affy, whose biological father had wanted her to go to university, still has no qualifications and her future looks unpromising. This realist play has much in common with other plays commissioned by Clean Break, such as Winsome Pinnock's *Mules* (1996), in that it focuses on young women, and sees their victimisation, usually at the hands of men, as part of repeated cycles of deprivation. These young women are both worldly-wise and world-wary, with dreams of better lives thwarted by socio-economic realities, and a lack of sustained support structures, including, importantly, parental ones.

Sanctuary (2002)

First performed at the National Theatre's temporary Loft space as part of the *Transformation* season on 29 July 2002, Hettie Macdonald's production of *Sanctuary* generated intense debates, not least because of its subject matter, namely the ways in which the Christian church, and indeed England, provide sanctuary for people from other countries who have been involved in atrocities and genocide. A two-act play, it belongs to an increasingly large body of work engaging with the question of ethnic conflict and its aftermath.[14] It features a former pastor from Rwanda on the run for his part in the killing of Tutsis in 1994, an Afro-Caribbean war photographer who witnessed these killings and has been tracking this pastor down, and a man from Kashmir who saved his daughter from being slaughtered by Indian soldiers but failed to protect his wife from rape and murder. These men, and a mixed-race girl born in England but who is avoiding her mother and the mother's latest abusive male partner, find refuge in a quasi-Edenic churchyard, supported by a woman vicar, Jenny, and her mother Margaret, widow of an army doctor with whom she travelled the world. Michael Billington described 'Gupta's attempt to bring all these refugees together in one place [. . .] somewhat contrived' but admired the play for 'rub[bing] our noses in global reality'.[15] Gupta herself has said that her play was inspired by a stay in Kashmir in 1988:

> The day we left, there was some kind of a disturbance and gun shots were heard ringing out. Since then, thousands of innocent civilians have died in the war [. . .] I wanted to write a play that dealt with one of those many thousands of civilians.[16]

Utilising a realist form, the play moves between different time frames: the here and now of the sanctuary versus the there and then of the time of violence when all sanctuary, and the sanctity of the church as sanctuary, proved ineffectual against the onslaught of ethnically motivated genocidal atrocities. The play gradually reveals the histories of the three men, haunted by their memories and by what they did, raising questions of violence, (self-)sacrifice, justice and redemption. It is the women in the play who put a temporary stop to the persecution and killings that haunt the play, even as the churchyard, the men's temporary sojourn and a symbolic haven, is itself condemned to a make-over that will see it re-emerge as a leisure complex, thus signifying the banalisation of life and death in contemporary global culture.[17]

Fragile Land (2003)

First performed at the Hampstead Theatre on 25 March 2003, this two-act play centres on a group of six youngsters, four boys and two girls, in multicultural London where everybody is connected to somewhere else, including the one white boy, named Fidel by his left-wing, cross-culturally eager parents. Realist in its language, the play moves between the outside of an Indian sweet shop, where the various characters hang out, and three dream sequences. These sequences are intended to make real the fears of Tasleema (a young Asian woman who worries that her father might send her back to Bangladesh), Hassan (an Afghani refugee remembering the destruction of his family by the Taliban) and Omar (a Muslim boy who creates trouble in school by giving a knife to another kid who then uses it against kids who bully him). Although Kate Bassett found the dream sequences 'dire', 'the play clearly went down a bomb with the young people in the audience', according to Michael Billington.[18] Gupta, too, has commented on the play's success with its audiences.[19] One reason for this is Gupta's ability to convey both the lives of young people and the language they use to express their experiences. Drug-taking is commonplace: Asian girl Lux is described as 'expertly roll[ing]' (p. 52) weed in her hand and sniffing it to test its quality as she buys a 'ten quid bag' (p. 51) off Omar. Sexual come-ons, and one-upmanship among the boys are standard fare. But underneath all the swearing, banter and horseplay lurk anxieties about their futures that the young-sters themselves – who have either been deprived of their parents through war and displacement, or who are overly controlled or seemingly abandoned by them and their generation – have little sense of or faith in. They do not want their parents' life, which they regard as all work and no reward, but they also feel unsupported and unwelcome in the fragile land that is Great Britain, where they are the objects of constant rejection. In a distressing, skunk-fuelled exchange between Quasim and Omar, Quasim is accused of having 'impure blood' and being 'half and half . . . a dilution' (p. 49). His retort, 'I'm the new blood. The future belongs to people like me – mixed races, dual identity, double heritage . . .' (p. 50) is laughed off by the others, not least by Omar who veers between Muslim machismo and the desire to 'do the right thing' by his mates in distress. But, as Benedict Nightingale put it, 'If you want to feel optimistic about race relations in multi-ethnic Britain, *Fragile Land* may not be the play for you.'[20]

Gladiator Games (2005)

Gladiator Games was commissioned by Sheffield Theatres, and first performed at the Crucible Theatre Studio on 20 October 2005, before transferring to the Theatre Royal Stratford East. The play takes its title from a practice alleged to have occurred at Feltham Young Offenders Institute where prison officers supposedly put 'prisoners in a shared cell in the hope of racial violence or other conflict between them' (p. 93). Although the inquiry into the racially motivated murder of Zahid Mubarek, on which this two-act play is based, cleared the prison officers on this count, it also found that a series of major errors had occurred in the handling of Robert Steward, Zahid's killer, leading to Robert and Zahid being placed together in Cell Twenty-Eight. There Robert, who suffered from serious mental illness and was a known racist, 'clubbed Zahid to death with a table leg' (p. 35) on 21 March 2000, shortly before Zahid was due to be released. It took Zahid's family five years to get a public inquiry into what went wrong, and that inquiry's report had not yet been published at the time this play was first performed.

Gladiator Games is a docu-drama. In line with other such plays, it draws on verbatim witness statements and official documents from a public inquiry to call the state to account for its institutional failings, here related to prison regimes, institutionalised racism and the treatment of young offenders. Gupta also dramatises material from conversations she had with members of Zahid's family and in particular his uncle Imtiaz, because, as she put it,

> I've been struck by the fact that in lots of verbatim theatre you
> don't see the victims of the story [. . .] With Zahid Mubarek,
> I wanted to make sure that he was always at the centre of the
> story.[21]

Lyn Gardner described the published version of *Gladiator Games* as 'a model of good practice' because it explained 'the origins of almost every line', setting it against other such plays that merely 'confirm what most of us already largely think and know' and cajoling us 'into accepting that piece's particular bias as the truth and nothing but the truth'.[22]

The play intercuts direct addresses to the audience (signalled through the stage direction '*steps forward*') by witnesses at and commentators on the inquiry, and its antecedents, with dramatised interactions between the various characters, to unpack the events leading up to the assault on Zahid and his subsequent death. In this it partly moves away from the more conventional, declarative courtroom style of much verbatim theatre. The play indicts the British prison system for its failure to keep institutionalised young offenders safe, and for failing to provide adequate rehabilitative measures for those who are incarcerated.

Sugar Mummies (2006)

Sugar Mummies opened to mixed reviews when it was first performed at the Royal Court on 5 August 2006. While Lizzie Loveridge, for example, was broadly sympathetic to the play, Michael Coveney thought that its 'promising' topic of 'the pleasures and perils of female sex tourism' was 'never really deliver[ed] while skirting around various personal stories'.[23] Nicholas de Jongh viewed it as 'more soap than sugar' and 'sloppy'.[24] The play was commissioned by the Royal Court's artistic director Ian Rickson after he read 'feminist campaigner Julie Bindel's article on what was happening in Jamaica'.[25] The theatre sent Gupta to Negril, Jamaica, for a two-week research holiday (husband and three children in tow). She came away wanting to challenge her audience:

> Theatre audiences think they're very liberal, think they're political, and generally tend to be very white [. . .] I think a play like this will challenge their preconceptions [. . .] on one level [female sex tourism] might seem to be about women's liberation, it's really another form of colonialism.[26]

A two-act play, *Sugar Mummies* explores female sex tourism from the perspective of four female punters, three from the UK, one from the US, of varying class, age and racial backgrounds, as well as from the viewpoint of the Jamaican 'beachboys', who sell their bodies for cash. Unlike other such plays – for instance, debbie tucker green's *Trade* (2004) or Winsome Pinnock's *Talking in Tongues* (1991) – this play does not produce an easy white vs black, or black First World vs black Third World dynamic. Rather, a seemingly simple reverse gender politics (women exploiting men) is intersected with a complex racial structure (one female sex tourist is Afro-American, another mixed-race, two are white) that places the agenda strongly into the economic realm.[27] As white middle-aged Maggie concludes, 'He will always be financially beholden to you and eventually it drives men mad. They can't cope unless they are the bread-winners' (p. 122). Underlying this female sex tourism are the women's unfulfilled emotional yearnings, inflected by how women are positioned in First World countries where the combination of female emancipation and gender inequalities mars women's lives. Gupta's holiday romances remain temporary illusions that are soon shattered as compliments give way to the realities of economic need that structure the lives of the black boys the women are romanced by.[28]

Summary

Gupta's work emerged in the 1990s, a time variously described by Aleks Sierz as beset by a 'slump' and 'timidity'.[29] He argues that the new work that proliferated in this period frequently suffered from 'conservative and untheatrical ways' of articulating issues, beset by the 'hegemony of social realism and naturalism'.[30] Sierz's impatience with this, though not entirely unfounded, ignores some of the subtleties of the work referred to, which Janelle Reinelt seeks to tease out in her refusal of the generational differences that are often assumed to exist between groups of writers.[31] Gupta's work certainly bears traits of the hegemony of naturalism in terms of the language employed by her characters, the predominantly social realist settings of her plays, and her use of teleological narratives, including an emphasis on closure and the tying up of loose ends. However, she also presents reality with a twist, simultaneously ensuring that, in her words, the 'punters enjoy it' and pushing them out of their comfort zone.

Gupta's early plays centred strongly on Bengali contexts – one of the reasons why she was constructed as an Asian playwright. Gupta told Peter Billingham that initially she did not mind being labelled in this way: 'To begin with, because I was searching for and establishing my own identity, I didn't mind those labels in my early twenties [. . .] I'm very clear now [. . .] I'm a writer.'[32] But the post-categorical world that Gupta aspires to is a long way off, as clearly shown by the fact that all critical engagement with her work addresses the issue of her identity: Salman Sayyid's 2006 invention of 'BrAsian', an auditorily unappealing term that has unsurprisingly not been taken up, is but one of the more recent attempts to articulate South Asianness in a British context. Raminder Kaur and Alda Terracciano discuss Gupta's work under the banner of 'exile and cultural hybridism', thus harking back to the colonialities that her post-categorical aspirations are seeking to move beyond.[33]

More poignantly, perhaps, Gupta's exchanges with Billingham point to the ways in which individual and public life cycles as much as institutionalised imperatives shape a playwright's work. As a young woman, Gupta engaged intensely with her family's history, and her early plays therefore focused – as has been the case with much of her subsequent work – on issues of family, inter-generational relations, the clashes between past and present. From 2000 onwards, these issues moved into the contemporary urban British setting that has become the hallmark of her work. Here, the parental generation is frequently off-stage and sidelined, as issues of peer culture among younger generations are explored and explode. This reflects on the one hand Gupta's own life cycle and the fact that her three children have reached the teenage stage. But it also and equally importantly references the new, post-2000 geopolitical and neo-imperial realities: for example, Hassan, one of the characters in *Fragile Land*, is a refugee from Afghanistan, seeking asylum in Britain and hoping that marriage to Tasleema, who has a British passport, will save him from deportation. Similarly, in *White Boy*, Sorted is a young refugee from Sudan, like Hassan alone in the UK, and trying to survive in a political and socio-economic climate increasingly resistant to immigrants.

The realities with a twist that are portrayed in Gupta's plays take particular forms, of which I shall briefly address three: one twist is the invocation of the spiritual world in the form of the dead coming alive as they journey from this world into a (not 'the') next one. This is in many ways quite alien to contemporary Western stages, and the frequently unimaginative theatricalisation of this (which one could rationalise by suggesting the equivalence of the material and the immaterial worlds in these plays and their attendant imaginaries) is an expression of this alienation, as much as of the paucity of British stagecraft that is caught in the literalism rightly lamented by Sierz.[34] A second twist in Gupta's work is the pushing, especially from the perspective of South Asian communities, of socio-sexual taboos, including domestic violence, the reduction of women to the role of housewives, the end of patriarchalism, lesbianism, adulterous affairs, pre-marital sex, drug-taking among Asian youths, racism across ethnically diverse communities, youth violence, marrying across castes and classes (usually in the form of girls' 'marrying down', as in Gupta's adaptation of *Hobson's Choice*). Gupta forces her audiences, and particularly those of Bengali and other South Asian origins, to face up to the kinds of socio-sexual realities that are usually silenced in those communities.[35] In common with many plays by writers of South Asian origin, her work dramatises these social taboos while frequently maintaining a comic mode that sweetens the pill (her versions of both *The Country Wife* and *Hobson's Choice* end with Bollywood-style dancing, for example).[36] In fact, her adaptations of canonical classics such as these into British Asian contemporary contexts might be described, in Dimple Godiwala's terms, as one of the 'intercultural-postcolonial strategies' designed to 'destabilise and relocate authority and authenticity by altering power structures via revisionist performance'.[37] However, another revisionist way of considering these productions – which were highly successful with both white and Asian audiences – is to view them in terms of their appeal to 'universalist themes' (this now, of course, much-derided phrase) regarding familial, peer and romantic relations.

Perhaps her most important twist is her portrayal of multicultural groups of youths, routinely including Asian, black, mixed-race and white characters. This is, and remains, a highly unusual cast for any contemporary play, most of which centre firmly on one racial group, or at best straddle two. In this almost all contemporary theatre obeys the ontological imperative – you write what you are in ethnic or racial terms. This becomes immediately evident when one compares Winsome Pinnock's or Caryl Churchill's plays to Gupta's, and it holds not only for the ethnicity of their characters but more widely for the casting of plays – cross-racial casting still attracts significant attention precisely because it is rare. Across Gupta's plays of the 2000s, multicultural casts are the norm, whether in *Gladiator Games*, *White Boy* or in her version of *The Country Wife*. One might read this as the 'relaxation of boundaries' and a new form of crossover – though typically such resistance to normative categorisations usually occurs in relation to those commonly minoritised and mostly in the work of writers from minority communities, rather than on the part of the hegemonically normative.[38] In Gupta's plays, the portrayal of multi-cultural groups produces first an interesting levelling effect among the different racial groups since all of them are equally represented on stage. Secondly, this levelling is carried over into the characterisations of her key figures who all suffer equally from 'swagger'. In the female protagonists this takes the form of feistiness and a striving for liberation from certain traditional forms of femininity; in the male characters it is denoted through over-assertiveness, a tendency to dominance behaviour mingled with aggression, and the need to come across as sussed. It is a world not as in-yer-face as that of some other playwrights from the same period (the transgressions are not as high octane; the violence not as graphic; resolutions are almost always achieved) but it is possibly all the more knowing for it. It anchors those agendas in the everyday.

Importantly, Gupta's work engages in a gender politics that pays equal attention to the plights of women and men (a focus she shares with playwright Dolly Dhingra). In this she is again somewhat unusual: Roy Williams's theatre work, for instance, tends to focus on black male youths. Gupta's youths have gendered destinies; her girls tend to get what they want, while her lads get caught out. In *Inside Out*, for instance, Affy has a family and Di comes out of prison; though both face an uncertain future, they have survived their traumatic childhoods. In *White Boy*, by contrast, Victor ends up dead, Sorted is about to be arrested, the white boy is left without anybody; in *Gladiator Games*, too, of course, one of the central male characters is killed, the other remains severely disturbed. Many of Gupta's male characters, then, are representative of what I would describe as a form of urban beleaguered masculinity, utilising swagger to mask their uncertainties.

In 'Beyond Timidity?' Sierz argues that 'What new British theatre needs most is to shake off its habitual timidity and to explore the world's more dangerous shores.' He asks, 'Isn't it odd that there have been no British plays about global warming? Or corporate manslaughter? Or mixed-race identity?'[39] I'd like to suggest that for many, as Gupta's plays indicate, the more immediately dangerous shores are the domestic and estate fronts that they have to negotiate on a daily basis.

Primary Sources

Works by Tanika Gupta

Skeleton (London: Faber & Faber, 1997).
The Waiting Room (London: Faber & Faber, 2000).
Inside Out (London: Oberon, 2002).
Sanctuary (London: Oberon, 2002).
Fragile Land (London: Oberon, 2003).
Gladiator Games (London: Oberon, 2005).
Sugar Mummies (London: Obcron, 2006).
Meet the Mukherjees (London: Oberon, 2008).
White Boy (London: Oberon, 2008).

Secondary Sources

Aston, Elaine, 'A Fair Trade? Staging Female Sex Tourism in *Sugar Mummies* and *Trade*', *Contemporary Theatre Review*, Vol. 18, No. 2 (2008), pp. 180–92.

Bassett, Kate, 'Howl, Howl, Howl: It's Santa on the Prowl', *Independent*, 30 March 2003 <http://license.icopyright.net/user/viewFreeUct?fuid=ODc0MjzMQ%3D%3D>

Billingham, Peter, *At the Sharp End: Uncovering the Work of Five Contemporary Dramatists* (London: Methuen Drama, 2007), pp. 203–60.

Bindel, Julie, 'The Price of a Holiday Fling', *Guardian*, 5 July 2003 <http://www.guardian.co.uk/theguardian/2003/jul/12/weekend7.weekend1>

British Council, 'Tanika Gupta', *Contemporary Writers*, 26 November 2010, <http://www.contemporarywriters.com/authors/?p=auth568718EC050e418D7BTHO22ABB85>

Canton, Ursula, 'We May Not Know Reality, But It Still Matters: A Functional Analysis of "Factual Elements" in the Theatre', *Contemporary Theatre Review*, Vol. 18, No. 3 (2008), pp. 318–27.

Coussens, Catherine, 'Updating the Restoration Libertine in Tanika Gupta's Contemporary Adaptation of William Wycherley's *The Country Wife*', *Journal of Arts and Social Sciences*, Vol. 12 (2009), pp. 61–74.

Coveney, Michael, 'Sugar Mummies', *What's On Stage* website, 11 June 2006 <http://www.whatsonstage.com/reviews/theatre/london/E88211552>

Edmondson, Laura, 'Genocide Unbound; Erik Ehn, Rwanda, and an Aesthetics of Discomfort', *Theatre Journal*, Vol. 61, No. 1 (2009), pp. 65–83.

Gardner, Lyn, 'Write About an Arranged Marriage? No Way!', *Guardian*, 25 July 2006 <http://www.guardian.co.uk/stage/2006/jul/25/theatre1/print>

—, 'Does Verbatim Theatre Still Talk the Talk?', *Guardian Theatre Blog*, 7 May 2007, <http://www.guardian.co.uk/stage/theatreblog/2007/may/07/foreditorsdoesverbatim thea>

Godiwala, Dimple, 'Editorial Introduction: Alternatives within the Mainstream: British Black and Asian Theatre', *Studies in Theatre and Performance*, Vol. 26, No. 1 (2006), pp. 3–12.

—, 'Genealogies, Archaeologies, Histories: The Revolutionary "Interculturalism" of Asian Theatre in Britain', *Studies in Theatre and Performance*, Vol. 26, No. 1 (2006), pp. 33–47.

Griffin, Gabriele, *Contemporary Black and Asian Women Playwrights in Britain* (Cambridge: CUP, 2003).

—, 'What Mode Marriage? Women's Partner Choice in British Asian Cultural Representation', *Women: A Cultural Review*, Vol. 18, No. 1 (2007), pp. 1–18.

Gupta, Tanika, 'From Kashmir to Grange Hill', *Independent*, 28 July 2002 <http:77license.icopyright.net/user/viewFreeUse.act?fuid=ODc0MTA0Ng%3D%3D>

Halliburton, Rachel, 'Tanika Gupta: Interview', *Time Out*, 31 July 2006 <http://www.timeout.com/london/theatre/features/1771/Tanika_Gupta-Interview.html>

Kaur, Raminder and Alda Terracciano, 'South Asian/BrAsian Performing Arts', in Nasreen Ali, Virinder S. Klara and Salman Sayyid (eds), *A Postcolonial People: South Asians in Britain* (London: Hurst, 2006), pp. 343–57.

Loveridge, Lizzie, 'Sugar Mummies', *Curtain Up* website, 12 August 2006 <http://www.curtainup.com/sugarmummies/html>

Ponnuswami, Meenakshi, 'Citizenship and Gender in Asian Performance', in Elaine Aston and Geraldine Harris (eds), *Feminist Futures: Theatre, Performance, Theory* (Basingstoke: Palgrave Macmillan, 2006), pp. 34–55.

Reinelt, Janelle, 'Selective Affinities: British Playwrights at Work', *Modern Drama*, Vol. 50, No. 3 (2007), pp. 305–24.

Roy, Amit, 'Hanged Bengali Icon's Great-Niece Bags MBE', *Telegraph India*, 15 June 2008 <http://telegraphindia.com/1080615/jsp/frontpage/story_94140>

Sayyid, Salman, 'BrAsians: Postcolonial People, Ironic Citizens', in Nasreen Ali, Virinder S. Klara and Salman Sayyid (eds), *A Postcolonial People: South Asians in Britain* (London: Hurst, 2006), pp. 1–10.

Schlote, Christiane, 'Either for Tragedy, Comedy, History or Musical Unlimited: South Asian Women Playwrights in Britain', in Geoffrey V. Davis and Anne Fuchs (eds), *Staging New Britain: Aspects of Black and South Asian British Theatre Practice* (Bern: Peter Lang, 2006), pp. 65–86.

Sierz, Aleks, 'Beyond Timidity? The State of British New Writing', *PAJ: A Journal of Performance and Art*, Vol. 81, No. 3 (2005), pp. 55–61.

—, 'Reality Sucks: The Slump in British New Writing', *PAJ: A Journal of Performance and Art*, Vol. 30, No. 2 (2008), pp. 102–7.

—, '*Blasted* and After: New Writing in British Theatre Today', *Transcript 27: British New Writing*, Theatrevoice website, 16 February 2010 <http://www.theatrevoice.com/tran_script/detail/?roundUpID=43>

—, 'As Long as the Punters Enjoy It: In Conversation with Tanika Gupta', *New Theatre Quarterly*, Vol. 24, No. 3 (2008), pp. 260–9.

Svich, Caridad, 'An Advocate for Change: Tanika Gupta in Conversation with Caridad Svich', in Caridad Svich (ed.), *Trans-Global Readings: Crossing Theatrical Boundaries* (Manchester: MUP, 2003), pp. 99–104.

Notes

1. See British Council, 'Tanika Gupta'.
2. Lyn Gardner, 'Write About an Arranged Marriage? No Way!'.
3. This play was originally sent to Tawala theatre company who put Gupta in touch with Matthew Lloyd at the Hampstead Theatre. He acted as dramaturge to the play; it finally had two performances at the National Theatre Studio in 1995 (Aleks Sierz, 'As Long as the Punters Enjoy It', p. 261). See also Amit Roy, 'Hanged Bengali Icon's Great-Niece Bags MBE'.
4. Aleks Sierz, 'As Long as the Punters Enjoy It'.
5. Caridad Svich, 'An Advocate for Change', p. 100.
6. Tanika Gupta, 'Preface', *Inside Out*, p. 8.
7. Tagore was a cultural icon for her family.
8. Such figures include vampires, the golem, and the mechanical dolls of late-nineteenth-century *Kunstmärchen*.
9. The myth of Narcissus and its latterday version, Oscar Wilde's *Dorian Gray*, significantly, are both male.
10. Reviews in *Theatre Record*, Vol. XVII, No. 11 (1997), pp. 680–1.
11. Peter Billingham, *At the Sharp End*, pp. 211–12.
12. See Gabriele Griffin, *Contemporary Black and Asian Women Playwrights in Britain*, pp. 81–4, 115–23, 133–4.
13. Reviews in *Theatre Record*, Vol. XX, No. 11 (2000), pp. 696–9.
14. See Laura Edmondson, 'Genocide Unbound'.
15. Michael Billington, *Guardian*, *Theatre Record*, Vol. XXII, No. 15 (2002), pp. 1009–10.
16. Tanika Gupta, 'From Kashmir to Grange Hill'.
17. See Billingham, *At the Sharp End*, pp. 231–8.
18. Kate Bassett, 'Howl, Howl, Howl: It's Santa on the Prowl'; Michael Billington, *Guardian*, *Theatre Record*, Vol. XXIII, No. 7 (2003), p. 407.
19. Billingham, *At the Sharp End*, p. 221.
20. Benedict Nightingale, *The Times*, *Theatre Record*, Vol. XXIII, No. 7 (2003), p. 407.
21. Gardner, 'Write About an Arranged Marriage? No Way!'.
22. Lyn Gardner, 'Does Verbatim Theatre Still Talk the Talk?'. For another reading, see Ursula Canton, 'We May Not Know Reality, but It Still Matters'.
23. Lizzie Loveridge, 'Sugar Mummies'; Michael Coveney, 'Sugar Mummies'.

24. Nicholas de Jongh, *Evening Standard*, *Theatre Record*, Vol. XXVI, No. 16–17 (2006), p. 909.
25. Julie Bindel, 'The Price of a Holiday Fling'; Rachel Halliburton, 'Tanika Gupta: Interview'.
26. Halliburton, 'Tanika Gupta: Interview'.
27. This important issue was underplayed in Aston's reading of *Sugar Mummies*.
28. Reviews in *Theatre Record*, Vol. XXVI, No. 16–17 (2006), pp. 909–12.
29. Aleks Sierz, 'Reality Sucks'; 'Beyond Timidity?'.
30. Sierz, 'Beyond Timidity', p. 56; Sierz, 'Reality Sucks', p. 102.
31. See Janelle Reinelt, 'Selective Affinities'.
32. Billingham, *At the Sharp End*, pp. 206, 207.
33. Raminder Kaur and Alda Terracciano, 'South Asian/BrAsian Performing Arts', p. 343.
34. Sierz, 'Reality Sucks', p. 104. Sierz too readily lambasts the playwrights while saying little about the lack of creativity shown by both theatre directors and stage designers.
35. The most prominent example of this was the infamous case of the closing down of Gurpreet Kaur Bhatti's *Behzti* in December 2004. See also Billingham, *At the Sharp End*, p. 212.
36. Gabriele Griffin, 'What Mode Marriage?'. See also Catherine Coussens, 'Updating the Restoration Libertine', and Christiane Schlote, 'Either for Tragedy, Comedy, History or Musical Unlimited'.
37. Dimple Godiwala, 'Genealogies, Archaeologies, Histories', pp. 37, 39.
38. Aleks Sierz, '*Blasted* and After'.
39. Sierz, 'Beyond Timidity?', p. 60.

13 DAVID HARROWER

Clare Wallace

Knives in Hens; Kill the Old Torture Their Young; Presence; Dark Earth; Blackbird

Introduction

Along with David Greig and Gregory Burke, David Harrower is one of the most successful of the new Scottish playwrights to emerge in the mid-1990s. In an article surveying tendencies in contemporary Scottish theatre, Jean-Pierre Simard considers the 'triple prism' of dominant elements that characterise Scottish theatre today: the popular, the political and the poetic.[1] Certainly these tendencies can be identified to varying degrees in Harrower's plays, though perhaps the most prominent is the poetic impulse in his best work.

Born in 1966 in Edinburgh, Harrower's career started with the Traverse Theatre's production of *Knives in Hens* in 1995. The play captured the imaginations of audiences, directors and critics around the world, and has become, according to the National Library of Scotland, 'one of the most performed Scottish plays of all time'.[2] It has been widely translated and continues to be performed across Europe, America and Australia. In particular, the German premiere of the play, directed by Thomas Ostermeier at the Baracke am Deutschen Theater Berlin in 1997, won the Theater Heute Best Foreign Play (Critics' Award) and was pivotal in presenting Harrower's work to European audiences. Since then Harrower has produced a number of plays, though little to equal the stunning achievement of his debut work: *Kill the Old Torture Their Young* (Traverse, 1998), *Presence* (Royal Court, 2001), *Dark Earth* (Traverse, 2003) and *Blackbird* (Edinburgh Festival, 2005). His most recent pieces include *365* (NTS, 2008) and *Lucky Box* (Paines Plough, 2009). Among these, only *Blackbird* has won critical acclaim in any way comparable to *Knives in Hens*. Arguably *Blackbird*'s success lies in its fusion of the other two elements highlighted by Simard – the popular and the political. The play opened at the Edinburgh Festival in veteran German director Peter Stein's production and then transferred to the West End. Winner of the 2006 Critics' Awards for Theatre in Scotland Best New Play and the Laurence Olivier Award for Best New Play in 2007, *Blackbird* has placed Harrower back in the critical limelight. A steady stream of productions has since taken place in Europe and beyond.

Besides his own work, Harrower has also been responsible for numerous adaptations. He has expressed a fascination with antecedent playwrights and their formal choices, asking, 'Why they've written the plays they've written and what it was in response to'.[3] His adaptations include Pirandello's *Six Characters in Search of an Author* (2001), Büchner's *Woyzeck* (2001), Chekhov's *Ivanov* (2002), Fosse's *The Girl on the Sofa* (2002) and *Purple* (2003), Horváth's *Tales from the Vienna Woods* (2003), Schiller's *Mary Stuart* (2006), Brecht's *The Good Soul of Szechuan* (2008) and Schnitzler's *Sweet Nothings* (2009). This dimension of Harrower's creative output is a significant aspect of his contribution to the contemporary theatre environment in Britain and Scotland.

The Plays

Knives in Hens (1995)

Knives in Hens opened at the Traverse Theatre in Edinburgh on 2 June 1995. The work is a non-naturalistic, semantically open, three-hander that revolves around themes of language, literacy and agency. Set in an indeterminate pre-industrial rural space, Harrower describes the play – along with *Dark Earth* – as an 'investigation of [his] thoughts and feelings about Scotland'.[4] Yet in fact there is little to mark this work (in contrast to *Dark Earth*) as regionally specific, and undoubtedly this has been a contributing factor in its popularity across cultures and languages. What is remarkable about *Knives in Hens* is the powerful sense of linguistic choreography, compositional precision and poetic nuance. A recapitulation of the play's plot does little to communicate its effect, though Alison Croggon's description of the play as a fable is apt.[5] As Mark Fisher remarked in a review of the 2005 revival,

> It seems to hit you on a subconscious level, as if by stripping back the language and the setting to its most austere, the playwright has tapped into a source of elemental power. Like a dream, *Knives in Hens* is a play you feel. Articulation comes later and is never adequate.[6]

Nevertheless, the poetic qualities of the play text reward scrutiny, in particular the modalities of the literal and the figurative that frame its concerns.

Knives in Hens follows the gradual transformation of its central character, known only as Young Woman, as she moves from a state of brute existence to a self-aware and literate relation to her world. The other characters – Pony William, the ploughman who becomes her husband, and Gilbert Horn, the miller who becomes her lover – introduce her to experiences and knowledge that alter her identity. The play begins with the Young Woman interrogating and bluntly rejecting William's use of metaphorical language:

Young Woman I'm not a field. How'm I a field? What's a field? Wet. Black with rain. I'm no field. [. . .]
William Said you're like a field.
Young Woman Said I'm a field sitting here.
William Said you're like a field. Like a field.
Young Woman 'S the same.
William Nothing close, woman.
Young Woman If I'm like a field must be a field.
William (*laughs*) Don't have to be a thing to be like it. (p. 1)

While the scene serves to sketch the characters' relative sensibilities, it also unfolds a self-conscious metatheatrical set of possibilities concerning the power of words to create worlds. Despite the simplicity of the words here and their repetition, a multi-faceted linguistic negotiation is underway that underwrites the drama as a whole. Metaphorical relations are conventionally understood as a means of extending and transforming meaning. Here that process, so habitually taken for granted, is contested and thus spotlighted. First the Young Woman takes William's statement literally; notably his original statement is absent so he is forced to reiterate. She repeats what she hears, but her paraphrase renders the analogy a complex metaphor – stripped of the word 'like' which must then be explicitly reintroduced by William. William's simile is a much simpler form of comparison and has several obvious possible figurative meanings – woman as property, woman as fertile earth to be tended and planted by man, woman as a force of nature – though he fails to elucidate any of these. Implicit here and as the play progresses is not merely the power involved in naming, but the radical nature of metaphor that comprises analogy, but also violent collision of ideas, images and symbols.[7]

In the opening scene William exerts authority over the Young Woman through his superior command of language; nevertheless the lesson conveyed in the final line of the above quotation marks the Young Woman's initiation into a new level of verbal competence that complements her innate curiosity and strength of will. By the third scene William has made the Young Woman his wife, and despite his earlier eloquence, her practical functions as worker and as sexual object are clearly now what he most values. The woman's mouth is for eating, for sexually pleasuring her husband, not for naming the world around her. William discourages her from dangerous abstract thought and in a reversal of the dynamic of the first scene directs her towards the literal when he asks her to list her morning's activities.

Obliged to take their grain to the miller when William attends his horses, the Young Woman's encounter with Gilbert Horn is a rite of passage that endows her with a new sense of identity. The miller is demonised by the ignorant villagers as a parasite and sorcerer. Though initially paralysed by terror and hatred of the unknown embodied by Gilbert, the Young Woman's dialogues with him slowly extend her comprehension of the power of language to shape reality. During her second visit to the mill, Gilbert's literacy becomes the focus of the

Young Woman's fear, when he reveals to her his record book in which he writes daily events and his thoughts. Writing is for the woman an unnatural act that controverts the natural process of forgetting: "'S God puts things in your head and's him who takes them away. 'S sin to keep them' (p. 18). Here the clash of epistemologies on the cusp of the transition from a pre-literate to a literate world is subtly articulated. Gilbert challenges the woman to overcome her dread and use the skills she learned in school. A seminal moment in the play occurs when, with considerable effort, she defiantly writes her name. At this point she assumes an agency she has heretofore lacked; she names herself, and is no longer merely the wife of Pony William. Significantly though, her name is not revealed in the exchange between characters, Gilbert merely remarks: 'Tell you what, horse-wife. You're beautifully named' (p. 21).

The Young Woman's engagement with the literate world via the miller initially does not displace the superstitious conviction that he has cast a spell on her and the conflict between irrational and rational rages in her statements. Yet, as a result of this collision of worldviews, the Young Woman arrives at an uneasy enlightenment – an understanding of William's unfaithfulness is revealed by Gilbert, and some sense of her own power, as expressed in writing:

> This is me. I live now. [. . .] Every thing I see and know is put in my head by God. [. . .] His world is there, in front of my eyes. All I must do is push names into what is there the same as when I push my knife into the stomach of a hen. This is how I know God is there. (p. 26)

But most strikingly the woman's appropriation of the power of the written word, of naming, is analogous to a violent gesture. Something is killed as a result of this type of knowledge and a new reality is created. Superstition and a belief in evil magic give way to a more rational understanding of betrayal and a desire for revenge.

Following the community ceremony of rolling the miller's new millstone to the mill, William, Gilbert and the Young Woman finally share the stage space. His wife apparently unconscious as a result of exhaustion and alcohol, William discusses his attitude to her with the miller. Again the metaphors he uses are agricultural. The Young Woman and the Miller join forces, killing William with the old mill-stone before consummating their relationship. The Young Woman then resolves to perform the role of 'broken-hearted wife' (p. 38) in the community and Gilbert leaves the village. The twinning of the capacity for deceit with the acquisition of knowledge inevitably suggests the Fall of Man, an allusion that concludes the play with a resonant sense of ambivalence.

Kill the Old Torture Their Young (1998)

Harrower's second play could hardly have provided a greater contrast to the poetic impetus of *Knives in Hens*. *Kill the Old Torture Their Young* premiered on 12 July 1998 at the Traverse. Contemporary in focus, the play is set in an unnamed northern city in the UK that perhaps resembles Glasgow. Social alienation, urban isolation, post-modern identity and a crisis of belonging are its principal thematic strands. Composed of short scenes set in different nondescript urban locations, the play revolves around several small clusters of characters whose paths cross but whose lives fail to connect. The structure is a familiar device in narratives with some postmodern import, as is evidenced, for example, by David Greig's *The Cosmonaut's Last Message* which premiered the following year. Harrower's title derives from a song by Scottish grunge band Biffy Clyro and although it seems laden with in-yer-face promise, little by way of the expected provocation is delivered. Michael Raab describes the play as a 'diffuse city panorama' and ventures that the title was perhaps its best feature.[8]

A collage of interlocking and juxtaposed fragments is linked directly and indirectly to the return of a film-maker to his hometown after ten years. Robert Malloch has been successful in London and he wants to film a documentary about the city of his childhood. Each of the play's characters embodies forms of isolation, marginalisation and lack of belonging that bear tangentially on the film project. Darren, a young man who wants to be an actor but works at menial service sector jobs, manifests wildly disjointed moods oscillating between menace and extreme neediness. Heather, a receptionist at a television company, is a routine-bound office drone whose initiative does not extend beyond manipulating those weaker in her workplace and maintaining a strict after-work programme of badminton on Tuesdays, aerobics on Wednesdays, cinema on Thursdays and so on. It is not a little ironic that Malloch adopts her as his muse for the ill-fated documentary. Steven, Heather's boss, is a lonely divorcee wracked with a sense of his own powerlessness and indirection for which he compensates by talking too much and meddling in others' affairs. Angela, a failed artist, expresses her insecurity through an overly assertive desire to help others. Her elderly neighbour Paul callously rejects her efforts, preferring to live in isolation in his tenement flat with the fading memory of a time he spotted an eagle in the city. The rock star is a paper-thin cliché of the alienated traveller.

The city as a set of 'non-places', to use Marc Augé's term, is certainly applicable here.[9] And of interest is the guiding metaphor of the film-maker's desire to produce a creative document that would make these spaces and his memories of them signify. Yet what is in evidence is the extent to which such a project is the product of chance, luck and chaos. As stressed by Malloch himself, 'There's always going to be things I'll miss [. . .] I have to accept that' (p. 44). The failure of imagination and creativity that permeates the play provides an engaging concern, but its potential is only partially realised.

Harrower works the humour of his various scenarios with skill. Robert's somewhat pompous speech about the gift of inspiration with the very uninspiring Heather is juxtaposed with the rock singer thrashing out a new song in the adjoining hotel room. In a similar vein, the most richly humorous scene in the play occurs when Steven, while looking for Robert and the camera crew, encounters a solitary birdwatcher on a patch of open ground. Although the birdwatcher is unequivocal about his desire to be left alone, Steven is painfully oblivious:

> **Birdwatcher**   Some people can tell by looking at me that
> because I'm sitting here on my own it means I don't want

> to talk to anyone. I want to be let alone. This is why I
> come bird-watching. It's me and nobody else.
>
> **Steven**   I know exactly what you're saying.
>
> **Birdwatcher**   Do you? Good.
>
> **Steven**   I should find something like this to do on my own.
> Something to take my mind off things. (p. 28)

Admittedly, the comedy of failed communication here is finely wrought, and Harrower reveals his talent for dramatic irony and contemporary idiom. Yet these qualities ultimately fail to equip the play's investigation of postmodern ennui with complexity of plot or depth of character.

Presence (2001)

Presence opened at the Royal Court Theatre Upstairs on 19 April 2001. The play is a dialogue-driven piece set in Hamburg in 1960, dramatising the formative moments of the Beatles. In an interview Harrower claimed that it was 'his most well-crafted story yet – but to write it he has steeped his hands in some pretty murky waters'. His aim was to 'write about the dynamics of the band', and since the Beatles are such an important part of the fabric of British popular culture it is undoubtedly a subject that is an 'intriguing' one.[10] The play falters in its ambitions, however, primarily due to the conservative lifelessness of the chosen form. The naturalistic dialogue and linear, mono-dimensional plot fail to energise the material.

The play outlines the arrival of the band in Hamburg, their experiences of living in squalor, playing in a club, attempting to seduce girls, and their interaction with Marian, the manager of the club. Marian's attempts to keep the Liverpool lads out of trouble on the mean streets of Hamburg are met with disdain. Full of youthful bombast and led by the aggressively arrogant Paul, they disregard her efforts to guide them as to how to behave and how to perform. Pete, the only member of the group to speak a little German, develops a polite relationship with Marian and is increasingly distanced from the rest. The naïve George ineptly attempts to seduce a waitress, Elke, who is enthralled by American culture and wants to escape Germany. The group meanwhile develops an increasingly confrontational performance style incorporating jack boots and references to Hitler. Their historical ignorance and insensitivity are both stunning and unsympathetic. Pete's superior attractiveness becomes a bone of contention when Marian, angry that they have disobeyed her, tells the group that he should be their front man. As a result of breaking curfew the under-age George is sent home and the others are forced to follow suit. The closing scene portrays Marian writing Pete Best on the ceiling with soot and setting fire to his stage jacket.

The play adheres rather methodically to a lesser-known aspect of the history of the Beatles' inaugural experiences as a group struggling to establish themselves. The McCartney character is negatively portrayed and, peculiarly, Lennon never appears – indeed one review noted that 'the Beatles sans Lennon inevitably suggests Hamlet without the prince'.[11] Somewhat more interesting, for an English audience, is the flavour of German culture at the beginning of the 1960s as seen through the eyes of German women of different generations, though the usual Nazi skeletons in the closet get a routine rattle. The title points in a number of directions: stage presence, historical presence and, of course, the presence of original band members, like Best (the so-called Fifth Beatle). Generally, reviews of *Presence* were tepid, pointing to the limitations of its conventional form, plot and laddish repartee.

Dark Earth (2003)

According to Danièle Berton-Charrière, in 2003 the Traverse Theatre invited several dramatists to write on the theme of Britishness.[12] *Dark Earth*, which premiered at the venue on 25 July, was Harrower's response. As Ian Brown says, '*Dark Country* [sic] examines modern tensions between urban and rural, modern and atavistic in the shadow of the Antonine Wall.'[13] A lengthy three-act piece, it is an uneven work that hobbles between unfulfilled menace and comedy. Glaswegians Euan and Valerie get stranded in the Lowlands near the Antonine Wall when their car breaks down. In one of the play's moments of arch humour, the city dwellers pore over the map unable to locate themselves – 'We're on a fold, I think, if you can believe that' says Euan (p. 7). They are indeed on a fold in an almost Deleuzian sense where subjectivity is accounted for not within the conventions of interiority and exteriority but as a topology of folds that collapses 'a distinction between perceiver and perceived, virtual and actual, inside and outside'.[14] Valerie and Euan find themselves in contact with a Scotland that is simultaneously uncannily familiar and alien.

The couple are assisted by Petey, Ida and their twenty-year-old daughter Christine, who have a small farm nearby. Petey and Ida are jovial, if idiosyncratic, Christine is prickly and caustic. The city dwellers find themselves victims of Ida's hospitality and audience to Petey and Christine's fascination with the Roman and Scottish history of the area. With friction already overt between Euan and Valerie, the couple find themselves further at odds in their reactions to their rural hosts. Valerie is content to accept their hospitality and to stay the night, Euan is ill at ease and wants to leave as soon as possible. As the evening wears on, and with neither a mechanic nor a taxi in sight, Euan and Valerie stay. Whisky is drunk, songs are sung, stories are told and the following morning Petey takes Valerie to see the Wall, while Euan is subjected to a full Scottish breakfast. However, antipathies erupt when it becomes evident that Petey and Ida have offered their accounts to Valerie for inspection and Christine reveals that the farm has already been sold since they are virtually bankrupt. Ida's desire to reverse the sale and open a bed and breakfast causes Christine to storm out with plans to leave her parents to their fate. After some further confrontation, the Cauldwell family regroups and turn on Euan and Valerie. The play concludes with them hurling abuse at the 'freeloaders' and 'thieves' as Euan and Valerie drive off (pp. 107–8).

The resonances of the play's title are gestured towards by a definition that prefaces the text. Dark Earth is 'buried soil in archaeological excavation which often reflects prolonged periods of abandoned settlement; alternatively, deposits of silty soil reworked by earthworms to produce grassland' (p. 6). Both pertain to the symbolic terrain of the drama. Euan and Valerie in their failed attempt to locate some site of archaeological significance, unwittingly unearth something in the heart of their own country, an existence they fail to comprehend. Petey, Ida and Christine's obsession with the distant past is brought to the surface by the presence of the outsiders, and it is noteworthy that they treat that past as contiguous with the present. Thus Christine and Petey's argument over the status of Bonnie Prince Charlie is not a matter of historical debate, but of present loyalties. While their rather romantic attachment to the layers of history surrounding them is endearing, perhaps even poetic, in a much harsher sense the Cauldwells are living in the past. A more prosaic concern emerges in the second act when Christine reveals that the farm as a business is no longer a viable entity and in the third act when squabbles over accounts, the costs of bed and breakfast and discrimination against farmers are introduced. Regardless of longevity of the family's claim to their land, or of the fertility of their imaginations, the closing impression is of futility – the Cauldwells, buried in debt, are likely to become just another forgotten contour in the dark earth of the region. In concordance with this view Berton-Charrière reads the play as a political critique of forms of Scottish identity and the disintegration of the fiction of national unity into 'a constellation of egocentric, individual elements'.[15]

Reception of the play was relatively polarised. As Michael Billington remarks in his review, it 'eventually falls uneasily between economic parable and romantic myth'. He felt 'that Harrower had led us up the mystic garden path only to return us to the world of material fact. One is left with a strong sense of two mutually uncomprehending cultures.'[16] *Encore Theatre Magazine* by contrast describes the play as 'a tautly constructed thriller' and although admitting the final twenty minutes are less successful, claims 'the first act is one of the most perfect pieces of playcraft in years'.[17] Peculiarly, the *Evening Standard* described the play as a 'comedy of manners', while the *Culture Wars* reviewer praised it as 'an impressive piece, with an intricately crafted plot, generous characterisation, wonderfully subtle humour and an ambitious thematic scope'.[18]

Blackbird (2005)

A young woman in her late twenties and a man in his mid-fifties meet in an anonymous office staff common room. The young woman has sought him out after accidentally seeing his photo in a trade magazine. She seems to have come to confront him; he is anxious not to be alone with her in a closed room. It soon emerges that fifteen years previously the two had had a sexual relationship – when she was twelve, and he was forty. This is the scenario for *Blackbird*, which was commissioned for the Edinburgh International Festival and premiered at the King's Theatre on 15 August 2005, directed by Peter Stein. The combination of controversial subject matter, a major theatre festival and a high-profile director meant that *Blackbird* attracted considerable media attention and has since travelled extensively.

The play is partly derived from a 2003 child abuse case. Thirty-one-year-old American, Toby Studebaker, groomed a twelve-year-old British girl over the internet before running away with her to Paris to have sex. After five days in Europe with Studebaker, the girl returned to her parents of her own will, while he was arrested and later jailed for abducting and sexually exploiting a minor. What appealed to Harrower was the way in which Studebaker 'still went through with going away with her as if he was thinking he would test the limits of the moral world'.[19] According to Stein, when he met Harrower with an early draft of the play he shared his own experience of 'a devouring love for a younger woman', encouraging the playwright to structure the work around 'a metaphor of love. It must be about leaving. That is the problem of love. It starts, then it dies. Or you leave.'[20] It is not insignificant that neither Harrower nor Stein uses the word paedophilia (in an interview for *Theatrevoice* the first word Harrower uses for the relationship is 'affair'; Stein prefers to talk about love). Studebaker notwithstanding, Nabokov's *Lolita* is the more immediate point of reference, even though Stein denies this.[21]

Throughout, the play sustains an acute level of ambivalence and emotional tension. Una's purpose in meeting with Peter, who now calls himself Ray, is unclear. Is she there to trap him, to oblige him to apologise, to kill him or to seduce him? His reaction to her is initially fearful and defensive. Harrower harnesses the dramatic energy of taboo as the characters reel through emotions ranging from rage to guilt to desire and disgust. The stark force of the dialogues, the potent sense of the inadequacy of language to capture complex and contradictory emotions and lapses into silence showcase Harrower's writerly aptitude, last fully witnessed in *Knives in Hens*. Pace is modulated not only by the varying nature of exchange, but also through the strategic use of monologue. In establishing their versions of the past, Una and Ray each deliver compelling, uninterrupted speeches. Una's precedes Ray's and is considerably longer – her voice was the one silenced by official authority before, now she is determined to be heard. Chillingly she describes her intense feeling of abandonment, rather than the expected sense of violation: 'You left me alone. Bleeding. You left me. You left me in love' (p. 59). The accusatory tenor of her monologue is countered by Ray's defence of his actions, his declaration of his intention to return. In reconstructing their memories and emotions, both Una and Ray figuratively return to the courtroom and dissect their actions in a manner impossible during the investigation and trial fifteen years previously.

What follows is arguably the play's *coup de théâtre* – there is an unexplained blackout. As Daniel Schlusser notes in his review of the Edinburgh and Berlin productions of the play, this moment can be rendered to produce powerfully differing effects. In Stein's production the sense that the blackout in the fictional world of the play functions as a metaphor for Una's situation in the past and present cystallised. In Benedict Andrews's Schaubühne premiere of the play the blackout was extended, leaving the audience in doubt as to whether there really had been a power cut, thus creating the feeling of 'disorientation and powerlessness' just articulated by Una in her monologue.[22]

Harrower furnishes the play with a number of suggestive images that expressively echo its themes. Most evident is the rubbish-strewn set which functions metaphorically to recall the emotional mess of the half-finished encounter that yokes the characters' destinies. Ominously the cathartic outburst as they kick the contents of the overflowing bin around the room segues into tentative sexual contact in the midst of the debris they have just scattered around. The gesture is physically initiated and then halted by Ray. Again, his actions can be interpreted in hugely divergent ways – is he just a pathetic older man suffering from impotence, is he actively tearing away from the past, or as Una brutally remarks, 'Am I too old?' (p. 81). The play's title also unfolds a set of polymorphous symbolic possibilities. In Biblical terms black birds, more specifically ravens, are associated with retribution and responsible for pecking out the eyes of sinners (Proverbs 30.17 and Isaiah 34.11). This chimes with Ray's discomfort at the beginning of the play when he compulsively rubs his reddened eyes. Albert Williams's review of the Chicago production of the play notes the use of Paul McCartney's 1968 song 'Blackbird', whose lyrics provide an apt account of the traumatised Una, as opening music.[23]

At the core of *Blackbird*'s disturbing energy is the radical unde-cidability of Una's character. The play is deliberately provocative in the questions it raises, yet ironically it is Ray, the paedophile, who emerges as the more readable, even mildly sympathetic, character. As she states herself, Una's whole life has been shaped by the experience. Ray's plea that he is 'entitled to something. To live' (p. 28), to forget, is ferociously rebuffed:

I did the sentence. I did your sentence. For fifteen years. I lost everything. I lost more than you ever did. I lost because I never had time to *begin*. [. . .] I *kept* my name. [. . .] I re-live it every day. (p. 28)

Even as the play delicately balances the characters' positions, the elliptical suggestion of the spurned female as mortal threat is naggingly present. Peter's illicit sexual desire for a child is softened by the suggestion that she was, like Lolita, wise beyond her years, a provocateur who led him astray. Stein asserts that 'it's a play about love', but then somewhat contradictorily goes on to claim that 'It's also about a world where 12-year-olds are treated as consumers, where advertising uses sex as a means of enticement and where kids have easy access to internet porn', introducing the suggestion of a social critique that is frankly absent both in the play and in his production of it.[24] Rather, the child Una is represented as endowed with adult agency and self-aware sexuality, while Peter's responsibility as an adult *not* to respond is obscured by the assertion of consensual love. When she returns as an adult, Una is a manipulative, damaged force of destruction. Notably Stein's production altered the play's conclusion. The littered office setting is removed and the final moments of the play are relocated to a car park where Una and Ray physically wrestle with each other in a dramatic finale. The closing image is of raw mortal combat. The play text offers a less sensational though more desolate conclusion, as Ray shoves Una aside as he flees to join his partner and her daughter. Perhaps inspired by Stein's directorial treatment, American director Stuart Carden remarked, 'In many ways, it's a car wreck of a play. You feel a simultaneous impulse to look and look away.'[25] Charged with grim visceral emotion, *Blackbird* is a mesmerising work.

Summary

No unifying set of concerns can be easily identified in Harrower's work. Consequently, although he is frequently mentioned in academic works on British or Scottish theatre, often this is little more than name-checking or brief explanatory discussion. Aleks Sierz, for instance, discusses Harrower's *Knives in Hens* in the final chapter of *In-Yer-Face Theatre*, focusing upon violence and language. Contrasting its aesthetics with 'in-yer-face' drama, Sierz describes how the play's violence is 'shrouded in words [. . .] the intense and sensuous language, and the production's restrained mime of the killing, distanced the audience'.[26] Jean-Pierre Simard likewise produced a reading of *Knives in Hens* focused on the poetic tools of initiation in a 2001 issue of *Études écossaises*. Dominic Dromgoole gives Harrower a chapter in *The Full Room*, offering an impressionistic account of *Knives in Hens*, and defending *Kill the Old Torture Their Young* as 'wholly original and wholly refreshing'.[27] More recently, Ian Brown's chapter on contemporary Scottish theatre in *The Edinburgh History of Scottish Literature* portrays Harrower as 'a leading member' of his generation and concisely surveys his plays with the exception of *Presence*, devoting most space to an appraisal of *Blackbird*. For Brown, Harrower deals – sometimes with bleak comedy – with the irresistible and irresoluble conflict between passion and accepted mores, the subversion of reason, the new rationalisations constantly invented to justify the unreasonable and the pain of the unachievable and deeply desired.[28]

Christina Wald, defining the term Trauma Drama, notes *Blackbird* among a burgeoning list of plays about sexual child abuse.[29] Caridad Svich, in a review of Joe Mantello's production of *Blackbird* in New York, also comments on the genre of the play as Trauma Drama, suggesting nevertheless that

it manages primarily by virtue of Harrower's forceful and elliptical way with language to skirt the queasy comfort of the familiar. For Harrower, as in his previous works [. . .], language is not in concert with but rather at odds with nature and the body. The erotic charge in his work, thus, comes from the disjunction between thought and action, and in inchoate and perhaps unreliable manifestation of feeling.[30]

Harrower's adept and evocative use of language is regularly highlighted in various reviews and is given some welcome sustained attention by Alison Croggon in her appraisal of a recent Australian production of *Knives in Hens*.[31]

In the work that pertains to Scotland what can be observed is a deconstructive attitude to existing notions of Scottish identity. As David Pattie contends, one might see the work of Harrower, Chris Hannan, Stephen Greenhorn, Gregory Burke and David Greig as:

creat[ing] a composite image, not only of Scotland, but also of the contemporary nation-state, that does not trade on the idea that a country's essential qualities can be revealed through the study of its people and the societies they create. Rather, their work tends to suggest that national and cultural identity is always in the process of formation, that it is always up for grabs, and that any attempt to arrive at a final definition of identity [. . .] will be doomed to failure.[32]

Pattie goes on to discuss *Dark Earth* in terms of a post-devolution need to re-map Scotland. The play's characters

> are forced into sharp opposition because the versions of Scotland they inhabit cannot be reconciled [and ultimately] the elements that split one Scotland from the other [are] not history or culture, so much as class and income.[33]

Questions of historical continuity and rupture, tradition and innovation and contemporary Scottish identity are teased out in various articles by Jean-Pierre Simard in his work on Scottish theatre and with respect to Harrower specifically, and by Danièle Berton-Charrière in an essay on *Dark Earth*.[34]

As a playwright and adaptor, Harrower's position within English and Scottish theatre seems assured. Since his debut he has had the strong support of the Traverse Theatre and a successful relationship with a number of major theatres in London. While this career in terms of his own writing has been a good deal more modest than the accomplishment of *Knives in Hens*, the immense success and publicity surrounding *Blackbird* has clearly rebooted his profile as a playwright of talent.

Primary Sources

Works by David Harrower

Knives in Hens (1995; London: Methuen Drama, 1997).
Kill the Old Torture Their Young (London: Methuen Drama, 1998).
Presence (London: Faber & Faber, 2001).
Dark Earth (London: Faber & Faber, 2003).
Blackbird (London: Faber & Faber, 2005).

Secondary Sources

Anon., 'Critics' Guide to the Fringe', *Evening Standard*, 1 August 2003 <http://www.thisislondon.co.uk/theatre/article-6036557-critics-guide-to-the-fringe.do>

—, 'Edinburgh Shrapnel', *Encore Theatre Magazine* website, 23 September 2003 <www.encoretheatremagazine.co.uk>

—, '12 Key Scottish Plays 1970–2010', National Library of Scotland, <www.nls.uk/Scottish-theatre/knives-in-hens/index.html>

Augé, Marc, *Non-Places: Introduction to an Anthropology of Supermodernity*, trans. John Howe (London: Verso, 1995).

Berton-Charrière, Danièle, 'Parcours et détours en Écosse *Dark Earth* de David Harrower', *Études écossaises*, No. 10 (2005), pp. 205–16.

Billington, Michael, 'I Don't Read New Work', *Guardian*, 15 August 2005 <http://www.guardian.co.uk/stage/2005/aug/15/theatre.edinburghfestival20055>

Brown, Ian, 'Staging the Nation: Multiplicity and Cultural Diversity in Contemporary Scottish Theatre', in Ian Brown et al. (eds), *The Edinburgh History of Scottish Literature Volume 3, Modern Transformations: New Identities (from 1918)* (Edinburgh: EUP, 2007), pp. 283–94.

Carter, Alice T., 'City Theatre Set to Ruffle Feathers with *Blackbird*', *Pittsburgh Tribune Review*, 11 November 2009 <http://www.pittsburghlive.com/x/pittsburghtrib/ae/theater/s_652702.html>

Colebrook, Claire, *Understanding Deleuze* (Crows Nest, NSW: Allen & Unwin, 2002).

Croggon, Alison, Review of *Knives in Hens*, *Australian*, 13 August 2009 <http://theatrenotes.blogspot.com>

Deleuze, Gilles, *The Fold: Leibniz and the Baroque*, trans. Tom Conley (Minneapolis: Minnesota UP, 1993).

Dromgoole, Dominic, *The Full Room: An A–Z of Contemporary Playwriting* (London: Methuen Drama, 2002).

Fisher, Philip, 'Interview with David Harrower', *Theatrevoice* website, 12 August 2005 <http://www.theatrevoice.com/listen_now/player/?audioID=328>

Jones, Sarah, 'Controversial Play Hits the West End', *Independent*, 12 January 2006 <http://www.independent.co.uk/arts-entertainment/theatre-dance/features/controversial-play-hits-the-west-end-522653.html>

Kellaway, Kate, 'The Director Who Invited His Whole Cast to Tuscany', *Observer*, 5 February 2005 <http://www.guardian.co.uk/stage/2006/feb/05/theatre>

Logan, Brian, 'I'm Tired of Telling Well Crafted Stories', *Guardian*, 18 April 2001 <http://www.guardian.co.uk/culture/2001/apr/18/artsfeatures>

Markham, Tim, Review of *Dark Earth*, *Culture Wars* website, 2003 <www.culturwars.co.uk/edinburgh2003/Edinburgh2003.htm>

Pattie, David, '"Mapping the Territory": Modern Scottish Drama', in Rebecca D'Monté and Graham Saunders (eds), *Cool Britannia: British Political Drama in the 1990s* (Basingstoke: Palgrave Macmillan, 2008), pp. 143–57.

Preminger, Alex, Frank J. Warnke and O. B. Harrison (eds), *Princeton Encyclopedia of Poetry and Poetics* (Princeton, NJ: PUP, 1965).

Raab, Michael, 'Kryptischer Schotte: Porträt David Harrower', *Die Deutsche Bühne*, Vol. 81, No. 5 (2010), pp. 45–7.

Schlusser, Daniel, 'Two Ways of Looking at *Blackbird*', *Realtime*, No. 71 (2006), p. 10.

Sierz, Aleks, *In-Yer-Face Theatre: British Drama Today* (London: Faber & Faber, 2000).

Simard, Jean-Pierre, 'Irrationel et étrange, outil poétique de l'initiation dans *Knives in Hens* de D. Harrower', *Études écossaises*, No. 7 (2001), pp. 83–96.

—, 'Populaire, politique et poétique réévaluer la réputation du théâtre Écossais', *Études écossaises*, No. 10 (2005), pp. 187–201.

—, 'Rupture et continuité, le théâtre Écossais au passage du millénaire', *Cycnos*, Vol. 18, No. 1 (2008) <http://revel.unice.fr/cycnos/index.html?id=1687>

Svich, Caridad, 'Ordinary Sites of Transgression', *PAJ: A Journal of Performance and Art*, Vol. 30, No. 2 (2008), pp. 88–92.

Wald, Christina, *Hysteria, Trauma and Melancholia: Performative Maladies in Contemporary Anglophone Drama* (Basingstoke: Palgrave Macmillan, 2007).

Williams, Albert, 'In David Harrower's *Blackbird*, It's Complicated', *Chicago Reader*, 23 July 2009 <http://www.chicagoreader.com/chicago/in-david-harrowers-blackbird-its-complicated/Content?oid=1165696>

Notes

1. Jean-Pierre Simard, 'Populaire, politique et poétique réévaluer la réputation du théâtre Écossais', p. 187.
2. Anon., '12 Key Scottish Plays 1970–2010'.
3. Philip Fisher, 'Interview with David Harrower'.
4. Ibid.
5. Alison Croggon, Review of *Knives in Hens*.
6. Mark Fisher, *Guardian*, 11 February 2005 <http://www.guardian.co.uk/stage/2005/feb/11/theatre1>
7. Alex Preminger, Frank J. Warnke and O. B. Hardison (eds), *Princeton Encyclopedia of Poetry and Poetics*, pp. 490–5, provides an extended survey of definitions and debates around this trope.
8. Michael Raab, 'Kryptischer Schotte', p. 45. Thanks to Natascha Brakop for the translation. a
9. Marc Augé, *Non-Places*, pp. 33–4.
10. Brian Logan, 'I'm Tired of Telling Well Crafted Stories'; Susannah Clapp, *Observer*, *Theatre Record*, Vol. XXI, No. 9 (2001), p. 526.

11. Michael Billington, *Guardian, Theatre Record*, Vol. XXI, No. 9 (2001), p. 528.

12. Danièle Berton-Charrière, 'Parcours et détours en Écosse *Dark Earth* de David Harrower', p. 205.

13. Ian Brown, 'Staging the Nation', p. 292.

14. See Gilles Deleuze, *The Fold*; Claire Colebrook, *Understanding Deleuze*, p. 54.

15. Berton-Charrière, 'Parcours et détours en Écosse *Dark Earth* de David Harrower', p. 216.

16. Michael Billington, *Guardian, Theatre Record*, Vol. XXIII, No. 18 (2003), 'Edinburgh Supplement', pp. 1099–100.

17. Anon., 'Edinburgh Shrapnel'.

18. Anon., 'Critics' Guide to the Fringe'; Tim Markham, Review of *Dark Earth*.

19. Kate Kellaway, 'The Director Who Invited His Whole Cast to Tuscany'.

20. Ibid.

21. Fisher, 'Interview with David Harrower'; Michael Billington, 'I Don't Read New Work'.

22. Daniel Schlusser, 'Two Ways of Looking at *Blackbird*'.

23. Albert Williams, 'In David Harrower's *Blackbird*, It's Complicated'.

24. Billington, 'I Don't Read New Work'.

25. Alice T. Carter, 'City Theatre Set to Ruffle Feathers with *Blackbird*'.

26. Aleks Sierz, *In-Yer-Face Theatre*, p. 208.

27. Dominic Dromgoole, *The Full Room*, p. 137.

28. Brown, 'Staging the Nation', p. 292.

29. Christina Wald, *Hysteria, Trauma and Melancholia*, p. 100.

30. Caridad Svich, 'Ordinary Sites of Transgression', p. 88.

31. Croggon, Review of *Knives in Hens*.

32. David Pattie, 'Mapping the Territory', pp. 144–5.

33. Ibid., pp. 154–5.

34. See Simard, 'Populaire, politique et poétique réévaluer la réputation du théâtre Écossais', and Berton-Charrière, 'Parcours et détours en Écosse *Dark Earth* de David Harrower'.

14 JONATHAN HARVEY

Peter Paul Schnierer

Beautiful Thing; Rupert Street Lonely Hearts Club; Guiding Star; Hushabye Mountain; Canary

Introduction

Jonathan Harvey was born in Liverpool in 1968 to parents working in welfare and education; he himself trained (and worked for some time) as a secondary-school teacher. His theatrical career took off early: *The Cherry Blossom Tree* won the Liverpool Playhouse/National Girobank Young Writers' Award in 1987 and was staged at the Playhouse that year. One year later, *Mohair*, an Ulster tragedy, was the first of his plays to be produced by the Royal Court Theatre, with *Wildfire* (1992) and *Babies* (1994) to follow. The latter won the *Evening Standard* Award for Most Promising Playwright and the George Devine Award; that year, Harvey also received a nomination for Lloyds Bank Playwright of the Year. Other early plays include *Catch* (1989), produced at Spring Street Theatre in Hull, *Tripping and Falling*, produced by the Glasshouse Theatre Company in Manchester in 1990, and *Lady Snogs the Blues* at the Lincoln Theatre Festival in 1991.

 Beautiful Thing, his greatest critical success to date, followed in 1993. It was staged at the tiny Bush Theatre in west London and became one of the key plays of the decade. The venue's artistic director, Dominic Dromgoole, describes its immediate impact:

> It was more as if some large hand took hold of the little black box the hundred people sat in, wrenched it out of the old Victorian building that surrounded it, took it out above London, above its theatrical and social context, and chucked

> it hard and high up into the stars, where it floated around for
> a couple of hours, exhilarated by the view.[1]

Harvey repaid the compliment by praising Dromgoole for having 'good taste. Good taste in scripts. Good taste in marrying writers with directors. Good taste in knowing which actors would suit the intimacy of the space.'[2] *Beautiful Thing* was a huge success, being made into a film in 1996, and exerting a strong influence on other emerging playwrights. Harvey's other plays, which usually feature a mix of funny one-liners and wry observation (often with the pervading theme of death), include *Boom Bang-a-Bang* (1995), *Rupert Street Lonely Hearts Club* (Contact, Manchester, 1995), *Swan Song* (1997), *Hushabye Mountain* (Hampstead, 1999), *Out in the Open* (Hampstead/ Birmingham Rep, 2001) and *Canary* (Liverpool/Hampstead, 2010). At the same time, his work has also concentrated on television, notably the three series of *Gimme Gimme Gimme* (BBC, 1999–2001) and the two seasons of *Beautiful People* (BBC, 2008–09). He wrote both scripts on his own; contributions to other shows include scripts for *Coronation Street* (ITV, 2004–07). Harvey also was responsible for the libretto of the Pet Shop Boys' musical *Closer to Heaven* (2001), a venture that met with almost universal panning by the critics; a typical comment was: 'What sinks the show is the crudity of Harvey's book.'[3] The musical did not bomb; it is characteristic of Harvey's work that continued success with the public is at odds with marked – and increasing – scepticism on the part of his reviewers. All his plays opened to mixed reviews; he satisfies neither the theatregoer in search of nothing but uncomplicated laughs nor the literary critic keen on postmodernist deconstructions. It is this middle ground that he occupies so well.

The Plays

Beautiful Thing (1993)

The first performance of *Beautiful Thing* took place on 28 July 1993 at the Bush Theatre. It was directed by Hettie Macdonald and won the John Whiting Award as well as being nominated for an Olivier and a Writers' Guild Award. It had 'particular cachet at the time of its production because of the campaign to reduce the age of homosexual consensual sex to 16'.[4] The play is the first in a series set in south-east London. To the playgoers in Shepherd's Bush as well as in the Donmar Warehouse, where the play was revived in 1994, and in the Duke of York's Theatre, where it saw its West End transfer later the same year, this location fairly reliably signals working-class conditions and characters, fruity speech and rude, fast wit as well as a world that has little to do with the rest of London. Here a young lad is reading from *Hello!*, a magazine peddling celebrity gossip:

> **Jamie**   [. . .] Her partner is another actor, but she is coy about revealing his name. Saturdays are spent shopping and eating out, and Sundays are set aside for catching up with old friends or taking long strolls on Hampstead Heath which her flat overlooks.
> *Pause.*
> **Ste**   That's north of the river, innit?
> **Jamie**   Mm. (p. 31)

The action of the play is set on the landing walkway of a Thamesmead council estate, with three doors leading into three off-stage flats – an ingenious version of the multi-door interiors of the drawing-room comedy. Three of the five characters are sixteen-year-olds: Jamie, Leah and Ste. Jamie's mother Sandra and her young lover Tony complete the on-stage cast; Ste's father Ronny is occasionally heard cursing but never appears. The plot is hardly more than one event; when Ste flees domestic violence Sandra offers him a share of Jamie's bed, and both boys quickly discover their homosexuality. The play ends with Sandra and the boys moving out of the estate, presumably into a future that is equally straitened economically, but sexually and socially more liberated and at ease.

The play was an immediate and resounding success. At first glance this is difficult to justify: its plot is flimsy, the story hardly original and its poetical appeal, if it has any at all, rests solely on the south-east London cockiness with which the characters banter, curse and make love. Yet this in itself provided a welcome counterweight to the incipient wave of cheerless theatre nasties of the time: the language of *Beautiful Thing* is rich with four-letter words, but these do not amount to the aggressive drone of an early Ravenhill play. They rather serve a form of good-humoured realism: while the play is not without its share of south-of-the-river clichés, its language carefully captures the inflections of Plumstead, Woolwich and Deptford. All partake in this; none of the characters is in any way linguistically handicapped. In fact, the sitcom writer's facility with one-liners is evident in the speech of almost all characters in any Harvey play. In *Beautiful Thing* one can almost quote at random:

> **Leah** It's disgustin', innit? When men dribble. You wanna use a cloth, Jamie.
> **Sandra** (*to* **Leah**) First decent thing you've said all day, girl.
> **Jamie** Shut up.
> **Tony** Men of the cloth. (*Sniggers.*)
> **Jamie** (*tuts*) Oh, shut up!
> **Sandra** Oi! Manners!
> **Jamie** Me mother never taught me none!
> **Sandra** Er, she taught you please and thank you and respect God's creatures, so keep your trap shut.
> **Jamie** Shut up.
> **Sandra** Shut up? Shut up? You're killing the art o'conversation you are.
> **Jamie** What conversation? No one gets a word in edgeways with you around.
> **Sandra** Inn'e a wit, eh? Inn'e a laugh? Eh? Makes me die he does.
> **Jamie** That IS the intention. (p. 41)

That is the way conflict is negotiated in Harvey's Thamesmead. Seen against the background of the theatre of Sarah Kane, Mark Ravenhill and Anthony Neilson, the most remarkable feature of *Beautiful Thing* (and Harvey's plays in general, with the most notable exception of *Canary*) is the simultaneous ubiquity and absence of violence. The play's characters continually threaten each other, give each other cuffs, punches and 'wallops', but these, even in the following scene, are the physical equivalent of their robust banter:

> *She slaps him across the face. He slaps her back. She lays into him, fists flying. He holds his hands up to his face, protecting himself. She's not giving up so he hits back. They fight like cat and dog, knocking* **Ste***'s washing over in the process. Finally* **Sandra** *is sitting on* **Jamie***'s chest, a fierce look in her eyes. This dissolves to tears. She weakens her grip.* **Jamie** *pushes her off. He goes and sits in one of the patio chairs.* (p. 45)

The real violence that motivates the play – the 'leatherings' Ste receives at the hands of his father Ronny and presumably of his brother Trevor, as well as the vicious beating Sandra once suffered – are only reported. Remarkably, for a coming-out play by a self-proclaimed gay writer of Harvey's stature, none of this violence is homophobic. In fact, much of the fairy tale colouring that divided critics is due to the benevolent attitude all on-stage characters take towards homosexuality. Far from triggering prejudice and hostility, Ste and Jamie's coming-out furnishes material for more verbal fireworks:

> **Sandra**   You're pissed.
> **Jamie**   No I'm not.
> **Sandra**   Pissed from a bloody gay bar!
> **Jamie**   How d'you know it's gay anyway?
> **Sandra**   Coz it's got a bloody great big pink neon arse outside of it. Jamie, I'm in the business, I get to know these things! (p. 70)

Harvey acknowledges the wishful thinking motivating the characterisation of Sandra; there may be such indulgent mothers, but she owes her existence to a sense that the stage can purvey a higher and more satisfactory truth than the world outside the theatre. In that sense, the ending is not so much camp as truthful:

> *The music turns up of its own accord, blasting out. A glitterball spins above the stage, casting millions of dance hall lights.* **Ste** *and* **Jamie** *are dancing.* **Leah** *and* **Sandra** *are dancing. The lights fade.* (p. 90)

Scenes such as these were the cause for the consensus emerging quickly from the critics, i.e. that the play is close to soapiness but well done. Lyn Gardner's description of it as an 'urban fairy tale' is indicative of the general esteem the play has been held in ever since;[5] Benedict Nightingale was the only one to cavil at the ending: 'The Harvey who wrote that is, I fear, a wishful thinker or didactic dreamer, not the disinterested observer he has hitherto seemed.'[6] Yes, but there is nothing inherently wrong with both dreams and didacticism; they have always been pillars of a theatre of empowerment – the former in the British tradition, the latter on the Continent. Together they allow the theatre to become a forum for what might be and what ought to be – the continuing revivals of the play document this undiminished appeal.

Rupert Street Lonely Hearts Club (1995)

After its initial run at the Contact Theatre, Manchester, where it opened on 27 September 1995, the play was transferred to the Donmar Warehouse in London. The Donmar has limited runs; successful productions need to clear the stage nevertheless after six weeks or so. If they are commercially viable for at least some more months they are moved to another venue, typically in the West End. The transfer of *Rupert Street Lonely Hearts Club*, directed by John Burgess, to the Criterion Theatre therefore is indicative of the public success it enjoyed. Even the critics were more lenient his time: it won the *Manchester Evening News* Award for Best New Play.

Rupert Street Lonely Hearts Club is set in east London, just a little to the north of the housing estates of *Beautiful Thing* and *Babies*, and quite a distance (in metropolitan terms) from the Kentish Town flat of *Boom Bang-a-Bang*. By then Harvey had established himself very much as a local-colour playwright, although it has to be noted that the sense of place that emanates from *Beautiful Thing* is less compelling in his later plays. This may have to do with his indoor settings: all we get to see of Rupert Street is the inside of a bedsit that might just as well be in Liverpool, where the two central characters come from, or New York, for that matter. Straightforward references apart, places are primarily evoked by the accents used, but even here the 'broad London accent' (p. 281) of one character is contrasted with those of another:

> **Clarine**, *twenty-eight, quite portly. She has a repertoire of different personalities, and although she is from Kidderminster, she speaks usually in either a London or a Rochdale accent.*
> (p. 281)

Clarine's unpredictable switchings between these personalities and voices constitute a focus of interest and mystery in an otherwise almost eventless play. It is perhaps the best example of Harvey's preference for unspectacular, even attenuated plots. In its seven scenes Shaun, a twenty-three-year-old hairdresser whose girlfriend is currently abroad, is variously visited in his bedsit by four other characters. Together, without ever fully spelling out their similarities, they make up the lonely hearts club of the play's title. George still has not fully come to terms with the separation from her boyfriend Malcolm, one of a group of physically absent characters. Shaun's elder brother Marti cannot find love in the darkrooms he frequents; the bondage harness he reveals upon changing his wet clothes can be seen as a symbol of hedonism but also of constraints and limitations – although Harvey's sense of theatricality ensures that there is scope for laughter, too. Similarly, when Marti's companion Dean enters, he '*is dressed up as Fifi Trixabelle La Bouche, glamorous sex kitten. His feminine get-up is convincing, but he has the voice of a navvy*' (p. 305). Again, Harvey generates much comic potential later in the play from this clash of signals: Dean combines camp mockery and sophistication with a set of crude right-wing prejudices in a way that can either be seen as sad floundering amid incompatible social expectations and personal needs, or as outrageous comedy.

> **Dean**   Yeah, well, if you vegetarians got off your fat arses and ate a bit o'meat instead o'being a bunch o'no-hope ponces, you'd be putting people in work. So I think you better think again before you start ramming paranoia down people's throats.
>
> **Shaun**   I don't impose my views on anyone.
>
> **Dean**   Good. Coz no cunt'd listen to you. This country's fed up of people like you. Do this, do that. You're a bunch o'champion wankers. No offence. (p. 315)

The fact that Harvey manages to keep the balance between these two extremes is one of the charms of this quiet, careful play. When Marti, in the final minutes, suddenly attempts to commit suicide by slitting his wrists, the act is almost unprepared yet uncontrived; evidently, we still know far too little about what makes these characters go on or despair. Marti, had he been left alone with his brother's shocked lethargy, would have died; their incessant re-enactment of old Hollywood weepies has made them jointly unfit for life in the present, it seems. As it is, Marti survives due to Clarine's decisive action, calling an ambulance and administering first aid simultaneously. The one character who seemed utterly in denial, fantasising about rats and performing rather dubious religious songs, suddenly faces up to the incontrovertible demands of reality. That is a strong ending.

Some reviewers found the play too melodramatic for their tastes, others were more indulgent: they frequently compared the play to film director Mike Leigh's work (whom Harvey admires) and saw darker, more compelling writing, still weak on plot but good on one-liners and occasional insight into characters.[7] That is a fair summary both of the play's effects and of the development Harvey's writing took from there.

Guiding Star (1998)

Harvey's most topical play was first performed in London, at the National Theatre's Cottesloe auditorium, directed by Gemma Bodinetz, on 11 November 1998, and thus almost ten years after the events that triggered it. In 1989, during the FA Cup semi-final between Liverpool and Nottingham at Hillsborough Stadium in Sheffield, ninety-six people were crushed to death when panic broke out in the crowd. The British tabloid the *Sun* disgraced itself by misreporting the alleged inhumanity of the survivors. This was the immediate incitement for Harvey's play:

> I knew the reality to be different and, in *Guiding Star*, wanted to show how the tragedy affected an ordinary family. An ordinary family where in fact no one died. Yet, nearly ten years later, Terry Fitzgibbon hasn't shaken off the haunting images from that day. That day has shaped his family's development ever since.[8]

These lines are almost sufficient as a plot outline. As always in Harvey's earlier plays the focus is less on outward action than on the mental and verbal reactions of a set of protagonists to the dramatic experiences of the past and the pressures held in store for them by their environment. Almost always, these are related to (homo-)sexuality; this play is no exception, although the coming-out plot revolving around Terry's son Liam is badly integrated and actually superfluous to the play's negotiation of trauma. Terry found his two young sons alive amid the Hillsborough wreckage; he may – inadvertently and unavoidably – have trampled another child in the crush. His neighbours Marni and Charlie lose their terminally ill teenage son Wayne in the first act; the entire rest of the play shows the gradual and painful process of measuring the enormity of grief – the coming to terms with it will come later, but it will probably come:

Charlie Death doesn't scare me.
Terry After all . . . that little lad. When we . . . I could tell

he was a young lad coz of his voice. Shouting for his mam. Me foot was on his chest. I couldn't see him. Then the safety barrier went and we all ended up on top of him. The life squoze out of him. Don't be funny about your Wayne, when . . . that poor fucking kid. (p. 48)

Straight or gay, in London or Liverpool, Harvey tends to put young people centre stage. Parents are frequent, too, as sometimes abusive, often supportive characters, but they are almost always enabling figures, there to further their offspring's plot. *Guiding Star* is different; here the parents have more stage time, are more eloquent, and they go to greater lengths to make sense of their world. Everybody in the play keeps referring to their own and other characters' ages, but somehow the biologically older ones seem more innocent and less cynical. While Terry's wife Carol needs a mirror to convince her that she is not eighteen any more, her seventeen-year-old son and his slightly older girlfriend have little truck with romantic moods:

Gina Well, what's that one called? The big bright fuck-off one at the top.
Laurence That's the guiding star.
Gina The what? Never heard of it.
Laurence So me dad says.
Gina Your dad? And you believe him? Feel a cunt for yeh.
(p. 66)

Harvey himself, in his Introduction to the play, has characterised Gina as 'spout[ing] the psychobabble she has heard on daytime confessional shows while completely unaware of the very real pain surrounding her'.[9] Yet Gina is not a caricature, nor is she a failed attempt by a gay playwright to engage with female psychology, but a credible portrait of a badly neglected young girl. The comparison with Kevin Elyot that is sometimes made in reviews of Harvey's plays – two contemporary gay writers of tragi-comic, conversation-heavy plays about gays in the time of AIDS – falls short when it comes to female characters; Harvey is much more interested in them and often shows them to be saner and more capable of compassion. A better comparison, odd as it may sound at first, is that with Sean O'Casey. Harvey's plays may not be full of paycocks, but they have their Junos.

As usual, the reviews were mixed. The adjective used most frequently to describe *Guiding Star* was 'mediocre' and one reviewer saw 'a play which rarely resists cheap tears, mawkishness, deadly clichés and the flamboyant wearing of hurt hearts on sleeves'.[10] Michael Coveney, however, called it 'one of the best new plays of the year'.[11] It certainly is Harvey's most compassionate one.

Hushabye Mountain (1999)

The play, directed by Paul Miller, was first performed in the Lyceum Theatre, Crewe, on 3 February 1999, before going on a national tour. *Hushabye Mountain* was a conscious departure:

> Sam [Mendes] instructed me to free my mind and take risks. My previous plays there had been one-set, five-actor plays. He told me to think bigger than this and so I did. With *Hushabye Mountain* I decided to play around with time, setting, reality, memories.[12]

Harvey certainly used the new opportunities, although the envisaged production by Mendes for the Donmar Warehouse eventually fell through. His play requires the cast to change roles constantly, mixing real characters with imaginary (yet not less efficacious) figures. To demonstrate the break between this play and its predecessors it is best to quote the list of dramatis personae in full:

Danny May, *thirty, a waiter from Liverpool who has recently died from an AIDS-related illness.*
Connor Bond, *late twenties, Londoner. Danny's boyfriend.*
Lee Bond, *early thirties, Connor's brother. A cycle courier.*
Lana Bond, *thirty. Liam's middle-class wife. A red-haired, anxious PR assistant.*
Beryl May, *fifty. Danny's mum.*

Ben, *twenty-three, northern gardener and part-time actor. Diagnosed HIV-positive in his late teens.*

Judy Garland, *a dark-haired actress and singer who could be thirty or sixty. Currently employed as the Keeper of the Stars in Heaven.*

Kevin, *early twenties, Glaswegian. Beryl's nurse.*

Julie Andrews, *a hotel chambermaid with exquisite diction.*

The Virgin Mary, *a chain-smoking Irish celebrity mum.*

Sister Bernadette, *an elderly deaf nun.*

Priest

Spirit of Esther Finnegan, *a stern primary-school teacher.*

Bird Woman, *a character from* Mary Poppins.

Two Pearly Gates Attendants

Two Dead People, *recent arrivals in heaven.* (p. 117)

The first four of these form the core of the play, which can, after all, be performed by a mere six actors. Again there is no plot to speak of. Flashbacks to happier days alternate with scenes in which the survivors try to cope with Danny's death. These scenes are intercut with fantastic exchanges at the Pearly Gates in which Judy Garland appears and offers her services as psychopompos (soul-guide) to Danny. She does not seem to be quite sure what she is doing, though, and certainly is less than omnipotent:

> *The overture from* Mary Poppins *starts to play. A bright light, then* **Connor** *and* **Lana** *appear, walking on the water, dressed head to toe in white, dressed as the attendants of the pearly gates. They carry clipboards. They look up to* **Danny** *and smile.*
>
> **Judy**   Has he been passed? Has he been passed?
>
> **Connor**   Danny! It's me! Connor!
>
> **Danny**   Connor!
>
> **Judy**   Hey! Who's fuckin' fantasy is this?! (p. 180)

This conflation of levels and the resultant destruction of verisimilitude do not yet amount to an example of the theatre of the absurd, but they offer a theatrical experience that was rare at the time. There are literary precursors: Lord Dunsany's *The Glittering Gate* exploited the comic possibilities of incongruous characters failing to enter heaven as early as 1909, and, of course, Tony Kushner's *Angels in America* can be adduced here. Still, in Harvey's work this departure from realism marks a new stage (one might argue that Clarine's hallucinations in *Rupert Street Lonely Hearts Club* are predecessors).

The technique of introducing film characters into plays other than stage versions of established movies is currently much in fashion. Harvey himself used the device in *Rupert Street Lonely Hearts Club* in order to highlight the discrepancy between unattainable possibilities and the constraints of the mundane. Thus the play's title, taken from a lullabye sung in *Chitty Chitty Bang Bang* (1968), sets its agenda:

> You know my problem? I believed all the hype. Not the usual shite. Get a semi-detached in suburbia, wife and kiddie and that's your key to eternal happiness. I believed the movies. The musicals. Everything's OK in the end. See? Even me dreams are tacky. (p. 202)

The play offers a more sophisticated argument than that, though. It contains one scene the critics did not bother with and which, while supernatural, is set neither in the quotidian surroundings of Connor, Lana and Lee nor at the Pearly Gates. It is in the hospital's Lady Chapel where Connor is granted a vision; the Sister Bernadette in the following excerpt is deaf:

> *He kneels down to pray and starts to cry. While he's not looking there is some movement around the shrine to the Virgin Mary. A secret door where her face is slides across and we see a woman's face peering through. It's like in* Carry On Screaming. *The woman,* **Mary**, *speaks with an Irish accent.*
> **Mary** The cheek of it. I'm not that ugly.
> **Connor** *looks up. He sees* **Mary**'s *face. He looks round to see if the* **Sister Bernadette** *is looking; she's got her head bowed in prayer.*
> **Mary** Pass us one o'them candles, quick.

Connor *gets up and passes a candle to* **Mary** *who has a ciggie hanging out of her mouth. He lights it and she smokes. He replaces the candle.*

[. . .]

Mary All a mother can give is unconditional love. A shoulder to cry on and an arm round you to steady you when you feel wobbly. What d'you reckon?

Connor Well, she never done that.

Mary But you did. From where I'm standing he had the best mother in the world.

Connor I thought that was you.

Mary For me son's sake he had you. Quick, I've got to go, the priest's coming. Remember what I said now.

She disappears and the painted face slides back. **Sister Bernadette** *gets up.*

Sister Every day I come and pray. For a sign from Our Lady. Like me namesake, Bernadette of Lourdes. A miracle. To get my ears back. Every day the same blank expression. May the Lord be with you, my child. (pp. 212–13)

The usual mixed reviews were in evidence again. The more tepid comments pronounced on the play's inordinate length and its ramshackle construction. Sheridan Morley damned with very faint praise when he called Harvey 'the touchy-feelgood dramatist of the post-Aids generation'.[13] Aleks Sierz, on the other hand, saw 'a gloriously imaginative and touchingly redemptive play'.[14] The one comment most applicable to Harvey's career in general comes from Charles Spencer, who said: 'It is promising, certainly, but you can't go on being promising forever'.[15]

Canary (2010)

Canary was first performed on 23 April 2010 at the Liverpool Playhouse in a production directed by Hettie Macdonald, who had already been responsible for the staging of *Beautiful Thing* seventeen years earlier. It subsequently transferred to the Hampstead Theatre in London. *Canary* is structurally very different from his earlier work: it requires twenty-eight individual characters as well as an unspecified number of gay and lesbian activists disguised as nuns, security guards and Ku Klux Klan members. The action of the play encompasses half a century – the earliest scenes are set in 1962; some of the prior events culminate in 2010. In between, there are scenes set in 1970, 1971, 1979, 1981, 1982, 1984, 1986, 1999, 2000 and 2009 or combinations of up to three of these years. The total number of scenes, spread over three acts and a prologue, is thirty-two; they combine to form four plotlines and a sequence of hallucinatory encounters. In addition, these subplots, while chronologically presented in themselves, are intercut; only once (Act II, Scenes Three and Four) is there a direct continuation. This sounds confusing, and although some of the ambiguities that are necessarily created by such a kaleidoscope can be (and have been) removed in performance, the fact remains that this is not a user-friendly play. Even within the individual plots there are occasional jumps, gaps and shifts of locale; to keep track of the text's possibilities requires repeated readings; diagrams of character constellations and time vectors also help.

Help to achieve what, though? Once the jump cuts have been made transparent, the story that emerges is essentially melodramatic: in 1962, policemen catch their young colleague Tom *in flagrante* with Billy – homosexual acts, even in private, were still illegal then in Britain. Tom's father, an influential police officer, destroys the evidence incriminating him, and while Tom embarks on a career that will eventually make him 'Police Commander for a prominent London Borough' (p. 7) Billy is sentenced to revulsion therapy and gets sent to a psychiatric hospital, where one Dr McKinnon treats him with disturbing images and nausea-inducing medication in a scene reminiscent of *A Clockwork Orange*, but based on research. Harvey says,

> Aversion therapy is really primitive: in the 1960s people convicted of so-called gross indecency would sometimes be given the choice of prison or a therapy cure. In the cure, they

used the same techniques as they used in Nazi concentration camps to change people's behaviour.[16]

Billy will become a gay activist, helping to disrupt a meeting run by Mary Whitehouse, a historical figure who fought for higher standards of what she saw as decency in the media. Decades later, both Tom and Billy's lives will be blighted and their careers end in failure because of the events of 1962. Tom's son Mickey will die of AIDS in 1986; Tom fails to confess his own sexuality to him in a moving deathbed scene. Tom will finally be exposed to the gutter press in 2010. Billy will have a chance meeting with Dr McKinnon, who turns out to be homosexual himself; he will tie him to a chair and stab him to death.

Apart from the theme of homosexuality, the material is that of the pathos-laden melodramas of the early nineteenth century: torture, crime, misguided parental and filial love, passion, the relentless approach of nemesis. One might even wish to see a neo-Jacobean revenge tragedy lurking somewhere in there. Reactivations such as these can serve the purpose of focusing a play's concerns; Stephen Jeffreys's *The Clink* (1990) made that point powerfully. In Harvey's case, the structural ambitiousness does not underscore, but undermines any such strategy. There is, to put it bluntly, no aesthetic or political point to chopping up an already sprawling plot (the above outline ignores three-quarters of the play's characters, including Tom's wife Ellie who does all the hallucinating). Harvey's technique here is reminiscent of experimental prose narrative on the one hand and television and film cutting on the other; his work on soaps and sitcoms has certainly influenced his playwriting. It is, therefore, no surprise to see that he has decided to extend his artistic range: his first novel, set among TV people, is announced for 2012 by Pan Macmillan.[17]

One should not write off the play in its entirety, though, just because its structure alienates without elucidation. Harvey's insistence on decency – not the Mary Whitehouse kind, but that built around tolerance – informs *Canary* just as it does all his plays, and his concern with and for the gay community is made plain even in the Introduction to the play:

I am passionate that the lesbians and gay men who went before me and fought for the relative liberties I have today should be remembered and thanked. I am passionate that the younger generation should not become complacent. (p. 5)

When Billy likens women and gay people to 'canaries in the mine' (p. 80) he becomes a spokesman for his author's convictions and fears. The broad canvas of *Canary* has prompted the majority of reviewers to compare it, mostly unfavourably, to Tony Kushner's *Angels in America*. That is not really helpful, because Kushner's play used the gay mode, as it were, to comment on national themes. Harvey, by contrast, only admits historical and political figures if they are of use to his argument that vigilance is still required – we get to meet and laugh at Margaret Thatcher and Norman Fowler. Yet these laughs, unlike Kushner's wistful humour, are cheap: When Mary Whitehouse introduces a fellow campaigner, she says, 'Lovely Colin Green there. What he does with his Mongoloid daughter brings tears to the eyes, it really does' (p. 9). This wouldn't have been out of place in a Joe Orton play from the 1960s; today it grates: 'It's hard to imagine a weaker target than extinct bigotry.'[18]

Summary

Harvey, in his work to date, has been a predictable playwright. He accepts and appreciates this: 'When people come to see one of my plays, they know what they are getting.'[19] His audience has come to expect English metropolitan settings, three or four youngish characters and their parents, their private tragi-comic dilemmas culminating in ominous or even lethal endings, gay coming-out of more or less lovable Everymen, in-jokes, more talk than action, in fact hardly any plot that Rattigan or Coward would have recognised. Neil Dowden summarises the balance of critical opinion on his achievement: 'Harvey has been criticised for being sentimental and insufficiently political, but his talent to engage and amuse audiences is undeniable.'[20] Equally predictably, the critics have followed the minute modifications of the pattern of his work with mounting exasperation; the increasing use of non-realistic material in his later plays has done nothing to allay their concerns. Perhaps they are right. When the comprehensive histories of theatre around the turn of the millennium will come to be written, his work from the late 1990s and 2000s will not merit a separate chapter. But he is not a theatre hack either – all of his plays, even the lesser ones only mentioned in passing here, are not without their attractions, and his gift for witty repartee, though less than that of a genuine humorist, is still more than the facility to write effective jokes. His plays show us believable characters in unspectacular circumstances – in other words, they show us ourselves, most of the time. They work best when they are unpretentious – and happily, *Hushabye Mountain* apart, they usually are. Harvey is also significant in the field of British new writing, with *Beautiful Thing* doing much to redefine what a gay play might be, and to promote positive images of gay sexuality, although at a cost which Andrew Wyllie calls 'its easy and undemanding optimism'.[21] Nevertheless, when the play transferred to the West End, it was attacked by the homophobic press as spearheading a 'plague of pink plays'.[22] In opposition to this bigotry, critic Nicholas de Jongh argues that '*Beautiful Thing* was revolutionary. It did away with a theatrical tradition in which gay men were usually depicted as middle-class, arty, adult, well-dressed and neurotic.'[23] Likewise, in the words of Alan Sinfield, 'the success of *Beautiful Thing* does suggest that the mainstream is changing', with West End audiences attracted by the comedy of the play.[24] Harvey's first play has also found favour with some feminists. In the context of plays by men which symbolically 'annihilate the mother', for example, Michelene Wandor argues that in the play 'the mother-figure [Sandra] not only does not have to be imaginatively annihilated, but can be integrated into the lives not only of the next generation, but into a world of young men and their defiant sexualities'.[25]

Harvey has enriched London theatre with made-to-the-moment fare that covers the middle ground between stand-up comedy (or agit prop, for that matter) and the sophistication of a Tom Stoppard or David Greig. David Tushingham's judgement, made as early as 1995, is still valid today: 'There may be subtler and more intellectual playwrights around than Harvey, but for sheer pleasure he is very hard to beat.'[26] Harvey is comparable to playwrights such as Billy Roche and Owen McCafferty from across the Irish Channel: at home in various media, concerned with the effects of threatening, uncontrollable developments on a small group of people who are essentially innocent, placing a strong emphasis on a sense of place. To have kept faith to that commitment for two decades, and with no sign of a let-up, is no mean achievement.

Primary Sources

Works by Jonathan Harvey

Plays One: Beautiful Thing, Babies, Boom Bang-a-Bang, Rupert Street Lonely Hearts Club (London: Methuen Drama, 1999).
Plays Two: Guiding Star, Hushabye Mountain, Out in the Open (London: Methuen Drama, 2002).
Canary (London: Methuen Drama, 2010).

Secondary Sources

Aragay, Mireia, Hildegard Klein, Enric Monforte and Pilar Zozaya (eds), *British Theatre of the 1990s: Interviews with Directors, Playwrights, Critics and Academics* (Basingstoke: Palgrave Macmillan, 2007).
Bradwell, Mike (ed.), *The Bush Theatre Book* (London: Methuen Drama, 1997).
Deeney, John, 'Lesbian and Gay Theatre: All Queer on the West End Front', in Mary Luckhurst (ed.), *A Companion to Modern British and Irish Drama 1880–2005* (Oxford: Blackwell, 2006), pp. 398–408.
Dowden, Neil, 'Harvey, Jonathan (Paul)', in Colin Chambers (ed.), *The Continuum Companion to Twentieth Century Theatre* (London: Continuum, 2002), p. 346.
Dromgoole, Dominic, *The Full Room: An A–Z of Contemporary Playwriting* (London: Methuen Drama, 2002).
Hampstead Theatre, Programme Note to *Canary* (London: Hampstead Theatre, 2010)
Sierz, Aleks, *Rewriting the Nation: British Theatre Today* (London: Methuen Drama, 2011).
—, 'Interview with Jonathan Harvey', 2001, In-Yer-Face Theatre website, <http://www.inyerface-theatre.com/archive9.html#b>

—, 'Interview: Jonathan Harvey.' *TheatreVOICE* website, 12 April 2010, <http://www.theatrevoice.com/listen_now/player/?audioID=840>

Sinfield, Alan, *Out on Stage: Lesbian and Gay Theatre in the Twentieth Century* (New Haven, CT: Yale UP, 1999).

Wandor, Michelene, *Post-War British Drama: Looking Back in Gender* (London: Routledge, 2001)

Williams, Charlotte, 'Pan Mac Acquires Debut from "Corrie" Writer', *The Bookseller*, 24 January 2011 <www.thebookseller.com/news/pan-mac-acquires-debut-corrie-writer.html>

Wyllie, Andrew, *Sex on Stage: Gender and Sexuality in Post-War British Theatre* (Bristol: Intellect, 2009).

Notes

1. Dominic Dromgoole, *The Full Room*, pp. 140–1.
2. Jonathan Harvey, no title, in Mike Bradwell, *The Bush Theatre Book*, p. 84.
3. Michael Billington, *Guardian*, *Theatre Record*, Vol. XXI, No. 11 (2001), p. 709.
4. John Deeney, 'Lesbian and Gay Theatre', p. 405.
5. Lyn Gardner, *Guardian*, *Theatre Record*, Vol. XIII, No. 16–17 (1993), p. 877.
6. Benedict Nightingale, *The Times*, *Theatre Record*, Vol. XIII, No. 16–17 (1993), p. 878.
7. See *Theatre Record*, Vol. XV, No. 23 (1995), pp. 1555–9.
8. Harvey, 'Introduction', *Plays Two*, p. x.
9. Ibid., p. xi.
10. Nicholas de Jongh, *Evening Standard*, *Theatre Record*, Vol. XVIII, No. 23 (1998), p. 1512.
11. Michael Coveney, *Daily Mail*, *Theatre Record*, Vol. XVIII, No. 23 (1998), p. 1514.
12. Harvey, 'Introduction', p. xi.
13. Sheridan Morley, *Spectator*, *Theatre Record*, Vol. XIX, No. 8 (1999), p. 492.
14. Aleks Sierz, *Tribune*, *Theatre Record*, Vol. XIX, No. 8 (1999), p. 492.
15. Charles Spencer, *Daily Telegraph*, *Theatre Record*, Vol XIX, No. 3 (1999), p. 180.
16. Harvey quoted in 'In Conversation: Playwright Jonathan Harvey Talks to Aleks Sierz about *Canary*', Programme Note, *Canary*, Hampstead Theatre, London, May 2010.
17. Charlotte Williams, 'Pan Mac Acquires Debut from "Corrie" Writer'.
18. Lloyd Evans, *Spectator*, *Theatre Record*, Vol XXX, No. 11 (2010), p. 628.
19. Aleks Sierz, 'Interview with Jonathan Harvey'.
20. Neil Dowden, 'Harvey, Jonathan (Paul)', p. 346.
21. Andrew Wyllie, *Sex on Stage*, p. 108.
22. Milton Shulman, 'Stop the Plague of Pink Plays', *Evening Standard*, 30 September 1994.

23. Nicholas de Jongh, in Mireia Aragay et al., *British Theatre of the 1990s*, p. 127.

24. Alan Sinfield, *Out on Stage*, p. 340.

25. Michelene Wandor, *Post-War British Drama*, pp. 226–7.

26. David Tushingham, *Time Out, Theatre Record*, Vol. XV, No. 15 (1995), p. 966.

15 TERRY JOHNSON

Stephen Lacey

Insignificance; Hysteria; Dead Funny; Cleo, Camping, Emmanuelle and Dick; Hitchcock Blonde

Introduction

Terry Johnson is a difficult man to classify. He does not sit easily in orthodox critical or professional categories, and his plays – uniquely in contemporary playwriting – combine often outrageous comedy with philosophical debate. Oddly enough, he has not received much critical attention from the academy. Perhaps his work is too popular. But his theatrical style is certainly distinctive. As Michael Billington has observed, he is 'that rare creature; a moralist with wit'.[1] He also writes across media, producing both original work and adaptations for the theatre, television and the cinema, and also enjoys a high-profile career as a theatre director. Director Dominic Dromgoole sums up his achievements:

> Terry Johnson has successfully created his own reality, a blend of what we know and what we dream, where he has the freedom to be truthful, to be philosophical, to be rhetorical and to let his own concerns, his own cruelties and his own cares float free.[2]

Johnson was born in 1955 near Watford, Hertfordshire, and educated at the Queen's School in nearby Bushey. He studied drama at the University of Birmingham, during which time he was taught playwriting by David Edgar. While finding his feet as a writer, Johnson worked as an actor in community theatre and with the Science Fiction Theatre of Liverpool. The latter was the creation of the late Ken Campbell, whose comic surrealism chimed in with Johnson's own. His first play, *Amabel*, premiered at the Bush Theatre in 1979. Concerning the painters Toulouse-Lautrec and Degas, *Amabel* established Johnson's enduring fascination with celebrity, creativity and death, and with the philosophical and moral dimensions of farce.

Amabel was followed in 1981 by *Days Here So Dark* for the new writing touring company Paines Plough. It was, however, Johnson's next play, *Insignificance* (Royal Court, 1982), with its mixture of iconic historical figures and intellectual debate, which brought him his first major theatrical success. Premiered at the Royal Court, the play was a critical and popular hit. It was nominated for Best Play and Johnson for Best Newcomer in the prestigious Society of West End Theatres Awards of 1982, and won its author a Most Promising Playwright in the Plays and Players Awards and the *Evening Standard* Awards. It was subsequently performed across the world. *Insignificance* was followed by a touring production of *Bellevue* in 1983, and *Unsuitable for Adults* (Bush Theatre, 1984). Johnson's next three plays were not particularly well received, but demonstrated his confidence with a range of settings and themes: *Cries from the Mammal House* (Haymarket, Leicester, 1984) was set in a failed private zoo and the island of Mauritius; *Tuesday's Child* (Theatre Royal Stratford East, 1986, co-written with Kate Lock) concerned the possibilities of immaculate conception in rural Ireland; and *Imagine Drowning* (Hampstead Theatre, 1991), set in rural Cumbria, represents a diverse range of characters seeking different kinds of personal redemption.

Johnson's next play, however, re-established him as a major playwright, with a command of theatrical form and intellectual and moral ideas. *Hysteria* (Royal Court, 1993) concerns Sigmund Freud at the end of his life, and continued Johnson's interest in major historical figures, unlikely collisions (Salvador Dali appears) and the intellectual possibilities of farce. It won the Olivier Award for Best Comedy in 1993 and the Writers' Guild Award for the Best West End Play on its transfer to the West End the following year. *Hysteria* was followed by two plays that provided different takes on Johnson's recurrent interest in comedy, sexual malaise and masculinity, but within a recognisably

British context: *Dead Funny* (Hampstead Theatre, 1992) and *Cleo, Camping, Emmanuel and Dick* (National Theatre, 1998). He also adapted Edward Ravenscroft's seventeenth-century comedy of sexual manners, *The London Cuckolds*, for the National Theatre (1998).

Since 2000, Johnson has been more preoccupied with adaptations – most notably *The Graduate* (Gielgud Theatre, 2000), which he also directed – and his work as a West End director. However, there have been two original plays, *Hitchcock Blonde* (Royal Court, 2003), and *Piano/Forte* (Royal Court, 2006), which both provide evidence of Johnson's continuing experiments with theatrical form and the power of obsession. As a director, Johnson's successes include *Elton John's Glasses* (1998), *La Cage Aux Folles* (2008–10), and *Prisoner on Second Avenue* (2010), all in London's West End. Throughout his career, he has also written for the screen, especially television. He adapted his *Insignificance* for the big screen in 1985, directed by Nicholas Roeg, and this became a cult film. His main television credits include an adaptation of Alan Ayckbourn's *Way Upstream* (BBC, 1987), the mini-series *The Bite* (Warner Sisters/ABC AUS, 1996), *Cor Blimey* (ITV, 2000) and *Not Only but Always* (Channel 4, 2004), about comedians Peter Cook and Dudley Moore. He is an Associate of the Royal Court Theatre.

The Plays

Insignificance (1982)

Albert Einstein meets Marilyn Monroe in a hotel in America in 1953. This startling conceit lies at the heart of *Insignificance* – which opened at the Royal Court on 8 July 1982 – and goes some way towards explaining its attraction to both audiences and critics. Its success was achieved against the grain of many of the concerns of theatre of the 1980s. As Rob Ritchie, then the literary manager of the Royal Court, noted, Johnson's early plays had 'a cheerful disregard for the pressing issues of the day – Thatcher, police corruption [. . .] the current obsessions at the Court'.[3] It is a play, however, about serious matters.

Monroe and Einstein are joined by Senator Joe McCarthy, the rabidly anti-communist Chair of the House Committee for Un-American Activities (in an early version, it was to be the reclusive millionaire Howard Hughes), and Monroe's first husband, the baseball player Joe DiMaggio. However, none of the characters is named as such, and they bear their generic titles throughout – 'The Professor', 'The Actress', 'The Senator', 'The Ballplayer'. The dramatic focus, therefore, is on their quasi-mythical status as contemporary icons as well as historically located individuals, which plays against the particularised realism of the hotel-room setting. Historical time, too, is emblematic, with the hearings of the House Committee and Monroe's famous photo shoot, where her white dress is blown around her waist by the hot air from a wind machine beneath a grating, as events within the time frame imagined for the play. The narrative occurs over one night and part of a morning, and is driven by the Professor's dilemma: will he testify to the House Committee as demanded by the Senator? (He does not.) While he ponders this, the Actress, pursued by her jealous husband, arrives and proceeds to demonstrate her (accurate) understanding of Einstein's special theory of relativity with the aid of a flashlight, two toy trains and a model of Charlie Chaplin. None of this is part of the historical record, of course, but is conjured up for the intellectual challenges and the moral and political dilemmas posed. It is also joyfully and hilariously playful, embodying the central themes of the play.

As explained by the Actress, the special theory of relativity is an enormously creative act of imaginative understanding, and the play is interested in different ways of knowing the world and the difference between facts, knowledge and understanding. The Senator prides himself on working his way through the dictionary, learning entries one at a time. His accumulation of words, divorced from their contexts, stands as a measure of a man driven by ambition, yet devoid of empathy and imagination. The Senator's word for the second day of the play is solipsism, the ultimate statement of narcissistic self-regard (and humour is gained from the Ballplayer challenging him to prove that he, the Ballplayer, does not exist beyond the Senator's need to invent him). For the Professor, the goal is truth. He chides the

Actress that she has learned without understanding: 'Knowledge is
nothing without understanding [. . .] You may know a great deal but
without understanding you will never know the truth' (p. 19). However, the Actress has her own ways of knowing and understanding,
which are implicit in her intuition and fierce independence of spirit:
'I understand I was born and that I'm still living' is part of her reply
(p. 20). Margaret Llewellyn-Jones has argued that *Insignificance* is
about 'the human need to establish a consistent and personal view that
makes sense of the world'.[4] It is also about attempting to exert control
over that world, to master its destructive unpredictability. In this way,
the theory of relativity is a beautiful and dangerous thing, and the
Senator is the enemy of knowledge and understanding as much as he
is of communism.

Insignificance, though an essentially optimistic play that asserts we
are all significant in the end, does not offer easy ways out. As the
Professor says, 'Smallness happens and aloneness happens but the
miracle is that insignificance doesn't happen' (p. 24). But he also
realises that Americans 'will not take *responsibility* for their world!'
(p. 59). The Professor must live with the fact that he was instrumental
in inventing the atom bomb (Einstein was a lifelong pacifist). The
Actress must live with the fact that she probably cannot have children
and that she will be trapped by the sexualised image that her fame has
created. Wildly funny as *Insignificance* undoubtedly is, its final
moments are unsettling. The Professor struggles against a terror that
continues to haunt him, for which he can find no words, and there is
a chilling moment 'out of time', in which an enormous explosion and
intense white light disrupt the space (p. 61). In this, Johnson reminds
us of the reality that his assured and hilarious invention has been
concerned with.

Hysteria (1993)

Hysteria opened on 26 August 1993 at the Royal Court, directed by
Phyllida Lloyd. Its subtitle is *Fragments of an Analysis of an Obsessional
Neurosis*, which indicates the play's Freudian concerns and that it will
be a kind of case study, though not of a conventional Freudian kind.

The play is set in Freud's London study in 1938, a precise moment in Freud's – and, indeed, Europe's – history, and blends historical fact with farcical invention. Freud is dying of throat cancer and is haunted by the fear that he may have suppressed his own analytical insights because they were too uncomfortable to acknowledge. Having argued that infantile fantasy was the cause of hysteria, he is confronted with evidence that it is sometimes the product of sexual abuse in childhood, and that his own father may have been guilty of it.[5] Freud's nemesis is Jessica, the daughter of one of his most widely known case histories, whose insistence that he accept that her mother was a victim of childhood sexual abuse, which was also inflicted on Jessica herself by her grandfather, drives the narrative. Into this situation comes Salvador Dali (in reality, Freud and Dali did meet briefly), who acts as a comic foil to the central confrontation, and Yahuda, Freud's physician, who represents the norms of social, and particularly Jewish, orthodoxy.

The narrative energy of *Hysteria* is provided by Jessica's insistence that Freud recognise his error and its appalling consequences (Jessica's mother committed suicide), and by Freud's increasingly farcical attempts to conceal Jessica's presence from Yahuda, with Dali as both accomplice and obstacle. Johnson presents us with the full panoply of farcical techniques, including lost trousers (Dali's), a half-naked Jessica, women's underwear, characters shut in a cupboard and increasingly implausible protestations offered as increasingly unlikely explanations of what is happening. Farce is the vehicle by which Freud's troubled unconscious mind erupts on to the stage, and in a spectacular theatrical *tour de force* Johnson has the solidly realist and accurate re-creation of Freud's study dissolve in a riot of surrealist imagery. The clock melts, the walls soften, a sexualised echo of Freud's daughter appears instead of Jessica, a 'Patriarch' (Yahuda) appears and strikes Freud on his diseased jaw and, as the stage directions tell us, *'grotesque images appear, reminiscent of Dali's work, but relevant to Freud's doubts, fears and guilts'* (p. 184). Freud's sisters, whose safe passage from Austria he was unable to ensure, are among the victims of Jewish persecution he must confront. When reality is restored, Freud asks Yahuda for morphine to relieve his agony, and the cycle begins again. Jessica is at the window, as she was near the beginning of the play, dripping wet and demanding attention.

In concluding *Hysteria* more or less as it began, Johnson establishes the play as a morphine-induced nightmare, in which Freud wrestles with his own guilt. The original text, published at the time of the first production, makes this apparent, beginning with Yahuda administering an injection. This was omitted from the production itself, and from the 2003 version published in the collected plays, suggesting that Johnson felt that the vertiginous uncertainty about the reality of what the audience is watching was more productive – we are asked to experience the hallucination without knowing at first that it is one. In fact, the dream state, which the cyclical play increasingly resembles, is also registered in a section where Jessica, with Dali's assistance, acts out her mother's case history. As Margaret Llewellyn-Jones has observed, the play-within-a-play, with its verbal punning and recapitulation, is a form of repetition and doubling that echoes Freud's work on the uncanny and is linked to repression and sexual crisis:

> The intense level of intertextual reference suggests Freud's writing on the 'Dream Work' in which he defines many of the creative techniques of language actually being used by Johnson here.[6]

At some moments, however, Freud embodies both history and his autobiography:

> Deeper than cancer. The past. And of all the years, the year I looked into myself is the one that has been killing me [. . .] The past, for the most part, has passed. I chose to think, not feel. (p. 185)

Dali's presence in the play is partly a reminder of the dream-like disturbances of reality that surrealist art created, and through which Freud experiences his own trauma. He also provides much of the comic energy of the play, being the butt of a great deal of the physical humour. It is ironic that Dali should be so at the mercy of the wild and disturbing comic devices that Johnson heaps on him, since his art was so controlled and meticulously executed: the author of the panic-inducing imagery that engulfs Freud is also a comic victim of it. As he says, 'Don't blame me for this; is nothing to do with. I tell you already; surrealism is dead. Besides; is impossible to understand' (p. 185). There has been some critical unease about the play, centring mainly on its farcical treatment of serious subject matter and its revisionist account of Freud's later years.[7] However, even critics who raised doubts about its comic tone recognised *Hysteria*'s exuberant but technically assured and highly controlled theatricality.[8]

Dead Funny (1994)

Johnson's next play, which opened on 27 January 1994 at the Hampstead Theatre, directed by the playwright, returned him to the contemporary world and to imagined, rather than reimagined, characters. More precisely, historical figures remain off-stage (though central to the action). *Dead Funny* is set in a suburban London living room in 1992, two years prior to its performance date. The timing is precise, since the action is precipitated by the deaths of real-life British comedians Benny Hill and Frankie Howerd. Hill's death is announced in Act One Scene One, with the rest of the play occurring a week later at a costume party to commemorate his life given by the Dead Funny Society, which consists of mostly male comedy fans. At the centre of the narrative are Richard, the Chair of the Society, and Ellie (Eleanor) his wife, who is desperate to have a baby. Richard, however, has no sexual desire for Ellie, and their sex life is reduced to fraught therapy-induced nude massages, one of which is painfully presented in Scene One. Other characters include Nick and Lisa, fellow society members and long-time friends, and Brian, a closet gay, whose coming out towards the end of the play is the one honest act among the deceptions.

Dead Funny works through paradox and reversal. On the one hand, those who are dedicated to comedy are not, by and large, funny. Nick, Brian and Richard may perform old Morecambe and Wise and Benny

Hill routines, but these are always framed by the dramatic context in which they occur, the increasingly fraught atmosphere of deceit and the threat of exposure, which makes them comic and painful in equal measure. Outside of the repeated jokes, the male characters have neither wit nor self-awareness. Lisa, the only woman in the society, lacks any sense of irony. When Ellie complains that she finds nothing funny any more, Lisa replies, 'Well Ellie, humour's a funny thing' (p. 228). The only truly funny character is Ellie, who refuses membership of the Society and is constantly rebuked for not having a sense of humour. Her role is pivotal and paradoxical, and she both embodies one of the central themes of *Dead Funny* – the pain at the heart of a diseased bourgeois marriage – and comments on it, providing a caustic viewpoint on the situation while being fully implicated in it. As Johnson noted,

> There's quite an old theatrical convention of having one extremely witty character [. . .] she paradoxically became the depressed character and all the others became the ones obsessed by comedy.[9]

The humour that the Dead Funny Society celebrates is the so-called traditional humour of smut and innuendo: one of Benny Hill's most familiar routines consisted of him as a bespectacled middle-aged man, chasing glamorous, scantily clad women, with a knowing wink to the (predominantly male) audience. *Dead Funny* exposes the male fear of sex and loss of potency in this kind of humour by focusing on men who admire and reproduce [sic] it. To Brian, it is 'good old bawdy innuendo' (p. 234), beyond malice and reproach. The anxieties it embodies, however, are played out by the characters: Richard has no desire for Ellie, but is having an affair with Lisa (we witness him screwing her over the sofa at the end of Act One, and in the first production, when they are interrupted, she did an astonishing somersault and landed with her knickers around her ankles), and Nick reveals that he cannot have children (it is suggested that his and Lisa's baby is actually Richard's). When proof of infidelity is offered, Richard and Lisa dismiss it as unimportant, as if it were simply a

Benny Hill sketch, while for Ellie and Nick the pain is acute.

The other great fear that comedy confronts is that of death. The death of Benny Hill occasions *Dead Funny* and is punned in its title. Also, Richard is a gynaecologist (the irony is not lost on Ellie) and the play opens with, according the stage directions, a '*torso*', a model of a human body, '*its organs spilled*' (p. 195) across the stage. To Richard, it is a reminder of his own mortality, and the image is one that haunts the rest of the play. In the closing minutes, Brian, who is grieving for the death of his mother, observes: 'All of a sudden everyone's dying. And you never expect it' (p. 297). Violence, pain and mortality are never far from the surface. When Ellie finally tells a show-stopping joke it's about Alzheimer's and AIDS (p. 268). The party in Hill's honour is accompanied by traditional, slapstick custard pies, which are eventually deployed with genuine venom, and finally Nick threatens Richard with a knife.

Dead Funny ends with a kind of renewal – not a restoration of the old order but the establishment of a new one. Richard leaves home, and Ellie and Brian establish a comfortable truce. The last line is Brian's: 'Well, you've got to see the funny side, haven't you?' (p. 298). This is the last paradox, since the play is, as many critics realised, not so much about seeing the funny side of life as about facing the reality that humour so often conceals.[10]

Cleo, Camping, Emmanuelle and Dick (1998)

Cleo, Camping, Emmanuelle and Dick was first performed at the National Theatre on 4 September 1998, in a production that Johnson also directed. It returns us to the territory of British comedy laid out in *Dead Funny* but this time real-life comics are re-created onstage. The play is set in the same and increasingly dilapidated actor's caravan between 1964 and 1978 and explores the relationships between several of the key actors who dominated the *Carry On* series of films: Sid James, Kenneth Williams, Imogen Hassell and Barbara Windsor, during the filming of four of the latter films, with each of the play's four acts corresponding to a film: *Carry On Cleo* (1964), *Carry On Camping* (1969), *Carry On Dick* (1974) and *Carry On Emmanuelle*

(1978). Much of the action concerns the fractious but dependent relationships between this central cast, with the developing real-life affair between James and Windsor providing the strongest narrative hook.

The very popular *Carry On* series ran from 1956 to 1978 (*Emmanuelle* was the last), each with the same cast (with a few variations) though not playing the same characters, and set mostly in a variety of institutions – hospitals, schools, the army. Known for a similar bawdiness and innuendo as the TV comics venerated in *Dead Funny*, the *Carry On* films were not well-regarded critically, despite their popularity (or perhaps because of it). Nevertheless, the play version was more highly regarded and it won Best Comedy in the Olivier Awards that year. It was, however, suggested by some critics that the play lacked metaphorical resonance. Comparing *Cleo, Camping, Emmanuelle and Dick* to *Dead Funny*, Mark Fisher noted that the former lacked the 'double perspective' of the latter, being only about this particular group of people.[11] Certainly, there are few references to the wider world in *Cleo, Camping, Emmanuelle and Dick*. Indeed, the play requires that its audience has knowledge of the original films and their characters, and are interested enough in them to care.

However, the characters are not unknown individuals, but come with a weight of cultural association. It is not simply that Sid is a celebrity, but that his celebrity status is imbued with a form of stereotyping that is located in the films but survives outside them.[12] The characters in *Cleo, Camping, Emmanuelle and Dick* are wearily aware of their public personae and have a complex relationship to them. The representation of Kenneth draws on Williams's well-known antipathy to the popular comedy that made him famous, while Sid knows that he is far too much like his lecherous onscreen self, and that what he really wants is not the endless trail of women who come to his caravan, but Barbara. The consequences of Sid's affairs are played out onstage in the character of Sally, his young assistant, who, it is suggested, is his illegitimate daughter (Johnson plays with this idea in *Dead Funny*, with Lisa cast in the role). But perhaps the most damaging consequence is that his obsession with Barbara is itself coloured by her persona as sex goddess. Of all the characters in this play, it is Barbara who has the most self-knowledge and the greatest awareness of how being 'Babs' Windsor has damaged her:

> **Barbara** Sid, when you look at me you don't see me you see Her. So when I look at you I see Her in your eyes. I try to be me when I'm with you but I'm not. She's there between us. And He's between us too: good old Sid. Yuck yuck yuck. When I'm with you, Sid, I don't know who the fuck I am. (p. 201)

Barbara's self-awareness, like Ellie's caustic wit, is an answer to the charge that the play is too much in love with its male characters. Certainly, it is Sid who dominates the narrative, and much of the humour comes from the banter between Sid and Kenneth, while much of the pain comes from their antipathy to each other (and Sid's homophobia). However, it is only Barbara who understands what is happening, because, as Kenneth says, 'You're the only person I know who likes themselves. The rest of us just grieve' (pp. 212–13).

As in many of Johnson's plays, there is a metatheatrical impulse in the play, which serves to remind the audience of its connection to its real-life subject. At the end of Act Two, a farcical series of events ends with the caravan tipping up, catapulting all the female characters – Barbara, Sally and Imogen – in various states of undress and into Sid's lap. The device is knowingly clever, but lacks some of the thematic and philosophical resonance of similar devices in previous dramas. Johnson's ultimate affection for the sometimes monstrous characters he presents, and the essential sadness of their decline, is caught in the final image of the play. Sid James died in 1976, and consequently does not appear in Act Four except at the end as a ghost, playing cards with Imogen Hassell, who committed suicide in 1980. Such sombre reflections appear also in some of the reviews of the original production, where Sheridan Morley called the play 'the best and bleakest comedy of the year' and John Peter styled it 'a boisterous but melancholy comedy'.[13]

Hitchcock Blonde (2003)

Hitchcock Blonde opened at the Royal Court on 2 April 2003, later transferring to the Lyric, Shaftesbury Avenue. Although many critics felt it lacked the emotional power of his other work, it does offer a deeper exploration of some characteristic themes.[14] Once more, Johnson opens up to scrutiny the inner life of an iconic historical character, here the eponymous film-maker Alfred Hitchcock. The key reference point is the famous shower sequence in his film *Psycho* (1960), in which Marion Crane/Janet Leigh is murdered, and one of the central narrative hooks is Hitchcock's problematic relationship with Leigh's body double (Hitch and Blonde in the play text), who stands in for all the blondes in Hitchcock's films. Johnson's approach, however, is to juxtapose this encounter with another, between a middle-aged film lecturer (Alex) and his young, blonde undergraduate assistant (Nicola), who are attempting (in 1999) to reconstruct a lost Hitchcock film from 1919 from largely decomposed film stock. The play moves between three periods, therefore, although 1919 is represented only on film (projected on to screens and surfaces in William Dudley's designs for the original production). Its concern with the techniques of filming is evident from its opening line of dialogue: 'Opening shot, first angle: her torso, the knife, twenty-one frames' (p. 3).

The central concern of *Hitchcock Blonde* is voyeurism and the power relationship it embodies, and the parallel between Hitch and Alex is one between different kinds of sexual power and a consequent emotional detachment. There are two blondes in the play for Hitch – the body double and the woman (later revealed as Alicia Arnold) who gradually emerges as the lost 1919 film is reconstituted. In both relationships, Hitch is revealed as a sexual manipulator whose predilection is to use the medium of film to pursue unconsummated sexual fantasies. The Blonde (1959) recalls the sexually charged nature of the filming of the *Psycho* scene to her husband; later, she is persuaded to play out a separate nude bathroom fantasy for Hitch's private camera. The recovered film from 1919 is an early presentiment of the voyeurism of the *Psycho* shower scene, and of all the other vicariously violent acts committed against women in Hitch's films subsequently, though without a murder. It is clear that it is in this private film, not meant for the rest of the world, that the seeds for Hitch's subsequent fascination with blondes, and of his near-sadistic treatment of them, lies. In the parallel plot, Alex's manipulation of Nicola is, in fact, consummated, although once he has bedded her, Alex becomes uninterested: the thrill is in the chase and the exercise of power.

In *Hitchcock Blonde*, voyeurism is a middle-aged male condition, linked to a sense of impending mortality. Indeed, death and near-death shadows the play. The 1959 Blonde attempts to murder her husband and enlist Hitch's help in getting rid of the body, only for the husband, inconveniently and unexpectedly, to wake up; Alex pretends that he has cancer and thus only a short time to live as a way of seducing Nicola; and the 1919 Blonde commits suicide (Hitch is her only mourner). Johnson admitted to an interviewer that the play had become, in the writing if not in its origins, a form of 'mid-life crisis drama', in which the middle-aged man falling in love with a younger woman had parallels in his own life.[15] Curiously, the play is marked by the absence of love, of the sheer abandonment of sexual desire, and Hitch and Alex's sexual emotions seem, on the page, to be held at arms' length. However, the same may not apply to the audience. Johnson often confronts the spectator with a theatrical image that embodies the theme of the play, and in *Hitchcock Blonde* audience members are asked to confront their own voyeuristic impulses, since, for much of the play, the 1959 Blonde (Rosamund Pike in the original production) is semi-nude, and when she is being filmed for Hitch's private amusement, completely naked. This was the subject of some comment in the press (in his adaptation of *The Graduate*, which had only recently closed, Johnson had sent first Katherine Turner and then Jerry Hall briefly naked on to the stage as Mrs Robinson). As a device, it aims to provoke thought about, rather than exploit, the inherently voyeuristic nature of spectating, although the fact that audiences were frisked for cameras in the West End suggests that the line between the two is often blurred.

Summary

Johnson is perhaps better known to a theatregoing public as the director of several award-winning, commercially successful plays attracting star casts, than as a dramatist. His work as a director, however, is of a piece with his writing, and in both he demonstrates a very practical awareness of the possibilities of theatre, which he seems to have acquired at an early stage in his career. All his major plays (and many of the minor ones) demonstrate a confident handling of dramatic form and theatrical effect, and this is evident in the demands he places on the ingenuity of designers and directors (including himself). Freud's gradually melting office in *Hysteria* which must then solidify, the interplay of real, stuffed and imagined animals in *Cries from the Mammal House* and the complex filmed sequences in *Hitchcock Blonde* are all significant challenges, yet integral to both the theatrical experience aimed for and the intellectual ideas explored. He also has an acute awareness of the way that his writing serves the actor. Commenting on how he approaches teaching students playwriting, Johnson said, 'Teach them to concentrate on through-line not literature [. . .] all early drafts are too literary. You can never tell if something works until an actor tells you.'[16] He is an enthusiastic champion of the analytical approach to rehearsal popularised by director Max Stafford-Clark and known as actioning, in which actors are encouraged to use transitive verbs as a means of plotting a character's journey through the play.[17] This approach becomes, in Johnson's hands, a way of ensuring a degree of realism and consistency in characters, who may be asked to play in otherwise non-realist dramas. Johnson's Marilyn Monroe or Sigmund Freud may be playfully reimagined, but they are fully realised, psychologically consistent characters, which helps to ground them in the reality of the audience's time and place.

Johnson's use of comic form is similarly grounded in a theatrical, as distinct from a literary, sensibility, one in which humour is the means by which ideas and themes are explored. At its most successful, Johnson's approach opens up a double perspective, in which comedy is used to unmask intellectual absurdities, while exposing the moral and philosophical dimensions of a comic device or view of the world: the Senator's comic duping of the Ballplayer in *Insignificance* recalls a classic clown double-act; and the slapstick custard pie fight in *Dead Funny* becomes genuinely violent. In one sense, *Dead Funny* is a paradigm of the way that humour functions in Johnson's plays, providing both form and central preoccupation. A distinction is drawn between jokes, which are present in the form of routines and gags from the society's much-loved comedians endlessly parroted by the members of the society, and humour as a way of seeing the world, embodied in Ellie's caustic and effective wit.

Cast formally in terms of farce, *Hysteria* is a particularly successful example of how comic form is inextricably linked to theme. Farce is essentially about loss of control, about concealment, disguise and panic. The physical buffoonery with which British farce is associated – the lost trousers, young women in older men's wardrobes, the not-quite infidelity – suggests that there is always something at stake: the moral status quo is threatened, though in its popular UK forms, it is nearly always restored. Johnson is, in fact, one of several writers who have attempted to refashion farce to serve a new purpose. He calls the moment of inspiration that animates his plays 'the car-crash', when two antithetical ideas collide.[18] Citing Joe Orton's *What the Butler Saw* (1969) and Michael Frayn's *Noises Off* (1982) as antecedents, Michael Billington argues that *Hysteria* is an 'intellectual farce', which explores 'the thin line between order and chaos'.[19] In *Hysteria*, order is equated to repression, and Freud's increasingly absurd attempts to prevent Yahuda discovering Jessica's identity are the signs of a man trying to prevent the inevitable – with consequences already noted. An order of sorts is re-established at the end of the play, although Johnson suggests that it will be temporary and that only Freud's death will bring closure.

It is significant that Johnson's exploration of comedy often places women in positions of strength, and this is connected to his concern with the problematic nature of male identity, especially in relation to questions of sex and power.[20] Men are frequently weak and morally and sexually damaged, with the consequences providing narrative energy: Richard's denial of Ellie and seduction of Lisa in *Dead Funny*,

Sid's obsessive womanising in *Cleo, Camping, Emmanuelle and Dick*, the power games of Hitch and Alex in *Hitchcock Blonde*. In this way, men frequently dominate the plays as subjects – although they often do not have the best lines – but there is a proto-feminist, if not post-feminist, counterbalance. Johnson's women are bold and articulate, never willing victims of the men who seek to control them, often seeing the reality of the situation more clearly even when they cannot change it: Marilyn, Jessica, Ellie, Barbara, the Blonde, Nicola – these are all strong and vibrant women, and it is not surprising that some of the most talented female actors in contemporary theatre have appeared in his plays. Johnson does not adopt an overt political or ideological stance, however, and has explained the moral and sexual power of (predominantly young) women in his plays in terms of Jungian psychology, as aspects of his 'anima', a projection of his own challenging and youthful self (although this is not incompatible with a more feminist response).[21]

One of Johnson's other recurrent concerns – it is one for which he has become particularly well-known – is his use of historical figures as the main characters in his plays. He is not entirely alone in this, and there is a trend in contemporary culture, which can be found across theatre, film and television, for exploring 'the real'; Johnson is displaying sound commercial instincts. The attraction is partly that historical figures come pre-packaged, with a set of expectations that can then be negotiated, if not subverted:

> Famous people provide the writer with a well-lit path towards his subject matter, even if he's not yet aware (and at the beginning I never am) what that subject matter might be. The same route beckons the audience with the intimation of a not entirely unfamiliar journey to a place that may turn out to be, in the scope of its vista, entirely unfamiliar.[22]

Many recent representations of actual people proceed from either a documentary impulse – the reconstructions of hearings and trials popularised by London's Tricycle Theatre, for example – or are biopics, retelling (or inventing) the 'real' person behind the public mask. Johnson's plays share something of the latter, though not much of the former, but the exploration of iconic historical figures in comic form makes his approach different. Also, he often takes highly over-determined figures, some of the most revered and mythicised people in twentieth-century history – Einstein, Monroe, Freud. It is the myth itself that is often the subject, rather than the person crushed by its weight. In fact, historical figures appear in his plays for different reasons and with different effects. *Hysteria*, for example, clearly intends to nail Freud for suppressing his knowledge of childhood sexual abuse among Vienna's bourgeoisie, and indeed his own family. And *Hitchcock Blonde* echoes film scholarship that draws attention to the director's unsavoury attitude to the women he cast. However, other plays use historical figures in order to make more general points. This has changed over time. *Insignificance*, for example, was revived in 2005 at the Lyceum Theatre, Sheffield, and seemed to be much more a play about the workings of celebrity and the way that it both imprisons those it holds up to the public gaze and deflects attention from deeper political forces. As Michael Billington has argued:

> What gives Johnson's play new topicality is its vision of an America where celebrity is a political instrument [. . .] in a society taught to worship celebrity, people will never question the power of the less visible.[23]

From this perspective, both the Actress/Monroe and the Professor/Einstein are in flight from the entrapments of their status, with no clear sense of their destination. Johnson is not a writer who offers solutions, or even poses questions in a rational and orderly way. He does, however, use a confident command of theatrical technique and dramatic form to explore problems that are personal to him, but which resonate across contemporary culture.

Primary Sources

Works by Terry Johnson

Plays One: Insignificance, Unsuitable for Adults, Cries from the Mammal House (London: Methuen Drama, 2005).

Plays Two: Imagine Drowning, Hysteria, Dead Funny (London: Methuen Drama, 2003).

Plays Three: The London Cuckolds, Cleo, Camping, Emmanuelle and Dick, The Graduate (London: Methuen Drama, 2004).

Hitchcock Blonde (London: Methuen Drama, 2003).

Piano/Forte (London: Methuen Drama, 2006).

Secondary Sources

Billington, Michael, *State of the Nation* (London: Faber & Faber, 2007).

Devine, Harriet, *Looking Back: Playwrights at the Royal Court, 1956–2006* (London: Faber & Faber, 2006).

Dromgoole, Dominic, *The Full Room: An A–Z of Contemporary Playwriting* (London: Methuen Drama, 2002).

Durant, Sabine, 'The Swim of Things: Terry Johnson Talks to Sabine Durrant About Journeying and the Troublesome Business of Writing Plays', *Independent*, 23 January 1991.

Johnson, Terry, 'Foreword', in Marina Calderone and Maggie Lloyd-Williams, *Actions: The Actors' Thesaurus* (London: Nick Hern, 2004), pp. xi–xii.

—, 'The Devil You Know', *Guardian*, 11 June, 2003 <http://www.guardian.co.uk/stage/2003/jun/11/theatre.artsfeatures1>

Jordan, Marion, 'Carry On . . . Follow That Stereotype', in James Curran and Vincent Porter (eds), *British Cinema History* (London: Weidenfeld & Nicolson, 1983), pp. 312–27.

Llewellyn-Jones, Margaret, 'Terry Johnson', in John Bull (ed.), *British and Irish Dramatists Since 1945*, Vol. 1 (Columbia, SC: Bruccoli Clark Layman, 2000), pp. 173–81.

Mangan, Michael, *Staging Masculinities: History, Gender, Performance* (Basingstoke: Palgrave Macmillan, 2003).

Masson, Jeffrey, *The Assault on Truth: Freud's Suppression of the Seduction Theory* (New York: Ballantine, 2003).

Rabey, David Ian, *English Drama Since 1940* (London: Pearson Education, 2003).

Rees, Jasper, 'You Have to Begin Undressing', *Telegraph*, 24 June 2003 <http://www.telegraph.co.uk/culture/theatre/drama/3597291/You-have-to-begin-undressing.html>

Ritchie, Rob, 'Introduction', in Terry Johnson, *Plays One* (London: Methuen, 2005), pp. ix–xii.

Roberts, Philip and Max Stafford-Clark, *Taking Stock: The Theatre of Max Stafford-Clark* (London: Nick Hern, 2007).

Taylor, Paul, 'Theatre: It's the Way We Tell 'Em', *Independent*, 6 April 1994 <http://www.independent.co.uk/arts-entertainment/theatre–its-the-way-we-tell-em-joking-apart-terry-johnsons-dead-funny-now-in-the-west-end-is-a-cannily-comic-look-at-how-we-use-and-define-humour-by-paul-taylor-1368231.html>

Notes

1. This quotation is used on the back cover of all three volumes of Johnson's *Collected Plays*.
2. Dominic Dromgoole, *The Full Room*, p. 158.
3. Rob Ritchie, 'Introduction', p. ix.
4. Margaret Llewellyn-Jones, 'Terry Johnson', p. 174.
5. This controversial view had been discussed by Jeffrey Masson in *The Assault on Truth*.
6. Llewellyn-Jones, 'Terry Johnson', p. 178.
7. Ibid.
8. Reviews in *Theatre Record*, Vol. XIII, No.18 (1993), pp. 965–9.
9. Paul Taylor, 'Theatre: It's the Way We Tell 'Em'.
10. Reviews in *Theatre Record*, Vol. XIV, No. 3 (1994), pp. 130–7.
11. Mark Fisher, '*Cleo, Camping, Emmanuelle and Dick*', *Guardian*, 8 February 2005 <http://www.guardian.co.uk/stage/2005/feb/08/theatre3>
12. See Marion Jordan, 'Carry On . . . Follow That Stereotype', pp. 318–19.
13. Sheridan Morley, *Spectator*, John Peter, *The Sunday Times*, *Theatre Record*, Vol. XVIII, No. 19 (1998), pp. 1223–5.
14. Reviews in *Theatre Record*, Vol. XXIII, No. 7 (2003), pp. 433–9.
15. Jasper Rees, 'You Have to Begin Undressing'.
16. Sabine Durant, 'The Swim of Things'.
17. See Terry Johnson, 'Foreword'. See also Philip Roberts and Max Stafford-Clark, *Taking Stock*.
18. Quoted in Harriet Devine, *Looking Back*, p. 185.
19. Michael Billington, *State of the Nation*, p. 351.
20. Johnson is not alone in this: see Michael Mangan, *Staging Masculinities*, and David Ian Rabey, *English Drama Since 1940*, for discussions of post-1980s drama and masculinity.
21. Terry Johnson, 'The Devil You Know'.
22. Ibid.
23. Michael Billington, *Guardian*, *Theatre Record*, Vol. XXV, No. 5 (2005), p. 316.

16 SARAH KANE

Ken Urban

Blasted; Phaedra's Love; Cleansed; Crave; 4.48 Psychosis

Introduction

Sarah Kane never committed an act of 'unspeakable Dadaism in the college dining hall', performed a 'spontaneous happening through a serving hatch to an audience of one', or worked as a roadie for the Manic Street Preachers, but Marie Kelvedon accomplished all three.[1] When Kane's *Crave* was given a public reading in March 1997, Kelvedon was Kane's *nom de plume*. Her fictitious biography might have shocked her critics, surprised, given the bleakness of her work, that she possessed a sense of humour. Her debut, *Blasted* (Royal Court, 1995), had made her notorious, so when she signalled a new direction in her writing, she wanted audiences to experience the play free from prejudice, and not as a new 'feast of filth'.[2]

Kane's identity would not remain a secret for long. In hindsight her use of a pen name for *Crave* reminds us of her many contradictions. Her plays feature scenes of shocking violence and cruelty, yet her work is not devoid of comic moments, and in their humour lies their humanity. Kane wanted people to focus on her work, not her. To that end, she left instructions that, after her death, no biographies were to be written, and she avoided answering questions about her personal life, especially her sexuality. Yet the kind of plays that Kane wrote invited biographical speculation. Indeed, her final play *4.48 Psychosis* (Royal Court, 2000) makes the audience imagine that the pain expressed in the text is the pain of its author. Kane herself enjoyed the spotlight, penning the occasional newspaper piece about her love of football or sex shows in Amsterdam. She felt her work did not require authorial exegesis, writing only a brief Afterword to the first publication of *Blasted*.[3] She bristled at explaining the meaning of her plays. Yet she gave numerous interviews in which she was open about the genesis of her work.

Born in 1971, Kane grew up in the village of Kelvedon Hatch, and became interested in theatre at a young age. She played Bradshaw in Howard Barker's *Victory* during her first term at Bristol University in 1989. She also directed plays by Shakespeare, Caryl Churchill, Samuel Beckett and Franca Rame. It was during this time that she first began writing. Her earliest piece *Comic Monologue* details the rape of the female speaker who is forced to perform oral sex on her boyfriend, and this man, like many of Kane's male characters, was both violent and kind to his victim. In April 1991, *Comic Monologue* was featured as part of a double-bill at the Hen & Chicken Pub in Bedminster and then later performed at the Students' Union in Bristol. During these early presentations, Kane performed the monologue herself. That August at the Edinburgh Fringe Festival, *Comic Monologue* was part of *Dreams Screams and Silences*. This evening of work featured short plays by Vincent O'Connell as well as a newer monologue by Kane. Taking its title from the Smiths song, *What She Said* details a bisexual torn between Deb and Howard, her two lovers. Kane directed *Dreams Screams and Silences* (with help from O'Connell and Sean Holmes), but did not perform either of her monologues. Next year, she returned to the Fringe Festival with O'Connell where her monologue *Starved* was performed as part of *Dreams Screams 2*. The newer monologue details the obsessive behaviour of a bulimic. It was at the 1992 Festival that Kane first saw Jeremy Weller's *Mad*, a devised piece by Jeremy Weller's Grassmarket Project about mental illness that featured non-actors, an 'experiential' approach that deeply influenced her as a writer. On 24 August 1993, all three of Kane's monologues were performed as a work-in-progress in an evening called *Sick* at the New End Theatre in Hampstead.[4]

Following her graduation from Bristol with a first-class honours degree in 1992, Kane enrolled in the MA programme in playwriting at Birmingham University, then run by David Edgar. It was during this year that the first draft of *Blasted* was completed. An excerpt of the play, up to the point where Ian yells, 'I am a killer' during oral sex, was staged at the university's studio theatre. It divided the audience, but the presentation secured Kane her agent Mel Kenyon. Kenyon had read Kane's monologues during her tenure as literary manager at the Royal Court, and, as Kane's agent, she brought *Blasted* to the Court, where it had a rehearsed reading on 29 January 1994. The Court programmed the play and her first professional production transformed Kane from an unknown into Britain's most notorious playwright.

Following the play's explosive run, Kane participated in the New Dramatists/Royal Court playwright exchange programme that brought her to New York in May 1995, where she worked on *Cleansed*. The following May, Kane directed her play *Phaedra's Love* at the Gate Theatre, and then returned to the Gate in October 1997 to direct Büchner's *Woyzeck*, which she considered 'one of the greatest plays ever written'.[5] Her short film *Skin*, directed by Vincent O'Connell, was broadcast on Channel 4 in 1997, and she became Writer-in-Residence at Paines Plough, where she developed *Crave*, which the company produced in August 1998. Not only were both *Crave* and *Cleansed* (Royal Court) produced in that year, but critical opinion about her work began to shift. Despite this success, Kane suffered from depression and committed suicide in 1999 at King's College Hospital. *4.48 Psychosis* was staged posthumously in 2000.

The Plays

Blasted (1995)

The first production of *Blasted*, directed by James Macdonald, opened on 12 January 1995 in the Theatre Upstairs, and was met with a torrent of negative reaction. 'This disgusting feast of filth,' announced Jack Tinker, a comment seconded by many of his peers: 'She isn't a good writer' (*Daily Telegraph*); 'Naïve tosh' (*Guardian*); 'Lacks even the logic of a dream' (*Independent on Sunday*); 'A truly terrible little play' (*International Herald Tribune*).[6] By 2001, however, when the Royal Court revived the play on its main stage, it was considered one of the most important plays of its decade.[7] Set in a hotel room in

Leeds, *Blasted* begins with the arrival of Ian, a racist and dying journalist, and Cate, a much younger woman plagued by fits. The opening moment sets up nicely the conflict between the two characters. Cate stares at the up-scale hotel room, '*amazed at the classiness*', while Ian mutters, 'I've shat in better places than this' (p. 3). The play initially tricks the audience into thinking that its subject is a gritty investigation of this pair's destructive relationship, but at the end of the play's second scene, the Soldier pushes his way into the room and shortly after, a mortar bomb blasts the hotel. Leeds becomes not a generic city in the north of England, but the site of a violent civil conflict. The Soldier rapes Ian and then eats his eyes. The violation of Ian is not simply an act of random violence. The Soldier's girlfriend was tortured and murdered, and the Soldier, in an act of mourning, imagines Ian to be his deceased love Col. 'You smell like her,' he tells Ian, 'same cigarettes' (p. 49). The soldier exhibits Freud's 'compulsion to repeat': he re-enacts Col's violation, but this time he takes on the active role, now the perpetrator of that violence with Ian's body standing in for his girlfriend, all in an attempt to overcome his grief.[8] He is not successful; he blows his brains out. Cate eventually returns to the hotel, first with a baby, and eventually with food and drink for the broken Ian. In light of the horrific violence of the conflict, Cate's simple act is one of startling generosity, and the play's final words, spoken by Ian, are 'Thank you' (p. 61).

When Kane first began the play, her initial intention was to focus the play on Ian and Cate's relationship. But witnessing the violence in Bosnia on the news changed her focus:

At some point during the first couple of weeks writing [*Blasted*], I switched on the television. Srebrenica was under siege. I was suddenly disinterested in the play I was writing. What I wanted to write about was what I'd just seen on TV.[9]

The attack on Srebrenica that caught Kane's attention was part of the largest mass murder in Europe since the systematic killings perpetuated by the Nazis. Rather than abandon the story of Ian and Cate, Kane felt that her play could draw an important parallel between the two situations: 'The logical conclusion of the attitude that produces an isolated rape in England is the rape camps in Bosnia, and the logical conclusion to the way society expects men to behave is war.'[10] Kane's play dramatises how Ian's treatment of Cate foreshadows the behaviour of the Soldier, and rather than imagining that violence happening in some distant country, the play brings the 'foreign' conflict to Leeds.

The final version of *Blasted*, however, contains no specific references to the Bosnian conflict. The Soldier is never given a name, and while he is not English, his nationality and ethnicity are unspecified. In the 2008 New York premiere of the play, actor Louis Cancelmi created an accent for the Soldier based on a number of countries in the Balkans; it was, in his words, 'distinctly foreign but not readily placeable'.[11] Like Pinter's political plays, *Blasted* indexes a specific incident of genocide, while at the same time striving for a universal theme. Kane's play is a response to the ethnic cleansing of the Bosnians, but it is not *about* that specific conflict. The play's ambiguity opens it up to many readings, and Kane's experimenting with form undoubtedly played a part in the initial hostility that greeted it. Critical realism, or verisimilitude with a clear point of view, was the dominant type of new play; in this kind of work, a play details an argument and is rooted in an identifiable world. *Blasted* refuses such safety nets. But it announced a powerful and shocking new voice in British playwriting.

Phaedra's Love (1996)

A commission from the Gate Theatre in London, Kane's second play was her riff on the Phaedra story, specifically Seneca's adaptation of Euripides. Kane directed the first production, which opened on 15 May 1996. To many critics, *Phaedra's Love* has been perceived as a problem play in the author's canon, especially for its final scene with its orgy of violence complete with a hovering vulture.[12] Some thought this was evidence of a puerile worldview. An excellent revival at the Barbican Pit in 2005, directed by Anne Tipton, helped to correct that initial perception.

In Kane's version, the focus is not on Phaedra, but instead the object of obsessive desire: her stepson Hippolytus. Kane updates the story to the world of a contemporary royal family whose hold over *hoi polloi* is fragile. The poor leave birthday gifts for Hippolytus, but quickly turn on him when there are accusations of immoral behaviour. Unlike Seneca's Hippolytus, Kane's protagonist is no chaste virgin, but an obese ennui-filled sexpot, desired by many, including his stepmother. Yet, Hippolytus spurns all his suitors after sex, because no one 'burns' him, save for Lena, whose name causes Hippolytus to become violent (pp. 83–4). We watch Hippolytus eat hamburgers, play with a toy car and masturbate into dirty socks. He is a nihilist who sees no value in the world. While other people 'live', Hippolytus feels he is just 'filling up time', waiting for something that will never happen (p. 79). He feels that everyone is a liar, and he has chosen a path of absolute honesty, no matter whom it hurts. Phaedra has an irrational desire to cure her stepson of his ennui, even though both the family Doctor and her daughter Strophe advise her to get over Hippolytus. But his malaise only makes Phaedra 'burn' for him more: 'Can't switch this off. Can't crush it. Can't. Wake up with it, burning me' (p. 71). She eventually consummates her desire, performing perfunctory oral sex on Hippolytus only to be notified by him afterwards that he has gonorrhoea: a different kind of 'burn' awaits poor Phaedra. She accuses Hippolytus of rape and kills herself. This accusation gives meaning to his existence. He does not refute it because he is, in essence, responsible for Phaedra's death, and to deny the rape would make him as hypocritical as the Priest that he mocks. In the orgy of rape and violence that closes the play, Hippolytus subjects himself to the angry mob who barbecue his genitals and disembowel him. That suffering gives his life meaning. He finally 'lives' instead of 'filling up time', and just before the vulture descends to make a meal of him, he wishes that 'there could have been more moments like this' (p. 103).

Kane referred to this play as a comedy, a fitting description given Hippolytus's darkly humorous lines. Hippolytus, upon hearing Phaedra's accusation, responds, 'A rapist. Better than a fat boy who fucks' (p. 88). A characteristic of comedy is its focus on the body, for in the comic scenario the body brings back to earth all of humanity's metaphysical ideals by reminding us of the body's grotesque truths. The body that dreams of spirit is also the body that shits. In the world of this royal family, Hippolytus's corporeality points out society's hypocrisy. The mob attacks Hippolytus for his immorality, only then to disembowel him in front of their children. Hippolytus's father, Theseus, mistakenly rapes his stepdaughter, Strophe, in anger at Hippolytus's actions, committing the crime of which Hippolytus is only falsely accused. Yet the ultimate irony is on Hippolytus himself: the world only has meaning when he takes his very last breath before becoming a meal for a bird.

Cleansed (1998)

Kane's third play *Cleansed*, directed by James Macdonald, received its premiere at the Royal Court on 30 April 1998. It was originally intended to form a trilogy with *Blasted* and a never completed play with the working title of *Viva Death*. The hints of naturalism in Kane's first play are abandoned completely. The language of the characters is stark, making individual lines open to numerous interpretations and allowing for little verifiable backstory. Kane modelled the structure of the play on *Woyzeck*. In *Cleansed*, as in Büchner's play, the scenes represent moments of emotional intensity, with little to no exposition to deflect from the scene's impact. Stage directions almost outnumber the lines of dialogue. One of the reviewers of the first production, touted as the most expensive in the Royal Court's history, said, 'Half the time the play could be an installation in an art gallery.'[13]

Cleansed's setting is a university that now acts as a halfway house for unwanted males, but whose restorative and pedagogical functions have given way to brutalising savagery. Like *Blasted*'s hotel room, this university reads as English (the characters' names, Robin's dialect) while at the same time, the play's story references a larger social world: the concentration camps of Nazi Germany, the ethnic cleansing campaign of the Serbs, the South African prison on Robben Island, even the fictional dystopia of Orwell's *Nineteen Eighty-Four*. Tinker, the would-be doctor-cum-drug dealer, observes his fellow undesirables and then inflicts unspeakable tortures on them. The character's name is undoubtedly a reference to Jack Tinker, the *Daily Mail* critic who helped make Kane infamous. Tinker takes over the role of university guardian following the death of Graham and uses that newfound power to torture the university's inmates: Rod and Carl, two men who express their love for each other on the college greens; Grace, who has come to retrieve the belongings of her dead brother Graham only to become one of Tinker's patients; and a young boy, Robin, who can neither write nor read. Tinker is no omnipotent force, however. He masturbates before a nameless stripper who performs for him in the university sports hall now converted into peep-show booths. Only in these moments can Tinker express any affection or compassion: 'Can we be friends,' Tinker asks the Woman, only to later promise her, 'I'll give you whatever you want, Grace' (pp. 121, 123). He projects Grace's identity on to this stripper because he desires Grace but knows that he cannot have her: she loves only her brother Graham. In many ways, Tinker is simultaneously controlled and dominated by the very institution that he presumably operates, subject to punishment even as he hands it out.

The violence of *Cleansed* surpasses even the spectacles of *Blasted*. Yet, the violence, since it was intended for the stage, reads as more metaphorical since the various dismemberments cannot be staged naturalistically. Arguably, the emotional core of the play is the relationship between Carl and Rod, the storyline featuring much of the play's most extreme violence. In this institution, the clichéd dream that a true lover should die, should he need to, for the other, becomes a harsh reality. Tinker tests the bonds of the lovers through fanatical tortures on Carl's body. Carl promises Rod that he would die for him, but Rod cannot return the promise: he knows what happens in this university. When Tinker has Carl tortured, Carl breaks his promise, crying out for Tinker to kill Rod, not him. Tinker spares them both, but cuts off Carl's tongue, so he cannot apologise for his betrayal. Carl continues to try and ask for Rod's forgiveness, and after every attempt, Tinker punishes Carl further: when Carl writes a message to Rod in the mud, Tinker cuts off his hands; when Carl performs a dance of love for Rod, Tinker cuts off his feet. In each instance, Rod watches, but cannot save his partner. Like Cate's laugh at the death of the baby in *Blasted*, Rod can only laugh when Carl suffers the loss of his feet because the pain is too incomprehensible to register. After witnessing such tortures, Rod, the cynical one who saw commitment as achievable only on a momentary basis, in turn, sacrifices himself for his partner. After a sequence in which Rod and Carl make love, Tinker demands that Rod make a choice: 'You or him, Rod, what's it to be?' (p. 142). Rod makes the promise that he couldn't before; he tells Carl that he will always love him, that he will never lie to him, never betray him. But Rod can only keep that promise through death; Rod tells Tinker, 'Me. Not Carl. Me,' and Tinker cuts his throat (p. 142). In his previous scene, Rod remarked that in the university, 'Death isn't the worst thing they can do to you' (p. 136).

Following Rod's death, Tinker cuts off Carl's penis and grafts it on to Grace in an effort to fulfil Grace's wishes to be her brother. But unlike Rod, Carl survives. In the play's final scene, Grace reaches a state of utter nihilism:

> Think about getting up it's pointless. Think about eating it's pointless. Think about dressing it's pointless. Think about speaking it's pointless. Think about dying only it's totally fucking pointless. (p. 150)

All activity, even death, no longer has any meaning. But in this place of despair, Grace can now thank her doctor and torturer Tinker, and reach out to touch Carl's stump. In their blurred gender identities (Grace looks like her brother, Carl wears Grace's clothes), there is a communion between the pair, suggesting that love can exist even in such horrific circumstances. But typical of Kane, '*blinding*' sunlight and the '*deafening*' squeaking of rats co-exists with that hopeful suggestion (p. 151). What awaits Carl and Grace: redemption or annihilation?[14]

Crave (1998)

First staged on 13 August 1998 at the Traverse Theatre in Edinburgh as part of the annual festival, *Crave* represents a change from *Cleansed*. Kane's fourth play was pared down linguistically, with the graphic imagery of the previous play nowhere to be seen. Kane took inspiration from Rainer Werner Fassbinder's play *Pre-Paradise Sorry Now* (1969), which combines short scenes 'about the fascistoid underpinnings of everyday life' with scenes featuring the serial killers Ian Brady and Myra Hindley, interrupted by occasional 'liturgical sections': Fassbinder noted that the scenes could be played in any order as long as the 'through-line can be followed'.[15] What Kane took from Fassbinder was the possibility of a play comprised of sound, devoid of standard ideas about character. Like Fassbinder, Kane designated her characters only by a single letter (A, B, C, M). The play also features a number of lines taken directly from Kane's early monologues as well citations from the Bible, Shakespeare and T. S. Eliot.[16]

Kane's play follows two couples. M is an older woman, who wants to have a child and pursues a relationship with B, a younger man who wants more than simply a sexual relationship. A is a paedophile obsessed with C, a younger woman who is traumatised by past events and eventually finds herself in ES3, a ward in Maudsley Hospital. When the story is parcelled out, the letters that designate each character can be seen to have meaning: A is the abuser, C is the child, while M is the would-be mother, and B is the boy. The text alternates between moments of dialogue where A and C, and M and B appear to speak to one another, and more presentational sections that are spoken directly to the audience. Yet the play's appearance on the page makes that division between dialogue and direct address ambiguous; there are no stage directions except for silences and beats, no designations indicating whom the speaker is addressing. As a result, the play cannot be conclusively divided up into dialogue or direct address. In fact, after A delivers a lengthy monologue in which he imagines his fantasy life with C, the moments of potential dialogue between M and B, and A and C that follow could, in fact, be a response to a line delivered by a member of the other couple; for instance, B's line 'The choice is yours' could be a response to C's line, 'Silence or violence,' though initially it does not appear as if the boy (B) and the child (C) know each other

(p. 187). Given the openness of the text and the lack of stage directions, there have been a variety of directorial choices. Vicky Featherstone's original production looked almost like a talk show, and with the exception of two of the speakers changing seats, the stage picture was fairly static. Randy Sharpe's production at New York's Axis Theatre in 2000 continued that tradition. The four actors stood in a line in dim light. This production did use video to situate the play in New York and the casting of Blondie's frontwoman Deborah Harry in the role of M brought a new level of irony to M's fear about being 'too old and cold and poor to dye [her] hair' (p. 165). Other productions have taken a different approach, incorporating a wide range of movement and dance.

Unlike Kane's previous work, the play garnered largely positive notices from the British press when the production transferred to the Royal Court in September 1998 before touring in Europe.[17] Sometimes the lack of violent images on stage was misinterpreted as a more positive vision from the author. Yet the opposite is true. At the play's end, the characters' quest to satisfy their desires is replaced by a death drive: B's line, 'Kill me', is followed by a series of lines by the four characters that sound like 'passing over': 'Free falling | Into the light | Bright white light' (p. 200). The political material that fuelled *Blasted* and *Cleansed* is replaced by the inward examination of an emotional state: craving for a lover only to be ultimately rejected by that lover. In performance, *Crave* can feel frustratingly static. No doubt, this reflects the state of the four characters, each of whom is unable to move forward. In places, *Crave* can feel too personal, too connected to the author's life to communicate to an audience. For instance, B's line '199714424' in the context of the play does not mean anything necessarily. Is it the patient number given to C when she is at ES3? If so, why is it B's line? Have they become friends? The number has personal meaning to the author, which she shared with the original cast, but Kane said, 'I have no intention of telling anyone else what it means.'[18] This refusal invites a large degree of autobiographical speculation, which continues to fuel websites and message boards devoted to Kane's work. Did Kane spend 144 24-hour days with a lover who broke her heart in 1997? One Dutch production substituted a local mobile number for the original line, but that alters the text in a way that changes its meaning: it is *not* a telephone number. The risk is that this line and others like it have no meaning, or meaning only in that they reflect Kane's own life, specifically her depression and suicide.

4.48 Psychosis (2000)

Kane's final play opened on 23 June 2000, directed by her long-time collaborator James Macdonald. In a kind of full circle, the production happened at the Royal Court Theatre Upstairs, the same venue where *Blasted* was staged five years earlier, except now Kane had been dead for fourteen months, and this time the critics praised the work.[19] Many initially viewed the play as a suicide note and, given the circumstances of this first production, it is not surprising. A number of lines sound as if they are to be delivered to Kane's friends and family after her death: 'look after your mum', or 'watch me vanish' (pp. 243–4). But as with all of Kane's work, it is a carefully crafted piece of writing inspired by a number of different sources: the writings of Antonin Artaud and the ideas of Roland Barthes, particularly *A Lover's Discourse*. The play is also an extension of the poetic style that was first used in *Crave*, but here Kane pushes those ideas further. The play does not designate the number of characters nor which characters speak which lines. In scenes of dialogue, however, there is a dash to indicate a change of speaker. The lines are also carefully laid out on the page to give a sense of delivery, as is common in poetry.

Given its complicated structure, *4.48 Psychosis*, on first glance, can appear to be more random than organised. The disparate sections might appear to have no story, but this is not the case. It can be helpful to discuss the play in terms that come from the visual arts. The play might appear to be a collage, but upon closer inspection, it is a montage. Critic David Graver describes the difference between the two terms:

> In *montage*, the disparate fragments of reality are held together and made part of the work of art by the work's constructive

principle. All elements are related rationally to the whole despite the obvious heterogeneity of their sources. In *collage*, the fragments of reality are not fully integrated into a representational scheme of the work of art.[20]

Kane's final play is a theatrical montage: it takes different types of language, monologues and scenes and brings them together under the 'constructive principle' of articulating the experience of a psychotic breakdown. Kane describes psychosis as a state in which 'you no longer know where you stop and the world starts', where the boundaries that we normally take for granted no longer hold.[21] Yet, as with a visual montage, the different registers of language in Kane's play are never fully integrated into a seamless whole since their differences remain.

Kane's final play can be read as a psychological exploration of a character similar to *Crave*'s C. The play's story concerns a patient who develops a relationship with their doctor, but is ultimately let down by them. The play alternates between scenes between these two figures and moments of interiority in which language tries to capture the experience of that fragile mental state. That intense focus can make an audience feel as if it is inside the mind of the character. Like her hero Beckett, who, actress Billie Whitelaw claims, 'actually put [a] state of mind on stage', Kane does not merely *describe* the experience of psychosis, but has the audience *experience* that psychotic state.[22] Given the openness of the text and the differences in the kinds of language that comprise the play, *4.48 Psychosis* has been staged in a variety of ways. In the original production, Macdonald was inspired by a line, 'Victim. Perpetrator. Bystander' (p. 231) and divided the text between three actors. Each of the actors took one of these identities. In 2005, Claude Régie's production came to the Brooklyn Academy of Music and his staging conceived of the play primarily as a monologue delivered by actress Isabelle Huppert, a kind of stand-in for Kane, with the Doctor figure appearing only in shadow.

Summary

Kane's stature has continued to grow since her death. In the academy, the critical literature on Kane's work continues to grow. Aleks Sierz and Graham Saunders were the first to consider her work in depth. Sierz, in his *In-Yer-Face Theatre*, contextualises Kane's work within the popularisation of the violent and sexually explicit aesthetic that dominated new playwriting in the 1990s, while in his book *'Love Me or Kill Me'*, Saunders provides a careful reading of each of her plays as well as helpful context in a series of interviews with actors and directors. Sierz, in his numerous essays since the initial publication of *In-Yer-Face Theatre*, has augmented his reading of Kane, now finding her more an anomaly in the world of British 1990s theatre, her interests more classical than those of her contemporaries.[23] *Blasted* remains the text most analysed in theoretical discussions of Kane's work. For example, Kim Solga's 2007 article focuses on Cate's offstage rape and uses feminist and Lacanian theories to argue that rape's status as both present and invisible is part of the play's radical critique of what realism cannot show. Other recent scholarship reads *Blasted* through Aristotle's ideas of tragedy (Elizabeth Kuti), Shoshana Felman's theories of trauma (Peter Buse) and Artaud's ideas of cruelty (Ken Urban).

Two writers – Elaine Aston and Steve Waters – point to provocative directions for Kane scholarship. Aston's chapter on Kane in her book *Feminist Views on the English Stage* is a significant re-reading of Kane as a feminist writer. Aston uses the theories of gender of Judith Butler and Hélène Cixous as well as the phenomenology of Bert O. States to rethink Kane's position in the tradition of British feminist theatre. Kane's complicated relationship with feminism and her refusal of the label 'woman writer' has often led to Kane being considered an honorary male, and hence, ignored or denigrated in studies of women playwrights, for instance, Michelene Wandor's dismissive and inaccurate discussion of *Cleansed* in her *Post-war British Drama*. Aston argues that Kane's work is a 'political and aesthetic invitation' for her audience 'to feel differently'.[24] In her careful readings of *Blasted*, *Cleansed* and *Crave*, Aston finds that Kane's plays articulate the suffering produced by 'oppressive gender positions', and more than just having an audience experience the nihilism that comes from masculinity's violence, Kane's vision of gender 'rests on the redemptive possibilities of love'.[25]

At the other end of the spectrum, the playwright Steve Waters's insightful essay 'Sarah Kane: From Terror to Trauma' looks at Kane's work as a form of 'terrorism'. For Waters, Kane's work features 'a passionate, almost pathological identification with pain and trauma and a concomitant desire to communicate the horror of pain in its own idiom'.[26] Her work attempts to 'communicate' true suffering and that leads Kane to repudiate any sense of redemption or catharsis, while simultaneously refusing theatre's humanistic tendencies to explain events with recourse to rational thought. While not cited by Waters, Anthony Kubiak's study *Stages of Terror* is an appropriate intertext here: Kubiak finds terrorism to be emblematic of tragedy from its ancient origins. Thinking of Kane's revision of the Greeks, Kubiak's ideas might prove illuminating in the context of Kane's work. Waters's essay also helps explain Kane's flat style of dialogue, which in plays like *Blasted* and *Cleansed* eschews any 'writerly' flourishes. Director Dominic Dromgoole commented that he did not think that Kane was a 'natural writer'.[27] In Waters's mind, that refusal of 'writerly-ness' is central to Kane's theatre. Her work does not develop significant 'voices' for characters like Ian and Tinker because she wants her plays 'to enact the banality of evil'.[28] In both Aston's and Waters's analyses, we can see future avenues of inquiry regarding Kane's canon.

Kane's work continues to be staged frequently at home and abroad. One only needs to visit some of the websites devoted to Kane to get a sense of the sheer number of productions that are offered each year. Her quick canonisation has inevitably led to some detractors who continue to find her work juvenile and lacking in nuance. But those same qualities also explain her broad appeal among young people. For those theatregoers looking for extended character development and easy-to-follow narratives, Kane will always be an acquired taste. But Kane's work satisfies the needs of a generation not raised on the well-made play, a generation that prefers raw emotion to traditional storytelling. The real issue is *not* converting those who don't like her work into true believers; the real threat facing Kane's work is the ossification of her oeuvre, transforming a career cut short into a narrative of completed artistic development.

Her plays are not perfect and the later plays still feel like experiments that future plays might have further refined. Maybe we should consider Kane's work a kind of 'rough theatre', to borrow a term from her playwriting peer David Greig, who wrote sympathetically about her work in his introduction to her *Complete Plays*. 'Rough theatre' is 'poetic rather than prosaic', 'childish and infantile', 'transcendent' and perhaps most importantly, it remains 'unfinished'.[29] Kane's theatre is rough because of its emotional directness; like the lyrics of Nine Inch Nails, the Smiths or Joy Division, it is simultaneously 'infantile' and 'transcendent' in the best possible way. In isolation, a line or lyric might appear juvenile, but its lack of irony, its call to emotion resonates when placed in a whole: that is the craft that makes such a line or lyric 'sing'. Kane's plays have their flaws, but that is part of what makes them interesting. There is a tension in all five of the plays between morality and ethics, between a clear black-and-white, and the more dangerous grey area that lies in between. For instance, *Blasted*, on the surface, is as moralistic about masculinity as Sarah Daniels's *Masterpieces* (1983): in both, men are potential rapists. Yet, Kane knew there was more to the story than that, so she made Ian horribly alluring: a rapist, a racist, yet fragile and human. The same is true of Tinker in *Cleansed*.

Thinking about her plays as 'rough theatre' also reminds us that the plays do not comprise a completed journey, but an interrupted one. There is a popular narrative that there was nowhere left for Kane to go after *4.48 Psychosis*, as if the trajectory from *Blasted* onwards was clearly defined: from the social to the interior to death. True, Kane said she wasn't sure where her work would take her. But what writer ever really is? It feels better to think of her plays as rough. The task ahead for the next generation of theatre-makers is to imagine where her work might have gone. For instance, how could Kane combine the political and social concerns of *Blasted* with the radical post-dramatic dramaturgy of *4.48 Psychosis*? I don't know the answer, but it makes her work feel more alive if I don't think of these plays as a closed system. It also serves as a painful reminder of what the world has lost now that we will never learn her answer to such questions.

Primary Sources

Works by Sarah Kane

Blasted, in Pamela Edwardes (ed.), *Frontline Intelligence 2: New Plays for the Nineties* (London: Methuen Drama, 1994), pp. 1–50.
Crave (London: Methuen Drama, 1998).
Complete Plays: Blasted, Phaedra's Love, Cleansed, Crave, 4.48 Psychosis, Skin (London: Methuen Drama, 2001).

Secondary Sources

Aston, Elaine, *Feminist Views of the English Stage: Women Playwrights, 1990–2000* (Cambridge: CUP, 2003).
Buse, Peter, *Drama and Theory: Critical Approaches to Modern British Drama* (Manchester: MUP, 2001).
Cancelmi, Louis, Personal Interview, New York, 15 June 2010.
De Vos, Laurens and Graham Saunders (eds), *Sarah Kane in Context* (Manchester: MUP, 2010).
Dromgoole, Dominic, *The Full Room: An A–Z of Contemporary Playwriting* (London: Methuen Drama, 2000).
Fassbinder, Rainer Werner, *Pre-Paradise Sorry Now*, in *Plays*, trans. Denis Calandra (Baltimore, MD: Johns Hopkins UP, 1985).
Freud, Sigmund, *Beyond the Pleasure Principle* (New York: Norton, 1961).
Graver, David, *The Aesthetics of Disturbance: Anti-Art in the Avant-Garde Drama* (Ann Arbor: Michigan UP, 1995).
Greenfield, Elana, 'Kane in Babel: Notes', *The Brooklyn Rail*, December 2008 <http://www.brooklynrail.org/2008/12/theater/kane-in-babel-notes-by-elana-greenfield>.
Greig, David, 'Rough Theatre', in Graham Saunders and Rebecca D'Monté (eds), *Cool Britannia: British Political Drama in the 1990s* (Basingstoke: Palgrave Macmillan, 2007), pp. 208–21.
Hattenstone, Simon, 'A Sad Hurrah', *Guardian*, 1 July 2000 <http://www.guardian.co.uk/books/2000/jul/01/stage>
Iball, Helen, *Sarah Kane's Blasted* (London: Continuum, 2008).

Kubiak, Anthony, *Stages of Terror: Terrorism, Ideology, and Coercion as Theatre History* (Bloomington: Indiana UP, 1991).

Kuti, Elizabeth, 'Tragic Plots from Bootle to Baghdad', *Contemporary Theatre Review*, Vol. 18, No. 4 (2008), pp. 457–69.

Morris, Peter, 'The Mark of Kane', *Areté*, Vol. 4 (2000), pp. 143–52.

Rabey, David Ian, *English Drama Since 1940* (Harlowe: Pearson Education, 2003).

Rebellato, Dan, 'Brief Encounter Platform', Public Platform with Sarah Kane, Royal Holloway, London, 3 November 1998 <www.rhul.ac.uk/drama/staff/rebellato_dan/>

—, 'Sarah Kane: An Appreciation', *New Theatre Quarterly*, Vol. 15, No. 59 (2001), pp. 280–1.

—, 'Sarah Kane before *Blasted*: The Monologues', in Laurens De Vos and Graham Saunders (eds), *Sarah Kane in Context* (Manchester: MUP, 2010), pp. 28–44.

Saunders, Graham, *'Love Me or Kill Me': Sarah Kane and the Theatre of Extremes* (Manchester: MUP, 2002).

—, *About Kane: The Playwright and the Work* (London: Faber & Faber, 2009).

Sellar, Tom, 'Truth and Dare: Sarah Kane's *Blasted*', *Theater*, Vol. 27, No. 1 (1996), pp. 29–34.

Sierz, Aleks, *In-Yer-Face Theatre: British Drama Today* (London: Faber & Faber, 2001).

—, '"We're All Bloody Hungry": Images of Hunger and the Construction of the Gendered Self in Sarah Kane's *Blasted*', in Elisabeth Angel-Perez and Alexandra Poulain (eds), *Hunger on the Stage* (Newcastle: Cambridge Scholars Publishing, 2008), pp. 268–79.

—, '"Looks Like There's a War On": Sarah Kane's *Blasted*, Political Theatre and the Muslim Other', in Laurens De Vos and Graham Saunders (eds), *Sarah Kane in Context* (Manchester: MUP, 2010), pp. 45–56.

Singer, Annabelle, '"I Don't Want to be This": The Elusive Sarah Kane', *TDR: The Drama Review*, Vol. 48, No. 2 (2004), pp. 139–71.

Solga, Kim, '*Blasted*'s Hysteria: Rape, Realism and the Threshold of the Visible', *Modern Drama*, Vol. 50, No. 3 (2007), pp. 346–74.

Urban, Ken, 'An Ethics of Catastrophe: The Theatre of Sarah Kane', *PAJ: A Journal of Performance and Art*, 69 (September 2001), pp. 36–46.

—, 'Commentary', *Blasted* (London: Methuen Drama, 2011), pp. 63–120.

—, 'Cruel Britannia', in Graham Saunders and Rebecca D'Monté (eds), *Cool Britannia: British Political Drama in the 1990s* (Basingstoke: Palgrave Macmillan, 2007), pp. 38–55.

—, 'The Body's Cruel Joke: The Comic Theatre of Sarah Kane', in Mary Luckhurst and Nadine Holdsworth (eds), *A Concise Companion to Contemporary British and Irish Drama* (Oxford: Blackwell, 2007), pp. 149–70.

Wandor, Michelene, *Post-war British Drama: Looking Back in Gender* (London and New York: Routledge, 2001).

Waters, Steve, 'Sarah Kane: From Terror to Trauma', in Mary Luckhurst (ed.), *A Companion to Modern British and Irish Drama: 1880–2005* (London: Blackwell, 2010), pp. 371–82.

Notes

1. The fictitious biography of Marie Kelvedon is in Sarah Kane, *Crave* (1998).
2. 'This Disgusting Feast of Filth' was the headline of Jack Tinker's review of *Blasted* in the *Daily Mail*, 19 January 1995. See *Theatre Record*, Vol. XV, No. 1–2 (1995), pp. 42–3.
3. See Pamela Edwardes, *Frontline Intelligence 2*, p. 50.
4. See Dan Rebellato, 'Sarah Kane before *Blasted*'.
5. Interview with James Christopher, October 1997 (quoted in Graham Saunders, *About Kane*, p. 42).
6. Reviews of *Blasted* in *Theatre Record*, Vol. XV, No. 1–2 (1995), pp. 38–43.
7. Reviews of the 2001 Royal Court revival of *Blasted*, *Theatre Record*, Vol. XXI, No. 7 (2001), pp. 418–23.
8. See Sigmund Freud, *Beyond the Pleasure Principle*.
9. Interview with Aleks Sierz, 18 January 1999 (quoted in Saunders, *About Kane*, p. 50).
10. Quoted in Tom Sellar, 'Truth and Dare', p. 34.
11. Louis Cancelmi, Personal Interview.
12. Reviews of *Phaedra's Love*, *Theatre Record*, Vol. XVI, No. 11 (1996), pp. 651–4.
13. Robert Butler, *Independent on Sunday*, *Theatre Record*, Vol. XVIII, No. 9 (1998), p. 566.
14. Reviews of *Cleansed*, *Theatre Record*, Vol. XVIII, No. 9 (1998), pp. 563–8.
15. Rainer Werner Fassbinder, *Pre-Paradise Sorry Now*, p. 128.
16. See Rebellato, 'Sarah Kane before *Blasted*'.
17. Reviews of *Crave*, *Theatre Record*, Vol. XVIII, No. 9 (1998), pp. 1152–4.
18. Dan Rebellato, 'Brief Encounter Platform'.
19. Reviews of *4.48 Psychosis*, *Theatre Record*, Vol. XX, No. 13 (2000), pp. 826–31.
20. David Graver, *The Aesthetics of Disturbance*, p. 31.
21. Rebellato, 'Brief Encounter Platform'.
22. Whitelaw describes Beckett's work in an interview screened before a repeat broadcast of *Not I* in January 1990 on BBC2 TV (http://www.ubu.com/film/beckett_not.html).
23. See, for example, Aleks Sierz, '"We're All Bloody Hungry"', and '"Looks Like There's a War On"'.
24. Elaine Aston, *Feminist Views of the English Stage*, p. 82.
25. Ibid., pp. 83, 89.
26. Steve Waters, 'Sarah Kane', p. 373.
27. Dominic Dromgoole, *The Full Room*, p. 162.
28. Waters, 'Sarah Kane', p. 379.
29. David Greig, 'Rough Theatre', p. 220.

17 KWAME KWEI-ARMAH

Lynette Goddard

Elmina's Kitchen; Fix Up; Statement of Regret; Let There be Love; Seize the Day

Introduction

Kwame Kwei-Armah was born in 1967 and grew up in Southall, west London, where he attended the Barbara Speake Stage School in Acton. His parents were from Grenada, but after tracing his ancestral line to Ghana he changed his name from Ian Roberts to Kwame Kwei-Armah in his early twenties as a deliberate refusal to carry the legacy of slavery around in his daily life and to ensure that his children and future generations of his family line would no longer carry the name of the slave master.[1] Kwei-Armah's public career began as an actor in the 1990s where he first became widely known for playing paramedic Finlay Newton in *Casualty* from 1999–2004 and as a contestant on *Comic Relief Does Fame Academy* in 2003. Appearances on BBC television discussion panels consolidated his role as a media pundit on black British arts and culture in the early twenty-first century, and he has also presented the documentary *Christianity: A History* (Channel 4, 2009) and the short series *On Tour with the Queen* (Channel 4, 2009).

Kwei-Armah wrote his first play *A Bitter Herb* (1999) while he was writer-in-residence at the Bristol Old Vic Theatre, but it was not produced until 2001, after productions of the soul musical *Hold On* (1999; originally titled *Blues Brother Soul Sisters*) at the Bristol Old Vic Theatre and *Big Nose* (1999; inspired by Rostand's *Cyrano de Bergerac*) at the Belgrade Theatre, Coventry, in which he played the leading role. *A Bitter Herb* centres on a racist murder in London, evoking memories of the case of teenager Stephen Lawrence,[2] and anticipates

Kwei-Armah's concern with urban violence in *Elmina's Kitchen*. Kwei-Armah made his London playwriting debut when Jack Bradley (then literary manager for the National Theatre) invited him to write a play at the National Theatre Studio. *Elmina's Kitchen* (National Theatre, 2003) became the first part of Kwei-Armah's triptych of plays set in black establishments, which also included *Fix Up* (National Theatre, 2004) and *Statement of Regret* (National Theatre, 2007). He became the first British-born black playwright to have a non-musical play staged in the West End when *Elmina's Kitchen* transferred to the Garrick Theatre in 2005. Towards the end of the decade, Kwei-Armah wrote and directed *Let There be Love* (2008) and *Seize the Day* (2009) for the Tricycle Theatre in Kilburn, London.

Kwei-Armah has rapidly become established as one of Britain's leading black playwrights. *Elmina's Kitchen* was shortlisted for an Olivier Award for 'Best New Play', and won the Charles Wintour *Evening Standard* Most Promising Playwright Award in 2004; the television version was nominated for a BAFTA. His international reputation has been secured with productions of *Elmina's Kitchen*, *Fix Up* and *Let There be Love* in the USA, and plans are afoot to translate *Elmina's Kitchen* into Arabic for performance in Pakistan and Israel.[3] Kwei-Armah completed an MA in Classical Narrative at the University of the Arts, London, in 2002, and he was awarded Honorary Doctorates from the Open University in 2008 and University of East London in 2009. He is committed to raising the profile of black British playwriting and was instrumental in initiating the development of a black play archive, which is housed at the National Theatre Studio. The Black British Theatre Archive is 'a major venture, in partnership with Sustained Theatre, to archive and record extracts from every African, Caribbean and Black British play produced in the UK in the last 60 years'.[4]

The Plays

Elmina's Kitchen (2003)

Elmina's Kitchen was first performed on the National Theatre's Cottesloe stage on 29 May 2003 (directed by Angus Jackson) and remains Kwei-Armah's most successful play. The original cast and director made a screenplay adaptation, which was aired on BBC4 in 2003, and the 2005 national tour (with Kwei-Armah taking over the leading role) visited the Hackney Empire, the Birmingham Rep and the West Yorkshire Playhouse before becoming the first non-musical play by a British-born black playwright to be mounted in the West End when it transferred to the Garrick Theatre. Three productions have been staged in the USA including Chicago and at the Center Stage Theatre in Baltimore, Maryland in 2005, which was directed by August Wilson's director Marion McClinton.

Elmina's Kitchen is a realist drama depicting inter-generational conflicts between fathers and sons as a basis from which to examine the urgent social issue of 'black-on-black' violence and gun crime and explore how black men negotiate their environment and overcome their circumstances. The play is set in Elmina's Kitchen, '*a one-notch-above-tacky West Indian food takeaway restaurant in "Murder Mile" Hackney*' (p. 3) named after central character Deli's mother and Elmina's Castle in Ghana, 'the oldest slave fort on the West African coast, built in 1492 [. . .] where enslaved Africans were kept until the European ship was ready to bring them to the new world'.[5] Kwei-Armah highlights contemporary 'black-on-black' violence as one of the detrimental legacies of slavery that continues to disadvantage black people today, particularly black boys and men who are noted in the programme as being 'excluded from school three times as often as their white counterparts for the same offences', as suffering higher rates of unemployment and as being disproportionately represented in Britain's prisons.[6]

Elmina's Kitchen represents three generations of black fathers and sons – second-generation British-born central character Deli, who runs the café, his third-generation teenage son Ashley (who has recently become a father himself) and his Caribbean father Clifton who has returned to England for the funeral of his other son Dougie, who was killed on the day he was released from prison. Local Yardie gangster Digger also frequents the café and his presence keeps the local protection racketeers at bay. Digger's version of black macho behaviour grounded in criminal activity and his unrelenting aggression and violence is contrasted with first-generation West Indian door-to-door salesman Baygee, an old-timer who appreciates the simple things in life, like sharing rum, humorous banter and calypso songs with Clifton, and is critical of 'the new set of Yardies that eating up Hackney. They giving children BMWs, who could compete with that, eh?' (p. 24). Their diversity is characterised through individual speech patterns, which reflect their multiple identifications within a (black) British context. Deli's London accent is interspersed with occasional patois, especially when angry, Ashley speaks the contemporary street talk of London's urban youth, and the West Indians Baygee and Clifton have Caribbean accents. '**Digger** *is from Grenada but came to England aged fourteen.* [. . .] **Digger**'*s accent swings from his native Grenadian to hard-core Jamaican to authentic black London*' (p. 4) and Anastasia '*Although black British, she too swings into authentic, full-attitude Jamaican at the drop of a hat*' (p. 15).

Kwei-Armah's plays are primarily concerned with black masculinity, thus women tend to figure in minor roles as wives, girlfriends or potential love interests. A huge picture of Deli's deceased mother Elmina hangs on the wall of the café, but the only female character seen on stage is Anastasia, who arrives in the first scene and cheekily asks Deli for a job, helping him to transform the dingy and dated takeaway into 'Elmina's Plantain Hut', a thriving business in a newly renovated space at the start of the second act. Her potential for making a positive impact on the predominantly male environment is short-lived, however, as both Deli and his father pursue her as a love interest and she is forced to leave the café, marking the beginnings of the play's descent towards a tragic dénouement.

The plot revolves around the inter-generational conflicts arising from Deli's futile efforts to prevent his teenage son Ashley from being drawn towards a life of crime. Deli is a reformed criminal who tries to ensure that his son chooses the right path, but Ashley condemns his father's hard work and honest living ethic as weak, and seeks the materialist symbols of high status – the latest designer fashions and a top-of-the-range sports car – and respect on the streets, which he thinks he can gain more rapidly by dropping out of college, becoming a runner for Digger and working his way up the criminal chain, rather than through legal means. Kwei-Armah wrote the play as a warning for his then ten-year-old son about the dangers of aspiring towards the glamorised gun violence represented in gangsta rap culture, to enforce the point that there is no need to conform to peer pressure of 'badness'. Such warnings prevail in the images of black men prematurely losing their lives that recur throughout the play. Anastasia has lost her teenage son, and Deli's brother Dougie is killed as they await his arrival on release from prison. A final stark reminder of the inherent risks of a gangster lifestyle is delivered in the last scene as Ashley is gunned down and murdered by Digger. After discovering that Ashley was responsible for an arson attack on rival shopkeeper Roy's shop, Deli reports the crime to the police, making a deal to save his son from prison by testifying against Digger. Becoming an informer is seen as the ultimate betrayal of brotherhood and in a final act of retribution Digger instructs Ashley to shoot his father. But while the teenager stands with his gun poised Digger shoots him in the back first, leaving the closing image of a father kneeling over his son's lifeless body as a brutal reminder of the dangers of a gangster's lifestyle.

Digger Alright, now point the gun at your punk-arsed dad. The one that gets beat up and does nothing, has his business near taken away and does nothing, but then informs on a brother man to the other man for what? [. . .] Is this the type of people we need in our midst? Weak-hearted, unfocused informers? No, I don't think so. Do you, Ashley?

Ashley's *hands are shaking a little. After a beat.* [. . .]

Ashley No.

Digger OK then, raise the gun, point it.

Ashley *does.*

Digger Good. Is your finger on the trigger?
Ashley Yes.
Digger Good.
Digger *pulls out his gun and shoots* **Ashley** *dead.*
Deli Nooooooooooooooooooooooooooooooooooooo.
Digger *looks to* **Deli**.
Digger Yes. Ah so dis war run! (pp. 94–5)

Elmina's Kitchen was commended as one of a new wave of plays by black British writers that probed beneath news headlines to provoke consciousnesses about the state of the nation and was especially praised for portraying serious issues with warmth, sensitivity and humour, 'bringing a human face to London's gang violence and showing how easy it is to make the wrong choice when struggling to survive'.[7]

Fix Up (2004)

Fix Up was first produced at the National Theatre's Cottesloe on 16 December 2004 (directed by Angus Jackson) and has also been produced in Italy and New York.[8] Kwei-Armah continues his concern with history and the politics of progress for black people in contemporary Britain and the impact of the past on the present. The play brings together a range of characters who debate contrasting opinions on race, culture and heritage and the fundamental question about the need to understand history and heal the past in order to secure a better future. It is 'Black History Month [. . .] in "Fix Up" a small, old-school "Black conscious" bookstore' (p. 3) in Tottenham, north London, where the shelves are crammed with books and African statues and carvings that reflect the Afrocentric politics of owner Brother Kiyi, but the shop is empty and the CLOSING DOWN SALE sign hints at its future. Although Kiyi struggles to make the money, he remains committed to the political project of the bookshop as a resource for remembering black history, to the extent that he has forged volumes of books that he passes off as authentic slave narratives. Kiyi is a father figure to the community, loaning out books to ensure that they are read, using slave narratives to teach 'care-in-the-community patient' Carl (p. 4) how to read, and letting political militant Kwesi use the upstairs room free of charge to hold meetings of his activist All-Black African Party, which is organising reparations for slavery events. Kiyi's best friend Norma regularly pops in for a chat, to continue an ongoing game of draughts and advises him on how best to secure the future of the bookshop.

The naturalistic trajectory of *Fix Up* is propelled by the arrival of a stranger whose presence impacts on all of the characters and disrupts the seeming harmony of the community. Mixed-race character Alice arrives in the first scene under the pretext of buying books to broaden her knowledge of black history and discover the 'black' part of her cultural heritage that she had not experienced growing up with her white adoptive family in Shropshire, but she also has a more pragmatic purpose to reveal Brother Kiyi as the black father who left her to be brought up in care. Alice's presence is used to raise questions about race, heritage and identity, acknowledging that people of dual heritage may well be one of the fastest-growing communities in Britain and considering some of the implications this might have for contem-porary race politics.[9] Kiyi's black consciousness politics are heavily informed by the speeches, lectures and manifestos of prominent black nationalist thinkers and political activists such as James Baldwin, Marcus Garvey and Claude McKay, whose tapes he listens to in the shop, but Alice draws attention to the inherent sexism and Afrocentrism of the black nationalist movement, and highlights Kiyi's attitudes towards mixed-race people as outmoded for the context of contemporary Britain, 'flawed by nostalgia, arrogance and a limited view of what "black" is in a Babylon where mixed race or (the PC term) "dual heritage" is the norm'.[10]

Fix Up stages debates about the routes of progress for contemporary black British people, centring primarily on the value of sticking to archaic political principles versus progressing through popular con-sumerism and questions about the merits of individual versus community gain. The lack of customers suggests there is no longer any desire for knowledge of black history in contemporary Britain, and the bookshop is under threat of being sold to developers and converted into a potentially more lucrative venture of luxury flats over a black hair care shop. The revelation that political activist Kwesi is behind the conversion plans is used to raise questions about how the quest for black liberation needs to adapt to the changing demands of a contemporary world. Kiyi exclaims, 'You can't replace history with hair gel' (p. 23), but Kwesi's rationalisation of his lucrative business venture opposes Kiyi's 'knowledge is power' ideals with a viable approach to empowerment through fiscal means.

> People don't – want – books. They wanna party, and look good, have the latest hairstyles, and nails and tattoos. That's where niggers be at, Kiyi. They ain't spending they money in here. Why should the other man take our money, Kiyi? That's why we powerless, 'cos we ain't where the money at. (p. 71)

Hair is a prominent motif in the play, underlining the commercial potential for converting the bookshop to a hair product store. Kiyi's full head of 'greying, unkempt locks' (p. 2) is a signifier of his Afrocentric political allegiance and sitting centre stage cutting off his locks as the bookstore is being dismantled around him at the end of the play symbolises a break with the past and the end of an era for his black radical politics. Norma wears a different wig in each of her appearances and her first concern on deciding to get involved in local politics is about where she can buy a new wig to wear at her inaugural election campaign meeting. Kiyi's comment that 'in the first months of trading no doubt more black folk will have passed through here than I'd have seen in my whole fifteen years' (p. 63) is an indictment of the possibility that 'black people today would rather have their roots done by a hairdresser than examined by a historian', as one astute reviewer put it.[11]

Reviews suggested that the dramatic potential of the play was undermined by the weight of the themes, causing contrived, melo-dramatic plotting and characterisation with unbelievable twists, particularly in the second half, as the loose ends are tied up. However, some of the more positive reviews indicated that *Fix Up* demonstrates Kwei-Armah's innovative contribution to contemporary British playwriting. For example, Helena Thompson writes: 'To his credit, Armah's understanding of traditional structure underpins a script that broaches issues rarely seen at the National. It is a combination that makes his message all the harder to ignore.'[12]

Statement of Regret (2007)

Statement of Regret was first produced at the National Theatre's Cottesloe on 14 November 2007 (directed by Jeremy Herrin) and an updated version was broadcast as 'The Saturday Play' for BBC Radio 4 on 18 July 2009. It explicitly tackles the issues of post-traumatic slave syndrome that are alluded to in Kwei-Armah's previous two plays, examining the legacy of slavery in the lives of black people in contemporary Britain and the vexed question of whether an apology should be made for the continued discrimination created by this troubled aspect of British history. A play directly addressing the effects of post-traumatic slave syndrome is undoubtedly the natural culmination of a triptych whose plays are concerned in some way with the legacy of slavery on black psyches.

Statement of Regret is set in a black policy think tank in 2007, the year in which Britain celebrated the bicentenary of the abolition of the slave trade, and was inspired by Tony Blair's 'statement of regret' that no apology would be made for slavery. The timing of the first production allowed for a more explicit examination of topical issues around debates about reparations for slavery, and a crucial exploration of how slavery may have created divisions between black people – most notably in creating animosity between those of West Indian heritage who were transported and enslaved and those of African descent. The characters debate the complexities of the reparation debate and question the impact of slavery on black race relations.

Kwaku Mackenzie is the West Indian Director of the Institute of Black Policy Research (IBPR), where he heads a team of intelligent and well-spoken workers who are mostly of African descent. The play opens with the think tank members gathering in their plush modern office to celebrate the recent government appointment of the first ever Minister for Race, which is immediately followed by a meeting to brainstorm ideas for their next agenda. The office colleagues represent a cross-section of black British society, including Africans and West Indians as well as one female and one gay employee, and ideas of a homogeneously united black community are countered by internal factions based on class, gender, sexuality, heritage, political leanings and personal ambitions. A key question is whether black institutions should be setting their agendas in relation to wider government initiatives, and whether they should maintain a separatist race agenda or be pursuing integration. The think tank was initially founded to address white racism, but outspoken Idrissa, Director of Research, highlights the need to respond to changing racial agendas by turning the debate inwards to self-criticism.

Kwaku believes that black political thinking can be rejuvenated by returning to the issue of the impact of slavery, which continues to manifest itself in a range of social ills. His workers criticise his ideas as old notions that blamed white racism for the disadvantaged experiences of black people in Britain, and suggest that there are more pressing intra-cultural issues, such as sexism, homophobia and domestic violence in black communities. A reparations agenda goes against the integrationist initiatives that were heavily pursued in British culture in the 2000s, emphasising divisions not only between blacks and whites, but also between African and Caribbean blacks. Kwaku compounds the conflicts with the controversial suggestion that any reparation for slavery should be given only to West Indians, who have borne the brunt of the atrocities of slavery and continue to be disadvantaged today. The second half of the play descends into the acrimonious trading of insults between Kwaku and his colleagues that features West Indian name-calling of Africans as savage 'jungle bunnies', 'African booboo, take the bone out of your nose' (p. 72) as defensive insults from feelings of being let down by African complicity in slavery, and African taunts of West Indians as lazy or 'cultureless' (p. 76) as a reflection of a sense of superiority towards those who are disenfranchised by a history of enslavement.

These political debates are refracted through personal family issues, particularly the legacy of passing on a heritage from father to son. Kwaku's alcoholism and grief for the recent death of his father affect his judgement and his relationship with his two sons – Junior, the legitimate son of his marriage to an African, and Adrian, the illegitimate son from his affair with a West Indian – which also emphasises the intra-cultural factions between Africans and Caribbeans in Britain. Adrian overcame growing up with a struggling single mother by doing well in school and gaining advanced university degrees, whereas Junior lived with his parents in a big house and received a private education, but is viewed as somewhat of a failure in his father's eyes because he did not go to university and identifies with black street culture. Kwaku's decision to employ Adrian as an office intern sets off a trail of repercussions in already fragile office politics, which culminate in the breakdown of relationships with his wife, legitimate son, and employees.

Kwei-Armah touches upon a range of pertinent political issues in *Statement of Regret*, such as separatism versus integration, divisions and hierarchies in British black communities, book knowledge versus work experience and life knowledge, and contemporary race and identity politics and potential directions for the future, thus cementing his reputation for provocatively staging debates about controversial subjects. The production received the most damning reviews of his plays so far, drawing criticism for cramming too many ideas into one piece and for unconvincing and underdeveloped personal stories – Kwaku's affair with his female co-worker, marital breakdown, and the eventual suggestion that his erratic, paranoid, aggressive, and forgetful behaviour is a sign of the onset of dementia. However, Michael Billington 'applaud[ed] the play for its honesty in tackling abrasive issues', Charles Spencer commended Kwei-Armah for 'being unafraid to wade in where more cautious writers might fear to tread' and Kate Bassett paid a big compliment by claiming that 'Kwei-Armah is now our black British David Hare. *Statement of Regret* is an illuminating state-of-the-nation play.'[13]

Let There be Love (2008)

Let There be Love was first performed at the Tricycle Theatre on 17 January 2008 (directed by Kwei-Armah), revived for a second production in August 2008, and also mounted at Center Stage Theatre, Baltimore, Maryland, in 2010. After the scathing reviews of *Statement of Regret*, the play was 'a type of healing' that got Kwei-Armah back to writing quite quickly, and was also a tribute to his mother, upon whom the main female character is based.[14] The play is set in the front room of elderly first-generation Caribbean migrant Alfred's home in north-west London, which is decorated in a conventional West Indian 1980s style with flowery wallpaper, a world globe trolley that opens up into a drink bar and a radiogram that he calls Lillie holding pride of place in the corner. At the start of the play, Alfred is a '*quintessential grumpy old man, a cross almost between Alf Garnett and Victor Meldrew*' (p. 260), a cantankerous xenophobe whose bigoted ideas about new immigrants as 'thieving the Englishman job' (p. 269) echo prejudiced attitudes that were once used against his generation of post-war Caribbean immigrants, a marked reminder of 'how quickly we forget: how the impulse to feel threatened by the next group to arrive in society overrode memories of the discrimination and pain we had ourselves suffered'.[15] Alfred has frosty relations with his two daughters; the elder, Janet (not seen in the play), has thrown him out of her house for being derogatory about her white husband and mixed-race child, and he fell out with his younger daughter Gemma when she left her male partner and became a lesbian, and she has not visited him for the past three years. The arrival of Polish cleaner Maria, whom Gemma employs to help Alfred while he recovers from an operation, is the catalyst towards healing the rift with his daughter and improving his fraught family relations.

Kwei-Armah uses the relationship between Alfred and Maria to explore issues of citizenship and the passing of the baton between older and newer migrants. Maria is in her late twenties and represents the next major generation of immigrants arriving in late-twentieth- and early-twenty-first-century England with similar hopes, dreams and aspirations as their predecessors, especially a belief in the idea that they would only stay long enough to make money and return home wealthy. Her aspirations are refracted through the reality of Alfred's generation's experiences – he is sixty-six years old and has lived in England for over forty-five years, and although he does not like to be called English, has a reverence for speaking the Queen's English, corrects Maria's 'broken English', and helps her to prepare for her citizenship test by teaching her about what it means to be 'British'.

Maria and Alfred immediately connect over missing 'home' and as his health and her living circumstances deteriorate, she moves in to live with him and the pair develop a warm and understanding platonic friendship that contrasts with the inter-generational conflict with his daughters. Like Kwei-Armah's earlier plays, it is memories and failure to heal past conflicts that is continuing to affect Alfred today, and with Maria's encouragement he faces up to the past by visiting Grenada to see his ex-wife and returns to England with a new lease of life as he looks to the future. Maria's effect leads to his redemptive trans-formation from a prejudiced old codger who resents the new immigrants to a forgiving man who eventually recognises her as the next generation to walk the path created by her predecessors, and acknowledges the inherent progress of the newer immigrants benefiting from the inroads of a pioneer generation that came before.

Let There be Love is a warm and poignant realistic comedy-drama that infers love and understanding as a fundamental basis for building and maintaining relationships. The quintessentially feelgood quality is underlined by playing Nat King Cole's versions of 'Let There be Love', and 'Let's Face the Music and Dance' at various points, culminating in Maria and Alfred sharing a final dance before he relaxes back into his chair and dies smiling peacefully as the lights and the music fade. Kwei-Armah wrote the play to examine the impact of new immigration in Britain, to show 'how much warmer, how much easier the country had become for immigrants, mostly due to the battles my parents' genera-tion – the *Windrush* pioneer generation – had fought and won'.[16] A number of pertinent themes are touched upon, including inter-generational conflict, racism, immigration, citizenship, sexual politics, domestic violence, terminal illness and assisted suicide, but this is a smaller and more intimate play with only three characters and makes a departure from the usual debate and didacticism of his writing style. Reviewers were generally surprised by the domestic focus of the piece when compared to Kwei-Armah's trilogy and some criticised the play for being contrived and excessively sentimental while others enjoyed the warm affection at the heart of the play.

Seize the Day (2009)

Seize the Day was first performed at the Tricycle Theatre on 22 October 2009 (directed by Kwei-Armah) in repertory with Roy Williams's *Category B* (2009) and Bola Agbaje's *Detaining Justice* (2009) as part of the venue's 'Not Black and White Season', a trilogy of plays exploring black Britain at the end of the first decade of the twenty-first century. Each playwright chose a topical theme, with Kwei-Armah drawing inspiration from the election of President Barack Obama as the first African American President of the USA to imagine what it would take for London to elect a black Mayor, which would amount to a symbol of progress of improved race relations in Britain. A realistic mode situates the play in relation to contemporary British society, referring to key black British political figures, past and present, including Bernie Grant, Diane Abbott, Paul Boateng and Trevor Phillips.

Seize the Day is the first of Kwei-Armah's plays to incorporate multiple settings, moving between a range of private, public and professional locations (living rooms, parks and offices) to bring together a focus on the domestic and the professional by contrasting the rising political career of reality television star presenter and mayoral candidate, Jeremy Charles, with his turbulent personal life. Jeremy is in his mid-thirties and lives in a nice home with his white wife, but he is not happy in his marriage and is having a longstanding affair with a black woman. It is implied that he married a white woman as a symbol of status, but he feels that she does not support him in his career, and she experiences hostility from his black friends. A chance confrontation with urban teenager Lavelle is the catalyst for rethinking his stereotyped views of young black working-class masculinity. After witnessing what looks like a mugging while recording a live outside broadcast and slapping seeming perpetrator Lavelle to the ground, Jeremy undertakes to mentor the teenager, but he has much to learn from Lavelle about young black men's lives. Jeremy was born on a council estate and has risen to become a celebrity and recognised face in the community, but his choices are brought into question by Lavelle, who accuses him of losing touch with his 'ghetto roots' and not being true to his race. Their relationship provides a basis to address many of the racial issues that have resurfaced throughout Kwei-Armah's plays, including questions about the black community's responsibility for raising children better and solving urban youth problems.

Jeremy's celebrity status and profile increases following the broadcast of him hitting Lavelle, making this an opportune moment to stand to become London's first black Mayor, and the play maps issues of strategy, spin, public face and conspiracy that are at the heart of election campaigns. Alongside Jeremy are a range of other black middle-class characters who groom him for his role, helping him to develop the terms of a campaign that would attract both black and white voters. Jeremy does not want to emphasise racial issues and his political adviser Howard wants to market his crossover appeal, but there is increased pressure for him to address black issues, the argument being that if he as a black man does not tackle these issues then no one else will. Given that there are so few black people in highly influential positions in Britain, those who make it are often perceived to have a responsibility to highlight black issues.

Jeremy's values are contrasted with Lavelle's to raise concerns about the failure of black boys who identify with 'street' culture at the expense of pursuing a proper career. Jeremy criticises Lavelle's identification with black street style where his public image belies his capability. Lavelle gained eleven A-star grades for his GCSE exams, but rejected the opportunity to go to college, and talks 'street' slang interspersed with occasional big words. Lavelle learns about life choices and Jeremy rethinks his stereotypical perceptions about the black underclass. A meeting between the two men in the final scene demonstrates that they have started to understand and accept each other's life choices. Throughout the play, the contrast between Jeremy's white wife Alice and black lover Susan is simplistically drawn in terms of their sexual appeal, stereotypically of the black woman as a highly charged sexual being in contrast with an uptight white woman, though both female characters are heavily under-written. The suggestion that he married a white woman as a symbol of his upward social mobility is ironically reinforced in the final scene as Jeremy's increased racial awareness coincides with him separating from his wife, rejecting his mayoral campaign, and making plans for a future with Susan.

Seize the Day combines the prominent debates of Kwei-Armah's earlier work, incorporating domestic and institutional worlds and considering the impact of one on the other. Discussions throughout echo those heard in *Fix Up* and *Statement of Regret*, and, in a similar way to *Let There be Love*, the resolution in the final scene leaves a sense of hope for better understanding between diverse communities in Britain.

Summary

Gradually, Kwei-Armah's work has attracted attention from academics such as Deirdre Osborne, Geoffrey Davis, Amelia Howe Kritzer and David Lane.[17] He is an openly political playwright who writes as a 'catalyst for debate around themes that are pertinent to our communities and to our nation' and his 'diasporic black politics [are] influenced by the philosophies of Marcus Garvey and Malcolm X and the writings of James Baldwin and Amiri Baraka'.[18] While his playwriting influences include Edgar White and David Hare, he was particularly inspired to document black British experiences after seeing a production of August Wilson's *King Hedley II* (1999) in New York. His plays share Wilson's style of using naturalist plot conventions to examine history and explore how the past impacts on the present, especially looking at how legacies of slavery affect contemporary black men's psyches.[19] A key motif of Kwei-Armah's plays is the way that secrets, lies and the revelation of past indiscretions threaten to undermine the stability of characters who are dealing with unfinished business from the past.

Kwei-Armah updates identity-politics plays to account for the perspectives of two generations (second and third) that were both born in the UK and address other topical issues arising from the lives of black people in Britain today. A prominent trope throughout Kwei-Armah's oeuvre is a concern with black masculinity, depicting fathers and their children to symbolise a sense of legacy and heritage that metaphorically alludes to slavery, while highlighting the literal responsibilities that come with fatherhood and their role in teaching the successive generations how to follow in their footsteps. Kwei-Armah counters stereotypical ideas of absent and irresponsible black fathering by making fathers present and fundamental to creating the futures of their children.

Kwei-Armah also homes in on the intra-cultural tensions within black British communities, provocatively staging debates that draw inspiration from current affairs and issues, including 'black-on-black' violence, Blair's 'statement of regret', the election of President Obama, and Boris Johnson replacing Ken Livingstone as London Mayor, as well as themes of immigration and citizenship. He uses a conventional linear narrative structure where a stranger's arrival is the catalyst for the ensuing drama, and the plays are built using humour in the first half and pathos in the second as the conflict builds towards dénouements that see the characters' arguing and fighting reflected in messy stages and destroyed habitats. Careful and precise stage directions set up symbolism through location, décor and language use that capture the subtle inflections of various black accents to evoke diverse identities and identifications in the UK.

The institutional settings for Kwei-Armah's National Theatre triptych become forums for public debates on the topical issues at the heart of each play as the realistic sets are peopled with characters that could be drawn from everyday life in these habitats. Despite the realism of the settings, there is very little stage action as the focus is placed on dialogue. The centrality of debate is a particular quality of Kwei-Armah's writing that sees diverse characters arguing around the core issue, often disagreeing with each other about pertinent issues of race and progress, thus challenging homogeneous notions of black people by allowing a range of complex and contradictory ideas to surface.

One of the most significant inroads of Kwei-Armah's playwriting is the representation of a rarely seen black 'transitional class', departing from the trend for plays about 'urban' black teenagers that proliferated on the British mainstream stage during the early twenty-first century.[20] In the post-show talk for *Seize the Day*, Kwei-Armah stressed that he was not dealing with the black underclass, while also identifying his playwriting as metaphorically alluding to the arts and the place of black theatre in Britain.[21] His characters debate issues of cultural diversity that echo concerns for British arts institutions, questions about the relationship between black theatre and mainstream institutions, whether black theatre practitioners should maintain a separatist agenda or seek integration, and about what types of plays earn black playwrights a mainstream profile. He writes from the heart, about issues that matter to him, aiming to challenge stereotypical perceptions of black men, rather than seeking to appease the expectations of the producing houses. Kwei-Armah's determination to challenge legacies of slavery stems from his childhood vow to change his name after watching the televised version of Alex Haley's *Roots* (1997) at just twelve years old, which has continued throughout a playwriting career that is dedicated to writing political dramas that raise awareness about important issues of race, culture and heritage for black people in contemporary Britain. His success illustrates how he is fulfilling the challenge to write plays that are accessible to both black and white audiences, functioning in line with black aesthetics to reveal black humanity through art while creating awareness that could lead to social change.

Primary Sources

Works by Kwame Kwei-Armah

Plays by Kwame Kwei-Armah: A Bitter Herb, Big Nose, Hold On (previously Blues Brother, Soul Sister) (London: House of Theresa, 2001).

Plays One: Elmina's Kitchen, Fix Up, Statement of Regret, Let There be Love (London: Methuen Drama, 2009).

Not Black and White: Roy Williams Category B, Kwame Kwei-Armah Seize the Day, Bola Agbaje Detaining Justice (London: Methuen Drama, 2009).

Secondary Sources

Anon., '96: Kwame Kwei-Armah', *MediaGuardian 100 2010, guardian.co.uk* website, 12 July 2010 <http://www.guardian.co.uk/media/2010/jul/12/kwame-kwei-armah-mediaguardian-100-2010>

Davis, Geoffrey, 'This is a Cultural Renaissance: An Interview with Kwame Kwei-Armah', in Geoffrey V. Davis and Anne Fuchs (eds), *Staging New Britain: Aspects of South Asian British Theatre Practice* (Brussels: Peter Lang, 2006), pp. 239–51.

Elam, Harry J., Jr, *The Past as Present in the Drama of August Wilson* (Ann Arbor: Michigan UP, 2004).

Howe Kritzer, Amelia, *Political Theatre in Post-Thatcher Britain: New Writing 1995–2005* (Basingstoke: Palgrave Macmillan, 2008).

Kaneko Lucas, Valerie, 'Performing British Hybridity: *Fix Up* and *Fragile Land*', in Joel Kyortti and Jopi Nyman (eds), *Reconstructing Hybridity: Post-Colonial Studies in Transition* (Amsterdam: Rodopi, 2007), pp. 241–55.

Kasule, Samuel, 'Aspects of Madness and Theatricality in Kwame Kwei-Armah's Drama', in Dimple Godiwala (ed.), *Alternatives within the Mainstream: British Black and Asian Theatres* (Newcastle: Cambridge Scholars, 2006), pp. 314–27.

Kwei-Armah, Kwame, 'From Ian to Kwame: Why Slavery Made Me Change My Name', *Observer*, 25 March 2007 <http://www.guardian.co.uk/uk/2007/mar/25/humanrights.britishidentity>

—, 'Introduction', *Plays One* (London: Methuen Drama, 2009), pp. ix–xiv.

—, Personal Interview, London, 12 July 2010.

—, et al. 'Our Job is to Write About What is in Our Hearts', *Guardian*, 6 October 2003 <http://www.guardian.co.uk/stage/2003/oct/06/theatre.race>

Lane, David, *Contemporary British Drama* (Edinburgh: EUP, 2010).

Logan, Brian, '"Heart of Blackness": The Playwright Kwame Kwei-Armah Would Like to be the David Hare of Black British Theatre', *The Times*, 29 October 2007 <http://entertainment.timesonline.co.uk/tol/arts_and_entertainment/stage/theatre/article2748898.ece>

National Theatre, *Black British Theatre Archive at the NT*, <http://www.nationaltheatre.org.uk/51932/platforms/black-british-theatre-archive-at-the-nt.html>

—, *Elmina's Kitchen* Programme, May 2003.

Osborne, Deirdre, 'The State of the Nation: Contemporary Black British Theatre and the Staging of the UK', in Dimple Godiwala (ed.), *Alternatives within the Mainstream: British Black and Asian Theatres* (Newcastle: Cambridge Scholars, 2006), pp. 82–100.

—, '"Know Whence You Came": Dramatic Art and Black British Identity', *New Theatre Quarterly*, Vol. 23, No. 3 (2007), pp. 253–63.

Sierz, Aleks, 'Cooking Up a Storm', *Evening Standard*, 25 April 2005 <http://www.thefreelibrary.com/Cooking+up+a+storm%3B+Black+British+writing+is+thriving+in+the. . .-a0131910972>

Notes

1. Kwame Kwei-Armah, 'From Ian to Kwame', p. 18.
2. Stephen Lawrence was murdered in south-east London in April 1993 and the case became notorious for the police mishandling of the investigation, which failed to secure a conviction of the killers. However, the Stephen Lawrence Inquiry and its subsequent *Macpherson Report* had a major impact on race relations debates and legislation in the late 1990s and early 2000s.
3. Kwame Kwei-Armah, Personal Interview.
4. See *Black British Theatre Archive at the NT*. Sustained Theatre is an Arts Council-funded initiative established to promote connections and collaborations for a diverse arts sector in Britain. See <http://sustainedtheatre.org.uk/Home>
5. National Theatre, *Elmina's Kitchen* Programme.
6. Ibid.
7. Maddy Costa, *Guardian*, *Theatre Record*, Vol. XXIII, No. 11–12 (2003), p. 703.
8. Kwei-Armah, Personal Interview.
9. The 2001 British Census included mixed race as a separate category for the first time.
10. Benedict Nightingale, *The Times*, *Theatre Record*, Vol. XXIV, No. 25–26 (2004), p. 1695.
11. Patrick Marmion, *Daily Mail*, *Theatre Record*, Vol. XXIV, No. 25–26 (2004), p. 1696.
12. Helena Thompson, *Ham and High Express*, 7 February 2005.
13. Michael Billington, *Guardian*, Charles Spencer, *Daily Telegraph*, Kate Bassett, *Independent*, *Theatre Record*, Vol. XXVII, No. 23 (2007), pp. 1373, 1375.
14. Kwei-Armah, 'Introduction', p. xiv.
15. Ibid.
16. Ibid.
17. See Deirdre Osborne, 'The State of the Nation' and '"Know Whence You Came"', Geoffrey Davis, 'This is a Cultural Renaissance', Amelia Howe Kritzer, *Political Theatre in Post-Thatcher Britain* and David Lane, *Contemporary British Drama*.
18. *MediaGuardian*, '96: Kwame Kwei-Armah'; Deirdre Osborne, '"Know Whence You Came"', p. 253.
19. See Harry J. Elam, *The Past as Present in the Drama of August Wilson*.
20. See for example Roy Williams's *Fallout* (2003) and *Little Sweet Thing* (2005), Bola Agbaje's *Gone Too Far!* (2007) and *Off the Endz* (2010), and Levi David Addai's *93.2 F.M.* (2005) and *Oxford Street* (2008).
21. Post-show talk at the Tricycle Theatre, 29 October 2009.

18 ANTHONY NEILSON

John Bull

Normal; Penetrator; The Censor; The Wonderful World of Dissocia; Realism

Introduction

On the frontispiece of his *Plays One*, Anthony Neilson provides a playfully fictional biography that, ten years later, in *Plays Two* he equally playfully corrects: 'Contrary to previous biographies, he has no children yet, nor any of the things that an adult should.'[1] These joky accounts introduce what is an important strategy in Neilson's work, a deliberate confusion about the reliability of the text and those characters who stand witness in it, and a conscious avoidance of the conventional responsibilities of adulthood. In the face of a theatre that craves sincerity and a concern with 'truths', Neilson demands the right to retain an essentially childlike view of the world, albeit a frequently nightmarish view: to offer fantasy and uncertainty, where an audience conventionally seeks seriousness and fixity.

He was born in Scotland in 1967. His father, Sandy Neilson, is an actor and theatre director who was to direct one of his son's plays, *The Censor*, at Dundee Rep in 2002, and to appear in another, *Realism* (National Theatre of Scotland, 2006). His mother, Beth Robens, was an actress. He has described himself as 'a rehearsal room baby',[2] a point reiterated by Joyce McMillan:

> In a sense, radical thinking about theatre is part of Neilson's inheritance [. . .] and he spent a backstage childhood following his parents around the theatres and rehearsal rooms of the country, at a time of real creative ferment. When he was eight, John McGrath launched 7:84 Scotland; by the time he

was ten, his parents were appearing in plays by the hugely popular 1970s generation of playwrights led by Donald Campbell, Hector MacMillan and Tom McGrath.[3]

Neilson feels that the unconventional lifestyle of his parents 'instilled a questioning attitude' in him, but also a great sense of insecurity.[4] Until he was three, the family lived in a single room in Aberdeen, before moving to Edinburgh. 'I remember bailiffs and the constant threat of eviction [. . .] my mother having nervous breakdowns'.[5] The connection between childhood experience and later psychological problems is a recurrent theme in his work, for example in *Penetrator* (Traverse, 1993), but it would be foolish to regard the problems experienced by the characters in his plays as having the kind of relationship to the writer's own life that you might find, say, with the work of Sarah Kane. He says: 'If you've grown up in that situation, you don't have the same reaction to mental illness as other people do – you actually find it quite normal.'[6]

Neilson's schooling was troubled: he claims that he 'is one of those people that institutions feel they have to break'.[7] A brief interlude at the Royal Welsh School of Music and Drama led to him trying his hand as a playwright: 'thrown out [. . .] for insubordination [. . .] nothing to do that summer, so I entered a BBC young playwrights' competition, and won'.[8] *The Colours of the King's Rose* was transmitted in 1988, and he then wrote a stage play, *Welfare My Lovely*, its title playing on that of the classic Raymond Chandler crime novel. That same year, a second radio play, *The Fluttering of Wings*, was transmitted.

By then, he was living in London, but Scotland continued to beckon, and Neilson put his thoughts towards producing something that would attract Fringe attention and audiences.

> I knew the Edinburgh Festival very well and I knew that you needed a certain angle [so that] people skimming through the brochure would be drawn by your show.[9]

Normal (1991) not only kick-started his theatrical career but, with its careful deployment of disturbing images, this portrait of a serial killer has been claimed by many as the real starting point for 'in-yer-face theatre'.

That and, two years later, *Penetrator* established his reputation at the forefront of shock-fest theatre. It was a play that 'Sarah Kane was directly influenced by', seeing it at London's Finborough Theatre, the same venue where Neilson directed a reading of the first draft of Mark Ravenhill's *Shopping and Fucking*.[10] The performance is cheekily memorialised in *The Night Before Christmas* (Red Room, 1995), produced before *Shopping and Fucking* had its formal debut, but containing a character called Gary (as Ravenhill had borrowed this and other names from the pop group Take That) whose wife Lulu (another Ravenhill borrowing) had left him in 1993, the year that Take That had shared the number-one slot with Lulu with 'Relight My Fire', which is precisely what Gary wants his wife to do.

In 1994, *Year of the Family*, a macabre and taboo-busting 'celebration' of the European Year of the Family, played at the Finborough. *The Night Before Christmas* was one of five plays that Neilson, with his ambivalent notions about childhood, has located in whole or in part during this 'festive season', the others being: *Year of the Family*, *The Lying Kind* (Royal Court, 2002), *God in Ruins* (RSC, 2007), a reworking of the Scrooge story, and *Get Santa!* (Royal Court, 2010), a play for children. The year 1995 was a busy one for the playwright, who had plays at the Royal Court (*Heredity*), National Theatre Studio (*White Trash*) and on the Edinburgh Fringe (*Jeffrey Dahmer is Unwell*, a collaborative piece). In 1997, the Finborough was again the venue for *The Censor*; Neilson then took time out to write and direct *The Debt Collector* (Channel 4 Films, 1999), before returning to the stage with *Edward Gant's Amazing Feats of Loneliness* (Drum, Plymouth, 2002), a first attempt at the kind of surreally structured form he would present in its full glory in *The Wonderful World of Dissocia*. That same year saw the first performances of two of Neilson's most controversial plays, *Stitching* (Bush) and *The Lying Kind*, the latter of which failed to find critical acclaim. *Dissocia* opened at the Tron Theatre, Glasgow in 2004, before a later revival by the new National Theatre of Scotland, and *Realism* was a huge success at Edinburgh's Royal Lyceum Theatre.

Then came *God in Ruins, Relocated* (Royal Court, 2008) and, in 2009, the screenplay for a film version of *Normal: The Düsseldorf Ripper*, as well as *The Séance* at the National Theatre.

The Plays

Normal (1991)

Normal opened at the Pleasance, Edinburgh, on 7 August 1991. Like many of Neilson's plays, it was directed by its author. Although not his first staged play, it was the work with which Neilson really attracted public attention. Written consciously for a Fringe audience, it is a disturbingly imagined account of the triangular relationship between a young defence lawyer, Justus Wehner – virgin in every sense at the outset – his client, the infamous German serial killer, Peter Kurten – active in Düsseldorf between 1929 and 1930 – and the latter's wife.

In his 'Introduction' to *Plays One*, Neilson stresses the importance of the art of storytelling for a playwright. This emphasis is crucial. The violent elements, both verbal and physical, of *Normal* may have resulted in Neilson being installed as the forerunner of a 'New Brutalist' theatre that had yet to be conceptualised, but it was the gripping way in which the story was presented that held audiences. The play opens with the lawyer, Wehner, addressing the audience, whose presence he acknowledges at many key moments in the play. He speaks of 'the memory of a memory' (p. 4), giving promise of a story that will be presented by recall, and he tells us that he is prompted to speak by his experience of having taken his two children to an amusement arcade. What he then describes is represented on stage in a bizarre expressionist moving tableau, a Black Museum: a zombie-like figure moves in a halting clockwork movement towards an emergent swan; the man carries an outsized pair of scissors which he first raises and then thrusts towards the swan, before a blackout denies the completion of that particular part of the narrative. The full horror of the tableau's conclusion remains to be revealed at the end of the play, as in any good story. However, the implications are graphically clear. The machine presents its violent story only if money is fed into the slot: in paying to enter, the audience, too, are exhibiting a desire to see the horror dramatised on stage.

Normal consists of a number of individual scenes, not formally separated, other than through lighting cues, and they move seamlessly in and out of each other. The lawyer has been hired to prove that Kurten is insane, not normal, and therefore not answerable for his acts. He tells us why he has been selected for the job and why he feels unprepared for it:

> Still in my twenties, I was their most prided and precocious
> son and it's true
> I knew everything of the law.
> Little of life
> and less of love.
> But I knew everything of the law.
> The year was 1931. (p. 5)

We learn of the desperate economic condition of Germany at the time that Wehner is preparing for Kurten's trial. The psychological and the historical contextualisation are interlinked, and so begins the process of connecting Kurten's bestial acts to those of the period of German history that will follow his execution. Wehner makes the point explicitly in what is almost the last speech in the play:

> In the years that followed Peter's execution
> I
> and a great many 'normal' men
> were to do things we had never thought ourselves capable of.
> (p. 58)

Although the lawyer is ultimately unsuccessful in arguing the case for insanity, much of the narrative consists of the revelation of the deprived, and depraved, childhood of the killer, with the strong implication that there might well be psychological and social explanations for his murderous zeal. That is to say, he is presented both as a result of the social circumstances of his time and as an embodiment of them in a historical chain that will lead inexorably to the holocaust: as Kurten argues in one of his addresses to the audience, 'it is not just Peter Kurten that stands trial here | But society itself' (p. 18). However, the question of what is normal (sane) is not defined merely geographically – Kurten compares himself to London's Jack the Ripper – or historically – Neilson has his murderer echo Margaret Thatcher's words, 'There is no such thing as society' (p. 25); but, above all, it is not defined in terms of abnormal psychology, and it is this that gives the play its real power.

Kurten not only reveals the full history of his horrific journey to his present imprisonment but, in so doing, he draws the lawyer into a web of realisations and, eventually, admissions:

> I've had a mother and her daughter take turns at sucking my prick. Now tell me that doesn't cause even a slight 'frisson' in your liberal loins. (p. 16)

It is his role as a liberal man that makes Kurten's eventually accepted offer of his wife's sexual services initially compromising. That the wife, Eva, should have the same name as the childhood sweetheart that Wehner asks after in his increasingly desperate letters home makes the connection between the two men the stronger. However, it is when – in a terrifying nightmare enactment of subconscious desires – Wehner is directed by Kurten to violently attack and then kill Eva that Neilson really confronts his audience. He does this quite literally, invading the 'audience space' as Eva escapes from the stage and is dragged back to have her legs broken and finally dispatched with a hammer (p. 48). In performance, the effect of this sequence is intentionally disturbing. The murder is immediately followed with another dream sequence in which the roles are again swapped. Kurten is in court defending Wehner from the crime on the grounds of insanity, after which we return to the after-events of the real trial, in which a guilty verdict has been returned and the plea of insanity rejected, before the end of the tableau that had opened the play is brought to its terrible conclusion:

Wehner   [. . .] having found no victim in the Hofgarten
  he had
Kurten *raises his scissors.*
Wehner   he had cut
  the head
The scissors come down. **Frau Kurten** *drops her head. Red light*
bathes the stage.
  from a sleeping swan
  and drunk its gushing blood. (p. 57)

The lights fade and only Wehner delivering the epilogue that connects past with present is left. Its particular significance is that *Normal* differs from all Neilson's other plays in that it is set in an historically imagined past, a past that haunts the memories of more than just the lawyer.

Penetrator (1993)

Penetrator, which opened at the Traverse on 12 August 1993, was a very alarming take on the lives of contemporary young males. Like *Normal*, the play is concerned with a triangular relationship: in this case between the misogynistic Max (played by Neilson) and the more sensitive Alan, who share a shabby flat, and the unexpected visitor, Tadge, an extremely disturbed soldier-on-the-run, and once a school friend of Max's. The narrative is straightforward, its enactment terrifying. It is, in essence, a version of the 'invaded room' theatre model, but Pinter's protagonists were never confronted with anyone quite as scary as Tadge.

Although he makes his entrance in the fourth of the play's six scenes, we have unwittingly already seen Tadge hitching a lift in the rain at the opening, the one brief time that the action moves outside the flat. But even here, a voiceover 'deep and subhuman', recounts a pornographic fantasy about another hitchhiker's 'adventure':

My cock was like a truncheon in my jeans. I saw her looking
at it, licking her sluttish red lips. 'But if I'm giving you a

ride, you should do the same for me' she said smiling.
(p. 61)

This provides the link, takes us from a public to a private world, as the
lights go up into Scene Two, 'the living-room of a rented flat' (p. 62),
with the voiceover continuing as we see Max hunched up on the floor,
masturbating and ejaculating as he reads the magazine that is the
source of the voiceover's story. Given that the final words of the
voiceover in Scene One – 'I want you to shoot me' (p. 62) – are
associated with the visual sighting of the squaddie, they appear to have
a specifically male warfare resonance. However, this association takes
on a less straightforwardly heterosexual significance, when the
sentence is completed, this time not with the audience gaze on a male
soldier, but with Max's male gaze on a violently abused female object
of pornographic desire:

> I want you to shoot me full of your thick
> of your thick salty cum
> I want you to
> shoot – (p. 62)

Indeed, after Tadge has moved in on the pair, Alan's remark to Max,
'You've got a history with him' (p. 82), takes on a new significance
when, after a long process of interrogation, the latter is subsequently
made to recall an interrupted homosexual incident in childhood, all the
time with Tadge threatening Alan with a knife. It proves the final straw
for Alan, who grabs the weapon and screams at his friend to get rid of
the soldier. However, Neilson has carefully prepared for this moment.
Even before Tadge's arrival, there has been an uneasy tension in the
flat. Max and Alan have very little in common: they embody the polar
opposites of contemporary masculinity. Max, who has lost his
girlfriend and who will discover at a climactic moment in the play that
Alan has slept with her, demonstrates the point beautifully when
talking about a girl the pair had the previous evening:

Max She didn't seem to mind using the word *dickhead*. She didn't seem to mind using the word *bastard*, and think about the meaning of *that*.

Alan Yes, but nobody uses that literally.

Max (*nods*) The same with cunt. If I wanted to insult someone, why would I compare them to a vagina? It happens to be a part of the anatomy that I'm quite *fond* of, you know . . . She was just one of those fanny-bashers that Mikey collects so he can feel all right on. (p. 70)

Tadge embodies the worst excesses of the pornographic fantasies that Max gets off on, and what makes his stories of sexual violence perpetuated by himself and army colleagues the more disturbing is that he is quite unable to distinguish reality from fantasy. In contrast Max can make the distinction, as is evidenced in the chillingly comic Scene Four, when Max has Alan's teddy bears simulate copulation as he provides the pornographic dialogue. It is one of these bears that Tadge will later rip apart as part of his terrorisation of Alan, after a terrifying knife fight, which 'if done right uniquely shattering', Neilson writes in the text (p. 119).

However, despite his sexual boasts, Tadge regards himself primarily as a victim, haunted by false memories of an army-based organisation called the Penetrators who have tortured and sexually abused him. Although to Alan, in particular, his stay in the flat represents an extremely unpleasant and unwanted invasion, for Tadge it is seen as a much-desired return to the security of home and of childhood, his destruction of Alan's childhood teddy bear being the more significant in this context. And so it is that, as in Pinter's *The Caretaker*, one of the trio is ejected from the nest: in this instance it is, inevitably, Alan; and Max and Tadge conclude the action recalling their childhood and eating the chocolate Rolos that Alan had brought back for himself and Max at the beginning of the play. The final words are Tadge's and they demonstrate, above all, the impossibility of a return to a world of recalled, albeit falsely recalled, innocence: 'I used to like coming to your house', and over the ending the audience hear the Bee Gees singing 'How Deep is Your Love' (p. 117).[11]

The Censor (1997)

Neilson was born one year before the abolition of theatre censorship in Britain in 1968, and had taken a surprisingly early interest in the subject, at the age of ten writing repeatedly to the British Board of Censors, frustrated at not being allowed to watch the remake of *Invasion of the Body Snatchers*, and demanding to know what were the criteria for certification for films.[12] It was thus entirely fitting that he should be commissioned to write a play on the subject. *The Censor* premiered at the Finborough Theatre on 1 April 1997. Structurally, it is the simplest piece Neilson has written. The play is set in a gloomy basement, the 'shit-hole', a symbolically conceived underworld of filth, in which extreme pornographic films are pondered over by the main character, the Censor.

> **Censor** (*V/O*) It started with a pornographic film. And I
> swear to God, it was a porn film like any of the hundreds
> I'd seen. No: there *were* differences. [. . .] I put it down to
> the fact it was made by a woman. The film was hard-core
> and unpassable as it stood but she requested a meeting
> with me to challenge the ruling. (p. 245)

The action opens with the Censor and the female film-maker having clearly come to the end of their meeting, with the latter offering to undress in support of her cause. His insistence that she put her shirt back on is met with a blunt response, 'don't act so shocked: you spend all day staring at women's breasts' (p. 246). The woman alternates between sexually teasing the diffident man and insisting that, far from being a piece of typical pornography, her film contains a narrative that shows a couple at first unfamiliar with each other's bodies, but gradually becoming more and more adventurous in the security of their intimacy. It is a point that is lost on the Censor: 'Your film is just one sex scene after another. There's no plot, there's no character, there's no nothing' (p. 249). This will be one of six meetings between the two, with the sexual chemistry developing between them in a way that parallels the woman's analysis of her own film. At first refusing to plead a special case to allow the film to be issued without a certificate so that it can be screened in private clubs, by the fourth meeting he offers wine and she flowers, and by the fifth he is writing the plea. Physically, the attempted striptease at the outset is succeeded by two sessions of what an earlier generation might have described as heavy petting, before she offers to have sex with him: an offer he refuses, at which she suggests that, for some reason, he is impotent. The parallel between the two stories, that of the film and that of the play, is reinforced frequently. For example, in Scene Five, she invites him to 'put your fingers in me', an offer he at first refuses, invoking his token of office in a moment of unconscious irony: 'I won't be able to hold my pen' (p. 258). When he does as she asks, she proceeds to interpret her film story for him in a way that leads to a comic alliance between the two male protagonists:

> **Fontaine** Just hold it there. That's nice. [. . .] her strokes were erratic, random. [. . .] So that *means* . . . ?
> **Censor** Uh – that means – they haven't . . . done it . . . before?
> **Fontaine** This is the early part of the relationship. They're still learning about each other.
> Deeper.
> *He pushes his fingers deeper. She winces, laughing at his mistake.*
> Deeper into the *story* . . . (pp. 258–9)

These meetings are punctuated by brief dialogues with his wife, in which the non-sexual nature of their marriage is stressed, as is the fact that she is having an affair with an unnamed off-stage lover. Although these scenes are located in the text as in the couple's kitchen, the wife is actually omnipresent, sharing the same stage space as the other two, but only lit when she and her husband are talking. When we also realise that, unlike that in the 'shit-hole', the dialogue in the kitchen is continuous, not the product of different occasions, the question arises as to exactly how an audience is to interpret the story. That it is a love story of sorts is evident, and is stressed by the Censor at the end of Scene Five when talking about the contentious film, also allegedly a love story:

> **Censor** *Brief Encounter* is a story about two lovers, but you
> don't have to see Trevor Howard's penis thrusting in and
> out of Celia Johnson, do you?
> *Pause. She smiles.*
> But you'd like that wouldn't you? (p. 261)

That '*her smile infects him and he finds himself laughing*' is made the more significant when, after '*a moment*', Scene Six returns us to the kitchen with an opening question, 'What's funny?' (p. 261). Of course, it could simply be the recollection that is making him smile, but there is also the possibility that everything that happens in the play is essentially a product of his own fantasies and that the subterranean office is not just an underworld, but the site of the subconscious. This is further complicated by the fact that neither the Censor nor his wife is ever referred to by an individualised name: even the film-maker is never further personalised than by the 'Miss Fontaine' (a somewhat filmic creation, in itself) with which the Censor addresses her. This allows an opening up of the discourse into more general questions about male and female sexuality, desire and fantasy, in a manner most notoriously explored in Neilson's *Stitching*.

Miss Fontaine's insistence on tracing the roots of his impotence take the pair back to his childhood and, in the most controversial moment of the play, she squats and defecates on the floor, the 'shit-hole' receiving its ultimate tribute. Finally aroused, he responds to her sexually, only for her to announce her departure for America in the next and final meeting. The play ends with his wife telling the Censor that she has seen in her newspaper that Miss Fontaine has been murdered in New York. Clearly upset, his wife tries to comfort him, saying, 'We'll work it out. We always do' (p. 285) and a brief last scene has him in his office watching the film. '*And after a while, he smiles*' (p. 285): but at a memory or the prospect of the possibility of a new kind of relationship with his wife? It is impossible to decide.[13]

The Wonderful World of Dissocia (2004)

With *Dissocia* Neilson really established himself in the broader European surrealist/absurdist tradition that had been evident in his work as early as *Normal*, but which first found a real form in *Edward Gant's Amazing Feats of Loneliness! Dissocia* premiered on 28 February 2004, and is a play of two halves. In the first, and longer, of the two acts, Lisa is struck down by a mysterious illness that has possible attributes of a nervous breakdown or schizophrenia, and has a problem with her watch: it is always resolutely one hour slow. She has sent it off to be repaired, and the play opens with the arrival of a visiting Swiss clock-mender, who tells her that, as a result of confusions over international date-lines, the delayed take-off of her flight from New York and the end of British Summer Time: 'Your watch is not an hour slow, Lisa, *you* are' (p. 204). Despite the fact that, as we discover later, she is dressed for a date with her boyfriend Vince, she is persuaded to go on a visit to Dissocia where, the clock-man insists, her lost hour will be found. After a brief phone call and her response to an automated voice – 'If you wish to report a conspiracy, please press 1. If you think everyone would be better off without you, please press 2. If you wish to correct a temporal disturbance, please press 3' (p. 206) – the flat is immediately transformed into a mysterious lift. She descends, accompanied by four complete strangers, one of whom is loudly planning the details of a murder on his mobile phone, but Lisa is told that she is being 'rude' when she asks, 'Excuse me – are you all right?' (p. 207).

That the lift, which anyway includes a sideways move in its design, should be accompanied by a soundtrack that suggests it is more likely a tube train is – like the fact that the clock-maker bears a more than passing resemblance to Sigmund Freud – a cue to the audience that they are being privileged in being allowed to experience two levels of consciousness: the world as magically conceived by Lisa in her disturbed and untreated state and the mundane realities of a material world that intersects and interacts with the world of Dissocia but never succeeds in denying its existence.

Travelling through the country, Lisa encounters a bizarre set of characters that are conceived as both comic and threatening. These include a pair of Insecurity Guards whose dilemma echoes that of the Free Soldiers in Jarry's *Ubu Enchaîné*, who are punished for obeying orders. Also, Lisa, in a vain attempt to recover her hour in a Lost Property Office that, it transpires, is itself lost, meets a Laughter, who has lost his sense of humour and laughs hopefully at everything. She also encounters Inhibitions, Argument and Ticket, all of whom have lost their own attributes. In fact, Argument tries to convince her that the cruelty of a wild goose chase might merit the attentions of hunt saboteurs. Earlier, she has been confronted with a self-proclaimed scapegoat who wants to be 'blamed for things [he] had little, or nothing, to do with' (p. 232), but who turns out to be provided also with the traditional attributes of an ordinary goat and attempts to sexually assault her. It is an attack from which she is rescued by an already severely wounded Jane, an official from the Community Crime Initiative, who insists that 'I'm here to be beaten and anally raped for you' (p. 238), as a part of a programme to reduce the number of victims of crime. As so often in Neilson's work, mischievous humour and satire jostle for prominence.

Lisa learns that the country is at war with the Black Dog King, and that the Queen of Dissocia is in hiding. That 'black dog' was the name given by Winston Churchill to his fits of depression and that Lisa is later thought to be the missing Queen gives added stress to the way in which this magic world is one conjured up by the disturbed consciousness of our heroine. So, on occasions the sound cues and even parts of the dialogue are transparently derived from an off-stage sound system that can be associated with a parallel universe, and the boyfriend, Vince, even intrudes into the action briefly. That there is a dark side to Dissocia is important, as for all the trips in flying cars, and meetings with friendly talking polar bears (a bi-polar disorder joke), it is a world that is falling apart.

Neilson says that Lisa's party dress 'should be simple but bold in colour', indirectly suggesting the iconography of Dorothy's dress in *The Wizard of Oz* or Alice's in *Alice in Wonderland*, and these two works directly influenced the playwright.[14] Like Alice, the childlike Lisa is set loose in a world of would-be adult oppression, as well as of surreal fantasy, and all three works use the narrative structure of a journey, of a quest. In addition, the association with *The Wizard of Oz* gives added weight to the difference between the two acts of Neilson's play. Just as the film opens with the black-and-white (grey) world of Kansas (reality), before exploding into colour on Dorothy's arrival in Oz, so the two acts are differentiated. Where Act One is all brightness and colour, the notes for the second act stipulate that 'there should be no overt colour used in set design, costume or lighting' (p. 270). For the play concludes with a return to the hospital ward where Lisa is unwillingly receiving medication for her mental disorder. It is a world of a harsh reality certainly, but one that is presented as well-intentioned on the part of the attendant doctors and nurses. Surrealism gives way to naturalism, imagination to reality. Vince visits her and an uneasy truce is established. The play ends with Lisa asleep, with a reminder of Dissocia (a toy polar bear) in her arms. The final stage directions enforce what is anyway clear in performance: that whatever the merits of taking her medicine, the other world will never leave her: 'We hear music at last. Coloured lights play on her face [. . .] Dissocia still exists, caged within her head. There is little doubt that she will return to her kingdom' (p. 285).[15]

Realism (2006)

Where *Dissocia* had been concerned with the dream world of the mentally disturbed and highly imaginative Lisa, with *Realism* – which opened on 14 August 2006 – Neilson turned his attention to the tension between the real and the imagined worlds of a supposedly sane and ordinary man, Stuart, as he picks his way through just another Saturday. By the end of the play, when asked 'What did you do today?' he answers, 'Today?' (*Pause.*) 'Fuck all' (p. 355). The audience are privileged, however, to witness the scenarios enacted in Stuart's head, which mix reality and fantasy.

However, the audience is aware from the outset that whatever is to confront them in performance, it is only too evidently not 'normal'. Although the opening dialogue, in which Stuart declines his mate Paul's invitation to join him for a game of five-a-side football, is entirely naturalistic, it takes place in a large open-plan living space that incorporates all the different rooms without walls or doors, that slopes towards the audience, and is covered in sand in which all the expected items of furniture, the sofa, the fridge, the washing machine, the television, the lavatory are buried. Furthermore, though Paul is present in Stuart's space and active on stage, they are actually communicating by phone – an instrument that figures large in the narrative but is never present, lines of communication being erratic in this play. It is not long before a remembered dream intrudes and Stuart is confronted by the absent figures of his mother and father. This is but the start of a sequence of events in which the movement between the real and the imagined becomes more frenetic and more bizarre. Thus he is established at the outset as a perfectly ordinary guy, and both he and Paul bear the first names of the actors playing them: what is real and what is not?

At the end of the first scene, Stuart's mother alerts him to the presence of Israeli fighter planes in the sky, and the second scene concludes with him watching television while, unnoticed by him, around the room a war zone explodes into life, with people throwing themselves into the sand, seeking cover behind the appliances. Throughout the play, although his imagination takes him on wonderful journeys, he remains mired in his own room and in his own head. This does not prevent him from making a number of quite remarkable interventions in the world of communication, including an appearance on *Desert Island Discs* and a wonderful riposte to politicians of both right and left on the subject of the ban on smoking in public places that had just come into operation in Scotland: a riposte that results in the BBC announcer addressing the radio audience, 'I'm afraid we have no choice but to abandon this week's *Any Questions* due to a stunningly lucid intervention from a member of the public' (p. 310). Neilson scores a double hit when, after allowing Stuart a wonderfully obscene on-line destruction of a persistent cold-caller, his mother brings the nuisance through the door, an apologetic cripple, wheelchair-bound and with an IV drip.

Stuart's sense of himself as a one-man protest against commercialism and bureaucracy is given its most theatrical manifestation at the end of the first act. Angered on opening a letter with a council tax demand he believes he has already settled, he starts to sing 'What a bunch of cunts, what a bunch of cunts' (pp. 318–19). A troupe of dancers appears on stage, with the men blacked up as in the 1970s BBC television series, *The Black and White Minstrels* – 'a spectacularly incorrect show', as Neilson describes it – and a fully choreographed realisation of Stuart's lyrics ensues (p. 319). A Minstrel defends himself against Stuart's charge of racism, countering that 'It was your idea', as indeed it was (p. 319). The sequence epitomises Neilson's delight in the construction of bad taste and, hardly surprisingly, his investigation of Stuart's sexual fantasies reveals an altogether unexpected world of the imagination, involving as it does an incident in which his current on-off girlfriend masturbates his ex-flame while she is sat on the toilet attempting to accede to his demand that she pee in his presence.

The fact that Stuart is presented as an unremarkable man is what makes his creation of a stage full of absent characters the more hilarious and engrossing. These extraordinary events are simply the product of a very ordinary day, a testament to the untapped – if often embarrassing – resources of each member of the audience. The play concludes with a formal severance of the realms of reality and the imagination in a way that serves to underline their inter-connection. A box is flown in with all the kitchen furniture in its proper place. Stuart enters and starts to make a cup of tea; Angie briefly appears to empty the washing machine. Stuart drinks his tea and 'eventually the theatre empties' (p. 355). The only remaining clue to the previously disclosed other-world comes from Angie's discovery that '*a stray red sock has caused the whites to come out pink*' (p. 355).

Summary

Although originally a playwright very much associated with the 'in-yer-face theatre' of the 1990s, Neilson's later work, while never losing its potential to shock audiences, looks back to an earlier tradition of surrealist and absurdist drama. In his 'Foreword' to the original *Dissocia* play text, he rejects 'in-yer-face theatre' and embraces absurdism.[16] The way in which he works, directing his own plays, largely creating his experiential effects in the rehearsal process, is vital to his examination of the relationship between the conscious and the subconscious roots of human behaviour. For his plays are all about the process of exploration, a process that yields results that cover the full range of human behaviour, from the most unpleasant to the downright farcical. Whatever insights Neilson has to offer, comedy is never very far away, whether it be the black humour of the condemned man's cell in *Normal* or the absurdity of a son addressing a mother who is in the washing machine in *Realism*.

His work is never overtly political in the sense of that generation of playwrights dating from 1968 whose work I discuss in *New British Political Dramatists*. In *Realism*, for example, he appears to be making a comment about Israeli imperialism, but adds a note to his text: 'At the time of writing, in 2006, Israel had invaded Lebanon. Substitute a more topical/timeless reference if necessary' (p. 297). But neither does it espouse the non-political line of Ionesco, for example. Neilson's characters live in a real world, and are confronted by the problems of that world. There is nothing of the preacher about him, and if there is a single most important political impulse underlying his work it is towards individual anarchism.

Neilson is now solidly established as one of the major writers of what can be acknowledged as a remarkable generation of playwrights. Rightly selected by Aleks Sierz as one of the three playwrights chosen for extensive analysis in *In-Yer-Face Theatre*, he has also attracted attention from other quarters. For example, director Dominic Dromgoole points out that 'a sense of threat' hovers over his plays, and that 'sex is a weapon constantly wielded, often by women against men', while David Ian Rabey describes how his work typically 'lays out a confrontational, insistent and socially contradictory physicality', staging the 'unsettling immediacy of the physical presence'.[17] Other accounts (such as those of Ian Brown, Trish Reid and Adrienne Scullion) place him in the context of Scottish theatre. Since his emergence, Neilson has gone on to plough a very individual course and, whatever he offers in the future, what is certain is that audiences will continue to be shocked and disturbed, amused and delighted, sometimes confusingly all at the same time.

Primary Sources

Works by Anthony Neilson

Plays One: Normal, Penetrator, Year of the Family, The Night Before Christmas, The Censor (London: Methuen Drama, 1998).
Plays Two: Edward Gant's Amazing Feats of Loneliness!, The Lying Kind, The Wonderful World of Dissocia, Realism (London: Methuen Drama, 2008).
Stitching (London: Methuen Drama, 2002).
The Wonderful World of Dissocia and *Realism* (London: Methuen Drama, 2007).

Secondary Sources

Aragay, Mireia et al., *British Theatre of the 1990s: Interviews with Directors, Playwrights, Critics and Academics* (Basingstoke: Palgrave Macmillan, 2007).
Barnett, Laura, 'Portrait of the Artist: Anthony Neilson, Playwright', *Guardian*, 3 March 2009 <http://www.guardian.co.uk/culture/2009/mar/03/anthony-neilson>
Brown, Ian, 'Alternative Sensibilities: Devolutionary Comedy and Scottish Camp', in Berthold Schoene (ed.), *Contemporary Scottish Literature* (Edinburgh: EUP, 2007), pp. 319–27.
Bull, John, *New British Political Dramatists* (Basingstoke: Palgrave Macmillan, 1984).
Cavendish, Dominic, 'I Want to Disturb People', *Daily Telegraph*, 16 August 2004 <http://www.telegraph.co.uk/culture/theatre/drama/3622348/Edinburgh-reports-I-want-to-disturb-people.html>
D'Monté, Rebecca and Graham Saunders (eds), *Cool Britannia: British Political Theatre in the 1990s* (Basingstoke: Palgrave Macmillan, 2007).
Dromgoole, Dominic, *The Full Room: An A–Z of Contemporary Playwriting* (London: Methuen Drama, 2002).
Logan, Brian, 'Anthony Neilson: Promise? I was Showing That Years Ago', *Independent*, 24 November 2002 <http://www.independent.co.uk/arts-entertainment/theatre-dance/features/anthony-neilson-promise-i-was-showing-that-years-ago-600950.html>
McMillan, Joyce, 'Reality Bites for a Rebel with a Cause to Explore', *Scotsman*, 11 August 2006 <http://findarticles.com/p/news-articles/scotsman-edinburgh-scotland-the/mi_7951/is_2006_August_11/reality-bites-rebel-explore/ai_n34363728/>
Neilson, Anthony, 'Foreword', *The Wonderful World of Dissocia* and *Realism* (London: Methuen Drama, 2007), no pgn.
Rabey, David Ian, *English Drama Since 1940* (Harlow: Longman, 2003).
Ravenhill, Mark, 'I Want to Stay Pure', *Guardian*, 26 August 2004 <http://www.guardian.co.uk/stage/2004/aug/26/theatre.edinburghfestival20042>

Reid, Trish, '"Deformities of the Frame": The Theatre of Anthony Neilson', *Contemporary Theatre Review*, Vol. 17, No. 4 (2007), pp. 487–98.

Scullion, Adrienne, 'Devolution and Drama: Imagining the Possible', in Berthold Schoene (ed.), *Contemporary Scottish Literature* (Edinburgh: EUP, 2007), pp. 68–77.

—, 'Theatre in Scotland in the 1990s and Beyond', in Baz Kershaw (ed.), *The Cambridge History of British Theatre Volume 3: Since 1895* (Cambridge: CUP, 2004), pp. 470–84.

Sierz, Aleks, *In-Yer-Face Theatre: British Drama Today* (London: Faber & Faber, 2001).

Stark, Kathleen, 'Battlefield "Body": Gregory Burke's *Gagarin Way* and Anthony Neilson's *Stitching*', in Hans-Ulrich Mohr and Kerstin Machler (eds), *Extending the Code: New Forms of Dramatic and Theatrical Expression* (Trier: WVT, 2004), pp. 171–9.

Taylor, Paul, 'Anthony Neilson: Gut Feelings', *Independent*, 27 November 2002 <http://www.independent.co.uk/arts-entertainment/theatre-dance/features/anthony-neilson-gut-feelings-605488.html>

Notes

1. Anthony Neilson, *Plays Two*, p. ix.
2. Quoted in Aleks Sierz, *In-Yer-Face-Theatre*, p. 65.
3. Joyce McMillan, 'Reality Bites for a Rebel with a Cause to Explore'.
4. Sierz, *In-Yer-Face-Theatre*, p. 66.
5. Ibid.
6. Ibid.
7. Ibid.
8. Laura Barnett, 'Portrait of the Artist: Anthony Neilson, Playwright'.
9. Quoted in Sierz, *In-Yer-Face-Theatre*, p. 68.
10. Brian Logan, 'Anthony Neilson: Promise? I was Showing That Years Ago'; Mark Ravenhill, 'I Want to Stay Pure'.
11. Reviews of *Penetrator* in *Theatre Record*, Vol. XIII, No. 21 (1993), p. 1151; Vol. XIV, No. 1 (1994), pp. 38–9.
12. See Paul Taylor, 'Anthony Neilson: Gut Feelings'.
13. Reviews of *The Censor* in *Theatre Record*, Vol. XVII, Nos 7; 12; 18 (1997), pp. 407; 712–14; 1132–4.
14. Dominic Cavendish, 'I Want to Disturb People'.
15. Reviews of *The Wonderful World of Dissocia* in *Theatre Record*, Vol. XXVII, No. 7 (2007), pp. 383–6.
16. Anthony Neilson, 'Foreword'.
17. Dominic Dromgoole, *The Full Room*, p. 215; David Ian Rabey, *English Drama*, p. 197.

19 JOE PENHALL

Margarete Rubik

Some Voices; Love and Understanding; Blue/Orange; Dumb Show; Landscape with Weapon

Introduction

Joe Penhall was born in 1967 in Surrey; the family emigrated to Australia in 1976. At the age of twenty, Penhall returned to London, taking various odd jobs and finally working as a reporter for local London newspapers. He then became involved in the Royal Court Young People's Theatre, where he was taught by, among others, April De Angelis, Hanif Kureishi and Caryl Churchill.[1] The Royal Court, indeed, was to prove decisive for both his artistic training and for the launching of his career.

His first work, however, premiered on the fringe. It was a one-act drama about friendship, exploitation and violence, called *Wild Turkey*, and was performed during the 1993 London New Play Festival at the Old Red Lion Theatre. He then wrote *Some Voices*, which was given a reading at the Battersea Arts Centre in 1993, but was turned down by the Bush, the National and the Hampstead theatres. However, it caught the attention of Royal Court artistic director Stephen Daldry, who put it on at the Royal Court Upstairs in 1994 in a season that culminated with Sarah Kane's *Blasted* in 1995. Penhall's play was a commercial and critical success: it won the Thames Television Bursary and the John Whiting Award in 1995, and was performed in France and New York. In 2000 Penhall wrote the screenplay for the film version (Film Four).

Pale Horse, about a man's inability to deal with bereavement, followed in 1995, again at the Royal Court, and also went to Europe and New York. In 1995 Penhall became writer-in-residence at the

National Theatre, where he worked with playwright Stephen Jeffreys.[2] The Bush put on *Love and Understanding* in 1997. The less successful *Bullet* was performed at the Donmar in 1998. His greatest success to date, *Blue/Orange*, was staged at the National Theatre in 2000 and won the *Evening Standard* Best Play of the Year Award (2000), the Critics' Circle Theatre Award for Best Play (2000) and the Olivier Award for Best New Play (2001). In 2004 Penhall returned to the Royal Court with *Dumb Show*. His last play to date, *Landscape with Weapon*, was put on at the National in 2007.

In between, Penhall has worked for television and has been in increasing demand as a screenwriter. He dramatised Ian McEwan's *Enduring Love* (Pathe, 2004), Jake Arnott's *The Long Firm* (BBC, 2004) and Cormac McCarthy's *The Road* (2929 Productions, 2009) for the big and small screens. In 1996 he wrote a short film about schizophrenia, *Go Back Out*, which was broadcast by BBC2, for whom he also directed *The Undertaker* (2005) and wrote the detective series *Moses Jones* (2009).

The Plays

Some Voices (1994)

Some Voices, which opened in Ian Rickson's Royal Court studio production on 15 September 1994, deals with schizophrenia, one of the last taboos in our society. It was inspired by an experience that had haunted Penhall for years: a friend who seemed mad was in fact suffering from schizophrenia.[3] The title hints at the acoustic hallucinations said to be typical of schizophrenia, but also indicates that a voice is given to people normally silenced in our society.

In the play, Ray, a schizophrenic, is released from an asylum in compliance with legislation of the Conservative government recommending the discharge of mental patients into what was called Care in the Community. His brother Pete, who takes him in and is supposed to make Ray take his medication, regularly report to a psychiatrist and prevent him from getting into trouble, is driven to his wits' end by the responsibility he has assumed. Ray is a likeable but emotionally unstable young man and all he wants is a life of harmless fun, but he refuses to take pills that work like 'a smack on the head with a claw-hammer' (p. 8), and randomly lapses into aggression. He saves Laura, a young woman, from abuse by Dave, her thuggish boyfriend, and falls in love with her. The idyll, however, is short-lived. Laura withdraws, frightened by his verbal outbreaks and mental illness. She herself, however, also harbours a potential for violence: when Ray saves her from a further attack and possibly death by hitting Dave on the head with a hammer, she cudgels her abuser several more times until he sustains brain damage. In the end, Pete instals his disabled brother in a hostel and is gently teaching him the simple pleasures of cooking a tasty omelette.

What looks like bleak tragedy is actually laced with black humour, the characters' language ranging from slang to poetic intensity. The two acts are structured chronologically but intertwine three strands of action: the strained but basically loving relationship between the brothers, Ray's affair with Laura, and finally the appearance of Ives, an escaped inmate of the asylum, who ends up dead on the streets. The play moves from one climax to another in quick succession, putting the spectators 'through a relentless emotional knockabout', exhausting them, 'because that's what schizophrenia does to you. [. . .] I was dragging people beyond their sense of endurance.'[4] Horseplay gives way to violence and vice versa. When Ray threatens to ignite himself and Pete manages to coax a lighter from him five times, this may look like farce, were it not for the real threat Ray poses to himself and others.

Penhall arouses understanding and compassion for Ray's plight without sentimentalising his condition. Schizophrenia may (also) be a 'symbol of urban alienation', but Ray is undoubtedly ill, although spectators are baffled as to how ill or dangerous he actually is.[5] We sympathise with his annoyance that an over-anxious Pete 'worries I might accidently enjoy myself' (p. 40) and with his refusal to deaden his sensibilities with anti-psychotic drugs, only to be shocked subsequently at his wish to gun down Pete's noisy neighbours in their fancy cars and to kill himself. Ives's sad death on the streets is a potent reminder of what might happen to Ray without professional care.

Despite Penhall's criticism of the policy of emptying mental homes, however, hospitalisation and sedation with drugs is no solution either.

Ray is not the only character who seems mad. Ives is seriously deranged and given to apocalyptic speeches, but voices a touching critique of institutional – and social – callousness:

> **Ives** They pretend to care – they profess to know how to be in
> the business of caring, which to me . . . is no different to a
> butcher professing to know how to operate on the brain.
> (p. 5)

Dave is pathologically jealous and abusive; Laura has no qualms about bashing in his head; and Pete, an icon of normality, is driven frantic by responsibilities for which he is not qualified and complains in all earnestness that Ray helped an abused woman: 'Never get involved. [. . .] That's not your problem' (p. 29).

Penhall himself had lived in Shepherd's Bush, west London, where the play is set, and

> felt strongly that newspaper articles weren't enough to convey
> the true misery and loneliness of schizophrenia, unemploy-
> ment, redundancy, alcoholism, domestic violence and
> everything else that was going on around me.[6]

The play he wrote instead took off: *The Sunday Times* hailed *Some Voices* as 'the most thrilling playwriting debut in years'.[7]

Love and Understanding (1997)

After the 'angst-ridden, dark' early works, Penhall wanted his new play – which opened at the Bush on 30 April 1997, directed by Mike Bradwell – 'to be lighter and funnier than the others. Frivolous even. [. . .] I wanted articulate, witty characters for a change. I was tired of grand, easily identifiable drama about madness and death.'[8] For his plot, he turned to his own experience of 'friends from old drifting in, drinking, taking my money'.[9] He was also struck by his experience as a reporter that reactionary politicians were always more 'articulate and floridly quotable' than the 'vaguely well-intentioned' representatives of the Labour Party, and although Richie in the play is not a Tory, the play does contrast his manipulative eloquence to his friend's honest plodding.[10] The power of rhetoric to convince and charm was later taken up again in *Blue/Orange*. The play also has a literary model: it reverses the situation in Pinter's *Homecoming* by making 'mad bad Richie' return from America to his 'square friends' in London.[11]

Richie turns up out of the blue at the door of his best friend, blithely disregarding the fact that Neal and his partner Rachel, chronically overworked doctors, need to spend time alone to work through a rough patch in their relationship. Richie wheedles money from Neal, helping himself to drugs from the hospital's refrigerator and unscrupulously playing off his two hosts against each other. He makes Neal look boring to Rachel, and Rachel querulous to Neal, while both are fascinated by Richie's supposedly glamorous life. In the end, the couple split up, with Neal quitting his stressful job, cynically adopting the frivolous values on which his irresponsible friend seems to thrive, and throwing Richie out of his flat. It remains doubtful whether Neal and Rachel will ever get together again.

Penhall carefully made several scenes of the play mirror one another: thus, in the two bedroom scenes in Acts One and Two, Richie at first voyeuristically spies on the couple through the bedroom door, while later Neal from the same position catches Rachel and Richie in bed together. In addition, in a series of similar scenes, one character misrepresents to another what the third one supposedly said or did, with Richie alternately ganging up with one of the lovers against the other. Neal and Rachel are both offended by the supposed unkindness and betrayal of their partner, unaware that they are doing the very same thing. Their gullibility is farcically exaggerated, as is Richie's amazing insolence.

Penhall uses a firework of humour often based on Richie's completely unexpected or inappropriate replies. Drugs are 'a form of self-medication' and his friend is a 'spoilsport' (p. 178) because he refuses to give him morphine. Richie is egomaniac, selfish and unscrupulous – but he is also a flamboyant charmer.

> **Neal** I'm thinking people like him are having all the fun.
> Even when he's not having fun he does it better than me.
> (p. 227)

Rachel, who is nostalgic about her carefree student days and dreams of a trip around the world, for which Neal, worrying about his job and mortgage, shows no interest, is attracted to the dazzling world of adventure Richie seems to symbolise and is torn, as Penhall puts it, between 'the simultaneous lusts for freedom and stability'.[12]

Neal's idealism and boring normality are pitted against Richie's mendacious charisma and cynicism, although – as is typical of Penhall – things are not quite so unequivocal. For all his bravado, Richie's life is in reality anything but glamorous: he is an unsuccessful journalist and seems to have no other friends. Aleks Sierz sees in the play 'two sides of masculinity in crisis': Richie is too insincere and Neal too repressed.[13] Besides, not only Richie, but also Neal and Rachel are oblivious to each other's needs, and Richie's insight into the self-destructiveness of Neal's anxiety is sound enough, even though he turns the whole thing into a joke.

> **Richie** If you don't care enough you're a bad doctor and if
> you care too much you'll go insane and be no use to
> anyone etcetera. It's a dilemma. And the answer's very
> very simple. [. . .] You're not cut out to be a doctor.
> Maybe you should try something a little less cut-throat.
> Like show business. (p. 194)

None the less, Penhall clearly champions Neal's unfashionable virtues over Richie's alluring irresponsibility. By the end of the play Neal has become a cynic himself, is on the dole and drinking furiously. He may have become less vulnerable emotionally, but the audience will hardly think this a change for the better.

Blue/Orange (2000)

With *Blue/Orange*, which opened in the Cottesloe space at the

National Theatre on 7 April 2000, directed by Roger Michell, Penhall
returned to the topic of schizophrenia and the drama of ideas. The
play, which he had thought about for seven years and then wrote
down without much revision, was greeted with rave reviews in the
London papers.[14] It was hailed as 'Britain's best new play' since
Michael Frayn's *Copenhagen* (1998) and 'thrillingly original', 'one of
the best new plays in the National's history', 'a mind-blowing must
see'.[15] Penhall wanted it to say 'something that nobody else was saying,
and that needed to be said, and seen by as many people as possible'.[16]

The title refers to young black patient Christopher's delusion that
oranges are blue, and 'the slash [. . .] between two colours represents
the fracture in personality that stereotypically defines schizophrenia'.[17]
The play is set in an asylum, where he is about to be released after his
twenty-eight days of observation. However, Bruce, the young
psychiatrist in charge, is having second thoughts and wishes to retain
him in hospital because he suspects him of being schizophrenic. His
consultant Robert thinks this is a misdiagnosis resulting from cultural
prejudice and wants to dismiss Christopher into Care in the
Community to free up hospital beds for new patients. Their controversy turns increasingly acerbic until the well-being of the patient has
been forgotten in each psychiatrist's furious attempt to gain the upper
hand. The quarrel continues right to the end, although Bruce is likely
to be dismissed at Robert's instigation.

The three acts are tightly structured, constantly reversing the
relationship between the characters. Thus in Act One Bruce examines
the patient, but by the end of Act Three he himself faces an examination for professional misdemeanour. Christopher is torn between
denial of his illness and a wish for a cure, between the wish to go home
(Acts One and Three) and the wish to stay (Act Two) – possibly
because he has internalised Bruce's anxiety. Thoughtless remarks
made by the two doctors in the course of the play incriminate them in
the last act, when Bruce is charged with racism because he repeated
Christopher's self-assessment of being an 'uppity nigga' (pp. 9, 20,
88), and a metaphor Bruce used to explain transference causes
Christopher's delusion of literally thinking Bruce's thoughts.

The riveting effect of the play depends on constantly forcing us to reassess both the patient and our sympathies. Penhall gives both doctors a case and involves us in an insoluble moral conundrum. Bruce at first seems an inflexible, intolerably patronising young control freak, so we side with Robert, a disciple of R. D. Laing's anti-psychiatry movement and an admirer of Allen Ginsberg, who believes that white doctors' diagnoses of mental illness in ethnic minorities may have a strong ethnocentric bias and seems benign and liberal. But then he reveals himself as an irresponsible careerist who acts out of self-interest and expediency, whereas Bruce seems to be genuinely worried about Christopher. Throughout the play our sympathies fluctuate, until we realise that both care less about the patient than about winning their power struggle. Christopher, however, is no mere pawn over whom the two specialists argue. He himself slyly sets the two doctors upon each other.

Right to the end it remains unclear whether he is schizophrenic or only has borderline symptoms. Bruce suspects serious mental illness because Christopher claims he is the son of Idi Amin and that oranges are blue. But the seemingly implausible story of his parentage might just possibly be true. And although the blue oranges are, for Bruce, 'classic hallucinatory behaviour' (p. 45), Robert gloatingly points out that Eluard wrote a surrealist poem entitled 'Le Monde est Bleu comme une Orange' (p. 45) and that there is a children's book called *Tintin and the Blue Orange* (p. 46) – which destabilises our conviction that such idiosyncrasy must necessarily be a sign of madness. When it transpires in Act Three that Christopher also claims Muhammad Ali as a father, we are shocked but still unable to gauge whether he needs to be confined or could cope on his own. True – he has delusions and is easily influenced – but does this make him a case for extended hospitalisation?

As in *Some Voices*, Penhall is entirely unsentimental about mental illness and liberally employs black humour. Christopher can be sharp and witty, modulating between articulateness and slang, irony and naïveté. It is unclear whether he really takes several metaphors and jokes literally or just pretends to, and whether he really does not remember why he should not drink coffee or is just trying to provoke Bruce.

In the main, the play consists of a battle of arguments between the two psychiatrists, in which they use professional jargon, rhetorical dexterity and every dirty trick they know in their fight for power. As in *Love and Understanding*, witty and silver-tongued Robert has an advantage over the less articulate Bruce, who tends to lose emotional control more easily.

> **Robert** It's a matter of 'opinion'. And I'd be loath to resection the boy on a basis of a difference of opinion. It's semantics. And right now, Doctor, my semantics are better than yours so I win.
> **Bruce** I can't live with that diagnosis.
> **Robert** *You* don't have to. (p. 28)

While the doctors' quarrel is conducted with urbane malice at first, it gets completely out of hand in Act Three, when Robert and Bruce abuse each other and the patient. Such is the fury of the quarrel that occasionally all three characters sound mad.

For twenty years, the *Spectator* wrote, there has not been 'a better or more enthralling drama about the world of mental health'.[18] The play addresses a host of contentious issues: madness and the problematic policy of Care in the Community; racism and cultural prejudice; and professional rivalry. Its power is due to Penhall's 'refusal to give simple answers to difficult questions'.[19]

Christopher's case raises, for instance, the question about why African males are much more likely to receive a schizophrenia diagnosis than white males. Might behaviour acceptable in the minority culture seem lunatic only to Anglo-Saxon psychiatrists and might supposed madness thus be simply a matter of cultural difference? Robert's research into the cultural element in people's behaviour and institutionalised cultural prejudice is cutting-edge and relevant, but it is compromised by his selfish motives: by following government guidelines on desectioning he hopes to further his career. He also wants to use Christopher as an object of research, entirely disregarding the fact that the patient comes from Shepherd's Bush and thus a theory of cultural difference cannot really apply to him. He means to send him out into the Care of the Community, although Christopher has no community to go to and no one to care for him. Robert thus 'appropriates essentially liberal notions [. . .] for reactionary means'.[20]

However, he often has a point. As a follower of the anti-psychiatry movement Robert argues that mental illness is socially constructed and that anger, depression and paranoia are 'maybe [. . .] the only *suitable* response to the human condition' (p. 33). His antagonist Bruce smugly calls Laing a '*madman*' (p. 33), but Christopher's belief that people stare at him and harass him, which Bruce takes as proof of his mental illness, might well be a natural result of society's racism. Indeed, just because you are paranoid does not mean they are not after you.

> **Robert** It's just occurred to me that when Chris talks about his 'neighbours', he might not mean literally 'the people next door'. Do you, Chris? Nor would you mean 'sibling' should you allude to a 'Brother'. [. . .] Neighbours is Everybody, isn't it? People in the street giving you a wide berth. Women on escalators holding their handbags that little bit tighter as you pass. People looking straight through you as if you're not even there. Football hooligans. Skinheads. Throwing bananas. Your work-mates. Bruce and I can only guess at the horror of suffering from acute paranoia and being one of the culturally oppressed minority. (pp. 111–12)

Bruce, deeply convinced that a release would be disastrous for the patient, fails to appreciate the social stigma attached to a diagnosis of schizophrenia. Here, as at several other points in the play, Penhall paradoxically uses the dubious Robert as his mouthpiece:

> **Robert** Schizophrenia is the worst pariah.
> One of the last great taboos.
> People don't understand it.
> They don't want to understand it.

It scares them.

It depresses them.

It is not treatable with glamorous and intriguing wonderdrugs like Prozac or Viagra.

It isn't newsworthy.

It isn't curable.

It isn't heroin or Ecstasy.

It is not the preserve of rock stars and supermodels and hip young authors.

It is not a topic of dinner-party conversation.

Organised crime gets better press.

They make *movies* about junkies and alcoholics and gangsters and men who drink too much, fall over and beat their woman until bubbles come out of her nose, but schizophrenia, my friend, is just not in the phone book. (p. 54)

The alternatives of either long-term hospitalisation or sending the patient out into the streets both seem equally unattractive. As in *Some Voices*, the problem seems to be the unavailability of sheltered accommodation, which could perhaps help him find his way in a hostile society. Although highly critical of the policy of saving money on hospital beds at the expense of patients, Penhall does not indict mental asylums or the medical profession in general. He 'uses the medical trade as a metaphor for the vanity, self-deception and ostentatious certainty' of professionals in power.[21]

Dumb Show (2004)

Dumb Show – which opened at the Royal Court on 2 September 2004, directed by Terry Johnson – is an acerbic satire on entrapment journalism. Two unscrupulous journalists disguise themselves as bankers to entrap the gullible Barry, a declining TV comedian possibly modelled on Michael Barrymore, into indiscretions which they record with a hidden camera and microphone. They flatter, cajole and egg him on, until he offers the woman drugs and sex, whereupon they blackmail him into making a confession to their tabloid. The ensuing scandal results in his show being axed. None the less, after the death of his estranged wife, Barry is willing to meet Liz once more, to put a new sentimental spin on his enduring conjugal love beyond the grave, in the hope of a sizeable fee and possibly the chance of a new career.

Penhall walks a tightrope between black comedy and tragedy. The two acts trace Barry's decline from swaggering vanity to aggression and despair, until he finally adapts to the rules of the game. In contrast to the sophisticated language used by the educated characters of *Blue/ Orange* or *Love and Understanding*, the style is flat, full of repetition, cliché, hypocritical moralising, primitive flattery and fake sympathy, imitating the banality of the tabloid style which Penhall was familiar with from his days as a journalist. A passage where Liz and Greg deliberate whether the story of Barry's drug abuse and desertion by his wife would sell better as melodrama or moral outrage serves as a good example.

> **Greg** In *his* pain he turned to . . .
> **Liz** Unable to *face* it he regrettably found himself turning to . . .
> **Greg** Yes, yes, but only because of *her* pain . . .
> **Liz** Absolutely. Or: he didn't even care.
> **Greg** How do you mean?
> **Liz** Maybe he didn't even feel any pain. That's the kind of person he is. They had everything *and yet* . . . even as she lay dying, he was in a five-star luxury hotel snorting large amounts of fucking hard drugs . . . eh? Propositioning young *women*. Eh?
> **Greg** O-ho. Cynical.
> **Liz** People like cynicism. (pp. 182–3)

Even Barry's gags are lame – although occasionally he does muster genuine wit, as in the quip 'If Jesus Christ were alive today you'd be going through his *bins*' (p. 170). That the play is none the less funny is due to the moral obtuseness of the two journalists and their complete unawareness that their moral indignation most appropriately applies to themselves. They pretend to work in the public interest. After blackmailing him, they assure Barry that 'we don't want you to feel you're being pressured here. [. . .] We're absolutely sensitive' (p. 161) and advise him not to 'take it personally' (p. 159).

Some critics have complained that the play tells us nothing new about tabloid (im)morality and, because of the utter contempt we feel for the two sleazy journalists, fails to explore 'the real conflict between necessary investigation and unwarranted intrusion' and 'lacks the moral dilemmas that make for gripping drama'.[22] In return, Penhall complained that reviewers were always looking for a darker message but that he simply wanted to write a 'funny play about a funny guy and the mess he gets himself into'.[23] Although Barry is vain and greedy, his vulnerability arouses pity. But the play also shows that 'there is a symbiotic relationship between the prey and the predators' and that the insatiable interest in scandal and the private lives of celebrities on the part of the public makes us complicit in such tabloid stings.[24]

Landscape with Weapon (2007)

In *Landscape with Weapon* – which opened on 29 March 2007 at the National Theatre's Cottesloe space, directed by Roger Michell – Penhall returns to staging a moral dilemma, namely the moral responsibility of the scientist. Dan is shocked when he learns that his brother Ned, a genius inventor, has designed unmanned air vehicles, so-called drones, which no longer need GPS but rely on each other to navigate and can hence be sent down tunnels or into houses to pick out specified human targets. When Ned belatedly develops moral qualms because the Ministry of Defence retains a controlling share of the intellectual property and means to split it with the Americans, who might then sell the weapons to their allies, he refuses to sign the contract, but is duped and pressured into compliance, and then made redundant. In revenge, he programs a bug into the system, sabotaging his own prototype. However, the Secret Service tracks him down and forces him to give up the programming code. He ends up a mental wreck like Pinter's Stanley, paranoid and with the

Stockholm syndrome, desperately trying to atone by offering to make beautiful toys – as Leonardo da Vinci, another designer of weaponry, did.[25]

The first of the two acts concentrates on the relation of the two brothers and their dispute about the drones. Because Ned had to sign a gagging order, information about what he is actually up to is only revealed gradually, to the mounting horror of his pacifist brother. While Ned proudly defends his invention as a paradigm shifter, his brother Dan recognises his invention as a weapon of mass destruction – although Dan is ill qualified to take the high moral ground, given that he semi-legally injects his rich patients with botox. In Act Two, focusing on his negotiations with the commercial head of the weapons factory and the Secret Service agent, Ned has radically changed his mind. The play presents a variety of arguments for and against the design of new weapons and the scientist's responsibility. However, as is typical of Penhall, there is also a lot of humour, ranging from witticisms to slapstick, when the two brothers wrestle and throw food at each other. At other points, Ned waxes absurdly poetical about his inventions: 'It'll make guided missiles look like nutcrackers . . . it'll be like a symphony in the sky!' (p. 20).

In spite of generally friendly reviews, most critics complained that Ned's initial naïveté is incredible and his 'Damascene conversion comes a little late in the play'.[26] Indeed, his belief that the military will finance his research but not control the product or that in such a business political expediency will not take precedence over a fair deal is simple-minded. 'Where did you train – *Disneyland*?', the cynical intelligence officer asks (p. 64). Whether spectators will think the 'dice are too loaded' for genuine ethical debate depends on their moral beliefs.[27] Although there are some plausible arguments for production (the right to defend oneself against aggression, terrorists killing hostages and using civilians as a shield), the weight of the objections is overwhelming: 'It's a shame that Penhall couldn't make the debate more disconcerting for the National's liberal audience.'[28]

Ned initially tries to defend the weaponised drones as deterrents and means of eliminating collateral damage, but he cannot rule out mistakes, quite apart from the danger of their getting into the wrong hands. Besides, with such technological superiority, the West will never have to negotiate.

> **Ned** As long as we have swarming technology and weaponised UAWs we'll never work with people, never negotiate, never make any effort to find a real solution to their misery, never consider cultural and religious antecedents, we're just going to bring out the big guns and move on to the next war. (p. 60)

To be sure, responsibility for launching weapons will ultimately lie with politicians and military commanders; Ned, however, is not worried about legal liability, but about his own conscience. Scientists are not unmoved when their inventions are used for mass killings – as is exemplified, for instance, by Robert Oppenheimer, who was conscience-stricken when the atomic bomb he had helped invent was dropped on Hiroshima and Nagasaki. This is what makes the commercial director of the factory so horrifying – she thinks that producing the drones will be 'fun' (p. 38). What saved da Vinci was perhaps the good luck that his weapons were never made – so '[h]e never had to worry about . . . consequences' (p. 82).

Summary

Penhall is a difficult dramatist to classify. He does not belong to a school and does not wish to be pigeonholed. His plays are concerned with diverse themes, some intending to 'shift people's preconceptions', while others merely wish to entertain.[29] His early plays gained him a 'tough guy reputation' and Aleks Sierz put him into the 'Battered and Bruised' chapter of his *In-Yer-Face Theatre*, but such tags unduly foreground the use of physical violence, which is absent from all later plays, which focus much more on moral dilemmas. Nor can the term 'naturalism' adequately describe his style. Criticism that his figures occasionally do not behave the way people would in reality

(Why does Neal not throw Richie out earlier? Would Bruce really dare to abuse his superior?) miss the point. His characters are larger than life and either move towards farce (as in *Dumb Show* or *Love and Understanding*) or, more often, towards what he calls 'heightened naturalism' or 'poetic realism'.[30] Penhall's 'dialectical imagination' makes him consummate at dramatising moral dilemmas. He is at his best when he ascribes convincing arguments to both antagonists, which makes it impossible for the audience to take sides and constantly forces them to reassess the characters – splendidly realised, for instance, in *Some Voices* and *Blue/Orange*, not quite so successfully in *Landscape with Weapon*.[31]

Despite his brilliant ability to enter the minds of both antagonists, he always conveys a strong sense of moral conviction, of right and wrong, but without resorting to preaching. At a time when playwrights, as he claims, are encouraged to write 'paeans to depravity', such an attitude 'risks seeming old-fashioned, as traditionally lefty as the conservative structure of his plays. Yet Penhall's stance is precisely a critique of postmodern culture's attitude that "anything goes".'[32] So firmly has he become associated in critical perception with problem plays about moral conundrums as his hallmark that these expectations become a kind of 'albatross' for him whenever he decides to write less meditative plays, such as *Dumb Show*, in which he was 'just poking fun at show biz because I have been immersed in it for the last four years'.[33] He is also annoyed when he is tied down and connected to one particular theme and milieu, the unprivileged underclass. 'I felt like I was becoming a tool of the Left.'[34]

Penhall's early 'stories from dark places' do display an interest in and sympathy with the underdogs of society, the misfits and losers (Ben in *Wild Turkey*, Ray in *Some Voices*, Charles in *Pale Horse*, Christopher in *Blue/Orange*), but increasingly he has moved into the milieu of more educated and articulate figures (the middle-class family in *Bullet*, the doctors in *Love and Understanding* and *Blue/Orange*, engineers and top managers in *Landscape with Weapon*), although his own diagnosis that his plays generally 'involve a straight man and a misfit' embodying 'the conflict between freedom and responsibility, permissiveness and home

making' still holds basically true: Ray is contrasted to Pete, Richie to
Neal, Ned to Dan, Christopher to the doctors.[35] 'All my plays are
about the impulse towards freedom': characters want to escape from
their jobs, relationships and mental condition; but escape and
liberation also involve dangers.[36]

'More than acceptance, everybody in my plays wants understanding,' Penhall claims, echoing one of his play titles.[37] Indeed, he
makes us understand people on the margins of society, but he never
sentimentalises his figures. He is also aware that 'one of the key
components to characterisation is paradox'.[38] All his plays contain
sharp social criticism and are, as Penhall affirms, 'implicitly political in
that they attack a set of assumptions on which society is founded'.[39]
Landscape with Weapon takes an explicit stance against the American
Military-Industrial Complex and the involvement of the West in
illegal wars.

His plays display a high command of technique and are carefully
composed, constantly modifying and regrouping their original con-
figurations. They are all set in London (Shepherd's Bush is a frequent
location), generally featuring few characters: three in *Blue/Orange*,
Love and Understanding and *Dumb Show*, four in *Landscape with
Weapon* and *Wild Turkey*; only three early plays contain larger casts.
Women used to be in the background and were often cast as victims
(Laura, the mother in *Bullet*), but in his two most recent plays, *Dumb
Show* and *Landscape with Weapon*, he has portrayed strong women
who are ruthless and power-hungry.

Despite their sober subject matter, all his plays are black or tragic
comedies involving generous doses of humour but also passages of
poetic richness. There is witty repartee, but more often laughter is
aroused by unexpected answers, inappropriate responses, the dramatic
irony of characters unaware that they are indicting themselves through
what they say. Critics have praised his 'superb ear for cadence,
hesitation and emphasis' and have compared his 'laconic style', with
its 'undercurrents of unease' transcending 'prosaic naturalism'
with that of the young Pinter.[40] Like Pinter, Penhall is keenly aware of
the power verbal dexterity confers, as well as its ability to charm,
threaten and twist the truth through rhetoric. He is wary of spin and

usually gives such verbal sophistication to silver-tongued egotists such as Richie and Robert, whom he contrasts with more ingenuous characters like Neal and Bruce, who, in spite of their honesty, come across as gauche and humdrum in comparison to their urbane antagonists. He has also been compared to Mamet, who also dramatises the power play between characters, the moves and counter-moves, in fights to gain the upper hand. Moreover, Penhall remembers being impressed by a performance of Miller's *Death of a Salesman* as a boy.[41] Years later, he wrote his own version of the corrosive effect of a man's redundancy on his family in *Bullet*. The relationship of the brothers in Miller's drama, too, struck an autobiographical chord, as did Shepard's *True West*.[42] Relationships between brothers figure prominently in some of Penhall's own works (*Some Voices*, *Bullet*, *Landscape with Weapon*). In addition, he acknowledges a variety of further influences: Beckett's 'exasperated absolutism', Chekhov, Büchner's *Woyzeck*, Raymond Carver's alienated, bemused characters suddenly bursting into loquaciousness.[43] All of these authors write about 'lost people' and 'personal, subjective, existentialist dilemmas', unlike mainstream theatre; Hare, in contrast, writes about politicians and the Establishment, which is not a sphere of Penhall's abiding interest.[44]

Throughout his career, reviewers have, with few exceptions, admired both Penhall's intriguing subjects and his technical finesse. Charles Spencer in 1998 even thought that, compared to Sarah Kane, Penhall might prove 'the more enduring talent', although, unlike hers, his plays are devoid of 'theatrical exhibitionism'.[45] This, of course, remains to be seen. Penhall's last play was put on in 2007. It will be interesting to see in what direction he will move in the future.

Primary Sources

Works by Joe Penhall

Plays One: Some Voices, Pale Horse, Love and Understanding, The Bullet (London: Methuen Drama, 1998).
Plays Two: Blue/Orange, Dumb Show, Wild Turkey (London: Methuen Drama, 2008).
Landscape with Weapon (London: Methuen Drama, 2007).

Secondary Sources

Aragay, Mireia, Hildegard Klein, Enric Montforte and Pilar Zozaya (eds), *British Theatre of the 1990s: Interviews with Directors, Playwrights, Critics and Academics* (Basingstoke: Palgrave Macmillan, 2007).

Devine, Harriet, *Looking Back: Playwrights at the Royal Court, 1956–2006* (London: Faber & Faber, 2006).

Howe Kritzer, Amelia, *Political Theatre in Post-Thatcher Britain: New Writing 1995–2005* (Basingstoke: Palgrave Macmillan, 2008).

Johnson, Terry, 'Introduction', in Joe Penhall, *Plays Two* (London: Methuen Drama, 2008), pp. ix–xiv.

Klein, Alvin, 'Dr Kafka and Dr Beckett Will See You Now, Sir', *New York Times*, 1 August 2004 <http://www.nytimes.com/2004/08/01/nyregion/theater-review-dr-kafka-and-dr-beckett-will-see-you-now-sir.html>

Penhall, Joe, 'Introduction', in Joe Penhall, *Plays One* (London: Methuen Drama, 1998), pp. ix–xv.

Sierz, Aleks, *In-Yer-Face Theatre: British Drama Today* (London: Faber & Faber, 2001).

—, 'Interview with Joe Penhall (two parts)', *Theatrevoice* website, 31 January 2005 <http://www.theatrevoice.com/listen_now/player/?audioID=264>, <http://www.theatrevoice.com/listen_now/player/?audioID=263>

Notes

1. See Mireia Aragay et al., *British Theatre of the 1990s*, p. 77, and Harriet Devine, *Looking Back*, p. 242.
2. Aragay, *British Theatre of the 1990s*, p. 84.
3. See Penhall, 'Introduction', p. x.
4. Aleks Sierz, *In-Yer-Face Theatre*, pp. 211, 214.
5. Ibid., p. 214.
6. Penhall, 'Introduction', p. x.

7. John Peter, *The Sunday Times, Theatre Record*, Vol. XIV, No. 19 (1994), p. 1143.

8. Aragay, *British Theatre of the 1990s*, p. 80, and Penhall, 'Introduction', p. xii.

9. See Aleks Sierz, 'Interview'.

10. Penhall, 'Introduction', p. xii.

11. Aragay, *British Theatre of the 1990s*, p. 83.

12. Penhall, 'Introduction', p. xii.

13. Aleks Sierz, *Tribune, Theatre Record*, Vol. XVII, No. 10 (1997), p. 653.

14. See Devine, *Looking Back*, pp. 247–8.

15. Alistair Macaulay, *Financial Times*; John Peter, *The Sunday Times*; Roger Foss, *What's On, Theatre Record*, Vol. XX, No. 8 (2000), pp. 480, 482.

16. Devine, *Looking Back*, p. 245.

17. Alvin Klein, 'Dr Kafka and Dr Beckett Will See You Now, Sir'.

18. Sheridan Morley, *Spectator, Theatre Record*, Vol. XX, No. 8 (2000), p. 479.

19. Aleks Sierz, *Tribune, Theatre Record*, Vol. XX, No. 8 (2000), p. 484.

20. Penhall, in Sierz, 'Interview'.

21. Michael Billington, *Guardian, Theatre Record*, Vol. XX, No. 8 (2000), p. 480.

22. Michael Billington, *Guardian, Theatre Record*, Vol. XXIV, No. 18 (2004), p. 1117.

23. Devine, *Looking Back*, p. 246.

24. Michael Billington, *Guardian, Theatre Record*, Vol. XXIV, No. 18 (2004), p. 1117.

25. See Benedict Nightingale, *The Times, Theatre Record*, Vol. XXVII, No. 7 (2007), p. 398.

26. Michael Billington, *Guardian, Theatre Record*, Vol. XXVII, No. 7 (2007), p. 396.

27. Susannah Clapp, *Observer, Theatre Record*, Vol. XXVII, No. 7 (2007), p. 399.

28. Jane Edwardes, *Time Out, Theatre Record*, Vol. XXVII, No. 7 (2007), p. 398.

29. Devine, *Looking Back*, p. 249.

30. Penhall, in Sierz, 'Interview'.

31. Sierz, *In-Yer-Face Theatre*, p. 214.

32. Ibid.

33. Penhall, in Sierz, 'Interview'.

34. Devine, *Looking Back*, p. 245.

35. Penhall, 'Introduction', p. xv; Sierz, *In-Yer-Face Theatre*, p. 212.

36. Aragay, *British Theatre of the 1990s*, p. 78.

37. Penhall, 'Introduction', p. xiv.

38. Terry Johnson, 'Introduction', p. x.

39. Aragay, *British Theatre of the 1990s*, p. 88.

40. Johnson, 'Introduction', p. ix; Charles Spencer, *Daily Telegraph, Theatre Record*, Vol. XVIII, No. 7 (1998), p. 444.

41. Devine, *Looking Back*, p. 241.

42. Penhall, in Sierz, 'Interview'.

43. See Penhall, 'Introduction', p. xi.

44. Aragay, *British Theatre of the 1990s*, p. 84.

45. Spencer, *Daily Telegraph, Theatre Record*, Vol. XVIII, No. 7 (1998), p. 444.

20 WINSOME PINNOCK

Elizabeth Sakellaridou

Leave Taking; Talking in Tongues; Mules; Can You Keep a Secret?;
One Under

Introduction

Winsome Pinnock is the most prominent black British female
playwright and the first to have her work produced at the National
Theatre. She is of Caribbean origin and was born in 1961 in Islington,
London, where her parents had moved as immigrants from Jamaica in
1958. She graduated from Goldsmiths College with an MA degree in
English and Drama. Her subsequent admission to the Royal Court's
Young Writers Group in 1986 and the encouragement of Hanif
Kureishi, director of the group, helped her start a writing career
through a rehearsed reading of her first play, *A Hero's Welcome*, in the
Royal Court Theatre Upstairs. This play was then revised for a full
production at the Royal Court (1989) by the Women's Playhouse
Trust and was nominated for the Susan Smith Blackburn Award.
Three more plays of hers, *A Rock in Water* (1989), *Talking in Tongues*
(1991) and *Mules* (1996) were staged at the Royal Court, while the
National Theatre mounted a revival of *Leave Taking* (1994–95), the
play which had received the George Devine Award in 1991, and
premiered her new youth play *Can You Keep a Secret?* (1999). Despite
her undoubted recognition by the mainstream, however, Pinnock is
very sceptical about the audience politics of both the Royal Court and
the National Theatre. In an interview in 1997 and in a short essay on
black British theatre in 1999 she expresses her disappointment with
these institutions' failure to introduce effective mixed-audience
policies. It is therefore not accidental that, despite the Royal Court's
continuing interest, she considers Jules Wright and the Women's

Playhouse Trust as the most important vehicle for first productions of her work. It is equally suggestive of her equivocal feelings towards the mainstream that her last three plays – *Water* (2000), *One Under* (2005) and *IDP* (2006) – all premiered at the Tricycle Theatre, whose major aim is to attract new audiences and support black and Asian writers. Indeed, *Water* involves an ambitious portrait of the artist as a nationwide success. Sporadically, her work has also been produced in other places: *The Winds of Change* (Half Moon, 1987) and *Picture Palace* (Women's Theatre Group, 1988).

She has also worked for BBC Television. Her TV credits include scripting for *Chalk Face*, *EastEnders*, *South of the Border* and the screenplay *Bitter Harvest*. To radio drama she has contributed the adaptations of *Indiana* by George Sand and *Let Them Call It Jazz* by Jean Rhys, and the original plays *Her Father's Daughter* and *Water* (the latter adapted from her own stage play). She has been writer-in-residence at the Royal Court Theatre, the National Theatre Studio, Clean Break Theatre/Holloway Prison and the Tricycle Theatre. She has also been Visiting Lecturer at various British universities, including Cambridge. She has received the George Devine Award, the Thames TV Playwrights' Scheme Award for 1991, and the Unity Theatre Trust Award.

The Plays

Leave Taking (1987)

Pinnock's stage debut was the production of *Leave Taking* at the Liverpool Playhouse Studio on 11 November 1987. The measure of its success is reflected in the number of subsequent revivals it has received. Despite her later development into a wide-ranging playwright, manifestly 'breaking down the door' that blocked black writers from entering the mainstream British dramatic canon, this play continues to be a favourite for drama anthologies, reference books and scholarly studies as a fine representative of black writing – contrary to Pinnock's own wish to stress its 'universality' and the audience's identifying with the characters 'irrespective of their class or race'.[1] This play and *Talking in Tongues*, its thematic sequel, are presumably her most autobiographical ones, about the schizoid agony of forging a black British identity:[2]

> That's based on when I was growing up. If you ask anybody my age, they'll say, 'They never told us anything about where they came from, how they lived.' And in *Leave Taking*, in my own life I suppose, the silence was to do with a sense of shame. The sort of poverty they came from was shameful, they thought. And there was a desire for their children to be British, and therefore to forget about the past. I remember being told off if I spoke with a West Indian accent. 'Don't. You're British. Speak English.' I understand this because it's about fitting in, integrating and getting on. If you didn't you'd be an outsider. But the play was about celebrating those things that people were ashamed of.[3]

This sharp psychic pain led her to dramatise the story of Enid, a first-generation immigrant from Jamaica, who left her poverty-stricken mother and country without even a proper 'leave taking', in order to settle down in Britain and start a new life and a family of her own in her host country, to which she has given in faith her whole self. The tag attached to her is 'Miss English'. Ironically, of course, it is her two English-born daughters Del and Viv who know this culture from the inside and respond to it, whereas she has trouble in suppressing her Jamaican roots both in language and in mentality.

Leave Taking is a strikingly female play, emphasising a matrilinear ascendancy within the family, stretching back from the two daughters and their mother Enid to the abandoned grandmother in Jamaica, reinforced by the emblematic presence of Mai, the wise old Jamaican woman and clairvoyant, who is the British-Caribbean Mama substitute for the three younger women. Her advice is typical: 'Look, lady, if is man you come 'bout you might as well go straight home' (p. 145). Men are practically absent since Enid is an abandoned wife and the daughter Del faces an anonymous, unwanted pregnancy, while the only man in the play, Enid's brother Broderick, is an ineffectual drunk.

There is a neat symmetry in the way the characters conceive history, tradition and social reality.[4] A dual tension is felt all along. The importance of tradition is pitted against the urge for change and innovation; the necessity of roots stands against the need for 'leave taking'; historical memory is as much sought for as historical amnesia is thought to be healing; a voyage out to the abandoned homeland is as desirable as an inner journey to the self is indispensable. Enid is a complex character with complex ideas about the migrant experience. When she says that 'England be good to me' (p. 152) she is celebrating her own capacity to adapt to her new environment and her ability to bring up her daughters as English. But although Broderick agrees with her, he also points out that living in England for thirty years, and working in a car factory, has not prevented the UK authorities from treating him as an 'alien' and getting him to pay for the privilege of staying in the country (p. 152). The characters themselves can be neatly classified between those who are immovably anchored in the black tradition (Mai and Broderick) and those who are in an equivocal, transitory situation (Enid and her two daughters). Within this second group, Enid represents the first-generation immigrant, who tries to suppress her cultural past at all costs and assimilate into the host culture for the full benefit of social recognition and material acquisition; but in the course of the play she realises she has become an 'empty shell' (p. 189) and is immersed in melancholia. The daughters, each in their own way, react ambivalently to British culture – both feeling a yearning, a reclaiming instinct for black culture. All three, at the end of the play, display a hope for change; a dynamic for the forging of a hybrid identity; a reconciliation with the self and the others, after a long period of agony and negotiation. Mai and Broderick are given up as obsolete and irrelevant.

Beyond the racial struggle, so vividly depicted in the play, it is the centrality of motherhood (so integral to the black tradition) that undoubtedly defines the play as one highlighting black femininity and has justifiably attracted the attention of feminist studies.[5] An additional strength of the play that heightens its complexity is its sensitivity to social upgrading and the role of education in this process. In a manner reminiscent of the dialectical struggle between the two sisters in Caryl Churchill's *Top Girls* (1982), Pinnock sets up her own strong class and race dialectic by inventing some strong scenes between Del, Viv and Enid, in which they talk over all their suffering as they are torn between social opportunity and family obligation.

This exciting black play of the 1980s vindicates its historical importance as a significant play in the rise of black British writing – a phenomenon which Pinnock has celebrated in her essay 'Breaking Down the Door'. The reviews were positive, but one must not overlook the more reserved opinion expressed by the *Financial Times*, 'Would this kind of social realism be interesting if *Leave Taking* were about whites? Surely not. But it serves in part as a documentary. It makes some black issues more real to all of us.'[6] In the white critic's cool view one can spot, from the other side of the racial divide, Pinnock's own resentment at her labelling as a black woman playwright.

Talking in Tongues (1991)

Talking in Tongues is a real turning point in Pinnock's work not only as her sixth, middle play in a total of eleven but, more crucially, because it concludes dynamically all her previous search into the historical trauma of black immigration in Britain, while also making a decisive move towards reconciliation with her hybrid position in European and British culture. The play is based on an actual trip that Pinnock took with her mother to Jamaica, the country of her origin; but her treatment of the material is detached enough from personal experience to allow the creation of dramatic characters credible for themselves. Talking about her authorial discipline, Pinnock warns: 'We must not let our guilt or anger – however justified – get in the way.'[7] The play premiered at the Royal Court Theatre Upstairs on 28 August 1991 and had an overall warm welcome.[8]

Pinnock has analysed with impressive lucidity her intentions. She spells out the political agenda she had endorsed since the beginning of her career, taking now a more polemical stance on the double oppression of black femininity in a white European environment. Her pain and rage are emphasised in her motto: 'The black woman is still seen as the mule of the world.'[9] The author is equally outspoken in her afterword to the published play text. The play's wide success must be attributed mainly to the author's stylistic and ideological maturity, after years of revisiting the themes of black migration and identity in her previous work. The strong physical staging, under the direction of Hettie Macdonald, also contributed to its success.

The plot of the play follows the painful journey of a young black Londoner, Leela, to her ancestral roots after the betrayal of her black husband with a white woman. The first act includes scenes from a mixed-race party in London, where Leela is a social misfit on the verge of a breakdown. However, a prologue and an interlude, both presenting glimpses from a remote black culture, create a different context for the audience, in which Leela's psychological disturbance can be viewed in a different spectrum of normalcy. The prologue consists of a long monologue (in Jamaican Creole) by a young native, Sugar, as she is giving Leela a massage. Sugar narrates the story of three native women who practised secret rituals of communion with the divine spirit while in ecstasy. The interlude consists of the story of a black hermaphrodite, Irma, who makes a surrealistic appearance to the unhappy Leela at the London party, comforting her with her own cool acceptance of her sexual hybridity. The cultural displacement presented by the two stories adds a surrealistic tone to the play, questioning and unsettling the realistic 'normalcy' of the London scenes. The audience becomes conscious of an alterity in body language and codes of communication that escaped the Eurocentric optics of the first act.

The second act transfers the heroine, Leela, and her female friend, Claudette, to Jamaica, in pursuit of another reality that eluded them in their British environment. After a number of encounters with natives and European visitors, however, the two young women become disillusioned about the purity of an ancient black culture they looked for in order to empower themselves. Leela's awakening to a crude, fragmented and hybridised reality is most dramatic. After an act of ritualistic, symbolic violence against a sleeping white woman, Kate, on whose body she projects all her vengeful bitterness for the multiple humiliation of her black femininity, she suffers an epileptic seizure, during which she has bodily convulsions and starts talking in tongues. When her body releases all its stored-up tension, Leela is a reborn being, ready to embrace her hybrid identity as a second-generation West Indian Brit and even to accept the friendship of the white woman she had just assaulted. The whole plotline corresponds to Pinnock's claim: 'I remain committed to integration but it's going to be an uphill struggle. We can't form relationships that do not acknowledge the treacheries of history.'[10] The end of the play, particularly, achieves what she always yearned for: a reconciliation with her interstitial position as a black female British writer. In this sense, it puts forward a new (Brechtian) female bonding across race, which confirms the 'healing' of black trauma that critic Elaine Aston has rightly spotted in the play.[11]

The complexity of the black vision and its dramatic economy have made *Talking in Tongues* an exemplary text for analysis in several recent studies that focus on black British writing, including issues of post-coloniality, black feminism, migration and interstitiality of the black subject. All these studies prove the multi-perspectivity of the play and highlight its intellectual value. What should be equally stressed, however, is its performative dynamic, which clearly explodes the Eurocentric realism, whose typology Pinnock has on the whole followed as a writer (not always to her credit). As I have suggested elsewhere, through the plight of her protagonist Leela, but also through the stories of Sugar and Irma, she introduces a somatic language, performative by nature, which links directly to the black Caribbean tradition and points to a new authentic theatre language, alien to European theatre practice.[12] Similarly, Aston underlines Pinnock's 'collision' with Eurocentric naturalism and refers to Meenakshi Ponnuswami's theory of the diasporic aesthetic to substantiate her argument.[13]

Generally, *Talking in Tongues* shows Pinnock at the crossroads of her artistic career. It is a conclusion and a farewell to the tormenting memories of the West Indian history of migration and an opening to a new, wider understanding of the problems of contemporary multicultural societies and global capitalism.

Mules (1996)

After her bitter statement that the black woman is still seen as the 'mule of the world', the title of her following play *Mules* (which premiered at the Royal Court Theatre Upstairs on 25 April 1996) came as no surprise.[14] This play was commissioned by Clean Break Theatre Company (whose aim is to develop theatre by and for women prisoners). Pinnock wrote it after a period of research in Holloway Prison and Jamaica. This commission was no easy task and the playwright explains her difficulties while 'negotiating [her] own role in creating a play for a prison audience'.[15] Despite her specific instructions she needed to detach herself 'as an outsider and, therefore, as a commentator'.[16] Choosing for her theme the exploitation of young black women as 'mules' in drug trafficking, she found herself in the double bind of this type of crime, which could also be seen as 'a kind of rebellion', as an escape from victimisation.[17] Pinnock clarified the fine line she had crossed from the initial commission by focusing on a dangerous aspect of the play: 'the joy of transgression, the joy of criminality.'[18] Luckily, the result of this authorial digression was all to the play's advantage: it broadened its scope and rescued it from the pitfalls of mandatory morality.

The plot of the play traces the recruiting of hopeless, young black women for drug smuggling to Europe and follows them through the perils of the job: mugging, imprisonment and death. The major story concerns two young sisters from Jamaica, who give up a life of no prospects in Kingston for the false promises of Bridie, a glamorous native woman who seems to have escaped the ghetto and shot to the top. The play opens with a sharp scene in the London office, where Bridie plays boss. Bridie's celebratory scene is soon followed by her downfall, when she is next seen as a bloody heap on the ground. 'She's nothing but a mule,' announce her colleagues and they turn away to pursue their own fatal course (p. 67). The two Jamaican sisters' lot is equally depressing. Lyla lands back in Kingston, despite one successful mission, while her sister Lou ends up in an English prison, together with another one of Bridie's recruits. After serving her three years, Lou returns to Jamaica to join willy-nilly her sister Lyla in the lowest menial job available: working in the fields – ironically, in a ganja plantation!

Pinnock's heroines do not only sacrifice their right to family life and maternity to professional success like Churchill's white protagonist in *Top Girls*. Here their sexuality is fully trapped as their genital zone is actually hired for the promotion of the deadly drug trade rather than new life in the world. Gabriele Griffin aptly talks about 'sexploitation genitally focused' while Aston refers to female 'recolonization'.[19] Both terms suggest the full exploitation of the black female body by the neocolonial global economy.

Pinnock complicates her main story with three subplots, thus giving a dire collective picture of the fate of young black females in ex-colonies and the English metropolis, although her main focus remains the neocolonial state of Jamaica. Yet, despite all this interlocked gender and race trouble, Pinnock insists that race is not an issue in the play. In a related interview she blamed the reviewers for seeing it as a black play.[20] *Mules* was initially written for a mixed cast but was finally staged with three black actresses for all twelve roles. This casting partly explains why critical opinion was divided concerning the importance of race in Pinnock's writing. Lynette Goddard and Aston, for instance, overlook race for a broader survey of the exploitation of women by 'global capitalism'.[21] On the contrary, Griffin and Bernhard Reitz recall the author's steady preoccupation with blackness throughout her career, thus agreeing with the majority of the reviewers.[22]

Another point of disagreement in the play's reception is its ending, which finds Lyla and Lou stooping in the fields with no prospect for a better life. 'We will never leave the ghetto,' announces Lou; and Lyla has no better answer than a Chekhovian urge to 'finish this piece of work so that we can go home early' (p. 71). Of all critics, Griffin seems to be closest to the ambiguities of the play, its 'unresolved problematic'.[23] What Reitz and Jeremy Kingston have mistaken as a touch of moral uplifting towards a happy ending must have been the female bonding, which, despite the pressures of stern materialism that have hardened the women, still permeates the play as the only sign of empowerment.[24] From this point of view, the maternal instinct and the issue of surrogate motherhood (a recognisable motif in Pinnock's plays) certainly reflect perennial cultural images from the black tradition. This imagery, although less central in *Mules*, is further reinforced by references to rituals of black spiritualism and healing, thus confirming the, albeit peripheral, role that race still plays in Pinnock's dramaturgy. Especially the scene with the 'bad girls' appearing like elfish 'creatures' and the one with Bridie performing her piece of magic when luring her naïve recruits with a torrent of coins, although they may bring to mind yet another Churchill play, *The Skriker*, are undeniably vested in the black spiritualist tradition and culture.

Cultural diversity has helped the writer give this play a freer form. Although *Mules* basically follows the post-Brechtian aesthetic of the socialist theatre of the 1970s and 1980s, the black spirit of migration, emancipation and visionary longing creates a special atmosphere of movement, transience and transcendence to alternative spaces – a sensation also transferred to the fast-changing, fluid stage setting and acting.

Can You Keep a Secret? (1999)

This play was a commission for the National Theatre's BT Connections youth theatre project, and first staged at the Cottesloe space on 7 July 1999. It is a one-hander, consisting of seventeen scenes. It concerns the racial killing of a black boy by a white youth and the ordeal of the latter's girlfriend, who had witnessed the murder, until she decides to break her silence and testify to the police, thus risking rejection from her community.

After a number of works on the issue of black immigration in Britain, Pinnock now concentrates on the third generation of immigrants, observing youth culture in general and the conditions that enhance violence. Race is still crucial for the central characters but it is of no consequence for the rest. Besides, the two black families involved (the victim's and his girlfriend's) enjoy a higher middle-class status. On the contrary, the white families (those of the offender and his girlfriend) are given a lower social and cultural profile. The situation between blacks and whites appears not only relaxed but also somehow reversed. Yet, in the course of the play one realises the irony behind the high profile of the prospective black victim – an aspiring art student who provocatively proclaims a 'New world order: The Niggers Rule OK and you, my dear Nancy Boy, are the new victim' (p. 99). The play backsteps into racism before reinstalling hope for reconciliation.

The piece opens with young Kate and Aleysha waiting to go to the movies with their boyfriends. The purpose of the scene is obviously to establish a common language between the white and the black girl; to stress sameness rather than difference. The girls are presented as 'ordinary young Londoner[s]', as Pinnock stressed, referring to the real story on which she based her script (p. 138). Ambition in the young is now pursued across gender and race. The same applies to other values: family life, parental care etc. One can also discern a trusting attitude to social institutions, the police included. Thus, the police inspector is presented as a sympathetic and supportive man: a guardian angel in the public sphere.

The story is presented in a linear narrative. Although location varies, there is an austere action distribution among the characters, an overall classical dramatic design with a carefully written dialogue that bridges all the gaps. *Can You Keep a Secret?* follows all the clichés of the well-made play. There are just two stratagems in the whole script which attempt to break the realist conventions. The first is the introduction of a character called Weirdboy – a surrealist intervention of a witness, external to the plot and scapegoat to the action. The second is the persistent reappearance of Derek, the murdered black boy, as a ghost to Kate – the white girl who had witnessed his death – as an anti-realist technique in the Shakespearean tradition.

In one interview, Pinnock discloses her major theme: the nature of a guilty conscience, the dilemma and the consequences of withholding and of telling the truth. There are also psychological and philosophical implications concerning mortality, memory, secrecy, loyalty, truth-telling. It is the darker side of life, as the Inspector explains, which finds the youth vulnerable and unprotected. Underneath these general considerations, however, one discerns the reopening of the black trauma, which was at the core of Pinnock's earlier work. A member of the black gang makes extensive use of the history of black immigration. Its pessimistic conclusion upsets the racial equilibrium suggested at the beginning of the play:

> And us – just when we were beginning to take things for granted, now we can see that things are going to be just as tough for us and that we're going to have to fight just as hard as they did. (p. 114)

The whole conception of the play sounds conventional, promoting the role of theatre as a vehicle of change, as having a strong corrective or utilitarian function. Pinnock's own words in a related interview suggest as much (p. 41). It has an obvious political agenda, offering moral advice and an optimistic, uplifting message. It is a play of empowerment and positive action, rather naïve in the final female bonding between Kate and Aleysha under the approving gaze of the dead youth. The benign ending matches the Inspector's function as a sort of benevolent divinity helping out the young. One can trace a number of transcendental images and personifications of good and evil forces from the rich English literary stock from Shakespeare to T. S. Eliot.

Despite its brevity and its conventional structure, *Can You Keep a Secret?* is pivotal in the development of Pinnock's dramaturgy. Written after her migration plays, it shows the wider concerns that preoccupy her and reflects in practice her ambition to be accepted beyond the labels attached to a black female writer. It also suggests an attempt to experiment with anti-naturalist forms, even though these may have been borrowings from the European theatre tradition. Her own reference to myth in her interview accompanying the play text suggests as much.

One Under (2005)

One Under is the play that achieves most fully Pinnock's long-term ambition to transcend the limitations of race and integrate into

English tradition. It is her most existential play in the mode of Beckett and Pinter, and was first presented at the Tricycle Theatre on 7 February 2005. A young man, Sonny, is killed when he throws himself under a tube train. The train driver, Cyrus, after his shock, abandons his settled family life and starts a long journey into the self and the world. On the way he meets other people experiencing similar situations of loss and dispossession: parents abandon or lose children and vice versa. The general mood of mournfulness for the emptiness and inscrutability of human life may be Beckettian but the specific pattern of lost children, parents and siblings and the quest for recovering them may also strike a Shakespearean chord. However, Pinnock concretises and complicates the social and familial situation in ways closer to a Pinter setting. Loneliness and insecurity as well as the struggle for communication and for emotional and spatial possession show an obvious Pinter influence. The women – Nella, Zoe and Christine – appear as possessive as any Pinter female character; and Cyrus, the uprooted male protagonist, tries to lay claim on spaces that do not belong to him – not unlike Pinter's miserable Davies in *The Caretaker* (1960). The haunted and haunting nature of the characters, their delusions, guilts and insecurities, can also recall similar moods in Pinter's world.

Two nocturnal scenes in Act Two can be considered especially Pinteresque in essence, which project elusive emotional states to the territorial setting, thus transcending the naturalistic structure of the play. The first imaginary transformation concerns a momentary vision of London as 'a different animal at night', recalling a Caribbean experience (p. 62). The second is a lengthier moonlight scene in Nella's garden, where her foster son, the suicidal Sonny, makes the same sepulchral appearance as the dead daughter Bridget in Pinter's metaphysical play *Moonlight* (1993). Sonny already has a spectral quality around him when still alive; when he is truly gone, 'he's left his shadow behind' (p. 40). Pinnock ensures that the dead man's voice is heard repeatedly on his answering machine when his friends or family visit his empty flat. A poetic, saturnine mood is already anticipated in the opening epigraph of the text 'Bereavement can overshadow life: the dead can destroy the living' (p. 1).

More echoes from Pinter – this time from *Ashes to Ashes* – are added when Christine denies her story about a lost child with an aporetic 'What woman? What kid' (p. 68), which places her in the same unsettling position as Pinter's deluded heroine Rebecca in the aforementioned play. All these influences indicate Pinnock's ambition to broaden her human scope and expand on her themes; to probe into deeper psychic and intellectual domains and enter lyrical moods.

It is certainly an exaggeration to call *One Under* a Greek tragedy, as one reviewer suggested.[25] On the contrary, there is some substance in the criticism of other reviewers about the writer's 'overstating'; or writing a 'stilted' or 'tepid' dialogue; or creating an over-elaborate plot.[26] Despite such objections, however, it is vital to stress the merits of the play. 'Urban' and 'metropolitan' are some of the qualifiers critics attached to the characters' lifestyle. Especially Charles Spencer is categorical about Pinnock 'never mention[ing] race issues once' and he hails the play as 'the first "black" play [. . .] that accepts the multi-cultural nature of Britain today without finding any need to examine its stress fractures'.[27] This view is the highest praise for the play's achievement and is reflected in later, more radical gender and race studies. Goddard, for instance, concludes with a paean about the play's transcendence of race issues, adding also the author's self-assertive statement that 'at this point of my writing, I just love stories, I really love stories'.[28] Griffin, on her part, refers to this same interview in order to underline Pinnock's claim to her authorial licence to eliminate race specificity from her characters. After a lengthy speculation on the final mixed-casting choices of the production, the critic praises the black dramatist not only for presenting a 'post-empiric situation' but also for focusing on 'male vulnerability' – a new issue in Pinnock's writing.[29]

Summing up this controversial but stimulating play we need to point out that by embarking her black male protagonist on an existential journey of guilt, torment and self-knowledge, Pinnock transcends her race and gender barriers and addresses the enigmatic and tragic ordeal of human life in a much more complex way than in her previous, more predictable works. The migratory or diasporic aesthetic, which formed the basic thematic matrix of the black lives she depicted before, now becomes an expanded metaphor for every human's continuous quest through the riddles of life. Again, the only reservation one can have for the progress of Pinnock's art is the persistence of an old-fashioned naturalism which occasionally packs her work with unnecessary detail, over-structuring and complication. In its total dynamic, however, *One Under* is a positive step towards what Goddard has already celebrated as Pinnock's 'millennial stories': a step towards a postmodern aesthetic of un-knowledge and uncertainty.[30]

Summary

Pinnock has attracted the attention of many feminist and cultural critics, black and white alike, and her oeuvre has been the object of systematic scholarly study from various perspectives. Her early plays – *A Hero's Welcome, Leave Taking* and *A Rock in Water* – all centre on race, gender and migration, and deal with specific problems of displacement and citizenship involved in the formation of the migrant black identity. These plays belong to a thematic cycle that the author now considers concluded. *Talking in Tongues* in my view recapitulates, in a cathartic way, all the author's obsessions with the black migrant's legacy and opens her vistas to larger, worldwide issues. Indeed, studies of her work illustrate the breadth and depth of her intellectual pungency and ideological thinking. Aston's *Feminist Views on the English Stage* includes a short but astute presentation of Pinnock's work. With some reference to contemporary citizenship theory, Aston emphasises Pinnock's multicultural and integrationist politics and highlights her contribution to transnational feminism. Similarly, Goddard in her *Staging Black Feminisms* stresses Pinnock's 'universal outlook' – one that gets gradually detached from the specificities of black history and abandons didacticism. While Goddard notes Pinnock's 'migration narratives' she also hails her 'millennial stories'.[31]

Among the Pinnock critics, Griffin holds a special position because she has visited this British Caribbean writer's work repeatedly, each time from a different perspective. Griffin's scope ranges from the socio-economic problems of the immigrant subject ('Theatres of Difference'), to colonial memories ('The Remains of the British Empire'), to issues of black femininity, such as maternity and sexual exploitation (*Contemporary Black and Asian Women Playwrights in Britain*), to more radical aspirations for the acceptance of contemporary Britain as a diasporic space where black and Asian women playwrights are admitted as 'constitutive subjectivities'.

Other studies on a variety of cultural topics address aspects of Pinnock's politicised thought, such as the issues of motherhood (Jozefina Komporaly), displacement (Geraldine Cousin), and nomadic identities (May Joseph). Beyond all these compartmentalised views of Pinnock's theatre, there are two more theoretical voices that deserve mention. These are Meenakshi Ponnuswami and DeLinda Marzette, who both formulate a more general problematic around Pinnock's dramas. In her groundbreaking article 'Small Island People', Ponnuswami makes an important statement about the emergence of a new black aesthetic, which is based on the expressive codes of diaspora culture and sets out to examine the limits of postmodernism through a new type of ethnic syncretism. In this new theoretical scheme she tries to find a place for black women playwrights practising in Britain and she uses Pinnock as a test case to support her theory. Although often prescriptive, Ponnuswami has certainly pushed black theatre theory forward and her views are often quoted by other critics. Marzette's article 'Coming to Voice' creates a highly sophisticated theoretical nexus (ranging from Stuart Hall and Homi Bhabha to Derridean thought and Cixous's *entre-deux* concept), in which to place Pinnock's complex dramatic art. Both these scholars have contributed greatly to the development of a more comprehensive hermeneutical frame for Pinnock's multi-faceted work and a better appreciation of her sophisticated thought.

Other, earlier secondary sources which can be useful for a preliminary charting of the field are Elaine Savory's 'Strategies for Survival' and Mary Karen Dahl's 'Postcolonial British Theatre'. The titles of these essays can be keys to the thematic and aesthetic exploration of Pinnock's plays. One more recent study on the constitution of the fugitive identity by HollyGale Millette, entitled 'Exchanging Fugitive Identity', can be recommended because it focuses on the concept of bi-cultural competence and probes into the issue of culture learning (including both social skills and social values) – all problems that torment Pinnock's black migrant characters to a greater or a lesser degree. With all the rich critical and theoretical positioning in conversation with her work, Pinnock has doubly secured her position as the leading black British woman playwright not only in theatrical but also in intellectual terms, no doubt fulfilling the 'aesthetic presuppositions' that Reitz had called for as a challenging prospect for her future art.[32]

Primary Sources

Works by Winsome Pinnock

Leave Taking, in Kate Harwood (ed.), *First Run: New Plays by New Writers* (London: Nick Hern, 1989), pp. 139–89.

A Rock in Water, in Yvonne Brewster (ed.), *Black Plays: Two* (London: Methuen Drama, 1989), pp. 45–91.

A Hero's Welcome, in Kadija George (ed.), *Black and Asian Women Writers* (London: Aurora Metro Press, 1993), pp. 21–55.

Talking in Tongues, in Yvonne Brewster (ed.), *Black Plays: Three* (London: Methuen Drama, 1995), pp. 171–227.

Mules (London: Faber & Faber, 1996).

Can You Keep a Secret? in Suzy Graham-Adriani (ed.), *New Connections 99: New Plays for Young People* (London: Faber & Faber, 1999), pp. 93–141.

Water (unpublished typescript, British Library, 2000).

One Under (London: Faber & Faber, 2005).

IDP, in Nicolas Kent (ed.), *How Long is Never? Darfur: A Response* (London: Josef Weinberger, 2007), pp. 75–85.

Secondary Sources

Aston, Elaine, *Feminist Views on the English Stage: Women Playwrights 1990–2000* (Cambridge: CUP, 2003).

—, Interview, in Lizbeth Goodman and Jane de Gay, *Feminist Stages: Interviews with Women in Contemporary British Theatre* (Amsterdam: Harwood, 1996), pp. 121–7.

Cousin, Geraldine, *Women in Dramatic Place and Time: Contemporary Female Characters on Stage* (London: Routledge, 1996).

Dahl, Mary Karen, 'Postcolonial British Theatre: Black Voices at the Center', in J. Ellen Gainor (ed.), *Imperialism and Theatre* (London: Routledge, 1995), pp. 38–55.

Edgar, David, *State of Play: Playwrights on Playwriting* (London: Faber & Faber, 1999).

Goddard, Lynette, *Staging Black Feminisms: Identity, Politics, Performance* (Basingstoke: Palgrave Macmillan, 2007).

Griffin, Gabriele, *Contemporary Black and Asian Women Playwrights in Britain* (Cambridge: CUP, 2003).

—, 'Constitutive Subjectivities: Contemporary Black and Asian Women Playwrights in Britain', *European Journal of Women's Studies*, Vol. 10, No. 4 (2003), pp. 377–94.

—, 'The Remains of the British Empire: The Plays of Winsome Pinnock', in Mary Luckhurst (ed.), *A Companion to Modern British and Irish Drama: 1880–2005* (Oxford: Blackwell, 2006), pp. 198–209.

—, 'Theatres of Difference: The Politics of "Redistribution" and "Recognition" in the Plays of Contemporary Black and Asian Women Playwrights in Britain', *Feminist Review*, Vol. 84, No. 1 (2006), pp. 10–28.

Joseph, May, *Nomadic Identities: The Performance of Citizenship* (Minneapolis: Minnesota UP, 1999).

Komporaly, Jozefina, *Staging Motherhood: British Women Playrights, 1956 to the Present* (New York: Palgrave Macmillan, 2006).

Marzette, DeLinda, 'Navigating the Interstices in Plays by Winsome Pinnock', in Elizabeth Brown-Guillory (ed.), *Middle Passages and the Healing Place of History: Migration and Identity in Black Women's Literature* (Columbus: Ohio State UP, 2006), pp. 32–51.

Millette, HollyGale, 'Exchanging Fugitive Identity: William and Ellen Craft's Transatlantic Reinvention', in Cora Kaplan and John Oldfield (eds), *Imagining Transatlantic Slavery* (Basingstoke: Palgrave Macmillan, 2010), pp. 61–76.

Pinnock, Winsome, 'Breaking Down the Door', in Vera Gottlieb and Colin Chambers (eds), *Theatre in a Cool Climate* (Oxford: Amber Lane, 1999), pp. 27–38.

—, 'Interview', *Guardian*, 27 August 1991.

—, 'Interview with Jane Edwardes', *Time Out*, 7–14 December 1994, p. 129.

—, 'Influences: Winsome Pinnock, Playwright', *New Statesman and Society*, 27 January 1995, p. 21.

Ponnuswami, Meenakshi, 'Small Island People: Black British Women Playwrights', in Elaine Aston and Janelle Reinelt (eds), *The Cambridge Companion to Modern British Women Playwrights* (Cambridge: CUP, 2000), pp. 217–34.

Reitz, Bernhard, '"Discovering an Identity Which Has been Squashed": Intercultural and Intracultural Confrontations in the Plays of Winsome Pinnock and Ayub Khan-Din', *European Journal of English Studies*, Vol. 7, No. 1 (2003), pp. 39–54.

Sakellaridou, Elizabeth, 'Alternatives to Silence: Winsome Pinnock's *Talking in Tongues*', in Sabine Coelsch-Foisner et al. (eds), *Daughters of Restlessness: Women's Literature at the End of the Millennium* (Heidelberg: Winter, 1998), pp. 203–13.

Savory, Elaine, 'Strategies for Survival: Anti-Imperialist Theatrical Forms in the Anglophone Caribbean', in J. Ellen Gainor (ed.), *Imperialism and Theatre* (London: Routledge, 1995), pp. 243–56.

Stephenson, Heidi and Natasha Langridge, *Rage and Reason: Women Playwrights on Playwriting* (London: Methuen Drama, 1997).

Wright, Jules, 'Interview', in Lizbeth Goodman and Jane de Gay, *Feminist Stages: Interviews with Women in Contemporary British Theatre* (Amsterdam: Harwood, 1996), pp. 107–14.

Notes

1. Winsome Pinnock, quoted in Heidi Stephenson and Natasha Langridge, *Rage and Reason*, p. 49. 'Breaking Down the Door' is the name of an essay by Pinnock which gives a survey of black writing in 1980s Britain.
2. See Pinnock's interviews in the *Guardian* (1991); *Time Out* (1994); *New Statesman and Society* (1995); Stephenson and Langridge, *Rage and Reason*.
3. Winsome Pinnock, quoted in Stephenson and Langridge, *Rage and Reason*, p. 49.
4. Gabriele Griffin in *Contemporary Black and Asian Women Playwrights in Britain* notices the 'symmetrical positioning of the characters' (p. 36), which she also represents graphically with diagrams in her discussion (pp. 36–63).
5. See Jozefina Komporaly, *Staging Motherhood* and DeLinda Marzette, 'Navigating the Interstices in Plays by Winsome Pinnock'.
6. Alastair Macaulay, *Financial Times*, *Theatre Record*, Vol. X, No. 18 (1990), p. 1006.
7. Winsome Pinnock, 'Interview', *Guardian*.
8. Reviews of *Talking in Tongues*, *Theatre Record*, Vol. XI, No. 18 (1991).
9. Pinnock, 'Interview', *Guardian*.
10. Ibid.
11. Elaine Aston, *Feminist Views on the English Stage*, p. 130.
12. Elizabeth Sakellaridou, 'Alternatives to Silence', pp. 207–8.
13. Aston, *Feminist Views on the English Stage*, p. 131.
14. Pinnock, 'Interview', *Guardian*.
15. David Edgar, *State of Play*, p. 59.
16. Ibid.
17. Pinnock, Interview, *Rage and Reason*, p. 52.
18. Edgar, *State of Play*, p. 59.
19. Griffin, *Contemporary Black and Asian*, p. 213; Aston, *Feminist Views on the English Stage*, p. 136.
20. Pinnock, quoted in Stephenson and Langridge, p. 52.

21. Aston, *Feminist Views on the English Stage*, p. 136, and Lynette Goddard, *Staging Black Feminisms*, p. 65.

22. Gabriele Griffin, 'The Remains of the British Empire', p. 205, and Bernhard Reitz, '"Discovering an Identity Which Has been Squashed"', p. 47.

23. Griffin, *Contemporary Black and Asian*, p. 222.

24. Reitz, '"Discovering an Identity Which Has been Squashed"', pp. 48–9; Jeremy Kingston, *The Times*, *Theatre Record*, Vol. XVI, No. 9 (1996), p. 546.

25. John Peter, *The Sunday Times*, *Theatre Record*, Vol. XXV, No. 3 (2005), p. 162.

26. Mark Cook, *Evening Standard*; Brian Logan, *Guardian*; Sharon Garfinkel, *What's On*; Paul Taylor, *Independent*, *Theatre Record*; Helen Chappell, *Tribune*, *Theatre Record*, Vol. XXV, No. 3 (2005), pp. 163–4.

27. Charles Spencer, *Daily Telegraph*, *Theatre Record*, Vol. XXV, No. 3 (2005), p. 163.

28. Goddard, *Staging Black Feminisms*, p. 193.

29. Griffin, 'The Remains of the British Empire', pp. 200, 207.

30. Goddard, *Staging Black Feminisms*, p. 192.

31. Ibid.

32. Reitz, '"Discovering an Identity Which Has been Squashed"', p. 54.

21 MARK RAVENHILL

Caridad Svich

Shopping and Fucking; Some Explicit Polaroids; Mother Clap's Molly House; Product; The Cut; Shoot/Get Treasure/Repeat

Introduction

Born in 1966 and raised in west Sussex, Mark Ravenhill has emerged not only as one of his generation's most provocative playwrights since the debut of his controversial play *Shopping and Fucking* (Royal Court, 1996), but also as a central figure to the field of new writing in contemporary British theatre. He studied English and Drama at Bristol University, then moved to London, where he worked first as assistant administrator at the Soho Poly Theatre, and then as its workshop director in 1989–91. In 1990 he was diagnosed as HIV-positive, and in 1993 his boyfriend died from complications related to AIDS. Illness and death are frequent subjects in his work, and although his work is rarely directly autobiographical, the spectre of disease haunts his writing.[1]

Seeing Ravenhill's ten-minute play *Fist* at the Finborough Theatre in 1995, Max Stafford-Clark, director and founder of Out of Joint theatre company, encouraged him to forge ahead with his idea of documenting the values of his generation and speaking to them in their own language. Out of this passion came the play that, alongside Sarah Kane's *Blasted* (1995), would mark a new chapter in British playwriting: *Shopping and Fucking*. In 1997 Ravenhill became the literary director of the new writing company Paines Plough and also wrote the play *Faust is Dead* for Actors Touring Company under Nick Philippou's direction. His next two plays, *Handbag* (ATC, 1998), again directed by Philippou, and *Some Explicit Polaroids* (Out of Joint, 1999), directed by Stafford-Clark, capped a rewarding part of his career. In 1998, Ravenhill collaborated with Hillary Fannin, Stephen Greenhorn and Abi Morgan on *Sleeping Around*, and was the recipient of the *Evening Standard* Award for Most Promising Playwright for *Handbag*.

Ravenhill's twenty-first-century works have become more experimental in their structural design and more abstract in their conception. Key works from the past decade include *Mother Clap's Molly House* (National Theatre, 2000), *Product* (Paines Plough, 2005), *The Cut* (Donmar Warehouse, 2006), *Pool (No Water)* (Frantic Assembly, 2006) and *Shoot/Get Treasure/Repeat* (Paines Plough, 2008). In 2009, his *Over There* was staged at the Royal Court and he collaborated with British drag artist Bette Bourne on her life story, *A Life in Three Acts*, which Ravenhill co-scripted, directed and co-performed with Bourne in Edinburgh, London, and on a world tour. His adaptation of Terry Pratchett's novel *Nation* premiered at the National Theatre under Melly Still's direction. In the autumn of 2010, *Shoot/Get Treasure/Repeat* was staged by director Claus Peymann at the Berliner Ensemble under the title *Freedom and Democracy I Hate You*.

While a majority of his plays are about young, queer, defiant characters and Ravenhill has never been closeted about his sexuality, in November 2007 in an essay in the *Guardian*, he announced he would concentrate on writing about heterosexual characters for a while. Current work includes *The Experiment* (2009), developing a music-theatre work with composer Conor Mitchell for singer Marc Almond to perform entitled *Ten Plagues* (2010), and directing a live broadcast of his forty-minute television drama *Ghost Story* for the Sky Arts channel on 16 June 2010.

Ravenhill has also translated Xavier Durringer's *A Desire to Kill on the Tip of the Tongue* (1997) and Luis Enrique Gutierrez Ortiz Monasterio's *The Girls of the 3.5 Floppies* (2004). He has also written for young people – *Totally Over You* (National Theatre, 2003), *Citizenship* and *Scenes from Family Life* (2007). Other plays in his extensive repertoire include the verbatim project *North Greenwich (for the Dome)*, the radio play *Feed Me* (2000), and the screenplay *Lost and Found*. He was appointed artistic associate at the National Theatre in

2002, is a regular cultural commentator for the *Guardian*, and a passionate advocate of new writing. Of all the dramatists who rose to fame during the moment of 'in-yer-face theatre', Ravenhill has sustained the most diverse career thus far.

The Plays

Shopping and Fucking (1996)

Shopping and Fucking was picked up by Stafford-Clark for further development at the National Theatre Studio in June 1996. In less than three months, the play found its way to a production at the Royal Court Theatre Upstairs on 1 October 1996. Composed of thirteen scenes, *Shopping and Fucking* presents snapshots of increasingly disconnected moments of human behaviour – specifically of a quintet of young, wasted bottom-feeders (named after the band members of the pop group Take That and the singer Lulu) – revolving around work and sex in which every moment can be reduced to a transaction. Revelling in staccato Mametian rhythms and Pinteresque menace, Ravenhill at heart seems to be making a plea for a world in which love can transcend the violence and hatred of a society that has been run into the ground by the consumerist values of a wayward class – a plea that has run consistently throughout his body of work ever since. The character of Robbie expresses one of the play's central themes in a speech, inspired by Jean-François Lyotard's *The Postmodern Condition* (1978), which recognises the decimation of grand narratives in a postmodern age.

> I think we all need stories. We make up stories so we can get by. And I think long ago there were great big stories. Stories so big you could live your whole life in them. The Powerful Hands of God and Fate. The Journey to Enlightenment. The March of Socialism. But they all died or the world grew up or grew senile or forgot them, so now we're making up our own stories. Little stories. (p. 66)

Influenced mainly by US novels – Bret Easton Ellis's *Less than Zero* (1985) and Douglas Coupland's *Generation X* (1991) – *Shopping and Fucking* is written in an ironic, quite cynical tone, befitting the sensibility of its generation. Although the play is comprised of a cast of five, the main focus is on Mark, a heroin addict who is trying to break his habit. Introduced as one part of a mysterious trio living in a relatively bare flat, the play follows Mark on a journey into a loveless urban hell where he encounters Gary, a hard-edged teenage rent boy with whom he has a series of increasingly bitter transactions. The play shifts back and forth between Mark and Gary, and the other members of the trio: Robbie, who has a deep crush on Gary, and Lulu, who deals Ecstasy as one of the ways to stay afloat in this drowning world. Rounding out the cast is an elusive character named Brian, who is nominally Lulu's boss, but also serves as a kind of choral figure in the text, commenting on the play's themes each time he appears. It falls upon Brian to deliver the blunt ad-line that encapsulates the play's central message.

> Civilisation is money. Money is civilisation. And civilisation – how did we get here? By war, by struggle, kill or be killed. And money – it's the same thing, you understand? The getting is cruel, is hard, but the having is civilisation. (p. 87)

The crux of the play is a tormented scene of violence and it places the audience as voyeur to the outré actions presented on stage. As I mention in my essay 'Commerce and Morality in the Theatre of Mark Ravenhill', Ravenhill wants to call attention to the voyeur in all of us, who is turned on/turned off by intimations of sex and violence.[2] It is a position in which he will place his audience time and again throughout his career, challenging them to be scandalised by a culture weaned on tabloids and instant celebrity, to laugh at the preening narcissism of empty lives consumed by endless shopping, and to mourn the illness of societies rent apart.

When the play premiered, several critics, including Michael Billington of the *Guardian* and Jack Tinker of the *Daily Mail*, mentioned the scenes of rape and rimming in the piece but didn't dwell on these stage actions.[3] Instead their attention focused on Ravenhill's worldview: his blunt dialogue and sexual gestures positioned alongside themes of social alienation, the vacuity of consumerist culture, and ever-deepening socio-economic class divide. Dan Rebellato places *Shopping and Fucking* within a historical framework of new writing that centres on the decline of the left in British society, and focuses instead on a new kind of political theatre that goes against the state-of-the-nation play favoured in a previous generation by playwrights such as David Edgar and David Hare. Rebellato stresses Ravenhill's ability to look at youth stranded in micro-narratives they can barely understand:

> The myriad permutations of fucking and shopping in the play reflect in a fairly precise way the fate of desire under capitalism [. . .] The play continually reminds us that money is a poor prophylactic for desire, that no matter how hard capitalism may threaten to turn all encounters into economic trans-actions, our need for love can never be fully expressed in economic terms.[4]

The play received two West End runs, a national and international tour and dozens of productions around the world. Ravenhill's deft moral critique of a nation without a centre, hard-wired to globalisation's network of multinational corporate deal-mongering, touched a cultural nerve.[5]

Some Explicit Polaroids (1999)

Some Explicit Polaroids was first performed on tour as an Out of Joint production on 30 September 1999. It tells the story of a former revolutionary left political activist named Nick, who is released from prison after fifteen years for kidnapping and torturing a venture capitalist named Jonathan. Nick finds a city and country that has seemingly abandoned the radical political fervour of his youth, and has replaced it instead with excessive consumerism and a relatively disengaged outlook on public life. Structured as a ten-scene portrait of societal chaos, the play presents a series of dialectical encounters between Nick and his past flames, new and old acquaintances, and class enemies. Ravenhill walks Nick and his characters through the shifting political landscape of London after the flashy rhetoric of Prime Minister Tony Blair's rise to power has lost its initial, aspirational appeal to the citizenry, and the realities of a slowly vanishing liberalism have set in. Egalitarian in its ability to share the burden of blame for the decline of the left and the failure of socialism to effect the kind of socio-economic and political progress once envisioned by idealists on either side of the Iron Curtain, *Some Explicit Polaroids* is a play that illustrates the compromises made by many people. The youngest character is a Russian rent boy named Victor. Ravenhill allows him to describe his hatred of socialism:

> Everything falling to pieces. The buildings ugly and falling down. The shops ugly, empty. The ugly people following the rules and mocking and complaining when they think no one is listening. [. . .] This progress. Big fucking lie. (pp. 270–1)

Inspired, in part, by Ernst Toller's *Hoppla! Such is Life* (1927), which also features a Rip Van Winkle concept, *Some Explicit Polaroids* is one of Ravenhill's angriest plays. Ravenhill does not wax nostalgic for the Nicks of this world. Neither does he exonerate those who have readjusted their political beliefs, and carried on in society. The play skewers its British and Euro-trash characters and is deeply mournful about their state at one and the same time. It is also one of Ravenhill's most overtly personal plays. Tim, the HIV-infected character, who downloads porn and hires Victor for casual sex, slowly deteriorates throughout the play after illness strikes, and two of the piece's most emotional scenes are set in the hospital.

> I want communists and apartheid. I want the finger on the nuclear trigger. I want the gay plague. [. . .] I want to know where I am. Since I was nineteen, I've known that, you know? I knew where everything was heading. (p. 288)

While reading *Some Explicit Polaroids* through an autobiographical lens is not useful critically, certainly the fact that Ravenhill suffered the loss of his long-time partner to illness contributes to the emotional veracity of these scenes.

Working in quick jolts, the play detonates a society and a character – in this case, Nick – who has little left in the end with which to recover. The acuteness of Ravenhill's ability to dissect his own culture with his ironic writing also reflects his deep passion and love for Britain. So much coolly focused rage at the declining values of a country makes Ravenhill an impassioned moralist and humanist. He gives the character of Jonathan, the venture capitalist, a clear-headed speech of justification toward the play's end that maintains the equivocal nature of the play's tensile lines of action:

> I think we both miss the struggle. It's all been rather easy for me these last few years. And I start to feel guilty if things come too easily. But really money, capitalism if you like, is the closest we've come to the way that people actually live.
> (p. 311)

In *Some Explicit Polaroids*, as he wrestles with Nick's re-entry into London, lap dancer Nadia's odd co-dependent attachment to Nick, Tim's consensual subjugation of Russian sex slave Victor, Helen's mid-level political activism, and Jonathan's necessary estrangement from his former captor, Ravenhill lays bare a society in inevitable decline. Patrice Pavis stresses that *Some Explicit Polaroids*

> can be seen to illuminate a whole period, its power relations and the respective camps of winners and losers [. . .] It attempts to explain the world, to clarify links between personal and political motivations. Through his sense of the group, Ravenhill is able to disentangle the various narrative threads on a number of simultaneous levels, to offer a plot that has both tension and excitement, and to tell a human story using all the resources of dramatic art.[6]

Pavis compares Ravenhill's reach and scope in this play to Ibsen. His reading of *Some Explicit Polaroids* in some ways reinforces, however, the conventional social realist reading of the work, yet also expands the view to place the playwright within a wider tradition of world drama, speaking of Ravenhill in the same breath as Shakespeare, especially in regard to the manner in which he works with speech and action.[7]

Some Explicit Polaroids was received moderately well by UK critics when it premiered. Much of the response was similar in lauding the play for its emotional poetry while indicting it for its soft political stance.[8] If *Some Explicit Polaroids* feels elegiac, despite its angry tone, this is not unintended. Towards the end of the play the former kidnapper and prisoner Nick and Jonathan finally meet. Although on opposite political sides, their dialectical encounter, positioned as the play's structural climax, reveals that they have more in common than perhaps either of them would like to believe. Rebellato points out,

> As Jonathan offers Nick the use of his shower, a curious sensuousness curls onto the stage, as if their bodies had found a nostalgic equilibrium in their mutual understanding.[9]

Mother Clap's Molly House (2001)

Mother Clap's Molly House is Ravenhill's first play with songs. Initially developed with students at the London Academy of Music and Dramatic Arts in 2000, the play premiered professionally, with music by Matthew Scott, at the Lyttelton Theatre, National Theatre, on 24 August 2001 under Nicholas Hytner's direction. It was Ravenhill's first production at the National, and, sporting a cast of fourteen-plus playing multiple roles, it was his largest cast play.

The first half of the play is set in the eighteenth century and diagrams the machinations of Mrs Tull, played in the original production by Deborah Findlay, a widow who has inherited her husband's dress hire shop for whores, and who, out of economic necessity and avarice, sets up a molly house or gay club (where men meet in private to dress up, dance together and have sex) and becomes its madam. The second half of the play is set in 2001 in a London apartment where two men stage a gay orgy, dutifully recorded by one of the guests on his camcorder. Ravenhill is clearly linking the gleeful, hedonistic brio of the eighteenth century's commercialised sex culture with the more insidious, fetishised rites of pleasure conducted for the camera's eye in the modern capitalist state. The bitterly elegiac tone that suffused *Some Explicit Polaroids*, while not as evident in this play's bawdy rapturously Hogarthian first half, is fully present in the play's second half, which becomes progressively grim. Overseeing all are the characters of the deities God and Eros, both of whom comment on the action and frame the play's mercantile and Dionysian nature.

Similar in spirit to *Handbag*, in which Ravenhill reimagines Wilde's *The Importance of Being Earnest* (1895), *Mother Clap's Molly House* is a play about the end of one era and the beginning of another, and how the past has paved the way for the actions of the future. There is a cultural amnesia at work in Ravenhill's plays. Characters live with ghosts of their past but somehow cannot claim them. Characters are destined to repeat actions and mistakes and lessons learned are soon forgotten. In the play's second act, Tom (played by the actor who was Martin, Tull's apprentice, in the first act), states:

> Well, I know this is mad but I feel like the Old Me was living in the Olden Days. History and that. Really, really old-fashioned. All scared and no sex and no drugs. And Now there's New Me – and I'm like totally Today. I'm Now. Do you know what I mean? Time machine. Two months. I've travelled hundreds of years into the future. Only the future's like now. I mean, look at me. Clubs. E. Shagging all sorts of blokes. It's great. (p. 64)

One of the rare joys of *Mother Clap's Molly House* is that the character of Mrs Tull is someone who makes use of her past and her inheritance and changes her course of action in life. Brash and upfront, Mrs Tull is the play's heart in the same way that Mother Courage is the heart of Brecht's play. The loss of Mrs Tull's voice in the second half of the play, save for the end sequence, is one of the piece's nagging losses. For Ravenhill there is no place for her in the postmodern age.

> Old woman Tull – that's her wanting, that is. And I dun't
> want no more of that foolish bitch no more. And Mother
> Clap. She's gone too. Goodbye to her. Dun't need me mollies
> a-skipping and a-fucking around me no more. Good game
> while it lasted and it filled me purse fit to bursting. So now we
> can move on. (p. 105)

The unresolved contradictions inherent in the play's actions are
revealed in the play's binary structure. The mollies of the play's first
half revel in their carnal pleasures. The second half is post-AIDS and
there is a sense of sadness evident through every transaction, however
explicit and trained each is for the camera's relentlessly cool gaze. At
the end, Eros joins the dancing mollies as they go from the eighteenth
century and enter the frenzy of a rave club. A sharp, ecstatic release of
energy and pulsing bodies is the play's final image: an image both
liberating and elegiac at one and the same time.

Critically, the play received mixed to positive reviews at its premiere.
Michael Billington in the *Guardian* called it 'an astonishing work to
find at the National Theatre or anywhere else for that matter', while
Michael Coveney in the *Daily Mail* was enthusiastic in his response to
seeing Ravenhill's 'rabid, raw talent exposed on the large Lyttelton
stage and given the full works with glorious costumes, lighting – and
an audience ready to cheer or to boo'.[10] Perhaps due to the size of its
cast, and its musical and production demands, it is one of the least
performed of Ravenhill's works on the global theatre circuit.

Product (2005)

Product was presented by Paines Plough at the Traverse Theatre under
Lucy Morrison's direction. Marking Ravenhill's debut as an actor in
his own work, the play is a deceptively slight satire about the movie
industry. It centres on a writer, James, and his relentless pitch to a B-
movie starlet named Olivia, who wants to kick her career into gear
with a serious project that will showcase her talent. While the
ostensible subject of *Product* is tired, its execution bristles with energy,
wit and flair. The movie industry is an easy target for satire, yet

Ravenhill manages to make the desperate spin of writer James thoroughly engaging. Writing for the solo voice (although the play is a two-hander, Olivia is entirely silent) for the first time, Ravenhill's monologue is a neo-Orwellian dissection of the culture of fear, its genius, and how spin has become a studied art in Western societies delivering products ready-made for consumption and aimed at the lowest common denominator.

The play begins with a story within a story. James tells Olivia about a scene in the proposed film script: an Anglo-Saxon woman on an aeroplane sees a Middle Eastern man pull a knife from his jacket to slice open a croissant. They address each other. A love story in the world haunted by the spectre of terrorism ensues. A story is told of desperate against-all-odds love and danger, Hollywood-style. The writer is careful to note throughout that product placement is key. A world of surfaces is on display. Everything in the representation of reality is a product on the market. As James describes the script to Olivia, and the story becomes more and more intensely, yet subtly ludicrous, it becomes clear that James is testing not only himself on how effectively he can sell his creative 'product', but also how he can win Olivia to accept the idea that what he has in hand for her is the role of a lifetime.

Product's running time is about an hour – the writing is spare and wittily dry. Yet, its power in its compressed performance time is disarming. Ravenhill is writing here about writing, about the act of performance itself, and the kinds of narratives audiences have been conditioned to accept and believe in for years. He is also writing about the kinds of narratives that have taken hold in the consciousness of Western society after 11 September 2001.

> Europe is to be torn apart. The Hague. The Reichstag. Tate Modern. Suicide bombing. Each of these men is to be stuffed and strapped with explosives and then at midday tomorrow they will carry off buildings and people and nothing but misery and devastation will follow. (p. 65)

In *Product*, everything and everyone in and out of the central conceit of the story is a product and a commodity, readily sold, consumed and in the end, easily disposable. The former lover of the script's heroine died in the Twin Towers. A West meets East vengeance drama is set to play itself out. The story that the writer spins is a mish-mash of culturally assembled fragments that collide and swirl around one another to fabricate an outrageously manufactured construct – the script's showdown finale is a nightmare sequence set in Disney World Europe:

> These are good people, these are good, fat, happy, bright people. Queueing, eating, riding people. These are your people. What are you doing? What are you doing? [. . .] We're all just dead people in the Magic Kingdom of Life. (pp. 67–8)

Product is a bracing piece, and it is not a surprise at all that it was well received when it first played in Edinburgh and wherever it has played since.

The Cut (2006)

The year 2006 saw three Ravenhill premieres in the UK: *The Cut*, *Citizenship* and *Pool (No Water)*. *The Cut* is a play that examines the constantly shifting binary between good and evil. Ravenhill has never been afraid of taking on big ideas and grand schemes. His works are ambitious and driven by a desire to communicate cautionary tales, moral tales, wake-up stories for a generation sleepwalking through their lives. In *The Cut*, Ravenhill, whose work is rife with complicated stories of absent, abusive, exploitative father figures and abandoned teenagers and children, writes about a father figure who is part of a regime that condones and promotes his abusive behaviour, and who is ultimately held accountable for it.

The Cut premiered at the Donmar Warehouse on 22 February 2006. The production starred Sir Ian McKellen as Paul and Deborah Findlay as his wife Susan. The play contains three scenes, which are set in different spaces. The first scene is between Paul and John in a room in an office. Paul is in a high-to-mid-level official position in government. John is his willing subject. Paul's job is not immediately clear in the first few moments, but soon it is apparent that he is a government-sanctioned torturer who administers the cut, which eliminates individual desire and historical memory, and that John wants the procedure to take place.

> There's no history. All that struggling to move forward, to expand, to progress. That's gone away. And there's no society. All the prisons and universities have fallen down or exploded. Or maybe they never were. It doesn't matter. [. . .] Darkness is light. Void is everything. You are truth. (p. 18)

The second scene is at home and shows Paul's relationship with his wife and house servant Mina. There is no discussion of his work when he is at home, although there is tension. Paul is unusually rattled by the day's events. His wife tries to console him. Their relationship is strained and filled with bitterness and resentment. She reveals that their son Stephen has written, and that the letter has awakened her somehow to the reality of Paul's job. She confronts him. He tries to avoid her. She persists. He breaks down. Then she challenges what she interprets as his desire for empathy from her:

> You've never been the sort of man who cries. All the time I've known you. The last lot. The new lot. The generations. You've never been the sort that cries. How can I make love to you? How can I make love to a man who cries? Who shuts his eyes and cries and cries? [. . .] Of course you're sorry. We're all sorry. But we still have to eat. (p. 41)

The scene ends in an impasse. The final scene is between Paul and his son Stephen. Time has passed. Paul is in jail as a result of the cut being banished from a new government. Stephen confronts the father. It is a day of reckoning. The tone of the scene is casual but its aspect is nearly Biblical:

> So – this is the bright new future. This is the new world. Kids who can't tell the difference between a lie and the truth. Oh

son. Oh son, I would weep but there's no more fucking tears.
(p. 49)

The father stays in the dark, and lets his son go out into the world, into the light. At a running time of ninety minutes, *The Cut* is a sleek and economical piece of theatre. Its world is familiar yet somewhat at a remove. It is set in a world that thrives on the efficiency of its surveillance, and its ability to divorce home and leisure spaces from the consequences of those of the workplace. This is the thinly veiled world of extraordinary rendition during the Blair–Bush years. *The Cut* is a powerful and elegantly disturbing play, yet critically the piece received a lukewarm response. Most of the critics repeatedly used the word 'obscure' to describe it and on the whole tended to fault the piece for its lack of social realism.[11] The play is not place- or time-specific, but its aim is decidedly not social realism. Peter Billingham notes that *The Cut* is distinguished from earlier Ravenhill plays by its

> construction of dramatic character and a significant change to a more conventional, less episodic Ibsenesque dramatic narrative structure. [. . .] What is important is the question of what defines theatre as 'political' in terms of the interplay between dramatic form, aesthetics and ideological intention. [. . .] *The Cut* by implication examines this political and ideological dilemma from a position of bleak, cynical pessimism.[12]

Shoot/Get Treasure/Repeat (2008)

In March 2007, Ravenhill suffered a particularly severe epileptic fit and was hospitalised. The coma had left him with acute memory loss, but he accepted a commission from Paines Plough artistic director Roxana Silbert to write a play a day for the Edinburgh Fringe Festival. As he describes it in an article, he wanted to write a

> big piece that would capture our urge to bring our model of freedom and democracy to the world, even as we withdraw

into more and more fearfully isolated groups at home. But I didn't want to have a grand narrative with linking plots and characters. I wanted this global theme to be glimpsed through 16 fragments.[13]

The result was *Ravenhill for Breakfast*, presented as a play a day each morning at the Traverse Theatre in August 2007. It won a Fringe First Award. Excerpts from each play were published in the *Guardian* daily, and shortly after the sixteen plays were assembled under the new title *Shoot/Get Treasure/Repeat*. From 2–30 April 2008 the plays were staged around London at diverse venues by the Gate Theatre, the National Theatre, Out of Joint, Paines Plough, the Royal Court and BBC Radio 3.[14] A seventeenth play, *Paradise Regained*, was commissioned by the Golden Mask festival in Moscow and presented at the Royal Court in September 2008.

 Shoot/Get Treasure/Repeat, with its video-gaming title and quest-like staging strategy in London, is appropriately epic. The titles of each short play come from a pre-existing masterpiece: 'The Odyssey', 'War and Peace', 'The Mikado', etc. The entire cycle of plays examines the effects of war, in Iraq, Afghanistan and the Middle East, and on the domestic home front(s). Each play is twenty minutes in length. If staged together in one sitting, the plays would run for six hours. It is Ravenhill's most overtly ambitious work for the theatre. It is also a cycle that contains some of his most violent and surreal stage images and actions. In 'The Odyssey', the dictator is 'kicked to death by the chorus, and the male members of the chorus urinate over the corpse. Once this is done, the female members apply make-up to his face' (p. 184). In 'Crime and Punishment' an unnamed Soldier interrogates an unnamed woman. The piece's tension is suspended between the woman's fear and the soldier's increasing demand for love. At the end of the interrogation the soldier cuts the woman's tongue out and declares

9:47 a.m. I have cut out detainee's tongue. My mission is pointless. Nobody loves me. Now I must choose if I shoot out my brains. Maybe there is love in another place, maybe if we

invade again then a woman will say [. . .] or maybe it is better
to shoot now. I wish I had an order from a superior. [. . .] But
there is no order from above. The choice is mine. This is
democracy. This is what we call democracy. Democracy – I
hate you. (p. 94)

Written in an open manner, and recalling in its experimental nature
some of Martin Crimp's work, especially his seminal *Attempts on Her
Life* (1997), *Shoot/Get Treasure/Repeat* is divided into choral sections,
monologues and dialogic sequences. Margherita Laera states that

Ravenhill explores the effects of politics and ideology over
the characters' bodies and language practices. He exposes the
repercussions of war and the effects of the society of
the spectacle on our relationship and biological functions
such as eating, dreaming and having sex.[15]

Alternating between choral odes and individual episodes, the cycle
engages in themes of war, love, death, fear and sacrifice. Although war
writ large is its overarching theme, sacrifice is its strongest thematic
thread, befitting the ritualistic aspect of the cycle.

Staged as a treasure hunt of sorts in and around London, inter-
activity was key in its conception and design. Audiences were asked to
engage at different levels, depending on which venue was staging the
specific piece(s). They were free to select which play to choose to see
when. They could also see them in and out of order, shuffling plays as
if they were tracks on an iPod. The site-responsive stagings of the cycle
are unique in Ravenhill's work. None of his plays prior or since (thus
far) has been staged unconventionally in London. With the rise of
more and more site-specific, responsive and immersive work produced
in London in the last five to seven years (for example, work produced by Shunt, Punchdrunk, and so on), *Shoot/Get Treasure/Repeat*
could also be seen as part of a larger, innovative trend towards
exploring alternative ways of seeing, and participating in and
marketing theatre events in the UK.

Summary

While he is undeniably linked to the 1990s Cool Britannia youth aesthetic, Ravenhill's plays are fuelled by a moral impulse that links him to a tradition of writing that is much more classical in its nature. Influenced by ancient Greek drama, the plays of Oscar Wilde, Brecht and contemporary pop culture, Ravenhill's mannerist plays examine gender, class and the social-political climate in which his characters live, and how the transactions of daily life shape British and global culture. The intersection of commerce and sex (queer and straight) are central concerns of his early plays. In his first decade as a dramatist in the twenty-first century, his work has become more concerned with the effects of globalisation on local and immediate lives, figures of authority and how they wield power to corrupt their citizenry, and the role of art and how it speaks to culture, if at all.

In an essay for the *Independent*, Ravenhill wrote about the influence of Edward Bond on his work:

> I was 20 when I first read Edward Bond's play *Saved*. For the first time, I discovered a playwright who was my contemporary. Bond had stripped away all of the conventional rhetoric of British theatre. The characters communicated in terse, demotic lines. The action progressed as much through a series of stark visual images as it did in words. His was a world I instantly recognized.[16]

Ravenhill has proved in an already impressive body of work that ranges from *Shopping and Fucking* to *Ghost Story* that his dramatic project is less about scandal, shock and awe than about unnerving his audience and crossing boundaries of authority and moral licence in order to expose the licentiousness of the times. In his essay 'A Tear in the Fabric', Ravenhill explains his artistic mission:

> I've always written against moral relativism. [. . .] To write against our ironic, easy going times, where any hierarchy of values has melted away, to stage something that makes an

audience say, 'That is wrong' – that is definitely something I've delighted in doing.[17]

The essay goes on to describe the murder of three-year-old James Bulger in February 1993 by two ten-year-old boys. Ravenhill recalls the impact that the surveillance images of the abduction had on him and how the story took hold of his imagination particularly because this was a crime against a child committed by other children.[18]

Ravenhill's work has attracted sustained critical attention from emerging and established theatre scholars and critics and reviewers. Aleks Sierz notes in *In-Yer-Face Theatre* that Ravenhill was one of the first dramatists to recognise that the

> blank fictions of American culture – with their emphasis on the extreme, the marginal and the violent – applied equally to today's Britain, [and] that Ravenhill has blended the bleakness of 'apocalypse culture' with more traditional humanistic concerns.[19]

Dan Rebellato, in his Introduction to Ravenhill's *Plays One*, positions the author as a dramatist whose vision is

> elliptically but recognizably social, even socialist. He addresses not the fragments but the whole, offering us not just some explicit polaroids but the bigger picture.[20]

Patrice Pavis in his essay on Durringer and Ravenhill states that Ravenhill

> draws on a profounder and more disturbing disreputability and reveals real bodies, historic conflicts, existing contradictions, and forces the audience to reconstruct a political story that goes well beyond the aspect of sexual provocation.[21]

Michael Billington says that *Shopping and Fucking* was the 'one play that defined the theatre of the 1990s'.[22] David Edgar has pointed out that *Shopping and Fucking* was an example of British theatre's focus on 'masculinity in crisis'.[23] Rebellato aptly notes that the long line of surrogate and absent fathers in Ravenhill's work is indicative of the 'disappearing paternalism' of the welfare state in the post-Thatcher era.[24] Peter Billingham dedicates a chapter to Ravenhill in his book *At the Sharp End* and assesses his dramatic project as one distinguished by

> a contemporary political and moral sensibility that is often in active resistance to what he perceives as the listless vacuity of many postmodern narratives.[25]

Amelia Howe Kritzer, David Ian Rabey, Michelene Wandor and Clare Wallace have also written about his work.[26] Enric Monforte interviewed Ravenhill for the *British Theatre of the 1990s* collection.[27] In short, while Ravenhill continues to be associated with the moment of 'in-yer-face theatre', despite his admitted scepticism concerning the label, critics who persist in seeing Ravenhill only through the *Shopping and Fucking* lens will in time come to realise that his project as a writer goes beyond the subjects of sex and commerce. Ravenhill writes to make sense of a blasted universe: blasted but not broken. It is this degree of inexorable hope (against hope) that sets his work apart.

Primary Sources

Works by Mark Ravenhill

Sleeping Around, co-written with Hillary Fannin, Stephen Greenhorn, and Abi Morgan, (London: Methuen Drama, 1998).

Plays One: Shopping and Fucking, Faust is Dead, Handbag, Some Explicit Polaroids (London: Methuen Drama, 2001).

Mother Clap's Molly House (London: Methuen Drama, 2001).

Totally Over You (London: Samuel French, 2003).

Pool (No Water) and *Citizenship* (London: Methuen Drama, 2006).

The Cut and *Product* (London: Methuen Drama, 2006).

Shoot/Get Treasure/Repeat (London: Methuen Drama, 2008).

Over There (London: Methuen Drama, 2009).

A Life in Three Acts, written with Bette Bourne (London: Methuen Drama, 2009).
The Experiment, unpublished play text, 2009.
Ghost Story, unpublished play text, 2010.

Secondary Sources

Aragay, Mireia, Hildegard Klein, Enric Montforte and Pilar Zozaya (eds), *British Theatre of the 1990s: Interviews with Directors, Playwrights, Critics and Academics* (Basingstoke: Palgrave Macmillan, 2007).

Billingham, Peter, *At the Sharp End: Uncovering the Work of Five Contemporary Dramatists* (London: Methuen Drama, 2007).

Billington, Michael, *State of the Nation: British Theatre Since 1945* (London: Faber & Faber, 2008).

Croall, Jonathan, *Inside the Molly House: The National Theatre at Work* (London: National Theatre Publications, 2001).

Deeney, John F., 'National Causes/Moral Clauses?: The National Theatre, Young People and Citizenship', *Research in Drama Education*, Vol. 12, No. 3 (2007), pp. 331–44.

D'Monté, Rebecca and Graham Saunders (eds), *Cool Britannia? British Political Drama in the 1990s* (Basingstoke: Palgrave Macmillan, 2008).

Edgar, David (ed.), *State of Play: Playwrights on Playwriting* (London: Faber & Faber, 1999).

Howe Kritzer, Amelia, *Political Theatre in Post-Thatcher Britain: New Writing 1995–2005* (Basingstoke: Palgrave Macmillan, 2008).

Laera, Margherita, 'Mark Ravenhill's *Shoot/Get Treasure/Repeat*: A Treasure Hunt in London', *TheatreForum*, No. 35 (2009), pp. 3–9.

Pavis, Patrice, 'Ravenhill and Durringer, the *Entente Cordiale* Misunderstood', trans. David Bradby, *Contemporary Theatre Review*, Vol. 14, No. 2 (2004), pp. 4–15.

Rabey, David Ian, *English Drama Since 1940* (Harlow: Longman, 2003).

Ravenhill, Mark, 'A Tear in the Fabric', *TheatreForum*, No. 26 (2005), pp. 85–92.

—, 'My Pink Fountain Pen Has Run Dry', *Guardian*, 12 November 2007 <http://www.guardian.co.uk/culture/tvandradioblog/2007/nov/12/mypinkfountain penhasrund/>

—, 'The Playwright Explains Why He's Drawn to His Gritty, Uncompromising Works', *Independent*, 10 January 2008 <http://www.independent.co.uk/arts-entertainment/ theatre-dance/features/mark-ravenhill-the-playwright-explains-why-hes-drawn-to-his-gritty-uncompromising-works-769307.html>

—, 'My Near Death Period', *Guardian*, 28 March 2008, <http://www.guardian.co.uk/ stage/2008/mar/26/theatre>

Rebellato, Dan, 'Introduction', in Mark Ravenhill, *Plays One* (London: Methuen Drama, 2001), pp. ix–xii.

—, 'Introduction', in Mark Ravenhill, *Shopping and Fucking* (London: Methuen Drama Student Edition, 2005), pp. viii–ix.

—, 'The Cut and Its Critics: Ravenhill's Ethical Politics', presented at Ravenhill 10 Conference, Goldsmiths College, University of London, 11 November 2006.

Sierz, Aleks, *In-Yer-Face Theatre: British Drama Today* (London: Faber & Faber, 2001).

Svich, Caridad, 'Commerce and Morality in the Theatre of Mark Ravenhill', *Contemporary Theatre Review*, Vol. 13, No. 1 (2003), pp. 81–95.

Wallace, Clare, *Suspect Cultures: Narrative, Identity and Citation in 1990s New Drama* (Prague: Litteraria Pragensia, 2006).

Wandor, Michelene, *Post-war British Drama: Looking Back in Gender* (London and New York: Routledge, 2001).

Notes

1. Mark Ravenhill, 'A Tear in the Fabric', p. 88.
2. Caridad Svich, 'Commerce and Morality in the Theatre of Mark Ravenhill', p. 83.
3. Aleks Sierz, *In-Yer-Face Theatre*, pp. 127–9.
4. Dan Rebellato, 'Introduction', pp. viii–ix.
5. Reviews of *Shopping and Fucking*, *Theatre Record*, Vol. XVI, No. 20 (1996), pp. 1244–8.
6. Patrice Pavis, 'Ravenhill and Durringer', p. 6.
7. Ibid., p. 8.
8. Reviews of *Some Explicit Polaroids*, *Theatre Record*, Vol. XIX, No. 21 (1999), pp. 1354–6.
9. Rebellato, 'Introduction', *Plays One*, p. xviii.
10. Reviews of *Mother Clap's Molly House*, *Theatre Record*, Vol. XXI, No. 18 (2001), pp. 1082–92.
11. Reviews of *The Cut*, *Theatre Record*, Vol. XXVI, No. 5 (2006), pp. 228–32.
12. Peter Billingham, *At the Sharp End*, p. 151; see also Dan Rebellato, 'The Cut and Its Critics'.
13. Mark Ravenhill, 'My Near Death Period'.
14. Reviews of *Shoot/Get Treasure/Repeat*, *Theatre Record*, Vol. XXVIII, No. 8 (2008), pp. 396–8.
15. Margherita Laera, 'Mark Ravenhill's *Shoot/Get Treasure/Repeat*', p. 4.
16. Mark Ravenhill, 'The Playwright Explains Why He's Drawn to His Gritty, Uncompromising Works'.
17. Ravenhill, 'A Tear in the Fabric', p. 91.
18. Ibid.
19. Sierz, *In-Yer-Face Theatre*, p. 151.
20. Rebellato, 'Introduction', *Plays One*, p. x.

21. Pavis, 'Ravenhill and Durringer', p. 15.
22. Michael Billington, *State of the Nation*, p. 359.
23. David Edgar, *State of Play*, p. 27.
24. Rebellato, 'Introduction', *Plays One*, p. xiii.
25. Billingham, *At the Sharp End*, p. 135.
26. See Amelia Howe Kritzer, *Political Theatre in Post-Thatcher Britain*, David Ian Rabey, *English Drama Since 1940*, Michelene Wandor, *Post-war British Drama* and Clare Wallace, *Suspect Cultures*.
27. See Mireia Aragay et al., *British Theatre of the 1990s*.

22 PHILIP RIDLEY

Dan Rebellato

The Pitchfork Disney; The Fastest Clock in the Universe; Brokenville; Vincent River; Mercury Fur

Introduction

Philip Ridley was born in 1964 in Bethnal Green in the East End of London, the area that has provided the settings for nearly all of his plays. In addition to being a playwright, Ridley is a poet, novelist, painter, photographer, screenwriter, children's author, performance artist, librettist, songwriter and film director. The origin of this prolific diversity lies in his childhood when, stricken with chronic asthma and alienated from school, he was largely self-educated. His father made him a board to fit his chair on which he would have books, art materials, paper and pens, and he would spend his days in this 'art capsule' moving fluidly between reading, drawing, writing and imagining.[1] When he applied to St Martins School of Art, his subject was nominally painting, but in fact he continued to explore many art forms, forming his own theatre company for which he wrote texts, music, designed costumes and painted sets. There he also started writing and performing monologues, two of which were complementary: one centred on a character who was afraid of everything ('I'm afraid of going out. I'm afraid of cats. I'm afraid of dogs. I'm afraid of shadows. I'm afraid of Americans. I'm afraid of friends') and the other on someone who was not afraid of anything ('I love the feel of explosions. I love the feel of radiation on my skin. I love the feel of acid on my eyes. I love the feel of being raped. I love the feel of being attacked. I love the feel of blood dripping on another person').[2] Soon Ridley began to wonder what would happen if these characters met, a chain of thought that led to his first play *The Pitchfork Disney*.

This play, opening in 1991 at the Bush Theatre, achieved full houses and outraged critics, with its apparently amoral fusion of violence and sexuality, realist setting and intense verbal imagery.[3] Ridley, coming from a visual arts background, was influenced as much by surrealist film-makers such as Luis Buñuel and Jan Švankmajer, or painters such as Francis Bacon, as by any playwright, and was hard for the critics to place. Similarly, for much of his career, he has been dogged by moralistic responses that pay scant attention to the image structures in his work. Ridley's contemporaries at art school were the Young British Artists who gained acclaim and notoriety in the mid-1990s for their similarly iconoclastic and unnerving clashes of beauty and scandal. Many of the images in Ridley's plays sit comfortably alongside such artworks as Damien Hirst's *For the Love of God* (2007) – a human skull encrusted with diamonds.

In Ridley's play *Leaves of Glass* (Soho Theatre, 2007), the young, troubled artist Barry has an exhibition of his drawings but when his moralistic mother dismisses them as twisted and pornographic ('All those screaming faces. The tears. That's not sex as I know it', p. 247) it falls to Barry's brother to defend him: 'They're a sequence. You see? Individually they don't make much sense. Composition's all fucked up. [. . .] But when you put them next to each other and . . . it'll start to balance out. Make sense' (p. 254). The same is true of Ridley; looking at the repeated motifs, the developing shape of his playwriting, the clear groups of plays make it easier to identify the profound ethical and political dimensions of his work.

Ridley's plays so far fall loosely into three distinctive groups. His first three plays, *The Pitchfork Disney* (1991), *The Fastest Clock in the Universe* (Hampstead Theatre, 1992), and *Ghost from a Perfect Place* (Hampstead Theatre, 1994) share a fascination with violence, a distinctively gothic and claustrophobic sensibility, and are, in particular, marked by their exotically named characters – Sherbet Gravel, Cosmo Disney, Torchie Sparks – and long set-piece monologues, often on fantastic themes. Although they have been referred to as an 'East End trilogy', they wear their East End references very lightly. The second group of plays, often produced at the National Theatre, begins with *Sparkleshark* (1997) and includes *Fairytaleheart* (1998), *Brokenville*

(2003), *Moonfleece* (2004) and *Karamazoo* (2004). These plays are mainly written for young people and all feature storytelling at their heart; they range from a monologue – *Karamazoo* – to a large-cast play like *Moonfleece*. Ridley has called this group 'the Storyteller Sequence' and has plans for it to number seven plays.[4] The third group comprises *Vincent River* (Hampstead Theatre, 2000), *Mercury Fur* (Paines Plough, 2005), *Leaves of Glass* (2007) and *Piranha Heights* (Soho Theatre, 2008). These plays, while still rich in metaphor and verbal imagery, take a step towards realism: the character names are more everyday, the locations are more realistically sketched in, and there is a stronger sense of psychological depth to the characters, with a particular – perhaps autobiographically inspired – focus on brotherly relationships.

The Plays

The Pitchfork Disney (1991)

In a dilapidated house in a derelict landscape, a twin brother and sister, Presley and Haley Stray, fearful of the outside, sustain themselves on fantasies, medication and chocolate. Into this world come the beautiful and terrifying Cosmo Disney and his hideous and terrifying associate the Pitchfork Cavalier. Presley is clearly attracted to Cosmo, but Cosmo has designs on Haley.

The play was startling on its first appearance for its immense theatrical confidence and its lack of an explicitly moral authorial voice, two qualities that seemed, when it opened on 2 January 1991, contradictory. Indeed, the play is structured around opposites – the shabby surroundings and Cosmo's red glittery jacket, the childlike obsessions of the twins and the intruder's adult sexuality, the fairytale elements and the brutality of the physical acts: a broken finger, Cosmo swallowing a live cockroach. Previously, the major waves of British new playwriting had been explicitly political. But *The Pitchfork Disney* does not identify the form of society, even the nature of the world outside the room in which it is set. Cosmo aggressively accuses Presley of being homosexual and Haley repeats xenophobic clichés about foreigners, but what Ridley thinks of this homophobia and racism is ambiguous. This led some critics to say of this play – as they would say of many others – that Ridley was politically disengaged, perhaps even salaciously exploiting the horrors being portrayed. In the words of Dominic Dromgoole, the Artistic Director of the Bush Theatre, the critics were horrified by a play that had 'no politics, no naturalism, no journalism, no issues'.[5] But to others – like me, who saw the play fresh out of university – it offered a ferociously funny and unsettling vision of a 1990s culture shot through with uncertainty, absence and loss.

Strikingly absent from the play are the parents. Parents are absent in nearly all of Ridley's plays: *Vincent River, Leaves of Glass, Piranha Heights, Fairytaleheart* and *Karamazoo* take place in the shadow of a parent's death; in others, parents are absent or unmentioned. In some ways this reflects the proximity of Ridley's story-worlds to fairytales, which are filled with parents losing or abandoning their children, children sent to wicked stepmothers and cruel stepfathers, lured by wolves and witches, imprisoned in cottages and castles. This parental absence is not always an unambiguous disaster; in many of the plays, they present an opportunity for young people to free their imaginations beyond the boring constraints of adult society.

Here, though, the absence of parents is traumatic. Haley and Stray continually rehearse memories of an impossibly idealised and extremely conventional family, quite at odds with the eerily dysfunctional and shattered world in which they now live, but where have the parents gone? The play does not say explicitly, but there are sufficient repeated motifs in the pair's stories to suggest that they died at the hands of a serial killer and that Haley and Presley's imaginations and memories have been shattered and fragmented by this trauma. In Presley particularly, one sees a fearful, eroticised fascination for the killer, even identification with him. There are repeated phallic images that almost always become images of castration, suggesting a kind of horrified excitement at adult sexuality. For example, Presley's story about finding a snake and cooking it (p. 19), and, more literally, the huge erection that 'scrapes across the tarmac' becoming 'grazed and cut, leaving a trail of blood behind me' in Presley's long dream (p. 66).

More broadly, the loss of the parents is symptomatic of a broader loss of authority; four times, Presley describes the world outside to Haley as 'black. A sheet of dark cloud obscures everything. No heaven visible': a phrase which takes on an almost metaphysical sense of loss.[6] These characters live in a world where all meaning, certainty, authority and perhaps morality have gone. They are forced to rely on poorly remembered scraps of childhood memories. Even the characters' names – Disney, Presley, Haley – suggest fragments of a shattered popular culture.

This parental absence connects with a profound sense of loss and abandonment, often worked through visually in the surroundings of the plays. The 'old and colourless' (p. 5) room of *Pitchfork* is joined by *Fastest Clock*'s 'dilapidated room above an abandoned factory in the East End of London' (p. 93), and the burned-out room of *Ghost from a Perfect Place* with one window which 'reveals a pitch-black night beyond' (p. 181). *Vincent River* takes place in 'a run-down flat' (p. 9), and *Mercury Fur* and *Moonfleece* in derelict flats in neglected estates. *Fairytaleheart* transpires in 'an abandoned community centre' (p. 9), *Sparkleshark* on the rooftop of a tower block among 'discarded household furniture, piles of rubbish and various scattered detritus' (p. 71), and the characters of *Brokenville* converge in 'a ruined house: no ceiling, near-demolished walls, smashed windows, stairway [. . .] Everything damaged by some nameless catastrophe' (p. 3).

Individually, these evoke particular conditions; together they suggest a profound vision of social calamity. This vision is expressed most clearly in *Brokenville* in which the survivors of that 'nameless catastrophe' have literally lost their memories of the recent past, even of who they are. They tell each other stories and slowly, through these elliptical allegories, grope intuitively towards a reconstruction of what happened. The stories they tell portray a society marked by narcissism and greed, damaged by self-interest and the incapacity of the powerful to love and be loved. In 1991, these were vices often associated with the rightward turn of British politics. While one can easily see the catastrophe suffered by the worlds of *Pitchfork* and *Brokenville* as nuclear, military, terroristic or environmental, they are also open to interpretation as a way of thinking through the effects felt by those altruistic cultures of community, welfare and solidarity of a decade of

Conservative government, in Britain embodied in that group of policies known as 'Thatcherism'.

This is not to say that *The Pitchfork Disney* can be simply decoded as an allegory for conventional political topics. It is crucial to understanding Ridley's work that he is drawn to ambiguity and abstraction, to imaginative metaphor rather than literal reference. He has precisely *not* written an explicitly anti-Thatcher play or a savage indictment of homophobia. His plays do acknowledge, without censorious commentary, the simultaneous pleasure and discomfort audiences can feel in witnessing sexual and violent acts on stage, their possibly mixed feelings about complex issues about identity and multiculturalism. While it may draw on moral or political anxieties it cannot be reduced to simple commentary. *The Pitchfork Disney*, more than any other play, marks the transition from the political convictions of 1980s theatre to the profound ambiguities of the 1990s.

The Fastest Clock in the Universe (1992)

Ridley's next play was already half-written when *The Pitchfork Disney* made its debut. Watching the play every night was undoubtedly an intense education in theatre craft that he drew on to complete *The Fastest Clock in the Universe*, which opened at Hampstead Theatre, in north London, on 14 May 1992. In an interview with Jane Edwardes, he explained

> The experience of doing *Pitchfork* was a revelation to me. It was the most direct contact I had ever had with an audience. I sat through twenty performances and saw twenty different plays. It was a revelation to hear people scream when Cosmo ate the cockroach, to see them nearly moved to tears. I went straight out of doing that into writing *The Fastest Clock*.[7]

The lesson he learned was about the virtues of developing a more causally coherent structure for the play: 'By being that disciplined with myself, it's given me a greater freedom to be more baroque in other areas that really excite me.'[8]

The move to a more carefully plotted structure did not mean compromising the outrageousness or the surreal imagery. An older and a younger man, Captain Tock and Cougar Glass, whose relationship seems to be occasionally sexual, share a flat. Cougar is thirty but, in denial of his advancing years, is throwing a party to celebrate his nineteenth birthday. He has befriended a teenage boy, Foxtrot Darling, and it appears that he plans to seduce or rape him under the guise of the celebration. But when Foxtrot appears with a pregnant girlfriend, Sherbet Gravel, in tow, the evening darkens, ending with Cougar's violent assault on the young woman, causing her to miscarry.

Fastest Clock is typical of Ridley in several respects, one of which is in the age range of the cast. Foxtrot is sixteen years old while the elderly neighbour, Cheetah Bee, is eighty. The very old and the very young fill Ridley's plays. In *Ghost from a Perfect Place*, the characters range from twelve to seventy; in *Vincent River* the two protagonists are seventeen and fifty-three; *Brokenville*'s inhabitants range from a ten-year-old to an eightysomething. This has in part an explanation in the childhood origins of Ridley's creativity: isolated from his peers by being withdrawn from school, he spent a great deal of time listening to stories told by older members of his family:

> I could sit there – I still can – for hours and listen to people tell me stories about their childhood. My great-grandmother was still alive and she could remember Queen Victoria. My aunt could remember stories of Jack the Ripper. And then my parents would tell stories of the Kray Twins. So this whole dark, glittering mythology of East London was my life's blood and I did stories about that and pictures about that.[9]

This simultaneous experience of childhood and age remains a wellspring for Ridley's mature creativity. In the experience of the plays themselves, however, the older and younger characters seem to be those with greater access to imagination and the power of story.

In *Fastest Clock*, the extremes of age difference are a development from the irreconcilable oppositions that, as we have seen, also structured *Pitchfork*. In these early plays, these oppositions create an effect that has affinities with the artistic mode known as 'the grotesque'. The term emerged in the sixteenth century, at first to describe some aspects of Roman decoration that mixed plant, animal and architectural motifs in apparent disregard for 'natural order' or any kind of realism. It has subsequently been applied to artworks that employ caricature, vulgarity and extremes of disharmony and horror. In the late twentieth century, a more precise definition was offered in an influential study by Wolfgang Kayser who argued that what was unsettling about these modes was that 'the grotesque is the estranged world'.[10] By that he meant that the grotesque took aspects of our familiar world and transformed it in a way that unsettles our ordinary sense of things and suggests that 'the categories which apply to our world view [have] become inapplicable'.[11] For the critic Philip Thompson, a way of characterising this is to see the grotesque as

> *a fundamentally ambivalent thing, as a clash of opposites*, and hence, in some forms at least, as an approximate expression of the problematic nature of existence. It is no accident that the grotesque mode in art and literature tends to be prevalent in societies and eras marked by strife, radical changes or disorientation.[12]

Ridley's work displays just this ambivalence and these clashing opposites and, as can be seen in the critical response at least, generates deep tremors of anxiety in the audience. These are not merely between narrative elements (the very old and very young, for example, and in this play between homosexual and heterosexual), but they are aesthetic (extremes of beauty and ugliness), stylistic (realist settings and surreal imagery), and moral too, in the repeated juxtaposition of infantile and adult sexuality. In *Fastest Clock*, the play does not underline for us that Cougar's actions are immoral: if anything, the experience of the play is an increasing discomfort deriving from simultaneously experiencing mounting horror at Cougar's plan alongside a sense that the play's farce structure is encouraging us to will Cougar on. As Ridley has said more recently, the play owes a great deal to the English tradition of high comedy: 'I've always thought it's set up like a classic Noël Coward two-act comedy. Instead of "Rupert" wanting to seduce "Sophia", it's Cougar wanting to rape Foxtrot.'[13]

Brokenville (2003)

Brokenville had a long gestation, beginning its life as *Cavesongs* while Ridley was still at St Martins; it then became *Apocalyptica*, performed as a work-in-progress during the run of *Fairytaleheart* at Hampstead Theatre in 1998. In May of the following year, it was performed for five nights under the title *Brokenville* by a cast of Kosovan refugees in St George's Church, Dagenham, directed by Benjamin May. Ridley revised the play again in 2002, when asked for a second time to contribute to the National Theatre's Connections programme of plays for young people, and the play was performed at the National's Cottesloe Theatre in July 2003. It is a key play in the 'Storyteller Sequence' and Ridley imagines that it would be the last of the plays in that series. It is also a key play in Ridley's career.

It is set in a ruined house after an unnamed catastrophe, where a group of young people and an elderly woman slowly gather. There is a very young child, traumatised and anxious, whose book of fairy stories has been almost destroyed. The assembled group take turns improvising and acting out stories both to calm the child's fears and somehow to make sense of the horrors that have befallen them all.

Stories have always played a central role in Ridley's dramaturgy. In *Pitchfork*, there are several set-piece monologues, one of them, Presley's horrified account of a recurring nightmare, lasting five pages (pp. 65–9). In *Fastest Clock*, the image of the title is expressed as the conclusion to a elaborate fairy story told by the Captain. In *Ghost from a Perfect Place*, Travis Flood is an East End gangster returned from many years away to promote his autobiography, and the play hinges on the different stories that all the characters tell to make sense of their lives. *Leaves of Glass* is driven by the attempts of three characters to impose their stories on each other.

It is in the Storyteller plays where story takes on the task of generating the dramatic action. In all of these plays, the act of telling a story is what moves the play from its beginning to its end. In *Karamazoo*, a teenager's way of coping with the loss of a parent is to remember and retell the stories they used to make up. In *Sparkleshark*, a young boy is menaced by the other kids on the estate and – Scheherazade-like – finds himself compelled to tell stories to avoid being harmed. In *Moonfleece*, it is only by listening to a storyteller that the true story of a family tragedy can be articulated. Gideon and Kirsty, in *Fairytaleheart*, use stories both to express their upset at their parents' new relationships and also to find and express a kinship between themselves. Stories for these characters are therapeutic, sources of deception and opportunities for magic, and one of the ways we make sense of the world. Crucially, *Brokenville* is a play about story's links to theatre. The play moves from storytelling to drama, as the stories begin to be animated, the broken refugees begin to regain a sense of character. It is a play that shows the role that theatre can have in generating a sense of community, shared history, memory and identity.

Key is the ability of story and theatre to allow us to confront our fears and emerge better armed against them. In *Fairytaleheart*, Gideon expresses this through the image of a tribe menaced by a monster in the jungle who deal with this threat by telling each other stories about it around the campfire (pp. 26–9). This image is echoed in *Brokenville* with the characters building a makeshift campfire in the ruins of the house and telling their stories round it. As the play begins, the characters have suffered a traumatic catastrophe so decisive that they can barely remember who they are; like kids in a playground, they give each other nicknames based on appearance – 'Satchel', 'Quiff', 'Bruise' and so on. As these shattered characters begin to tell their story, we seem to be hearing an allegorical account of the destruction of their society. The group tells five stories, all set in a magical world of Kings, Queens, Princes, Dragons and Witches. None of the stories can be precisely turned into a realistic account of the calamity, but the picture is painted of a society rendered brutally unequal by the narcissism and selfishness of its rulers, ruined by warfare and neglect. Once the stories are told, the child ends the play by announcing that he is no longer scared.

The sentiment is understandably simplified in this play for young people but this is a structure that may be found throughout Ridley's work. His interest in violence and taboo imagery is precisely that the theatre gives us a chance 'to open a few doors to point out that these things go on so that we can consider and experience them'.[14] In *Leaves of Glass*, Barry describes a suicide bombing but does so as if it were a painting: 'There was all this burning wreckage around him. The flames were all cadmium yellow and vermilion' (p. 232), suggesting that aesthetic perception may be a way of coping with the horrors of ordinary life. Barry shares with Vincent in *Vincent River* – and Ridley himself – a childhood fascination with images of atrocity: images of Auschwitz, Hiroshima, and of Kim Phúc, the girl famously photographed fleeing from a village in Vietnam, napalm burning her skin.

Ridley's attraction to the East End – or at least what he calls 'my mythical East End'[15] – is in its simultaneous beauty and harshness, its wealth of experience and its material poverty; in particular, Ridley is drawn to the harsh vividness of the way language is used: 'There's a caustic beauty, the beauty of battery acid on metal, a real sulphuric beauty to East London images and I've always been really attracted to that.'[16] The art of storytelling is a form of aesthetic reframing that takes you beyond conventional moral responses to something subtler, more plural.

Vincent River (2000)

Ridley's first adult play for six years, which premiered on 6 September 2000, marked a striking change of direction. Gone are the baroque character names, the fabulist set-pieces. *Vincent River* is a two-hander for Anita and Davey, a middle-aged woman and a young man. Anita's son, Vincent, has recently been killed by a gang in a disused railway station that was a well-known gay cruising area and Davey says he found the body while taking a shortcut with his girlfriend. What slowly, painfully emerges through their halting and awkward conversation is that Davey and Vincent were briefly lovers and Davey had been the one who persuaded Vincent to go there for sex at the station.

Vincent River is a *tour de force* of simple, almost classical playwriting. As in a Greek tragedy, the extremes of action take place offstage and the two characters are like messengers reporting these events. Anita's story, which parallels Vincent's, is of her ostracism by the community after she became pregnant by a married man. The play is not long, probably no more than ninety minutes in length, and its action, as in most of Ridley's plays, proceeds in real time without a break; none the less, it manages to express both a forty-year history of attitudes to sexuality in the East End and a more intimate story of two people coming together in shared grief. The dramaturgical mechanism is equally elegant: one character who desperately wants to tell his story but doesn't know how, another who needs to hear his story but doesn't know why; the one wanting the details of a man's death, the other wanting the details of his life.

It would be an exaggeration to say that *Vincent River* is whole-heartedly realistic, let alone naturalistic. The play has Ridley's characteristic intensity of expression and delight in strong verbal images and there is a striking moment – perhaps one of the few moments of overt physical action in the play – when Davey draws Anita into his story, pushing her to confront precisely the nature of their relationship by playing Vincent's part in their first sexual contact. As the young man and older woman caress each other and kiss, it feels like a moment of intense ritual, both characters wanting the act of performance to bring his lover and her son back.

Vincent River is perhaps the first of Ridley's plays that directly presents a gay character. Although there are homoerotic moments in the first three plays, the plays do not seem to place much emphasis on identity politics. This play tells the story of Davey's burgeoning sexuality and does so with delicacy and sympathy. Perhaps it does so because it is based, Ridley says, on the story of someone he knew at art school who died in similar circumstances to Vincent. As such, this marks a turn towards more personal subject matter. While it would not be helpful to think of any of Ridley's plays as autobiographical, it is hard to avoid seeing the relationships between brothers that run hauntingly through *Fastest Clock*, *Mercury Fur*, *Leaves of Glass*, *Piranha Heights* and *Moonfleece* as reflecting Ridley's own family relationships. More precisely, in *Leaves of Glass* and *Piranha Heights* one brother is a solid family man, the other an artist, a relationship that resembles Ridley's published descriptions of his own sibling relationship.[17] What seems to go along with this closer, more personally searching period of his plays is a much greater interest in individual psychology which is first seen in *Vincent River*.

There may be many reasons for this turn away from the style of his early plays. Ridley himself has suggested that dissatisfaction with one's own work is an important driver in his development, citing the artist Philip Guston who, at several points in his career, abruptly abandoned his techniques, subject matter and artistic affiliations to find new ones, refusing to settle into a style. It may also be that some of the things that were so distinctive in the first plays were now much more commonplace in the theatre, after the wave of new British playwrights that emerged in the mid-1990s, on whose work Ridley had a conscious or unconscious influence. In *Leaves of Glass*, two characters reflect on seeing a play (which sounds like a parody of an 'in-yer-face' drama):

> **Debbie**   She was in that play. Remember?
> **Steven**   No.
> **Debbie**   The raped girl thing.
> **Steven**   What raped girl thing?
> **Debbie**   Soldiers burst into that girl's house. Raped her. Shot her. And the girl's parents. Then set fire to the whole caboodle and went back to base camp calm as cucumbers.
> (p. 219)

The comically inadequate description and the banal reflection on the play's purpose – 'What people are capable of, eh? Awful. Makes you think' (p. 219) – perhaps indicates that, in writing *Vincent River*, Ridley was interested in a seeking a less sensational approach to his audience and a calmer, more reflective response. His next play, however, would be an altogether different story.

Mercury Fur (2005)

In an abandoned council flat, two brothers are preparing a party. This is not a usual party, however. The service that Elliot and Darren provide is to make wealthy people's dreams come true. This week's party guest has hired them to provide him with a young boy, referred to only as the 'party piece', dressed as Elvis, that he can torture and kill with a meat hook for his sexual pleasure. The moral horrors within the flat are matched by social turmoil without; gangs roam the streets, society is collapsing, and it is rumoured that a foreign government plans to carpet-bomb the country into submission.

The play began to gather hostile responses before it took the stage on 10 February 2005, in a production directed by John Tiffany. Ridley's publisher, at Faber & Faber, refused to publish it. His friends stopped talking to him after reading it. Although this was widely discussed before the production opened, the critics were still shocked: Charles Spencer, writing in the *Daily Telegraph*, described the play as 'a poisonous piece' by a writer 'turned on by his own sick fantasies and is offering no more than cheap thrills', while Michael Billington in the *Guardian*, in more moderate tones, condemned the play for offering 'fashionable nihilism' and 'more shocks than enlightenment'.[18]

Mercury Fur is indeed an extremely shocking play, but it shocks by painting a vivid portrait of a society sufficiently like ours to be recognisable but exaggerated just enough to see the hollowness of our world in a new light. It is, in the artistic sense, a grotesque piece of work – or, rather, a piece of grotesque work. One of the most haunting inventions of the play is the drug culture it represents; most people in the play are addicts, but the way they take them in *Mercury Fur*'s world is by swallowing butterflies genetically modified to be narcotic. It's an image that is, characteristically, both beautiful and about the wanton destruction of beauty. The play suggests that these psychotropic drugs have been distributed by the government as another attempt at social control, an idea drawn from persistent stories that the CIA flooded black neighbourhoods with drugs, as a means of destabilising the emergent civil rights movements. More immediately, though, the play is shot through with the paranoia and fear that characterised the 'war on terror', America's and Britain's response to the terrorist attacks of 11 September 2001. Although its writing pre-dated the invasion of Iraq and the subsequent revelations of abuses at Abu Ghraib in Baghdad, the play captures the atmosphere of state brutality, weaponised government, and the images of social disorder around terror attacks. And, as ever, Ridley is drawing on these contemporary anxieties in order to dispel their debilitating power: 'What I did in *Mercury Fur*, I did for a reason. I like putting people on a ghost train, but I guide them safely through the other end; I don't want to keep them there, I want to take them on a ritual of exorcism.'[19]

More surprisingly, perhaps, Ridley has suggested that the play is less about violence than it is about love:

> It is [. . .] about what we do for love and what happens if there is a lack of love. I was interested in what happens to a society if we lose our memories and language disintegrates. One of the things that separates us from the animals is our ability to tell stories. I wanted to explore what happens when we are all robbed of our personal narratives.[20]

Indeed, as this passage suggests, *Mercury Fur* revisits some of his earlier work. The emphasis on the importance of stories from the Storyteller Sequence and other plays; the curious loss of memory in *Pitchfork* and *Brokenville*; the emphasis on love in *Fastest Clock*. Indeed, the procurement of the 'party piece' is, in some ways, only a hideous extension of the deception and attempted seduction of Foxtrot Darling in the latter play.

In *Mercury Fur*, the collapse of historical narrative is brought to the fore in the characters' persistent scrambling of modern history into a peculiar amalgam of misplaced fact, rumour and pornographic fantasy (for example, p. 114). It suggests a connection between the moral vacuity of the present and these people's inability to remember the past. It is a play that demands a sense of history and a sense of responsibility, not a play that delights in their absence. Indeed, unlike most of Ridley's plays, the main characters develop a moral conscience through the course of the action. At the crucial moment, Darren and Elliot decide to protect the 'party piece' from the Party Guest, and as the government forces start bombing the city, Darren repeatedly urges his brother to say he loves him.

Summary

Ridley has divided critics, but critics aren't the only audience for his work and his plays have always attracted enthusiastic audiences. He has always had his champions, and is often described as a 'visionary' and a 'prophet', unparalleled for the range and intensity of his work.[21] He has had strong ongoing relationships with theatres like the National, Hampstead and the Soho (though the failure of the Royal Court to stage his work says something about his refusal of social realism and explicit political commentary). Aleks Sierz described him as the best British playwright of the last twenty years.[22] His plays, despite their mixed British responses, have been acclaimed across the world; since its British premiere, *Mercury Fur*, for example, has been constantly in performance somewhere in the world. His work has also attracted some of the best actors of the age: Billie Whitelaw in *The Krays*, Rupert Graves in *The Pitchfork Disney*, John Wood in *Ghost from a Perfect Place*, Deborah Findlay in *Vincent River*; similarly, he has shown a canny ability to write parts that discover the great actors of the future; Jude Law, Chiwetel Ejiofor, Helen Baxendale, Viggo Mortensen, Ben Whishaw and Brendan Fraser all performed in Ridley's plays and films early in their careers.[23]

Twenty years after the premiere of *The Pitchfork Disney*, revivals of his plays have met increasingly receptive critical attention. A revival of *Fastest Clock* at Hampstead Theatre in 2009 was greatly admired, without a hint of the horrified reactions it received in 1992. If there were criticisms, they were generally that the production wasn't shocking enough. Even more strikingly, a new production of *Mercury Fur* in February 2010 saw a complete turnaround of critical opinion, with Lyn Gardner in the *Guardian* finding it 'almost unbearable to endure and yet so compelling you can't stop watching, Ridley's play is, for all its disturbing violence, fiercely moral and tender'.[24] Part of the reason for Ridley's acceptance is that the theatrical experiences he pioneered have become more widespread and more easily understood. The baroque violence of the first plays was taken up by playwrights such as Anthony Neilson in *Penetrator* (1993), Sarah Kane in *Blasted* (1995) or Jez Butterworth in *Mojo* (1995), and perhaps too by the film director Quentin Tarantino.[25] In both *Blasted* and *The Pitchfork Disney*, there is a faint suggestion that the nightmare unfolding before us is taking place in the dreams of the play's female character. *Mojo* is populated by the dandified, cutlass-wielding gangsters of *The Krays* and *Ghost from a Perfect Place* (and even borrows Cosmo Disney's glittering jacket). Meanwhile the emotionally blank, ancient children of Mark Ravenhill's *Shopping and Fucking* (1996) come straight from *The Pitchfork Disney*. In both plays, too, main characters are named, surreally, after pop music stars. Martin McDonagh's *The Pillowman* (2003) and Dennis Kelly's *Debris* (2003) show the effect of Ridley's gothic plays on the contemporary theatrical imagination; elements of *Mercury Fur* are, no doubt unconsciously, echoed in Simon Stephens's *Motortown* (2006). The influence may be felt even more widely. BBC television comedy group The League of Gentlemen may owe a small debt to Ridley in their mixture of comedy and genuine horror. And in another successful comedy series, *Little Britain*, its most famous character, Vicky Pollard, is said to live in a district called 'Darkly Noon' (taken from Ridley's 1995 film, *The Passion of Darkly Noon*).

And finally, a small but significant body of more considered critical writing has begun the process of offering a more rigorous exposition of Ridley's work. Aleks Sierz's *In-Yer-Face Theatre* offers a reading of *Ghost from a Perfect Place* that details the accusations of gratuitousness but argues that Ridley places the violence in a social and historical context and the ending, dismissed by some as sentimental, actually represents the political possibility of change.[26] Ken Urban's essay 'Ghosts from an Imperfect Place' offers a subtle and sophisticated argument that shows the dependence of the characters in Ridley's first three plays on nostalgia and a refusal to accept the present or the future. He notes the contemporary significance of this because of Conservative governments' ideological dependence on nostalgia.

Urban shows that while the first two plays end by expelling those figures that pose a threat to this nostalgia, in the third, nostalgia is exposed for its inadequacy and a new story is made possible. Andrew Wyllie in his book, *Sex on Stage*, places Ridley alongside Harold Pinter but suggests that Ridley outstrips Pinter in his 'harsh vision of sexuality'.[27]

Ridley's vivid and arresting plays marked the first signs of a move away from explicit political commentary towards a new emphasis on ambiguity, metaphor and the employment of harsh, vivid and often beautiful imagery to provoke reflection on the state of our common life, the values we live by, and the limitless powers of the imagination.

Primary Sources

Works by Philip Ridley

Plays One: The Pitchfork Disney, The Fastest Clock in the Universe, Ghost from a Perfect Place (London: Methuen Drama, 1997).

Plays Two: Vincent River, Mercury Fur, Leaves of Glass, Piranha Heights (London: Methuen Drama, 2009).

Two Plays for Young People: Fairytaleheart, Sparkleshark (London: Faber & Faber, 1998).

Brokenville, in *Shell Connections 2003: New Plays for Young People* (London: Faber & Faber, 2003), pp. 1–85.

Moonfleece (London: Methuen Drama, 2010).

Secondary Sources

Cripps, Charlotte, 'Cultural Life: Ben Whishaw, Actor', *Independent*, 4 July 2008 <http://www.independent.co.uk/arts-entertainment/films/features/cultural-life-ben-whishaw-actor-859382.html>

Cunningham, John, 'The Men They Couldn't Hang a Label on', *Guardian*, 3 January 1991.

Dromgoole, Dominic, *The Full Room: An A–Z of Contemporary Playwriting* (London: Methuen Drama, 2002).

Edwardes, Jane, 'Shudder Play', *Time Out*, 13 May 1992.

Eyre, Hermione. 'Philip Ridley: The Savage Prophet', *Independent on Sunday*, 'The Sunday Review', 28 October 2007.

Gardner, Lyn, 'The Devil Inside', *Guardian*, 'G2', 9 February 2005.

Gilbey, Ryan, 'Viggo Mortensen: A Method Actor in Middle Earth', *Independent*, 14 December 2001 <http://www.independent.co.uk/arts-entertainment/films/features/viggo-mortensen-a-method-actor–in-middleearth-748054.html>

Kayser, Wolfgang, *The Grotesque in Art and Literature* (Bloomington: Indiana UP, 1963).

Kemp, Gary, *I Know This Much is True: From Soho to Spandau* (London: HarperCollins, 2009).

Rabey, David Ian, *English Drama Since 1940* (London: Longman, 2003).

Ridley, Philip, Personal Interview, London, 30 April 2010.

Sierz, Aleks, *In-Yer-Face Theatre: British Drama Today* (London: Faber & Faber, 2001).

—, '"Putting a New Lens on the World": The Art of Theatrical Alchemy', *New Theatre Quarterly*, Vol. 25, No. 2 (2009), pp. 109–20.

—, 'Philip Ridley: Our Theatre's Polymath Genius', *Time Out* Theatre Blog, 24 September 2009 <http://www.timeout.com/london/connect/theatre/blog/146/philip-ridley-our-theatres-polymath-genius>

Thomson, Philip, *The Grotesque* (London: Methuen Drama, 1972).

Travers, Peter, 'Review of *The Reflecting Skin*', *Rolling Stone*, 10 May 2008 <http://thereflectingskin.wordpress.com/2008/03/10/a-review-that-sums-it-all-up>

Urban, Ken, 'Ghosts from an Imperfect Place: Philip Ridley's Nostalgia', *Modern Drama*, Vol. 50, No. 3 (2007), pp. 325–45.

Wyllie, Andrew, *Sex on Stage: Gender and Sexuality in Post-War British Drama* (Bristol: Intellect, 2009).

—, 'The Politics of Violence after In-Yer-Face: Harold Pinter and Philip Ridley', in Craig N. Owens (ed.), *Pinter et Cetera* (Newcastle: Cambridge Scholars, 2009), pp. 63–77.

Notes

1. Aleks Sierz, ' "Putting a New Lens on the World" ', p. 110.
2. Philip Ridley, Personal Interview.
3. *Theatre Record*, Vol. XI, No. 1 (1991), pp. 11–14.
4. Ibid.
5. Dominic Dromgoole, *The Full Room*, p. 241.
6. Ridley's first three plays have been published in a number of different editions, with small variations. Although Ridley considers the Faber edition of *Plays One* published in 2002 to be definitive, this is no longer available, so references are to the Methuen Drama edition.
7. Jane Edwardes, 'Shudder Play', p. 113.
8. Ibid.
9. Ridley, Personal Interview.
10. Wolfgang Kayser, *The Grotesque in Art and Literature*, pp. 184–5.

11. Ibid.
12. Thompson, *The Grotesque*, p. 11, original emphasis.
13. Ridley, Personal Interview.
14. Ridley quoted in Edwardes, 'Shudder Play', p. 113.
15. Ridley quoted in John Cunningham, 'The Men They Couldn't Hang a Label on', p. 22.
16. Ridley, Personal Interview.
17. Sierz, '"Putting a New Lens on the World"', pp. 112–13; Ridley, *Plays Two*, pp. xxxvii–iii.
18. *Theatre Record*, Vol. XXV, No. 5 (2005), pp. 280, 279.
19. Ridley quoted in Hermione Eyre, 'Philip Ridley: The Savage Prophet', p. 35.
20. Ridley quoted in Lyn Gardner, 'The Devil Inside', p. 11.
21. See Eyre, 'Philip Ridley: The Savage Prophet' or Peter Travers, 'Review of *The Reflecting Skin*'.
22. Aleks Sierz, 'Philip Ridley: Our Theatre's Polymath Genius'.
23. See Charlotte Cripps, 'Cultural Life', and Ryan Gilbey, 'Viggo Mortensen'.
24. *Theatre Record*, Vol. XXX, No. 4 (2010), p. 180.
25. In his autobiography, the singer Gary Kemp, who played Ronnie Kray in *The Krays*, recalls Tarantino admitting that when preparing *Reservoir Dogs* (1992) he was influenced by the sleekly stylish presentation of the gangsters in that film (pp. 269–70).
26. Aleks Sierz, *In-Yer-Face Theatre*, pp. 44–5.
27. Andrew Wyllie, *Sex on Stage*, p. 78.

23 SIMON STEPHENS

Christopher Innes

Herons; Country Music; Motortown; Pornography; Punk Rock

Introduction

Born in 1971, Simon Stephens is a contemporary of the 1990s 'in-yer-face theatre' playwrights: the same age (he points out) as Martin McDonagh, and slightly younger than Mark Ravenhill or Joe Penhall.[1] At the same time he is highly conscious of beginning his writing career later than this group. Although the eighth or ninth play Stephens had written, *Bluebird* was his first play to be staged at the Royal Court's Young Writers Festival in 1998 – a sign of his arrival. Today he tends to gloss over his first two plays, staged in Edinburgh during the Fringe Festival, and to mark the beginning of his career with *Bluebird*, because this allows him to categorise himself as part of the post-millennial and post-in-yer-face generation of playwrights, whose main output was staged after 2000. As he comments:

> In my plays the family is quite central [. . .] If you look at the 'blood-and-sperm' plays, as the German critics call them, the family is defined by its absence. Apart from Martin McDonagh's plays, where the bonds are perverse, you never see parents and children on stage together in those plays.[2]

Coming from Stockport – his play *Port* (Royal Exchange, Manchester, 2002) refers to the city – and educated in an all-boys comprehensive school – which finds its analogue in the Stockport grammar school of his *Punk Rock* (Lyric Hammersmith, 2009) – Stephens had his political awakening during the 1984–85 Miners' Strike. This became the defining moment of his political consciousness, although now Stephens sees himself as part of a generation defined by Thatcher's reign as prime minister, believing in the value of the individual rather than the collective identity and communal action embraced by the previous generation of British political playwrights such as David Hare or Howard Brenton. Instead he sees himself as continuing the tradition of intense individualism celebrated in the plays of John Osborne. Stephens's teenage rebellion took the form of punk music. He started a band called Country Teasers – influenced by New York rock musicians such as Alex Chilton or Jonathan Richman, who founded the first proto-punk garage rock band – and music has been central to his plays, as well as informing the titles of *Country Music* (Royal Court, 2004) and *Punk Rock*. Other influences include American films by directors such as David Lynch and Martin Scorsese, with Paul Thomas Anderson's 1999 movie, *Magnolia*, being referenced in Stephens's Heathrow plays, *Lullaby Burn* and *Wastwater* (Royal Court, 2011).

He has traced some aspects of his dramatic approach to his university training as a historian, commenting that

> the characters in my plays carry the burden of the past around with them [. . .] the historian, like the dramatist, fixates on behaviour and its causes and its consequences.[3]

Some of his university plays were taken to the Edinburgh Festival in 1992; as a result Stephens moved to Edinburgh, then two years later made the move to London, where he now lives. A schoolteacher, he then, following the success of *Bluebird*, became writer-in-residence at the Royal Exchange Theatre in Manchester, and in 2000 was appointed Resident Dramatist at the Royal Court. At that point he had never read or seen any plays by either Edward Bond or Sarah Kane: two of the iconic Royal Court playwrights. As Stephens remarks:

> I was too embarrassed to admit it [. . .] I read *Blasted* and *Saved* on the same day, just at the start of my residency. I remember it absolutely as a visceral shock and was unable to move after reading both plays.[4]

His plays, *Herons* (Royal Court, 2001), *One Minute* (Crucible, Sheffield, 2003) and *Christmas* (Brighton Pavilion, 2003), demonstrated his developing skills.

Then Ian Rickson, artistic director of the Royal Court, commissioned him to work with male prisoners and produce a play based on the experience (*Country Music*). Stephens set up playwriting workshops at Wandsworth and at Grendon Prison, an institution for long-term serious offenders, mostly serving life sentences. He also brought in actors and a director to stage extracts from the plays the prisoners had written. Since then, Stephens has continued to teach playwriting in prisons, and at schools, as well as working with the Royal Court's Young Writers' Programme up to 2005; in 2006 he became the first Resident Dramatist at the National Theatre; and in 2009 he was appointed Associate Artist at the Lyric Hammersmith by new artistic director Sean Holmes. His *On the Shore of the Wide World* (Royal Exchange, Manchester, 2005) won a prestigious Olivier Award and his *Motortown* (Royal Court, 2006) and *Harper Regan* (National Theatre, 2008) further established his reputation. He has also developed an international standing, with some of his plays (most notably *Pornography*) being first performed in Germany. He has also collaborated with other playwrights, with *Supernova* (Latitude, 2009) co-written with Tayshan Cushnie, and *A Thousand Stars Explode in the Sky* (Lyric Hammersmith, 2010) co-written with David Eldridge and Robert Holman. His prolific output includes the monologue *Sea Wall* (Bush Theatre, 2008), *Heaven* (Traverse Theatre, 2009), *Canopy of Stars* – part of the Tricycle Theatre's *The Great Game: Afghanistan* season (2009) – and *The Trial of Ubu* (2010).

The Plays

Herons (2001)

The music in *Herons* comes from Rebel. 'Can I Pass?' opens and closes the play, as well as recurring at key points in the action, with lyrics that clearly relate to the situation of the adolescent protagonist, who has to navigate the world of urban gangs. For Stephens the title is not a reference to Ibsen's *The Wild Duck* or Chekhov's *The Seagull* but 'a metaphor for an impossible escape, but there's a kind of latent savagery to it as well'.[5] In the play, which opened on 18 May 2001 at the Royal Court Theatre Upstairs in a production directed by Simon Usher, the pastime of fourteen-year-old Billy and his father, Charlie, is fishing in the canal, and the herons are predatory competitors. Charlie has bought a gun to shoot them, though the only time it gets used (unloaded) is when Billy challenges a threatening bully, Scott.

The scenes, separated only by a dimming of the stage lights, described as '*almost imperceptibl[e]*' (p. 172), present a story in which Billy (in a reversal of the usual father–son relationship) tries to protect Charlie, who has witnessed the murder of a young girl, committed by Scott's elder brother and his gang, and informed the police. Now imprisoned, they are threatening revenge, a menace channelled through Scott and his teenage gang. Billy, fishing and writing down everything he sees in a notebook, attracts the attention of Scott's girlfriend, Adele, who is converted to his side by the poetic quality of his perceptions: '"Some of the people look like sticks. They look like they could snap. They have nodules in odd places." I think that's very true' (p. 214). As in Stephens's other plays, alcoholism is a key element, with Billy describing his mother as 'a wino. A pisshead. A cruel drunken bitch' (p. 209), who arranged to have his father badly beaten, and smashed Billy's head against a radiator, so that he was forced to take refuge with his father. Violence is endemic: standing up to Scott, in defence of his father and the murdered girl, gets Billy badly beaten up and anally raped on stage with a beer bottle. Yet even a vicious bully like Scott is presented as '*scared*' (p. 209), being driven to violence by fear; and when Billy takes revenge, he breaks the cycle of violence by using the gun to reveal the psychological weakness under Scott's brutal exterior. The play ends with a long moment of stillness: Billy, flanked by Charlie and Adele, staring out front (over the canal) and exchanging occasional glances, after Billy has declared his intention to leave.

Billy You can come with me if you want to but I'm definitely, I'm just definitely going.

Charlie Right.

Billy I'm going to go to Southend, I think. Or Brighton. Or Portsmouth. Somewhere where there's sea. (p. 232)

Herons also has a strong environmental focus – the first statement of a theme that will surface frequently in Stephens's work – with parallels between nature and people, '*a looming damaged oak tree*' (p. 154), one of the permanent scenic pieces on the stage, being echoed both in Charlie, who is described as a '*hulking damaged man*' and Scott, the tormentor of his son, also described as '*deeply damaged. He has a vulnerability which manifests itself in cruelty*' (p. 153), and with Billy's analysis of the gang mentality:

I think I know why they were so scared. I think that they realized what I realized when I saw Scott like that. The way that things are wonderful. They way that colours work. The sound of things and the way they smell [. . .] But they couldn't handle it. So they got frightened. And I started to figure out how everything joins up. (pp. 228–9)

The world of the gangs is one of debris and litter, fouling the nature that they despise, in an extended hate-sequence aimed at Billy as the 'Nature boy' (p. 204). Critical reception of the play was positive, with Michael Billington in the *Guardian* describing his achievement as 'graphically acknowledging the nihilistic cruelty of east end school-kids', while balancing an account of 'damaged characters' with 'a potent lyricism'.[6]

Country Music (2004)

Speaking of *Country Music*, which opened at the Royal Court Theatre Upstairs on 24 June 2004 in Gordon Anderson's touching production, Stephens has commented that this style of song is

> prisoners' music. It's traditionally white man's blues. And if
> you hear the songs of Johnny Cash or Hank Williams [. . .]
> their songs are about working people's lives and often about
> violence [. . .] I mean the amount of songs Johnny Cash wrote
> about killing people and going to prison for it – the play and
> those songs operate absolutely in the same territory.[7]

As signalled in the title, country music also provided the structure of
the play, with its extremely simple scenes echoing the bald stories of
the genre, and the repetition at the end mirroring the way country
music ends with a refrain of the opening verse. Clearly based on
Stephens's experiences at Grendon, where the Royal Court production of the play was given a single performance that according to
Stephens the inmates found 'deeply moving', the play opens with the
eighteen-year-old Jamie together with his fifteen-year-old girlfriend,
Lynsey, talking about his latest exploit: stealing the car they are sitting
in, an under-powered Ford, which he dreams of driving like 'Mad
fucking Max' to 'Bomb it. Fucking overtaking and everything' (p. 79).
The gap between reality (the car) and delusive fantasy is a key to the
play. There are references to Jamie having 'glassed' (attacked with a
broken bottle) someone called Gary, then stabbing a sixteen-year-old
kid in the pub and stealing a bottle of tequila, a pack of cigarettes and
some chips – all of which he offers to Lynsey. When he then suggests
breaking into the coin machines in laundromats, to finance a night in
a hotel, she goes along with the fantasy. But when he calls for home
invasions, she tries to save him from himself – already having been
arrested he is likely to be sent away to Borstal (the prison for under-
age offenders) – by giving himself up to the police and admitting his
offences, and his response is to hit her across the face.

The next scene is in Grendon prison itself: in the visiting room,
where Jamie's younger brother (now nineteen, double the age he was
in the first scene) has come to tell him that Lynsey has left, with his
daughter, and won't give her new address. During their conversation
we learn that Jamie was indeed sent to Borstal for attacking Gary and
stabbing the teenager, and then when he came out Jamie killed a boy
who seemed to be sexually abusing his brother, which is why he has

now been incarcerated in Grendon for over five years. We learn that it is because he hit Lynsey that she has now found someone else. We are also told about the casual but extreme violence of the prison system, in a story about guards beating up a prisoner in his cell, which is clearly designed to echo, indeed exceed, the violence of the prisoners.

In Scene Three, nine and a half years later, after his release, his seventeen-year-old daughter, Emma, has come to visit Jamie. We learn that his daughter has lied about him, rejecting him: 'I've got a dad. It's not you' (p. 126) – and does not even share the memories he has of being with her as a child. He imagines bright futures for her: office manager, and when she tells him the one thing she wants is to fly a plane, his response is: 'I think that's brilliant, that. That stops me breath' (p. 129). Yet both are equally unrealistic, since Emma is a dental receptionist without education – which is an even stronger underlining of the gap between actuality and fantasy that characterises this play. As Stephens remarks, this is a play about 'chances not taken. [. . .] Defined by one moment' all the prisoners, whether hardened criminals in Grendon or young offenders, 'were unable ever to redefine themselves as anything else. There was something awful about this that I wanted to dramatise.'[8] The point indeed is made explicit, with Jamie's wish to 'go back in time. Turn my body back in time. Screw myself up into a, I don't know, a knot and go back and not do it. I have tried' (p. 127).

The final scene, the coda, is idyllic: Jamie and Lynsey lying on a hill in the sunshine. This is in fact a prequel. We learn why Jamie had attacked Gary – he found him making love to his mother in the family bed, betraying her second husband, the father of his younger brother – but this has not yet happened, and the sexual play between them is free and positive. It clearly demonstrates what his violence has destroyed and the potential happiness of ordinary life – home, garden, a trip to Margate (which is a recurrent trope in Stephens's plays) – that Jamie's actions effectively make impossible. Yet it also shows that all his violence, however misplaced, has had a generous motive, his first assault, then the murder, both being committed to protect his younger brother, and to save his mother. Although some of the reviewers made jokes about the lack of banjos and rhinestones in the play, it was widely appreciated, with the *Daily Telegraph*'s Charles Spencer concluding: 'In its hauntingly desolate way, his drama can indeed stand comparison with the best and darkest of Hank Williams and Johnny Cash.'[9]

Motortown (2006)

For Stephens, this was his breakthrough play. A reaction to the war in Iraq, where – as Stephens remarked – 'British soldiers literally have no idea who their enemy is any more, leaving them in a morally chaotic state', it deals with the reaction of a returned soldier, Danny, and his reaction to the society for which he fought, with its disrespect for all that he represents, and complete lack of moral standards: an absence that unites 'homeland' with war zone.[10] Stephens's play counters what he saw as a delusory moral superiority in the anti-war campaigners, and his aim was 'to write, as honestly as I could, about England' reflecting – as in almost all his work – a culture that is 'dark and contradictory and violent'.[11]

Motortown opened on 21 April 2006 at the Royal Court in a production directed by Ramin Gray. Although its epigraph is taken from Heiner Müller's *Mauser* (1975, a *Lehrstück* about revolutionary violence and terror during the civil-war period in Russia), this play was influenced by Georg Büchner's fragmented nineteenth-century classic about a cruel and vicious military system, and its effect on a soldier who kills his woman. And indeed it echoes the major elements in *Woyzeck*'s action. Other influences Stephens has pointed to are films: Martin Scorsese's *Taxi Driver* (1976) and Mike Leigh's *Naked* (1993). Motortown is of course Dagenham, the centre of the British auto industry, which ties in with the war-for-oil aspect of Iraq. Rejected by his one-time girlfriend, Marley, and alienated from his family – a drunken, abusive father and his autistic brother, Lee – Danny buys a replica revolver from Tom, a friend who sends him to Paul, a contact who can transform it from a harmless pellet gun to firing real bullets. While his gun is being re-engineered, Danny meets Paul's fourteen-year-old black girlfriend, whom he abducts, takes to Foulness Island (which also houses the military base where he was trained), terrorises, tortures in a replay of searching female suicide bombers in Basra, pours petrol over, and finally shoots, photographing each turn with his cell phone. With her body in the trunk of his car, Danny stays at the Northview Hotel in Southend for the night, where he falls in with a couple from London who try to seduce him into a sexual threesome, then winds up back where he started in his brother's Dagenham apartment, having confessed to the killing. Lee points out that he may be unable not to tell the police; Danny initiates sexual contact with his brother, who has never before had any physical contact, then demands he cut his hair; and the lights fall as Lee turns on the clippers. The extreme simplicity of this plot in just eight scenes is bleak, with no complicated psychological analysis, and expressed in short declarative sentences, all of which emphasises the brutality of the action. And this simplicity is accentuated by the use of only first names for the characters, which also helps to universalise the drama.

As in *Country Music*, but here presented explicitly as a cliché, normality is envisioned by Danny as

> a day trip. [. . .] Go up Southend. Go to the seaside. Get a few drinks at the Northview. Look out to sea. Go and ride on the fairground. (p. 150)

Lee passes up the offer. Tom doesn't take it seriously. But Jade is unable to refuse, and what happens at 'the seaside' completely undermines the cliché. Another of the key themes in the play is defined by the gun engineer, who characterises himself, and society as a whole, as unable to 'tell the difference any more between what is real and what is a fantasy' (p. 169). This is certainly epitomised in Danny, whose emotional connection to Marley turns out to be completely make-believe: she hasn't seen him since school, and has had another boyfriend 'for years' so that Danny's desire for kids and a family car with tea in the morning (the other concept of normality, also present in *Country Music*) is literally a fantasy. And Danny plays on others' inability to perceive the truth, picking up suggestions from Tom to pass himself off to Paul as a special-effects specialist for James Bond films, and to the hotel couple as an arranger of firework displays. But the depth of his own confusion between reality and fantasy is shown immediately following Jade's very graphic death, when Danny continues to speak to her corpse, in a diatribe against the anti-war protesters, even asking her whether he is stammering.

Stephens has also adapted *Motortown* for a film script, which gave him a different angle on the play. He points out:

> One of the things I realized about Danny in the adaptation, although I think this still holds water for the play, is that a lot of his sense of alienation was exacerbated by a desire to belong to a collective identity, and a dissolution of the possibility of that. So probably his disaffection and disillusionment with the army not being what he'd hoped, exacerbated his alienation and isolation.[12]

Indeed the picture we are given of Danny is that of a person who has lost all connection to society: alienated from the other soldiers in Basra (because, he claims, he alone tried to obey the rules), he hates or despises his family, has imaginary relationships with the women he knows, where the only real connection is extreme violence; he rejects the wider population of Britain, whom he identifies with the anti-war protesters whom he excoriates. As he says to the couple in the hotel: 'I come back home. It's a completely foreign country' (p. 200). But this is also a general aspect shared by most of the other characters. The gun engineer Paul presents himself as a philosopher, but his view of the world is completely negative. He characterises the poor as myopic, racist and homophobic, and the wealthy as addicted to hardcore porn on the internet: 'The family unit seems like an act of belligerence. *All* long-term relationships are doomed or ironic' (p. 171). And this is indeed evidenced by the married couple in the hotel searching for sexual partners, as by his own relationship with a fourteen-year-old girl. For Paul the apocalypse is here – too many people, all consumers of resources, not enough oxygen or water:

> We'll continue to eat it all up and eat it all up and eat it all up until the only thing we've got left to fucking eat, Danny, the only thing we've got to eat is each other. (p. 174)

Yet, Stephens has continually rejected the notion that there are 'bad people' and stated that 'every individual has the capacity for redemption.'[13] Even though Danny repeats this apocalyptic vision to the hotel couple, the ending shows him redeeming himself in a way that, however marginal, is meaningful – very much like the ending of Bond's *Saved*, where in the alienated family Len starts mending a chair: an ending also almost directly echoed in the ending of his *On the Shore of the Wide World*, where the family share a mundane task: laying the dinner table – in connecting with his brother, breaking through Lee's autistic physical isolation, and the final image of a communal action: letting his brother clip his hair. Critics were split about the play, with some praising it for being against the war and some lauding the way it criticised the anti-war movement.[14]

Pornography (2007)

First performed at the Hanover festival and at Deutsches Schauspielhaus, Hamburg, in June and October 2007, *Pornography* reached the British stage about a year later, when it opened on 28 July 2008 at the Traverse Theatre, Edinburgh, in Sean Holmes's production. This was a sign of the play's perceived immediacy, although at least one critic found it 'a curiously oblique work' that by avoiding any mention of Muslims became 'a craven cop-out'.[15] *Pornography* was written just three weeks after the 7 July 2005 bombings in the London Underground. In many ways it is a companion piece to *Motortown*. Both are examinations of British society, centred on an absence: the war in Iraq, and here the bombing itself, which is only ever mentioned circumstantially. Even the leader of the suicide bombers, while giving precise details about how the four bombers get up to London and the different tube lines they will be taking, presents this as an ordinary day and does not mention anything but the size of his rucksack – no mention of Islam or Iraq: just bleakly derogatory comments on the countryside his train passes, or ordinary people he meets. Between each scene there is a stage direction: '*Images of hell. They are silent.*' Yet only in the final scene, which is a reading of fifty-two mini-obituaries, does the bombing get mentioned; and then only twice, in number twelve who sent a text message 'twenty-one minutes before the first blast' and number forty-two: 'the only Afghan national to be killed in the bombings' (p. 279). Up to that point, while it is clear something catastrophic has happened, we are expected to fill in the blank.

The same sort of absence occurs in *One Minute*, where the expected elements of a detective story (discovery of body, identification of suspect, arrest, confession, court case) are all missing,[16] but in *Pornography* Stephens accentuates this, both by omitting any names for the different characters – the scenes are all monologues, or duologues with dashes indicating a new speaker – and by creating an elaborate structure around this gap. Firstly, the scenes are presented in a reverse numbering, like a countdown, although the effect of the bombing is referred to in every one, except the central scene with the bomber. As Stephens points out in his Introduction, the structure is based on Shakespeare's 'Seven Ages of Man' by melancholy Jacques in *As You Like It*.[17] Already in its original context a speech about the meaninglessness of life, Stephens adds point to the different 'ages' by making each centre on a moral transgression. In the opening, the infant is the sole focus of his mother – who betrays her employer by leaking a research report to a rival firm. The schoolboy here gets a crush on one of his teachers, stalks her, attempts blackmail, and when rejected reveals himself to be rabidly racist and fascist. Finally he fantasises that she would have been 'on the tube [. . .] when a young man with a backpack climbed on' (p. 231). For the lover we get a man whose sister (or, in one German production, brother) comes to stay, and seduces him into an incestuous passion, which, as they boast, is 'against every rule that has ever been written by anybody in the whole of human culture' (p. 239). The longest of the scenes, this is the most explicit demonstration of the social problem Stephens sees as the cause of the bombing. They objectify the faces of people interviewed on television:

> It's always hilarious. You'll see them talking about their loss. Maybe their child has been abducted. Or they lost a lover in a terrorist attack. [. . .] Tears well up in their eyes. And what we

do is we stay with them. [. . .] We hold them in our gaze for a good twenty seconds before the cut. It has become a formula. (p. 232)

Jacques's soldier is represented by the leader of the suicide bombers on his way to London, while the Justice becomes a university teacher, meeting an ex-student half his age, whom he offers a bed for the night, then rapes. Old age is an eighty-two-year-old woman, forced to walk home right across the city because of the tube closures following the bombing. The final scene – the seventh age, 'mere oblivion [. . .] sans everything' – is a list of mini-biographies, with number forty-three being blank, one for each of the real victims of 7 July 2005.[18] In the German premiere these were each read out; in the first British production, they were projected on to the back wall of the stage after the curtain call. And indeed, despite the careful symbolic structure for the play as a whole, Stephens sees it as being completely open, so that 'it can be staged in any order using any number of actors'.[19]

With respect to his title for the play, stressing that the suicide bombers are typical of the dysfunctional British society of the time, Stephens explains:

I was haunted by what the bombers were going through on that final day. It struck me that at the heart of their action was an alienation from the people they were going to kill and from themselves. This seemed to be symptomatic of a consumerist culture, which objectifies everyone and everything. And objectification also sits under the production and consumption of pornography. I think we're living in pornographic times.[20]

Like the lovers of Scene Five, the old lady watches porn movies, and tells us that the television 'coverage of the war in Iraq [. . .] offers me the same kind of thrills as do exciting video games' (p. 269). However, Stephens also shows that the shocking nature of the bombing has a salutary effect. It makes the brother reject his incestuous relationship with his sibling; most strikingly, it creates connection for the elderly woman, whose life up to then seems to her like a hallucination, isolated and solipsistic – 'I don't see anybody. I don't speak to anybody. And God, the fucking horror if I were forced to [. . .]' (p. 269) – then in sharp contrast, she drops in, uninvited, on a stranger's barbecue and begs a meal of chicken, which is willingly given to her. Set against the obituaries that follow, it is a sign of unambiguous hope.[21]

Punk Rock (2009)

Punk Rock opened at the Lyric Hammersmith on 3 September 2009, directed by Sarah Frankcom. Inspired by early-twentieth-century plays about teenage sexual awakening, particularly Ferdinand Bruckner's *Pains of Youth* (1929, directed at the National Theatre by Katie Mitchell earlier in 2009, in a version by Martin Crimp), *Punk Rock* is also a reply to Tom Stoppard's *Rock 'n' Roll* (Royal Court, 2006). In Stephens's play the music is also a form of punctuation between the scenes, but here the style is anything but mainstream (as it is in Stoppard). For Stephens, 'rock music's the music of dissent, of dissidence, of the alternative and the forbidden';[22] and the punk rock movement combined a sexual craving for chaos with political alienation in an art school tradition that for all of its proletarian icons was the middle-class music of the 1970s and 1980s, and therefore particularly 'appropriate for the world of the play'.[23] But the songs here also relate to the action, 'Kerosene' by Big Black – a song about a teenage arsonist burning down a town – introducing the nihilism and self-destructiveness of these elite sixth-form school kids, or 'Loose' by the Stooges as a description of the image they want to project, and 'Fell in Love with a Girl' by the White Stripes to encapsulate the catalytic effect of the arrival of a newcomer – Lily, a sexually mature self-abuser – while 'Touch Me I'm Sick' by Mudhoney introduces the climactic scene of violence, and Daniel Johnston's 'Desperate Man Blues' heads the prison-hospital coda.

The sexual insecurities, patterns of bullying and abuse and culture of silence in these sixth-formers, all compounded by the tension of mock A-level exams and the unexpected death of a sympathetic schoolmaster, play out in hyper-naturalistic scenes set in the school library, with exact times for the start of each episode: starting on *'Monday 6 October, 8.31 a.m.'* (p. 5) – climaxing on *'Tuesday 11 November, 8.57 a.m.'* (p. 82).[24] The group includes a badly bullied, semi-autistic, precocious genius, Chadwick, about whom one of the other pupils, William, forecasts:

> He should stand up to it. Stick his chin out. I wish he would. I've seen it happen. [. . .] People like him who get so much abuse and then one day. Pop. (p. 24)

Ironically it is William who breaks. Fantasising about being a government spy on Muslim youth, about being an orphan, about a million-dollar legacy from his supposedly dead father – and about a relationship with Lily, who has in fact chosen another boyfriend – as a defence against feelings of worthlessness and self-disgust, William, watched by us, gradually comes apart: moments of confusion, missing his history exam, unable to remember a simple word like 'tired', suffering from a crippling headache, hearing 'banging' noises that no one else is aware of. Then he appears with a pistol, hearing voices. He shoots the bully Bennett together with his girlfriend, plus the boy Lily has chosen instead of him – but spares Lily (whom he has warned to stay away from school that day) and Tanya, a fat girl who has been a target of bullying, while Chadwick escapes.

Despite this apparent motivated targeting, William rejects all the standard explanations for his actions:

> See, the main question people have been asking me is why I did it? [. . .] I did it because I could. I did it because it felt fucking great. (p. 99)

Yet, as a context for this massacre, there is a forecast of a social and ecological apocalypse, into which the shooting fits:

> **Chadwick** Everything good human beings ever make is built on something monstrous. Nothing lasts. We

certainly won't. [. . .] You know what will define the next
two hundred years? Religions will become brutalized;
crime rates will become hysterical; everybody will become
addicted to internet sex; suicide will become fashionable
[. . .] The oceans will rise. The cities will flood. [. . .]
Species will vanish for ever. Including ours. (p. 69)

This apocalyptic diatribe is carefully orchestrated: it is the moment
when Chadwick does finally stand up to the bully – ending with 'So if
you think I'm worried by you calling me names, Bennett, you little,
little boy, you are fucking kidding yourself' (p. 69) – and the young
audience at the opening night stood in their seats and cheered. The
critical response was more measured, but enthusiastic enough to
persuade the Lyric Hammersmith to stage the play again in September
2010.[25]

Summary

Gradually, more and more is being written about Stephens. In one
article, Dan Rebellato appreciates the motif of the 'moment of pure
sincerity' in his work and its 'unabashed and guileless' characters.[26]
Amelia Howe Kritzer's *Political Theatre in Post-Thatcher Britain* has
an analysis of *Herons* 'from a generational standpoint' and David
Lane's *Contemporary British Drama* includes a section on his work.[27]
Pornography is briefly analysed in the chapter on structure in
playwright David Edgar's *How Plays Work*.[28] This growing interest
may be partly because he has developed his career by incorporating, as
Pornography illustrates, naturalistic elements in a more complex
structure. The more formal this structuring, the more open Stephens's
directions. So the 'Seven Ages of Man' countdown can be played in
any order, and the same principle is expanded in the Heathrow plays,
Lullaby Burn and *Wastwater*, where each is a series of three short plays,
with the last appearing in both, designed to be performed in different
variations. Or there may be a symbolic subtext, as in *Harper Regan*
where the female protagonist's journey of self-discovery is also a

mythic quest, informed by intense readings of Euripides. At the Hamburg performance her odyssey was presented as a dream in which the characters doubled: her husband becoming the racist journalist she attacks in a bar, her daughter reappearing as a hospital nurse, her boss doubling for the man she has sex with – and the idyllic ending when Harper returns to her home is deliberately ambiguous: either signalling a bright-lit future for this damaged family, or a delusion where patterns of destructive behaviour will be repeated (pp. 101–2). Stephens's plays are characteristically open-ended, which some reviewers have seen as an avoidance of resolution, although ambiguity is also the element that allows the minimalist hope that characterises almost all his endings to surface in the bleak landscape of his plays.

Indeed Stephens's carefully orchestrated structures are accompanied by other techniques to break naturalistic illusion: as for example, keeping all the actors on stage throughout the performance; characters observing the scenes of others, in both *One Minute* and particularly *On the Shore of the Wide World*. The other major element that modifies the naturalistic surface of Stephens's plays is his use of music, which serves him as reference and structuring principle; and he has commented that the central tension, which emerges in all his plays, is 'between the musicality and the content'. Starting with theme songs, as in *Herons*, this expands to frame the action in *Country Music*, and conditions our response in *Punk Rock*. Even in *Pornography* recurring quotations from Coldplay's 'Yellow' help to focus the action. Indeed, *Marine Parade* (2010) is co-written with Mark Eitzel, a musician Stephens admired when running his band, and is intended as a prototype for reviving musical theatre: 'synthesizing [. . .] without bastardizing the theatrical element or the musical element'.[29] So the text offers a series of short scenes of contrasting lovers – from a youth with a fourteen-year-old girl, to a middle-aged couple, who had an adulterous fling in the same hotel twenty years earlier and are now breaking up because of the man's guilt over leaving his first wife – interspersed with songs and lyrics that both reveal deeper emotions of the characters singing, and also generalise their situations.

Stephens's themes are frequently autobiographical, *Bluebird* being a direct response to expecting his first child, while *Herons* combined the experience of teaching teenagers in Essex and Dagenham with wheeling his eighteen-month-old son Oscar 'up and down the Grand Union Canal [. . .] always finding the moments when the herons landed on the bank somewhat astonishing'.[30] There are also auto-biographical echoes in the origin for the suicide bomber in *Pornography* – Manchester (rather than Leeds), passing through Stockport, a journey Stephens himself has taken; and Stockport is the setting for several plays, including *Port, On the Shore of the Wide World, Punk Rock* and even provides the journey's end of *Harper Regan*.

Another major theme is ecology and the environment, running from *Herons* through *Punk Rock* to *Marine Parade* and the Heathrow Plays, and in the consistency of its expression represents a direct authorial message. Global warming and social breakdown are united, but this apocalypse is also linked with the stars: the wonder of the natural universe, which is beyond the destructive reach of mankind. When asked to 'stun' his classmates, Chadwick, the one really intelligent – and bullied – schoolboy in *Punk Rock* counts up the number of stars: 'there are about a hundred billion stars in most given galaxies. That's ten thousand billion, billion stars in the universe [. . .]' (p. 18). Exactly the same reference is made in *On the Shore of the Wide World*; and at the end of *A Thousand Stars Explode in the Sky* all life on earth is ended by a stellar cataclysm. But elsewhere the stars are a symbol of hope, however ironic, as in the Coldplay 'song ['Yellow'] about looking at the stars [. . .] see how they shine for you' (p. 216) from the first Live Earth concert that immediately precedes the bombing in *Pornography*, or the theme song of *Marine Parade*, 'Every Falling Star'.

Stephens is one of the most prolific British playwrights, with fifteen plays staged in twelve years, and a further six completed in 2009–10. (He is also known for the speed with which he completes his plays: *Motortown* was written in just four days, and a comparatively long play like *On the Shore of the Wide World* in three weeks, although he explains that his plays have a long gestation period.) At the same time his combination of naturalistic characters with experimental structures, and the breadth of his themes along with the topicality of his dramatic subjects and the creative ambiguity that replaces political statements, make him one of the most important of today's British dramatists – and he is clearly still in mid-development.

Primary Sources

Works by Simon Stephens

Plays One: Bluebird, Christmas, Herons, Port (London: Methuen Drama, 2005).

Plays Two: One Minute, Country Music, Motortown, Pornography, Sea Wall (London: Methuen Drama, 2009).

On the Shore of the Wide World (London: Methuen, 2005).

Harper Regan (London: Methuen Drama, 2008).

Punk Rock (London: Methuen Drama, 2009).

A Canopy of Stars, in Nicolas Kent (ed.), *The Great Game: Afghanistan* (London: Oberon Modern Plays, 2009), pp. 229–50.

Secondary Sources

Cavendish, Dominic, 'Pornography? The Most Shocking Play of the Edinburgh Festival?', *Daily Telegraph*, 31 July 2008 <http://www.telegraph.co.uk/culture/theatre/3557508/Pornography-the-most-shocking-play-of-the-Edinburgh-Festival.html>

Devine, Harriet (ed.), 'Simon Stephens', *Looking Back* (London: Faber & Faber, 2006), pp. 255–64.

Edgar, David, *How Plays Work* (London: Nick Hern, 2009).

Howe Kritzer, Amelia, *Political Theatre in Post-Thatcher Britain: New Writing 1995–2005* (Basingstoke: Palgrave Macmillan, 2008).

Kellaway, Kate, 'How Simon Stephens' Plays are Galvanizing British Theatre', *Guardian*, 30 August 2009 <http://www.guardian.co.uk/stage/2009/aug/30/simon-stephens-theatre-punk-rock>

Lane, David, *Contemporary British Drama* (Edinburgh: EUP, 2010).

Lyric Hammersmith Theatre, *Punk Rock*, 2009 <www.punkrocked.co.uk>

Rebellato, Dan, 'Simon Stephens', *Contemporary Theatre Review*, Vol. 15, No. 1 (2005), pp. 174–8.

Sierz, Aleks, 'Interview with Simon Stephens', *TheatreVoice* website, 28 April 2006 <www.theatrevoice.com/listen_now/player/?audioID=394>

—, 'Interview with Simon Stephens (two parts)', *TheatreVoice* website, 20 October 2008 <www.theatrevoice.com/listen_now/player/?audioID=620>, <www.theatrevoice.com/listen_now/player/?audioID=619>

— (ed.), 'New Writing for Theatre: A Public Discussion', *Western European Stages*, Vol. 19, No. 1 (2007), pp. 37–48.

Stephens, Simon, 'Why I Wrote Motortown', Royal Court Education Pack, April 2006.

—, 'Keynote Address: Writing Black People', in Werner Huber, Margarete Rubik and Julia Novak (eds), *Staging Interculturality* (CDE 17; Trier: WVT, 2010), pp. 19–36.

—, Personal Interview, London, 3 February 2010.

—, Mark Ravenhill and Richard Bean, 'Debate on New Writing (three parts)', *TheatreVoice* website, 28 May 2004 <www.theatrevoice.com/listen_now/player/?audioID=169>, <www.theatrevoice.com/listen_now/player/?audioID=168>, <www.theatrevoice.com/listen_now/player/?audioID=172>

Notes

1. Simon Stephens, Personal Interview.
2. Ibid.
3. Ibid.
4. Ibid.
5. Ibid.
6. *Theatre Record*, Vol. XI, No. 11 (2001), p. 664.
7. Stephens, Personal Interview.
8. Simon Stephens, 'Introduction', *Plays Two*, p. xiv.
9. *Theatre Record*, Vol. XXIV, No. 13 (2004), p. 840.
10. Stephens, Personal Interview. See also Aleks Sierz, 'Interview with Simon Stephens', 2006.
11. Simon Stephens, 'Why I Wrote Motortown'.
12. Stephens, Personal Interview.
13. Ibid.
14. Reviews of *Motortown* in *Theatre Record*, Vol. XXVI, No. 9 (2006), pp. 488–91.
15. Charles Spencer, *Daily Telegraph*, *Theatre Record*, Vol. XXIX, No. 16–17 (2009), p. 877.
16. See Stephens, 'Introduction', *Plays Two*, p. xi.
17. Ibid., p. xviii.
18. Stephens, Personal Interview.
19. Stephens, 'Introduction', *Plays Two*, p. xix.
20. Aleks Sierz, 'Interview with Simon Stephens', 2008.
21. Reviews of *Pornography* in *Theatre Record*, Vol. XXVIII (2008), 'Edinburgh Supplement', pp. 1518–20, and *Theatre Record*, Vol. XXIX, No. 16–17 (2009), pp. 877–9.
22. Stephens, Personal Interview.
23. Lyric Hammersmith, *Punk Rock*.
24. These dates mean that the play takes place in 2008, and the main action spans precisely 37 days and 26 minutes.

25. Reviews of *Punk Rock* in *Theatre Record*, Vol. XXIX, No. 18 (2009), pp. 932–6.
26. Dan Rebellato, 'Simon Stephens', p. 175.
27. Amelia Howe Kritzer, *Political Theatre in Post-Thatcher Britain*, p. 113; David Lane, *Contemporary British Drama*, pp. 31–6.
28. David Edgar, *How Plays Work*, p. 114.
29. Stephens, Personal Interview.
30. See also Stephens, 'Introduction', *Plays One*, pp. viii–ix.

24 SHELAGH STEPHENSON

Peter Billingham

The Memory of Water; An Experiment with An Air Pump; Five Kinds of Silence; Mappa Mundi; Enlightenment

Introduction

Shelagh Stephenson is a playwright who, from the mid-1990s to the middle of the 2000s, attracted a substantial number of productions of her work and some critical interest. She was born in Tynemouth, Northumberland, in 1955, and read drama at Manchester University. Prior to her success as a playwright, she enjoyed a career as an actress both with the RSC and also with mostly supporting character roles in television drama, including the iconic British TV soap *Coronation Street*. Her first stage play, *The Memory of Water* (Hampstead Theatre, 1996), transferred to the West End, where it won an Olivier Award for Best Comedy in 2000. Following this, she wrote *Five Kinds of Silence* (originally broadcast on BBC Radio 4, 1996). Her second play, *An Experiment with an Air Pump* (1998), opened at the Royal Exchange Theatre in Manchester and was joint winner of the Peggy Ramsay Award. It subsequently transferred to the Hampstead Theatre and, along with *The Memory of Water*, went on to run at New York's Manhattan Theatre. In 2000 came her third play *Ancient Lights* (Hampstead) and her stage adaptation of her award-winning radio play *Five Kinds of Silence* was produced at the Lyric Hammersmith in the same year. In 2002, her screen adaptation of her first play – renamed *Before You Go* and starring Julie Walters – went on general release. It met with mixed reviews from the critics. Also in 2002 came *Mappa Mundi* (National Theatre), followed three years later by *Enlightenment* (Peacock, Abbey, Dublin). Her most recent plays are *The Long Road* (Soho, 2007) and *A Northern Odyssey* (Live Theatre,

Newcastle, 2010). *Enlightenment* was revived at the Hampstead in September 2010, directed by Edward Hall. She also has co-writer and co-producer credits on the critically well-received BBC4 television drama *Enid* (2010), starring Helena Bonham-Carter as the eponymous children's author Enid Blyton. Interestingly, given Stephenson's strong interest in the family and especially its female relationships, *Enid* explores a more challenging subtext to Blyton's life. The one-off film drama reveals an ambitious young woman who grows into an emotionally distant mother and manipulative wife. It offers a darker dimension to the hugely successful author, challenging the common perception of her as an anodyne chronicler of a class-ridden England now largely gone.

Hailed by the *Daily Telegraph* at the outset as 'clearly a dramatist to watch',[1] her output and reputation have stood the test of time. Director Dominic Dromgoole characterised her work as the exploration of 'families and love, zeal and betrayal with a warm compassion and a light wit'.[2] This successful career of recognition and productivity is sound evidence of the broad and positive appeal of her plays and their themes: especially family and relationships. While work such as the excellent *Five Kinds of Silence* is very challenging in its interrogation of themes relating to domestic abuse, Stephenson has a gift for capturing the nuances and indeed pathos of contemporary life. This is clearly expressed in her Introduction to *Plays One*, where she states:

> Looking back over the plays it's clear to me that whatever I thought I was writing about at the time, they are in fact all about death, dying, being dead, being afraid of death, being obsessed with it. I'm not sure why I set out to do this [. . .] As to why this may be, well, what else is there in the end?[3]

She has also been quoted as saying: 'We're all so obsessed with sex and it's so boring. It's so twentieth century. Death is the new sex.'[4] Stephenson's summary of her central concerns, death and mortality, are especially prevalent in *The Memory of Water* and *Mappa Mundi*, and are also a very useful defining signal for the stylistic and thematic diversity of plays such as *Five Kinds of Silence* and *Enlightenment*.

The Plays

The Memory of Water (1996)

With this play, first performed at the Hampstead Theatre on 11 July 1996, Shelagh Stephenson arrived on the British theatre landscape. This was a year when other contemporary British plays, as diverse as Martin McDonagh's *The Beauty Queen of Leenane* and Mark Ravenhill's *Shopping and Fucking*, had their premieres. Unlike those plays, and unlike those of another contemporary British female playwright, Sarah Kane, Stephenson's play is much more conventional and traditional in its language, characterisation and dramatic form. While the title might allude to and evoke something of the heightened poetic realism of David Greig, the play itself has more obvious allegiances with established playwrights such as Alan Ayckbourn and Alan Bennett. There is an almost post-Chekhovian pathos suffusing the piece alongside a wonderfully elliptical sense of the humorous in family life and mid-age relationships. In terms of a family drama dealing with difficult relationships in the context of the death of a parent, there is also an affinity with Tanika Gupta's *The Waiting Room* (2000).[5] In both Gupta's and Stephenson's plays, the death of a mother if not matriarch provokes the need for those facing the future without her to re-examine their own lives. Also of interest is that both playwrights employ the device of having the mother reappear posthumously to selected family members. Finally both writers wrote their respective plays following the death of one of their parents. In Stephenson's case it was her mother, with the playwright having four sisters.

Stephenson's play works best in terms of its direct and energetic exploration of the tensions within the lives of a middle-class English family. Three sisters return to their family home against the backdrop of their mother's death and funeral. Vi, the recently departed mother, opens the play in an aura of 1960s style and sexiness while her daughter Mary lies on what had been her parents' marital bed. However, Vi is now less bothered with her dresses or jewellery, but needs to confront her daughter about the fact that someone has been going through her bedside table. Inevitably, each daughter brings with her, as well as her neuroses, conflicting and competing memories of her family past. Mary is a doctor and Stephenson demonstrates her acuity and talent for a punishing comic one-liner when Vi, leafing through some of her daughter's books, comments:

> **Vi** *Head Injuries and Short-Term Changes in Neural Behaviour* [. . .] *The Phenomenology of Memory* [. . .] *Peripheral Signalling of the Brain.*
> *She puts them down.*
> Bloody hell, Mary. What's wrong with Georgette Heyer?
> (p. 4)

In addition, and this is where the play really works in terms of sharply focused pathos and nostalgia, the women bring with them occasional quasi-philosophical musings on life, death and mid-life crises. A good example of Stephenson's sense of the unknowingly absurd in the bric-a-brac of sisterly social intercourse comes in the opening act of the play where Mary and Teresa are in their mother's bedroom with its poignant furnishings of a disappearing petit-bourgeois social milieu. Even as Mary tries to hide under the bed sheets from this problematic journey down memory lane, a familial, emotional road crash is waiting to happen:

> *She tries to settle down in the bed, and pulls something out that's causing her discomfort: a glass contraption with a rubber bulb at one end* [. . .] **Teresa** *picks it up.*
> **Teresa** Oh, for God's sake . . . Is this what I think it is?
> **Mary** I don't know. What do you think it is?
> **Teresa** A breast pump.
> **Mary** I found it on top of the wardrobe. I think I'd like to have it.
> **Teresa** Why?
> **Mary** Because you've got the watch and the engagement ring.
> **Teresa** For Lucy. Not for me. For Lucy.

Mary   OK. So you want the breast pump. Have it. [. . .]
Teresa   You can't just take things willy-nilly.
Mary   You did.
Teresa   Oh, I see. I see what this is all about. (p. 7)

These interchanges work well both on their own terms and also with various other character clusters throughout the play. There's a strong sense in which the principal characters and their mid-life sparring sessions represent the narrative spine of the play. This results in a dramatic narrative that's principally based around effectively self-contained, quasi-humorous interludes which work exactly on their own episodic terms. Stephenson has an undoubted talent for the comic interchange with echoes at times of comedian Victoria Wood.

The background and context for the title of the play is symptomatic of Stephenson's need to entertain while suggesting a deeper subtext of insightful reflection upon life, death, marriage and families. Mary has an ongoing, illicit affair with a middle-aged man called Mike who in Ray Cooney style appears in her late mother's bedroom through the window after the most hilariously improbable, incident-fuelled journey to get to her former family home. Equally improbably, Mike decides to tell Mary of an anecdotal conversation relating to homoeopathy:

> They were doing these experiments with water, because they were researching the efficacy of homoeopathy, and what they came up with after months of apparently stringent tests was that you can remove every last trace of the curative element from a water solution and it will retain its beneficial effect [. . .] water had memory. You can dilute and dilute and dilute, but the pertinent thing remains. (p. 38)

This is expertly woven into the fabric of the play and enhances its characters, themes and their development with the following absurdly comic exchange, one that is dramatically well-timed – if rather clichéd:

Mike It's all complete bollocks, of course. Except . . . [. . .] I've got an erection. [. . .]
Mary We can't. We absolutely can't.
Mike No.
Mary It'll go away if we ignore it. (p. 38)

The play moves towards its own inexorable and rather sentimentalised conclusion. Stephenson's sense of the comic absurd and also her intrinsic celebration of a kind of generic 'northern no-nonsense' pragmatism undoubtedly had a strong appeal to an audience eager for recognisable characters and their all too recognisable dilemmas. The play walks a careful path between making us laugh or cry or confront some potentially more nuanced aspects of life's transience. The play effectively explores and achieves an assuredly distinctive and recognisable authorial voice. Through this, the play continues to enjoy phenomenal commercial success both in Britain and abroad, where in New York it attracted a strong following from within that city's gay community.[6]

An Experiment with an Air Pump (1998)

This play was inspired initially by Joseph Wright's 1768 painting, 'An Experiment on a Bird with an Air Pump'. It was first performed at the Royal Exchange Theatre, Manchester on 12 February 1998 and deploys two historical locations, separated by two hundred years: 1799 and 1999 with four contemporary characters, all of whom double with four of the seven characters from the earlier period. The action takes place in the same location, albeit separated by time. This allows Stephenson to explore in a dramaturgically stylised, neo-Brechtian way, the framing device of historicism: defamiliarising the present through the perspective of the past and familiarising the past through the recognisable lens of the present.

This is expressed most cogently through the opening visual motif and Ellen's opening speech. Ellen is aged forty and a scientist in the contemporary setting whose actress also plays the part of Susannah, Fenwick's wife, in the eighteenth-century setting. Apart from

Susannah/Ellen, the play opens with the chiaroscuro-infused lighting of Joseph Wright's iconic painting, capturing as it does a sense of scientific marvel and wonder. This image of an almost beatific aura surrounding the people witnessing a groundbreaking experiment cleverly evokes the aura of the divine associated with the religious paintings of the Renaissance. The experiment discovered that life could not exist in a vacuum. This staging device also allows Stephenson to use a neo-Brechtian strategy of having the actress playing Susannah/Ellen to be first seen on stage dressed in the costume of loose trousers, t-shirt etc. We therefore have a 'double-exposure' of the actress playing Ellen-as-Ellen gazing upon the historical scene. This is further accentuated by two dressers appearing on stage to dress Ellen in full view of the audience in her eighteenth-century costume. As they do so, Ellen addresses the audience directly:

> I've loved this painting since I was thirteen years old. I've
> loved it because it has a scientist at the heart of it, a scientist
> where you usually find God. Here, centre stage, is not a saint
> or an archangel, but a man. Look at his face, bathed in
> a celestial light, here is a man beatified by his search for
> truth. [. . .] Who would not want to be caught up in this
> world? Who could resist the power of light over darkness?
> (pp. 139–40)

The play's opening provides its audience with a continuing if subliminal reminder that history is itself something which is 'staged' and also offers the associated view that they, as well as the actors and actresses, are co-performers and co-participants in its unfolding. Stephenson further explores these possibilities and the play develops into an intriguing if at times complex dramaturgy. This can sometimes result in the dialogue employed by her characters in the eighteenth century seeming slightly overburdened; they are in some sense aware of the wider, post-historical significance of their speech and actions. This is evidenced in the following extract between Fenwick, Armstrong (a young scientist and physician) and a young Roget, scientist and future compiler of the classic *Thesaurus*.

Fenwick is critical of a botanist of the kind common at that period:

Fenwick We're talking about New Year's Eve for God's sake. The last night of the century. Has this fact bypassed these people? We want something worthy of the past and fired by visions of the future. We want to [. . .] march towards a New Jerusalem with all our banners flying. [. . .] If he's to lead us into a new century we're all doomed.

Armstrong With respect, I think you confuse a personal antipathy towards Reverend Jessop with the quality of his proposed lecture.

Fenwick Rubbish, one look at the man is enough to tell you he's a complete fool. He sets out with a premise and trims the world to fit it. What he practises is not science, but a branch of theology.

Armstrong Objectivity is paramount in these things, you said so yourself, sir. One set of prejudices is as dangerous as another. I think that's how you put it.

Roget And besides, you've not read the paper. I think you'll find there's not a mention of God in it anywhere – (pp. 144–5)

This admirably ambitious play sometimes has to work hard to retain consistency of thematic focus and narrative development. Genetics, eugenics, British imperialism, issues pertaining to feminism and disability, patriarchy, and sexual exploitation all jostle for our attention. This results sometimes in rather too much happening dramatically as ideas intrude upon the play, threatening occasionally to counteract dramatic dynamics, tempo and theatricality. When this happens the play can become too transparently a debate between the past and the present. Furthermore this can lead to a potentially improbable synchronicity of incidents and events. A good example of this is in the plotline, where we are faced with the implied sexual abuse of Isobel, a servant with a twisted spine and an impressively drawn character of the earlier historical narrative. She subsequently commits suicide when she becomes aware that Armstrong's apparent romantic attraction to her is no more than a cynical guise for his own quasi-scientific viewing of her as a specimen. The delineating of Isobel as having victim status is an unexpected consequence of Stephenson's deeper concern to explore a dialectic between gender politics and a discourse of disability. Armstrong ultimately utilises her body for surgical dismemberment in the name of science: a potentially dark premonition of eugenics and the Nazis. As powerful as this story undoubtedly is, it is also in some respects problematic, given Stephenson's aim of making a strong statement via a feminist revisiting of history and gendered power relations. Thus Isobel is constructed in such a way that she seemingly naïvely believes Armstrong when he declares love to her as a guise for his actual motives. It's with a melodramatic flourish, therefore, that Isobel is seen first to hide unnoticed by Armstrong and Roget and then '*runs off, stifling a cry*' (p. 221) when the former discloses those motives:

Armstrong   I flatter her, look suitably love struck when she
    comes into a room, I call her beautiful –
Roget   But why? –
Armstrong   And eventually I get her into the sack.
Roget   That would seem to be a logical, if cynical
    progression. It's not in itself an explanation. (p. 220)

After Armstrong then boasts to Roget that he has had an erection on seeing Isobel's naked, twisted body, one feels uncomfortably close to the caricature of a melodramatic villain. The play ends with a dramatically powerful reinforcement of this complex play's dark subtext with Tom's 'I keep thinking about the dead girl [. . .] Missing ribs. [. . .] I don't understand' with Ellen's obliquely self-reflective response 'I don't suppose we ever will' (p. 230). As the contemporary characters disappear for the last time, characters from the past reappear in the context of Isobel's funeral. Stephenson articulates in robust dialogue the past's impossible facility to see itself from the future's perspective:

Fenwick So this is how we're seeing out the century. Not the way we'd imagined it, not with a flurry of trumpets and beacons blazing. I thought it would be a golden night [. . .] and instead, this. Groping blindly over the border in fog of bewilderment. The future looks less benign now, Isobel. We're a little more frightened than we were. (p. 231)

Susannah's (by implication, Ellen's) concerned response articulates a neo-melodramatic but deeply felt pathos: 'I don't understand . . . I don't understand . . .' (p. 231). The play's final dramatic strategy offers a darkly theatrical resolution based on the visual metaphor of the play's opening: the painting is restaged but with Isobel in her coffin replacing the bird in the air pump.

An Experiment with an Air Pump represents an ambitious experiment on Stephenson's part to write not only a history play but also a history play that offers a post-mortem of the ideological contradictions intrinsic to a revolutionary historical period. In the end the play is subtly political in its feminist, liberal treatment of gender and disability. In its wider meta-perspective of an engagement with notions of history and the dialectics of scientific and religious faith and morality, it adopts a challenging and provocative perspective.[7]

Five Kinds of Silence (2000)

This play was first broadcast on BBC Radio 4 and won the Writers' Guild Award for Best Original Radio Play in 1996. It was adapted for the stage and presented at the Lyric Hammersmith on 31 May 2000.[8] It is Stephenson's strongest and most distinctive piece, and is of compelling and remarkable contrast to the dramatic style, language, form and concerns of *The Memory of Water*. The plays are so different in tone, texture and theatrical resonance that they serve as clear evidence of Stephenson's facility as a dramatist.

Stephenson wrote *Five Kinds of Silence* after learning of a grim, true-life story of a dysfunctional family in Burnley, Lancashire, an economically deprived area in north-west England. The play explores, with a degree of dramaturgical freedom and dark élan, a story of savage domestic violence and sexual abuse inflicted by the character Billy on both his wife and two daughters. The play has something of a contemporary, urban Jacobean tragedy informing its structure and texture. There is also a terrifying inevitability about the formation and evolution of Billy as an embodiment of patriarchal violence, its consequences for his wife and daughters and – ultimately – for him. Not surprisingly given its origins in radio, it is the play's richly textured, muscularly poetic language that most defines it. Furthermore it is in Stephenson's courageous journey into the heart of darkness that is Billy's tormented and destructive inner world that the play has its finest moments. It opens with a powerful monologue which is given a Büchner-style paranoiac intensity through the framing of the revisiting of a dream:

> **Billy** One night, I dreamt I was a dog. The moon was out, I could smell it. Ice-white metal smell. [. . .] The tarmac road made my dog teeth tingle, it was aniseed, rubber, and then the lamp-posts, studded with smells they were. [. . .] And the stars pierced my dog nose like silver wires. A woman came out of her house [. . .]. She didn't look at me, just walked straight on by, thought I was just a dog. [. . .] you think I'm a dog but I'm Billy [. . .]. I'm at my own door now. I don't need to see it, it comes to meet me, a cacophony, the smells are dancing towards me, the smells of home. (p. 99)

Stephenson captures with impressive expertise the internal, fractured alienation of Billy through his evocation of himself as a dog, a creature of raw instinct and brute power. Immediately after this viscerally disturbing opening, Billy is dead – shot by his daughters. The play then explores through a nuanced sequence of almost filmic jump-editing the past and the present: the descent of Billy into becoming a brutalised and brutalising man. Simultaneously Stephenson offers a narrative of post-murder scenes in which there is a montage of conversations and encounters between the sisters Susan and Janet with both their mother, Mary, and also psychiatrists and the police. When questioned by one of the psychiatrists, who suggests to Susan: 'I wonder if sometimes you deny what you feel,' Susan answers: 'We killed him. He's dead. We feel better now. There's nothing you can do about any of it' (p. 114).

Immediately following this sequence, in which Susan adds that 'If you had to live inside our heads for five minutes you'd go mad and die. Best we deal with it ourselves,' Billy 'returns' like some *deus ex machina* from purgatory (p. 115). It is in this long monologue that Stephenson dares to evoke the soul-destroying impact of the conditions of alienated labour made even more extreme in times of war. There is a kind of homoerotic attraction for Billy in the fetishised signifiers of warfare with all of its subliminal violence:

> **Billy** Our town is full of soldiers. There's a war on. I like the shine on their boots, I like the sound they make on the cobbles, harsh and strong, it sets my teeth tingling. They are polished and trim and neat these men, belted and tucked and ready for action. Already I'm hooked. [. . .] I'm beside myself with longing. [. . .] One of them shows me his kit [. . .] and then a quivery ripple shivers across my groin. I am at home here. I am in paradise here. [. . .] He lets me hold his gun. I imagine shooting all the people in our street, pop, pop, pop. [. . .] I imagine the look on their faces, stupid, caught by surprise. [. . .] I am laughing, shivers run up and down my spine, my feet are going like Fred Astaire. (p. 115)

Here in this litany of dangerously displaced psychotic desire Stephenson captures with clipped and assured linguistic texture the queasy orgasmic ecstasy of not only Billy but all men conditioned to a state-authorised love affair with violence. It's a reminder of the inner struggle between a fractured Eros and dominant Thanatos and Stephenson exudes a macabre poetics in her counterpointing of the sensuality intrinsic in the iconic cultural motif of Fred Astaire dancing (the staccato tap of his toe) and the 'pop, pop, pop' of Billy's libidinous imagined shooting spree.

The play weaves its dark meandering narrative to a concluding sequence in which we revisit and reconfront the daughters' murdering of their father. The final dialogue interweaving the voices of Mary, the mother, with Janet and Susan, the daughters, has the quality of a catechism of unspoken desire – or guilt? – expressed as a masquerade of their future domesticity:

Susan We can start a new life now.
Janet We've got a maisonette.
Mary We plan to have pink carpets.
Susan And a dog.
Janet We've got four bedrooms. (p. 134)

Mappa Mundi (2002)

Mappa Mundi is the name given to a famous thirteenth-century map of the world which is round and positions Jerusalem at the centre of the known world. Stephenson's play premiered at the Cottesloe, National Theatre, on 24 October 2002, but received disappointingly mixed reviews.[9] In this play, she returns in one sense to her first play in that her chosen territory is the world of family life with all of its attendant causes for celebrations, but also generational and gendered tensions and complications. It is a very satisfying and successful excursion into this territory and builds well and convincingly on her earlier play. In this it is characterised by some of the multiplicity of issues and storylines evident in both *The Memory of Water* and *An Experiment with an Air Pump*. Stephenson successfully 'maps' the complex and tragic-comic aspects of family life in a movingly nuanced way in this later play and consequently is able to allow herself the time, and the confidence perhaps, to explore some of the central characters in impressive detail.

The play's opening is celebratory and exhilarating with a group of black dancers and a band that perform under a backdrop of enlarged family photographs as well as an eighteenth-century map. This evokes immediately and with potent visual and aural theatricality not only the world of a family and its past, but also an imperialist, colonial past in dialectic conjunction with our post-colonial world of cultural and ethnic diversity.

The dancing is brought to a halt by the benign appearance of Sholto, a black lawyer in his late thirties. This exuberant framing device is an entry into the British family, we discover, and its central protagonists who will drive the central engine of the play's plot, narrative and themes. Jack, an old-fashioned northern patriarch, is asleep in a hammock in the garden when his son Michael enters, who is in his forties. Jack is tetchily combative with both his son and his thirtysomething daughter Anna, who enters the fray. It quickly becomes clear that the sense of celebration signalled in the opening framing device is to be Anna's marriage to Sholto. A priest, Father Ryan, has also come along to discuss the wedding, which signals the Catholic background to the family. It transpires that Ryan might also have a passing interest in Jack, whose health is not good. Stephenson cleverly uses Anna and Michael's response to Jack's latent racist stereotypes to counteract any easy empathy for the older man:

> **Jack** Sholto. What a stupid name.
> **Anna** If you say that once more –
> **Jack** Sholto. He's probably from one of those cargo cults, is he?
> **Anna** That's Polynesia, Dad. He comes from Leicestershire.
> **Jack** I mean originally. Before they came over here.
> **Michael** They don't have cargo cults in the West Indies.
> **Jack** They do, they worship Prince Philip. Big fella belong Missis Quinn. [. . .]
> **Anna** If you start this in front of Sholto and his mother –
> **Michael** We'll have you put in a home.
> **Jack** You'd like that.
> **Michael** A dog's home. (p. 7)

It transpires in Act One that Michael is an actor. There is then a further theatrical 'in-joke' referring rather knowingly to some of Stephenson's more controversial 'in-yer-face' contemporaries when Jack with a sense of confrontational mischief seeks to shock Father Ryan and his adult children in one masterstroke:

> **Jack**   If a policeman called you a cunt, you could sue him. But with an actor, it's water off a duck's back. It's cunt this and cunt that all the time in the theatre. Apparently. They mean it affectionately. So he says.
> **Michael**   Sorry about this Father Ryan.
> **Jack**   Causing a bit of a scene am I?
> **Anna**   Just behave will you?
> **Jack**   Cunt. If you say it enough, it takes the sting off it.
>   (p. 14)[10]

The character of Jack is Stephenson's funniest comic creation, and also the one who is most wonderfully engaging and believable. This reflects an impressively subtle and nuanced layering of character. In particular she clearly enjoys fusing and playing with character traits and textures that range from the ageing *agent provocateur* through to the pathos of an old man who knows – despite his anarchic mischief and belligerence – that he is facing death. This allows Stephenson the means by which to undercut the comic with a sharp-edged dramatic scalpel and for some of the philosophical musings that often felt imposed in her earlier play *The Memory of Water* to be woven even more seamlessly into the fabric of the play. This is nowhere more evident than towards the end of the play when Father Ryan shares with Jack that he is leaving the church:

> **Jack**   Help yourself to another.
> **Father Ryan**   Thanks Jack, I will.
> **Jack**   So, what do you want? D'you want to assuage me with the consolations of religion and the sure and certain knowledge of the Resurrection?
> **Father Ryan**   Not at all. [. . .]

Jack I thought that was your bloody job. Go on. Tell me I'll be up there with the angels and a bottle of Scotch by the end of the month. [. . .]

Father Ryan D'you think you'll see Rose again, Jack? D'you think she's waiting for you on the other side?

Pause

Jack D'you want the truth? No.

Pause

Father Ryan Neither do I. (p. 92)

Other narrative themes are developed as Stephenson tries to integrate issues around a contemporary multicultural Britain and mixed-race marriage. Jack's collection of maps includes one which Anna believes relates the family to the slave trade with Africa. With dark irony, and simultaneously a clear attack upon the neoliberal, progressive idealisation of the past, what the map seems to prove is that Jack and therefore the family are descended from plantation owners. But the motif of the map and the mapping of human lives and the history of slavery seems secondary to the spine of the play, which is Jack's journey into a deeper acceptance of his mortality. While the playwright comes close to over-sentimentalising Father Ryan's response to the gift of the map that the adult children have given to Jack, the old curmudgeon's reply is absolutely edged with a quiet, sad and belated life-realisation that is credible and moving:

Jack Did you see the map they gave me? The map of my life?

Father Ryan I did. I don't know why but it made me cry.

Jack I thought when I saw it, is that all there is? Is that all I was? Because I know in my heart there are other things that don't fit in there. There were other things in my life that no-one knows about. But the map is the life I mostly lived. There's another one in my head, but what I lived was that. And it choked me because that was my real life and I realised how small it was. And I can't change it now. There are no more choices to make. (p. 94)

Enlightenment (2005)

Enlightenment was first produced at the Abbey Theatre, Dublin, on 3 March 2005. The play's dark and complex themes touch the nerve of contemporary, predominantly middle-class concerns about dysfunctional families and problematic relationships, both married and filial. There is also an overriding anxiety that hovers over the play like some postmodern Furies about identity and otherness. Lia and Nick, a fortysomething professional couple, are facing the anguish and alienation of having lost contact with their son, who has been back-packing abroad in his gap-year, prior to university. Desperate for reassurance, Lia first employs a psychic adviser to discover where their son is and whether he is still alive. As the play develops through a web of postmodern narrative strategies, the couple are drawn into a night-marish vortex of existential doubt and occult paranoia. Their journey seems to reach a destination that will resolve their tragic dilemma with the arrival of Adam, a young man who claims to be their son. In the remaining half of the play, the parents re-embark upon another roller-coaster ride of elation, despair and ultimately sinister dénouement when Adam reveals himself as a lover of their son and, in classical Oedipal fashion, an amoral bisexual traveller who offers sex to Lia: 'I'd like to fuck you too. Then I'd really feel part of the family' (p. 94). This penultimate scene ends with Lia attacking him and knocking him unconscious, and the play ends with a disturbing sense that there will be no end for Lia and Nick's overwhelming anxiety about the fate of their son. Like a bleak Ionesco anti-resolution, the couple continue to enact a catechism of doubt and despair. At the end of the final scene, this is punctuated by their phone ringing:

> **Lia** Don't answer it.
> *The phone keeps ringing.*
>   It won't be him.
> *The phone keeps ringing. They both look at it for a long time.* **Lia**
> *can bear it no longer. She jumps up and grabs the phone.*
>   Hello?
> *Fade down lights.* (p. 98)

This play undoubtedly conveys a strong sense of contemporary fear of a threatening world beyond the confines of domesticity and the presumed known. Here is a world in which beneath the seeming social and moral coherence of family life lies a stratum of alienating fracture and dissonance. In this meta-territory identity is problematic, desire dangerous and a problematic past haunts and disrupts a vertigo-inducing present. To accentuate this gothic nightmare sense of the theatre of the absurd, Stephenson sets the play in a stridently non-naturalistic setting which carries with it a subliminal quality of a laboratory in which the subjects for interrogation and investigation are a human couple. Stephenson cleverly and wittily conspires to create a sense that it is we, the audience, who are their voyeuristic auditors. In September 2010, the new director of the Hampstead Theatre, Edward Hall, chose *Enlightenment* as his directorial premiere at the theatre. Significantly some critics were appreciative of its dark social and cultural contemporary resonances:

> Shelagh Stephenson's play is simultaneously recognisable – granola, telly, middle-class absurdity – and wonderfully odd, reflecting chaos theory, non-locality and Jungian synchronicity with casual brio [. . .] It's a seat-gripping ride.[11]

Summary

Stephenson is a playwright whose career as a writer began rather later than that of some of her contemporaries, who, unlike her, were associated with the 'in-yer-face theatre' genre of 1990s British theatre. Her relatively late arrival on the playwriting scene was pre-dated by substantial acting experience, especially in television. This has clearly had an influence upon her work and especially her successful family-based comedy dramas such as *The Memory of Water* and *Mappa Mundi*. The former brought her almost immediate commercial and popular success and it seems as if she has tried to return to that successful formula in later plays. Her adaptation of *The Memory of Water* into the film *Before You Go* also received mixed if mostly disparaging reviews. Her most recent plays have returned to the darker, experimental territory within her oeuvre with *Enlightenment* and *The Long Road* tracing a sharply contrasting existential strand in her work back to what is her strongest piece to date, *Five Kinds of Silence*. Her most recent work has been the Newcastle-based production of her unpublished play *A Northern Odyssey* (2010) which makes a return to the historical drama genre of *An Experiment with an Air Pump*, exploring the visit of a nineteenth-century American genre painter to the Northumberland coast one hundred years ago, a real event currently enjoying a centennial celebration in north-east England.

Stephenson's body of work embodies both the popular and commercially successful with the more darkly esoteric and experimental in a way that is both impressive and intriguing. Yet despite, or maybe because of, the enthusiasm of the reception of her popular debut play, she has attracted little interest from academics or critics. Although she has an entry in Susan Croft's compendium of female dramatists,[12] there have been few mentions of her work in the recent histories of contemporary playwriting. Steve Jones's 'Commentary and Notes' to the Methuen Student Edition of *The Memory of Water* is the only major account of her work.[13] Nevertheless, Stephenson is a writer who has an undoubted flair for the comic within ordinary family life and a strong sense of pathos. This is both a positive quality in some of her most popular work while also sometimes limiting more challenging character development and thematic exploration. Compared to some of the major female dramatists, she lacks the left-field awareness or focus of Caryl Churchill or Sarah Daniels, although *Five Kinds of Silence* brings her closest to those writers, especially Daniels's feminist classic *Masterpieces* (1983). In terms of her more immediate female counterparts, her work is different from that of Sarah Kane, but in her historical dramas there is some interesting comparison with Heidi Thomas, for example.

Stephenson's most successful plays, especially *The Memory of Water*, reflect a post-Thatcher, Blairite society and culture in which many middle-class professional women were engaged by the challenges of squaring their economic freedom and personal empowerment with the demands of family and the past. It is to that neoliberal consensus of post-feminist women and their personal relationships that her work finds its most extensive and popular audience. In plays such as *Five Kinds of Silence* she explores a darker, parallel universe of women struggling to survive against the brutalisation of patriarchy. It's a cause for celebration that she has had this relative freedom to explore that challenging post-feminist territory. With *Enlightenment* and *The Long Road* she gives evidence that that journey into a heart of darkness is still important to her. In the penultimate scene of *Mappa Mundi*, Jack and Father Ryan continue their frank but painfully liberating conversation of their agnosticism:

> **Jack**   D'you think there's another version of my life out there where different choices were made?
> **Father Ryan**   Would you like that, Jack?
> **Jack**   More than anything.
> **Father Ryan**   Then I hope so. (p. 94)

Stephenson has proved to be a distinctive and sensitive cartographer of the social and cultural territory of Britain from New Labour through to current times. Through her plays, she endeavours to explore the possibility of different choices. We should remain grateful for her distinctive dramatic voice and enduring compassionate humanity.

Primary Sources

Works by Shelagh Stephenson

Plays One: The Memory of Water, Five Kinds of Silence, An Experiment with an Air Pump, Ancient Lights (London: Methuen Drama, 2003).

Mappa Mundi (London: Methuen Drama, 2002).

Enlightenment (London: Methuen Drama, 2005).

The Long Road (London: Methuen Drama, 2008).

Secondary Sources

Billingham, Peter, *At the Sharp End: Uncovering the Work of Five Contemporary Dramatists* (London: Methuen Drama, 2007).

Croft, Susan, *She Also Wrote Plays: An International Guide to Women Playwrights from the 10th to the 21st Century* (London: Faber & Faber, 2001).

Dromgoole, Dominic, *The Full Room: An A–Z of Contemporary Playwriting* (London: Methuen Drama, 2002).

Jones, Steve, 'Commentary and Notes', in Shelagh Stephenson, *The Memory of Water* (London: Methuen Drama Student Edition, 2008).

Keblowska-Lawniczak, Ewa, 'Adaptations of Visual Material: Paintings, Drawings and Maps', in Monkia Pietrzak-Franger and Eckart Voigts-Virchow (eds), *Adaptations: Performing Across Media and Genres* (CDE 16; Trier: WVT, 2006), pp. 129–41.

Sierz, Aleks, *In-Yer-Face Theatre: British Drama Today* (London: Faber & Faber, 2001).

—, 'Shelagh Stephenson', 'A–Z', *In-Yer-Face Theatre* website <www.inyerface-theatre.com/az.html#s>

Stephenson, Shelagh, 'Introduction', *Plays One* (London: Methuen Drama, 2003), p. ix.

Notes

1. Charles Spencer, *Daily Telegraph*, *Theatre Record*, Vol. XVI, No. 15 (1996), p. 928.
2. Dominic Dromgoole, *The Full Room*, p. 253.
3. Shelagh Stephenson, 'Introduction', *Plays One*, p. ix.
4. Quoted in Aleks Sierz, 'Shelagh Stephenson'.
5. See Peter Billingham, *At the Sharp End*, pp. 228–31.
6. Reviews of *The Memory of Water* in *Theatre Record*, Vol. XVI, No. 15 (1996), pp. 925–8.
7. Reviews of *An Experiment with an Air Pump* in *Theatre Record*, Vol. XVIII, No. 4 (1998), pp. 216–17.
8. Reviews of *Five Kinds of Silence* in *Theatre Record*, Vol. XX, No. 11 (2000), pp. 669–72.
9. Reviews of *Mappa Mundi* in *Theatre Record*, Vol. XXII, No. 23 (2002), pp. 1499–504.
10. See also Aleks Sierz, *In-Yer-Face Theatre*, p. 31.
11. Libby Purves, *The Times*, *Theatre Record*, Vol. XXX, No. 20 (2010), p. 1125.
12. Susan Croft, *She Also Wrote Plays*, pp. 245–6.
13. Steve Jones, 'Commentary and Notes', pp. v–xxiv.

25 ROY WILLIAMS

Deirdre Osborne

The No Boys Cricket Club; Lift Off; Sing Yer Heart Out for the Lads; Fallout; Days of Significance

Introduction

Roy Williams is the most prolific indigenous black dramatist in contemporary British theatre. Writing from a standpoint which is distinct from the migrant sensibilities of previous generations of black writers in Britain, Williams represents aspects of contemporary culture as drawn from black citizens' experiences. He is of a generation which has achieved and sustained a mainstream visibility denied to their dramatist forebears, although this has yet to translate into substantial international profiles. From the mid-1990s, Williams has penned plays continuously, consolidating his place in the canon of British theatre history.

Born in Fulham, London, in 1968, the much younger child in a family of four siblings, he has always lived in London. When Williams was two, his father left the family for the United States. The son's childhood was a time of isolation: 'I spent my youth feeling detached, not just from my family, but from nearly everyone.'[1] Attending the Henry Compton Comprehensive Secondary School, by his own admission he 'was a bully and was bullied'.[2] School was not a stimulating experience for him: 'I had a real struggle just listening. I used to daydream, fly into my imagination.'[3] This detachment and self-immersion aids his creative hot-housing. When writing a new play he sometimes realises he has neither seen nor 'spoken to anyone else for days on end'.[4]

As Williams achieved good grades in English but did poorly at other subjects, his mother secured a private tutor for him – Don

Kinch, actor, writer and director with the black theatre Staunch Poets and Players – who introduced Williams to live theatre, confirming his desire to act. After leaving school at sixteen, working at McDonald's, Safeway, and in various warehouses for a year, he joined a performing arts course at Kingsway College. From there he went to the Cockpit Youth Theatre, and gained his first professional acting job with the Theatre Centre. Working with playwright Lin Coghlan, among others, he attended Noel Greig's evening Writers' Workshop and obtained his Equity Card.

Williams recalls that copious, but critical television watching as a youth alerted him – even before his involvement with theatre – to crucial aspects of plot, form and structure. However, a novel was his first inspiration. 'I was reeled in when I first read *Of Mice and Men* by John Steinbeck. When I finished reading that I knew I wanted to be a writer.'[5] His key drama influences were plays by Barrie Keeffe (*Sus*, 1979) and Nigel Williams (*Class Enemy*, 1978).[6] *Luke 4 Gary*, his first play, written on his mother's typewriter while he was a teenager, motivated him to undertake a writing degree at Rose Bruford College (1992–95). His final-year, full-length play, *The No Boys Cricket Club*, gained him a first-class degree. Staged at the Theatre Royal Stratford East (1996), it received Writers' Guild and TAPS Writer of the Year Award nominations. Within two months of graduating, he experienced further success with his radio play *Homeboys* (BBC Young Writers Festival, 1995). Since then, awards have adorned Williams's career: the Alfred Fagon Award (1997), the John Whiting Award (1998), an EMMA (1999) for *Starstruck*, the George Devine Award (2000) for *Lift Off* and the South Bank Show Arts Council Decibel Award and Screen Nation Award for *Fallout*. His plays have been revived regionally, in prison-theatre contexts, and by drama schools.

As a prominent dramatist, Williams has not distanced himself from his connections to young people's theatre. *Offside* (BBC Television) won a BAFTA for Best Schools Drama (2002). Other commissions for this audience include *Slow Time* (2005) and *Baby Girl* (2007) for the National Theatre, and *There's Only One Wayne Matthews* (2007) for Polka Children's Theatre. Further radio plays include *Tell Tale*

(2002) and adaptations of two E. R. Braithwaite novels: *To Sir, with Love* (1959) in 2007 and *Choice of Straws* (1965) in 2009. For the stage, he adapted Colin MacInnes's 1959 novel *Absolute Beginners* (Lyric Hammersmith, 2007) as well as penning *Days of Significance* (RSC, 2007). Notwithstanding the rural setting of his early play, *Josie's Boys* (Red Ladder, 1996) or those featuring Jamaican contexts – *The No Boys Cricket Club* (1996), *Starstruck* (Tricycle Theatre, 1998) and *The Gift* (Birmingham Rep, 2000) – Williams's dramatic oeuvre is firmly urban-centred. His prolific output includes *Local Boy* (Hampstead Theatre, 2000), *Clubland* (Royal Court, 2001), *Little Sweet Thing* (New Wolsey, 2005), *Joe Guy* (Tiata Fahodzi, 2007), *Category B* (Tricycle Theatre, 2009) and *Sucker Punch* (Royal Court, 2010). His screenplay of *Fallout* was aired as part of the *Disarming Britain* season on urban gun and knife crime (Channel 4, 2008). In the same year, Williams received further establishment recognition with the award of an OBE for services to drama.

The Plays

The No Boys Cricket Club (1996)

Williams's juvenilia of Caribbean-related plays begin with this professional debut, which opened on 24 May 1996, initiating his artistic relationship with director Indhu Rubasingham. His earlier work centralises the immigrant generation and later plays, indigenes' issues – something Williams recognises.

> My body of work is in two halves: the early plays were very reflective and personal where characters reflected on the past; my later plays are more objective, commenting on what's going on now.[7]

The Caribbean location (paradoxically) is symbolic of the Old World while Britain is the New. Sport (in this instance cricket) is used as one lens by which to evaluate degrees of belonging in contemporary urban culture, something he revisits in *Sing Yer Heart Out for the Lads*, *Joe Guy* and *Sucker Punch*.

In 1990, the right-wing MP Norman Tebbit fused explicitly the connection between cricket and white Britishness in his infamous 'cricket test', when he asked, 'Which side do they cheer for? [. . .] It's an interesting test. Are you still harking back to where you came from, or where you are?'[8] Williams subverts both the assumptions of whiteness and maleness through Abigail and Maisie, young cricketers who migrated from Jamaica to London and who now, in their early fifties, are confronted with the legacies of that decision. He represents a particularly uncompromising vision of diasporic (dis)inheritance in a London working-class community beset by domestic violence, neighbourhood fracas, male profligacy and drug dealing – a marked contrast to 1950s Kingston. As contemporary Kingston is a crime-ridden, impoverished city, Williams's play implies the primary affirming space for his protagonists lies in their nostalgic pre-migratory past, which mirrors the fantasy of accessing pre-colonialism; both acts of the imaginary. The play also asks, in the fantasy Young Abi's words, 'What happened to my dream?' (p. 61).

Critics failed to appreciate the play's colonial critique and ongoing repercussions, as inherited by British-born black citizens. Nick Curtis observes, 'It marks a decent but unspectacular opening innings for Williams on a major stage [. . .] he's clearly got talent, but needs a few more practice strokes.'[9] This unanimity in affirming Williams's important subject matter sat alongside observations that the play required more drafts, and remarks about audience reactions. Williams thus encountered the demand for instant expertise faced habitually by black British writers, while reviewers, encountering culturally unfamiliar material, could not assume their accustomed majority viewpoint as audience members.

The play's formal and generic experimentation reveals how, initially, Williams's style was not social-realist. Soundscapes palpably evoke character's interior lives. Concurrent audio-text and spoken dialogue verbally intertwine past and present. The conceit of a character's younger and mature versions in conversation dramatises whimsically an inter-generational communion beyond displacement and identity distortions. However, the migratory sensibility of prior national and cultural origin is also one that was imperially forged. Emigration promised amelioration to colonial disenfranchisement and the play voices reassessments of such hopes.

Lift Off (1999)

Lift Off, which premiered at the Royal Court Theatre Upstairs on 19 February 1999, was inspired by Williams's *temoignages* of west London teenagers. He explains

> Before the likes of Ali G came along, I used to see white kids,
> all around Ladbroke Grove talking and acting like black kids.
> They were not being rude, or offensive, they were absolutely
> genuine, reacting and responding to the world they were
> living in. I knew there was a play there.[10]

Typical Williams motifs converge in this play: urban inter-racial relationships between young people, racism and its effects upon them; the fluidity of possible cultural affinities relational to socio-racial identities; young people's traumatising by peers; adult inadequacy to sustain emotionally, support or encourage youth into maturity, and the intense compensatory (but insufficient) bonds they form with each other.

While Williams's later dramatis personae are racially specified, *Lift Off*'s cast is young people: Mal, Tone (with incarnations Young Mal and Young Tone), and Carol (Tone's younger sister), Rich and Hannah. Only Rich is detailed as '*a young black schoolboy*' (p. 163). The reader discerns the characters' ethnicities through the dialogue – a fact instantly apparent visually in performance – opening to scrutiny just what informs these socio-cultural categories of blackness and whiteness. Williams dramatises its absorption as shaping his young characters' relationships to surrounding society and their individual behaviours.

Their generally unrelenting, unpalatable behaviour can be difficult to digest. Through Mal and Tone's exchanges, Williams channels crude racialised remarks on sexuality, cultural credibility and social expectations.

Mal Wat yu expect me to say? 'Bredren, check out Tone's piece, shame on us all!' I was jealous. So how's it feel? [. . .]

Tone Yu have got a bigger dick. Nuff girls fancy yu. Even my little sister's up for it now. [. . .]

Mal [. . .] Yu carry on like there's sum big magic secret.

Tone Well there must be.

Mal There aint. (pp. 197–8)

Williams's artistic palette creates little subtlety in its metaphorical application of colour value to his dramatic canvas. Such representations face awkward positioning in theatre history. Black people's presence on the British stage until the late twentieth century has ranged from non-existent to one-dimensional, topical rather than typical (if registered at all) in non-black dramatists' plays. Negative representations by black writers can validate the socio-cultural stereotyping that persists in press and political arenas, prime mediators to public consciousness concerning Britain's black citizens. John Stokes argues: 'Because he works so close to the street, Williams shares his topics with the tabloids.'[11] These tabloid-redolent representations are what Williams contests, yet is then paradoxically unable to write beyond, due to his subject matter and the dramatic language he has forged, which is based on his own version of street vernacular. While Williams asserts his right (remembering the historically constricted opportunities for black dramatists) to tackle any subject he wishes, he nevertheless is exposed to pigeonholing via commissioning, critical expectations and censure for perpetuating a narrow range of black people's experiences.

In *Lift Off*, complexity is gleaned from the characters' implied backstories. These form an unnerving accompaniment to their harsh interactions. School is an irrelevant backdrop to their lives. Healthy aspirations are non-existent. They are fixed in abusive cycles of emotional impoverishment (which they then display to each other). Ventriloquists and imitators of culture, they lack agency to change their circumstances. Beneath the bluster and bombast of the patois-imbibed street vernacular, lie narratives of difficulty and open-endedness rather than neat conciliation – or hope. Williams remarked:

> It's hard for black men in particular to find themselves without having the weight of stereotypes thrown at them. [. . .] They're faced with 'all black people are athletic, all black people are good movers, they're good singers, they're good dancers, they've got big dicks' – all that rubbish.[12]

The play's title invites multi-significance: lifting off (not forcing), to reveal or expose contents; the launching pad into adulthood; releasing something trapped under a concealing label. Critic Dominic Cavendish observes: 'A desire for honesty underpins all his work, even if that means potentially causing offence,' as Williams explained to him:

> Before I write a line I often take a deep breath, knowing the risks involved, but I think: I have a responsibility to tell the best story I can and if I'm going to write about young black kids getting into crime and gun culture then I've got to put it down.[13]

This reveals a perspectival lacuna, not only in how a predominantly white British theatregoing public experiences representations of blackness, but also in the world of young people, subjects scapegoated habitually by Britain's media. Williams's work attempts, with questionable success, to refashion this.

However, non-conforming characters invariably are futureless. Like *Fallout*'s murdered schoolboy Kwame, Rich dies. His suicide is linked to the torment he suffered from Young Mal and Young Tone, through humiliation and verbal annihilation.

Mal Yu little spas Rich. [. . .] Yu aint nuttin man. [. . .] He aint black. Fuck knows wat he is. (pp. 234–5)

Rich rejects subscribing to a generalised category of violence attributed to black men, which he has suffered from his father (revealed when he cries 'get off me Dad!', p. 171, as Young Tone wrestles him against his will). While his death interrupts the continuation of violence, or future laced to perpetuating the grim legacy ascribed to black males, it is self-sacrificial. Identity definition is intimately bound to cultural stereotypes, as derived from racialised masculine characteristics. Tone (white) not only ventiloquises black-associative street talk, but also engages in cultural cross-dressing aiming to reproduce Mal's hyper-sexualised version of black masculinity. Hannah, a racist white girl who deplores Tone's exogamy, identifies this false consciousness:

> **Hannah**   You're not black though.
> **Tone**   I might as well be right.
> **Hannah**   Looked in the mirror lately? [. . .] There must be something seriously missing in your life if you think acting like them is going to fill it in for you. (p. 209)

Mal is a provocative character. His inveterate misogyny and homophobia range from his attitude to his mother, 'The fuckin bitch. [. . .] She has to open her mout whenever she feel' (p. 216), to other people's mothers, 'Yer mum sucks dicks for a livin' (p. 165), to groping women in clubs. He has sex with under-age Carol, Tone's sister, on the grounds that, 'her arse was all nice and fit man, wat was I supposed to do? Am I a batay bwai?' (p. 231). He abusively rejects Carol when he learns of her pregnancy, 'Getting yerself pregnant man, yu stupid bitch. [. . .] Ca' yu aint nuttin but a fuckin little whore. *Exits*' (p. 225).

Black culture is displayed by a set of distinctive attributes mimicked by white youth, yet the aspirational element of this imitation does not alter grass-roots social discrimination. When the malignant Mal is revealed as having malignant blood cancer, incurable because of his race (not enough black male bone marrow donors are registered), this points to a greater disenfranchisement of black people within Britain. The play connects to other works dramatising health issues in the black British dramatic canon: Maria Oshodi's *Blood, Sweat and Fears* (1988) and Benjamin Zephaniah's *De Botty Business* (2008). Believing he will die from leukaemia, Mal belatedly values Rich (the misfit in the misogynistic, desensitised world of one-upmanship). He fancifully converses with the dead Rich in a generic annexe outside Williams's prevailing signature of social realism, as Abi and Maisie interacted with their younger selves. This *volte-face* can test an audience's sympathy. Emotional brutality and callousness chafes against exercising compassion towards a young life short-changed for social health failings. Although Keith Peacock asserts that 'His own race will let him die', it is worth remembering his death will eventuate from a mesh of social factors caused by the racist-impelled legacy of second-class citizenship for black settlers and indigenes in modern Britain.[14]

Yet, Mal has a loving mother, who, Carol reminds him, is 'worried about yer' (p. 216). The denigration of mothering, its absence or powerlessness, and the misogyny towards feminine qualities (often parading as feistiness which is soon traduced) is a feature of Williams's corpus. *The No Boys Cricket Club* celebrates female friendship but bleakly represents the mothering of sons: Abigail's son deals crack, Maisie's son dies. In Williams's British-based plays, male–male cross-generational conflict remains of paramount importance. Women characters function as the catalysts by which to explore a primacy of male–male contestations in families and friendships.

Sing Yer Heart Out for the Lads (2002)

As part of the National Theatre's *Transformation* season, this play opened in The Loft on 2 May 2002 and was revived with a semi-promenade staging at the Cottesloe (2004). The play shows football fans gathering in a working-class, south-west-London pub for the England versus Germany World Cup qualifying game (2000) which England lost. Writing in response to the event, Williams establishes himself as a contemporary if not contemporaneous chronicler of British culture.[15] He dramatises a debate of narrow, white-centred nationalism versus the new claimants, indigenous black citizens, in relation to the broader base of antipathy to Germany sustained since the Second World War. Williams employs duologues to tread a fine line between conversation and didacticism. Alan, white, mid-fifties, racist rhetorician, is set against ex-soldier Mark, black, early thirties:

> **Mark** I'm English.
>
> **Alan** No you're not.
>
> **Mark** I served in Northern Ireland. I swore an oath of allegiance to the flag. [. . .] How English are you? Where do you draw the line as to who's English? I was born in this country. And my brother. You're white, your culture comes from northern Europe, Scandinavia, Denmark [. . .]
>
> **Alan** The fact is, Mark, that the white British are a majority racial group in this country, therefore it belongs to the white British. (p. 218)

The exchange typifies James Vernon's 'troubling slippage between "England" and "Britain"' which is, as Krishan Kumar observes, 'one of the most enduring perplexities of English national identity. How to separate "English" from "British"?'[16] Saying English and meaning British or, saying British but implying English, presents a conundrum of identities, necessitating decoding – both by the play's characters and by the audience, who may or may not find these viewpoints to coincide with those they bring to the performance. The English/British dichotomy suggests the inclusion/exclusion dynamic wherein patriotic emotion is somehow attached to England and its associations with whiteness, not Britain, a contrived conglomerate of geo-political contingencies. In this equation black British can never be English or part of its self-appointed hegemony within the countries and islands of the United Kingdom. Richard Hoggart's observation that 'Presumably most groups gain some of their strength from their exclusiveness, from a sense of people outside who are not "Us"' is fused in the play to a post-imperial definition of nation which excludes non-white citizens.[17]

Of the premiere, David Benedict wrote, 'the National is aspiring to the condition of pub theatre' and 'while it's salutary to be presented with unpalatable facts about society [. . .] facts alone are not what drama is for'.[18] Contrastingly, John Peter found 'the comedy is brutal. It can make you ashamed when you laugh. That's the point. The theatre is a ruthless teacher.'[19] The assumed dialogical relationship between white-male critic and staged play is tested by Williams's material. His comedy (located in his characters' expletive-ridden repartee) is generally overlooked by reviewers whose responses reveal cultural unawareness of both vernacular and black-centred experiences. Experiential newness tends to be perceived as social didacticism where a panacea to social dysfunction is expected from the playwright.

This play reveals the complexities of disenfranchisement by virtue of class affiliations shared by black and white citizens, paralleled to fading English sovereignty (symbolised in the demise of English football internationally) and its outdated xenophobic projections. Barry, Mark's younger brother's notable entrance, '*the flag of St George painted all over his face*' (p. 37) and tattoo of the British bulldog, invites scrutiny of how far the marking of jingoistic nationalism on one's body can only ever be a form of mimicry or scarification for black citizens – given racism's grim ideological and material legacy.

However, Williams also dramatises Barry's ludicrousness. He is marginalised and reviled by white racists for being black, yet embraces and imitates their xenophobia towards German people (frozen conveniently in that nation's most reprehensible historical period). Williams parodies the so-called English reserve which, via football fervour, is transformed into aggressive male group hysteria – hooliganism – that negatively distinguishes English football supporters. Repellent aspects of Englishness are displayed and interlocked through German-hating and black-hating prejudice. As the hyper-sexualised character Mal was politically powerless in the world of *Lift Off*, so too are the hyper-racists of this play. Lawrie exclaims: 'They're gonna walk over us, like everyone else!' (p. 180) Defeat in football elides easily into retaliation against perceived enemies in his immediate environment: 'If those cunts can't do it on the pitch, we can, we will! We're England!' (p. 180) – an impotently delusive, post-Empire, post-devolution, battle cry.

Barry, the most zealous supporter of them all, punctuates Act Two with his refrain, 'ENGERLAND', and chanting 'ENGERLAND! ENGERLAND! ENGERLAND! [. . .] Stand up if you won the war!' (p. 208), a claim he inherits, given the considerable (and until recently historically overlooked) contributions of black service personnel to the defeat of Nazi Germany. He savours his participation in hooliganism, boasting anecdotally:

> I backed you and Lee up when those bunch of Dutch fans tried to have a pop, we kicked every bit of shit out of them. Then we roared, right into their faces, England! (p. 209)

The grass-roots racism dramatised in Alan's obvious sway over his white counterparts is problematised by his semi-mentoring of Barry as a footballer. They might form a class-based and geographically close-knit community, but the sense of dispossession, of being eclipsed (as England has been), is voiced through corrosive racism. Suzanne Scafe observes, 'The black enemy within and the German enemy without are conflated slowly' through narratives of failure, envy and resentment.[20] Alan deplores the present-day economic superiority of nations who lost the war, for Mark all conversations confirm racial prejudice and pub landlady Gina's father Jimmy yearns for the days of 'the older blacks' over 'those fucking black kids from that estate' and 'the immigrants' (p. 187).

Rather than simply a black–white antagonism, characters are equally shaped by the green-eyed monster. Mark and Gina's ex-relationship, supplanted by Lee and Gina's former relationship and Lee's and Mark's friendship, have suffered from unresolved jealousies and resentments not derived from racial tensions, suggesting Richmond's prophetic 'the question of racial differences is incidental to the much larger problem of cultural conflict and social change'.[21] Ultimately, Mark's murder by Gina's son Glen cements the binarism, mirroring not only two football sides but Hoggart's 'Us' and 'Them' dichotomy. Unlike football, there is no going home after the murder. The pub symbolises an island of embattled whiteness surrounded by angry black youths. Closing with '*Sound of police sirens approaching*' (p. 235), Williams aurally evokes the bitter history between an institutionally racist police force, and black citizens' experiences of a criminal (in)justice system. The empathic, enigmatic final exchange between the mutually bereaved: Barry (face paint erased), and Lee, '**Lee** (*to* **Barry**) Don't lose yourself' (p. 235), suggests co-recognition of the legacy of angry retaliation to prejudice, and the struggle to negotiate identity and self-worth as separate from this.

Fallout (2003)

Fallout, which opened on 12 June 2003, is an 'incendiary play' which dramatises a racially related homicide investigation.[22] Hot-tempered black policeman Joe confronts white colleagues' liberal hypocrisy and the gang culture glorification now reigning where he was raised. Inter- and intra-cultural and racial differences converge in this scorching exploration of losing connections to one's cultural roots and the ever-diminishing chances of obtaining justice for a murdered African teenager. The fallout gestures to the stage-world murder's brutal ramifications and a wider consequentialist context of trans-generational displacement and social disenfranchisement. Director Ian Rickson described Joe as an epic figure, a kind of prodigal son returning to his kingdom.[23] However, Joe's alienation from his community of origin and professional context, and his inability to exact respect from the young people he is desperate to bring to justice (and even redeem), becomes a portrait of a man who is anything but commanding. Ultz's décor, a disembowelled Royal Court main house, placed the stalls audience behind wire cages and circle audience looking down upon the action, creating a fishbowl effect or suggesting that the cast were under surveillance, a familiar objectification experienced by black people in white-dominated society.

Fallout marked definitively (and controversially) Williams's presence as a leading neo-millennial playwright. As Sarah Compton describes, 'Roy Williams's new play opens with a gang of black kids running away from kicking another boy to death.' She praised the play:

> Williams is brave enough to take us into the lives of the killers, not to exonerate them, but to reveal the circumstances that make them behave as they do, to explore the corruption wrought by a sense of exclusion, of thwarted ambitions, of a false equation of toughness and cool. At the same time, he tackles the effects of political correctness in the police force and the police's inability to nail the boys they know are guilty.[24]

Black cultural commentators tended to disagree. Darcus Howe voiced disapprobation towards this representation of blackness, noting audience composition as 'almost wholly white except for four or five blacks including myself', where: 'This was not a slice of real life, but of low life sketched by the playwright for the delectation of whites.'[25] As he 'almost vomited' because of the playwright's dubious offering, white critic Toby Young's abjection interchanged theatricality with actuality: 'I left the theatre sickened by its savagery – and its accuracy.'[26] As Yasmin Alibhai-Brown has pointed out, the tendency for white critics' misguided praise of the culturally unfamiliar rewards stereotyping rather than encouraging artistic experimentation.[27]

Evoking Mal's diatribe against a generalised African worker in *Lift Off*, intra-racism between African and Caribbean-origin antecedents is identifiable in *Fallout*, but Williams avoids confronting these tensions (which implicitly catalyse the murder), stating that the focus is 'the political correctness that had been the response to the exposure and acknowledgement of institutional racism'.[28] His dramatised ghetto reveals teenagers marooned in a demographic bereft of moral guidance. They form substitute attachments spiked by ferocity and desensitisation. Flashpoints of male violence arise as black male characters become trapped in cul-de-sacs of circumstances which they perceive as demeaning and emasculating. Estate life and the consequences of poverty and social marginalisation govern the lives of teenagers and peripheral characters, such as Manny, the gang leader, or Dwayne's father, a vagrant addict. Manny is a device to expose Dwayne's vulnerability, providing a sub-textual indication of the extreme emotional and probable socio-economic deprivation characterising Dwayne's life up to the point of Kwame's murder.

> **Manny** Yu my Bwoi. Good bwoi, Junior.
>
> **Dwayne** Wat?
>
> **Manny** Wat?
>
> **Dwayne** Wat yu juss call me? [. . .]
>
> **Dwayne** Junior is yer son, who live up by Shepherd's Bush, my half-brudda, [. . .] live wid his two little sistas, Tasha and Caroline, yer daughters . . . Remember dem? Nuh, it muss be Anton yu remember, yer son who live up by Dagenham way. Or is it Stuart, my little brudda, who live two minutes away . . . Nuh, nuh, it muss be the latest one, dat lickle baby wid the stupid name, Kenisha. (p. 90)

Staging dispossession opens Williams to charges of writing depressing material devoid of suggesting 'any way of changing this reality'.[29] Harry Derbyshire declares that 'each fictional circumstance is designed to shed light on the world outside the play', confirming Suzanne Scafe's observation of white critics' reception, 'like so much Black expressive art, it is more valued as polemic than as theatre'.[30]

Days of Significance (2007)

In his mid-thirties, Williams took up global issues and explosive current affairs to explore contemporary youth morality. *Days of Significance* – which opened on 10 January 2007 at the Swan Theatre, Stratford-upon-Avon – is not an intertext of *Much Ado About Nothing*, although the characters' stichomythic verbal duels resonate with Shakespeare's play. Its tripartite structure encompasses an English market town and Iraq. Prior to leaving on a tour of duty, two young soldiers join their friends on a drinking binge. The characters' ignorance and moral dysfunction symbolise the fallacy of the West's moral high ground over those it deems terrorists. As Shakespeare filtered critiques of his contemporary political context through geo-historical displacement to investigate English Renaissance society, so too does Williams engage with recent issues concerning youth culture, binge-drinking and social alienation in a globalised world.

War is an age-old arena in which masculinity is tested, a public display of state-enacted violence that becomes glorified and enshrined in national consciousness. While the militarism of Shakespeare's era might now be uneasiness at waging war, its residual associations as a route to manhood remain. Jamie, accused of torturing Iraqi prisoners, represents the dehumanisation and unquestioning allegiance to superiors that is vital militarily, but disturbing in civilian life. His threat to his girlfriend Hannah, 'I could kill you right now', aligns its literal possibility with his disclaimer: 'It was an order!' (p. 264). Automatic military loyalty is at odds with any personal civilian relationship: 'Grass on my mates? Dishonour myself as well as my unit? You really don't know me, Hannah' (p. 265). His inarticulateness circumvents any explanation for torture. A rhythmic anaphora, 'I dunno, I dunno, I dunno why I did it [. . .] I dunno, I dunno, I don't fucking know. We juss lost it' (p. 266) underscores his emotional limitations. Mantra-like, it protects him from personal responsibility. 'I' becomes the group identity of 'We', the unit survival strategy for soldiers.

Williams purposely defied commissioning expectations that he would write a play for black characters.[31] Its two published versions (the second with a rewritten final act adding a wedding and reversing the seduction dynamic between Lenny and Hannah) evince the pressure that contemporary black British dramatists can face. As Caryl Phillips identifies, 'A lot of artists aren't given a chance to evolve . . . You need a period of gestation which is usually quite long.'[32] Influential (white) broadsheet reviewers have begun to point out that hastiness, leading to a lack of depth, characterises Williams's latest writing, insinuating that his prolific production may not best serve his artistry. According to Phillips, 'The danger is that white people will cut you off if you don't do what they want you to do.'[33] Although established, Williams remains fearful that each play will be his last and noted his frustration of not having enough time to finish his final approved version of *Days of Significance*:

> in-between Stratford and the Tricycle [its London venue], I did rework the play. When we had to get the play in to be published we were still working on it. So even the second published version is not the finished version.[34]

This relates to Williams's fixity in a commissioning cycle which restricts aesthetic experimentation. The consequence (perhaps) of his too-prodigious output is a static rather than protean stage language. John Stokes notes of *Days of Significance* (2007) that the restrictions 'of street talk finally become apparent, and with them a dilemma facing the writer. [. . .] At key moments his words turn flaccid, like symptoms of a spent cultural force.'[35]

Summary

Williams inherits British theatre's legacies: drama and performance that has consistently restricted and even erased black people's presence and input until the mid-twentieth century. He *has* experienced a degree of having his work revived (essential to longevity) and toured nationally in studio spaces but has not, as yet, enjoyed a West End transfer. Praising Williams as an inspirational presence, Caryl Phillips calls him 'perhaps the most adventurous, and certainly the most prolific, black dramatist to emerge in Britain in recent years'.[36] Naming collaborative partnerships as essential to the development of the British playwright – a dynamic in which white (male) theatre practitioners are well-versed, Phillips exemplifies Harold Pinter/Peter Hall, Edward Bond/Bill Gaskill, David Edgar/Trevor Nunn, while noticeably omitting the directorial longevity of Paulette Randall, Indhu Rubasingham and Michael Buffong in relation to black dramatists.[37]

Williams writes from an empathic, responsive and principled standpoint, evident in the many interviews, after-show talks and educational material in which he remains a committed participant. As part of the Monsterist group, he lobbied against the small cast sizes, inadequate budgets and confinement to studio spaces which have been viewed as adversely affecting contemporary writing. He noted recently the movement's obsolescence:

> I think we all agreed okay we will make our points and then we'll leave, otherwise we'll come across as a bunch of whinging playwrights. But thankfully theatres have got the message and more and more writers have been encouraged to write bigger plays.[38]

British theatre historiography shares much historically with race relations discourse,

> a discourse *about* a largely silenced other, a discourse in which, to borrow from Gayatri Chakravorty Spivak, the subaltern could not speak, except within the epistemological framework imposed by academic experts.[39]

Williams's motivation has been to fill a perceived cultural vacuum in British theatre, 'Question: "Why do I write what I write?" Answer: "Because no-one else is." '[40] However, his sex-gender schematics generally fulfil Bidisha's observation that 'misogyny is the strongest passion on earth', which in a theatre context means 'producers and editors (of both sexes) are still mysteriously unwilling to go anywhere near talented non-white women writers, except in the most tokenistic and belittling way' – parallelling non-white male writers' characterisations of women and white male critics' unchallenging reception of these characterisations.[41]

There is little scholarly material on Williams. What exists is primarily by white scholars or is confined to identity politics themes, examining the plays as dramatic literature without concurrent performance analysis. Aleks Sierz references Williams as New Writing in non-academic surveys and journalistic interviews. Williams's traceable evolving aesthetic goes unrecognised in Keith Peacock's comparative work. Harry Derbyshire's discussion of *Fallout* is filtered through a multicultural prism, delivering a sociological reading divorced from aesthetics as though the play is a direct refractor of the social world only, and not the world of the theatre. Its performance semiotics ignored, as well as influential sources of reception (only one theatre review is cited), the play becomes a case study for sociological readings. Janelle Reinelt comparatively discusses *Days of Significance* as part of her aim to contest 'a series of characterisations that have produced a different, dampened impression of contemporary British writing'.[42] Aware (unlike Peacock and Derbyshire) that audiences in all their experiential variegation exist in theatre-making, Reinelt proceeds to discuss the play using a Performance Studies approach and chronological plot retelling.

Notable essays on Williams include those by Elizabeth Barry and William Boles (who contextualise his early work, discussing it comparatively through aesthetic investigation) and pioneering black British academic Suzanne Scafe (who interrogates the socio-cultural circumstances of spatial occupancy in Britain's theatre venues and its relationship to a dramatist's vision). As initiatory forays into a developing critical mass, the articles' publication sites – an uneven and not easily obtainable hardback book also addressing Asian work, and an alternative press paperback – have not helped their dissemination or permeation of cultural records and scholarship. They have become obscured by other frameworks in an almost palimpsestic fashion. Interplay of literary criticism and performance analysis is vital for the emergence of an appropriate critical lexicon. No area better demonstrates this necessity than the work of Black British dramatists as they challenge prevailing theatrical, socio-cultural and linguistic assumptions and certainties.

Walter Ong notes, 'The spoken word does have more power to do what the word is meant to do, to communicate.'[43] Williams's distinctive stage language (while not approaching the experimental virtuosity of debbie tucker green) enables experiential representation of characteristically marginal voices in British theatre. As Williams asserts,

I am a playwright full stop [. . .] I don't write because I am
black, I write because I am a writer [. . .] Black playwright,
coloured playwright, brown playwright, whatever. Just as long
as they don't miss out the word playwright.[44]

Primary Sources

Works by Roy Williams

Plays One: The No Boys Cricket Club, Starstruck, Lift Off (London: Methuen Drama, 2002).
Plays Two: The Gift, Clubland, Sing Yer Heart Out for the Lads (London: Methuen Drama, 2004).
Plays Three: Fallout, Slow Time, Days of Significance, Absolute Beginners (London: Methuen Drama, 2008).

Secondary Sources

Alibhai-Brown, Yasmin, 'Black Art Can be Bad, Just Like Art by Whites', *Independent*, 2 May 2005 <http://www.independent.co.uk/opinion/commentators/yasmin-alibhai-brown/yasmin-alibhaibrown-black-art-can-be-bad-just-like-art-by-whites-489793.html>
Anon., *Fallout* Education Pack, Royal Court Theatre, 2003.
Barry, Elizabeth and William Boles, 'Beyond Victimhood: Agency and Identity in the Theatre of Roy Williams', in Dimple Godiwala (ed.), *Alternatives within the Mainstream: British Black and Asian Theatre* (Newcastle: Cambridge Scholars, 2006), pp. 297–313.
Bidisha, 'Shine the Spotlight on Every Shade of Black', *Observer*, 4 November 2007.
Bridglal, Sindamani, 'Profile of Caryl Phillips', *Artrage*, No. 1 (1982), pp. 3–6.
Cavendish, Dominic, 'Man of the Match', *Daily Telegraph*, 19 April 2004.
Compton, Sarah, 'Black British Drama Takes Centre Stage', *Daily Telegraph*, 9 July 2003.
Derbyshire, Harry, 'Roy Williams: Representing Multicultural Britain in Fallout', *Modern Drama*, Vol. 50, No. 3 (2007), pp. 414–34.
Fisher, Dan, 'Split Between Britain, U.S. Seen as "Inevitable"', *Los Angeles Times*, 19 April 1990.
Hoggart, Richard, *The Uses of Literacy* (London: Transaction Publishers, 1992).
Kennedy, Maev, 'Youth Takes Centre Stage in National's Quest for Relevance', *Guardian*, 9 April 2002.
Kumar, Krishan, *The Making of English National Identity* (Cambridge: CUP, 2003).

Ong, Walter, 'Word as Sound', in Peter Elbow (ed.), *Landmark Essays on Voice and Writing* (Davis, CA: Hermagoras, 1994), pp. 19–34.

Osborne, Deirdre, 'The State of the Nation: Contemporary Black British Theatre and the Staging of the UK', in Christoph Houswitschka and Anja Müller (eds), *Staging Displacement, Exile and Diaspora* (CDE 12; Trier: WVT, 2005), pp. 129–49.

—, '"I ain't British Though / Yes You are. You're as English as I am": Belonging and Unbelonging in Black British Drama', in Ulrike Lindner et al. (eds), *Hybrid Cultures, Nervous States: Britain and Germany in a (Post)Colonial World* (Amsterdam: Rodopi, 2010), pp. 203–27.

Peacock, D. Keith, 'The Question of Multiculturalism: The Plays of Roy Williams', in Mary Luckhurst (ed.), *A Companion to Modern British and Irish Drama: 1880–2005* (Oxford: Blackwell, 2006), pp. 530–40.

—, 'Black British Drama and the Politics of Identity', in Nadine Holdsworth and Mary Luckhurst (eds), *A Concise Companion to Contemporary British and Irish Drama* (London: Blackwell, 2008), pp. 48–65.

Phillips, Caryl, 'Lost Generation', *Guardian*, 23 April 2005.

Reinelt, Janelle, 'Selective Affinities: British Playwrights at Work 1', *Modern Drama*, Vol. 50, No. 3 (2007), pp. 305–45.

Richmond, Anthony H., *The Colour Problem* (Harmondsworth: Penguin Books, 1955).

Rickson, Ian, Personal Interview, London, 23 April 2004.

Scafe, Suzanne, 'Displacing the Centre: Home and Belonging in the Drama of Roy Williams', in Joan Anim-Addo and Suzanne Scafe (eds), *I am Black/White/Yellow: An Introduction to the Black Body in Europe* (London: Mango, 2007), pp. 71–87.

Sierz, Aleks, 'Beyond Timidity: The State of British New Writing', *PAJ: A Journal of Performance and Art*, Vol. 27, No. 3 (2005), pp. 55–61.

—, '"What Kind of England Do We Want?": Interview with Roy Williams', *New Theatre Quarterly*, Vol. 22, No. 2 (2006), pp. 113–21.

Stokes, John, 'Unofficial Rules of the Game', *The Times Literary Supplement*, 6 November 2009, p. 17.

Vernon, James, 'Review: Englishness: The Narration of a Nation', *Journal of British Studies*, Vol. 36, No. 2 (1997), pp. 243–9.

Waters, Chris, '"Dark Strangers" in Our Midst: Discourses of Race and Nation in Britain, 1947–1963', *Journal of British Studies*, Vol. 36, No. 2 (1997), pp. 207–38.

Williams, Roy, 'Spread the Word (Twilight Zone)', Talk, Morley College, London, 22 May 2005.

—, Personal Interviews, London, 24 October 2004 and 10 March 2010.

—, Talk, Goldsmiths, University of London, 24 October 2005.

—, Monsterists Panel, Birkbeck, University of London, 14 May 2009.

Wu, Duncan, *Making Plays: Interviews with Contemporary British Dramatists and Their Directors* (Basingstoke: Palgrave Macmillan, 2000).

Notes

1. Roy Williams, 'Spread the Word (Twilight Zone)', 2005.
2. Roy Williams, Talk, Goldsmiths, 2005.
3. Aleks Sierz, '"What Kind of England Do We Want?"', p. 113.
4. Williams, Talk, Goldsmiths, 2005.
5. Roy Williams, Personal Interview 2010.
6. Roy Williams, Personal Interview 2004.
7. Ibid.
8. Dan Fisher, 'Split Between Britain, U.S. Seen as "Inevitable"'.
9. *Theatre Record*, Vol. XVI, No. 11 (1996), p. 681.
10. Williams, 'Spread the Word (Twilight Zone)'.
11. John Stokes, 'Unofficial Rules of the Game'.
12. Williams, Personal Interview 2004.
13. Dominic Cavendish, 'Man of the Match'.
14. Keith D. Peacock, 'The Question of Multiculturalism', p. 533.
15. The play 'is based on the experience of the playwright Roy Williams, who found himself the only black man in a pub that night and was gradually intimidated out of it' (Maev Kennedy, 'Youth Takes Centre Stage').
16. James Vernon, 'Review: Englishness', p. 249; Krishan Kumar, *The Making of English National Identity*, p. 1.
17. Richard Hoggart, *The Uses of Literacy*, p. 48.
18. *Theatre Record*, Vol. XXII, No. 9 (2002), p. 556.
19. Ibid.
20. Suzanne Scafe, 'Displacing the Centre', p. 81.
21. Anthony H. Richmond, *The Colour Problem*, p. 13.
22. Deirdre Osborne, 'The State of the Nation', p. 130.
23. Ian Rickson, Personal Interview, 2004.
24. Sarah Compton, 'Black British Drama Takes Centre Stage'.
25. *Theatre Record*, Vol. XXIII, No. 11–12 (2003), pp. 756–60; Vol. XXIII, No. 13 (2003), p. 861.
26. Ibid.
27. Yasmin Alibhai-Brown, 'Black Art Can be Bad, Just Like Art by Whites'.
28. Anon., *Fallout* Education Pack.
29. Aleks Sierz, 'Beyond Timidity: The State of British New Writing', p. 59.
30. Scafe, 'Displacing the Centre', p. 81.
31. Williams joked that the RSC had contracted more black actors than usual in anticipation of casting specifications (Roy Williams, Monsterists Panel).
32. Sindamani Bridglal, 'Profile of Caryl Phillips', p. 6.
33. Ibid.
34. Williams, Personal Interview 2010.

35. Stokes, 'Unofficial Rules of the Game'.
36. Caryl Phillips, 'Lost Generation'.
37. Duncan Wu exemplifies the white male hegemony dominating British theatre in his pairings of male writers and directors. Women, black or Asian practitioners are excluded.
38. Williams, Personal Interview 2010.
39. Chris Waters, '"Dark Strangers"', p. 219.
40. Williams, 'Spread the Word (Twilight Zone)'.
41. Bidisha, 'Shine the Spotlight on Every Shade of Black'.
42. Janelle Reinelt, 'Selective Affinities: British Playwrights at Work 1', p. 305.
43. Walter Ong, 'Word as Sound', p. 21.
44. Williams, 'Spread the Word (Twilight Zone)'.

INDEX

abandonment 255, 428–9
Abbey Theatre (Dublin) 482
absence 17, 51, 56, 89, 90, 91, 92, 99, 157, 185, 428–9, 455–6
abuse, sexual 171–6, 473–4, 476
　domestic xiv, 185–6, 195, 236, 265, 332, 335, 476–8, 485–6
　see also paedophilia
Agbaje, Bola xiv, 336
AIDS xviii–xix, 166–8, 175, 177, 178, 189–90, 192, 278
Akhtar, Anwar 11, 12
Albany Empire 103
Albee, Edward 150
　Three Tall Women 9
Alibhai-Brown, Yasmin 500
alienation xix, 78, 127, 208, 236, 248, 365, 380, 407, 502
Almeida Theatre (London) 50
Ambassadors Theatre (London) xii
ambiguity 49, 50, 96, 133, 153, 185, 308, 430, 442, 461–3
Anderson, Gordon 449
Ansorge, Peter 55
anxiety 18, 132, 368, 369, 432, 482
Apollo Theatre (London) 54
Appiah, Kwame Anthony 16–17
Arts Council ix, x, xi
Aston, Elaine 55, 317–18, 389, 391, 397
Atlantic Club, Soho 43
Atlantic Theater (New York) 50
Augé, Marc 249
authenticity 77, 111, 132, 237
Ayckbourn, Alan 3, 9, 468

Bacon, Francis 426
Barker, Howard xv, 216
　Victory 305
Barry, Elizabeth 505
Bartleet, Carina 117
Bartlett, Mike xiv
Bassett, Kate 333
Battersea Arts Centre 110
Baudrillard, Jean 86, 89
Baxendale, Helen 440
Bayley, Clare 148
Bean, Richard xiv, xvii, **1–18**
　The Big Fellah 3
　England People Very Nice xvi, xxi, 2, 3, **11–15**, 16
　The English Game 3
　The God Botherers xvi, 3, **7–9**
　Harvest 2, 3, **10–11**
　The Heretic xx
　Honeymoon Suite 2, 3, **9**
　House of Cards 3
　In the Club xvi, 3

The Mentalist 3
Mr England 3
Of Rats and Men 2
Paradise for Fools 2
Pub Quiz is Life 1
Smack Family Robinson 3, **6–7**, **17**
Toast 1, 2, **4–5**
Under the Whaleback xviii, 1, 2, **5–6**
Up on Roof 1
Beckett, Samuel 79, 82, 89, 177, 316, 380, 395
　Happy Days 79
　Waiting for Godot ix, 76
Benedict, David 496–7
Benjamin, Walter 98
Bennett, Alan 468
Bent, Simon 148
Berkeley, George 97
Berkoff, Steven: *East* 146, 147
Berton-Charrière, Danièle 251, 253, 259
Billingham, Peter 213, 216, 235, 416, 421
Billington, Michael 5, 56, 88, 116, 147–8, 230, 253, 284, 299, 301, 333, 406, 412, 420, 438, 449
Birc, Anna 126
Blandford, Steve 56
Bodinetz, Gemma 271
Boles, William 505
Bond, Edward 419, 503
　Saved x, 153, 419, 446, 455
Bourne, Bette 404
Bradley, Jack 4
Bradwell, Mike xii, 366
Brecht, Berthold xv, 65, 78, 190, 207, 216–17, 225, 419
Brenton, Howard 71, 75, 125, 446
Brown, Ian xii, 251, 257–8, 360
Bruckner, Ferdinand: *Pains of Youth* 458
Bryden, Bill 25
Büchner, Georg: *Woyzeck* 306, 310, 380, 452
Buffini, Moira xix, 2
Buffong, Michael 503
Bull, John 12, 16
Buñuel, Luis 426
Burgess, John 110, 268
Burke, Gregory xiv, xvii, xx, **22–39**, 258
　Battery Farm 23
　Black Watch xvi, xx, 22, 23, **31–5**
　Debt 23
　Gagarin Way xvi, 22, **23–6**, 37–8, 39, 217
　Hoors 23, **35–7**, 38
　Liar 23
　On Tour 23, **29–31**, 38
　The Straits 23, **26–9**, 38
Burke, Kathy 187
Bush Theatre (London) x, xii, xiii–xiv, 7, 144, 145, 146, 163, 164, 263–4, 265, 285, 364, 366, 426

CONTRIBUTORS

Elaine Aston is Professor of Contemporary Performance at the University of Lancaster, UK

Peter Billingham is Head of the Department of Performing Arts, University of Winchester, UK

Nicole Boireau is Emeritus Professor of English Literature at Paul Verlaine University of Metz, France

John Bull is Emeritus Professor of Film and Drama at the University of Reading, UK

Rebecca D'Monté is Senior Lecturer in Drama at the University of the West of England, UK

Lynette Goddard is Senior Lecturer in Drama and Theatre at Royal Holloway, University of London, UK

Gabriele Griffin is Professor at the Centre for Women's Studies at the University of York, UK

Christopher Innes is Distinguished Research Professor at York University, Toronto, Canada

Stephen Lacey is Professor of Drama, Film and Television at the Cardiff School of Creative and Cultural Industries, University of Glamorgan, Cardiff, UK

Martin Middeke is Professor of English Literature at Augsburg University, Germany, and Visiting Professor of English at the University of Johannesburg, South Africa

Deirdre Osborne is Lecturer in Drama and Theatre Arts at Goldsmiths, University of London, UK

Anette Pankratz is Professor of British Cultural Studies at the Ruhr-University, Bochum, Germany

David Pattie is Reader in Drama and Theatre Studies at the University of Chester, UK

Dan Rebellato is a playwright and Professor of Contemporary Theatre at Royal Holloway, University of London, UK

Janelle Reinelt is Professor of Theatre and Performance Studies at the University of Warwick, UK

Margarete Rubik is Professor of English Literature at the University of Vienna, Austria

Elizabeth Sakellaridou is Professor of Drama at the Department of English, Aristotle University, Thessaloniki, Greece

Graham Saunders is Reader in Theatre Studies at the University of Reading, UK

Peter Paul Schnierer is Professor of English Literature at the University of Heidelberg, Germany

Aleks Sierz is Visiting Professor at Rose Bruford College and teaches at the London branch of Boston University, UK

Caridad Svich is a US-based playwright, translator, critic, and Associate Editor of *Contemporary Theatre Review*

Ken Urban is a playwright and director and teaches at Harvard University, USA

Eckart Voigts-Virchow is Professor of English literature at Siegen University, Germany

Christina Wald is Assistant Professor at Augsburg University, Germany

Clare Wallace is Senior Lecturer in Irish and British Literature and Irish and Intercultural Studies of English at Charles University Prague, Czech Republic

The editors are grateful to all of the above, to the efficient and friendly staff at Methuen Drama, and many others. Our greatest debts of gratitude for their diligent work on various stages of the manuscript are owed to Lisa Haubeck, Georg Hauzenberger, Julia Peter and Katja Utz.